Competition Law

The International Library of Essays in Law and Legal Theory
Second Series
Series Editor: Tom D. Campbell

Titles in the Series:

Freedom of Speech, Volumes I and II
Larry Alexander

Privacy
Eric Barendt

Comparative Legal Cultures
John Bell

Contract Law, Volumes I and II
Brian Bix

Corporate Law
William W. Bratton

Law and Democracy
Tom Campbell and Adrienne Stone

Legal Positivism
Tom D. Campbell

Administrative Law
Peter Cane

International Trade Law
Ronald A. Cass and Michael S. Knoll

Sociological Perspectives on Law, Volumes I and II
Roger Cotterrell

Intellectual Property
Peter Drahos

Family, State and Law, Volumes I and II
Michael D. Freeman

Natural Law
Robert P. George

The Creation and Interpretation of Commercial Law
Clayton P. Gillette

Competition Law
Rosa Greaves

Chinese Law and Legal Theory
Perry Keller

Constitutional Law
Ian D. Loveland

Law and Legal Interpretation
D. Neil MacCormick and Fernando Atria

Human Rights
Robert McCorquodale

Anti-Discrimination Law
Christopher McCrudden

Medical Law and Ethics
Sheila McLean

Mediation
Carrie Menkel-Meadow

Environmental Law
Peter S. Menell

Criminal Law
Thomas Morawetz

Law and Language
Thomas Morawetz

Law and Anthropology
Martha Mundy

Gender and Justice
Ngaire Naffine

Law and Economics
Eric A. Posner

Japanese Law
J. Mark Ramseyer

Restorative Justice
Declan Roche

Constitutional Theory
Wojciech Sadurski

Justice
Wojciech Sadurski

The Rule of Law
Frederick Schauer

Regulation
Colin Scott

War Crimes Law
Gerry Simpson

Restitution
Lionel D. Smith

Freedom of Information
Robert G. Vaughn

Tort Law
Ernest J. Weinrib

Rights
Robin West

Welfare Law
Lucy A. Williams

Competition Law

Edited by

Rosa Greaves

Allen & Overy Professor of Law
Durham European Law Institute, University of Durham, UK

Routledge
Taylor & Francis Group
LONDON AND NEW YORK

First published 2003 by Dartmouth Publishing Company and Ashgate Publishing

Reissued 2018 by Routledge
2 Park Square, Milton Park, Abingdon, Oxon OX14 4RN
711 Third Avenue, New York, NY 10017, USA

Routledge is an imprint of the Taylor & Francis Group, an informa business

A Library of Congress record exists under LC control number: 2001099642

ISBN 13: 978-1-138-70846-4 (hbk)
ISBN 13: 978-1-138-70841-9 (pbk)
ISBN 13: 978-1-315-19973-3 (ebk)

Contents

PART IV COMPETITION LAW AND THE GLOBAL ECONOMY

Acknowledgements

The editor and publishers wish to thank the following for permission to use copyright material.

ABA Publishing for the essay: Frank H. Easterbrook (1985), 'Vertical Arrangements and the Rule of Reason', *Corporate Counsel's Annual – 1985*, pp. 461–98. Reprinted from *Antitrust Law Journal*, **53**, pp.135–74. Copyright © 1984 American Bar Association.

Kansas Law Review for the essay: Spencer Weber Waller (1994), 'Neo-Realism and the International Harmonization of Law: Lessons from Antitrust', *Kansas Law Review*, **42**, pp. 557–604.

Kluwer Law International for the essays: Alex P. Jacquemin (1970), 'The Criterion of Economic Performance in the Anti-Trust Policies of the United States and the European Economic Community', *Common Market Law Review*, **7**, pp. 205–25; Bastiaan van der Esch (1980), 'E.E.C. Competition Rules: Basic Principles and Policy Aims', *Legal Issues of European Integration*, **2**, pp. 75–85; Valentine Korah (1980), 'Concept of a Dominant Position within the Meaning of Article 86', *Common Market Law Review*, **17**, pp. 395–414. With kind permission of Kluwer Law International.

O'Brien Center for Scholarly Publications for the essays: Robert H. Lande (1982), 'Wealth Transfers as the Original and Primary Concern of Antitrust: The Efficiency Interpretation Challenged', *Hastings Law Journal*, **34**, pp. 67–151. Copyright © 1982 Hastings College of the Law; Rudolph J. Peritz (1989), 'The "Rule of Reason" in Antitrust Law: Property Logic in Restraint of Competition', *Hastings Law Journal*, **40**, pp. 285–342. Copyright © Hastings College of the Law.

Oxford University Press for the essay: Richard Whish and Brenda Sufrin (1988), 'Article 85 and the Rule of Reason', *Yearbook of European Law*, **7**, pp. 1–38. Copyright © 1988 Richard Whish and Brenda Sufrin. Reprinted from *Yearbook of European Law*, **7**, 1987 edited by F.G. Jacobs (1988) by permission of Oxford University Press.

Sweet & Maxwell Limited for the essays: Sonya Margaret Willimsky (1997), 'The Concept(s) of Competition', *European Competition Law Review*, **1**, pp. 54–7; Barry E. Hawk (1988), 'The American (Anti-Trust) Revolution: Lessons for the EEC?', *European Competition Law Review*, **9**, pp. 53–87; Paul Torremans (1996), 'Extraterritorial Application of E.C. and U.S. Competition Law', *European Law Review*, **21**, pp. 280–93; Christopher Bright (1993), 'Article 90, Economic Policy and the Duties of Member States', *European Competition Law Review*, **6**, pp. 263–72; Anthony Gardner (1995), 'The Velvet Revolution: Article 90 and the Triumph of the Free Market in Europe's Regulated Sectors', *European Competition Law Review*, **2**, pp. 78–86; Trevor Soames (1996) 'An Analysis of the Principles of Concerted Practice and Collective

Dominance: A Distinction without a Difference?', *European Competition Law Review*, **1**, pp. 24–39. Copyright © 1996 Trevor Soames, Norton Rose; Rosa Greaves (1998), 'The Herchel Smith Lecture 1998: Article 86 of the E.C. Treaty and Intellectual Property Rights', *European Intellectual Property Review*, **20**, pp. 379–85; Daniel Glasl (1994), 'Essential Facilities Doctrine in EC Anti-Trust Law: A Contribution to the Current Debate', *European Competition Law Review*, **6**, pp. 306–14; Thomas Sharpe (1987), 'Predation', *European Competition Law Review*, **8**, pp. 53–76; Pierre-Emmanuel Noël (1997), 'Efficiency Considerations in the Assessment of Horizontal Mergers under European and U.S. Antitrust Law', *European Competition Law Review*, **8**, pp. 498–519; Ignacio De León (1997), 'The Dilemma of Regulating International Competition under the WTO System', *European Competition Law Review*, **3**, pp. 162–77. Copyright © Sweet & Maxwell & Contributors.

Tulane Law Review Association for the essay: David J. Gerber (1987), 'Law and the Abuse of Economic Power in Europe', *Tulane Law Review*, **62**, pp. 57–107. Copyright © 1987 Tulane Law Review Association.

University of Chicago, Law School for the essay: Richard A. Posner (1977), 'The Rule of Reason and the Economic Approach: Reflections on the *Sylvania* Decision', *University of Chicago Law Review*, **45**, pp. 1–20. Copyright © 1978 University of Chicago.

University of Pennsylvania Law Review for the essay: Robert Pitofsky (1979), 'The Political Content of Antitrust', *University of Pennsylvania Law Review*, **127**, and a Commentary by Louis B. Schwartz entitled '"Justice" and other Non-Economic Goals of Antitrust', pp. 1051–81.

Every effort has been made to trace all the copyright holders, but if any have been inadvertently overlooked the publishers will be pleased to make the necessary arrangement at the first opportunity.

Preface to the Second Series

The first series of the International Library of Essays in Law and Legal Theory has established itself as a major research resource with fifty-eight volumes of the most significant theoretical essays in contemporary legal studies. Each volume contains essays of central theoretical importance in its subject area and the series as a whole makes available an extensive range of valuable material of considerable interest to those involved in research, teaching and the study of law.

The rapid growth of theoretically interesting scholarly work in law has created a demand for a second series which includes more recent publications of note and earlier essays to which renewed attention is being given. It also affords the opportunity to extend the areas of law covered in the first series.

The new series follows the successful pattern of reproducing entire essays with the original page numbers as an aid to comprehensive research and accurate referencing. Editors have selected not only the most influential essays but also those which they consider to be of greatest continuing importance. The objective of the second series is to enlarge the scope of the library, include significant recent work and reflect a variety of editorial perspectives.

Each volume is edited by an expert in the specific area who makes the selection on the basis of the quality, influence and significance of the essays, taking care to include essays which are not readily available. Each volume contains a substantial introduction explaining the context and significance of the essays selected.

I am most grateful for the care which volume editors have taken in carrying out the complex task of selecting and presenting essays which meet the exacting criteria set for the series.

TOM CAMPBELL
Series Editor
Centre for Applied Philosophy and Public Ethics
Charles Sturt University

Introduction

Competition law, or 'antitrust law' as it is known in the United States (US), was absent from the first series of *The International Library of Essays in Law and Legal Theory*. This is not surprising since competition law/antitrust law, as a separate body of law, is very much a creation of the twentieth century and grew only into maturity in the latter half of that century. This area of law consists of rules adopted by states, such as the US, or supranational organizations, such as the European Community (EC), in order to regulate the activities of economic entities (private or public) in competitive markets. These activities embrace agreements or arrangements between undertakings, conduct by undertakings in dominant market positions, mergers, unfair practices (e.g., dumping) and aid granted by states to certain undertakings.

The legislative history of antitrust law in the US is founded in the Sherman Act, adopted by the US Congress in 1890 in order to deal with the trusts that controlled and consolidated American industry at the end of the nineteenth century. Thus antitrust legislation in the US was enacted just after their industrial revolution. In the early part of the twentieth century the American Supreme Court adopted rules such as the 'rule of reason' and the 'per se' rules[1] which have resulted in the modern law of antitrust. The Clayton Act and the Federal Trade Commission Act, adopted in 1914, completed the initial legislative package. As far as Europe is concerned, competition law is a post-Second World War legal phenomenon which flourished with the establishment in 1957 of the European Economic Community (now known as the EC). Although it is often stated that the origin of competition law in Europe was a consequence of the US's influence on post-war Germany, the influence of the neo-liberalism pre-1950s movement in Germany should not be underestimated.[2] The establishment of the European Economic Community in 1957 gave German thinkers an ideal opportunity to introduce innovative competition rules (Articles 81–90 of the European Community Treaty (EC Treaty))[3] into the new legal order they had created (European Community law) to deal with the restrictive practices and problems that arise from the exercise of economic power. The scope of these rules have been supplemented by secondary legislation[4] and by the interpretative rulings of the European Court of Justice (ECJ) resulting in a body of law known as 'EC competition law'. The EC Treaty envisaged the establishment of a common market based on four fundamental freedoms concerning the key factors of production (goods, persons, services and capital) and on the operation of common rules such as the competition rules. Thus, unlike the situation in the US where antitrust law was enacted long after free interstate trade had been established, EC competition law is an important element in the fundamental goal of establishing free movement of goods and services between member states. Article 3(f) of the EC Treaty requires the European Community to create a system ensuring that competition in the common market is not distorted.

As the 'common market' – now renamed the 'single European market' or the 'internal market' – has grown in importance, the usage of the term 'competition law' has become more common than 'antitrust law' in legal writing outside the US. The term 'competition law' is very much a European one which has enabled economic theories to be put into practice within the context of a political goal of economic integration in Europe. However, as markets become global, academic lawyers and practitioners argue for the creation of a World Competition Authority under the auspices of the World Trade Organization. Should the idea come to fruition, I have no doubt that 'competition law' rather than 'antitrust law' will be the term used globally. Thus the title of this volume is *Competition Law*. However, given that there are significant differences in competition law concepts between the US and the EC, the terms 'US antitrust law' and 'EC competition law' have been used accordingly when commenting on specific practices or concepts pertaining to these two jurisdictions.

Chosen Structure and Overview

The task of selecting essays for this collection has been harder than anticipated. European literature in particular tends to respond to specific problems which are raised in competition cases rather than to engage in theoretical or jurisprudential academic debate. Most of these works are problem-solving short pieces or critiques of judicial application of competition rules. They are written by academics, practitioners or policy makers, thus providing a variety of perspectives, and they are published in designated specialist journals, such as the *European Competition Law Review*, which are accessible to the legal profession.

American antitrust scholarship on the other hand, is extensive and focused on economics and antitrust policy. These articles are lengthy, published in a variety of university law reviews as well as in specialist journals such as the *Antitrust Law Journal*. The major influence in the United States in the second half of the twentieth century was the Chicago School's scholarship.[5] The Chicago School followers maintain that the only goal of antitrust policy and law is market efficiency, that is, the maximization of consumer welfare. Furthermore, rigorous economic analyses were applied by followers of the School to test the propositions in antitrust laws and to understand the impact of business practices on consumer welfare. The School's ideas were expounded by such writers as Bork, Easterbrook and Posner.

There are several well-known books on competition law. A non-exhaustive list would include: *The Anti-trust Paradox: A Policy at War with itself*;[6] *Antitrust Law: An Economic Perspective*;[7] *Antitrust and the Bounds of Power*;[8] *Law and Competition in The Twentieth Century Europe: Protecting Prometheus*;[9] *Competition Policy in the European Community*;[10] *EC Competition Law*;[11] *Monopoly Law and Market*;[12] and *The Rule of Reason in Antitrust Law*.[13]

Although notions of what is antitrust in the US differ significantly from those in the EC, EC competition law owes much to US antitrust law. As developments in US antitrust law have had, and continue to have, an important influence on the development of competition law in Europe and worldwide, articles have been selected from both sides of the Atlantic. Thus, under several headings I have selected works from both American and European perspectives. As competition law is a form of common law, it is not surprising that articles written by Europeans or Americans contain discussions or analyses of case-law decisions.

The collection focuses on the following aspects of competition law: the objectives and nature of competition law; the scope of competition law; selected legal concepts and challenges in competition law; and the global application of competition law. The collection does not include literature on state aids. Although state aids are of particular concern to EC competition law, they are beyond the scope of this volume.

Part I The Objectives and Nature of Competition Law

In the US there has been an ongoing debate as to the objectives or goals of antitrust law and policy.[14] In Europe the key objective of competition law, namely market integration, has never been seriously challenged. Willimsky (Chapter 1) provides a brief introduction to the underlying concepts of competition law and explains the basic characteristics of the two leading schools of thought, namely Chicago and Brussels. The policy differences between the US and the EC are then developed in Hawk's essay (Chapter 2). In both jurisdictions, politics play a significant role.

The Economic Concerns of Competition Law

Competition law is in a class of its own. It is generally agreed that it is shaped by economics but there is less agreement as to whether economics alone plays the vital role. Since it was in the US that the first antitrust legislation was adopted, American commentators have had the principal lead in evaluating the role of economics in the development of antitrust law. Many leading specialists (Areeda and Turner, 1980; Bork, 1978; Posner, 1976) argue that maximization of economic efficiency (consumer welfare) is the only goal and any other criteria is without legal foundation.[15] However, other commentators maintain that other goals are of equal importance. A critical review of these two schools of thought is given in Lande's essay (Chapter 3). Lande rejects both views and expresses his own theory that the primary goal of the drafters of the US antitrust legislation was to prevent 'unfair transfers of wealth from consumers to firms with market power' (Chapter 3, p. 68). An exhaustive evaluation of the economic goals of US antitrust law is undertaken by Lande.

The objective of competition law in the European context was never in doubt. Although maximization of efficiency was an important goal to a Europe devastated by war in the middle of the twentieth century, other policies such as political stability, integration of national markets and the protection of small and medium-sized enterprises, were (and remain) of equal concern. However, conflict between maintaining competition and achieving market efficiency has emerged. The conflict only arises where the business practice lessens competition (i.e., increases market power) but also produces economies (i.e., market efficiency). Jacquemin (Chapter 4) examines the constraints (legal and economic) on the US and the EC competition authorities in dealing with these situations where market efficiency and market power consequences coexist. The differences are explored. American tradition condemns any combination or agreement which increases market power, whilst in the EC the public interest prevails at least in the case of restrictive agreements (Article 81(3) EC Treaty). The only limit is to be found in abuses of a dominant position which are condemned.

The Political Concerns of Competition Law

Competition law is a hybrid type of law. The legislative measures and the judicial rulings implementing these measures reflect political goals expressed as competition *policy*. The policy seeks to prevent unfair acquisition of market power by undertakings, without being over-protective of competitors. The legislation therefore seeks to prevent restrictive agreements or concerted practices between undertakings (e.g., s1 Sherman Act, UK 1998 Competition Act and Article 81(1) EC Treaty), to prevent undue acquisition of power by undertakings through mergers, monopolization of markets (e.g., s2 Sherman Act and s7 Clayton Act) or through the abuse of a dominant position (Chapter 2 prohibitions UK 1998 Competition Act and Article 82 EC Treaty).

The major difference between US Antitrust law and EC competition law in dealing with restrictive agreements between undertakings is that under EC competition law, the prohibition (Article 81(1) EC Treaty) is mitigated by provision for administrative exemptions (Article 81(3) EC Treaty) based on public interest, efficiency and competition.[16]

Under this section, Pitofsky's essay, and the commentary by Schwartz that follows (Chapter 5), consider the political content of antitrust law, focusing on mergers as a means of illustration. Pitofsky starts with political values and how non-economic concerns are manifested in US legislation on mergers (s7 (as amended) Clayton Act). This is followed by an evaluation of how political concerns influence the development of rules applied to horizontal mergers. The author demonstrates that US antitrust law, although primarily concerned with economic considerations, is also dependant on political values. Schwartz's commentary strongly supports Pitofsky's argument and highlights examples where considerations of 'justice' have prevailed.

As far as the European Community is concerned, political and economic values are two sides of the same coin. The EC competition rules are complementary to the establishment of the common market and the removal of state barriers to trade. In his essay van der Esch (Chapter 6) focuses on the comprehensive character of these rules and on how the basic severity of them is mitigated by the possibility of an exemption being granted in the public interest and according to the conditions set out in Article 81(3) EC Treaty.

The Extraterritoriality Application of Competition Law

A controversial issue giving rise to much academic debate has been the question of the extraterritoriality application of competition law. As markets become global, undertakings accused of anti-competitive behaviour may not always be established or have a presence in the state where the consequences of that behaviour are felt. Public international law confers state jurisdiction on the basis of nationality or territoriality principles.[17] Thus other solutions were developed. The US favours the 'effects doctrine' whilst the EC has adopted the 'implementation doctrine'. Torremans (Chapter 7) considers how these two doctrines fit within international law principles and discusses critically the cooperation agreement signed between the EC and the US which is aimed at preventing clashes between these two regimes.

Part II The Scope of Competition Law

The scope of competition law is wide-ranging, covering primarily cartels, mergers and abuses of positions of market power. However, two matters are particularly interesting. As far as the US is concerned, there has been much debate as to whether antitrust law should be applied to vertical restraints, whilst in the EC an interesting question is to what extent public undertakings in member states are immune from the application of competition law.

Vertical Restraints

The debate on vertical restraints has been carried out in the US more rigorously than in Europe.[18] Although, in the early sixties, the European Court of Justice (ECJ) interpreted Article 81(1) EC Treaty as to apply to vertical agreements,[19] the issue became academic once the European Commission (the EC's competition authority) adopted legislation to exempt most of these agreements from the prohibition of Article 81(1).

Proponents of the Chicago School, such as Easterbrook (Chapter 8), argue strongly that only where restrictive dealings arise out of a cartel situation should antitrust laws be applied. In his essay, Easterbrook is highly critical of judicial reasoning in US decisions. He argues that most vertical arrangements are pro-competitive. Posner's essay (Chapter 9) on the '*Sylvania* Decision' centres on a crucial issue, namely, how resale price maintenance and non-price restrictions in distribution agreements are considered under US antitrust law. These restrictions had been treated as being illegal per se until the US Supreme Court ruling in *Sylvania*. The US Supreme Court accepted for the first time that a rule of reason approach was the correct one, thus taking into account the argument that restrictions imposed by manufacturers on their distributors are often intended to prevent free-riders and to enhance the manufacturer's interbrand competition, rather than to encourage the distributors to gain monopoly profits.

Public Undertakings and State Aids

What is the effect of EC competition law on the freedom of member states? Both Bright (Chapter 10) and Gardner (Chapter 11) consider the relationship between the EC competition law and public monopolies or undertakings on whom special or exclusive rights have been granted by member states. This is a delicate issue in the European context where community law claims supremacy over national law. The EC Treaty provides a compromise in Article 90. Although member states are free to confer such rights, the undertakings themselves must operate within what is permitted by EC competition law unless the assigned tasks are being undertaken in the 'general economic interest'. This is often referred to as 'public mission' exemption. In interpreting this provision, the ECJ has made several inroads in limiting the opportunities for undertakings to rely on this derogation. Gardner analyses most of these key rulings.

Part III Selected Legal Concepts and Challenges in Competition Law

The Rule of Reason and Per Se Rules

There are many unresolved legal issues/concepts in competition law which are still being debated. The selection of topics for this section is purely a personal choice. Apart from the 'rule of reason' and 'per se' rules and the defence of efficiency in merger investigations, all other issues considered in this section are primarily concerned with the development of competition law in Europe.

As far as 'per se' illegal practices are concerned, there is a very limited role for them in EC competition law. In view of the multiple goals of EC competition law, it is impossible to identify certain types of practices which can never be justified. If there are beneficial effects, they may well be exempted for a limited period of time. In the US, per se prohibitions are a prominent feature of the enforcement system.

From a European point of view one of the most fascinating issues has been the application of the 'rule of reason' rule by the American judiciary as an analytical tool to identify unreasonable 'restraint of trade' conduct. This is an ongoing debate on both sides of the Atlantic.[20] In Chapter 12, Peritz demonstrates how the US Supreme Court shifted its analysis of antitrust cases to a 'rule of reason' approach. As far as EC competition law is concerned the jury is still out. However, Whish and Sufrin (Chapter 13) argue strongly and persuasively that such an approach should be resisted in the development of EC competition law.[21]

Dominance, Concerted Practices and Joint Dominance

The drafters of Articles 81 and 82 EC Treaty and the ECJ opted for a *sui generis* vocabulary for EC competition law which inevitably has led to new legal concepts such as 'dominance' and 'concerted practices'. The concept of dominance is unique to EC competition law. Specific rules have been devised by the European Commission with approval from the ECJ on how to determine whether an undertaking is in a dominant position for the purposes of Article 82. Korah (Chapter 14) not only authoritatively analyses the concept but she is also critical of the perceived absence of consideration by the European enforcers of the competitive pressures that come from outside the market defined as relevant.[22] In Chapter 15, Soames evaluates the case-law jurisprudence of two concepts: concerted practices and joint dominance. These concepts are distinct and different but their application may in some circumstances overlap. The European Commission sees the extension of joint dominance as a possible solution to the problem of controlling oligopolies. Oligopolies cause many problems to competition authorities who fear that high prices will be maintained to the disadvantage of consumers. But how far and when should competition authorities interfere in an oligopolistic market?[23] Often, oligopolies emerge in markets which have high entry barriers due to the costs of infrastructure provision, ownership of intellectual property rights or simply efficiency which has resulted in a few undertakings controlling the market.

The final matter considered in this section of the collection relates to the relationship of intellectual property rights and Article 82 EC Treaty (Greaves, Chapter 16). Protecting the ownership of intellectual property rights is extremely important for the EC as a player in the global market. However, there can be significant conflicts between the rights conferred by the ownership of intellectual property and competition law particularly in the exercise of those rights. Intellectual property rights are powerful marketing tools in the hands of undertakings in dominant positions.

Essential Facilities Doctrine

The essential facilities doctrine is an example of an attempt to deal with industries where infrastructure costs or ownership of intellectual property rights makes it almost impossible for competitors to enter the market where the owner of the infrastructure or intellectual property right operates. A typical example is in the transport industry where the owner of a port facility will usually also operate maritime services from that facility. It is unlikely that the owner of the port will allow a competitor to use its facilities to offer competing maritime services. The doctrine was formulated in the US.[24] As far as the EC competition law is concerned, the issue is perceived in terms of the importance of market access for all competitors on equal terms (Glasl, Chapter 17). Thus, in Europe, references have not been made by the ECJ to the essential facilities doctrine as such but to 'third party access'. This is another example of the ECJ being determined to develop EC competition law concepts for community law rather than to import them from the US.

Abuse

Another pure EC competition law concept is that of 'abuse'. Having a dominant position is not anti-competitive. It is the abuse of that position which is prohibited by Article 82 EC Treaty. A thorough analysis of this concept is undertaken by an American scholar (Gerber, Chapter 18). Since the concept of abuse of economic power is not familiar to US lawyers, Gerber in his essay analyses its origins and comments on its application by the European Commission and the ECJ. One of the most difficult abuses the European competition authorities have had to consider is predatory pricing, and whether it is a legitimate business practice. In Chapter 19, Sharpe discusses the economics of predation and how it can be determined.[25]

Efficiency Defence in Mergers

Mergers have also caused a number of difficulties to competition authorities in trying to apply efficiency goals as the only or main objective of competition law. Noël (Chapter 20) undertakes a comparative assessment of how the defence of efficiency in merger situations has been considered by EC and US competition authorities. Unlike in the US, an efficiency defence is not a formal part of the standards of appraisal contained in the EC Merger Regulation. This is an area for development and only recently has the European Commission considered the defence.

Part IV Competition Law and the Global Economy

EC competition law has reached a degree of maturity that has persuaded the European Commission to propose decentralization of EC competition law to the national competition authorities of the member states. However, as markets become global (and the undertakings operating on those markets tend to be multinationals) and more and more states adopt national competition laws, there is a growing call for the regulation of anti-competitive practices to be carried out at global level. The World Trade Organization (WTO) system is already in place to regulate international trade and is an obvious candidate to take on the role of World Competition Authority. De León (Chapter 21) explores this possibility whilst Weber Waller (Chapter 22) critically analyses the transferability of national law from a number of perspectives and proposes a 'neo-realist' approach to harmonizing international economic (antitrust) law.

Notes

1 *Standard Oil Co.* v *United States*, 221 U.S. 1 (1911).
2 Gerber, D.J. (1994), 'Constitutionalizing the Economy: German Neo-Liberalism', *American Journal of Comparative Law*, **42**, pp. 25–84 and Oliver, H. (1960), 'German Neoliberalism', *QJ Econ*, **lxxiv**, pp. 117–49.
3 ex-Articles 85–94. The EC Treaty articles were renumbered after the Treaty of Amsterdam, 1997. Most of the essays in this collection will refer to the original numbering.
4 For example, Council Regulation 4064/89, OJ 1989 L395/1 (the Merger Regulation); Commission Regulation 240/96 OJ 1996 L31/2 (Transfer of Technology Agreements); and Commission Regulation 2790/99 OJ 1990 L336/21 (Vertical Agreements).
5 Posner, Richard A. (1979), 'The Chicago School of Antitrust Analysis', *University of Pennsylvania Law Review*, **127**, pp. 925–52 provides a useful historical perspective of the Chicago and Harvard Schools; Sullivan, Laurence A. (1994/95), 'Post-Chicago Economics Economists, Lawyers, Judges and Enforcement Officials in a Less Determinate Theoretical World', *Antitrust Law Journal*, **63**, pp. 669–81.
6 Bork, R. (1993), New York: The Free Press.
7 Posner, R. (1976), Chicago: University of Chicago Press.
8 Amato, G. (1997), Oxford: Hart Publishing.
9 Gerber, D. (1998), Oxford: Clarendon Press.
10 McLachlan, D.L. and Swann, D. (1967), Oxford: Oxford University Press.
11 Goyder, D.G. (1998), 3rd edn, Oxford: Clarendon Press.
12 Fejo, J. (1990), Kluwer.
13 Joliet, R. (1967), The Hague: Martinus Nijhoff. Joliet was one of the first European academics to argue for market analysis under the EC competition rules.
14 Blake, H.H. and Jones, W.K. (1965), 'In Defense of Antitrust', *Columbia Law Review*, **65**, pp. 53–87 provides an historical review of the debate on goals of antitrust; Posner, R.A., n.5.
15 Strong support for this proposition is to be found in the Chicago School of Antitrust which had a major influence in the direction taken in US antitrust enforcement. See generally, Posner, R.A., n.5.
16 NB there is no possibility of exemption for an abuse of a dominant position under the EC competition rules. However, the EC Treaty rules do not prohibit positions of dominance, only the 'abuse' of those positions. Specific legislation had to be adopted in order to regulate concentrations/mergers which might lead to a position of dominance.
17 See Slott, P.J. and Grabandt, E. (1986), 'Extraterritoriality and Jurisdiction', *Common Market Law Review*, **23**, pp. 545–65.
18 For an historical and detailed discussion of the tension between US competition policy and common law property rights, see Peritz, Rudolph J. (1988–9), 'A Genealogy of Vertical Restraints Doctrine', *The Hastings Law Journal*, **40**, pp. 511–76.
19 Cases 56 and 58/64, *Consten & Grundig* v. *Commission*, [1966] E.C.R. 299.
20 See Bork, R. (1965), 'The Rule of Reason and the Per Se Concepts: Price Fixing and Market Division', *Yale Law Journal*, **75**, pp. 3273–475, where he argues for the adoption of a doctrine of ancillary restraints rather than the per se rules applied to price fixing and market division agreements.
21 See also, Forrester, I. and Norall, C. (1984), 'The Laicization of Community Law: Self-help and the Rule of Reason: How Competition Law is and could be Applied', *Common Market Law Review*, **21**, p. 11.
22 An economist's assessment can be found in Baden Fuller, C.W. (1979), 'Article 86 EEC: Economic Analysis of the Existence of a Dominant Position', *European Law Review*, **4**, pp. 423–41.
23 Posner, Richard A. (1969), 'Oligopoly and the Antitrust Laws: A Suggested Approach', *Stanford Law Review*, **21**, pp. 1562–1606.
24 Areeda, Phillip (1990), 'Essential Facilities: An Epithet in Need of Limiting Principles', *Antitrust Law Journal*, **58**, pp. 841 et seq.

25 For an American context, see, Areeda, P. and Turner, D. (1974/75), 'Predatory Pricing and Related Practices under Section 2 of the Sherman Act', *Harvard Law Review*, **88**, pp. 667–733 and Scherer, F.M. (1976), 'Predatory Pricing Under Section 2 of the Sherman Act', *Harvard Law Review*, **89**, pp. 868–903.

Part I
The Objectives and Nature of Competition Law

[1]

The Concept(s) of Competition

Sonya Margaret Willimsky

There are a number of concepts which underlie competition policy and which form the theoretical premise upon which regulatory provisions are based. This analysis seeks to offer a brief introduction to the main strands of thought in this area which make competition a political, legal and economic chameleon.

"Antitrust policy", Robert Bork observed, "cannot be made rational until we are able to give a firm answer to one question: What is the point of the law—what are its goals?" The "battle for the soul of antitrust", as Eleanor Fox once put it, continues. This analysis will elaborate on the theoretical premise of the concept of competition and consequently examine the approach taken by the Chicago School of Thought and the European Union. It will be demonstrated that competition has no single unifying objective and that there are a variety of objectives pursued in its name. As Sir Leon Brittan stated: "Indeed, it can be said that a positive competition policy should not be determined in isolation; it must be related to and integrated with economic, industrial and also social policy."

Competition is the principal regulator of commercial forces in a capitalist market, presuming that individual competitors' motivating force derives from the pursuit of self-interest. The struggle for superiority in the market place is defined by the objective to persuade consumers on grounds of quality and value to make a particular purchase.

Competition policy is deeply embedded in the way one views human nature and the role of society and the state. The liberal view of the state and man, driven by self-interest as the supreme motivating force, favoured a more classical model of competition. Posner, for example, clearly favoured the view of individuals as rational maximisers of wealth. To advocate a more regulatory and interventionist model would, according to this view, unnecessarily interfere with the proper quasi-Darwinist pursuit for superiority and the natural selection of the most efficient market participants. It is believed that only selection, as expressed through consumer choice, would lead to an equilibrium of demand and supply and hence further the interests of society as a whole. Adam Smith's "invisible hand" as opposed to the very visible hand of the state would, according to this view, lead to the best overall solution.

Marxist social theory and the way human nature is perceived leads to the diametrically opposed view of competition. It would necessarily lead to a system whereby political and economic strands of thought would inevitably be closely intertwined with the perception of man as only one part of a greater web of society. Of course, it has to be remembered that even the crudest capitalist systems present a framework with a number of highly complex social, economic and political strata. However, the underlying value base is freedom as opposed to actual social equality and social justice and this general principle forms the foundations of commercial activity, assuming that the commercial and political ends are not separable. Experiments currently undertaken by China to combine a free or at least more liberal or open economy with a view of human nature which, ideologically, should be embedded in a restrictive, quasi-communist system, have to be observed with great interest.

It is generally accepted that competition policy may have important political goals and that an "unhealthy" (*i.e.* cartelised) economy may facilitate the establishment of totalitarian regimes. Hitler, for example, rose to power with the help of German cartels. In 1938, President Roosevelt stated: "The liberty of a democracy is not safe if the people tolerate the growth of private power to a point where it becomes stronger than their democratic state itself."

The basic ideological premise about human nature also has to be viewed in context with the objectives of competition. "Perfect competition" is a goal in which economic recourses are allocated between different goods and services in exactly those quantities which reflect consumer demand, reflected in the price consumers are prepared to pay for goods. This basic utopian ideal is, of course, very difficult to attain and some would even question whether it would be desirable to pursue in any case.

There are, for example, sectors which ought to be "inefficient", be it for economic reasons (for example agriculture) or for reasons of safety, such as transport. Sometimes, for R&D purposes, for instance, experts in a particular field have to be granted "time out" from the competitive race in order to develop new drugs, etc., in situations where the drive for efficiency would not allow for such an investment in terms of time and money.

Allocative efficiency is also a term which denotes a state of a market in which resources are allocated precisely in accordance with consumer demand. Pursuant to the neo-classical theory, it is presumed that under allocative efficiency, where competition is perfect, a producer will increase output to the point at which marginal cost and marginal revenue, the net addition to revenue of selling the last unit, coincide. Consequently, a reduction in his own output cannot affect the market price and so there would be no reason to limit it.

Productive efficiency is achieved when a producer is unable to sell above cost: if he did, he would lose customers. He would of course not sell below it, presuming that each producer wishes to maximise profits. If a producer were to charge above cost, other competitors would enter the market in the hope of undercutting the other competitors, charging below price and therefore acquiring a large market share. Eventually, the point will be reached where price and average cost of producing goods coincide, *i.e.* price would not rise above cost. The combined effect of allocative and productive efficiency is that society's wealth is maximised.[1]

"Workable competition" describes a system where the objectives set out above have not been attained, but a state of affairs has been reached which comes close to the "ideal".

Chicago versus Brussels

The main schools of thought today in terms of competition policy are the Chicago and the Brussels school of thought. The Chicago school of thought developed in the 1950s and proclaims that economic efficiency should be the sole pursuit of the competitive process and antitrust policy should only seek to prevent the inefficient allocation of recourses. Socio-political considerations ought to be excluded from competition policy and a "pure" approach to the maximisation of efficiency taken. The Chicago model, for example, views practices such as predatory pricing, tie-ins or resale price maintenance not as anti-competitive but as beneficial to the consumer. This view was particularly popular in the Thatcher/Reagan era; a competition policy impregnated with socio-political considerations was in fact viewed as "uncritical sentimentality". The main goal, as Ernest Gellhorn stated, for Chicago economists has to be "assuring a competitive economy".

A comparative study between the two schools of thought may however only be embarked upon if the historical background is appreciated. The European Union is involved in an unprecedented, *sui generis* attempt to integrate a market of greatest political, economic, social and cultural diversity.

The E.U. pursues a policy which is to a far greater extent interventionist, with the fundamental, broad objective of market integration underlying all policy considerations. There are a number of Chicago arguments which the Commission firmly rejects, such as the Chicago view that very low predatory pricing is beneficial to consumers. The Commission is generally far more concerned about entry and expansion barriers and their potential to hinder intra-community trade.

E.U. policy is therefore not about efficiency *per se*, as Commissioner Sutherland stated: "Competition is [. . .] not to be pursued for its own sake, but rather because it is an instrument for promoting a harmonious and balanced expansion, and an accelerated raising of standards of living." He stated that the Commission's approach is, on the one hand, flexible towards pro-competitive forms of co-operation between enterprises, such as R&D agreements. On the other hand, he added, restrictive measures aimed at hindering the realisation of a unified market will not be tolerated, but will be sanctioned with effective fines.

Brussels is consequently concerned with a more "balanced" view of competition. Small and medium-sized enterprises, for example, are shielded from the harsher elements of the markets, and the principle of "free competition" is deeply embedded in the Preamble to the Treaty of Rome. As Karel van Miert recently pointed out: "Competition, fiscal and social policy all belong together".

It is also interesting to note that, for example, the Coase Theorem presumes that irrespective of legal provisions, the parties will always reach the same efficient result provided that the transaction costs are zero. According to this theory, competition policy as such, be it Chicago and Brussels, would be irrelevant provided that the parties are free to conduct their own affairs. Competition policy may therefore be not only irrelevant but also dangerous given that producers may seek to abandon markets altogether in order to avoid straitjackets in the economy.

1 See Paul Auerbach, *Competition, The Economics of Industrial Change*.

Monopolies

Generally accepted both in the Chicago and in the Brussels school of thought is that monopolies are undesirable. A monopolist is, to an extent, immune from the forces of competition, a state of affairs which leads to allocative inefficiency, "dead-weight loss" and "x-inefficiency".[2] A monopolist is able to increase price by reducing the volume of his own production and, since the aggregate output determines price via the relationship of supply and demand, increase his profits. This would lead to allocative inefficiency since he will reduce output and therefore output would be lower than it would have been within a framework of perfect competition. The firm furthermore becomes "x-inefficient" since productive efficiency will generally also be lower than it otherwise would have been, given that it is unlikely that costs will be held to the lowest possible level. Liebenstein, who coined the term, therefore referred to a situation in which resources are channelled to the right product, but in a less productive way than they would otherwise have been.

However, Schumpeter offered an interesting insight into how "big" might be "beautiful". He demonstrated that there are dynamic advantages to monopolies. Aside from the aspect of the economics of integrated research, Schumpeter stated that "'within big units . . . (conscious) policy towards demand and taking a long-term view towards investment becomes possible." Also, one may argue that the legitimate goal, almost the *raison d'être* of competition, is the struggle for market leadership and hence a dominant position in a market *per se* appears to demand appraisal rather than antitrust intervention!

A fundamental question in this context is of course always whether, when a particular market is examined more closely, there are any barriers to entry. If there are not, even a dominant position or oligopolistic structure does not necessarily have to be cause for concern.

Oligopolies

Professor Wish argued that:

> The main argument against oligopoly is that the structural conditions of the market in which oligopolists operate are such that they will not compete on price and will have little incentive to compete in other ways; furthermore the theory of oligopolist interdependence asserts that they will be able to earn supra-competitive profits without entering into the type of collusive agreements generally proscribed by competition law.[3]

An oligopolistic market is one which is characterised by the presence of a small number of key players in the market. A structure which is typical in oligopolistic markets is such that the group of oligopolists do not compete with each other on price or in other ways, although, of course, in some markets, competition is intense. The theory of oligopolistic interdependence sets out various reasons for the "invisible bond" between the privileged few. Because of their interdependence, oligopolistic markets are very stable and subsist in a quasi-competition free vacuum. They are tied to one another in price, marketing and any other form of behaviour which would have an appreciable effect on the market. Unilateral actions would either force an oligopolist out of the circle or force the others to match. Parallel pricing strategies, therefore, are more the result of a heightened sense of awareness of each other's presence than necessarily evidence of a concerted practice or anti-competitive agreement.

Oligopolistic structures may only be combated by means of a structural attack on the particular market or a policy which would make parallel pricing unlawful *per se*. Galbraith stated that: "The final problem of anti-trust policy . . . is its inability to make satisfactory contact with oligopoly" and it is argued that competition policy should focus more on oligopolies than on possible monopolies, which are much easier to destroy. Direct regulation of oligopolies may first of all not be possible in a free market and would be very cumbersome and bureaucratic. E.U. competition policy in particular fails to address oligopolies and it appears that other systems, in particular the almost ad hoc U.K. system, seem to be more suitable to deal with this problem, if one views oligopoly as a problem at all. Again, the issue of foreclosure of markets has to be looked at more closely.

Conclusion

Which direction the Janus-like phenomenon of competition will look in future remains to be seen. The general trend of liberalisation and deregulation appears to favour the Chicago view, but other concerns such as stability and a "healthier" economic structure which also allows for a solid base of small

2 As first used by Liebenstein.

3 Wish, *Competition Law* (3rd edn), p. 468.

and medium-sized undertakings also add a powerful voice to the debate.

The author would at this stage conclude that principles, objectives and policies ought to be borne in mind when looking at particular legislative enactments or judicial interpretation and that competition is much more than a race or regulation of a race. Competition policy, in particular in view of E.U. developments, will remain a fascinating topic, and the competition for the "soul of antitrust" continues.

SONYA MARGARET WILLIMSKY
Haarmann, Hemmelrath & Partner
Düsseldorf and Warsaw

[2]

The American (Anti-trust) Revolution: Lessons for the EEC?

Barry E. Hawk

In the last ten years US anti-trust law has undergone a veritable revolution with a shift from strict rules to more tolerant case law and a highly relaxed enforcement posture on the part of the competent Federal Government agencies. This revolution has generated criticism of EEC competition law[1] as outmoded and insufficiently reflective of the 'new economic learning' in the United States which is largely responsible for the American revolution. For example, Commission and Court decisions have been condemned for failing to take sufficiently into account free rider and other asserted justifications for vertical restraints. Appeals for a 'rule of reason' under Article 85(1) frequently cite the trend away from per se rules in the United States towards the rule of reason.

A comparative examination of the development of EEC and US law over the last 10 to 20 years places these and other criticisms in a better perspective. Many criticisms of EEC law fail to recognise or give sufficient weight to important and in some cases dispositive differences in statutory language, policy objectives and enforcement institutions and mechanisms. This article describes those differences with the modest hope that this will provide a firmer basis on which to assess EEC law.

EEC competition law was born in 1958 of transatlantic parents. Its European mother was the basic Treaty goal of market integration. Its father (or godfather) was US anti-trust law and theory which influenced the drafting of Articles 85 and 86 through German law and thought. The US father has had considerably less

This article is based on a paper delivered at the Centre for Commercial Law and Applied Legal Research, Monash Law School, Melbourne, July 1987.

The author would like to thank Karen Banks, Valentine Korah, Giuliano Marenco, John Temple Lang and Michel Waelbroeck for their comments. Any infelicities of expression and errors in judgment remain the author's.

1 This article discusses only the competition provisions of the EEC Treaty and not the competition provisions of the ECSC Treaty.

influence over the upbringing of its offspring than the mother. Indeed, the father abandoned many of the strict disciplinary rules it held in 1958 in effect leaving the many-roomed anti-trust mansion of his ancestors for a leaner and more modern-designed dwelling.

Given the parentage of the EEC's competition law and the fact that both regimes concern anti-competitive business practices, the EEC and the US face many of the same legal and economic questions, such as the definition of abusive or monopolising behaviour and the definition of a restraint or restriction of competition. In many instances the EEC and the US have arrived at much the same answers, for example, with respect to horizontal exchanges of price and cost information and to criteria for membership in a group of competitors or access to a competitively necessary facility.

But many other legal and economic questions have received different answers for several reasons. First, policy considerations or objectives differ. For example, the EEC mother objective of market integration results in stricter rules on vertical territorial restrictions than presently exist under US law. Second, the EEC's notion of 'competition' includes political and social values (like fairness) which are now de-emphasised where not excluded from contemporary US anti-trust analysis. Again, this usually results in stricter EEC rules. Third, there are statutory or textual differences which not only express policy differences but also entail significant differences in enforcement and analysis. For example, the unfortunate bifurcation of Article 85 into paragraph (1) and paragraph (3) grossly complicates, with little or no redeeming virtues, both the formulation and enforcement of specific rules. Fourth, the revolution in US anti-trust law in the last ten years brought about by changes in accepted economic thinking (notably but not exclusively through the ascendancy of the so-called Chicago school of anti-trust thought) has magnified the differences between EEC and US anti-trust.

Policy Differences

EEC market integration goal

The primary goal of EEC competition policy is that of the EEC Treaty itself — the promotion of integration of the separate economies of the Member States into a unified 'common market'. Elimination of private practices that interfere with market integration is the first principle of EEC competition law. There is no analogue in US anti-trust law. This difference reflects the markedly contrasting economic realities where the EEC faces language and cultural differences, multiple currencies, shifting exchange rates, etc. EEC rules are thus stricter with respect to a broad range of agreements and practices, such as territorial restrictions along national boundaries and export bans. Under US law territorial restrictions in distribution agreements or in patent and know-how licences are generally upheld as reasonable unless the supplier enjoys significant market power or the restrictions further resale price maintenance.[2] The EEC market integration goal is also reflected in the types of business behaviour held to constitute an abuse of a dominant position under Article 86. For example, unjustified price disparities in different Member States may constitute an abuse.[3] Again, geographic price discrimination is examined under more tolerant US anti-trust rules.

The integration goal can also result in more permissive EEC rules than their US counterparts. To mitigate the risk that formerly isolated smaller and medium-sized firms may find it difficult to compete successfully with larger firms located both within and outside the Community, the Commission has not only tolerated but actually encouraged certain forms of co-operation among competing small and medium-sized firms. That is, the integration goal predisposes the Commission to accept certain horizontal agreements, especially those involving firms from different Member States, a predisposition unknown in U.S anti-trust law. Thus specialisation agreements that might not pass muster in the US have been approved in the EEC on the basis, among others, that they encourage co-operation and firm integration across Member State boundaries.[4]

The market integration goal not only results in different and generally stricter specific rules than US anti-trust law. The goal also results in a different analysis of certain agreements and practices. The market integration goal frequently prompts the Commission and the Court to condemn a practice without the depth of economic analysis seen in some recent US decisions. The EEC makes no enquiry into market power (effect on interbrand competition) or possible economic justifications or efficiencies before condemning export bans. This failure may reflect the EEC's willingness to sacrifice distribution efficiencies in order to advance market integration, that is, accept possible short-term efficiency losses to achieve perceived long-term gains from a single market. If such a policy judgment has been made, it is not clear from the decisions which rarely even acknowledge the possibility of trade offs between efficiency losses and integration gains.

2 For further discussion of vertical restraints, see below — Vertical Restraints. There are also significant differences between the EEC and the US anti-trust rules governing patent and know-how licensing. These are not examined in this article because of space constraints and not because of their lack of importance. For further discussion of patent and know-how licensing, see B. Hawk, *United States, Common Market and International Antitrust*, chapter 11 (2nd edn 1987).
3 See *United Brands v Commission*, 1978 ECR 207, CCH paragraph 8429. For further discussion, see below — Monopolisation and Abuse of Dominant Position.
Parallel citations of EC Court of Justice and Commission decisions to the Common Market Reporter (CCH) are given where available.
4 See, for example, *Sopelem/Vickers*, OJ L70/47 (13 March, 1978), CCH paragraph 10, 014 (specialisation between British and French microscope manufacturers).

56 THE AMERICAN (ANTI-TRUST) REVOLUTION? — [1988] ECLR

The EEC analysis appears to some observers as inadequate when compared with US anti-trust analysis. In the United States there is no market integration goal underlying anti-trust law and distribution efficiencies are not trumped in this way. Thus US anti-trust analysis lacks the complexity and attendant tensions engendered by the market integration goal. This must be borne in mind when comparing EEC and US anti-trust analysis critically. Indeed, one of the most, if not the most, important issues facing the EEC is how to resolve the tension between the market integration goal and the more traditional 'competition' goals many of which the EEC and United States share.

Contrasting 'competition' policies in the EEC and the US

Both the EEC and the US recognise the promotion of competition as a principal (and in the United States the exclusive) policy objective. There are, however, significant and growing contrasts between the EEC and US laws that result from two differences in the formulation of or what is understood by 'competition' policy. First, non-economic political or social values have always played a larger role in EEC law than in US law. Second, the economics component of competition policy in the two systems now differs considerably given the ascendancy of the Chicago school and the general shift in prevailing economic theories in the United States.

Social and political objectives of anti-trust policy. Social and political values play a far greater role in EEC anti-trust law than in US law. The Commission has stated in several annual reports on competition policy that social and human demands may require modification of results otherwise mandated on purely economic grounds such as allocative efficiency. The most important implication is the rejection of allocative efficiency as the exclusive legal standard or policy objective. At the minimum, distributive concerns (for example, transfer of income from consumers or re-sellers to producers) are included in addition to consumer welfare defined in terms of efficient allocation of resources. Although distributive concerns may be viewed as economic values, they also enjoy a social and political dimension particularly where they are emphasised or used as independent bases (that is, independent from allocative efficiency concerns) to condemn or regulate business practices. Viewed more broadly, however, these non-efficiency EEC policy objectives reflect social or political concerns for individual traders, fairness in the market-place, equality of opportunity for all commercial operators and the legitimate interests of workers, users and consumers.[5] For example, these broader policy concerns are seen in Article 86's

5 See, for example, Commission, Ninth Report on Competition Policy 9 to 11 (1980).

prohibition of dominant firm behaviour that unfairly exploits other traders.[6] A less transparent example is an arrangement's favourable effect on employment. Such an effect may be accepted more readily in the EEC than in the US as justification for a challenged agreement, although employment and labour factors are not unknown in the United States (at least at the prosecutorial as opposed to the adjudicatory stage)[7] and employment effects are rarely discussed in Commission decisions.[8]

EEC policy considerations of fairness, protection of buyers from exploitation and direct regulation of prices and access contrast sharply with current US anti-trust law which emphasises economics (and then only allocative efficiency and not distributive concerns) and protection of competition and not competitors. In the past social and political values have also played prominent roles in the enforcement of US anti-trust law.[9] Since the 1970's, however, US anti-trust has shifted towards a greater emphasis on economics. Indeed, the Justice Department would banish political and social values entirely from anti-trust analysis. Although the Supreme Court has not gone this far, it has clearly retreated from the populist days of the 1960's. Certainly economic values are accorded far greater weight than social or political values as can be seen in several Supreme Court decisions[10] and in the lower courts' increased reluctance to condemn vertical restraints.[11]

6 See below — Monopolisation and Abuse of Dominant Position.
7 For example, see *Lancaster Colony*, Trade Reg. Rep. (CCH) paragraph 21,538 (FTC 1978) (consent decree); *FTC v Weyerhaeuser Co.*, 1981–2 Trade Cas. (CCH) paragraph 64,263 (DC Cir. 1981) (acquisition's creation of employment in a depressed area one factor in affirming a district court's refusal to preliminarily enjoin the acquisition).
8 In *Metro I* the Court opined that employment effects were a consideration in the granting of exemptions under Article 85(3). See *Metro-SB-Grossmarkte GmbH v Commission*, [1977] ECR 1875, CCH paragraph 8435.
9 See, for example, *Brown Shoe Co. v United States*, 370 US 294, 315 to 16 (1962).
10 See *Matsushita Electric Industrial Co. v Zenith Radio Corp.*, 106 S. Ct 1348 (1986); *Continental TV Inc. v GTE Sylvania Inc.*, 433 US 36, 53 n.21 (1977); *National Society of Professional Engineers v United States*, 435 US 679 (1978). *Professional Engineers* held that an agreement among engineers not to negotiate or discuss fees before a prospective client selected an engineer for a particular project violated section 1 of the Sherman Act. The asserted justification for the agreement was that discussion of fees would be contrary to public health, safety and welfare; that is, such discussions before selection would lead to deceptively low bids and would tempt engineers to do inferior work. This was an asserted safety justification for an arrangement that would ordinarily be subject to the per se ban on price fixing. Judge Stevens rejected the safety justification, stating that under the rule of reason the inquiry is confined to consideration of impact on competitive conditions. Invocation of the traditional populist values continues to appear occasionally, particularly in section 7 merger cases. See *Cargill Inc v Montfort of Colorado Inc.*, 104 S.Ct 484 (1986).
11 See below — Vertical Restraints.

As with the market integration goal, the EEC social and political values both result in stricter anti-trust rules than in the United States and introduce far greater complexity into the anti-trust analysis and formulation of anti-trust policy. This situation cannot be expected to change. Social and political values will probably continue to play a more important role in EEC anti-trust law than in US law for several reasons. First, values such as fairness and protection of individual competitors are expressed in the language of the Treaty itself. In the United States open-ended statutes permit considerable cyclical variation in interpretation by the courts and enforcement authorities.[12] Second, centralisation in a single institution — the Commission — of the formulation and execution of different Community policies permits an easier integration of narrower microeconomic competitive concerns like allocative efficiency with broader economic, social and political concerns such as industrial policy and foreign economic policy. Third, it is highly doubtful whether the reasons for abandoning social and political values in US anti-trust law will be found persuasive in the EEC. One reason commonly offered for that abandonment is that predictable anti-trust rules cannot be derived from vague concepts like fairness. Another is that rules derived from fairness concepts frequently mask distributive concerns that in turn reduce or harm allocative efficiency. The latter reason is arguably mooted by the distributive concerns expressed in the text of Articles 85 and 86. The former reason presents a more formidable obstacle to the inclusion of social and political values in a primarily economics-based anti-trust or competition law. As seen below in connection with refusals to deal by dominant firms, fairness considerations tend to be dispositive without any inquiry into whether efficiencies may justify the refusal.[13]

Economic objectives of anti-trust policy. The issues of whether economics provides the exclusive framework for anti-trust law and whose economics are nicely illustrated by the shifts in anti-trust theory in the United States during the last 30 years.

In the late 1950's when EEC anti-trust was in its infancy, US anti-trust law was entering its most expansionary period. This expansion resulted from a convergence of the prevailing economic theory and the prevailing social or political values. The economic theory prevailing at the time was highly distrustful of large firms and concentrated markets. Strong inferences of anti-competitive behaviour and performance were drawn from high market concentration. Significant barriers to entry were generally presumed to exist. Production and distribution efficiencies were either disregarded or in some

12 For a comparison of the US and German anti-trust laws in this respect, see Hawk, Book Review of Maxeiner, *Policy and Methods in German and American Antitrust Law: A Comparative Study*, in 82 Am. J. Intl L. 208 (1988).
13 See below — Monopolisation and Abuse of Dominant Position.

perverse cases affirmatively invoked to invalidate business arrangements such as mergers.[14] This economic theory coincided with political or social populist attitudes that favoured deconcentration of markets, diffusion of economic power, freedom of opportunity for individual traders and freedom of consumer choice.[15] The case law reflected this convergence with broad per se prohibitions of many horizontal and vertical arrangements and strict scrutiny of most agreements and practices, including all types of mergers.

This inhospitality towards private arrangements came under increasing criticism in the 1970's. This criticism rested both on developments in economic theory (the so-called 'new learning') and shifts in political and social values. The principal critics were members of the Chicago school of anti-trust analysis popularised by Bork[16] and Posner,[17] now judges on the federal courts of appeals for the DC and 7th Circuits. In 1981 the Justice Department warmly embraced the Chicago school approach with the accession of William Baxter to the head of the Antitrust Division.[18] The Chicago school, using price theory analysis, de-emphasises market structure, 'concentration', and 'barriers to entry' and makes allocative efficiency the exclusive anti-trust policy objective. Previously accepted political and social values — like protection of small traders and deconcentration of markets as a political end in itself — are rejected. Chicago school adherents generally view barriers to entry as low and assume that potential competitors, suppliers and buyers have perfect information about their profit-making and cost-saving opportunities. They approach market power with a scepticism that more than merely transitory market power exists. They reason that the market has comparative advantages over courts in correcting market imperfections and the effects of anti-competitive and predatory behaviour.[19] The anti-trust policy implications are enforcement limited to traditional cartel behaviour and large horizontal mergers that raise risks of collusion or single firm exercise of market power.

Criticism of the inhospitality tradition was not limited to Chicago school adherents. Economists who did not subscribe to the general Chicago school agenda and premises sorely criticised the courts and enforcement agencies for failing to recognise distribution and production efficiencies, notably transaction cost efficiencies.[20] A growing consensus among most economists counselled a

14 See *FTC v Proctor & Gamble Co. (Clorox)*, 386 US 568 (1967).
15 For one sympathetic summary of these political and social values, see Pitofsky, 'The Political Content of Antitrust', 127 U. Pa L. Rev. 1051 (1979).
16 See R. Bork, *The Antitrust Paradox* (1978).
17 See, for example, R. Posner, *Antitrust Law* (1976).
18 The Federal Trade Commission also embraced the same approach in 1981 with the appointment of James Miller as Chairman.
19 See Easterbrook, 'The Limits of Antitrust', 63 Texas L. Rev. 1 (1984).
20 For example, see Williamson, 'Assessing Vertical Market Restrictions: Antitrust Ramifications of the Transaction Cost Approach', 127 U. Pa L. Rev. 953 (1979).

more permissive position toward many agreements and practices (such as vertical restraints[21] and exercise of intellectual property rights[22]) because of efficiencies and offsetting justifications such as the avoidance of free riding.

These developments in economic theory resulted in significant shifts in the case law.[23] The first dramatic example came in the 1977 Supreme Court decision in *GTE Sylvania*[24] where the Court reversed the *Schwinn* per se rule[25] and held that vertical non-price restrictions are generally subject to the rule of reason, relying expressly on the writings of Chicago school commentators. The Supreme Court has also stated on several occasions in the last ten years that the anti-trust laws are intended to protect competition and not individual competitors[26] and that economic values are accorded predominant if not exclusive weight as compared with social and political values.[27] Lower courts have been increasingly tolerant of vertical restraints,[28] co-operative arrangements and joint ventures among competitors[29] and mergers.[30]

21 In the 1980's this resulted in a reversal of enforcement policy. For example, the Justice Department in 1984 issued Vertical Restraints Guidelines which are quite tolerant of non-price restrictions. 1985 Trade Reg. Rep. (CCH) 687, pt.II. The Justice Department also favours relaxation of the per se ban on resale price maintenance. See amicus brief of the Government in *Monsanto Co. v Spray-Rite Service Corp.*, 465 US 752 (1984). See below — Vertical Restraints.

22 See, for example, Lipsky, 'Current Antitrust Division Views on Patent Licensing Practices', 50 Antitrust L. J. 515 (1981).

23 Although the relaxation of US anti-trust law in the last ten years cannot be attributed entirely to developments in economic theory, much of the case law does reflect those developments. Broader shifts in political concerns are also relevant. See Kaplow, 'Antitrust, Law and Economics, and the Courts', 50 Law & Contemp. Probs. (forthcoming).

24 *Continental TV Inc. v GTE Sylvania Inc.*, 433 US 36 (1977)

25 *United States v Arnold, Schwinn & Co.*, 388 US 365 (1967).

26 See, for example, *Reiter v Sonotone Corp.*, 442 US 330 (1979). Harm to individual firms, competitors and consumers remains relevant, however, in determining whether an unlawful restraint of trade or monopolisation has occurred. See *FTC v Indiana Federation of Dentists*, 106 S. Ct 2009 (1986); *Aspen Skiing Co. v Aspen Highlands Skiing Corp.*, 472 US 585 (1985); *Fishman v Estate of Wirtz*, 807 F.2d 742 (7th Cir. 1986).

27 See, for example, *National Society of Professional Engineers v United States*, 435 US 679 (1978); *Continental TV Inc. v GTE Sylvania Inc.*, 433 US 36 (1977).

28 See, for example, *Valley Liquors, Inc., v Renfield Importers Ltd*, 822 F.2d 656 (7th Cir. 1987); *Assam Drug Co. v Miller Brewing Co.*, 798 F.2d 311 (8th Cir. 1986); *Westman Comm'n Co. v Hobart Int'l Inc.*, 796 F.2d 1216 (10th Cir.1986).

29 See, for example, *National Bancard Corp. v VISA USA*, 779 F.2d 592 (11th Cir. 1986) (price agreements lawful as reasonably ancillary to national credit card system); *Rothery Storage & Van Co. v Atlas Van Lines Inc.*, 792 F.2d 210 (DC Cir. 1986), *cert. denied*, 107 S.Ct 880 (1987) (territorial restrictions lawful as reasonably ancillary to broader arrangement); *Polk Bros Inc. v Forest City Enterprises Inc.*, 776 F.2d 185 (7th Cir. 1985).

30 See, for example, *United States v Siemens Corp.*, 621 F.2d 499 (2d Cir. 1980)

There has been a reaction on both political and economic grounds to some of the so-called new learning described above. Traditionalists argue that the Chicago school's exclusive emphasis on allocative efficiency is an inappropriate political and not economic judgment.[31] Arguments couched in economic terms can mask political values and judgements. Thus it is fair to conclude that the Chicago school assertion of allocative efficiency or 'consumer welfare' in the narrowest sense as the exclusive anti-trust standard does not itself rest on economics but rather on political grounds or on an assessment that predictable and least costly anti-trust rules cannot be derived from non-economic policy considerations. As argued above, the EEC already refuses to chain competition law to allocative efficiency.

More relevant to the EEC is the reaction of economists, lawyers and anti-trust cognoscenti who criticise on purely economic grounds the Chicago school and the 'new learning' of the 1970's and early 1980's. This *nouvelle vague* of critics argues that the Chicago school approach suffers two serious related flaws, among others: it is too static and it unduly assumes information symmetries. According to these critics, traditional price theory which underlies much of the Chicago school analysis may underestimate the dynamic aspects of many business practices, particularly strategic behaviour like price and non-price predation.[32] For example, predation through reputation as a price predator and false signalling of costs may be viable and rational strategies that perhaps should be judged under legal standards different from the cost-based rules accepted or applied by the majority of US courts. As to non-price predation, the *nouvelle vague* of economists argues that predation and exclusion of competitors may be rationally and profitably accomplished through raising rivals' costs.[33] Raising rivals' costs may be more credible than traditional predatory pricing claims for several reasons that avoid Chicago school objections. The strategy does not necessarily impose

(conglomerate merger); *Stroh Brewing Co. v Malmgren*, 1982–1 Trade Cas. (CCH) paragraph 64,670 (W.D. Wis. 1982) (horizontal merger); *United States v Black & Decker Mfg Co.*, 430 F. Supp. 729 (D. Md. 1976) (conglomerate merger).

31 See, for example, Fox, 'The Politics of Law and Economics in Judicial Decision Making: Antitrust as a Window', 61 NYU L. Rev. 554 (1986).

32 See, for example, Hovenkamp, 'Antitrust Policy After Chicago', 84 Mich. L. Rev. 213 (1985); Kaplow, 'Extension of Monopoly Power Through Leverage', 85 Colum. L. Rev. 515 (1985); Krattenmaker & Salop, 'Anticompetitive Exclusion: Raising Rivals' Costs to Achieve Power over Price', 96 Yale L.J. 209 (1986); Williamson, 'Antitrust Enforcement: Where It's Been, Where It's Going', 27 St. Louis U. L.J. 289 (1983). For a spirited defence of the Chicago school approach and an equally spirited counter attack, see respectively Easterbrook, 'Workable Antitrust Policy', 84 Mich. L. Rev. 1696 (1986) and Hovenkamp, 'Rhetoric and Skepticism in Antitrust Argument', 84 Mich. L. Rev. 1722 (1986).

33 See, for example, Krattenmaker & Salop, above Note 32. For discussion and criticism of the raising rivals' costs theory, see Calkins, 'Comments on Presentation of Steven C. Salop', 56 Antitrust L.J.65 (1987).

higher costs on the predator than on the victims and the strategy does not necessarily require a long period of recoupment of the initial investment in the predation strategy.[34] The *nouvelle vague* of criticism, if ultimately accepted, would probably result in stricter anti-trust rules.

What will be the effect on EEC competition policy of the Chicago school 'new learning' and the possible counter-revolution of the *nouvelle vague*? The revolution in US economic thought has already had some effect in the Community in the limited sense that the Commission and the Court of Justice increasingly face arguments and asserted justifications resting on Chicago school analysis and emphases on efficiency considerations. More importantly, the softening in the last several years of the EEC position toward patent and know-how licensing reflects the influence of recent US developments.[35]

However, the Commission, and less certainly the Court, have largely resisted the Chicago school approach and the revolution in US law will not be duplicated in the EEC for several reasons, primarily because the policy and textual differences seen above significantly constrain a complete embrace of the Chicago school. The inclusion of distributive concerns, fairness and other social and political values in EEC competition policy make it almost inconceivable that the Community will ever embrace allocative efficiency as the exclusive policy standard. The market integration goal will continue to trump short-term efficiency arguments; for example, a free rider justification for export bans will not be accepted as a basis for an exemption, at least until the tension or conflict between market integration and short-term distribution efficiencies is addressed.

The time lag in the Community with respect to developments in economic thought on the other side of the Atlantic may prompt the EEC to leapfrog past static price theory analysis to the more dynamic theories about strategic behaviour and predation currently being developed in the United States. Indeed, the Commission's approach to predatory pricing in *ECS/AKZO*[36] evidences a rejection of static cost-based tests, although the decision hardly articulates a theory comparable to those seen in the *nouvelle vague*.

34 See Ordover, 'What the "New Learning" Has to Offer', in ABA Antitrust Section, Antitrust Magazine 5 (July 1987).
35 See B. Hawk, *United States, Common Market and International Antitrust*, ch. 11, (2nd edn 1987). For the contrasting views of two Commission officials in 1982 and 1986, compare Johannes, 'Technology Transfer Under EEC Law — Europe Between the Divergent Opinions of the Past, and the New Administration: A Comparative Law Approach', in 1982 Fordham Corp. L. Inst. 65 (B. Hawk ed. 1983) (strict), with Guttuso, 'Know-How Agreements', in 1986 Fordham Corp. L. Inst. 481 (B. Hawk ed. 1987) (tolerant).
36 OJ L374/1 (31 December, 1985), CCH paragraph 10,748. See below — Monopolisation and Abuse of Dominant Position.

Enforcement Differences

Any comparison of EEC and US anti-trust law must recognise the glaring contrast between the highly centralised EEC enforcement system and the highly decentralised US system.

In the EEC anti-trust enforcement is centralised almost exclusively in the Commission. The Member State role is almost entirely advisory and the Court of Justice provides the only judicial review of Commission decisions, although the proposed court of first instance will bring a welcome intermediate review tribunal.[37] Although private actions for damages in Member State courts are theoretically possible, few have been brought. Thus judicial enforcement is largely limited to the Court of Justice, although actions in Member State courts are growing in importance.

The situation in the United States is completely different. Private actions now play the dominant role outside the merger area. The availability of contingency fees, treble damages and class actions explain the marked difference with the EEC. Justice Department enforcement is now limited to hard-core cartel behaviour (horizontal price fixing and market division) and large horizontal mergers raising risks of collusion or single firm exercise of market power. Federal Trade Commission activity is largely limited to large horizontal mergers and anti-competitive practices encouraged or authorised by state bodies. State anti-trust enforcement is growing because the states perceive that federal enforcement has evaporated. Increased enforcement at the state level, either of the federal anti-trust laws or of state anti-trust laws, would raise many of the constitutional or institutional issues arising in the EEC in connection with the relationship between EEC competition law and Member State competition law.[38]

Considerable differences in procedure also exist. Viewed in extreme terms, the two systems stand in stark contrast. EEC procedures are more informal than those under US anti-trust law. Procedural safeguards and fact-finding protections are not as extensive. The EEC's lack of evidentiary rules, including rules concerning presumptions and burdens of proof, is particularly troublesome. The vertical conspiracy problem points up one of the most important weaknesses in the EEC system — the absence of evidentiary rules and procedures concerning burden of proof.[39] These are particularly crucial where credibility is a major

37 For a discussion of the proposed court's jurisdiction in competition cases, see Temple Lang, 'The Impact of the New Court of First Instance in EEC Antitrust and Trade Cases', in 1987 Fordham Corp. L. Inst. (B. Hawk ed. 1988) (forthcoming).
38 See, for example, Stockmann, 'EEC Competition Law and Member State Competition Laws', in 1987 Fordham Corp. L. Inst. (B. Hawk ed. 1988) (forthcoming).
39 See below — Notion of Agreement in Vertical Arrangements.

factor. The proposed Community court of first instance should introduce needed reforms in these areas.

United States procedures have not been free of criticism, particularly with respect to uncertainty, excessive costs and litigation delays associated with enforcement of US anti-trust law. In 1979 the National Commission to study the anti-trust laws focused on a number of procedural and institutional deficiencies.[40] The recent Georgetown Study examined in some depth private anti-trust actions.[41] Uncertainties in the rules have been particularly marked during the last ten years of transition from the traditional economic and social anti-trust policy objectives to the prevailing ones. For example, the movement away from per se rules to the rule of reason has reduced predictability in the near term, although courts are responding by attempting to formulate structured or truncated rules of reason that are more predictable and less costly.[42]

In sum, both systems reflect cultural and jurisprudential attitudes and both suffer from the excesses of those attitudes. Given the differences in underlying attitudes, there is probably less room for cross-fertilisation in the areas of procedure and enforcement mechanisms than is the case with substantive analysis. The chief exceptions are rules of evidence, allocation of proofs and procedural protections where the EEC might well benefit from a study of the advantages and disadvantages of US anti-trust enforcement.

Restraint of Trade/Restriction of Competition

A major dispute under EEC law concerns the definition of prevention, restriction or distortion of competition under Article 85(1).[43] Many commentators criticise the Commission's penchant to avoid any serious analysis of an agreement's actual competitive harms and benefits (for example effect on prices or output) by finding that 85(1) applies simply on the basis of a restriction on the freedom of

40 See *Report of the National Commission for the Review of Antitrust Laws and Procedures* (1979).

41 See, for example, *Symposium*, 74 Geo. L.J. 999 to 1236 (1986).

42 See below — Restraint of Trade/Restriction of Competition.

43 See, for example, Korah, 'The Rise and Fall of Provisional Validity — The Need for a Rule of Reason in EEC Antitrust', 3 Nw. J. Intl L. & Bus. 320 (1981); Steindorff, 'Article 85 and the Rule of Reason', 21 Common Mkt L. Rev. 639 (1984); Van Houtte, 'A Standard of Reason in EEC Antitrust Law: Some Comments on the Application of Parts 1 and 3 of Article 85', 4 Nw. J. Intl L. & Bus. 4978 (1982).

For a recent debate and contrasting views by a Commission official and by a critic, compare Schroter. 'Antitrust Analysis under Article 85 (1) and (3)', in 1987 Fordham Corp. L. Inst. (B. Hawk ed. 1988) (forthcoming) with Waelbroeck, 'Antitrust Analysis under Article 85(1) and 85(3), in *ibid.*

one of the parties and/or third parties. This debate has significant practical implications and raises questions about the relative importance and roles of the Commission, national courts and anti-trust counsel in the interpretation of Article 85(1).[44] A broad definition of restriction of competition under Article 85(1) shifts most of the inquiry over to Article 85(3) where only the Commission has the power to grant exemptions, thus requiring notification and excluding national courts from the more important part of the anti-trust analysis.[45]

United States anti-trust law is relevant to this debate not only because it may offer useful lessons to the EEC. US anti-trust law has also been made relevant by critics who call for a 'rule of reason' under Article 85(1). As seen below, the long history of the rule of reason in the United States reveals numerous ambiguities and analytical problems many of which US courts have only begun to address. These ambiguities and problems do not argue against a fuller economic inquiry under Article 85(1). They do counsel that the debate about Article 85(1) will produce more heat than light if the participants propose a rule of reason solution without taking the US experience into account.

The United States and the EEC take very different approaches to defining respectively restraint of trade under section 1 of the Sherman Act and restriction of competition under Article 85(1). US courts generally reject restraint on freedom of the parties to a contract or third parties as sufficient to establish a section 1 restraint of trade.[46] The Supreme Court reasons that such a definition would be overly broad and could literally cover most if not all contractual agreements on the reasoning that the contract contains provisions which limit or 'restrict' the freedom of the parties as it existed prior to the contract.[47] An effect

44 See Forrester & Norall, The Laicization of Community Law — Self-Help and the Rule of Reason: How Competition Law Is and Could be Applied, in 1983 Fordham Corp. L. Inst. 305 (B. Hawk ed. 1984).

45 See B. Hawk, above Note 35, at 76 to 87 (2d edn 1987).

46 Foreclosure of competing suppliers or buyers is relevant to the evaluation of many vertical restraints, such as tie-ins and exclusive dealing (exclusive purchase) agreements. The requisite foreclosure is frequently found without an inquiry into actual effects on prices or output. This does not mean, however, that the restriction on freedom concept has been adopted in these cases. Rather it means that effects on prices and output are not the only kinds of anti-competitive effects recognised under section 1's definition of restraint of trade.

47 For example, the Supreme Court has stated:

> There can be no doubt that the challenged practices of the NCAA limitations on, among other things, number of television appearances of each member of defendant association constitute a 'restraint of trade' in the sense that they limit members' freedom to negotiate and enter into their own television contracts. In that sense, however, every contract is a restraint of trade, and . . . the Sherman Act was intended to prohibit only unreasonable restraints of trade.

National Collegiate Athletic Association v Board of Regents of University of Oklahoma, 468 US 85 (1984).

on competition is necessary; harm to the plaintiff or a particular trader is not sufficient. This is clearly accepted. Less clear is what must be proved or is meant by effect on competition. This in turn leads to the US distinction between per se unlawful restraints of trade and agreements subject to the rule of reason under which agreements can be adjudged reasonable or unreasonable. Certain agreements are deemed per se unreasonable restraints of trade under any circumstances on the ground that they almost invariably harm competition through higher prices and reduced output without any redeeming pro-competitive benefits.[48] The list of per se offences has been reduced to price fixing (both horizontal and vertical) and horizontal market division and customer allocation. Boycotts and tie-ins are now per se unlawful only under certain limited conditions.[49] Moreover, some recent decisions indicate an increasing reluctance to condemn as per se unlawful restrictions concerning prices and markets even among competitors where the restrictions are not 'naked' — that is, where they are ancillary to an efficiency-enhancing arrangement.[50] Under the per se rule no inquiry is made into the actual competitive effects of the challenged agreement which is declared unlawful on its face. More specifically, the court does not examine defendant firms' market power, does not define the market (at least not with any precision) and does not evaluate asserted benefits of the agreement. Thus the per se rule provides several advantages, notably predictability of legal rules, provision of a bright-line deterrent to undesirable conduct and reduced judicial and enforcement costs. The per se rule also partially rests on the notion that courts may be inappropriate fora to resolve the complex economic issues involved.

The rule of reason analysis is far more complex and less defined. As 'classically' formulated in 1918 in *Chicago Board of Trade*, an elaborate inquiry must be made, including the history of the industry, the parties' intent, benefits and harms of the challenged practices, etc.[51] This open-ended definition of the rule of reason permits consideration of so-called economic evidence[52] and more traditional evidence such as the intent of the parties. The tests applied under the general rubric of the rule of reason have varied considerably as to the comprehensiveness of the market analysis required. Many decisions formulate the rule of reasón

48 See, for example, *Arizona v Maricopa County Medical Society*, 457 US 332 (1982) (price fixing).

49 See *Northwest Wholesale Stationers v Pacific Stationery & Printing Co.*, 105 S. Ct 2613 (1985) (boycotts); Jefferson Parish Hospital Dist. No. 2 v Hyde, 466 US 2 (1984) (tie-ins).

50 See, for example, *R.C. Dick Geothermal Corp. v Thermogenics Inc.*, 827 F.2d 407 (9th Cir. 1987); *Rothery Storage & Van Co. v Atlas Van Lines Inc.*, 792 F.2d 210 (DC Cir. 1986).

51 *Chicago Board of Trade v United States*, 246 US 231, 238 (1918). See also *Continental TV Inc v GTE Sylvania Inc.* 433 US 36, 49 (1986).

52 See Brunt, 'The Use of Economic Evidence in Antitrust Litigation: Australia', 14 Australian Bus. L. Rev. 261 (1986).

primarily in terms of purpose, effect and less restrictive alternatives.[53] Other decisions speak in terms of benefits and harms, with less or no emphasis on intent or purpose.[54]

Courts continue to struggle with the rule of reason. The shift away from per se rules to rule of reason analyses has intensified this struggle. Much of the doctrinal confusion arises from the Supreme Court's failure to re-examine the rule of reason for many decades. This situation has changed in the last ten years. In 1978 the Court declared that the rule of reason inquiry 'is confined to a consideration of impact on competitive conditions'.[55] Thus health and safety justifications or considerations unrelated to effects on the marketplace would appear irrelevant under the rule of reason.[56] More importantly, the Supreme Court has emphasised that there is frequently no clear bright line between the rule of reason and per se rules.[57] Thus the distinction between a per se rule and the rule of reason has been blurred considerably.

The shift away from per se rules has increased the complexity and costs of litigation and has reduced legal certainty. This has prompted courts, commentators and the Justice Department [58] to formulate truncated rules of reason which obviate the necessity of the court engaging in an elaborate market analysis in every case. In most cases this has worked in favour of defendants. For example, many lower courts use market power as a filter and dismiss rule of reason claims before trial where plaintiff fails to show that defendant(s) has significant market power.[59] However, the most recent two Supreme Court decisions to apply a quick look or truncated rule of reason affirmed that the challenged agreements were unreasonable.[60] In so doing, the Court held that plaintiff does not have to

53 See, for example, *Broadcast Music Inc. v Columbia Broadcasting System*, 441 US 1 (1979).
54 See, for example, *National Collegiate Athletic Association v Board of Regents of University of Oklahoma*, 468 US 85 (1984); *Rothery Storage & Van Co. v Atlas Van Lines Inc.*, 792 F.2d 210 (DC Cir. 1986).
55 *National Society of Professional Engineers v United States*, 435 US 679 (1978). See also *FTC v Indiana Federation of Dentists*, 106 S.Ct 2009 (1986).
56 Despite this statement, some lower courts since *Professional Engineers* have been reluctant to dismiss health and safety considerations entirely.
57 See, for example, *National Collegiate Athletic Association v Board of Regents of University of Oklahoma*, 468 US 85 (1984).
58 See, for example, *Ball Memorial Hospital Inc v Mutual Hospital Insurance Inc.*, 784 F.2d 1325 (7th Cir. 1986); *United States v Realty Multi-List Inc.*, 629 F.2d 1351 (5th Cir. 1980); P. Areeda, Antitrust Law 361 (1986); Easterbrook, *The Limits of Antitrust*, 63 Texas L. Rev. 1 (1984); Justice Department amicus brief in *National Collegiate Athletic Association v Board of Regents of University of Oklahoma*, 468 US 85 (1984).
59 See, for example, *R.C. Dick Geothermal Corp. v Thermogenics Inc.*, 827 F.2d 407 (9th Cir. 1987); *Rothery Storage & Van Co. v Atlas Van Lines Inc.*, 792 F.2d 210 (DC Cir. 1986); *Valley Liquors Inc v Renfield Importers Ltd*, 822 F.2d 656 (7th Cir. 1987).
60 *FTC v Indiana Federation of Dentists*, 106 S.Ct 2009 (1986); *National Collegiate Athletic Association v Board of Regents of University of Oklahoma*, 468 US 85 (1984).

prove defendant's market power (or probably define the relevant market) under certain not entirely clear circumstances.

In *NCAA* the Court refused to apply a per se rule to certain provisions in an agreement between an association of universities and television networks concerning the telecasts of college football games. The contracts imposed, among other things, limitations on the number of televised appearances by one school during the season and an absolute maximum on the number of televised games. The contracts also provided for minimum aggregate compensation which resulted in each school receiving the same fee for each national or regional television appearance. Several popular football powers challenged the restrictions. The Court held first that although agreements among competitors to restrict output are ordinarily subject to a per se rule, this was inappropriate because some restrictions were essential in order that the product (televised college football) be available at all. The Court went on to apply a truncated or 'quick look' rule of reason analysis under which the agreements were found to constitute unreasonable restraints of trade.

In applying its truncated rule of reason, the Court first found anti-competitive effects notably restrictions on output, higher prices and limitation of consumer choice. The Court then stated that no inquiry into market power is required where the challenged practice is a 'naked' restraint (that is, without redeeming competitive benefits). Finally, if anti-competitive effects are proved (and market power in the case of a non-naked restraint), then defendants bear a heavy burden of establishing competitive benefits as an affirmative defence — a burden that was not met.[61]

A truncated rule of reason was also made in *Dentists* where the Court upheld a Federal Trade Commission decision that an agreement by dentists not to provide x-rays to third party insurers as part of a fee review system was unreasonable. A per se rule was rejected on the grounds that the courts are slow to condemn rules of professional associations and the impact of the challenged practice was not immediately obvious. Under the rule of reason the Court asked first whether plaintiff had proved actual anti-competitive effects. The Court affirmed the finding of actual harms, although it emphasised primarily the limitation on consumer choice and the possible future effect on insurance premiums and

61 The Court rejected four asserted justifications: (1) there were no pro-competitive efficiencies in that the television plan did not enhance the competitiveness of college football; (2) the restrictions were not necessary to penetrate the market because college football had no competition; (3) the argument that the restrictions were necessary to protect live attendance at games was not proved and rejected in principle because it rested on the impermissible premises that competition between television and live attendance was undesirable; (4) the argument that the restrictions were necessary to maintain competitive balance among the teams was accepted in principle but held not proved.

medical cost-containment programmes.[62] The Court declared further that no elaborate inquiry into market power was necessary both on the *NCAA* rationale that the refusal was a 'naked' restraint and on a more persuasive rationale — that is, market power and market definition are relevant to determine whether conduct has the potential for causing genuine harm; if actual harms have been otherwise proved, then it is unnecessary to inquire into market power. Finally, the Court held that no efficiency-enhancing benefits or other justifications had been proved.[63]

Two principal conclusions can be drawn about the recent US decisions. First, the line between the per se rule and the rule of reason is increasingly blurred with courts applying 'quick look' per se rules and 'quick look' rules of reason.[64] Second, the major issue in the cases surrounds the circumstances in which inquiry into market power and market definition can be avoided. This issue is frequently addressed in the context of interpreting the Supreme Court opinions in *NCAA* and *Dentists*, particularly the definition of 'naked' restraint and the question whether 'naked' restraints are the only exception to the rule that market power (and market definition) are essential elements of the rule of reason analysis. These questions are often dispositive in cases involving horizontal restraints where characterisation of the challenged provision as not 'naked' may defeat plaintiff's claim where defendants lack market power.[65] Non-price vertical restraints are usually viewed as ancillary or non-'naked' and thus lack of the supplier's market power will preclude a finding of unreasonableness.[66]

Despite the ambiguities seen above, the struggle to refine the test for a restraint of trade under US law nevertheless compares favourably with the near anarchy under Article 85 engendered by inconsistent Commission and Court interpretations of restriction of competition under Article 85(1) and the bifurcation of what ideally should be a single anti-trust analysis into the double tests of Article 85(1) and Article 85(3). This *maudite* bifurcation presents a more serious obstacle to predictable and coherent rules than the current doctrinal confusion in the United States which may be a transitional phenomenon.

62 These 'anti-competitive' effects were more indirect and more uncertain than those proved in *NCAA*. At the least the Court in *Dentists* did not require plaintiff to establish significant effects on prices or output as is often suggested by Chicago school theorists. Indeed, the Court expressly stated that the FTC's failure to prove that higher prices resulted from the challenged practice was no defence.
63 The Court rejected a quality care justification in principle and as unproved.
64 For a decision applying a quick look per se rule to condemn a practice, see *General Leaseways Inc. v National Truck Leasing Association*, 744 F.2d 588 (7th Cir. 1984).
65 See, for example, *R.C. Dick Geothermal Corp. v Thermogenics Inc.*, 827 F.2d 407 (9th Cir. 1987); *Rothery Storage & Van Co. v Atlas Van Lines Inc.*, 792 F.2d 210 (DC Cir. 1986), *cert. denied*, 107 S.Ct 880 (1987); *Polk Bros Inc. v Forest City Enterprises Inc.*, 776 F.2d 185 (7th Cir. 1985).
66 See below – Vertical Restraints.

70 THE AMERICAN (ANTI-TRUST) REVOLUTION? — [1988] ECLR

The Commission frequently takes a radically broad view of what constitutes a restriction of competition within the meaning of Article 85(1). The emphasis in the Commission's reasoning, albeit not an exclusive one, is on interference with or limitation on freedom of either the parties to the agreement and/or of third parties. This position was taken early on[67] and this emphasis on limitation of freedom continues to appear in Commission decisions.[68] Under the restriction of freedom rationale, Article 85(1) captures a large number of agreements that raise little or no competitive concern in terms of price or output effects. Moreover, the restriction of freedom rationale provides the Commission with an extraordinarily wide discretionary tool to determine the applicability of Article 85(1). This effectively shifts most of the market analysis (that is, analysis of actual competitive harms and benefits) from Article 85(1) to Article 85(3).

The Court of Justice's interpretations of Article 85(1) are also not entirely consistent. The Court has not accepted unequivocally the restriction on freedom notion. The Court has declared in a growing number of judgements that certain provisions and obligations fall outside Article 85(1) even though freedom of the parties to the agreement or of third parties was clearly 'restrained' in any normal sense of the term.[69] The Court appears more willing than the Commission to require under Article 85(1) an inquiry into actual anti-competitive effects of a challenged agreement. However, such an inquiry has not always been required under Article 85(1).

In some judgments the Court adopts what might be termed the 'inherency' approach. Under this approach the overall arrangement is examined in the abstract to determine whether competitive *benefits* result. If so, then restrictions and obligations fall outside Article 85(1) where they are deemed 'inherent' to this arrangement. The inherency approach effectively operates as a per se rule of legality. For example, in *Metro I* the Court stated that Article 85(1) does not apply to selective distribution systems in which dealers are selected on the basis of

67 See, for example, *Consten & Grundig v Commission*, [1966] ECR 429, CCH paragraph 8046.

68 For example, foreclosure of competing suppliers and dealers resulting from an exclusive dealing contract has been described as a restriction of freedom of choice. See, for example, *Hennessy-Henkell*, OJ L 383/11 (31 December 1980), CCH paragraph 10,283. Agreements among competitors, such as joint purchasing, have also been held within Article 85(1) on the ground that freedom of choice of the members to purchase outside the joint venture was restricted. See, for example, *National Sulphuric Acid Association*, OJ L 260/24 (3 October 1980), CCH paragraph 10,246.

69 In *Société Technique Minière* the Court stated as early as 1966 that an exclusive distributorship agreement does not fall automatically within Article 85 (1) but that an analysis of the market and anti-competitive effects must be made before Article 85(1) can be found to apply. *Société Technique Minière v Maschinenbau Ulm GmbH*, [1966] ECR 429, CCH paragraph 8046.

qualitative objective criteria, non-discriminatorily applied, relating to the technical qualifications of the dealer and its staff and the suitability of its trading premises.[70] Similarly, in *Pronuptia* the Court declared that certain restrictions and obligations fall outside Article 85(1) because they are inherent in distribution franchises in the sense that they are necessary to achieve the two legitimate objectives of franchise systems.[71] The Court in *Pronuptia* engaged in little or no market analysis; that is, no reference was made to structural conditions (such as seller concentration, entry barriers or interbrand competition) or to actual anti-competitive effects.[72] This failure to inquire into the actual effects of the particular provisions at issue is partially explained by the procedural posture of the case, that is, the Court was simply answering questions referred to it by the national court.

The Court has also used an ancillary restraints approach under which restrictions and obligations fall outside Article 85(1) where they are reasonably necessary to achieve the purposes of a broader lawful arrangement.[73] The Commission also used an ancillary restraints approach to find that several provisions in a joint venture fell outside Article 85(1).[74] A series of decisions in the banking sector illustrate the Commission's ancillary restraints approach to pricing provisions which are part of larger exempted arrangements.[75] The

70 *Metro SB-Grossmarkte GmbH & Co. KG v Commission*, [1977] ECR 1875, CCH paragraph 8435. This statement cannot be explained on the basis of the freedom of choice notion, for the freedom of business choice of both parties (the selected dealers) and third parties (non-approved dealers) is restrained even by objective qualitative criteria in a selective distribution system. The Court declared simply that its conclusion that the qualitative selection distribution system did not fall within Article 85(1) was based on the nature of the products involved.
71 *Pronuptia de Paris GmbH v Schillgalis*, [1986] ECR 374, CCH paragraph 14,245.
72 In this respect *Pronuptia* is inconsistent with the trend toward an emphasis on interbrand competition in Commission and Court decisions dealing with other forms of distribution, particularly selective distribution.
73 The best example is the Court's judgment in *Remia BV v Commission*, [1985] ECR 2545, CCH paragraph 14,217 (covenant not to compete ancillary to sale of business).
74 *Mitchell Cotts/Sofiltra*, OJ L41/31 (11 February 1987), CCH paragraph 10,852.
75 In 1984 the Commission exempted a series of agreements concerning the international use and clearing of eurocheques. *Uniform Eurocheques*, OJ L 35/43 (7 February 1985), CCH paragraph 10,651. Two pricing provisions were found to fall within Article 85(1): foreign banks cashing the checks received a standard commission and no commission could be charged at the time of encashment by the foreign cashier or retailer. These two provisions were exempted on the ground, among others, that they were indispensable to attain the beneficial objectives of the overall system. For a US decision reaching the same result on much the same facts, see *National Bancard Corp. v VISA USA Inc.*, 779 F.2d 592 (11th Cir.), *cert. denied*, 107 S. Ct 329 (1986). In 1986 the Commission examined an entire range of agreements concluded within the national banking associations of Belgium, Ireland and Italy. *Belgische Vereniging der Banken/Association Belge des Banques*, OJ L 7/27

ancillary restraints approach differs from the inherency approach. Unlike the inherency approach the ancillary restraints approach does not operate as a rule of per se legality; rather a restriction is judged reasonable or unreasonable under the particular facts.

What lessons can the EEC draw from the recent US developments under section 1? The answer is mostly pessimistic because of the statutory differences, notably the bifurcation of Article 85.

First, Court of Justice judgments should not be too hastily characterised as embodying a US rule of reason analysis. Judgments like *Metro I*, *Maize Seed* and *Pronuptia* do indicate that the Court in an undefined set of cases requires an analysis broader than the Commission's restraint of freedom rationale. But despite the praise by many European commentators of recent Court of Justice judgments as introducing the 'rule of reason' into Article 85(1),[76] those judgments differ significantly from either the classic *Chicago Board of Trade* test or the truncated rule of reason articulated in *NCAA* and *Dentists*. Most US decisions require at the minimum inquiry into actual competitive harms and benefits, as well as definition of the relevant market and determination of defendants' market power (for example, amount of interbrand competition). The EEC judgments contrast with those US decisions requiring significant market power as a necessary condition of unreasonableness. Failure to recognise these differences worsens rather than advances the debate about the proper scope of Article 85(1).

Second, the bifurcation of Article 85 is the principal cause of the confusion about the definition of a restriction of competition under Article 85(1). Much of the analysis under the US rule of reason is reserved in the EEC for the exemption stage under Article 85(3). This results both from the differences in statutory structure and from the Commission's overly broad interpretation of Article 85(1). But the statutory difference is probably the more important, for it requires some analysis under Article 85(3) no matter how much flexibility or 'reason' one puts into Article 85(1). One possible way to reduce the present confusion in the EEC would be a unified analysis either through amendment of the Treaty (which is politically unlikely) or through amendment of Regulation 17 so as to grant national courts the competence to determine whether the Article 85(3) conditions

(9 January 1987), CCH paragraph 10,847; *Irish Banks' Standing Committee*, OJ L 295/28 (18 October 1986), CCH paragraph 10,829; *ABI*, OJ L 43/51 (13 February 1987), CCH paragraph 10,846. The decisions concerned primarily technical co-operation arrangements among banks. Pricing and analogous provisions were also discussed and some light is shed on the Commission's position toward ancillary pricing provisions. See B. Hawk above, Note 35, at ch. 8.

76 Several commentators have hailed *Pronuptia* as evidencing a rule of reason under Article 85(1). See Goebel, 23 Common Mkt. L. Rev. 683 (1986); Venit, 'Pronuptia: Ancillary Restraints – or Unholy Alliances', 11 Eur. L. Rev. 213 (1986). Korah is more circumspect. See Korah, 'Pronuptia – Franchising, The Marriage of Reason and The EEC Competition Rules', 8 Eur. Intell. Prop. Rev. 99 (1986).

for an individual exemption are met. The risk with the latter solution is possible interference with a uniform implementation of Community policies and interests which may require centralised competence in the Commission to the exclusion of the national courts. In sum, the underlying policy issue is whether the lack of intellectual coherence and the attendant potential loss of credibility in the EEC competition legal regime resulting from the present state of affairs poses a greater risk to the Community than devolution of the exemption power to the national courts.

Third, the EEC might well profit from the US emphasis on presumptions and allocations of proof in the recent analyses under section 1. The proposed court of first instance is in a well-placed and timely position to examine these issues.

Vertical Restraints

During the last 20 years the US and EEC positions towards vertical practices have altered courses considerably. In the late 1960's the US position was very strict. Today United States courts and enforcement agencies have become very tolerant toward vertical restraints (with the exception of resale price maintenance (RPM)). The history in the EEC is more complex. Vertical restraints that interfere with market integration, such as export bans and certain territorial restrictions, have been and continue to be condemned. Many other non-price vertical restraints, such as selective distribution and franchise agreements, are now viewed more tolerantly. Resale price maintenance remains prohibited in both systems.

In 1968 the Supreme Court ruled in *United States v Arnold, Schwinn & Co.* that territorial and customer restrictions on the resale (as opposed to consignment) of products was subject to a per se ban.[77] In 1977 the Court expressly overruled *Schwinn* in *Continental TV Inc. v GTE Sylvania Inc.* holding that non-price territorial and customer restrictions are subject to the rule of reason.[78] Since *GTE Sylvania* most territorial and customer restrictions have been upheld as reasonable. They have been found unlawful only where used to reinforce RPM or where the supplier enjoys significant market power. The former exception results from the still viable per se ban on RPM. The latter exception reflects the emphasis on interbrand competition as the focus of the inquiry on anti-competitive effects. Vertical restraints are also unlawful where a supplier or dealer cartel is proved.

The Reagan Administration has been very tolerant towards all types of vertical restraints, including resale price maintenance. The Justice Department argued in 1983 that the rule of reason should be applied to RPM.[79] In 1985 the Justice

77 388 US 365 (1967).

78 433 US 36 (1977).

79 See Amicus brief filed in *Monsanto Co. v Spray-Rite Service Corp.*, 465 US 752 (1984).

74 THE AMERICAN (ANTI-TRUST) REVOLUTION? — [1988] ECLR

Department issued Vertical Restraints Guidelines which declare per se lawful selective distribution, primary responsibility clauses, location clauses and profit passover clauses.[80] The Guidelines also articulate permissive standards to determine the reasonableness of exclusive distributorships, territorial and customer restrictions, exclusive dealing and tie-ins. Counter guidelines, setting forth far stricter tests, have been issued by the National Association of State Attorneys General.

This change in judicial and enforcement attitude results from shifts in economic theory which now emphasises distribution efficiencies that vertical restraints may bring. Vertical restraints are said to promote consumer welfare by reducing costs. The prevailing economic theory also assumes a communality of interest between suppliers and consumers. Supra-competitive prices by intermediate resellers are said to harm the supplier by reducing sales, with the resellers capturing any monopoly profits. The supplier wants the most efficient distribution of its products with the lowest retail prices for the combination of goods and services.

The most frequently asserted justification of many vertical restraints is the free-rider rationale. For example, territorial restrictions may prevent a lower-priced dealer from taking a free ride on the services offered by a higher-priced competitor, with the effect of deterring such services and ultimately depriving the consumer of this benefit. Although the free rider rationale and the economic premises of the laissez-faire school of vertical restraints have been challenged by some economists,[81] the majority of recent US decisions reflect the premises of that school.

EEC law stands in stark contrast. The EEC's prohibition of vertical agreements having the purpose or effect of isolating national markets distinguishes EEC from US law. There has always been and continues to be a per se-like rule with respect to *absolute* territorial restrictions along Member State boundaries. In the last several years, the Commission has also taken a stricter position toward some vertical restraints, notably exclusive distributorships, selective distribution and exclusive purchase or dealing agreements. This stricter position is reflected both in individual decisions and in the replacement block exemptions for Regulation 67/67 — Regulations 1983/83 and 1984/83.

The strict Commission position towards vertical restraints has been criticised

80 50 Fed. Reg. 6263 (1985).

81 See, for example, Comanor, 'Vertical Price-Fixing, Vertical Market Restrictions, and the New Antitrust Policy', 98 Harv. L. Rev. 983 (1985); Flynn, 'The "Is" and "Ought" of Vertical Restraints After *Monsanto Co. v Spray-Rite Service Corp.*', 71 Cornell L. Rev. 1095 (1986); Pitofsky, 'In Defence of Discounters: The No-Frills Case for a Per Se Rule Against Vertical Price Fixing', 71 Geo L.J. 1487 (1983); See generally Hay, 'The Free Rider Rationale and Vertical Restraints Analysis Reconsidered', 56 Antitrust L.J. 27 (1987).

by many commentators.[82] Critics assert that the EEC's predominant emphasis on intrabrand competition and the market integration goal sacrifices distribution efficiencies and harms interbrand competition. For example, free riding may be encouraged by the EEC's requirement or protection of parallel imports.[83]

The effect of the market integration goal and the continuing governmental and private barriers to trade between Member States makes EEC competition policy toward vertical restraints radically different from US anti-trust policy. One should not expect that the prevailing economic doctrine in the United States will bring about the *volte face* seen in US case law. The free rider rationale does not have the same influence in the EEC, at least where parallel imports are concerned. Moreover, the risk that vertical restraints may facilitate undetected and undetectable dealer or supplier cartels may be greater in the EEC where tacit collusion may be more common than in the United States.[84] None the less, resolution of the tensions between vertical efficiencies and interbrand competition on the one hand and market integration and distributive concerns on the other remains one of the most important issues in EEC anti-trust law.[85] The economics literature in the United States may provide the EEC with useful sources in attempting to achieve that resolution. The US case law will probably be less useful given the absence of the market integration goal in the United States.

Notion of Agreement in Vertical Arrangements

Article 85, like section 1 of the Sherman Act, requires the showing of an 'agreement' or 'concerted' practice. Horizontal agreements or concerted practices should be distinguished from vertical ones. The determination whether a concerted practice or agreement exists raises evidentiary and allocation of proof problems in essentially vertical situations significantly different from those seen where the parties compete at the same level. General definitions of agreements or

82 See, for example, Chard, 'The Economics of the Application of Article 85 to Selective Distribution Systems', 7 Eur. L. Rev. 83 (1982); Korah, 'Group Exemptions for Exclusive Distribution and Purchasing in the EEC', 21 Common Mkt. L. Rev. 53 (1984); Van Bael, 'Heretical Reflections on the Basis Dogma of EEC Antitrust: Single Market Integration', 8 Swiss Rev. International Competition L. 39 (1980).
83 See Gyselen, 'Vertical Restraints in the Distribution Process: Strength and Weakness of the Free Rider Rationale under EEC Competition Law', 21 Common Mkt. L. Rev. 647 (1984).
84 See Waelbroeck, 'Vertical Agreements: Is the Commission Right Not to Follow Current US Policy?', 25 Swiss Rev. International Competition L. 45, 49 (1985).
85 See Collins, 'Efficiency and Equity in Vertical Competition Law: Balancing the Tensions in the EEC and the United States', in 1983 Fordham Corp. L. Inst. 501 (B. Hawk ed. 1984).

concerted practices formulated in purely horizontal cases should not be blindly applied in mixed or purely vertical cases.

The US law on vertical agreements is in such a sorry state of confusion that the best lessons to be learned concern the pitfalls to be avoided. The principal reason for the disarray is the introduction of the *Colgate* doctrine[86] into an already highly complex area. Under *Colgate* a supplier has the right unilaterally to refuse to deal in the sense that it may announce in advance the terms and conditions on which it will supply (including recommended resale prices) and refuse to deal or cut off resellers not complying with those terms and conditions.[87] Any additional conduct probably takes the case out of the *Colgate* doctrine; for example, use of wholesalers and retailers to police a resale price maintenance system. Independent evidence of an agreement between the supplier and complaining dealer(s) ('vertical' conspiracy) or among complaining dealers themselves (horizontal dealers' cartel) excludes the *Colgate* doctrine because the refusal to deal is no longer 'unilateral'. The *Colgate* doctrine rests on two not entirely consistent bases: (1) the policy judgment that a general duty to deal should not be imposed on non-monopolists; and (2) the absence of an agreement. The latter causes the confusion because an 'agreement' would typically be inferred from the facts or conduct falling within the *Colgate* doctrine.

The resultant confusion is nicely illustrated in the courts'attempts to formulate the standard of proof necessary to establish that a supplier's refusal to deal or termination of a dealer was pursuant to an 'agreement' or not. The latest Supreme Court pronouncement came in *Monsanto Co. v Spray-Rite Service Corp.*[88] The Court stressed that it is crucial to distinguish unilateral action on non-price restrictions (which is evaluated under the rule of reason according to *Sylvania*) and price fixing arrangements (which are subject to per se treatment and treble damages). For a plaintiff to meet the burden of proving a vertical price fixing conspiracy, there 'must be evidence that tends to exclude the possibility that the manufacturer and nonterminated distributors were acting independently'.[89] In order to protect the policies underlying the *Sylvania* and *Colgate* doctrines, plaintiffs must establish more than the fact that termination came in response to distributor complaints. Otherwise, legitimate non-price restrictions or unilateral action might be deterred or penalised. Thus, the Court held that there must be 'direct or circumstantial evidence that reasonably tends to prove that the

86 *United States v Colgate & Co.*, 250 US 300 (1919).
87 *Russell Stover Candies Inc v FTC*, 718 F.2d 256 (8th Cir. 1983).
88 465 US 752 (1984).
89 *Ibid.* at 764.

manufacturer and others had a conscious commitment to a common scheme designed to achieve an unlawful objective'.[90]

Lower courts have applied the *Monsanto* standard in a number of cases, frequently with the result of summary judgment or pre-trial dismissal of the dealer termination claim.[91] In 1987 the Supreme Court granted *certiorari* to review the vertical conspiracy issue once again.[92]

The vertical conspiracy puzzle has appeared in EEC decisions, notably in connection with discriminatory use of facially neutral selective distribution systems to impede parallel imports and penalise price discounters and refusals to deal outside such systems in order to impede parallel imports.[93] For example, in *Ford Werke AG* the Court declared that a refusal to deal was not unilateral because it formed part of the contractual relations between Ford and its dealers.[94] The Court could have avoided this broad and somewhat strained definition of a concerted practice by affirming the Commission's denial of an exemption on the ground that the Commission may properly impose conditions on the granting of an exemption, including the doing or non-doing of unilateral action. Moreover, the finding of a horizontal agreement among the complaining British Ford dealers appears more plausible. Absent such a dealers' cartel, a US court would probably not have found the requisite agreement under the facts presented by the Commission to the Court in *Ford Werke AG*.

The vertical conspiracy problem points up one of the most glaring weaknesses in EEC competition law — the absence of evidentiary rules and procedures concerning allocation of proof. These are particularly crucial where credibility is a major issue, as in many dealer termination cases. The proposed Community court of first instance might introduce needed reforms in these areas.

90 *Ibid.* quoting *Edward J. Sweeney & Sons, Inc. v Texaco, Inc.*, 637 F.2d 105, 111 (3d Cir. 1980), *cert. denied*, 451 US 911 (1981). See *Matsushita Elec. Indus. Co. v Zenith Radio Corp.*, 106 S. Ct 1348 (1986) (summary judgment granted to defendant Japanese manufacturers on claims that they conspired to engage in predatory pricing to eliminate US competitors).

91 Compare the following decisions: *Lomar Wholesale Grocery Inc.* v *Dieter's Gourmet Foods Inc.*, 824 F.2d 582 (8th Cir. 1987); *Valley Liquors Inc. v Renfield Importers Ltd.* 822 F.2d 656 (7th Cir. 1987); OSC Corp. v Apple Computer Inc., 792 F.2d 1464 (9th Cir. 1986).

92 *Business Electronics Corp. v Sharp Electronics Corp.*, 780 F.2d 1212 (5th Cir. 1986). *cert. granted*, 107 S. Ct 3182 (1987).

93 *AEG-Telefunken v Commission*, [1983] ECR 3151, CCH paragraph 14,018. For further discussion, see B. Hawk, above Note 35, at 393 to 400.

94 *Ford-Werke AG v Commission*, [1985] ECR 2725, at paragraphs 14 to 26 CCH paragraph 14,144.

Monopolisation and Abuse of Dominant Position

Statutory differences

The monopolisation offence under section 2 of the Sherman Act and the abuse of dominant position provisions under Article 86 are similar in that both require substantial market power ('monopoly power' or 'dominant position') and anti-competitive or undesirable behaviour ('monopolising' or 'exclusionary' conduct or 'abuse'). Article 86, unlike section 2, sets forth a non-exhaustive list of abuses. This greater specificity of Article 86 provides more guidance to and constraints on the Commission and the EEC courts than exist in US law.

Contrasts in policy considerations and definitions of abusive or monopolising behaviour

The revolution in US anti-trust law described in section I also resulted in courts adopting a more sceptical attitude towards monopolisation claims. Some lower court decisions evidence an attitude that many business strategies that increase market share at the expense of rivals may help rather than harm consumers through efficiencies.[95] However, the almost exclusive emphasis on protection of competition and away from protection of competitors has been less important in monopolisation cases than it has been in other anti-trust cases. This is most clearly true if protection of competition is taken to mean that allocative efficiency is the exclusive anti-trust standard or value. The Supreme Court may be less willing than many of the lower courts to embrace efficiency as the sole standard or value in monopolisation cases[96] or anti-trust cases generally.[97] Harms to individual competitors and customers were considered by the Supreme Court in *Aspen*.[98] The Court affirmed a jury verdict of unlawful monopolisation where the defendant dominant firm discontinued dealing with the plaintiff-competitor without any accepted business justification. The Court described the requisite monopolising conduct as 'exclusionary', 'anti-competitive' or 'predatory'.[99] And

95 See, for example, *Berkey Photo Inc. v Eastman Kodak Co.*, 603 F.2d 263 (2d Cir. 1979), *cert. denied*, 444 US 1093 (1980); *Transamerica Computer Co. v IBM Corp.*, 698 F.2d 1377 (9th Cir.), *cert denied*, 464 US 955 (1983); *California Computer Prods v IBM Corp.*, 613 F.2d 727 (9th Cir. 1979).
96 See *Aspen Skiing Co. v Aspen Highlands Skiing Corp.*, 472 US 585 (1985).
97 See *FTC v Indiana Federation of Dentists*, 106 US 2009 (1986). But see *Matsushita Elec. Industrial Co. v Zenith Radio Corp.*, 106 S. Ct 1348 (1986).
98 *Aspen Skiing Co. v Aspen Highlands Skiing Corp.*, 472 US 585 (1985).
99 The Court also quoted Areeda and Turner's definition as conduct which (1) tends to impair opportunities of rivals, and (2) does not further competition on the merits or does so in an unnecessarily restrictive way. *Ibid.* at n.33, quoting P. Areeda & D. Turner, 3 Antitrust Law 78 (1978).

despite criticisms by many commentators and judges, courts continue to rely on evidence of defendant's intent to determine whether unlawful monopolisation has occurred.[100] Harm to consumer welfare may not be a necessary condition for unlawful monopolisation, because section 2 is also concerned with the competitive process and effects on competitive rivals.[101] Moreover, a *nouvelle vague* of economists is attempting to formulate dynamic, strategic-oriented economic theories to support claims of predation and other monopolistic behaviour.[102] In sum, the pendulum may be swinging again, that is, away from judicial scepticism toward monopolisation claims (which itself was a reaction against earlier decisions perceived as too strict).

Section 2 policy objectives are less defined than those under Article 86. It is safe to conclude, however, that the section 2 policies are probably narrower than those under Article 86. Many Article 86 policies are inconsistent with the efficiency orientation of section 2 seen in much of the recent US case law.

Three policy considerations can be gleaned from the text of Article 86 and from the Court of Justice's judgments. Two of those policy considerations play no role under section 2 — market integration and fairness. The third is less of a policy consideration than an attribute of Article 86 jurisprudence — the regulatory notion, that is, the tendency to use Article 86 to regulate directly dominant firms' prices and output. This notion plays a far lesser role, and in some cases no role whatsoever, under section 2. The Article 86 policy considerations of fairness and market integration and its regulatory notion prompt the EEC to characterise as an abuse conduct that would be viewed either neutrally or even favourably under section 2 because of the conduct's efficiency effects. These differences in policy considerations make particularly hazardous general critiques of Article 86 jurisprudence based on section 2 case law. Of course, the burgeoning economics literature remains highly relevant on both sides of the Atlantic.

The market integration goal is reflected in abuses involving discrimination against nationals of another Member State,[103] abuses perceived to have the effect

100 See, for example, *Aspen Skiing Co. v Aspen Highlands Skiing Corp.*, 472 US 585 (1985). Cf. *General Industries Corp. v Hartz Mountain Corp.*, 810 F.2d 795 (8th Cir. 1987) (intent heavily relied on to affirm jury verdict of attempt to monopolise). But see *Ball Memorial Hospital Inc v Mutual Hosp Insurance Inc.*, 784 F.2d 1325 (7th Cir. 1986) (intent accorded little weight).

101 For an excellent discussion of this issue, see *Fishman v Estate of Wirtz*, 807 F.2d 520 (7th Cir. 1986).

The more permissive position of US courts and enforcement agencies also rests in part on the policy premise that the consumer and the public interest are best protected by respect for freedom of action of private firms. This premise is not shared to the same extent in the EEC where Article 86 is interpreted as giving rise to strong presumptions that dominant firm conduct with exclusionary tendencies is contrary to consumer interest.

102 See above – Policy Differences.

103 See, for example, *GVL v Commission*, [1983] ECR 483, CCH paragraph 8910; *GEMA*, OJ L 134/15 (20 June 1971), CCH paragraph 9438.

of export bans or limitations on parallel imports,[104] and abuses involving unjustified price disparities among Member States.[105]

The second Article 86 policy consideration is fairness and protection of suppliers and buyers from dominant firms. Example (a) speaks of unfair trading conditions and example (c) speaks of discriminatory pricing that places disfavoured trading partners at a competitive disadvantage. Thus geographic price discrimination[106] and refusals to predisclose competitive information to competitors can constitute abuses under some circumstances.[107] In the United States primary line price discrimination (injury to competitors) constitutes unlawful monopolisation only where injury to competition is proved and secondary line price discrimination (injury to competitors of the favoured buyer) ordinarily does not establish a section 2 claim.[108] And the same IBM refusals to predisclose information about interfaces to new computer products which were challenged by the Commission were upheld as lawful by US courts.[109]

The fairness consideration is connected with the regulatory notion which also characterises Article 86 jurisprudence. Article 86 has been interpreted to prohibit 'exploitative' abuses, that is, conduct by a dominant firm that disadvantages buyers, suppliers or customers.[110] Thus 'excessive' prices[111] have been condemned as abuses and a broad duty to supply has been imposed on dominant firms[112] under Article 86. Article 86's prohibition of excessive prices and the imposition of a broad duty to supply competitors are regulatory in the sense that the competition authorities and courts directly regulate a firm's prices and access (and output). This contrasts with section 2 of the Sherman Act which does not prohibit excessive or monopoly pricing. Section 2 focuses instead on preserving

104 See, for example, *United Brands v Commission*, [1978] ECR 207, CCH paragraph 8429; *Hugin/Liptons*, OJ L22/23 (27 January 1978), CCH paragraph 10,007, *rev'd on other grounds, Hugin v Commission*, [1979] ECR 1869, CCH paragraph 8524.
105 See, for example, *United Brands v Commission*, [1978] ECR 207, CCH paragraph 8429.
106 *United Brands v Commission*, [1978] ECR 207, CCH paragraph 8429.
107 This was the Commission's position in its proceeding against IBM. See *IBM*, in Commission, Fourteenth Report on Competition Policy paragraph 94 (1985).
108 See B. Hawk, above Note 35, at 630 to 631. Price discrimination is also prohibited under certain circumstances by the Robinson-Patman Act. See *ibid.* at 632 to 634. However, recent decisions have developed more permissive standards even under the Robinson-Patman Act. See, for example, *Falls City Indus. Inc. v Vanco Beverage Inc.*, 460 US 428 (1983).
109 See *California Computer Prods Inc. v International Business Machines Corp.*, 613 F.2d 727 (9th Cir. 1979).
110 See Temple Lang 'Abuse of Dominant Positions in European Community Law, Present and Future: Some Aspects', in 1987 Fordham Corp. L. Inst. 25, 42 (B. Hawk ed. 1979).
111 *United Brands v Commission*, [1978] ECR 207, CCH paragraph 8429.
112 See, for example, *ICI & Commercial Solvents v Commission*, [1974] ECR 223, CCH paragraph 8209.

structures and conditions (and sometimes competitors) whereby market forces constrain price and increase output. Claims that excessive or monopoly pricing constitute section 2 monopolisation have been uniformly rejected by US courts on the grounds, among others, that this would eliminate the primary incentive to competition and innovation by denying monopoly profits and would subvert courts into price regulatory bodies.[113] And US courts appear far more willing than the Commission or the Court of Justice to uphold refusals to deal by dominant firms as incidental to efficiency-enhancing vertical integration.[114]

The major policy issue concerns the possible tension between efficiency considerations on the one hand and the Article 86 market integration and fairness policies on the other hand. To date that tension has largely been resolved in favour of the latter. Whether this will continue may depend on the EEC's willingness to acknowledge the tension and resultant possible trade-offs between allocative efficiency (or consumer welfare according to many economists) and protection of individual firms (or distributive concerns according to many economists). But even given the policy differences between Article 86 and section 2, the *nouvelle vague* of economic work on predation theories should prove useful in the EEC's analysis of those trade-offs.

Relevant market definition

Unlike the issues of abusive/monopolising behaviour, the EEC and US approaches to market definition have more in common than they have differences. A position can be 'dominant' within the meaning of Article 86 only if it is dominant in a relevant product and geographic market. This parallels the actual monopolisation offence of section 2 where monopoly power must exist within a relevant product and geographic market. In both regimes a two-step analysis to determine dominant position or monopoly power is ordinarily made; definition of the market and measurement of power within the previously defined market. This two-step analysis of market power suffers several infirmities, despite its administrative attractiveness. For example, market share may understate or overstate a firm's market power as where there are no or low barriers to entry. Most importantly, a blind emphasis on market share can misfocus the inquiry by minimising the primary objective (determination of market power) and by exaggerating the secondary objective (definition of a market).[115]

113 See, for example, *Berkey Photo Inc. v Eastman Kodak Co.*, 603 F.2d 263 (2d Cir. 1979), *cert. denied*, 444 US 1093 (1980).

114 See, for example, *Paschall v Kansas City Star Co.*, 727 F.2d 692 (8th Cir. 1984) (en banc).

115 For further discussion, see 1 B. Hawk, above Note 35, at ch.4.

82 THE AMERICAN (ANTI-TRUST) REVOLUTION?—[1988] ECLR

Before 1980 most decisions in the United States emphasised demand elasticity or substitutability in defining product markets. The primary focus was on price cross-elasticity of demand and, to a lesser extent, interchangeability of use. In recent years the economics literature and ultimately the case law have also looked to supply substitutability and entry barriers. Supply substitutability is included in the initial definition of the market, with the usual result of expansion of the market to include increased capacity of existing producers and, less certainly, entry of new producers. This recent emphasis on supply substitutability can be seen in the Justice Department's Merger Guidelines.[116]

United States courts have also developed the concept of submarkets which exist within the larger market. The 'relevant' market and submarkets are ultimately legal constructs constituting areas in which to assess a firm's market power. The submarket concept has been used by some courts to avoid choosing among possible markets in which to make that assessment. Many decisions have also been criticised for defining overly narrow submarkets in which market share, concentration ratios and other structural factors were sufficient to support a finding of liability.

The EEC approaches to product market definition are generally quite similar to the US approaches. Demand and supply substitutability are emphasised. Indeed, the *Continental Can*[117] judgment which emphasised supply substitutability anticipated the US courts in this respect. It is probably fair to conclude, however, that those economists who find market definition analysis in many US decisions wrong-headed if not primitive would probably find some EEC analyses even more wanting.[118]

There are several differences between the US and EEC. The EEC has rarely used a submarket concept, a point in its favour which many economists would applaud. Another important difference is the EEC's willingness to limit the market to a firm's own products,[119] a result which would produce the opposite

116 47 Fed. Reg. 28, 493–502 (1982). The Guidelines were amended in June 1984. 49 Fed. Reg. 26, 823 (1984).

117 *Europemballage & Continental Can Co. v Commission*, [1973] ECR 215, CCH paragraph 8171.

118 A prime example is *United Brands* where the Court affirmed the Commission's reasoning that because the 'young old and sick' had special needs, the product market was limited to bananas. *United Brands v Commission*, [1978] ECR 207, CCH paragraph 8429. No findings were made as to the percentage of banana purchases made by these three groups, a finding which would appear essential. See B. Hawk, above Note 35, at 545.

119 See, for example, *Hugin/Liptons*, OJ L22/23 (27 January 1978), CCH paragraph 10,007, *rev'd on other grounds*, [1979] ECR 1869, CCH paragraph 8524. A Swedish manufacturer of cash registers (Hugin) was found to have abused its dominant position in the market for spare parts for its own machines by refusing to supply them to a former distributor of its cash registers. Hugin had only 12 per cent of the market for cash registers in the Community, but a complete monopoly of the manufacture and sale of spare parts for its own machines.

reaction from many economists. Under US anti-trust law relevant markets are not generally limited to a supplier's own products.[120]

Geographic market definition is less developed than product market definition in both the EEC and the United States. The EEC definitions frequently fail to rest on any explicit economic analysis. There is a strong tendency to define markets along Member State boundaries. The effect of foreign competition and imports from non-Community suppliers on market definition has not yet been analysed in any detail under EEC law. This issue is presently the subject of numerous articles and extensive economic and political debate in the United States,[121] particularly with respect to mergers. The EEC might well benefit from a close study of this debate, particularly as it moves toward merger control.

Dominant position

'Dominant position' under Article 86 is the counterpart to 'monopoly power' under the actual monopolisation provision of section 2. Both require a showing of substantial market power. The language of neither provision offers much guidance, however, as to the requisite *degree* of market power necessary for a violation. Thus in both regimes predictable rules are hard to derive from the decisions which in turn makes comparisons even more difficult. Given these caveats, several tentative conclusions are offered. First, the EEC's general definition of dominant position is less rooted in price theory analysis than the general definition of monopoly power adopted by US enforcement authorities. Second, despite this theoretical difference, the courts in both regimes (and the EC Commission) now emphasise market share as a major factor, although the thresholds appear higher under section 2. Third, the courts in both the EEC and the US (and the EC Commission) look to many of the same non-market share factors in determining whether a dominant position or monopoly power exists, notably the existence or absence of barriers to entry, although again the US courts and agencies appear more willing to use low barriers or ease of entry to discount market share.

The Court of Justice has adopted a fairly consistent definition of dominant position in several judgments. In *Vitamins* the Court offered two related elements: power to *prevent effective competition* and power to *behave independently* of competitors and customers to an appreciable extent.[122] The emphasis on

120 See, for example, *Domed Stadium Hotel Inc. v Holiday Inns Inc.*, 732 F.2d 480, 488 (5th Cir. 1984); *Parsons v Ford Motor Co.*, 669 F.2d 308, 312 (5th Cir.), *cert. denied*, 459 US 832 (1982). But see *Heatransfer Corp. v Volkswagenwerk AG*, 553 F.2d 964, 979–81 (5th Cir. 1977), *cert. denied*, 434 US 1087 (1978).

121 See B. Hawk, above Note 77, at ch. 4F.

122 *Hoffman-La Roche v Commission*, [1979] ECR 461, at paragraphs 38 to 39, CCH paragraph 8527. See also *United Brands v Commission*, [1978] ECR 207, CCH paragraph 8429.

independence differs from economists' and most US courts' definition of monopoly power as the '"power to control prices or exclude competition."'[123] This is not to say that the EEC and US definitions are necessarily inconsistent. For example, the elasticity of demand facing a firm or the extent to which its price exceeds marginal cost is relevant to determine whether a firm has the 'power to prevent effective competition' under the Court of Justice's definition. But the Court's definition is not clearly rooted in price theory economics. This broader definition of dominant position, together with the Court's tendency in a number of early judgments simply to recite a litany of factors as showing dominance, may rest on policy differences between Article 86 and section 2. Article 86's emphasis on concepts like 'independence' may permit the EEC to emphasise fairness and the regulatory notion over the efficiency considerations emphasised under price theory analysis. The practical implication is a tendency to find a dominant position where a more focused economic analysis might indicate otherwise.

Despite this possible theoretical difference, both the US courts and more recent EEC Court judgments place great reliance on market share. In *Vitamins* the Court stated that a dominant position may be based on market share alone.[124] This trend indicates a convergence of EEC and US approaches. Although the Supreme Court and lower courts have warned against an overreliance on particular market share figures, most courts have regarded defendant's market share as the most important factor in determining existence of monopoly power. Market shares over 70 per cent have been commonly held to constitute monopoly power. Where market share falls in the middle range of the *Alcoa* formula (for example, between 50 and 70 per cent), the decisions are mixed.

The role of market share in the measurement of monopoly power has been the subject of considerable debate in the United States.[125] Market share may be a surrogate for more direct measurements of market power, such as the difference between price and marginal cost. Market share (with its attendant tendency to overemphasise market definition) is a necessary evil, given the many practical problems of the more direct measurements of market power. Given those difficulties, the courts' emphasis on market share as a surrogate is not surprising. The danger is reliance on market share as the exclusive measuring tool, for market share is also an imperfect tool which can reflect competitive ambiguities. As mentioned above, US courts and agencies increasingly look to barriers to entry as perhaps almost equally important in the analysis of monopoly power or of market power in merger cases.

123 See, for example, *United States v Grinnell Corp.*, 384 US 563, 571 (1966) quoting *United States v du Pont & Co.*, 351 US 377, 391 (1956).
124 *Hoffman-La Roche v Commission*, [1979] ECR 461, CCH paragraph 8527. The judgment does not specify a threshold figure. The Commission has stated, however, that a 60 per cent market share may raise a presumption of dominance. See Commission, *Ninth Report on Competition Policy*, paragraph 22 (1980).
125 See I B. Hawk, above Note 35, at ch.4.

US courts also consider non-market share evidence of monopoly power when it is brought to their attention by the parties. Courts have looked to a wide variety of non-market share factors as evidence of monopoly power: technological superiority resulting in cost advantages, price leadership, substantial economies of scale, relative size of competitors, performance of competitors, degree of entry barriers or barriers to expansion, pricing trends and practices, homogeneity of products, potential competition, stability of market shares over time, excess or 'super-normal' profits, creation of bottlenecks, entrenched customer preferences, large capital requirements, access to technical information and risk disparities. This list is not unlike the EEC laundry lists, such as market share, overall size, technological advantages or superiority, access to capital and raw materials, product and geographic diversification, vertical integration, limited number of purchasers, and a highly developed and specialised sales network. Both regimes would greatly benefit from cross-fertilisation of decisional law and literature on each side of the Atlantic.

Conclusion

What effect will the American anti-trust revolution have on EEC competition law and what lessons might the EEC draw from that revolution and the possible counter-revolution? The general answer is that the American revolution, at least in its more extreme form, will not be repeated in the EEC because of the policy and statutory differences between US and EEC law. However, the EEC might well profit from many of the developments in economic theory in the United States, particularly in the areas of vertical restraints, price and non-price predation and intellectual property. Useful lessons might also be drawn from recent US legal developments in the areas of vertical agreements, determination of a restraint of trade (rule of reason inquiry), and use of presumptions and allocation of burden of proof.

The market integration goal imposes a significant obstacle to a complete EEC embrace of the American revolution. This goal makes the economic analysis in the EEC more complex than in the United States, for US anti-trust analysis lacks the tensions engendered by the market integration goal. For example, it is uncertain whether the price theory models used under US anti-trust law provide the same precision in the EEC, at least without some modification. This is not to argue that price theory is irrelevant or unimportant under EEC competition law. One of the most, if not the most, important issues facing the EEC is how to resolve the tension between the market integration goal and short-term and perhaps even long-term efficiencies. The economics literature in the United States may be useful to the EEC in attempting to achieve that resolution. One lesson which the EEC might profitably draw from the American revolution is not so much from the results in the US case law but from the reasoning in the cases and the literature about efficiencies, notably distribution efficiencies, in order that the EEC can better identify and assess the possible economic or efficiency trade-offs (possible efficiency losses) of market integration-based rules.

A repeat of the American revolution in the EEC cannot be expected for another reason. Social and political values will almost certainly not be excluded from EEC competition law as they have largely been in the United States. The inclusion of distributive concerns, fairness and other social and political values in EEC competition policy make it almost inconceivable that the Community will ever embrace allocative efficiency as the exclusive policy standard. Values such as fairness and protection of individual competitors are expressed in the language of the Treaty itself. Centralisation in a single institution — the Commission — of the formulation and execution of different Community policies permits an easier integration of narrower microeconomic competitive concerns like allocative efficiency with broader economic, social and political concerns such as industrial policy and foreign economic policy. In the United States open-ended statutes and the traditional common law system permit considerable cyclical variation in interpretation by the courts and enforcement authorities.[126] The very different situation in the Community precludes radical shifts in EEC law and a repeat of the American revolution is precluded for this reason as well.

To the extent that inclusion or exclusion of non-economic values is a legislative matter, the EEC can make its own political judgment. However, the jurisprudential reasons for abandoning social and political values in US anti-trust law may alert the EEC to the potential disadvantages of basing competition rules on vague concepts like fairness that may mask distributive concerns that in turn reduce allocative efficiency. The US experience might focus the EEC's attention on the issue whether narrowing of the anti-trust analysis to allocative efficiency-based legal standards provides more predictable rules.

What lessons can the EEC draw from the recent US attempts to develop a more structured and predictable rule of reason under section 1? The first is an important but negative one, that is, that nondiscriminating appeals for a 'rule of reason' under Article 85(1) that fail to consider the ambiguities under the US rule of reason only further confuse the debate about the appropriate analysis under Article 85(1). Court of Justice judgments should not be too hastily characterised as embodying a US rule of reason analysis. Judgments like *Metro I*, *Maize Seed* and *Pronuptia* differ significantly from either the classic *Chicago Board of Trade* test or the truncated rule of reason articulated in *NCAA* and *Dentists*. The bifurcation of Article 85 is the principal cause of the confusion about the definition of a restriction of competition under Article 85(1). Much of the analysis under the US rule of reason is reserved in the EEC for the exemption stage under Article 85(3).

126 For a comparison of the US and German anti-trust laws in this respect, see Hawk, Book Review of Maxeiner, *Policy and Methods in German and American Antitrust Law: A Comparative Study*, in 82 Am. J. Intl L. 208 (1988).

Despite these statutory differences, however, the EEC might well profit from the US emphasis on presumptions and allocations of proof in the recent analyses under section 1.

Lessons might also be drawn with respect to the vertical conspiracy problem. One of the most glaring weaknesses in EEC competition law is the lack of clear evidentiary rules and procedures concerning allocation of proof. These are particularly crucial where credibility is a major factor, as in many dealer termination cases. The proposed Community court of first instance presents a timely opportunity for reforms in these areas and EEC law might benefit from US law, if only by avoiding the doctrinal confusion seen in the *Colgate-Monsanto* line of cases.

Finally, the counter-revolution brewing in the United States led by the *nouvelle vague* of economists may prove more attractive in the EEC than the more static price theory analysis of the traditional Chicago school, particularly the dynamic theories about strategic behaviour and predation currently being developed in the United States.

Barry E. Hawk
Fordham Law School
New York

The Economic Concerns of Competition Law

[3]

Wealth Transfers as the Original and Primary Concern of Antitrust: The Efficiency Interpretation Challenged

By ROBERT H. LANDE*

Considerable dispute over the goals of the antitrust laws has surfaced in scholarly commentary on the subject.[1] While it is unanimously agreed that Congress enacted these laws to encourage competition, disagreement continues over Congress' ultimate goals.[2]

---

* Attorney, Planning Office, Bureau of Competition, Federal Trade Commission. B.A., 1974, Northwestern University; J.D., 1978, Harvard University; M.P.P., 1978, John F. Kennedy School of Government, Harvard University.

The opinions expressed in this Article are solely those of the author and do not necessarily reflect the views of the Federal Trade Commission, of any individual Commissioner, or of the Bureau of Competition.

An earlier version of this Article appeared as an internal Federal Trade Commission document in January, 1979. This Article has profited from the comments of a number of lawyers and economists. Among those contributing were Richard Craswell, Kenneth Davidson, Kathryn Fenton, Eleanor Fox, Judith Gelman, James Hurwitz, Thomas Jorde, Heather Kirkwood, William Kovacic, Ronald Lafferty, Howard Marvel, Nancy Warder, and Richard Zerbe. I am especially grateful to Neil Averitt for his invaluable assistance with the introduction and the legislative history of the Federal Trade Commission, and, above all, to John Kirkwood for his assistance on the entire project.

1. For excellent summaries of the arguments regarding the wisdom of a large number of possible antitrust goals, see *Antitrust Jurisprudence: A Symposium on the Economic, Political and Social Goals of Antitrust Policy*, 125 U. PA. L. REV. 1182 (1977); *The Goals of Antitrust: A Dialogue On Policy*, 65 COLUM. L. REV. 363 (1965). For the history of this debate, see Blake & Jones, *In Defense of Antitrust*, 65 COLUM. L. REV. 377, 377-82 (1965).

2. Nor has the Supreme Court resolved this problem. *See* Reiter v. Sonotone Corp., 442 U.S. 330 (1979). The Court has stated on different occasions that the antitrust laws have a variety of goals. The Court has never made clear which goals were meant to prevail under what circumstances, or how conflicts among competing goals should be resolved.

Judicial uncertainty over the goals of the antitrust laws can be illustrated by Chief Justice Burger's opinion in *Reiter*. Some of the Court's language implies that the antitrust laws contain a strong preference for consumers: "It is in the sound commercial interests of the retail purchasers of goods and services to obtain the lowest price possible within the framework of our competitive private enterprise system. . . . Here, where petitioner alleges a wrongful deprivation of her money because the price of the hearing aid she bought was artificially inflated by reason of respondents' anticompetitive conduct, she has alleged an injury in her 'property'. . . . [The treble-damages remedy was passed] as a means of protecting consumers from overcharges resulting from price fixing." *Id.* at 339-43.

In the middle of this proconsumer pronouncement, however, the Chief Justice stated

The importance of this debate was eloquently expressed by Judge Robert Bork:

> Antitrust policy cannot be made rational until we are able to give a firm answer to one question: What is the point of the law—what are its goals? Everything else follows from the answer we give. Is the antitrust judge to be guided by one value or by several? If by several, how is he to decide cases where a conflict in value arises? Only when the issue of goals has been settled is it possible to frame a coherent body of substantive rules.[3]

The prevailing view is that Congress intended the antitrust laws only to increase economic efficiency.[4] Others, however, contend that Congress was largely motivated by a number of social, moral, and political concerns.[5] This Article presents a third view, one suggested by the antitrust laws' legislative histories.[6] This Article will argue that Congress passed the antitrust laws to further economic objectives, but primarily objectives of a distributive rather than of an efficiency nature.[7] In other words, Congress was concerned principally with preventing "unfair" transfers of wealth from consumers to firms with market power. This Article will also demonstrate that Congress in-

---

that the legislative debates "suggest that Congress designed the Sherman Act as a 'consumer welfare prescription' " (citing R. BORK, THE ANTITRUST PARADOX 66 (1978)). 442 U.S. at 343. Of course, Judge Bork concluded that the "consumer welfare prescription" embodied in the antitrust laws includes economic efficiency and excluded any concern with wealth distribution or any preference for consumers. R. BORK, THE ANTITRUST PARADOX ch. 2 (1978). (Judge Bork wrote the sources cited in this Article while he was still a professor.)

3. R. BORK, *supra* note 2, at 50.

4. *See* 4 P. AREEDA & D. TURNER, ANTITRUST LAW: AN ANALYSIS OF ANTITRUST PRINCIPALS AND THEIR APPLICATION 149 n.2 (1980); R. BORK, *supra* note 2; R. POSNER, ANTITRUST LAW: AN ECONOMIC PERSPECTIVE, (1976) (Judge Posner wrote most of the sources cited in this Article while he was still a professor.)

5. Historian Richard Hofstadter wrote that "[t]he goals of antitrust were of three kinds. The first were economic; the classical model of competition confirmed the belief that the maximum of economic efficiency would be produced by competition, and at least some members of Congress must have been under the spell of this intellectually elegant model, insofar as they were able to formulate their economic intentions in abstract terms. The second class of goals was political; the antitrust principle was intended to block private accumulations of power and protect democratic government. The third was social and moral; the competitive process was believed to be a kind of disciplinary machinery for the development of character, and the competitiveness of the people—the fundamental stimulus to national morale—was believed to need protection." R. HOFSTADTER, THE PARANOID STYLE IN AMERICAN POLITICS AND OTHER ESSAYS 199-200 (1965) [hereinafter cited as R. HOFSTADTER, THE PARANOID STYLE].

6. This Article will not, however, discuss what the goals of antitrust policy should be. It will merely attempt to ascertain the goals the Congresses that passed the antitrust laws were attempting to further.

7. For an explanation of the distributive and efficiency effects of market power, see *infra* text accompanying notes 23-58.

tended to subordinate all other concerns to the basic purpose of preventing firms with market power from directly harming consumers.

The efficiency view has been espoused by a number of leading commentators, who argue that the relevant legislative history and cases reveal only one goal, the maximizing of economic efficiency.[8] The use of social, political, or other nonefficiency criteria in antitrust analysis, they conclude, is not only unwise policy, but completely without legal foundation .[9] Sound analysis under this view consists solely of determining and implementing those actions within the scope of the antitrust statutes that maximize economic efficiency.[10]

A second group of analysts believe that in addition to enhanced economic efficiency, various social, moral, and political goals were important to the antitrust laws' framers. These goals include promotion of small business and creation of entrepreneurial opportunity,[11] encouragement of local control over business,[12] prevention of industrial concentration,[13] and the reduction of the political influence of large firms and promotion of individual liberty.[14] Not surprisingly, these commentators often disagree over the specific values to be considered,[15] and the nature of the role these goals should play.[16]

The view expressed in this Article is that the antitrust laws were

8. *See* 4 P. Areeda & D. Turner, *supra* note 4; R. Bork, *supra* note 2; R. Posner, *supra* note 4. Efficiency is defined and distinguished from other possible goals of antitrust policy *infra* at text accompanying notes 33-61.

9. One leading exponent of this view is Judge Bork. In chapter 2 of *The Antitrust Paradox*, he analyzes relevant legislative history with this question in mind. He concludes that there is no support in the legislative history of the antitrust laws for the use of other factors, and that the cases which indicate otherwise are incorrect. In addition, he identifies reasons apart from his analysis of the legislative history for eschewing objectives other than efficiency. R. Bork, *supra* note 2; *see also* remarks of William Baxter, Assistant Attorney General, Antitrust Division, United States Department of Justice: "The sole goal of antitrust is economic efficiency." Wall St. J., Mar. 4, 1982, at 28.

10. *See, e.g.*, R. Posner, *supra* note 4, at 8-22 (Judge Posner agrees with Judge Bork that antitrust laws should be used only to enhance economic efficiency, but differs with him over which actions will best achieve this. Compare, for example, Posner's approach to predation analysis, *id.* at 184-96, with Bork's approach, contained in R. Bork, *supra* note 2, at 144-60.).

11. Elzinga, *The Goals of Antitrust: Other Than Competition and Efficiency, What Else Counts?*, 125 U. Pa. L. Rev. 1191 (1977).

12. *Id.*

13. Arnold, *The Economic Purpose of Antitrust Laws*, 26 Miss. L.J. 207, 207-08 (1955).

14. Blake & Jones, *supra* note 1, at 382-84.

15. *Compare, e.g.*, Pitofsky, *The Political Content of Antitrust*, 127 U. Pa. L. Rev. 1051 (1979), *with* Schwartz, *"Justice" and Other Non-Economic Goals of Antitrust*, *id.* at 1076.

16. For example, Pitofsky, *supra* note 15, and Schwartz, *supra* note 15, disagree about whether noneconomic values should play a role only when the efficiency considerations are neutral or whether they can be balanced against efficiency considerations.

passed primarily to further what may be called a distributive goal, the goal of preventing unfair acquisitions of consumers' wealth by firms with market power. It should be stressed, however, that Congress did not pass the antitrust laws to secure the "fair" overall distribution of wealth in our economy or even to help the poor.[17] Congress merely wanted to prevent one transfer of wealth that it considered inequitable, and to promote the distribution of wealth that competitive markets would bring. In other words, Congress implicitly declared that "consumers' surplus"[18] was the rightful entitlement of consumers; consumers were given the right to purchase competitively priced goods. Firms with market power were condemned because they acquired this property right without compensation to consumers. This Article contends that the antitrust laws embody a strong preference for consumers over firms with market power.[19]

The Article begins by defining possible economic goals of the antitrust laws. Turning to the specific antitrust statutes, the Article first analyzes the legislative history of the Sherman Act to demonstrate Congress' motivations.[20] The Article next examines the legislative history of the Federal Trade Commission Act, concluding that its prohibi-

---

17. On balance, however, the redistribution effects of the antitrust laws probably favor the poor. *See infra* note 37. *See also* Elzinga, *supra* note 11, at 1194-96.

18. Consumers' surplus is the difference between the maximum amount that a consumer would pay and the price that he or she actually pays. Suppose that widgets are priced at $2.00, the competitive price. Marginal consumers of widgets would be willing to pay only this amount. Some consumers, however, would particularly desire widgets and willingly pay more—as much as $3.00. These consumers receive $1.00 in consumers' surplus when they purchase competitively priced widgets. If a monopolist gained control of the widget market and raised the price of widgets to $3.00, marginal consumers would no longer purchase widgets, and nonmarginal consumers would lose their surplus. The widget monopoly would acquire $1.00 of monopoly profits at the expense of widget consumers. For a more detailed definition, see E. MANSFIELD, MICROECONOMICS: THEORY AND APPLICATIONS 15 (4th ed. 1982); G. STIGLER, THE THEORY OF PRICE 78-81 (1966).

19. Thus, although Congress was strongly interested in increasing the size of the economic "pie" when it passed the antitrust laws, it was even more interested in ensuring its "fair" ownership. It should also be observed that all purchasers were to be protected, whether they were resellers, farmers or ultimate consumers. *See infra* note 123 & text accompanying note 137.

20. This Article will attempt to demonstrate that the Sherman Act was passed despite the possibility that its enforcement might impair, to a small degree, the efficiency of trusts, the form of industrial organization that in 1890 was thought to be most efficient. It argues that the legislative history shows that the Sherman Act was passed for a number of purposes: preventing monopolistic transfers of wealth from consumers to trusts, encouraging corporate productive efficiency in order that consumers would receive these benefits as well, reducing the social and political power of large aggregations of capital, and providing opportunities for small entrepreneurs. Congress' more minor goals were not, however, meant to interfere significantly with the right of purchasers to buy competitively priced goods.

tion against "unfair methods of competition" could be restated, with only some restriction in its intent or meaning, as a prohibition against "unfair" transfers of wealth.[21] A similar interpretation is then developed for the Clayton Act and its major extension, the Celler-Kefauver Antimerger Act.[22] Each of these discussions focuses upon Congress' distributive or wealth transfer goals, but also discusses Congress' efficiency goals and other goals so as to place the distributive objectives in proper perspective. Following the legislative history discussions, the Article uses the example of a horizontal merger to illustrate some of the differences that would result if distributive goals, in addition to or instead of efficiency goals, were considered in antitrust analysis. Incorporation of Congress' distributive goals into antitrust analysis would cause the antitrust laws to reach many more mergers and other monopolistic practices than does the present quest for efficiency in antitrust decisions.

Economic Effects of Monopoly Power: A Brief Overview

The observation that monopolies[23] cause increased prices and reduced output is hardly new. This conclusion finds expression in early English common law[24] and in classical economic theory. Adam Smith noted that "The monopolists, by keeping the market constantly understocked, by never fully supplying the effectual demand, sell their commodities much above the natural price, and raise their emoluments, whether they consist in wages or profit, greatly above their natural

21. The Federal Trade Commission (FTC) was charged, in § 5 of the Act, with preventing "[u]nfair methods of competition." 15 U.S.C. § 45(a)(1) (1914). The legislative history of the Act shows that certain methods of competition were considered "unfair," but not primarily because they might interfere with economic efficiency. Congress, in a single phrase, condemned both monopolies and fraud as "unfair" methods of competition primarily because each "unfairly" transferred wealth from consumers to firms with market power.

22. The Robinson-Patman Act, 15 U.S.C. §§ 13-13b, 21a (1976), is not discussed.

23. In this Article, the term "monopolies" will normally be used to include both individual firms with market power and cartels and trusts acquiring or exercising market power. This Article makes no distinction between single-firm and multifirm market power unless expressly noted.

24. *See* W. Letwin, Law and Economic Policy in America ch. 2 (1965). Even the Bible recognized the impact of monopolies. *See Isaiah* 5:8 ("Woe to those that add house to house/ And join field to field/ till there is room for none but you/ To dwell in the land"); *Proverbs* 11:26 ("He that withholdeth corn, the people shall curse him: but blessing shall be upon the head of him that selleth it."). For an elaborate discussion of the biblical attitude toward market power, see A. Levine, Free Enterprise and Jewish Law (1980), especially chapter 2, "Monopoly and Restraint of Trade."

price."[25] By the time the Sherman Act was passed, economists were able to prove that a monopolist pursuing its own best interests would normally follow this course of conduct.[26]

Modern economists have, of course, made many important advances in the theory of monopoly.[27] The most important development may be the modern analysis of the implications of monopoly self-interest, long recognized as including higher prices and restricted output. These effects can be divided into three categories. The first, allocative inefficiency, describes the misallocation of resources, which diminishes the total wealth of society. A second effect is a transfer of wealth from consumers to monopolists. The third involves the effect of monopolies, and antimonopoly statutes, on firms' productive efficiency. These three categories, the economic effects that might have caused Congress to legislate to prevent firms from obtaining or increasing market power, are examined here.

Allocative Inefficiency

Monopoly pricing reduces the total amount of wealth in society. Because a monopolist produces less than would be produced under competitive conditions,[28] some resources that would otherwise have been used to make the monopoly product will instead be used for other purposes, ones that consumers value demonstrably less.[29] This misallocation of resources results in diminished satisfaction of society's wants, and thus, in terms of what society values, a reduction of society's total

---

25. A. SMITH, AN INQUIRY INTO THE NATURE AND CAUSES OF THE WEALTH OF NATIONS 61 (Modern Library Ed. 1978) (1st ed. 1776).

26. For example, in his influential 1890 book, *Principles of Economics*, Alfred P. Marshall demonstrated that a monopolist will reduce supply to maximize profit: "The monopolist would lose all his monopoly revenue if he produced for sale an amount so great that its supply price, as here defined, was equal to its demand price: the amount which gives maximum Monopoly Revenue is always considerably less than that. It may therefore appear as though the amount produced under a monopoly is always less and its price to the consumer always higher than if there were no monopoly." 1 A. MARSHALL, PRINCIPLES OF ECONOMICS 484 (1st ed. 1890). Interestingly, Marshall also observed that the monopoly price nevertheless can be lower than the competitive price, particularly in the long run, because the monopolist can increase innovation without risking having to share the benefits of any advances made, be more efficient, waste less in advertising, or have greater access to capital. *Id.*

27. *See, e.g.*, E. MANSFIELD, *supra* note 18, chs. 10 & 11 (2d ed. 1975); F. SCHERER, INDUSTRIAL MARKET STRUCTURE AND ECONOMIC PERFORMANCE ch. 2 (2d ed. 1980).

28. E. MANSFIELD, *supra* note 18, at 277-92; F. SCHERER, *supra* note 27, at ch. 2; Stigler, *supra* note 18, at 78-81.

29. Firms operating in a competitive market are forced to use their resources in a manner that consumers desire most. Any deviation from competitive price and output decisions will result in consumer demand being somewhat less satisfied.

wealth. This effect is termed "allocative inefficiency."[30] Elimination of monopoly pricing would, *ceteris paribis*, increase society's total wealth and, therefore, increase consumer satisfaction.[31]

Economists have almost universally condemned the allocative inefficiency resulting from monopoly pricing.[32] Before one can understand why it is consistently viewed as "bad," however, the welfare criterion that will be used as the appropriate standard must be defined.

Modern economists almost universally use "Pareto optimality" as the appropriate welfare criterion.[33] Under this standard, a change that harms no one and improves the lot of at least one person in his or her

30. For a diagrammatic illustration of allocative efficiency, see *infra* text accompanying notes 290-91. For a formal proof that monopoly pricing leads to allocative inefficiency, see E. MANSFIELD, *supra* note 18, at 277-92; F. SCHERER, *supra* note 27, at ch. 2; Stigler, *supra* note 18, at 78-81.

31. E. MANSFIELD, *supra* note 18, at 277-92; F. SCHERER, *supra* note 27, at ch. 2; Stigler, *supra* note 18, at 78-81.

32. In particular it is condemned by scholars of both the "Harvard" and "Chicago" schools of analysis. *See* Sullivan, Book Review, 75 COLUM. L. REV. 1214 (1974); *see also* 4 P. AREEDA & D. TURNER, *supra* note 4; R. BORK, *supra* note 2; R. POSNER, *supra* note 4.

This unanimity of views explains the prominence of allocative efficiency in the antitrust literature. While it is theoretically very significant, there is evidence that it may be quantitatively less important. The first estimate of the loss to the American economy caused by monopolistic misallocations was presented by Arnold Harberger in 1954. If the results of Harberger's estimates were expressed in terms of 1982 dollars, they would be equal to approximately $12.00 per person per year. Harberger, *Monopoly and Resource Allocation*, AM. ECON. REV. 77 (1954). This estimate is based upon a variety of assumptions. It is hardly surprising that other economists arrive at different estimates, some of which are lower than Harberger's, while others are larger (some even by a factor of 50). Scherer's review of the evidence puts the figure "between 0.5 and 2 percent of the gross national product [between approximately $50 and $200 per person per year] with estimates nearer the lower bound inspiring more confidence than those on the higher side." F. SCHERER, *supra* note 27, at 464 (footnote omitted). The more important question is what the magnitude of this loss would be if there were no antitrust laws to act as both deterrent and corrective systems. It may be impossible, however, to formulate a meaningful estimate of this figure.

33. *See, e.g.*, E. MANSFIELD, *supra* note 18, at 57-8, 440, 459; E. PHELPS, ECONOMIC JUSTICE 12 (1973); F. SCHERER, *supra* note 27, at 595-96.

Other welfare criteria exist, *see* E. PHELPS, *supra*, at 12, and a few economists and philosophers reject the Pareto principle, considering it inadequate or irrelevant. For example, some believe that it is impossible to hold liberal (or libertarian) values, and at the same time accept the Pareto principle. *See* Peacock & Rowley, *Pareto Optimality and the Political Economy of Liberalism*, 80 J. POL. ECON. 476 (1972); Sen, *The Impossibility Of A Paretian Liberal*, 78 J. POL. ECON. 152 (1970). Like all welfare criteria, Pareto optimality ultimately is subjective; no one is compelled logically to accept it or its economic implications. As all modern economic analysis is based on one or another subjective welfare criterion, philosophically the results of any such analysis inherently are subjective. Nevertheless, it should be noted that Pareto optimality represents the theoretical underpinnings of almost all modern economic analyses of the effects of antitrust actions.

own opinion is considered an improvement.[34] The most commonly used version of Pareto optimality, however, recognizes that virtually any change is likely to harm at least one person. Thus, a Pareto improvement is usually defined to include a change that would benefit at least one person and would, through the use of transfer payments, simultaneously eliminate any harm to others.[35] Because all modern economic analysis is based upon this, or upon some other subjective welfare criterion, it must be observed that every result of "objective" modern economic analysis is, in some philosophical sense, subjective.[36] Economic theory has established that monopolies cause allocative efficiency and therefore violate Pareto optimality. Monopoly pricing, as measured under Pareto optimality, thus harms social welfare, unless some other characteristic of monopolies creates offsetting advantages.

In summary, monopoly pricing leads to allocative inefficiency that virtually every antitrust scholar criticizes as harmful to society. We now turn to a discussion of the other effects of monopolies and antimonopoly statutes.

Transfer of "Consumers' Surplus" from Consumers to Monopolists

The most visible and obvious result of monopoly pricing is a transfer of wealth from purchasers to the monopolist; consumers become poorer while the monopolist becomes richer.[37] The relative size of the

34. V. PARETO, MANUAL D'ECONOMIE POLITIQUE (1909). There are several variations and restatements of this principle. *See, e.g.*, E. PHELPS, *supra* note 33, at 12.

35. E. PHELPS, *supra* note 33, at 12. In fact, many economists assume that a transfer payment can be made so that all or most losers will be compensated. For this reason they ignore distributive results. Other economists recognize that certain public policy actions inevitably help some people and hurt others, and decline to make the necessary interpersonal comparisons of utility. For a superb general discussion of the disinclination of "positive" economists to consider distributive effects, see Horwitz, *Law and Economics: Science or Politics*, 8 HOFSTRA L. REV. 905 (1980).

36. *See supra* note 33.

37. Scherer concludes that "the redistribution associated with monopoly for the entire economy is . . . probably between 2 and 3 percent of GNP." F. SCHERER, *supra* note 27, at 471. Comanor and Smiley, in *Monopoly and the Distribution of Wealth*, 89 Q.J. ECON. 177 (1975), report that, if there had been no monopoly profits, the share of total personal wealth controlled by the wealthiest 2.4% of American families in 1962 would have been reduced from 40% to somewhere between 16.6 and 32%. *Id.* at 191-93. See the discussion in F. SCHERER, *supra* note 27, at 472-73.

It should be noted that wealth redistribution caused by monopolies does not always transfer wealth from poor consumers to rich stockholders. Monopolized products almost always will be purchased by at least some consumers who are richer than at least some stockholders. On balance, however, the redistributive effects of the antitrust laws would seem to favor the poor. But, as the legislative histories indicate, the legislators passing these laws were concerned with preventing transfers from consumers to monopolists and did not premise these statutes on redistribution from rich to poor. *See infra* notes 110-23, 181-90,

transferred wealth and the allocative inefficiency will vary considerably from case to case depending upon a number of factors.[38] Under market conditions most likely to be encountered, however, the transferred wealth usually will be between two and forty times as great as the accompanying allocative inefficiency.[39] Thus, the redistributive effects of market power generally exceed the allocative inefficiency effects by a substantial amount.

The two principal effects of monopolistic pricing, the transfer of wealth from consumers to monopolists and the decrease in allocative efficiency, are different in one fundamental manner: the latter represents a decrease in society's absolute wealth, while the former merely redistributes that wealth. As Professor Williamson has observed, "[t]his [redistributive] transformation of benefits from one form (consumers' surplus) to another (profit) is treated as a wash under the conventional welfare economics model."[40]

Nevertheless, this transfer of wealth raises a very controversial question: is the transfer a "good," "bad," or neutral result of monopoly pricing? The value-laden answer in large part is determined by whether anyone is thought to be entitled to the economic benefit of the "consumers' surplus." Under monopoly pricing, some consumers' surplus is acquired by the monopolist. Depending on one's perspective, one can be entirely indifferent to the result, or one can conclude either that the monopoly is "unfairly taking" property from consumers, or

---

267-74 & accompanying text. This redistributive process will also, of course, affect the total distribution of wealth in our society. For example, a yacht cartel with numerous stockholders might help to even the distribution of wealth, while a cartel that sells to poor people would probably act to skew the distribution. Questions concerning the fairness of the redistributive process are, however, different from questions concerning the initial or final distribution of wealth that the process produces.

38. These factors include the shape of the demand curve and the amounts by which the monopolist restricts output and raises prices.

39. Under certain standard assumptions the wealth redistribution can be shown to be exactly twice as large as the allocative inefficiency. These assumptions include a straight line demand curve and constant marginal costs. *See* Schmalensee, *Another Look at Market Power in Antitrust*, 95 HARV. L. REV. 1787, 1805 (1982). Under circumstances more likely to be encountered, the wealth transfer probably will be much larger relative to the allocative inefficiency. *See* Fisher & Lande, *Efficiency Considerations in Merger Enforcement*, 91 YALE L.J. — (1982).

40. Williamson, *Economies as an Antitrust Defense Revisited*, 125 U. PA. L. REV. 699, 711 (1977) [hereinafter cited as Williamson, *Economies Revisited*]. Areeda and Turner similarly wrote that their analysis of Williamson's merger example "assumes that the income transfer from consumers to producers is neutral." 4 P. AREEDA & D. TURNER, *supra* note 4, at 149 n.2. Landes and Posner wrote that "[w]e ignore possible distributional objections to monopoly, as both controversial and difficult to quantify." Landes & Posner, *Market Power in Antitrust Cases*, 94 HARV. L. REV. 937, 954 (1981).

that the monopoly is only reaping its just reward.[41]

The redistributive effects of monopoly power are clearly good or bad only with respect to the assumptions and welfare criteria that are used to evaluate them. Condemnation of the direct consumer impact of monopoly power is therefore normally and properly termed "subjective" or a "value judgment," because it is based upon a preference for consumers over monopolists.

This Article argues that Congress decided that consumers were entitled to the benefits of a competitive economic system. Consumers were deemed entitled to the "consumers' surplus" because Congress regarded the competitive scenario as the normal one.[42] Monopoly pricing represented a change from the norm which Congress condemned as an "unfair" taking of consumers' property.[43]

This congressional decision does not, moreover, violate the important principle of Pareto optimality. Before one can evaluate an improvement under the Pareto principle, the initial distribution of entitlements or property rights must be defined.[44] Assuming that Congress decided consumers were entitled to consumers' surplus, condemnation of monopolistic extractions of wealth does not violate Pareto optimality because the monopoly is unfairly taking property from consumers and, as a practical matter, no compensating transfer payments by monopolists to consumers are made.[45] Condemnation of monopoly pricing can thus be justified as the only practical method of preventing monopolies from "unfairly" taking property that, in the view of Con-

---

41. We could conclude, for example, that in order to provide firms the incentive to compete vigorously, we should permit them to earn monopoly profits.

42. It appears that Congress considered the distribution of wealth that would result if there were no monopolies as the more nearly "just" distribution. *See infra* notes 114-22, 181-90, 267-75 & accompanying text.

43. Not all of the consumers' surplus is taken by monopolies. Some is left with the consumers; some is destroyed (allocative inefficiency).

44. *See supra* note 33 & accompanying text.

45. Nor does allowing monopolization constitute a taking of property that could be substantially, even if not completely, rectified by transfer payments. If it could be shown that allowing monopolization helped 90% of society, and if 90% of the consumers harmed by monopolization could be compensated through transfer payments, society would almost certainly not condemn monopolization even though, strictly speaking, the change from competitive to monopoly pricing was not a Pareto change. The existence of allocative inefficiency, however, makes it extremely difficult to show that allowing monopolies generates more benefits than losses. Further, as a practical matter, the only way to make these transfer payments is through government regulation of the monopoly or through a complicated taxation and rebate plan, actions that are likely to cause so much waste and inefficiency that any gains from permitting monopolies would be dissipated. As it cannot be shown that most consumers would be compensated for their lost consumer surplus, the policy presumption should be in favor of allowing them to keep their property.

gress, belongs to consumers.[46]

Even if a condemnation of monopolistic transfers from purchasers to producers does violate Pareto optimality, this violation would not undermine the thesis of this Article. Pareto optimality, on which the condemnation of allocative efficiency is based, is itself a subjective standard which almost every modern economist is willing to accept.[47] No member of Congress, however, when subjectively designing or voting for any antitrust law, was, or is, under any compunction to be held to the Pareto principle. Similarly, it may or may not be wise social policy to design antitrust laws to prevent certain transfers of wealth; the decision, however, belongs to Congress.[48]

In summary, considerable controversy exists over the proper treatment of monopolistic transfers of wealth. This Article contends that Congress believed consumers were entitled to products priced at competitive levels and to the opportunity to buy the quantity of products a competitive market would offer. The Article argues that when Congress passed the antitrust laws it condemned the use of market power to interfere with these property rights or entitlements out of an explicit antimonopolistic, proconsumer bias.[49]

Productive Efficiency and Inefficiency

Monopoly power most directly affects the allocative efficiency and wealth distribution throughout our economy. However, monopolies have a host of other effects, positive and negative, on the productive

46. Further, the antitrust laws might not violate Pareto optimality if society believed that one way to prevent revolutions or the spread of communism or fascism was to prevent monopolistic transfers of wealth. *See infra* notes 125-42, 275-84 & accompanying text.

47. *See, e.g.*, E. MANSFIELD, *supra* note 18 at 457-60; E. PHELPS, *supra* note 33, at 12; F. SCHERER, *supra* note 27, at 595-96.

48. It is possible that many congressional actions violate the Pareto principle. For example, suppose that Congress believed that, in certain circumstances, a poor person valued a marginal dollar more than a rich person. Congress might judge that society as a whole could be made better off by taxing the rich to provide welfare payments. Congress' desire for equality or other notions of justice might at times prevail and override its desire for efficiency. Pareto optimality also might be rejected if Congress believed that the existing distribution of wealth was not a "fair" one. For example, suppose that a certain business practice, without taking any wealth away from anyone in absolute terms, produced a large increase in the yearly GNP, but gave the increase to the richest .01% of the population, or, alternatively, only to white Americans. Further, suppose that transfer payments, as a practical matter, could not be made. This business practice would satisfy Pareto optimality and yet, in the eyes of many, could be socially undesirable.

49. Congress believed that consumers, in other words, were entitled as a matter of right to the range of options that free competition would produce.

efficiency of an economy.[50] Whereas allocative efficiency concerns overall placement of resources in the economy, productive, or technical, efficiency refers to individual firms' use of their resources in the most effective manner. Productive efficiencies, whether in innovation, purchasing, manufacturing, marketing, distribution, or transportation, are crucial to any economy.[51]

Firms' desires to become monopolies can lead to important productive efficiency gains. The desire to earn monopoly profits often motivates businesses to compete energetically, to lower costs and prices, and to improve the quality of their product. Additionally, two or more firms often desire merger or combination to take advantage of large scale or multiplant economies, thereby improving their own efficiency and competitive posture. Any statute that, for other reasons, forbids or discourages mergers, the formation of monopolies, and even cartels, sacrifices these important advantages to some degree.

However, monopolies can simultaneously negatively affect productive efficiency. Sir John Hicks observed in 1935 that monopolists "are likely to exploit their advantage much more by not bothering to get very near the position of maximum profit, than by straining themselves to get very close to it. The best of all monopoly profits is a quiet life."[52] More recently, other economists have written that inefficiencies result when a monopolist is shielded from hard competition,[53] and that waste is caused by non-price competition to obtain monopoly profits.[54]

50. Productive efficiency is probably that type of efficiency which most commonly comes to mind when one thinks of business efficiency.

51. For more complete definitions of productive and allocative efficiencies, see E. MANSFIELD, *supra* note 18, at 1, 4-6; F. SCHERER, *supra* note 27, at 13-21.

52. Hicks, *Annual Survey of Economic Theory: The Theory of Monopoly*, 3 ECONOMETRICA 1, 8 (1935).

53. *See, e.g.*, Liebenstein, *Allocative Efficiency vs. "X-Efficiency,"* 56 AM. ECON. REV. 392 (1966). Professor Liebenstein argues that the motivations and incentives of workers and managers are different when their firm does not have to face competition: "In situations where competitive pressure is light, many people will trade the disutility of greater effort, of search, and the control of other peoples' activities for the utility of feeling less pressure and of better interpersonal relations. But in situations where competitive pressures are high, and hence the costs of such trades are also high, they will exchange less of the disutility of effort for the utility of freedom from pressure, etc." *Id.* at 413.

Similarly, monopolies can create "organizational slack" by tolerating inefficiency and waste. Without the discipline of competition, monopolies may have less incentive to cut waste and to search for ways to reduce costs. They may have the discretion to make only a comfortable profit and to tolerate a substantial amount of "fat" in their organizations and thus further waste society's resources. Some economists believe that it is "eminently plausible" that inefficiencies resulting from weak competitive pressures "are at least as large as the welfare losses from [allocative inefficiency]." *See* F. SCHERER, *supra* note 27, at 466.

54. Judge Posner hypothesized, "[A]n opportunity to obtain a lucrative transfer pay-

Similarly, some evidence suggests that the existence of monopolies might curtail overall research and innovation[55] or lead to other undesirable economic consequences.[56]

As this brief discussion demonstrates, monopolies both positively and negatively affect the productive efficiency of our economy. It thus becomes very difficult to know when the existence of monopolies, or, conversely, the existence of antitrust statutes, ultimately benefits society.[57] Further, because monopolies also create allocative inefficiency and affect society's distribution of wealth, an overall welfare-analysis of the desirability in various instances of permitting firms to obtain or retain monopoly power becomes extremely complex and involves subjective judgments that transcend conventional economic analysis.[58]

---

ment in the form of monopoly profits will attract real resources into efforts by sellers to monopolize, and by consumers to prevent being charged monopoly prices. The costs of the resources so used are costs of monopoly just as much as the costs resulting from the substitution of products that cost society more to produce than the monopolized product." R. POSNER, *supra* note 4, at 11. Judge Posner theorized that part or all of a firm's monopoly profits could be dissipated by its wasteful nonprice competition to achieve or protect its monopoly. In addition, he pointed out that this effect might also cause consumers or actual or potential competitors of the monopolist to waste resources as well. *Id.* at 11-12; *see also* Posner, *The Social Costs of Monopoly and Regulation*, 83 J. POL. ECON. 807 (1975). Professors Caves and Porter similarly believe that monopolies may channel their competitive activities into activities such as advertising to create entry barriers that help to preserve their monopoly position. Caves & Porter, *From Entry Barriers to Mobility Barriers: Conjectural Decisions and Contrived Deference to New Competition*, 91 Q.J. ECON. 241, 245-54 (1977). Of course, many economists do not believe that this occurs to a significant degree and believe that monopolies consequently continue to enjoy their full monopoly profits. *See supra* note 37. But if this effect does occur, some or all of the resources that otherwise are thought to be transferred from consumers to the monopolist instead would be wasted by the monopolist and would increase the absolute cost to society of monopoly power. *See generally* Rice & Ulen, *Rent-Seeking and Welfare Loss*, 3 RESEARCH L. ECON. 53 (1981).

55. *See, e.g.*, Kamien & Schwartz, *Market Structure and Innovation: A Survey*, 13 J. ECON. LIT. 1 (1975).

56. Some believe that monopolies overpay their executives or rank-and-file employees. See the discussion of those and other allegations in F. SCHERER, *supra* note 27, at 471-73. It is even possible that monopolistic redistributions of wealth might adversely affect employee-consumers' sense of justice and their feeling that they are obtaining their fair share of society's wealth. If so, the accompanying frustration could deaden work incentives and lead to a loss in productivity.

57. Even if monopolies benefit society by resulting in a net increase in society's wealth, and side payments (through the tax laws, for example) in theory could be made which would leave consumers better off despite the redistributive effects of monopolies, one could still justify having antitrust laws on the ground that side payments are, as a practical matter, too difficult to make.

58. The difficulties of analyzing the efficiency and distributive effects of monopoly power are illustrated by presenting an analysis of a horizontal merger that might yield productive efficiencies yet lead to a firm with monopoly power. *See infra* notes 287-309 & accompanying text.

However modern economists may resolve the issue, it is clear Congress has determined that, in certain circumstances, firms should be prevented from obtaining monopoly power. Keeping in mind the catalogue of possible economic effects of monopoly power and the possible economic reasons that Congress might have condemned these firms when it passed the antitrust laws, the following sections of this Article will examine the legislative histories of the major antitrust statutes to discern the true underpinnings of congressional intent.

Congressional Goals

It is axiomatic that when the words of a statute are clear and unambiguous, courts need go no further in their interpretation of that law.[59] Ambiguous, doubtful, or undefined words or phrases require interpretation, however, by reference to the statute's legislative history.[60] Examination of a legislative history generally seeks determination of legislative intent regarding particular applications of the statute. The analysis often goes one step further in an attempt to determine what legislative intent "would have been" had Congress considered situations never actually contemplated.[61]

59. "[W]hen words are free from doubt they must be taken as the final expression of the legislative intent, and are not to be added to or subtracted from by considerations drawn . . . from any extraneous source." Caminetti v. United States, 242 U.S. 470, 490 (1917).

60. Indeed, even the term "legislative history" needs clarification. The term can mean a narrow analysis of the history and progress of a bill in a legislative assembly. Alternatively, "legislative history" can mean an analysis of the condition of the times when the bill was passed, and an analysis of the factors which led to its passage. This Article uses the latter definition. For a more complete discussion of courts' reliance on legislative histories in interpreting acts, see Limbaugh, *Historic Origins of Anti-Trust Legislation*, 18 Mo. L. Rev. 215, 215-17 (1953); Posner, *Economics, Politics, and the Reading of Statutes and the Constitution*, 49 U. Chi. L. Rev. 263 (1982).

61. For example, in Bersch v. Drexel Firestone, Inc., 519 F.2d 974 (2d Cir.), *cert. denied sub nom.* Bersch v. Arthur Andersen & Co., 423 U.S. 1018 (1975), a case involving antifraud provisions of the Security Acts, Judge Friendly noted: "We freely acknowledge that if we were asked to point to language in the statutes, or even in the legislative history, that compelled these conclusions, we would be unable to respond. . . . Our conclusions rest on case law and commentary . . . and on *our best judgement as to what Congress would have wished if these problems had occurred to it.*" *Id.* at 933 (emphasis added). As Judge Bork noted, "[a] legislature may never address the issue of ultimate policy goals and yet write a law whose various categories and distinctions can be explained only by a particular policy. That policy may then quite legitimately be said to have been intended by the legislature, even though not a single member articulated it even to himself. A system of classifications has implications, and the legislature must be taken to intend not only what it says but also what is implied by what it does." R. Bork, *supra* note 2, at 57.

The Supreme Court, in Minnesota Mining v. N.J. Wood Co., 381 U.S. 311 (1964), quoted an earlier statement by Justice Holmes: "[I]t is not an adequate discharge of duty for courts to say: We see what you are driving at, but you have not said it, and therefore we

The antitrust laws are among the least precise statutes enacted by Congress. The central terms, including "competition," "unfair methods of competition," "conspiracy in restraint of trade," and "monopolize," are inherently vague and not self-defining.[62] One commentator has observed that antitrust legislation has, perhaps more than any other field, stimulated the courts to consider, as an interpretative aid, the history of the era that gave rise to the legislation.[63]

It is not possible to ascertain with certainty the original goals of the antitrust laws. Not only are there conflicting statements of legislative purpose, but it is often difficult to decide whether certain statements represent isolated, unimportant views[64] or infrequently mentioned but nevertheless significant motivating factors.[65] Therefore, this Article cannot hope to resolve every conflict, but it does attempt to generally reconcile the evidence to determine the common spirit, goals, policies, and purposes underlying the antitrust laws, and to develop an appropriate decisionmaking theory with which to analyze antitrust cases.[66] This judgment will by necessity be relative instead of absolute.

---

shall go on as before." *Id.* at 321 (quoting Johnson v. United States, 163 F. 30, 32 (1st Cir. 1908)).

62. No attempt will be made here to list those cases in which the courts have examined the legislative history of the antitrust laws in order to ascertain what Congress "would have wished" if the problems had occurred to it; such a list would be unbearably long. Good compilations of cases which examine the legislative histories of the antitrust laws, as well as comprehensive legislative histories of the antitrust laws can be found in E. KITNER, THE LEGISLATIVE HISTORY OF THE FEDERAL ANTITRUST LAWS AND RELATED STATUTES (1978); H. THORELLI, THE FEDERAL ANTITRUST POLICY (1955); 1 A. TOULMIN, TREATISE ON THE ANTI-TRUST LAWS OF THE UNITED STATES AND INCLUDING ALL RELATED TRADE REGULATORY LAWS 1-23 (1949).

63. Limbaugh, *supra* note 60, at 217.

64. An example of just such a remark in the FTC Act legislative history would, hopefully, be where Senator Kenyon quoted Senator Martine for the proposition that "everybody should be permitted to kill one lawyer and not be punished for it." 51 CONG. REC. 13,196 (1914).

65. Although it may be assumed that the legislators meant what they said during the floor debates, their statements might at times mask their true intentions. Further, some statements can be best classified as political rhetoric. For example, legislators might have stated that they condemn monopolization out of a concern for consumers when they actually were more concerned with providing small businesses fair opportunity to compete. Some Congress members might have supported weak antitrust legislation in order to protect large predators from stronger remedies. For a cynical view of relevant economic history see G. KOLKO, THE TRIUMPH OF CONSERVATISM (1973).

66. As Judge Bork noted in his examination of the legislative history of the Sherman Act, the task of ascertaining legislative intent should not be "an attempt to describe the actual state of mind of each of the congressmen who voted for the Sherman Act but . . . merely an attempt to construct the thing we call 'legislative intent' using conventional methods of collecting and reconciling the evidence provided by the Congressional Record." Bork, *Legislative Intent and The Policy of The Sherman Act*, 9 J.L. & ECON. 7, 7 n.2 (1966).

We can only make our most informed decision as to Congress' true intentions. And, although current antitrust decisionmakers have some degree of discretion in interpreting the antitrust laws, this discretion must be bounded by Congress' desires. This examination of congressional intent proceeds chronologically, because the earlier antitrust laws, and the Sherman Act in particular, laid out Congress' most fundamental antitrust policies.

The Sherman Act

From the language of the Sherman Act,[67] its legislative history,[68] and the history of late nineteenth century America,[69] it is clear Congress was concerned about those activities of trusts and monopolies that unduly restrained trade or caused a monopolization of interstate commerce. It is equally clear that with the Sherman Act " 'Congress was dealing with competition, which it sought to protect, and monopoly, which it sought to prevent.' "[70] These truisms do not, however, reveal why Congress passed the Sherman Act, or what goals it attempted to implement. If the goals of the antitrust laws are to be understood, the

Since most legislation is passed by a coalition whose members have very different interests, a complete reconciliation of every legislator's views is often impossible.

For the purposes of this Article, the historical methodology will be as follows: The statements that support a particular goal or policy will be identified, and given weight according to the relative importance of the speaker, and the strength of his sentiments. They will be balanced against opposing or contradictory legislative statements. If this calculation reveals a preponderance of evidence which favors a particular policy, then it will be assumed that the policy can be ascribed to Congress as a whole. If, however, there are only a few comments by less important legislators on a particular issue, the remarks will be cited but then ignored and it will be assumed that Congress did not articulate a policy toward that issue.

67. The Sherman Act condemns "[e]very contract, combination in the form of trust or otherwise, or conspiracy, in restraint of trade or commerce among the several States. . . ." Sherman Act, § 1, 26 Stat. 209 (1890) (current version at 15 U.S.C. § 1 (1976)). It provides punishment for "[e]very person who shall monopolize, or attempt to monopolize, or combine or conspire with any other person or persons, to monopolize any part of the trade or commerce among the several States. . . ." Sherman Act, § 2, 26 Stat. 209 (1890) (current version at 15 U.S.C. § 2 (1976).

68. For comprehensive sources on the legislative history of the Sherman Act, see E. KITNER, *supra* note 62; H. THORELLI, *supra* note 62; A. TOULMIN, *supra* note 62; Bork, *supra* note 66.

69. *See infra* notes 125-42 & accompanying text.

70. Standard Oil Co. v. Federal Trade Comm'n, 340 U.S. 231, 248-49 (1951) (quoting A.E. Staley Mfg. Co. v. Federal Trade Comm'n, 135 F.2d 453, 455 (7th Cir. 1943)). As the National Commission for the Review of Antitrust Laws and Procedures succinctly stated: "[T]he chief aim of government litigation under Section 2 of the Sherman Act is the dissipation of persistent monopoly power." NATIONAL COMMISSION FOR THE REVIEW OF ANTITRUST LAWS AND PROCEDURES, 1 REPORT TO THE PRESIDENT AND THE ATTORNEY GENERAL 158 (1979) [hereinafter cited as NCRALP REPORT].

crucial issue is the explanation behind Congress' effort to protect competition.[71]

This Article first attempts to demonstrate that the legislative history of the Sherman Act reveals a total lack of concern for allocative inefficiency. Trusts and monopolies were condemned principally because they "unfairly" extracted wealth from consumers. Productive efficiency also was an aim of the Act. Congress wanted the economy to function efficiently primarily to provide consumers the benefits of free competition. This section demonstrates, however, that in balancing the competing considerations, Congress condemned firms with monopoly power despite their acknowledged efficiencies, and with the knowledge that this condemnation might not maximize society's economic efficiency. Indeed, the evidence suggests that Congress was unwilling to subordinate its distributive-based distaste for trusts and monopolists to the goal of corporate efficiency when the efficiency gains would be retained by the monopolist. Moreover, this Article contends that the legislative history shows that Congress passed the Sherman Act because it believed that trusts and monopolies possess excessive social and political power, and reduce entrepreneurial liberty and opportunity.

Improving Economic Efficiency

Judge Robert H. Bork, who has written one of the most thorough analyses of the legislative history of the Sherman Act, contends that the drafters of the Sherman Act were preoccupied with economic efficiency rather than with any nonefficiency considerations.[72] Judge Bork argues that "[t]he whole task of antitrust can be summed up as the effort to improve allocative efficiency without impairing productive efficiency so greatly as to produce either no gain or a net loss in consumer wel-

71. A fascinating illustration of the intense debate over the goals of the Sherman Act is provided by Inglis v. ITT Continental Baking Co., 652 F.2d 917 (9th Cir. 1981). The court held that "[t]he relevance of the economic tests [for predatory pricing] so developed, however, must then depend in large part on whether allocative efficiency is a primary goal of the antitrust laws. As we see those goals, they are limited to the preservation of competition, and while one may assume that enhanced competition will lead to improvements in allocative efficiency, this may not always be the case. . . . Similarly, the search for allocative efficiency may lead one to accept conduct that is plainly anticompetitive. In any event, our objective is set by the antitrust laws and it concerns primarily the protection of competition." 652 F.2d at 936 n.20. Later, the court added that "[t]he antitrust laws were designed to protect competition, not solely to improve allocative efficiency." 652 F.2d at 939-40 (footnote omitted). Six months later, the same panel voted unanimously to amend its opinion by deleting all of the quoted material! Inglis v. ITT Continental Baking Co., Nos. 79-4207, 78-3604 (Feb. 10, 1982).

72. R. Bork, *supra* note 2, at 91.

fare."[73] Judge Bork asserts that the sole purpose of the Sherman Act was enhancement of "consumer welfare," a term of art he defined as the "maximization of wealth or consumer want satisfaction."[74] This view of "consumer welfare" includes maximum economic efficiency but excludes anything giving preference to consumers over monopolists or any concern with "unfair" transfers of wealth from consumers to monopolists. "Antitrust thus has a built-in preference for material prosperity, but it has nothing to say about the ways prosperity is distributed or used."[75]

Judge Bork asserts that this congressional mandate "requires courts to distinguish between agreements or activities that increase wealth through efficiency and those that decrease it through restriction of output."[76] He further asserts that there is "not a scintilla of support" in the Act's legislative history for "broad social, political, and ethical mandates,"[77] and explicitly rejects distributive issues as a possible area of antitrust concern.[78]

Judge Bork supports his conclusions by analyzing dozens of citations from the legislative history of the Act, relying most heavily upon the views of Senator Sherman, its primary sponsor.[79] These statements

73. *Id.*

74. Bork, *supra* note 66, at 7. The Court, beginning with Northern Pac. Ry. v. United States, 356 U.S. 1, 4 (1958), has condemned the misallocation of resources caused by monopoly pricing. In Reiter v. Sonotone Corp., 442 U.S. 330 (1979), the Court cited Judge Bork for the conclusion that the debates "suggest that Congress designed the Sherman Act as a 'consumer welfare prescription.'" *Id.* at 343. See the discussion of this case *supra* note 2.

75. R. Bork, *supra* note 2, at 90.

76. Bork, *supra* note 66, at 7.

77. *Id.* at 10. The only other value that he believes can be identified in the legislative history is the protection of small businessmen. He argues, however, that "this value was given a complementary (or incidental) but not conflicting role in relation to the goal of maximization of consumer welfare." *Id.*

78. R. Bork, *supra* note 2, at 111: "[I]t seems clear the income distribution effects of economic activity should be completely excluded from the determination of the antitrust legality of the activity. It may be sufficient to note that the shift in income distribution does not lessen total wealth, and a decision about it requires a choice between two groups of consumers that should be made by the legislature rather than by the judiciary." Interestingly, in his Sherman Act legislative history analysis, Bork observed that the argument in Congress for a rule against monopolistic mergers "derived in large measure from a desire to protect consumers from monopoly extortion. . . . Where producer and consumer welfare might come into conflict . . . Congress chose consumer welfare as decisive." *Id.* at 11. A concern with "monopoly extortion" would seem to be identical to the concern with the income distribution effects of economic activity which Bork says should be made by the legislature.

79. Judge Bork wrote that Senator Sherman "was by far the most articulate and thorough speaker on the question of what goals antitrust should serve. Those who spoke overwhelmingly agreed with his position on this issue. Disagreement was largely confined to questions of remedies and the constitutional reach of Sherman's measure." Bork, *supra* note

reveal overwhelming congressional concern with the activities of monopolies and trusts tending "to advance the price to the consumer"[80] and with practices effectively "destroying competition in production and thereby increasing prices to consumers."[81] Judge Bork thus makes a convincing case that these concerns were paramount and indeed represented the overwhelming weight of congressional opinion.[82]

Judge Bork then examines the proposition that Congress was concerned with "the preservation of efficiency,"[83] and finds support for the assertion that Congress, in passing the Sherman Act, did not mean to destroy existing efficient production methods.[84] In particular, he as-

---

66, at 45. "Sherman was the prime mover in getting antitrust legislation considered and pressed through the Senate . . . [and] though Sherman's bill was completely rephrased by the Judiciary Committee, of which he was not a member, the final bill in its substantive policy aspects, embodied Sherman's views." *Id.* at 14-15. For a description of the evolution of Sherman's initial bill into the Sherman Act, see *id.* at 13 n.9.

80. *Id.* at 16 (quoting remarks of Sen. Sherman, 21 CONG. REC. 2457 (1890)). In another example, Judge Bork cited § 1 of the bill that Sherman drafted. "[T]hat bill declared illegal two classes of arrangements, contracts, agreements, trusts, or combinations: (1) those made with a view, or which tend, to prevent full and free competition, and (2) those designed, or which tend, *to advance the cost to consumer of articles of commerce.*" *Id.* at 15 (citation omitted) (emphasis added). Judge Bork analyzes this language in the following manner: "Sherman employed these two criteria of illegality in every measure he presented to the Senate. The first test, which subjects all firms to market forces, is hardly a means of preserving social values that consumers are not willing to pay for. It can be reconciled only with a consumer-welfare policy. The second test is even more explicit. *The touchstone of illegality is raising prices to consumers. There were no exceptions.* Sherman wanted the courts not merely to be influenced by the consumer interest but to be controlled completely by it." *Id.* at 15-16 (citation omitted) (emphasis added).

81. 21 CONG. REC. 2558 (1890) (remarks of Sen. Pugh).

82. Bork, *supra* note 66. Judge Posner cited Judge Bork approvingly in summing up Congress' intent: "The framers of the Sherman Act appear to have been concerned mainly with the price and output consequences of monopolies and cartels . . . ." R. POSNER, *supra* note 4, at 23 (citing Bork, *supra* note 66).

83. Bork, *supra* note 66, at 26-31.

84. "Sherman took great pains to stress that his bill would in no way interfere with efficiency. . . . '[The bill] does not in the least affect combinations in aid of production where there is free and fair competition.' He stressed the legality of efficiency repeatedly, citing partnerships and corporations as two forms of combination which were efficiency-creating and therefore lawful. He said corporations 'ought to be encouraged and protected as tending to cheapen the cost of production.' He also praised the efficiency-creating corporate merger.

"Not once did Sherman suggest that courts should blunt or discourage efficient size or conduct in the interest of any social or political value. The only limit he urged to the creation of efficiency by combination was justified explicitly in terms of consumer welfare. He thought combinations of monopolistic size would not pass their efficiencies on to consumers:

" 'It is sometimes said of these combinations [the monopolistic trusts] that they reduce prices to the consumer by better methods of production, but all experience shows that this saving of cost goes to the pockets of the producer. The price to the consumer depends upon the supply, which can be reduced at pleasure by the combination.' Here again Sherman

serts that Congress did not intend to forbid monopolies attained solely through efficiency.[85] Criticizing the assertion that values other than efficiency should play a role in Sherman Act interpretation,[86] he concludes that "Congress' position with respect to efficiency cannot be explained on any hypothesis other than that consumer welfare was in all cases the controlling value under the Sherman Act."[87] In light of his definition of "consumer welfare," Judge Bork contends that Congress' only goal was to promote economic efficiency.[88] In summary, Judge Bork concluded that the Sherman Act was intended to improve economic efficiency and does not reflect any congressional concern with the effects of monopoly power on the distribution of wealth and other nonefficiency goals.

Allocative Efficiency

The efficiency-oriented view of the Sherman Act, as propounded by Judge Bork and others,[89] has initial appeal. No basis exists, how-

identified injury to consumers as occurring through restriction of output by firms with market control." *Id.* at 26-28 (citations omitted). Judge Bork's conclusions will be analyzed throughout this paper.

85. *Id.* at 28-31.

86. *Id.* at 39-42. For example, Judge Bork examines Judge Hand's assertions in United States v. Aluminum Co. of America, 148 F.2d 416 (2d Cir. 1945), that the Sherman Act should have as a goal the protection of small businessmen. He analyzes the legislative statements that Judge Hand relied upon, and concludes that while Congress certainly showed sympathy for small businesses insofar as they were hurt by the trusts, their concern never constituted an affirmative desire that the Act should seek their protection as an end in itself. Their protection, Judge Bork asserts, was thought to be an incidental benefit of the Act. Bork, *supra* note 66, at 39-42.

Judge Bork found only a single occasion upon which he believed that the Senators considered the preservation of small businesses as an end in itself, and concluded that "it is impossible to find even colorable language suggesting most of the other broad social or political purposes that have occasionally been suggested as relevant to the application of the Sherman Act." *Id.* at 41-42 (citation omitted). He backs up this assertion with a footnote in which he examines a few additional legislative statements which might support other nonefficiency goals and calls them "isolated remarks and shreds of casual rhetoric." *Id.* at 43 n.105. Judge Bork deliberately declines to consider the effects of the forces of populism that provided much of the impetus for the passage of the Sherman Act. *Id.* at 44 n.106.

87. Bork, *supra* note 66, at 26.

88. *Id.*; *see also* R. BORK, *supra* note 2, at 90-91.

89. *See supra* text accompanying notes 73-75. Areeda and Turner appear to come to essentially the same conclusion as Judge Bork, although they phrase it in less absolute terms. They identify "fairness" and "populist" goals as the principal nonefficiency goals that the antitrust laws might reach. But they conclude that "[a]s a goal of antitrust policy, 'fairness' is a vagrant claim applied to any value that one happens to favor. In our context, it may connote competition or its absence." 4 P. AREEDA & D. TURNER, *supra* note 4, at 21. They further conclude that these goals should play a role in antitrust analysis only insofar as they affect the efficiency of our economy: "In one set of meanings, competition promotes fair results in the sense of prices close to cost and multiple choices for buyers and sellers. Com-

ever, for their contention that Congress was concerned only with allocative efficiency. Indeed, it is unlikely that in 1890 many economists, much less legislators, understood the impact of monopoly power on allocative efficiency.

Judge Bork's review of the Sherman Act's legislative history conclusively demonstrates that Congress was preoccupied with the higher prices facing consumers as a result of monopolistic pricing.[90] Although he is correct to conclude that Congress was concerned with "consumer welfare,"[91] he incorrectly restricts the definition of this key term to economic efficiency.

The modern economist, Judge Bork asserts, knows that the only harmful result of monopoly pricing is its adverse effects on allocative efficiency;[92] therefore, in the interest of consumer welfare, the antitrust

petitive results are thus thought to be fair. Similarly, practices promoting competition are fair while those impairing it are not. . . . The promotion of fairness in these senses also promotes efficiency and progressiveness. But competitive processes and results are also called unfair by those who wish higher returns than competition gives them. . . . Here we note only that this conception of fairness is, of course, antithetical to both competition and economic efficiency." *Id.* at 21-22. They also asserted that "the weighing and resolution of conflicting interests and objectives would involve the courts in essentially political decisions for which there are no workable legal standards, and would often place them in a regulatory or supervisory role for which they are ill-equipped." *Id.* at 13.

Although they find some support for nonefficiency goals, Areeda and Turner nevertheless "concur with what we perceive to be the main thrust of the case law because . . . neither the statutes nor the legislative histories compel or even strongly suggest a different course of antitrust interpretation. If anything, they support the priority of competition and its efficiency goals." *Id.* at 12-13. In their view, promoting "non-efficiency goals over efficiency would be excessively costly, futile, and unadministrable." *Id.* at 24. They believe that "[o]nce antitrust rules are properly framed in terms of competitive and efficiency considerations, there is little room left for non-conflicting additional prohibitions; and avoiding conflict would require difficult if not elusive efficiency determinations that in many instances would otherwise be unnecessary. Accordingly, the contribution to populist goals from rules specially created to promote them would be far too small to warrant the inevitable legal difficulties, uncertainties, and enforcement costs they would involve." *Id.* at 30. Moreover, they think goals other than efficiency are inappropriate as antitrust standards even if they do not conflict with efficiency objectives. Areeda and Turner conclude that the Sherman Act's legislative history is vague, uncertain, seldom on point, abounding with casual language, and deserving of relatively little weight. *Id.* at 14-15. Interestingly, they do not appear to directly confront the wealth transfer issue. Although their merger analysis, for example, "assumes that the income transfer from consumers to producers is neutral," they do not directly discuss a possible concern with distributional questions. *Id.* at 149 n.2.

90. *See supra* notes 80-82 & accompanying text.

91. Bork, *supra* note 66, at 16. Judge Bork noted that "[t]he legislators did not, of course, speak of consumer welfare with the precision of a modern economist but their meaning was unmistakable." *Id.* at 10. Judge Bork also stated that "[t]he rules implied by the [consumer welfare] policy of [Congress] are alterable as economic analysis progresses. . . ." *Id.* at 47.

92. *See* R. BORK, *supra* note 2, at 90-91, 111; Bork, *supra* note 66, at 7, 9.

laws should be concerned only with improving allocative efficiency.[93] According to Judge Bork, the redistribution of wealth from consumers to producers is not an appropriate focus because it involves a value judgment and "could only rest upon a tenuous moral ground."[94]

Although modern economists often eschew economic value judgments, the 1890 Congress may have been more willing to make them. The legislative history of the Sherman Act indicates that Senator Sherman and other legislators condemned trusts for raising prices and restricting output,[95] but no evidence has ever been found to suggest that any legislator understood that monopoly pricing causes allocative inefficiency.[96] It is extremely unlikely that the legislators' distaste for monopoly pricing could have been based upon its impact on allocative efficiency: the concept of allocative efficiency was, at best, on the verge of discovery by leading economic theorists when the Sherman Act was passed.[97]

More importantly, leading economists of the day had very little

93. *See* R. BORK, *supra* note 2, at 90-91, 111; Bork, *supra* note 66, at 7, 9.

94. R. BORK, *supra* note 2, at 111. Judge Bork writes that "consumer welfare has no sumptuary or ethical component, but permits consumers to define by their expression of wants in the market place what things they regard as wealth." *Id.* at 90.

95. *See supra* notes 80-81.

96. *See, e.g.*, Bork, *supra* note 66.

97. Alfred Marshall, for example, devoted seventeen pages of the 1890 edition of *Principles of Economics* to a chapter entitled "The Theory of Monopolies" in which only one footnote discussed either allocative inefficiency or any incipient version of this concept. A. MARSHALL, PRINCIPLES OF ECONOMICS 466 n.1 (1890). Modern understanding of allocative efficiency is based, inter alia, on the assumption of Pareto optimality, first proposed in 1909. V. PARETO, *supra* note 34. Some of the precursors of this concept can arguably be found in Pareto's first major work, *Cours D'Economie Politique*, which was published in 1896-1897. *See supra* notes 33-35 & accompanying text. Not until 1938 did the first modern and rigorous discussion of allocative efficiency appear. Hotelling, *The General Welfare in Relation to Problems of Taxation and of Railway and Utility Rates*, 6 ECONOMETRICA 242 (1938). Even this path-breaking and influential discussion, concerned with allocative inefficiency resulting from improper taxation and incorrect railroad and public utility rate-setting, did not discuss the antitrust implications of allocative inefficiency.

Scherer noted that other nineteenth century economists discussed what we today term allocative efficiency insofar as it related to taxation and the government regulation of public utilities: "The notion of a 'deadweight welfare-loss triangle' entered the mainstream of Anglo-American economics in the first edition of Marshall's *Principles* [citation omitted]. An obscure English-language precursor was Jenkin, *On the Principles Which Regulate the Incidence of Taxes*, *reprinted in* READINGS IN THE ECONOMICS OF TAXATION 227, 233 (R. Musgrave & C. Shoup eds. 1959) (originally published in 1871). A variant of the concept can be traced to Dupuit, *On the Measurement of the Utility of Public Works*, *translated in* 2 INT'L ECON. PAPERS 83, 108 (A. Peacock, *et al.* eds. 1952) (originally published in French in 1844)." Scherer, *The Posnerian Harvest: Separating Wheat from Chaff*, 86 YALE L.J. 974, 977 n.20 (1977).

influence on the passage of the Act.[98] It is unlikely, then, that the legislators who passed the early antitrust laws were aware that monopoly pricing led to allocative inefficiency.[99] Nothing in the legislative history of the Sherman Act suggests that they were. No commentator has pointed to any economic testimony that referred to a concept resembling "allocative efficiency," nor is there the slightest evidence that any member of Congress was even remotely familiar with this type of welfare loss.[100]

Given the state of economic theory at that time, the assertion that legislators supporting the Sherman Act were influenced by considerations involving allocative efficiency is without credibility. Congressional distaste for the pricing and output consequences of monopoly pricing must therefore be rooted in other concerns. These concerns include the distribution of wealth between consumers and producers and, secondarily, the maintenance of productive efficiency, preservation of economic opportunities for small enterprises, and the concentration of economic, social, and political power in a few hands.

Productive Efficiency

Although the legislative history of the Sherman Act never alludes to any concept resembling allocative efficiency, it does repeatedly praise corporate productive efficiency and recognize that free competition leads to efficient competitors. The productive efficiency of free competition was especially encouraged when gains were passed on to consumers. Nevertheless, there is little basis for suggesting that the Sherman Act was passed primarily to improve or even to preserve pro-

98. It is worth remembering that the antitrust laws were passed by politicians, not economists. Professor Hofstadter observed that "[t]he Sherman Act was framed and debated in the pre-expert era, when economists as a professional group were not directly consulted by legislators. But even if they had been, they would have given mixed and uncertain advice." R. HOFSTADTER, THE PARANOID STYLE, *supra* note 5, at 200. Professor Stigler's conclusion is even more striking: "A careful student of the history of economics would have searched long and hard, on July 2 of 1890, the day the Sherman Act was signed by President Harrison, for any economist who had ever recommended the policy of activity combatting collusion or monopolization in the economy at large." Stigler, *The Economists and the Problem of Monopoly*, 72 AM. ECON. REV. 1, 3 (1982).

99. Indeed, the following analyses of the antitrust laws' legislative histories demonstrates that not even the most recent major antitrust law, the Celler-Kefauver Antimerger Act of 1950, was passed to enhance allocative efficiency. *See infra* notes 255-65 & accompanying text.

100. *See generally* R. BORK, *supra* note 2; Bork, *supra* note 66. One could, however, speculate about Congress' likely reaction had it known that trusts and monopolies caused allocative inefficiency. It seems reasonable to conclude that they probably would have used this as another reason to condemn them.

ductive efficiency; indeed, the trusts were viewed as extremely efficient. Rather, Congress wanted to pass a law for other purposes which hampered productive efficiency as little as possible.

Many scholars have suggested that the trusts existing in 1890 were efficient at production.[101] Even their harshest critics admit this.[102] Senator Sherman appreciated the efficiencies of large corporations generally:

> Experience has shown that they are the most useful agencies of modern civilization. They have enabled individuals to unite to undertake enterprises only attempted in former times by powerful governments. The good results of corporate power are shown in the vast development of our railroads and the enormous increase of business and production of all kinds.[103]

But congressional endorsement of trusts' efficient operations stopped when consumer prices rose, and the legislature withheld approval from combinations that, while yielding more efficient methods of competi-

---

101. *See, e.g.*, McGee, *Predatory Price Cutting: The Standard Oil (N.J.) Case*, 1 J.L. & ECON. 137 (1958); *see also* R. HOFSTADTER, THE PARANOID STYLE, *supra* note 5; Koller, *The Myth of Predatory Pricing: An Empirical Study*, 4 ANTITRUST L. & ECON. REV. 105 (1971).

It is unclear how much of monopoly efficiency can be ascribed to the fact that monopolies took the form of trusts, and how much merely came about because these trusts were often combinations of large, efficient corporations. It is unclear, in other words, how much of their productivity would have been lost if they were broken up. An important question to ask is whether Congress believed that it would jeopardize significant productive efficiencies when it broke up the trusts. Perhaps Congress wanted to achieve its other goals out of a belief that it could substantially assist consumers and at the same time only impair productive efficiency a modest amount.

102. Principally for this reason, some economists in the late 1800's believed that monopolies were, in balance, beneficial for society. *See* Letwin, *Congress and the Sherman Antitrust Law: 1887-1890*, 23 U. CHI. L. REV. 221, 238-39 (1956); *see also* R. HOFSTADTER, THE PARANOID STYLE, *supra* note 5; Stigler, *supra* note 98. At the same time, however, a minority of legislators held the belief that a lack of competition lowered productive efficiency. For example, Representative Fithian stated his belief that "skill is created and is stimulated by competition. A recent writer on political economy says: 'Wherever monopoly is dominant, the incentive for improvement and skill is deadened. It is only when competitors contend with each other for the favor of the consumer that they are stimulated to attract that consumer by presenting him with wares both skillfully and cheaply made.' " 21 CONG. REC. 4102 (1890). Representative Vest stated: "We know very well that competition always reduces prices. . . . I say if you let these two manufacturing interests compete together and create competition, you then secure lower prices to the consumer. That is the law of trade and that is the law of manufactures [sic] the world over." *Id.* at 2466.

Congress's dilemma became manifest in Mr. Dooley's comment on Teddy Roosevelt's early attitude towards the trusts: "The 'trusts,' says [Roosevelt], 'are heejoous monsthers built up be th' enlightened interprise iv th' men that have done so much to advance progress in our beloved country,' he says. 'On wan hand I wud stamp thim undher fut; on th' other hand not so fast.' " H. PRINGLE, THEODORE ROOSEVELT 172 (rev. ed. 1956).

103. 21 CONG. REC. 2457 (1890). "When corporations unite merely to extend their business, as connecting lines of a railway without interfering with competing lines, they are proper and lawful." *Id.; see also* remarks of Senator Sherman cited by Bork, *supra* note 84.

tion, also produced higher consumer prices. The trusts were condemned despite their efficiency in large part because they kept the fruits of such efficiency. As Senator Sherman pointed out in qualification of his praise for efficiency, "It is sometimes said of these combinations that they reduce prices to the consumer by better methods of production, but all experience shows that *this saving of cost goes to the pockets of the producer*."[104] Congressional condemnation of monopolistic extractions of wealth was so strong that it is even unlikely that Congress meant to provide an exception for a monopoly based solely upon superior efficiency.[105]

---

104. 21 CONG. REC. 2460 (1890) (emphasis added). Senator Sherman and others expressed similar views elsewhere. The Senator, for example, commented that "[the courts] will distinguish between lawful combinations in aid of production and unlawful combinations to prevent competition and in restraint of trade . . . ." *Id.* at 2456. He also said, "If they [the Standard Oil trust] conducted their business lawfully, without any attempt by these combinations to raise the price of an article consumed by the people of the United States, I would say let them pursue that business." *Id.* at 2469.

Representative Mason also condemned the trusts despite their efficiencies: "Some say that the trusts have made products cheaper, have reduced prices; but if the price of oil, for instance, were reduced to 1 cent a barrel it would not right the wrong done to the people of this country by the "trusts" which have destroyed legitimate competition and driven honest men from legitimate business enterprises." *Id.* at 4100. A slightly different sentiment was expressed by Senator Edmunds: "Although for the time being the sugar trust has perhaps reduced the price of sugar, and the oil trust certainly has reduced the price of oil immensely, that does not alter the wrong of the principle of any trust . . . because in the long run, however seductive they may appear in lowering prices to the consumer for the time being, all human experience and all human philosophy have proved that they are destructive of public welfare and come to be tyrannies, grinding tyrannies, that have sometimes in other countries produced riots, just riots in the moral sense, and so on." *Id.* at 2726. Moreover, none of the citations to the legislative history presented by Judge Bork confronted this trade-off. None suggested allowing higher prices to consumers in order to improve, or even to preserve, corporate efficiency. *See supra* note 84.

105. The controversy over whether Congress wanted to prohibit a monopoly achieved entirely by skill and efficiency comes largely from an exchange at the very end of the Sherman Act debates. Senator Kenna asked: "Is it intended by the committee, as the section seems to indicate, that if an individual . . . by his own skill and energy, by the propriety of his conduct generally, shall pursue his calling in such a way as to monopolize a trade, his action shall be a crime under this proposed act? . . .

"Suppose a citizen of Kentucky is dealing in shorthorn cattle and by virtue of his superior skill in that particular product it turns out that he is the only one in the United States to whom an order comes from Mexico for cattle of that stock for a considerable period, so that he is conceded to have a monopoly of that trade with Mexico, is it intended by the committee that the bill shall make that man a culprit?" 21 CONG. REC. 3151 (1890).

Senator Edmunds gave a direct response to Senator Kenna's hypothetical: "[I]n the case stated the gentleman has not any monopoly at all. He has not got the possession of all the horned cattle in the United States. . . . He has not done anything but compete with his adversaries in trade, if he had any, to furnish the commodity for the lowest price. So I assure my friend he need not be disturbed upon that subject." *Id.* at 3151-52. Senator Edmunds' response indicates that he believed that no monopolization was involved in the

Although Congress was aware that trusts and monopolies raised

---

hypothetical, so he did not really consider the need for an exception for a firm that achieved its monopoly solely by skill.

Senator Hoar then gave his well-known answer: "[I]n the case put [by Senator Kenna, if] . . . a man who merely by superior skill and intelligence, a breeder of horses or raiser of cattle, or manufacturer or artisan of any kind, got the whole business because nobody could do it as well as he could was not a monopolist, [unless] it involved something like the use . . . [of unfair] competition, like the engrossing, the buying up of all other persons engaged in the same business." *Id.* at 3152. Senator Edmunds then provided the final answer to Senator Kenna's question: "I have only to say . . . that this subject was not lightly considered in the committee, and that we studied it with whatever little ability we had, and the best answer I can make to both my friends is to read from Webster's Dictionary the definition of the verb 'to monopolize': 1. To purchase or obtain possession of the whole of, as a commodity or goods in market, with the view to appropriate or control the exclusive sale of; as, to monopolize sugar or tea.

"Like the sugar trust. One man, if he had capital enough, could do it just as well as two. 2. To engross or obtain by any means the exclusive right of, especially the right of trading to any place, or with any country or district; as, to monopolize the India or Levant trade.

". . . [W]e were not blind to the very suggestions which have been made, and we thought we had done the right thing in providing, in the very phrase we did, that if one person instead of two, by a combination, if one person alone, as we have heard about the wheat market in Chicago, for instance, did it, it was just as offensive and injurious to the public interest as if two had combined to do it." *Id.* The Sherman Act, forbidding any person to "monopolize or attempt to monopolize," was then passed by the Senate. *Id.* at 3153.

This crucial segment of the debate deserves careful consideration. It would seem that Senators Hoar and Edmunds provided opposite answers to Senator Kenna's question. Senator Hoar clearly did not consider a firm to be guilty of "monopolization" if it "got the whole business" by skill and efficiency alone. Senator Edmunds, however, defined "to monopolize" as merely "[t]o engross or obtain by any means . . . ." Edmunds intended that "if one person . . . did it, it was just as offensive and injurious to the public interest as if two had combined to do it." Edmunds clearly condemned every monopoly, although by his first response he did not consider the hypothetical situation given to describe a monopoly. Thus, it would appear that these statements should be construed as offsetting one another although, if a judgment had to be made, since Senator Edmunds spoke last and was one of the main sponsors of the bill, his statements could perhaps be said to carry greater weight. The fact that this discussion took place at the very end of the Sherman Act debate could very well mean that it embodied Congress' final view on the subject. However, these statements were also less able to be corrected or opposed by Senator Sherman or other legislators.

An alternative reading of this dialogue, which accepts Senator Hoar's comments and distinguishes or downplays Senator Edmunds' reply is, of course, possible. Under this interpretation, an exception would exist for monopolies achieved by efficiency alone. One possibly could conclude that Congress' desire to avoid discouraging innovation and industriousness outweighed its general distaste for monopoly pricing. Of course, Congress would not extend this exception to firms that combined in order to generate productive efficiencies, perhaps because its experiences with trusts led it to conclude that their true motive was probably to eliminate competition, rather than increase efficiency.

In addition, single-firm monopolization based on superior efficiency often involves lower prices to consumers during the period when the firm is attempting to increase its market share. By contrast, monopolization by merger or conspiracy, not based upon internally generated efficiencies, generally involves no short-term benefits to consumers. Thus, the long-term monopoly overcharges might have weighed more heavily in the multiple firm case

prices and restricted output, the legislators were unaware that this caused allocative inefficiency.[106] They thought that monopolies were relatively efficient producers and that breaking them up could decrease productive efficiency.[107] Yet, Congress enacted the Sherman Act largely to prohibit and condemn them.[108] Clearly, the chief economic concern was not productive efficiency;[109] if Congress' main goal was to encourage that form of industrial organization that was, in 1890, most efficient, it would have praised the trusts, not condemned them. Rather, the Sherman Act was intended to insure that consumers obtained their "fair share" of the benefits of free competition.

Protecting Consumers from Unfair Transfers of Wealth

In the legislative debates over the Sherman Act, Congress clearly condemned the use of market power to raise prices and restrict output.[110] This condemnation, however, did not arise from concern with allocative efficiency. The debates strongly suggest that Congress condemned trusts and monopolies because they had enough market power to raise prices and "unfairly" extract wealth from consumers, turning it into monopoly profits.[111]

---

and might have prompted Congress to condemn it even when it was based upon superior efficiency.

Nevertheless, if the main thrust of the statute is kept in mind, including Congress' basic condemnation of monopoly pricing despite a potential sacrifice of efficiency, the Sherman Act does not appear to provide an exception for the efficient monopolist.

106. *See supra* notes 80-84, 95-100 & accompanying text.

107. *See supra* notes 101-03 & accompanying text. It is unclear just how much of a loss in productivity Congress would have been willing to tolerate in order to break up the trusts. An extreme case of the recognition that it might sometimes be necessary to sacrifice productive efficiencies in order to achieve other goals is exemplified by the court's divestiture order in United States v. United Shoe Machinery Corp., 110 F. Supp. 295 (D. Mass. 1953), *aff'd per curiam*, 347 U.S. 521 (1954). *See* Averitt, *Section 5: Structural Remedies in Competition Cases under the Federal Trade Commission Act*, 40 OHIO ST. L.J. 781 (1979) [hereinafter cited as Averitt, *Structural Remedies*].

In a merger context the Supreme Court came to a similar conclusion: "Possible economies cannot be used as a defense to illegality. Congress was aware that some mergers which lessen competition may also result in economies but it struck the balance in favor of protecting competition." Federal Trade Comm'n v. Procter & Gamble, 385 U.S. 568, 580 (1967).

108. A possible exception to this general desire to prohibit monopolies may have been that provided for an "efficient monopolist." *But see supra* note 105.

109. It should be noted that while Congress was also concerned about small businesses, this concern was based upon a preference for small businesses as an end in itself, rather than upon the belief that protecting small businesses was a good way to increase the total efficiency or wealth of the economy. *See infra* notes 143-53 & accompanying text.

110. *See supra* notes 80-84, 95-100 & accompanying text.

111. *See* 21 CONG. REC. 2461 (1890). On July 10, 1888, Sherman offered a resolution, which was adopted without debate, condemning certain trusts and other business arrangements which "tend to foster monopoly or to artificially advance the cost to the consumer of

In the legislative debates, Congress discussed at length price increases by trusts and the resulting higher consumer prices.[112] For example, Senator Sherman, defending the bill's constitutionality, asked that Congress protect the public from trusts that "restrain commerce, turn it from its natural course, increase the price of articles, and therefore diminish the amount of commerce."[113] From this and other similar evidence Judge Bork correctly concluded, "The touchstone of illegality is raising prices to consumers. There were no exceptions."[114]

The debates strongly suggest that higher prices to consumers were condemned because they unfairly extracted wealth from consumers and turned it into monopoly profit. For example, during the debates Senator Sherman termed monopolistic overcharges "extortion which makes the people poor," and "extorted wealth."[115] Congressman Coke

---

necessary articles of human life. . . ." 19 CONG. REC. 6041 (1888). Sherman stated: "This bill does not seek to cripple combinations of capital and labor, the formation of partnerships or of corporations, but only to prevent and control combinations made with a view to prevent competition, or for the restraint of trade, or to increase the profits of the producer at the cost of the consumer." 21 CONG. REC. 2457 (1890); *see also id.* at 2461 (1890). Sherman added: "The law of selfishness, uncontrolled by competition, compels it to disregard the interest of the consumer." *Id.* He termed consumers subject to monopolistic pricing "unfortunate victims." *Id.*

Representative Heard stated: "We know that by such means the trusts which control the markets on sugar, nails, oils, lead, and almost every other article of use in the commerce of this country have advanced the cost of such articles to every consumer, and that without rendering the slightest equivalent therefor these illegal conspiracies against honest trade have stolen untold millions from the people." *Id.* at 4101.

112. *See supra* note 84.

113. 21 CONG. REC. 2462 (1890). Sherman also stated: "The sole object of such a combination is to make competition impossible. It can control the market, raise or lower prices, as will best promote to selfish interests . . . . Its governing motive is to increase the profits of the parties composing it. The law of selfishness, uncontrolled by competition, compels it to disregard the interest of the consumer. It dictates terms to transportation companies, it commands the price of labor without fear of strikes, for in its field it allows no competitors. Such a combination is far more dangerous than any heretofore invented, and, when it embraces the great body of all the corporations engaged in a particular industry in all of the States of the Union, it tends to advance the price to the consumer of any article produced." *Id.* at 2457.

114. Bork, *supra* note 66, at 16.

115. 21 CONG. REC. 2461 (1890). On July 10, 1888, Sherman had offered a resolution, adopted without debate, which condemned certain trusts and other business arrangements which "tend to foster monopoly or to artificially advance the cost to the consumer of necessary articles of human life . . . ." 19 CONG. REC. 7 (1888). Sherman also stated that "[t]his bill does not seek to cripple combinations of capital and labor, the formation of partnerships or of corporations, but only to prevent competition, or for the restraint of trade, or to increase the profits of the producer at the cost of the consumer." *Id.* at 2457. Sherman added: "The law of selfishness, uncontrolled by competition, compels it to disregard the interest of the consumer." *Id.* Sherman termed consumers subject to monopolistic pricing "unfortunate victims." *Id.* at 2461.

referred to the overcharges as "robbery."[116] Representative Heard declared that the trusts, "without rendering the slightest equivalent," have "stolen untold millions from the people."[117] Congressman Wilson complained that the beef trust "robs the farmer on the one hand and the consumer on the other."[118] Representative Fithian declared that the trusts were "impoverishing" the people through "robbery."[119] Senator Hoar declared that monopolistic pricing was "a transaction the direct purpose of which is to extort from the community . . . wealth which ought to be generally diffused over the whole community."[120] Senator George complained that "They aggregate to themselves great enormous wealth by extortion which makes the people poor."[121]

Congress condemned monopolistic overcharges in strong moral terms, rather than because of their efficiency effects.[122] Purchasers, whether resellers[123] or ultimate consumers, were entitled to purchase

116. *Id.* at 2614.

117. *Id.* at 4101 (emphasis added). The full quotation reads: "We know that by such means the trusts which control the markets on sugar, nails, lead, and almost every other article of use in the commerce of this country have advanced the cost of such articles to every consumer, and that without rendering the slightest equivalent therefore these illegal conspiracies against honest trade have stolen untold millions from the people."

118. *Id.* at 4098.

119. *Id.* at 4103. (Fithian was reading, with apparent approval, a letter from a constituent.)

120. 21 CONG. REC. 2728 (1890).

121. 21 CONG. REC. 1768. Senator George continued: "Then making this extorted wealth the means of further extortion from their unfortunate victims, the people of the United States, they pursue unmolested, unrestrained by law . . . . [They] have extorted their ill-gotten gains from the poor and then used the money thus obtained to complete the ruin of the people." *Id.* Senator George also complained that consumers were being robbed. *Id.* at 3150. He complained that the trusts were able to "fleece and rob the people." *Id.*

The Supreme Court has also used similar language. In Albrecht v. Herald Co., 390 U.S. 145, 153 (1967), the Court implied that it was an antitrust goal to "protect the public from price gouging by firms with monopoly power . . . ." *See also* Reiter v. Sonotone Corp., 442 U.S. 330, 339-43 (1979), discussed *supra* note 2. In Buckley v. Valeo, 424 U.S. 1, 262 (1976), Justice White, in dicta in a separate opinion concurring in part and dissenting in part, stated that "the antitrust laws are aimed at preventing monopoly profits and price fixing, which gouge the consumer."

122. Perhaps Congress was expressing more concern about preventing redistributions of wealth because they were relatively observable and certain. Efficiency gains, on the other hand, were probably more speculative in nature, and there was no guarantee that monopolists would pass them on to consumers.

123. Senator George, for example, recognized: "An advance in price to the middlemen is not mentioned in the bill, for the obvious reason that no such advance would damnify them; it would rather be a benefit, as it would increase the value of the goods he has on hand. He buys to sell again. He buys only for profit on a subsequent sale. So whatever he pays he receives when he sells, together with a profit on his investment; and so of all of them, including the last, who sells directly to the consumer. The consumer, therefore, paying all the increased price advanced by the middlemen and profits on the same, is the party neces-

competitively priced products. Members of Congress also condemned the unequal distribution of wealth resulting from monopolistic overcharges.[124] The legislators decided that competitive prices were "fair" whereas monopoly prices were not; therefore, consumers were entitled to own that quantity of wealth known today as "consumer surplus." The unfair prices, in effect, robbed consumers of that wealth. As a result, Congress was willing to risk some immediate efficiency losses in order to benefit consumers ultimately. Congress was willing to pass the Sherman Act in large part in an attempt to prevent such "unfair" transfers of wealth from consumers to monopolies.

Other Goals

Curbing the Social and Political Power of Trusts and Monopolies

Evidence also suggests that more than economic considerations motivated Congress to curb the power of trusts and monopolies. Although the concerns discussed thus far relate to the economic power of monopolies and trusts, Congress was also motivated by a desire to curb the social and political power of large businesses. This additional purpose is demonstrated by analyzing the history of the Sherman Act in light of the economic, social, and political context in which the law was passed.

The legislative history demonstrates that Congress condemned monopolies in part because they increased the cost of goods to consumers. Logic would seem to indicate that pressure from consumers burdened by higher prices contributed to the passage of the Sherman Act. This cannot be the complete explanation, however, because just prior to the passage of the Act, price levels in the United States were stable or

---

sarily damnified or injured." 21 CONG. REC. at 1767. He complained however, "The intent to advance the price to the wholesale or retail dealer alone will not do; it must be to advance it to the consumer. This leaves unpunished and perfectly lawful all these combinations which have proven so disastrous, that have for their object a decrease in the price to be given to the producer, and also those speculative movements now so common by which there shall be a temporary advance in the market, to last till a day not far off, when there shall be a settlement." *Id.* These quotations also suggest that the existence of middlemen should not nullify consumers' right to purchase competitively priced goods.

124. 21 CONG. REC. 2728 (1890). Senator Sherman stated: "The popular mind is agitated with problems that may disturb social order, and among them none is more threatening than the inequality of condition of wealth, and opportunity that has grown within a single generation out of the concentration of capital into vast combinations to control production and trade and to break down competition." *Id.* at 2460.

Senator George expressed a similar concern: "Is production, is trade, to be taken away from the great mass of the people concentrated in the hands of a few men who, I am obliged to add, by the policies pursued by our Government, have been enabled to aggregate to themselves large, enormous fortunes?" *Id.* at 2598.

slowly decreasing.[125] In 1890, American consumers paid less for goods than at almost any time since the end of the Civil War.[126]

Despite the then-recent rise of trusts, this phenomenon of falling prices is easily explained. The first trusts of any significance probably did not achieve their full power until a few years before passage of the Act.[127] Although some trusts did raise prices in the years immediately before 1890, overall consumer prices decreased dramatically from the end of the Civil War until approximately 1884, when they leveled off.[128] In addition, the last half of the nineteenth century witnessed a

125. Prices were falling, whether measured by the consumer price index, the cost of living index, or the wholesale price index. For example, in the generation between the end of the Civil War and the enactment of the Sherman Act, the consumer price index went down by 41%. Not only were prices falling on the average, they were falling for products in many of the industries that were cartelized, such as fuel and lighting (by 66%), metal and metal products (by 60%), textiles, chemicals and dyes, sugar, leather, food, spirits, building materials, etc. 1 U.S. BUREAU OF THE CENSUS, U.S. DEP'T OF COMMERCE, HISTORICAL STATISTICS OF THE UNITED STATES, COLONIAL TIMES TO 1970, at 201-11 (Bicentennial ed. 1975) [hereinafter cited as BUREAU OF THE CENSUS].

126. *Id.*

127. W. LETWIN, *supra* note 24, at 69-70, picks 1887 as the year of the formation of the first significant trusts. Other scholars pinpoint the start of the first great trusts and merger waves at different years. *See, e.g.*, D. MARTIN, MERGERS AND THE CLAYTON ACT 4 (1959) (concluding that the movement started in 1879, with the formation of the Standard Oil trust); OPPENHEIM & WESTON, FEDERAL ANTITRUST LAWS, CASES AND COMMENTS 317-23 (1967) (concluding that the first "merger movement" began after 1890). Regardless of the precise date that the first significant trusts were formed, it is generally agreed that they were stronger after 1890 than before it, and that the peak of the merger movement occurred after 1890.

128. The consumer price index and the cost of living index reveal that prices had not, on the average, started to increase by the time the Sherman Act was passed.

	Consumer Price Index (1967=100)	Cost of Living Indices (1913=100)			Wholesale Price Indices (1910–1914=100)	
		Federal Reserve Board Estimate	Burgess Estimate	All Commodities	Fuel & Lighting	Metals & Metal Products
1890	27	78	67.8	82	72	123
1889	27	78	67.8	81	71	116
1888	27	78	67.5	86	72	121
1887	27	76	65.4	85	70	119
1886	27	76	65.3	82	70	110
1885	27	75	64.6	85	72	109
1880	29	80	71.3	100	92	166
1875	33	86	81.2	118	128	175
1870	38	91	92.5	135	134	200
1865	46	102	108.1	185	214	306

1 BUREAU OF THE CENSUS, *supra* note 125, at 201-11.

great industrial revolution;[129] large-scale production, new technology, and increased production speed resulted in tremendous efficiencies.[130] The industries that spawned some of the most notorious trusts also benefitted most from the new efficiencies. As a consequence, prices often fell despite the existence of the trusts.[131]

Falling prices during this period in fact contributed to the formation of the trusts. Viewing falling prices and increased production with alarm, producers sought to arrest this trend by combining or entering agreements to stabilize or raise prices, restrict output, and suppress competition.[132] This trend was only beginning, however, by 1890. Most large and significant trusts were formed or achieved full power after and in spite of the passage of the Sherman Act.[133]

While prices might have fallen more rapidly had the trusts not attempted to halt their decline,[134] it seems unlikely that consumers would strongly condemn the trusts only because prices were not dropping as rapidly as they should have been.[135] It is possible that even though overall prices were stable or decreasing, Congress or the public could have focused their attention on those prices that were rising and concluded that trusts were, on the whole, causing higher prices. It is more likely that other factors were at work. Consumers probably were angered less by the reduction in their wealth than by the way in which the wealth was extracted.

The legislative history reveals that a major factor leading to the passage of the Sherman Act was a congressional desire to curb the power of trusts. While Congress was concerned about the uses of this power to raise prices and restrict output, it also desired, as an end in

129. The expansion of the railroads transformed the United States into one economic entity. Industrial growth and innovation were rapid and immense, creating tremendous advances in transportation, communication and distribution. *See* A. CHANDLER, JR., THE INVISIBLE HAND: THE MANAGERIAL REVOLUTION IN AMERICAN BUSINESS 250-59 (1977).

130. A. CHANDLER, JR., *supra* note 129, at 250-59.

131. *See supra* note 128. *See also infra* text accompanying note 133.

132. *See* R. HOFSTADTER, THE AGE OF REFORM, ch. 6 (1969) [hereinafter cited as R. HOFSTADTER, REFORM]; W. LETWIN, *supra* note 24, at 139.

133. *See* R. HOFSTADTER, REFORM, *supra* note 132, ch. 6; W. LETWIN, *supra* note 24, at 139.

134. It is uncertain whether in 1890, monopolies and trusts were responsible for more price *rises* than price *declines*. They did bring capital, large-scale production, organization, and modern technology to industry. Price reductions resulting from these efficiencies could have outweighed the price increases resulting from their monopoly power.

135. Trust decisions to raise prices often achieved great notoriety. Their efficiency gains were, of course, relatively invisible. In retrospect, it seems that a trust could have made a good case that its existence was in the public interest by merely pointing to the consumer price index.

itself, the prevention of accumulation of power by large corporations and the men who controlled them. Alarm over corporate aggrandizement of economic, social, and political power pervaded the debate.[136] The legislators feared not only the economic consequences of monopoly power, but potential social disruptions as well.[137] Moreover, this apprehension has been recognized repeatedly by courts interpreting the legislative history of the Act.[138]

---

136. As Senator Sherman warned, "[If] we will not endure a king as a political power we should not endure a king over the production, transportation, and sale of any of the necessaries of life. If we would not submit to an emperor we should not submit to an autocrat of trade, with power to prevent competition and to fix the price of any commodity." 21 CONG. REC. 2457 (1890). This theme runs throughout Senator Sherman's opening remarks. "If the concentered powers of this combination are entrusted to a single man, it is a kingly prerogative, inconsistent with our form of government, and should be subject to the strong resistance of the State and national authorities." *Id.* He framed the issue in the following manner: "The point for us to consider is whether, on the whole, it is safe in this country to leave the production of property, the transportation of our whole country, to depend upon the will of a few men sitting at their council board in the city of New York." *Id.* at 2570. Sherman further stated: "The popular mind is agitated with problems that may disturb social order, and among them none is more threatening than the inequality of condition of wealth, and opportunity that has grown within a single generation out of the concentration of capital into vast combinations to control production and trade and to break down competition. These combinations already defy or control powerful transportation corporations and reach state authorities. They reach out their Briarean arms to every part of our country. They are imported from abroad, Congress alone can deal with them, and if we are unwilling or unable there will soon be a trust for every production and a master to fix the price for every necessity of life." *Id.* at 2460. Senator George expressed a similar fear, asking, "Is production, is trade, to be taken away from the great mass of the people and concentrated in the hands of a few men . . . ?" 21 CONG. REC. 2598 (1890).

137. Senator Hoar warned that "[t]he complaint which has come from all parts and all classes of the country of these great monopolies, which are becoming not only in some cases an actual injury to the comfort of ordinary life, but are a menace to republican institutions themselves, has induced Congress to take the matter up." *Id.* at 3146 (1890). *See also supra* text accompanying note 104.

Senator Sherman wanted to protect the "industrial liberty of the citizens," *id.* at 2457, and believed that trusts caused inequality of wealth and opportunity that "may disturb social order." *Id.* at 2460. In his strongest statement expressing fear of corporate power, he cautioned that "[t]hey had monopolies and mortmains of old, but never before such giants as in our day. You must heed their appeal or be ready for the socialist, the communist, and the nihilist. Society is now disturbed by forces never felt before." *Id.* at 2457.

138. Perhaps the most famous expression of this recognition was Judge Hand's citation to the above-quoted remarks of Senator Sherman, in United States v. Aluminum Co. of America, 148 F.2d 416 (2d Cir. 1945): "We have been speaking only of the economic reasons which forbid monopoly; but, as we have already implied, there are others, based upon the belief that great industrial consolidations are inherently undesirable, regardless of their economic results. In the debates in Congress Senator Sherman himself . . . showed that among the purposes of Congress in 1890 was a desire to put an end to great aggregations of capital because of the helplessness of the individual before them." *Id.* at 428. In one of the first major Sherman Act cases, Standard Oil Co. v. United States, 221 U.S. 1 (1911), Chief Justice White offered a similar explanation: "The debates . . . conclusively show . . . that

A review of the social history of the period illuminates the reasons underlying Congress' alarm. The post-Civil War period saw a rural agricultural nation transformed into an increasingly urban and industrial society. Work patterns changed. By the end of the Civil War individual yeoman farmers had all but vanished. In their places stood entrepreneurs and commercial farmers who shipped their goods to markets and then used the resulting cash to purchase goods from small businesses.[139] Thus, traditional independence gradually changed into interdependence.

With the rise of trusts, interdependence became impotence. Decisionmaking was transferred from traditional power centers to the great industrialists. Self-reliant farmers, business owners, and local leaders became dependent on the discretionary power of a few very rich men. Local control of society ended as numerous small power centers were swept away by the new class, one perceived as greedy and evil.[140] This transfer of power generated hostility towards the trusts and resulted in

---

the main cause which led to the legislation was the thought that it was required by the economic condition of the times, that is, the vast accumulation of wealth in the hands of corporations and individuals, the enormous development of corporate organization, the facility for combination which such organizations afforded, the fact that the facility was being used, and that combinations known as trusts were being multiplied, and the wide-spread impression that their power had been and would be exerted to oppress individuals and injure the public generally." *Id.* at 50; *see also* United States v. South-Eastern Underwriters Ass'n, 332 U.S. 533, 553-54 (1944). Another early Supreme Court interpretation of the Sherman Act's legislative history, United States v. Trans-Missouri Freight Ass'n, 166 U.S. 290 (1897), came to the same conclusion: "[Trading combination] may even temporarily, or perhaps permanently, reduce the price of the article traded in or manufactured. . . .

"[I]t is not material that the price of an article may be lowered. It is in the power of the combination to raise it. . . . Nor is it for the substantial interests of the country that any one commodity should be within the sole power and subject to the sole will of one powerful combination of capital." *Id.* at 323-24; *see also* Appalachian Coals, Inc. v. United States, 288 U.S. 344, 359 (1933); United States v. American Can Co., 230 F. 859, 901 (D. Md. 1916).

139. For a concise discussion of the myth of agrarian independence and the emergence of industrial society, see R. HOFSTADTER, REFORM, *supra* note 132, chs. 1-2.

140. *Id.* ch. 6. Professor Letwin provides a concise description of the public attitude just before the passage of the Sherman Act: "The great fervor against trusts . . . was for the people living at the time nothing so sudden or strange. It was simply a familiar feeling raised to a high pitch, intense because the speed with which new trusts were being hatched made it seem that they would overrun everything unless some remedy were found soon. The general disposition of the public was not in doubt. There were numerous objections to the trusts. . . . Trusts, it was said, threatened liberty, because they corrupted civil servants and bribed legislators; they enjoyed privileges such as protection by tariffs; they drove out competitors by lowering prices, victimized consumers by raising prices, defrauded investors by watering down stocks, put laborers out of work by closing down plants, and somehow or other abused everyone. The kind of remedy that the public desired was also clear enough; it wanted a law to destroy the power of the trusts." W. LETWIN, *supra* note 24, at 70.

political pressure on Congress to pass antitrust legislation.[141]

The political and social evils of accumulated power, recited in the legislative debates and reiterated by the cases and historians, probably engendered more public resentment toward the trusts than did an isolated rise in prices during an era of stable and declining prices.[142] The congressional complaint, therefore, was directed not solely at the effects of monopoly power—higher prices and poorer consumers—but also at the process that produced them. The Sherman Act was intended not only to achieve competitive prices but also to restructure the economy in ways insuring a "fair" process for economic, social, and political decisionmaking by reducing the unfairly accumulated power of the trusts.

Protecting Small Businesses

Congress also expressed concern for preserving business opportunities for small firms.[143] The opportunity to compete has been viewed as particularly important for small entrepreneurs, perhaps because of

141. Certain exceptions to the Sherman Act were almost certainly not enacted in order to increase economic efficiency, but were probably provided in order to transfer power, and perhaps wealth, toward unions and states and in order to curb the social and political power of the trusts. *See generally* Noll, *Antitrust Exemptions: An Economic Overview* in NCRALP REPORT, *supra* note 70, at 168-70. The exceptions have the overriding purpose of promoting such political goals as federalism and the regulatory power of the states. *See, e.g.*, Parker v. Brown, 317 U.S. 341 (1943). One "exception" to the reach of the Sherman Act concerns the right to petition the state legislatures by a combination attempting to influence legislation and thereby produce a monopoly or other restraint of trade. *See, e.g.*, Otter Tail Power Co. v. United States, 410 U.S. 366 (1973); United Mine Workers v. Pennington, 381 U.S. 657 (1965); Eastern R.R. Presidents Conference v. Noerr Motor Freight, Inc., 365 U.S. 127 (1961). The antitrust laws also exempt labor unions from their coverage. *See generally* L. SULLIVAN, HANDBOOK OF THE LAW OF ANTITRUST 723-31 (1977).

142. *See supra* notes 125-26, 128 & accompanying text. A recent analogy might be found in the reaction of the American public to the recent rise in the price of petroleum. If the public had perceived that prices were rising because oil was getting scarce and expensive to produce, the public certainly would have become unhappy insofar as this meant that consumers would have to pay more for their gasoline and would, as a consequence, be poorer. But it is difficult to feel anger if one believes that price increases are caused "legitimately" by the impersonal factors of supply and demand. By contrast, the fact that the petroleum price increases were dictated by a small group of men acting at their own discretion angered people. The American public felt helpless before OPEC. There was great uncertainty over what OPEC might do next, and resentment that a small group of men had the power to make decisions that drastically affected everyone's life. The "unfairness" of the way that the price increases came about, in addition to their amounts, helped cause the public anger towards OPEC.

143. In the opening debates on the Act, Senator Sherman stated: "It is the right of every man to work, labor, and produce in any lawful vocation and to transport his production on

their vulnerability to predatory activities.[144] Carrying this goal to its extreme, Representative Mason alone would have condemned trusts even if they lowered prices to consumers because they could financially ruin small businesses.[145]

Judicial statements of congressional intention to assist small businesses have been frequent.[146] Courts have even occasionally viewed

---

equal terms and conditions and under like circumstances. This is industrial liberty and lies at the foundation of the equality of all rights and privileges. . . .

". . . .

"But, they say, competition is open to all; if you do not like our prices, establish another combination or trust . . . . [But] when the combination already includes all or nearly all the producers, what room is there for another?" 21 CONG. REC. 2457, 2460 (1890). This sympathy for the welfare of small businesses was also expressed in the Sherman Act debates by Senator George: "It is a sad thought to the philanthropist that the present system of production and of exchange is having that tendency which is sure at some not very distant day to crush out all small men, all small capitalists, all small enterprises. . . . So now the American Congress and the American people are brought face to face with this sad, this great problem: Is production, is trade, to be taken away from the great mass of the people and concentrated in the hands of a few men . . . ?" *Id.* at 2598. Senator George also stated that "[b]y the use of this organized force of wealth and money the small men engaged in competition with them are crushed out; and that is the great evil at which all this legislation ought to be aimed." *Id.* at 3147. See also the remarks of Senator Pugh concerning the freedom of competitive fairness as a policy to be furthered. *Id.* at 2558.

144. Hofstadter characterized this type of concern as one that was both "psychological and moral. It sprang from the conviction that competition has a disciplinary value for character, quite aside from its strictly economic uses. America was thought to have been made possible by the particular type of character that was forged by competitive individualism, a type that had flourished in the United States because competitive opportunities had been so widespread that alert men could hardly fail to see them, to grasp and use them, and hence, to be shaped by them. The American male character was believed to have been quickened and given discipline by the sight and pursuit of opportunity. For this process to take place it was important that business be carried on fairly . . . and that newcomers be able to enter the game as entrepreneurs. . . .

"The economic order was not merely an apparatus for the production of goods and services; it was a set of rules for forging good conduct." R. HOFSTADTER, THE PARANOID STYLE *supra* note 5, at 209.

145. "Some say that the trusts have made products cheaper, have reduced prices; but if the price of oil, for instance, were reduced to 1 cent a barrel, it would not right the wrong done to the people of this country by the 'trusts' which have destroyed legitimate competition and driven honest men from legitimate business enterprises." 21 CONG. REC. 4100 (1890).

146. For example, in Charles A. Ramsay v. Associated Bill Posters, 260 U.S. 501, 512 (1922), the Supreme Court held that "[t]he fundamental purpose of the Sherman Act was to secure equality of opportunity and to protect the public against evils commonly incident to destruction of competition through monopolies and combinations in restraint of trade." *See also* United States v. Topco Ass'n, 405 U.S. 596, 610 (1972). This same general purpose has also found expression in the doctrine that group boycotts and concerted refusals by traders to deal with other traders constitute violations of the Sherman Act, even if price competition is unaffected. *See, e.g.*, Klor's Inc. v. Broadway-Hale Stores, 359 U.S. 207 (1959); Fashion Originators' Guild v. Federal Trade Comm'n, 312 U.S. 457 (1941); Eastern States Retail Lumber Dealers' Ass'n v. United States, 234 U.S. 600 (1914). It has also found expression in

congressional interest in protecting small businesses as overriding its consumer-oriented goals.[147]

Despite clear judicial recognition, close examination reveals relatively little support in the legislative history, beyond the few references above, for the "small producer" rationale.[148] Although there are a few statements suggesting that the protection of the opportunity of small business to compete was one motivating factor for the legislators, these statements do not imply that protection of small businesses was meant to override other goals.[149] Congress probably did not intend to go fur-

the Court's preferences for individual "enterprise and sagacity." Associated Press v. United States, 326 U.S. 1, 15 (1945).

147. The most famous exposition of the view that the Sherman Act was passed in order to preserve small businesses even if this might result in higher prices to consumers is probably that put forth by Judge Hand in United States v. Aluminum Co. of America, 148 F.2d 416 (2d Cir. 1945): "[Congress in passing the Sherman Act] was not necessarily actuated by economic motives alone. It is possible, because of its indirect social or moral effect, to prefer a system of small producers, each dependent for his success upon his own skill and character, to one in which the great mass of those engaged must accept the direction of a few. . . .

"Throughout the history of these statutes it has been constantly assumed that one of their purposes was to perpetuate and preserve, for its own sake and *in spite of possible cost*, an organization of industry in small units which can effectively compete with each other." *Id.* at 429 (footnote omitted) (emphasis added). The desire to preserve opportunity for small businesses is perhaps explained by the belief that small businessmen were "worthy men" who lived productive and honest lives. This sentiment was powerfully expressed in United States v. Trans-Missouri Freight Ass'n, 166 U.S. 290, 323-24 (1897), where the Court stated: "Trade or commerce under [circumstances of artificially reduced prices] may nevertheless be badly and unfortunately restrained by driving out of business the small dealers and worthy men whose lives have been spent therein, and who might be unable to readjust themselves to their altered surroundings. Mere reduction in the price of the commodity dealt in might be dearly paid for by the ruin of such a class, and the absorption of control over one commodity by an all-powerful combination of capital." *See also* Fashion Originators' Guild v. Federal Trade Comm'n, 312 U.S. 457, 467 (1941);

An even more striking example of judicial interpretation occurred in a different context in Brown Shoe Co. v. United States, 370 U.S. 294 (1962), where the Court referred to the congressional desire to protect "viable, small, locally owned businesses," even though this might result in "occasional higher costs and prices." *Id.* at 344. *See infra* text accompanying note 254.

148. *See supra* text accompanying notes 143-44. The courts appear to cite repeatedly the same few references. For example, to support the conclusion reprinted *supra* in note 147, Judge Hand relied on the remarks of Senator Sherman and Senator George, *supra* note 143. United States v. Aluminum Co. of America, 148 F.2d at 428-29.

149. Only Representative Mason expressed an intent to protect small businesses at the expense of consumers. *See supra* text accompanying note 145. There are perhaps a small number of overlooked statements that support Representative Mason's view. In addition, some of the proconsumer statements may have disguised the desires of a few members of Congress who really favored aid to small businesses. But a few isolated statements do not represent the intent of Congress. Nor can they establish the policy or spirit of the Sherman Act. This is especially true because Representative Mason's views run counter to the strong consumer orientation of the Sherman Act.

ther than establishment of an economic system providing free opportunities for entry and enough producers to ensure vigorous competition, a system in which no company became large enough to dominate.[150]

Additionally, the congressional intent to assist small businesses can be interpreted as promoting distributive, rather than efficiency, considerations. Passage of the Sherman Act may have been intended, in part, to transfer wealth to small businesses. The legislative history does not indicate, however, that Congress intended to help small businesses as a means of improving the overall efficiency of the economy. The debate suggests only a possible intent to assist small businesses as an end in itself, not as a means of increasing total economic output.[151]

Sympathetic to the plight of small businesses harmed by trusts, Congress expressed a desire to create an environment in which small businesses could effectively compete. It can fairly be said that one of Congress' goals was to assist small businesses; although consumers' interests were meant to be paramount, and conflicts between the welfare of consumers and small businesses were generally to be resolved in favor of consumers, Congress' desire to help small businesses certainly extended to those circumstances in which small businesses would be

150. Of course, sentiments in the legislative history denouncing large trusts and monopolies and those praising small businesses are closely related. In the views of Professors Kaysen and Turner, "The legislators were well aware of the common law on restraints of trade, and of the power of monopolists to hurt the public by raising price, deteriorating product, and restricting production. At the same time, there was at least equal concern with the fate of small producers driven out of business, or deprived of the opportunity to enter it, by 'all powerful aggregations of capital.' There was no obvious inconsistency in these two interests. One could readily have identified free access and large numbers of comparatively small producers with competitive processes, and in turn have identified competitive processes derived from such market structures with beneficial economic results for the public at large. Or, to short circuit the proposition, one could have equated beneficial economic results with the protection of large numbers of small independent producers." C. KAYSEN & D. TURNER, ANTITRUST POLICY 19 (1959). Nevertheless, the two concepts are not identical. For example, one might fear the economic, social, or political power of IBM and desire that it be split into five parts. Each part would be a multibillion dollar enterprise and one of the largest companies in a huge industry. Splitting IBM into five companies could help small computer companies to compete. Alternatively, however, the five new companies could drive smaller computer companies out of business. One could desire to split up IBM because of its size and power, regardless of, or even in spite of, the effect that this would have on small computer companies.

151. Even large businesses were entitled to protection from predation. At one point Senator George complained, "If some great manufacturer has been injured by an advance in the price of his raw material he can sue, but the poor man, the consumer, the laborer, the farmer, the mechanic, the country merchant, all that large class of American citizens who constitute 80 per cent of our population and who are the real sufferers will have no opportunity of redress, and the bill, so far as they are concerned, will be a snare and a mere delusion." 21 CONG. REC. 3150 (1890).

helped but consumers would not significantly suffer.[152] Despite the wishes of Representative Mason,[153] however, this expression of sympathy did not amount to a congressional directive to assist small businesses in ways conflicting with the essential purpose of the Act, the protection of consumers.

Summary

Congress passed the Sherman Act to further a number of goals. Its main concern was with firms acquiring or possessing enough market power to raise prices artificially and to restrict output. Congress' primary aim was to enable consumers to purchase products at competitive prices. Artificially high prices were condemned not for causing allocative inefficiency but for "unfairly" transforming consumers' wealth into monopoly profits. All purchasers, whether consumers or businesses, were given the right to purchase competitively priced goods. All sellers were given the right to face rivals selling at competitive prices.

Concurrently, Congress was interested in encouraging efficient behavior in firms. Congress wanted a competitive economy to encourage the greater efficiencies resulting from competition. Efficiency gains were particularly desired when benefits passed through directly to consumers. A concern with productive efficiency could not, however, explain why Congress passed the Sherman Act. Congress condemned the relatively efficient trusts and monopolies for redistributive reasons. With the unlikely possibility of an exception for the "efficient monopolist,"[154] monopolizing conduct was not permitted merely because it pro-

152. Reconciliation of these interests can be illustrated through an analysis of a hypothetical case of predatory pricing. Assume that a firm lowered prices to below marginal cost in the short run, destroyed equally efficient competing small firms, and then increased prices to the monopoly level for an extended period. Because successful predation would hurt both consumers and small businesses, it would be condemned under either rationale. Suppose, however, that the predation attempt was unsuccessful because, although the below-cost pricing secured a monopoly position for the predator, as soon as it attempted to price above cost new competitors entered the market and eroded its market power. Unsuccessful predation would not hurt consumers; moreover, because they obtained below-cost goods for a short term, they benefited. However, small firms in the industry were destroyed by the unsuccessful predation attempt. While Congress desired that consumers not pay monopoly prices, at no point did Congress desire for consumers to be able to purchase goods below the competitive price. Consumers are entitled to competitive prices, not low prices. Unsuccessful predation should, therefore, be condemned out of a desire to protect small businesses.

For a legal and economic overview of predation, see Hurwitz & Kovacic, *Judicial Analysis of Predation: The Emerging Trends*, 35 VAND. L. REV. 63 (1982); Hurwitz, Kovacic, Sheehan & Lande, *Current Legal Standards of Predation*, in STRATEGY, PREDATION, AND ANTITRUST ANALYSIS (S. Salop ed. 1981), and the sources cited therein.

153. *See supra* note 149.

154. *See supra* note 105.

duced efficiency gains for the monopolist.

The Act also involved efforts to decentralize economic, social, and political decisionmaking to ensure that narrow private interests would be unable to override the public good flowing from free competition. The corporate power that the free market inadequately curbed was the target of the Act. Thus, the Act was also aimed at curbing the social and political power of large corporations and at encouraging opportunities for small entrepreneurs to compete, both thought to flow from the desired economic order as expressed in the Act.

The Sherman Act, the first antitrust law, set the tone for future antitrust legislation. Subsequent antitrust laws represented either extensions of the same ideas to different economic arenas, or attempts to better implement the same fundamental principles.

The Federal Trade Commission Act

Section 5 of the Federal Trade Commission (FTC) Act proscribes "[u]nfair methods of competition,"[155] a largely undefined prohibition against such traditional antitrust conduct as cartels and monopolization,[156] and against such consumer protection problems as fraudulent or coercive business practices.[157] Neither this phrase nor any of its component words, however, are defined in the Act. The same controversy and uncertainty that arose over the goals of the Sherman Act similarly cloud the meaning of "unfair methods of competition." The dominant view is that the FTC Act and the Sherman Act have identical, efficiency-oriented antitrust goals.[158] A minority of commentators, however, believe that the FTC Act was passed for a variety of social and political purposes.[159]

A third view is warranted. Although efficiency was a significant concern of the FTC Act, this Article argues that the overriding goal of section 5 was the prevention of transfers of wealth from consumers re-

155. FTC Act, 15 U.S.C. § 45(a)(1) (1976).

156. Averitt, *The Meaning of "Unfair Methods of Competition" in Section 5 of the Federal Trade Commission Act*, 21 B.C.L. Rev. 227 (1980) [hereinafter cited as Averitt, *Unfair Methods*].

157. Averitt, *The Meaning of "Unfair Acts or Practices" in Section 5 of the Federal Trade Commission Act*, 70 Geo. L.J. 225 (1981) [hereinafter cited as Averitt, *Unfair Acts or Practices*].

158. If both statutes were directed to maximize the economic efficiency of our economy it stands to reason that the two statutes should be interpreted identically, and that they would differ only in the scope of their coverage.

159. *See supra* notes 1, 11-16.

sulting from "unfair methods of competition."[160] For example, when monopolies force consumers to pay more for their goods or when fraudulent practices lead consumers to purchase goods they do not really want, wealth is "unfairly" transferred from consumers to firms with market power.[161]

The Congress that passed the FTC Act endorsed the Sherman Act's prohibitions, but feared that that law was inadequate.[162] The report of the Senate Committee on Interstate Commerce noted that "[a]ll agree that while the Sherman law is the foundation stone of our policy on this question, additional legislation is necessary."[163] Thus, the objective of both statutes was the same: the prevention and curtailment of monopoly power.[164] The legislative history of the FTC Act shows it

---

160. The framers of the FTC Act also had a variety of administrative goals, which will not be discussed in this Article.

161. The case of *In re* Allied Corp., File No. 811 0191, FTC (Dec. 8, 1982), directly confronted the wealth transfer issue. FTC Chairman James C. Miller stated that he endorsed the proposition, advanced by agency economists, that elimination of potential monopoly overcharges should *not* be counted as a law enforcement "benefit" when the agency does cost/benefit analyses. Such monopoly overcharges, said Miller, are merely "revenue transfers." F.T.C. Watch No. 158, Jan. 14, 1983, at 1. Commissioner Clanton, however, joined by Commissioners Bailey and Pertschuk, stated his belief that "preventing such transfers is one of the goals of the antitrust laws." *Id.* at 3.

162. The Senate Committee on Interstate Commerce expressed this idea in its 1913 report advocating additional antitrust legislation. The committee was of the opinion that the Sherman Act "should stand as the fundamental law upon the subject, and that any supplemental legislation for more effectual control and regulation of interstate and foreign commerce should be in harmony with the purpose of the existing statute." S. REP. NO. 1326, 62d Cong., 3d Sess. 2 (1913).

163. *Report of the Senate Comm. on Interstate Commerce*, S. REP. NO. 597, 63d Cong., 2d Sess. 8 (1914). As a consequence, the FTC was empowered to implement the Sherman Act. The Senate Committee on Interstate Commerce stated: "The proper enforcement of the Sherman Law also requires vigilant supervision which is most effectively obtained by a body in continual touch with the business organizations in the various industries." *Id.* at 1. This can also be illustrated by one of the final House debates involving Representative Frederick C. Stevens, a leading FTC sponsor:

> REPRESENTATIVE MADDEN. Do the conferees understand, and wish to have the House understand, that this does away with the Sherman Law?
>
> REPRESENTATIVE STEVENS. Not at all; it expressly does not. It is a method of enforcing it and making it more effective and preventing its misuse.

51 CONG. REC. 14,934 (1914).

The FTC was also charged with improving upon the Sherman Act's prohibitions by preventing monopolies in their incipiency. *See* Averitt, *Unfair Acts or Practices, supra* note 157, at 242-51. The FTC Act also had the explicit goal of preventing those practices which violated the spirit of the other antitrust laws. *See id.* at 251-71. *See generally* Averitt, *Unfair Methods, supra* note 156.

164. As Representative Morgan succinctly stated, "Monopoly is the evil we wish to control. Competition is the thing we wish to maintain." 51 CONG. REC. 8855 (1914). There was, however, a vocal minority that advocated a mixture of cooperation and competition. Senator Lippitt, for example, stated: "Cooperation in trade is a living, vital force that can

was enacted to better accomplish the goals of the Sherman Act,[165] and to extend Sherman Act principles to one significant new arena: "unfair" or "immoral" business behavior.[166]

The remainder of this section examines the legislative history of the FTC Act to determine what Congress meant by "competition" and by "unfair methods of competition." First, a review of the evidence demonstrates that the FTC Act was directed at insuring that corporate productive efficiency was both enhanced and passed on to consumers. The Article next argues that Congress' primary goal was prevention of "unfair" transfers of wealth caused by market power. The evidence also shows that, on balance, Congress did not want its distributive goals to be sacrificed for other objectives. Finally, the evidence relating to morality goals, the goal of curbing the noneconomic power of trusts and monopolies, and the goal of promoting the competitive position of small businesses is examined.

Improving Economic Efficiency

The dominant view of the FTC Act goals proposes that the Act, properly construed, should be concerned only with maximizing "consumer welfare,"[167] that is, with encouraging productive efficiency and

---

not be neglected, and the problem therefore that has to be intelligently met in the legislation on that subject if the situation is to be put upon a permanent basis is in some way to clearly formulate into law the intermediate ground between an unlimited and unregulated and destructive competition on the one side and an unregulated and unlimited cooperation on the other." *Id.* at 13,216.

165. Representative Morgan offered a very comprehensive early view of the Act's goals. *Id.* at 8854.

166. This prohibition on certain business behaviors, combined with the desire to prevent particular transfers of wealth, gives rise to and provides the goals behind the efforts of the Bureau of Consumer Protection. *See infra* text accompanying notes 213-15 & 221-28. Indeed, Congress' very use of the term "unfair" to modify "competition" strongly suggests a purpose for the prohibition that may be desired as moral, social or political, but in any case does not seem to be primarily efficiency oriented.

167. *See* R. BORK, *supra* note 2, at 51. Bork cautions, "We are compelled, I think, to accept this definition of 'competition'. . . . Very likely this is the primary value Congress had in mind when it used the word. Moreover, because 'competition' as a shorthand expression for consumer welfare enables us to employ basic economic theory, it avoids the pitfalls inherent in the other definitions surveyed. . . . [A]s will be shown . . . only this reading is consistent with other indicia of congressional intent and with the requirements of the judicial function." *Id.* at 61.

It is interesting to note that Bork considers and rejects four possible alternative meanings of competition:

"1. 'Competition' may be read as the process of rivalry. This is a natural mode of speech . . . . [Y]et it is a loose usage and invites the further, wholly erroneous conclusion that the elimination of rivalry must always be illegal.

"But this identification of competition with rivalry will not do for antitrust purposes. It

with minimizing allocative inefficiency. Judge Bork states that the mandated drive to enhance "consumer welfare" focuses on maximum economic efficiency and excludes such distributive concerns as "unfair" transfers of wealth from consumers to monopolists.[168]

The prevailing view, however, is not supported by the record. Familiarity with allocative efficiency did not increase substantially from 1890 to 1914, even among economists, who had little influence on the passage of the Act, much less among legislators.[169] No mention of any concept resembling allocative efficiency appears in the legislative history of the FTC Act.[170] On the other hand, the legislative history places considerable emphasis on preserving and even increasing corporate productive efficiency.[171]

---

makes rivalry an end in and of itself, no matter how many or how large the benefits flowing from the elimination of rivalry.

"2. 'Competition' may be read as the absence of restraint over one person's or firm's economic activities by any other person or firm. So viewed, competition is the absence of . . . 'bondage'. . . . This is not a useful definition, however, for the preservation of competition would then require the destruction of all commercial contracts and obligations.

"3. 'Competition' may be read as that state of the market 'in which the individual buyer or seller does not influence the price by his purchases or sales. . . . This is an enormously useful model for economic theory, but it is utterly useless as a goal of law. . . . For the law to move either national markets . . . or local markets . . . as close as possible to the model of perfect competition . . . would entail an unbelievable loss in national wealth for no particular purpose.'

"4. 'Competition' may be read, in a meaning closely related to the one just discussed, as the existence of 'fragmented industries and markets' preserved 'through the protection of viable, small, locally owned business.'" *Id.* at 58-60.

168. *See supra* text accompanying notes 72-89.

169. While the concept was known to economists, the theoretical underpinnings of allocative efficiency were mostly undeveloped in 1914. *See supra* notes 91-100 & accompanying text; A. MARSHALL, *supra* note 26, at 395-410 (8th ed. 1920) (reprinted 1961). Professor Stigler, discussing the influence of economists on the 1914 legislation, concluded, "I am unwilling to believe that economists . . . had any appreciable influence on antitrust legislation." Stigler, *supra* note 98, at 6.

170. None of the scholars who advocate allocative efficiency as the goal of antitrust laws have been able to point to any remarks in the Act's legislative history that indicate an understanding of the concept.

171. The statement that perhaps most strongly supports a major role for efficiency in § 5 analysis came from Senator Hollis: "Fair competition is competition which is successful through superior efficiency. Competition is unfair when it resorts to methods which shut out competitors who, by reason of their efficiency, might otherwise be able to continue in business and prosper. Without the use of unfair methods no corporation can grow beyond the limits imposed upon it by the necessity of being as efficient as any competitor. The mere size of a corporation which maintains its position solely through superior efficiency is ordinarily no menace to the public interest." 51 CONG. REC. 12,146 (1914). It should be noted that Senator Hollis was not one of the Act's principal sponsors. Nor did he explicitly confront the problem that even efficient firms may charge monopolistic prices. Despite his failure to confront the tradeoff between monopolistic overcharges and efficiency, however, his state-

Undoubtedly efficiency concerns were meant to play a major role in section 5 analysis, but remarks of a number of legislators suggest that efficiency was not Congress' sole objective. Their views imply that Congress was primarily concerned with preserving those efficiency benefits that flowed directly to consumers.[172] For example, Senator Cum-

---

ment nevertheless provides support for the view that efficiency should play a strong role in § 5 analysis.

Senator Robinson, quoting William H.S. Stevens, a leading economist of the times, provided a similar definition: "Nearly all normal business men can distinguish between 'fair competition' and 'unfair competition.' Efficiency is generally regarded as the fundamental principle of the former—efficiency in producing and in selling, while oppression or advantage obtained by deception or some questionable means is the distinguishing characteristic of 'unfair competition.'" *Id.* at 12,248. Professor Stevens expressed a similar opinion shortly after the Act was passed: "*[T]he interest of the public lies in securing the best goods at the lowest prices or, translated into other terms, in a competition of productive and/or selling efficiency*. In other words, the power given to the Trade Commission under section 5 is the power to prevent those methods which do not constitute a competition or productive and/or selling efficiency." W. STEVENS, "UNFAIR COMPETITION," A STUDY OF CERTAIN TRADE PRACTICES 236 (1917) (emphasis in original). Stevens continued that "a competition of productive and selling efficiency is, in the last analysis, practically synonymous with the public interest." *Id.*

Further, the 1913 Senate Committee on Interstate Commerce stated that it "believes that the progress of the world depends in a large measure upon that fair, reasonable rivalry among men which has hitherto characterized the advances of civilization. S. REP. NO. 1326, 62d Cong., 3d Sess. 13 (1913). Representative Morgan wanted the Act "[t]o enable us to assure all the benefits and advantages of the large industrial unit and escape the evils and dangers thereof. . . . [t]o relieve doubt and uncertainty to business, develop trade, encourage commerce, and promote enterprise. . . ." 51 CONG. REC. 8854 (1914). Additional concern for efficiency can be found in the earliest proceedings of the FTC, which noted its desire in making rulings and orders "to promote business efficiency and, within the limits of practicability, to cooperate with the business world in developing the best standards of commercial ethics." FEDERAL TRADE COMMISSION ANNUAL REPORT 26 (1916).

172. One early exchange openly revealed a preference for consumers, and explicitly stated that the purpose of the Act was not to help corporations:

> MR. BARTLETT. [The bill for the creation of the Federal Trade Commission] is in the interest of the people and not in the interest of the corporations.
>
> MR. STEVENS. . . . This must all be done with an eye single to the welfare of the people, and not in the interest of anyone who may desire these modifications. . . .
>
> MR. BARTLETT. And the course which the gentlemen suggest is not a course that is in the interest of the corporations, but in the interest of the people themselves.

51 CONG. REC. at 8852 (1914).

Representative Frederick C. Stevens, a House manager of the bill and a leading member of the conference committee that produced the final version that was eventually enacted, addressed this issue at the beginning of the debates: "The people have the right to look to us to ascertain what evils there really are and what remedies may be necessary, and at the same time preserve the inestimable blessings of our system of government and the wonderful efficiency and progress of our business affairs. This measure—by regulating efficiency of our organizations and institutions *so that the people can get the benefit of that efficiency*, can maintain a prosperity for the masses of our people, can assure them that their Government continues for their benefit, can assure stability and harmony and in such way conduce to the general satisfaction with our institutions." *Id.* at 8852 (emphasis added). This same inter-

mins, one of the bill's two main sponsors and the author of the influential "Cummins Report,"[173] applauded the efficiencies associated with large firms. He warned, however, that "[w]hatever those economies and efficiencies may be, they must . . . stop short of one thing, that is, the power to rule that field of commerce which they attempt to occupy."[174]

Even some opponents of the FTC Act based their opposition on the potentially negative impact on consumers of the inefficiencies that the Act would require.[175] The ultimate goal of the opposition was also

---

pretation also seems to be suggested by Representative Stevens toward the end of the debate: "In the economic field the Commission should assist the business concerns of this country along the lines demanded by the American people of efficiency and fairness. Then, while it is done, the pubilc [sic] also wants to know that with this efficiency will equally go fairness in the distribution of the benefits of such organization and work." *Id.* at 14,938. Representative Stevens also stated: "[W]e want these men who have accomplished so much and are capable of so much to realize that there is a responsibility upon them as American citizens, that they receive a part of the blessings of our institutions, and that they must yield something and do something for the common welfare and not try to grab it all for themselves." *Id.* at 8853.

173. S. REP. No. 1326, 62d Cong., 3d Sess. (1913).

174. 51 CONG. REC. 11,456 (1914). Cummins continued, "[T]here is no business field in this country so small but that it ought to be occupied by at least two enterprises, whether individual or corporate." *Id.* at 11,455-56; *see also* the remarks of Senator Newlands, 51 CONG. REC. 11,109 (1914).

The minority view expressed in the 1914 Report of the House Committee on Interstate and Foreign Commerce seems to take a similar position. This view would seem to allow corporations to keep the benefits from their efficiency advantages to the extent that these profits are not attributable to harm to consumers: "Any advantage large corporations have over small corporations or individuals through lower costs of production they are entitled to, but they should be prevented from an unfair use of the power that comes from their size alone." H.R. REP. No. 533, pt. 2, 63d Cong., 2d Sess. (1914).

175. Senator Lippitt extolled the efficiencies of monopolies because, in his opinion, they resulted in lower prices for consumers: "I believe that they enable the farmer and the consumer to buy goods at a cheaper price than they can be sold without some form of efficient organization." 51 CONG. REC. 13,306 (1914). Similarly, Senator Weeks stated that "there are a great many combinations which have reduced prices as a result of the combination, and that therefore they have been for the public good." *Id.* at 12,732. Senator Lippitt later stated that the FTC should not be created because it would achieve the opposite of its stated goal. He believed that it would make corporations less efficient, and that these losses would be passed on to consumers: "I have no doubt myself that it will add millions and millions of dollars to the cost of production of the articles used in the trade of the United States, and I am sorry that there is not somewhere some more definite information to be obtained upon this very important phase: for the ultimate result of such expenditures must undoubtedly be borne by the consumers of the articles as an addition to the already burdensome cost of living." *Id.* at 13,213. Lippitt later quoted a speech by Victor Morawetz, delivered at the second annual meeting of the Chamber of Commerce of the United States, Washington, February 12, 1914: "[S]ome contracts and combinations of that character are necessary to secure economy and efficiency in production and in trade and to preserve strong and healthy competition at home and in foreign markets. If such contracts or combinations involve no

achieving the lowest possible prices for consumers.[176] They differed with the sponsors of the FTC Act only about the method which would best achieve this goal.

The legislative history of the FTC Act thus indicates that Congress wanted efficiency to play a major role in section 5 analysis.[177] Several statements even suggest that efficiency was meant to be the only goal of the Act, or, at least, should not be sacrificed in the pursuit of any other goal.[178] But most statements suggest that economic efficiency was only one of the legislators' concerns and, further, that Congress wanted to ensure that purchasers received their "fair" share of these efficiency benefits.[179] The evidence suggests, moreover, that the majority of the legislators subordinated their appreciation for corporate efficiency to their distaste for monopoly overcharges. The bulk of the legislative history indicates that efficiency should be a factor in section 5 analysis only when its benefits accrue primarily to consumers, and not to trusts or monopolies. That is, Congress was not willing to sacrifice consumers' direct monetary interests in order that monopolists might become richer. Thus, the 1914 Congress, like the Congress that passed the Sherman Act, strongly limited the role of efficiency in antitrust analysis.[180]

Protecting Consumers from Unfair Transfers of Wealth

The legislative history of the FTC Act makes clear that Congress

elements of oppression of others, and if they do not put an end to healthy competition in any branch or [sic] trade or commerce, they should not be prohibited." *Id.* at 13,218.

176. *Id.* A cynic viewing these remarks, however, might speculate that they showed concern for obtaining the lowest possible prices for consumers in part because this seemed to be a useful tactic to prevent the creation of the FTC.

177. Congressional remarks concerned only productive efficiency. Although members of Congress did not consider the problem, it seems reasonable to believe that they would have been concerned with allocative inefficiency had they confronted it. *See supra* notes 89-100.

178. *See supra* note 171 and sources cited therein.

179. *See supra* notes 172, 174-76 and sources cited therein.

180. Although the debates show more discussion of efficiency in 1914 than in 1890, the role of efficiency in § 5 analysis seems to be identical to the role it was intended to play in Sherman Act analysis. *See supra* notes 95-108 & accompanying text. Under each statute there are some statements which imply a very strong or even dominant role for efficiency. The remarks by Senator Hoar in the Sherman Act debates, *supra* note 105, and Senators Hollis and Robinson in the FTC Act debates suggest this view. *See supra* note 171. In each statute's legislative history, however, the weight of the evidence suggests that efficiency was meant to be only one factor in the overall welfare analysis, and that efficiency concerns were not meant to prevail in those cases where they helped cause higher prices for consumers. Under the majority view, Congress' goal was both to increase firms' efficiency and to insure that the benefits of modern productivity were directly passed to consumers.

wanted to insure the existence of free competition and to prevent the use of market power to extract unfairly the entitlements or property rights Congress had decided belonged to consumers. Congress' dominant interest was to allow consumers to purchase their goods at competitive prices[181] without sacrificing other consumer interests such as optimal product quality.[182]

Congressional motives in condemning artificially high consumer prices were no different in 1914 than in 1890; Congress' redistributive concerns were paramount. Senator Newlands, the Act's main sponsor and the Chairman of the Senate Committee on Interstate Commerce, framed the issue as a concern for "unreasonable and extortionate prices."[183] Senator Lane identified the danger as

> [t]he fraud and the theft which is being practiced upon the people of this country . . . which mulct the people of this country out of hundreds of millions of dollars each year . . . [The people] are also being compelled to pay arbitrarily fixed and unjustly high prices for what they consume, they are being robbed . . . .[184]

The Minority Report of the House Committee on Interstate and Foreign Commerce complained that "[t]he common people are staggering under the burden they bear as a result of contributing extortionate

181. The goals of "protecting consumers against the high prices and [guarding] the interests of employees" were expressed by the House in H.R. REP. NO. 533, pt. 1, 63d Cong., 2d Sess. 14 (1914) (quoting from the *Preliminary Report of the Industrial Commission*, submitted to Congress in 1900). Senator McCumber even wondered if the only goal of the FTC Act was to control unfair competition whether or not the public obtained their goods "cheaper than they did before." 51 CONG. REC. 13,232 (1914). The Senate Committee on Interstate Commerce wanted to keep "within limited bounds the activities of a multitude of price-fixing associations in different branches of business, which, together with the great trusts, have been potent causes of the present high cost of living." S. REP. NO. 597, 63d Cong., 2d Sess. 9 (1914).

Congress specified competitive rather than low prices out of a recognition that a would-be monopolist might attempt to use predatorily low prices to drive out competition and then price at a monopoly level. Senator Reed presented a typical predatory pricing hypothetical: "It has been charged that . . . [the Standard Oil Company] goes into a trade territory which is occupied by a rival, drops the price of its products below their actual cost, and thus crushes and destroys the competitor, meantime selling in other communities at a higher price and gaining profits there, and out of those profits gained in other places sustaining itself, while it is selling goods at a loss in the community where their rival is located. When he is crushed it puts up the price. Now, that could be condemned under the provision I have drawn." 51 CONG. REC. 13,231 (1914). *See infra* notes 200 & 203.

182. *See, e.g.*, remarks of Senators Cummins and Lippitt. 51 CONG. REC. 11,106 (1914).

183. *Report of the Senate Committee on Interstate Commerce, Appendix: Statement by Sen. Newlands*, S. REP. NO. 597, 63d Cong., 2d Sess. 23 (1914). Newlands also spoke in terms of an "unfair or unreasonable price." *Id.*

184. 51 CONG. REC. 13,223 (1914).

profits to the trusts and monopolies."[185] Further, the stated goals of Representative Morgan were "[t]o minimize the power of the large industrial corporation to concentrate wealth, and to maximize its power as an agency for the equitable distribution of wealth [and] allay public suspicion and distrust, remove prejudice and secure the people from unjust tribute levied by monopolistic corporations."[186]

Even opponents of the Commission recognized redistribution as a central goal.[187] The legislative history indicates that opponents hoped to secure competitively low prices for consumers, opposing the bill in part because in their opinion it would cause productive inefficiencies that would raise consumer prices.[188]

These remarks suggest that Congress was overwhelmingly interested in securing competitive prices for consumers.[189] Congress' descriptive use of the terms "exactions," "extortionate profits," "theft," and "looting" is evidence of its great displeasure and suggests congressional condemnation of supracompetitive prices not because they caused allocative inefficiency, but rather because they "unfairly" transferred wealth from consumers to producers. Although price was the touchstone of congressional concern, Congress had broader aims as well.[190] As the next section indicates, these goals were primarily social and ethical in nature.

---

185. H.R. REP. NO. 533, pt. 3, 63d Cong., 2d Sess. 5 (1914) (minority report) (Rep. Lafferty's views).

186. 51 CONG. REC. 8854 (1914). *See also supra* text accompanying notes 173-74.

Even though Congress sought to protect consumers of particular products, it sometimes was concerned with products that might be inputs for other products. Senator Borah, referring to an instance of predatory pricing, explicitly named "those who should be benefited under the law of competition—that is, the consumers or users of these agricultural implements." *Id.* at 11,232.

187. Senator Burton, for example, stated that "no one here—I can speak with confidence for the entire Senate—would put one obstacle in the way of punishing dishonesty, of preventing oppression, of prohibiting exactions." 51 CONG. REC. 14,792 (1914).

188. *See supra* remarks of Senator Lippitt in text accompanying note 175.

189. *See* exchange between Representatives Bartlett and Stevens, *supra* note 172.

190. As Senator Cummins noted, prices were not Congress' only concern: "We often go wrong, I believe, in assuming that because a great corporation, a vast aggregation of wealth, can produce a given commodity more cheaply than can a smaller concern, therefore it is for the welfare and the interest of the people of the country that the commodity shall be produced at the lower cost. I do not accept that article of economic faith. I think we can purchase cheapness at altogether too high a price, if it involves the surrender of the individual, the subjugation of a great mass of people to a single master mind." 51 CONG. REC. 12,742 (1914).

Other Goals of the FTC Act

Preventing Unethical Business Practices

Congressional use of the word "unfair" to describe the types of competition it wanted to prohibit strongly suggests that the goals of section 5 include moral or ethical elements. The Act's legislative history strongly supports the conclusion that Congress wanted to prevent certain practices not because of any effects on efficiency or wealth distribution but because Congress considered them inherently unethical.[191] The desire to eliminate immoral practices was based, in part, on the belief that monopolies often resulted from immoral business behavior.[192] The FTC, it was believed, would become the "social machinery which will protect the individual from oppression and wrong."[193] Even the bill's critics thought the prohibition was, in part, an ethical one.[194] Thus, the legislative history leads to the conclusion that moral or ethical concerns helped inspire congressional use of the term "unfair."

The debates list several trade practices or conditions that the legislature considered "unfair;" monopolies created by unfair tactics were

---

191. Senator Newlands, for example, defined the parameters of "unfair competition" to include "every practice and method between competitors upon the part of one against the other that is against public morals . . . ." *Id*. at 11,112. Newlands wanted legislation to prevent "practices that shock the universal conscience of mankind." *Id.* at 12,980.

Senator Newlands strongly believed in the desirability of establishing standards of business ethics: "[I]t would be utterly impossible for Congress to define the numerous practices which constitute unfair competition and which are against good morals in trade, for we are beginning to realize that there is a standard of morals in trade or that there ought to be." *Id.* at 11,084. He stated the objective of Congress to be "simply to maintain by law good morals in business as in other matters." *Id.* at 11,108.

192. "Monopoly commences in insidious ways, by practices that are against good morals and constitute violations of individual rights for which the individual can have an action at law or in equity, but rights which the individual, because of his poverty or of his insignificance is often unable to assert against these great organized powers." *Id.* at 12,030. Newlands believed that his prohibition would cover everything Congress wanted and would "have such an elastic character that it [would] meet every new condition and every new practice that [might] be invented with a view to gradually bringing about monopoly through unfair competition." *Id.* at 12,024.

193. *Id.* at 11,109.

194. Senator Reed, a leading opponent of the Act, unsuccessfully proposed an amendment to redefine § 5 as follows: "The term unfair competition is hereby defined to embrace all these acts, devices, concealments, threats, coercions, deceits, frauds, discriminations, dishonest practices, false representations, slanders of business, and all other acts or devices, whether of like nature with those herein enumerated or not, done or used with the intent or the effect of which is to destroy or unreasonably hinder the business of another or prevent another from engaging in business, or to restrain trade or to create a monopoly." *Id.* at 13,310.

only one such example.[195] Many of these practices could be condemned because they led to monopoly power and eventually to the "unfair" extraction of wealth from consumers. Other practices could be prohibited because they unfairly harmed small businesses. With respect to these practices, characterizing section 5 concerns in terms of morality instead of consumer impact or small business protection might be historically correct, but makes little or no difference in the outcome of these cases.

Many of the practices mentioned in the debates might not lead to monopoly power,[196] but may have been considered malum in se.[197] Certain predatory practices, such as blowing up a competitor's plant or industrial espionage, are as obviously immoral as fraud or coercion,[198]

---

195. Senator Robinson presented the longest list of unfair practices that appears in the 1914 debates:

1. Local price cutting.
2. Operation of bogus "independent" concerns.
3. Maintenance of "fighting ships" and "fighting brands."
4. Lease, sale, purchase, or use of certain articles as a condition of the lease, sale, purchase, or use of other required articles.
5. Exclusive sales and purchase arrangements.
6. Rebates and preferential contracts.
7. Acquisition of exclusive or dominant control of machinery or goods used in the manufacturing process.
8. Manipulation.
9. Black lists, boycotts, white lists, etc.
10. Espionage and use of detectives.
11. Coercion, threats, and intimidation.

Id. at 11,230.

In addition, the Democratic Platform of 1912 favored "the prevention of holding companies, of interlocking directors, of stock watering, of discrimination in price, and the control by any one corporation of so large a proportion of any industry as to make it a menace to competitive conditions." REPUBLICAN CAMPAIGN TEXTBOOK 1912 at 272 *reprinted in* G. HENDERSON, THE FEDERAL TRADE COMMISSION 16-17 (1924). Similarly, the Progressive Platform for that year favored strengthening the Sherman Law by "prohibiting agreements to divide territory or limit output; refusing to sell to customers who buy from business rivals; to sell below cost in certain areas while maintaining higher prices in other places; using the power of transportation to aid or injure special business concerns; and other unfair trade practices." T. ROOSEVELT, PROGRESSIVE PRINCIPLES, appendix at 319, *reprinted in* G. HENDERSON, *supra*, at 17.

196. *See supra* note 195. Of course, § 5 has a strong incipiency mandate. *See supra* note 163 for a brief definition of incipiency mandate.

197. Some members of Congress may have viewed even cartels and monopolies themselves as malum in se. Senator Newlands suggested that certain practices were against "the laws of God." 51 CONG. REC. 11,086 (1914) (quoting State v. Central Lumber Co., 24 S.D. 136, 153 (1909)).

198. The legislators often referred to blatantly predatory acts which are relatively rare today. For example, early in the debates Senator Newlands stated that it had been proven that the National Cash Register Company "had men in the employ of their rivals, that they

and were condemned without regard to their effects on efficiency, distribution, small businesses, or consumers.

The primary impact of the ethical mandate of the statute has been the creation of the Bureau of Consumer Protection. It is possible to characterize this Bureau's concern with fraudulent, deceptive, and coercive practices solely as another manifestation of congressional condemnation of unfair transfers of wealth from consumers to producers.[199] It seems at least equally likely that Congress considered conventional consumer protection problems to be matters of morality and, for this reason, the object of prohibition.[200]

As a practical matter, however, unethical or immoral conduct has rarely been a factor in FTC antitrust enforcement.[201] Only blatantly unscrupulous practices, such as bribery or industrial sabotage, condemned by society under any circumstances, are challenged by the

---

had every form of espionage and detection, and that they even resorted to bribery of the employees of the rival concerns." *Id.* at 11,108.

199. It should also be noted that these practices generally lower economic efficiency. For example, coercive or fraudulent transactions can lower business confidence or individual incentive and might thus decrease the total stock of goods produced by the economy. It must be emphasized, however, that such practices were not condemned because of their efficiency effects.

200. This point is illustrated in the following exchange between Senator Lippitt and Senator Cummins:

> SENATOR LIPPITT. [I]f the competition is of such high character as to reduce the price to the public, it is going to be a very difficult question to say that it is injurious to the public. I presume he means it is unfair to the public, it is injurious, and that because in some way it will ultimately result in higher prices to them, but if the competition results in lower prices to the public, it is fair to them?
>
> MR. CUMMINS. Not always—If one goes into a store and desires a certain thing and through a misrepresentation, such as I have indicated, he takes another thing he is injured, and the people generally are injured if the same thing is practiced on them, without regard to the price, without regard to the quality of the goods involved.

51 CONG. REC. 11,106 (1914).

201. Only in Federal Trade Comm'n v. Keppel & Bro., Inc., 291 U.S. 304 (1933), and Federal Trade Comm'n v. Sperry & Hutchinson, 405 U.S. 233 (1972), did the Court rely upon moral or ethical objections as the basis for finding an antitrust violation. In *Sperry & Hutchinson* the Court referred with approval to the factors that the FTC may consider "in determining whether a practice that is neither in violation of the antitrust laws nor deceptive is nonetheless unfair: (1) whether the practice, without necessarily having been previously considered unlawful, offends public policy as it has been established by statutes, the common law, or otherwise—whether, in other words, it is within at least the penumbra of some common law, statutory, or other established concept of unfairness; (2) whether it is immoral, unethical, oppressive, or unscrupulous; (3) whether it causes substantial injury to consumers (or competitors or other businessmen)." *Id.* at 244-45 n.5. For a detailed discussion of this case, see Averitt, *Unfair Methods, supra* note 156.

FTC on ethical grounds alone.[202] Otherwise, immoral or unethical practices are challenged only when the practice is one that unfairly transfers wealth from consumers to producers, unduly harms small businesses, or causes economic inefficiency.[203] As a prescriptive matter, it rarely makes a difference whether congressional displeasure with certain practices is characterized by distributive preferences for consumers or small businesses, or by ethical considerations.[204] Under either explanation Congress has directed that these practices be prohibited.[205]

Curbing the Social and Political Power of Trusts and Monopolies

The FTC Act also was inspired by congressional interest in curbing the social and political power of large trusts and monopolies although this factor is less significant than in the Sherman Act debates. Nevertheless, as historian Richard Hofstadter has noted, the trusts and monopolies inspired "a fear founded in political realities—the fear that the great business combinations, being the only centers of wealth and power, would be able to lord it over all other interests and thus to put

202. *See* Federal Trade Comm'n v. Sperry & Hutchison, 405 U.S. 233 (1972); Federal Trade Comm'n v. Keppel & Bro., Inc., 291 U.S. 304 (1933).

203. The Act was also designed to help firms that were subjected to unfair business practices. For example, Senator McCumber inquired, "Here are two manufacturers selling their articles in competition with each other in a certain territory. One of the manufacturers advertises that his goods are produced by the most modern methods, that they are in every respect as good or better than those of his competitor, and that he will sell them 25 per cent cheaper than his competitor. We will assume that that public statement is false and untrue, that it is absolutely unfair, but the result has been that the competitor in that field has reduced the price of his product to meet the competition, and the public are getting his goods 25 per cent cheaper than they did before. Under that condition can not the man or corporation who has been compelled to reduce the price of his product by reason of that competition go before this commission and insist that his competitor's goods are not as good as his and that the competition is unfair, and ask an injunction against the continuance of that claim for the goods of the competitor?" 51 CONG. REC. 13,232 (1914). Senator Reed answered: "Certainly . . . the Senator has stated a very strong case, a case in which bad morals were involved, in which falsehood was involved, and yet the effect was to promote competition, and hence promote the general welfare." *Id.* Even though prices would fall in the short term, the behavior described by Senator Reed would probably not promote long-term competition and general welfare.

204. For certain immoral acts, however, differences would still remain. If the acts were blatantly immoral, such as industrial espionage, murder, or destroying a competitor's plant, it seems doubtful that the FTC should even allow the defendant to attempt to justify its actions on economic grounds. The FTC should be able to ban such blatantly immoral practices by a per se approach.

205. Although there were certainly views to the contrary, the legislative history also seems to suggest that Congress meant to condemn immoral practices in part because they harmed other businesses. In addition to the quotations presented in this section, some of the statements *infra* in notes 210-11 & accompanying text suggest this.

an end to traditional American democracy."[206] One Minority Report of the House Committee on Interstate and Foreign Commerce deplored the "unfortunate state of the Union" because "[f]ifty men in the United States control, through interlocking directorates, 40 percent of the wealth of the country."[207]

This fear was echoed throughout the debates.[208] Congressman F.C. Stevens stated:

> Vast wealth has been accumulated, especially in the hands of a few, irresponsible except to their own consciences and sense of justice and patriotism, and these powers have become so concentrated and involved that disentanglement is extremely difficult.
>
> From this situation the great mass of our people have a very just apprehension that this wealth, and power growing out of it, may be not only used to the detriment but also may be a potential source of injury and oppression.

He also advocated the creation of the FTC because "[t]he people will not be afraid of mere size if it knows that an able and wise and powerful commission is guarding their interests . . . ."[209]

Strong statements by Congress notwithstanding, the strident rhetoric that pervaded the Sherman Act debate was largely missing. Because the FTC Act was, in large part, an attempt more effectively to accomplish the Sherman Act's goals, it is not surprising that most speakers debated ways to fine-tune existing antitrust law, rather than declare that Congress should do something about the powerful trusts. The same problems may have existed in both 1914 and 1890, but the contemplated solution in 1914 was more ameliorative than innovative.

---

206. *See* R. HOFSTADTER, REFORM, *supra* note 132, at 277. "At bottom, the central fear was fear of power and the greater the strength of an organized interest the greater anxiety it aroused. Hence it was the trusts, the investment banking houses, the interlocking directorates, the swollen private fortunes that were most criticized." *Id.* at 241.

207. H.R. REP. No. 533, pt. 3, 63d Cong., 2d Sess. 5 (1914) (minority report) (Rep. Lafferty's views).

208. *See, e.g.*, 51 CONG. REC. 8850 (1914). Senator Newlands, commenting on the "Cummins Report," S. REP. No. 1326, 63d Cong., 3d Sess. xii (1913), added that "we find that the trusts are more powerful today than when the antitrust act was passed and that the evils have grown up so interwoven with the general business of the country as to make men tremble at the consequence of their disruption." S. REP. No. 1326, 63d Cong., 3rd Sess. 19 (1914) (additional views of Sen. Newlands, quoting a speech he made in the Senate, Jan. 11, 1911). For a discussion of the "Cummins Report," see Averitt, *Unfair Methods, supra* note 156, at 231-32. Senator Kenyon feared that "[i]f we are going to concede, after all these years, that this Government is powerless to destroy monopoly, then we have got to concede that monopoly is powerful enough to destroy this Government . . . ." 51 CONG. REC. 13,158 (1914); *see also id.* at 13,211 (remarks of Sen. Lippitt); *id.* at 8850 (remarks of Rep. F.C. Stevens).

209. 51 CONG. REC. 14,938 (1914).

Protecting Small Businesses

A number of statements in the legislative history of the FTC Act imply that direct protection of small businesses was an explicit goal of the Act.[210] There were also suggestions that competition was the only object of the statute.[211] It seems most likely that Congress' primary goal

210. For example, Senator Newlands expressed a desire to stop any practice that tended "to injury of a competitor unfairly." *Id.* at 12,980. Senator Reed articulated the purposes underlying the FTC Act as follows: "We are trying to keep the doors of competition open in this land. We are trying to keep the highways of opportunity unobstructed. We are trying to keep it so that the feet of the men of today may travel along an open path, so that all may have a fair chance to gain a livelihood and to embark in business." *Id.* at 13,231; *see also id.* at 13,232 (statement of Sen. McCumber), 12,932-33 (statement of Sen. Lewis).

Congressman F.C. Stevens stated, "Vast wealth has been accumulated, especially in the hands of a few, irresponsible except to their own consciences and sense of justice and patriotism, and these powers have become so concentrated and involved that disentanglement is extremely difficult. "From this situation the great mass of our people have a very just apprehension that this wealth, and power growing out of it, may be not only used to the detriment but also may be a potential source of injury and oppression." *Id.* at 8850. Further, he advocated the creation of the FTC because "[t]he people will not be afraid of mere size if it knows that an able and wise and powerful and patriotic commission is guarding their interests . . . ." *Id.* at 14,938.

Senator Lane feared that if the proposed legislation were not artfully crafted, "every small and honorable dealer may be put to intentional and infinite annoyance or driven out of business by his larger or more crafty rival." *Id.* at 13,223. Senator Burton felt, "In our business life there must be a free field for all, and along with this tendency toward operations on an enormous scale no policy should be adopted or allowed under which equality of opportunity shall be destroyed or the deserving competitor driven out of business." *Id.* at 14,792; *see also id.* at 12,980 (remarks of Sen. Newlands).

These quotations suggesting a moral objective to the Act also show that businesses, in addition to consumers, were objects of the Act's protections. *See supra* notes 191-205 & accompanying text.

211. "Where there is a practice or a class of practices which has for its main purpose an injury to the public by eliminating competition which ought to exist in the public interest, in such cases it is a fraud on the public, both as to purpose and results. If it be for the public interest to preserve healthful competition, then it is our duty to provide the means for it." 51 CONG. REC. 14,937 (1914) (statement of Rep. Stevens); *see also id.* at 14,936-38.

Senator McCumber agreed with Representatives Stevens and Bartlett, *see* their discussion *supra* note 172, about the intended beneficiaries of the Act: "I would like to vote for a trades commission bill the object of which would be to facilitate trade, insure honest competition, and insure a competition that would be beneficial to the public and not interfere with any competition that does not concern the public at large." *Id.* at 13,303.

Senator Cummins emphasized the specific aims of the Act: "The unfairness must be tinctured with unfairness to the public, not merely with unfairness to the rival or competitor. . . . We are not simply trying to protect the people of the United States, and of course, there must be in the imposture or in the vicious practice or method something that has a tendency to affect the people of the country or be injurious to their welfare." *Id.* at 11,105. This cannot, however, be fully reconciled with Senator Cummins' later statement that "we must do something to preserve the independence of the man as distinguished from the power of the corporation; that we must do something to perpetuate the individual initiative. We often go wrong, I believe, in assuming that because a great corporation, a vast aggregation of wealth, can produce a given commodity more cheaply than can a smaller concern, therefore

was preventing harm to the general public by prohibiting those practices that harmed small businesses to the extent that the practices harmed competition in general. Congress was certainly concerned with providing equal opportunity for small entrepreneurs and with condemning unfair business methods, in part, because of the effect of such methods on small businesses.[212]

Although some members of Congress supported the protection of small businesses as an end in itself, it appears that Congress did not intend to protect small businesses if higher prices for consumers resulted. Interpreting the statute as a directive to aid small businesses only when this aid does not interfere with any of Congress' other goals is more consistent with the general import of the FTC and Sherman Acts.

Antitrust and Consumer Protection Synthesis

As previously discussed, the antitrust concerns embodied in the FTC Act were based primarily upon distributive concerns.[213] A similar argument can be made concerning Congress' consumer protection goals. That is, Congress did not condemn practices such as fraud because they were inefficient;[214] rather, it considered them to be unfair transfers of wealth from purchasers to sellers.[215]

Congress' intentions perhaps could be characterized as an implicit and unconscious attempt to promote competition by preventing specific types of market failures. This characterization is appropriate because a basic assumption underlying the Act was that the free market, when functioning properly, would best structure and "regulate" the Ameri-

---

it is for the welfare and the interest of the people of the country that the commodity shall be produced at a lower cost. I do not accept that article of economic faith. I think we can purchase cheapness at altogether too high a price, if it involves the surrender of the individual, the subjugation of a great mass of people to a single master mind." *Id.* at 12,742.

212. The first stages of a monopolization plan often harm small businesses and aid consumers. Only the advanced stages of monopolization, when prices have been raised above competitive levels, are likely to harm consumers. Condemnation of monopolization in its incipiency thus primarily stems from a concern with the welfare of small businesses. *See also supra* note 156.

213. *See supra* notes 181-89 & accompanying text.

214. Of course, one could justify a prohibition against fraud on efficiency grounds. *See, e.g.*, Darby & Karni, *Free Competition and the Optimal Amount of Fraud*, 16 J.L. & ECON. 67 (1973). The important point, however, is that Congress did not do so.

215. For example, Senator Reed referred to a case in which one man had "copied another man's goods" and concluded that the copier "was taking advantage of the other man's art and genius and ability. He was, in effect, stealing the other man's ideas." 51 CONG. REC. 12,023 (1914); *see also* remarks of Senator Reed, *id.* at 12,026.

can economy.[216] While in the long run the operation of the free market might erode every cartel or monopoly, or force companies engaging in fraud or other anticompetitive practices to go out of business, by 1914 Congress recognized that, in the short run, the free market did not always function perfectly. With the advantage of hindsight, one might well conclude that the FTC was established because of a congressional belief that such factors as false information,[217] imperfect or incomplete information,[218] free rider problems,[219] or insufficient resources[220]

216. Senator Newlands, in an appendix to the 1914 Report of the Senate Committee on Interstate Commerce, stated that Congress "desires to maintain by governmental action if need be, the full competitive system and to rely chiefly on competition as the regulator of corporate business." S. REP. No. 597, 63d Cong., 2d Sess. 26 (1914) (appendix). See also the comment by Representative Morgan, *supra* in the text accompanying note 190. In his address of January 20, 1914, President Wilson gave his early view that the FTC should be established so that it would function "only as an indispensable instrument of information and publicity, as a clearing house for the facts by which both the public mind and the managers of great business undertakings should be guided, and as an instrumentality for doing justice to business where the processes of the courts or the natural forces of correction outside the courts are inadequate to adjust the remedy to the wrong in a way that will meet all the equities and circumstances of the case." Address by President Wilson on Trusts and Monopolies, H.R. DOC. No. 625, 63d Cong., 2d Sess. 6 (1914). Wilson was saying that the FTC should act only when the "natural forces of correction" were inadequate due, to use his example, to imperfect information, which is an example of and cause of market failure.

Representative R.B. Stevens also framed the issues in these terms: "[I]f we are to rely on the theory of competition to protect the public from the power of large corporations, it is imperative that the Government shall see to it that competition is on fair and equal terms." Report of the House Committee on Interstate and Foreign Commerce, H.R. REP. No. 533, pt. 2, 63d Cong., 2d Sess. 1 (1914) (minority views, delivered by Rep. Stevens). In addition, the Senate Committee on Interstate Commerce noted in its February 26, 1913 report: "Interference with free competition was generally but not necessarily a restraint of trade, for there were some restrictions that could be put upon competition and upon competitors that left the competitive force as an adequate protection to the people." S. REP. No. 1326, 62d Cong., 3d Sess. 3 (1913).

217. The 1914 House Commerce Committee report stated: "The publicity secured by the governmental agency should be such as will prevent the deception of the public through secrecy in the organization and management of industrial combinations or through false information. Such agency would also have at its command the best sources of information regarding special privileges or discriminations, of whatever nature, by which industrial combinations secure monopoly or become dangerous to the public welfare." *Report of the House Committee on Interstate and Foreign Commerce*, H.R. REP. No. 533, pt. 1, 63d Cong., 2d Sess. 4 (1914) (*quoting* the *Final Report of the Industrial Commission*, submitted to Congress in 1902, vol. 19, at 650-51); *see also* the views of President Wilson, *supra* note 216.

218. Congress believed that if the FTC provided the necessary information, imperfect markets would often correct themselves. The House Report on the bill that later became the FTC Act suggested that publication of excessively high business profits would encourage other firms to enter the industry, thus lowering prices. H.R. REP. No. 533, 63d Cong., 2d Sess. 3 (1914). One businessman testified that the publication of profit levels would cause businesses to keep prices low in order to avoid attracting new competition. Testimony of Wadill Catchings, *Hearings Before the House Comm. on Interstate and Foreign Commerce*, 63d Cong., 2d Sess. 52 (1914). Other members of Congress also stated their belief that the

caused the free market to protect inadequately consumer welfare in the short term. Congress believed that in these circumstances FTC intervention to correct market failures, performed prudently, could prevent unfair transfers of wealth from consumers to producers, improve economic efficiency, and otherwise improve "consumer welfare."

With the one prohibition against "unfair methods of competition" of section 5, Congress attempted to stop "unfair" transfers of wealth caused by such divergent practices as predation and fraud.[221] The mar-

---

publication of profit information would invite entry, thereby obviating the need for antitrust enforcement. *Id.* at 65, 204-05, 220. It was also stated that the publication of the "special privileges or discriminations" used to gain monopolies would ensure private actions which would bring them to an end. *See* H.R. REP. NO. 533 at 4-5; *see also* 51 CONG. REC. 8843, 8858, 8980-81, 8983, 8985 (1914). The 1914 House Commerce Committee Report stated that reports issued by the FTC would lead to an "elevated business standard and a better business stability." *Report of the House Committee on Interstate and Foreign Commerce*, H.R. REP. NO. 533, pt. 1, 63d Cong., 2d Sess. 3 (1914). Congress also quoted, with approval, the Preliminary Report of the Industrial Commission, submitted to Congress in 1900: "The larger corporations—the so-called trusts—should be required to publish annually a properly audited report showing in reasonable detail their assets and liabilities, with profit and loss; such reports and audit under oath to be subject to Government inspection. The purpose of such publicity is to encourage competition when profits become excessive, thus protecting consumers against too high prices and to guard the interests of employees by a knowledge of the financial condition of the business in which they are employed." *Id.* at 4.

219. In Federal Trade Comm'n v. Klesner, 280 U.S. 19 (1929), the Court held that "[t]o justify filing a complaint the public interest must be specific and substantial. . . . Sometimes, because, although the aggregate of the loss entailed may be so serious and widespread as to make the matter one of public consequence, no private suit would be brought to stop the unfair conduct, since the loss to each of the individuals affected is too small to warrant it." *Id.* at 28. For the FTC's proceedings, see 5 F.T.C. 24 (1922).

In the Sherman Act debates, Senator George challenged the practical effect of such consumer protectionism: "Will any single one of those men who have been thus wronged to the amount of ten, fifteen, twenty, or fifty dollars bring a separate suit? How can he maintain it? He is to employ a lawyer; he has to go to a distance of from 100 to 500 miles, perhaps to a distant State, to maintain his suit. Who will do it? I ask Senators to stop and reflect who will do it? Not one of them. If some great manufacturer has been injured by an advance in the price of his raw material he can sue, but the poor man, the consumer, the laborer, the farmer, the mechanic, the country merchant, all that large class of American citizens who constitute 90 percent of our population and who are the real sufferers will have no opportunity of redress, and the bill, so far as they are concerned, will be a snare and a mere delusion." 21 CONG. REC. 3150 (1890). For a definition of the "free rider" problem used in the context of an important area of antitrust concern, resale price maintenance, see Telser, *Why Should Manufacturers Want Fair Trade?*, 3 J.L. & ECON. 86, 91-92 (1964).

220. Senator Newlands, for example, stated his belief that private antitrust suits would not eliminate unfair competition because "[t]he suit of an individual against a strong combination is the contest of a lilliputian against a giant." 51 CONG. REC. 11,083 (1914).

221. Federal Trade Commission Act of 1914, ch. 311, § 5, 38 Stat. 717. The statute was subsequently amended to add the prohibition against "unfair acts or practices." *Id.* (codified as amended at 15 U.S.C. § 45(a)(1) (1976)). Interestingly, Congress did not always use such terms as "fraud," "predation," and "price discrimination" to stand for totally separate problems. The following exchange, which occurred toward the end of the House debates,

ket failures that section 5 was meant to correct, however, can be classified into two general categories, a distinction developed in collaboration with my colleague, Neil Averitt.[222] Congress was primarily concerned with market failures that were external to consumers and restricted or distorted consumers' available options. Those are the traditional antitrust concerns and are the responsibility of the Bureau of Competition of the FTC.[223] At the same time, however, Congress wanted to prevent market failures that occurred internally to consumers and affected their ability to choose freely and rationally among the options the market presented. This latter category is the area of concern of the FTC's Bureau of Consumer Protection.[224] These two main departments of the FTC were designed to work together to provide two levels of protection for consumers, addressing both internal and external market failures, thereby ensuring that consumers received the full

---

illustrates the close linkage between the competition and consumer protection missions of the statute.

> MR. COOPER. Suppose a corporation worth $100,000,000 should advertise that it would sell and that it does actually sell its product to one consumer in a certain town for 50 cents, and should advertise that it would not sell and does refuse to sell to any other in that town or in that State for less than $1?
>
> MR. STEVENS OF MINNESOTA. That is clearly fraud. . . . [S]uch an act might have a result to greatly injure the public by interfering and destroying competition, which the public needs, and that is the purpose of such discrimination. To that extent the injury and intent and result would be a fraud upon the public, now known to the law and under the jurisdiction of this bill.

51 CONG. REC. 14,936 (1914). A short time later Representative Cooper inquired whether there would be any fraud if a corporation "sells its product below cost throughout a certain county or perhaps an entire State, but does not increase the cost of the product to consumers in any other community or State." Representative Stevens replied: "Mr. Speaker, our bill does meet the situation, in this way: Where there is a practice or a class of practices which has for its main purpose an injury to the public by eliminating competition which ought to exist in the public interest, in such cases it is a fraud on the public, both as to purpose and results." *Id.* at 14,937.

Because of our current view that fraud and these antitrust concerns are separate problems, Representative Stevens' views might seem somewhat puzzling. Perhaps he was condemning both types of action as a "fraud on the public" because each "unfairly" took consumers' property.

222. *See* Averitt, *Unfair Acts or Practices, supra* note 157, at 281-84.

223. The work of the Bureau of Competition (BC) comes under the broad heading of antitrust; it deals with monopolization, cartels, resale price maintenance, mergers, and similar issues. *See generally* Averitt, *Unfair Methods*, *supra* note 156.

224. The Bureau of Consumer Protection (BCP) prevents or redresses a number of practices that directly injure consumers, such as fraud, deception, the provision of insufficient consumer information and unfair credit practices. *See generally* Averitt, *Unfair Acts or Practices, supra* note 157.

benefits flowing from a competitive market.[225] No consumer choices were to be artificially impeded.

The Bureau of Competition and the Bureau of Consumer Protection normally are thought of as performing substantially different functions. It is tempting to think of these functions as being very different and only related on the most general and abstract level, insofar as both Bureaus ultimately attempt to improve consumer welfare. Both the antitrust and consumer protection missions, however, were originally authorized by the single prohibition against "unfair methods of competition." The Congress that used this single phrase to establish one Commission to deal with both kinds of problems surely considered them to be closely related.

Both the Bureau of Competition and the Bureau of Consumer Protection were created to prevent certain "unfair" transfers of wealth and to enhance economic efficiency.[226] These goals are sought whenever

225. It should be noted that these two levels of protection do not perfectly correspond to the respective functions of the BC and the BCP that have evolved over time.

The following chart attempts to illustrate the synthesis of the FTC's purpose with the advantage of hindsight. A modern observer might state that the goals of both the BC and the BCP are virtually identical, including, primarily, the prevention of certain "unfair" transfers of wealth and, secondarily, the enhancement of economic efficiency and other goals.

A UNIFIED APPROACH TO § 5

Goals (The same for each half of the statute)	*When*? Whenever there is a market failure	*What* should be prevented or corrected?
	Bureau of Competition	
—prevent unfair transfers of "consumers' surplus" —encourage economic efficiency, especially if the benefits accrue to consumers	external to the consumer, and caused by —imperfect information —free rider problems —others	A. The manifestations —monopolies —cartel, etc. B. The market failure should be directly corrected
	Bureau of Consumer Protection	
—prevent immoral business competition —promote entrepreneurial opportunity	internal to the consumer, and caused by —imperfect information —free rider problems —a lack of free will —others	A. The manifestations —fraud —coercion, etc. B. The market failure should be directly corrected

226. The primary difference is that the BC is also concerned with reducing the social and political power of large corporations. The other goals overlap. For example, even

there are market failures that interfere with the operations of the free market.[227] In these cases the FTC may either correct the market failure directly or intervene in the market and undo the anticompetitive effect of the failure.[228]

Congress' overall mission in passing the FTC Act was to strengthen and improve the Sherman Act, and to better implement its competition goals. Congress viewed "competition" as the rule of the marketplace that would best achieve and enhance "consumer welfare," as Congress defined the term. Congress charged the FTC with carrying out its wishes in a faithful manner, subject to a crucial constraint: the FTC can act only when the free market does not function properly, and only when the FTC, by acting, is likely to improve consumer welfare.

The FTC Act is a more forward-looking and flexible statute than is the Sherman Act. It also encompasses a more expansive range of trade practices, such as unethical or fraudulent business practices. But its ultimate goals were identical to those of the Sherman Act.

The Clayton and Celler-Kefauver Acts

Experience with the Sherman Act and the Supreme Court decision in *Standard Oil Co. v. United States*[229] led Congress to conclude that additional antitrust legislation was necessary.[230] In enacting the FTC and Clayton Acts, Congress made two virtually simultaneous responses.[231] The FTC Act, as we have seen, reflected the belief that since it was impossible fully to specify in advance all of those practices which might harm competition, it was necessary to enact a broad prohibition and to leave the implementation specifics to an administrative

though the prevention of immoral acts is normally thought of as a BCP concern, immoral acts can also constitute predatory practices.

227. Many market failures, such as imperfect information, can trigger violations of either half of the statute, corresponding to both the BC and the BCP. Others, however, such as the absence of free will, seem more closely linked to only one half, either the BC or the BCP.

228. For example, suppose that a monopoly has arisen through "unfair methods of competition." The FTC might be forced to intervene directly into the marketplace and impose structural relief. But if, to use the suggestion often made in the legislative history, *see supra* note 218, publishing the profits earned by the monopolist would be likely to cause entry into the market which would erode the monopoly, structural relief might not be necessary.

229. 221 U.S. 1 (1911).

230. For a more detailed discussion of the effect of this case, see Averitt, *Unfair Methods*, *supra* note 156.

231. The FTC Act was enacted September 16, 1914, and the Clayton Act, October 15, 1914. In the FTC Act debates Senator Lippitt stated: "Here is the judiciary bill, the Clayton bill; they are all involved together. The instant you pass this bill you have got to go on and consider the Clayton bill, which is interlocked with it." 51 Cong. Rec. 13,164 (1914).

agency.[232] The Clayton Act[233] reflected a congressional desire to prohibit specific practices believed to be harmful. Several legislators believed that the Clayton Act was duplicative and unnecessary because the broad prohibitions of the FTC Act encompassed all the specific interdictions contained in the Clayton Act.[234] Nevertheless, the prevailing view was that the Clayton Act was justified as a way of insuring that a number of particular practices would be banned.[235] This approach also led, in 1950, to the primary restatement and extension of the Act, the Celler-Kefauver Antimerger Act.[236]

The Clayton Act

Section 7 of the Clayton Act prevents firms from acquiring rival companies where "the effect of such acquisition may be substantially to

232. As Justice Brandeis eloquently observed in a dissenting opinion in Federal Trade Comm'n v. Gratz, 253 U.S. 421, 434 (1920), "The Clayton Act . . . was framed largely with a view to making more effective the remedies given by the Sherman Law. The Federal Trade Commission Act . . . created an administrative tribunal, largely with a view to regulating competition."

The passage of the Clayton Act was an election promise of the Democratic Party under the leadership of Woodrow Wilson who stated in 1913 that society was sufficiently familiar with the processes and methods of monopoly and restraints of trade so that legislation could be passed to deal with price discrimination and other unfair trade practices. *See* W. PATMAN, COMPLETE GUIDE TO THE ROBINSON-PATMAN ACT 7 (1968).

233. 16 U.S.C. § 12 (1914). For a more detailed account of the legislative history of the Clayton Act, see W. LETWIN, *supra* note 24, ch. 7; D. MARTIN, *supra* note 127; 2 A. TOULMIN, *supra* note 62, ch. 1.

234. For example, Senator Newlands, the principal sponsor of the FTC Act, stated: "[The Judiciary Committee] can, if it chooses, taking the view that is entertained by the Interstate Commerce Committee, conclude that section 5 covers all the various practices that in the common vernacular are termed 'unfair competition,' and having come to that conclusion, the Judiciary Committee can, if it chooses, leave out all legislation with reference to specific practices which are today regarded as unfair competition, or they can put them in, according to their pleasure." 51 CONG. REC. 12,030 (1914); *see also id.* at 15,829 (remarks of Sens. Borah and Culberson).

235. Senator Clapp expressed what very well might have been Congress' final opinion on this proposition: "[T]hose things that may be made plain, upon which we are generally agreed, should be prohibited. We should prohibit them, and then leave the Commission with that territory to work in which we are unable to cover by specific cases." *Id.* at 14,259.

236. 15 U.S.C. §§ 18, 21 (1950). Another major amendment was the Robinson-Patman Act, 15 U.S.C. § 13 (1936), which prohibited certain forms of non-cost-justified price discrimination between businesses that purchase the same goods where the effect of such discrimination may be substantially to lessen competition or to tend to create a monopoly. Space does not permit a full examination of the goals of the Robinson-Patman Act. It is relatively certain, however, that the Act was not passed solely to increase economic efficiency, although efficiency was mentioned as a legislative goal. *See, e.g.*, Committee on the Judiciary, H.R. REP. NO. 2287, 74th Cong., 2d Sess. 306, 368 (1936). The legislators also stated that their intent was not to cause higher prices for consumers. *Id.* at 368-69. Congress was probably more concerned, however, with the financial status of small businesses.

lessen competition, or to tend to create a monopoly."[237] The overall purpose of the Act, stated in the Senate Judiciary Committee's report on the final bill, was to prevent such mergers in their incipiency.[238] The legislators explicitly expressed their desire for competition.[239] Congress, in other words, wanted to implement essentially the same goals as those embodied in the Sherman and FTC Acts.

More specifically, Congress wanted to stop the formation of monopolies that might engage in supracompetitive pricing that, in Congress' opinion, unfairly transferred consumers' wealth to monopolists. Some advocates pressed for passage of the Clayton Act because some firms otherwise would have "the power to arbitrarily control prices and thus exact unjust profits from the people."[240] The remarks of one Senator expressed a desire to protect consumers and to encourage corporate efficiency in the belief that these benefits would be passed on to consumers: "The chief purpose of antitrust legislation is for the protection of the public, to protect it from extortion practiced by the trust, but at the same time not to take away from it any advantages of cheapness or better service which honest, intelligent cooperation may bring."[241]

Thus, Congress remained preoccupied, as it was when it passed the Sherman and FTC Acts, with the redistributive effects of market power. While it wanted to achieve its direct consumer impact goals, Congress wanted to accomplish them in a manner that did not unduly sacrifice corporate efficiencies, largely because that sacrifice could harm the public. This evidence,[242] although somewhat limited, when analyzed in light of the general proconsumer, procompetition goals of the

237. 15 U.S.C. § 18 (1914).

238. "Briefly stated, the bill, in its treatment of unlawful restraints and monopolies, seeks to prohibit and make unlawful certain trade practices which, as a rule, singly and in themselves, are not covered by the Act of July 2, 1890, or other existing anti-trust acts, and thus, by making these practices illegal, to arrest the creation of trusts, conspiracies, and monopolies in their incipiency and before consummation." Senate Judiciary Report, *quoted in* United States v. United Shoe Machinery Co., 264 F. 138, 162 (E.D. Mo. 1920), *aff'd*, 258 U.S. 451 (1921).

239. For example, Representative Morgan stated that "the one thing we wish to maintain, and retain and sustain, is competition. We want to destroy monopoly and restore and maintain competition." 51 CONG. REC. 9265 (1914).

240. *Id.* Representative Hamlin stated: "The only reason why trusts and combinations are declared illegal is because they are organized and operated for the express purpose of more effectively exploiting the people by taking advantage of their necessities and controlling the price of those necessities to the consumers, as well as the purchase price which they have to pay for the raw material." *Id.* at 9556. Senator Cummins wanted to protect "the people against the rapacity and the avarice of monopoly . . . ." *Id.* at 14,256.

241. *Id.* at 14,223 (remarks of Sen. Thompson).

242. *See supra* text accompanying note 241. In addition, see *infra* text accompanying note 245 (remarks of Sen. Borah).

antimerger laws, suggests that a merger should be prohibited, despite potential gains in efficiency, if that merger is likely to create a firm with market power that could adversely affect consumers.

Other evidence suggests that Congress was also motivated by concern for the social and political power possessed by large corporations, based on the fear that the mere existence of this power had the potential to cause social disruption. One Representative, for example, condemned the discretionary political power of men like J.P. Morgan:

> [A]ll of the power represented by this wealth is lodged in the hands of a few men. Can anyone doubt the danger which such concentration permits?
>
> . . . It is useless to say that the power represented will never be used to the detriment of the American people. . . . [I]t is too great a power to be concentrated—it affords too great a temptation to frail humanity.[243]

Congress also worried that the concentrated wealth and power of those who controlled large corporations could threaten the very fabric of the nation. The House Committee Report accompanying section 8, which deals with interlocking directorships, warned that "[t]he concentration of wealth, money, and property in the United States under the control and in the hands of a few individuals or great corporations has grown to such an enormous extent that unless checked it will ultimately threaten the perpetuity of our institutions."[244] Acknowledging the possibility that antimerger legislation might sacrifice corporate efficiency, one Senator nevertheless strongly condemned monopolies and trusts

243. 51 CONG. REC. 9186 (1914) (remarks of Rep. Helvering). *See also* remarks of Senator Cummins, *id.* at 14,536.

244. H.R. REP. No. 627, 63d Cong., 2d Sess. 19 (1914). Representative Kelly echoed this fear: "Enterprises with great capital have deliberately sought not only industrial domination but political supremacy as well . . . . Great combinations of capital for many years have flaunted their power in the face of the citizenship, they have forced their way into politics and government, they have dictated the making of laws or scorned the laws they did not like, they have prevented the free and just administration of law. In doing this they have become a menace to free institutions and must be dealt with in patriotic spirit without fear or favor." 51 CONG. REC. 9086 (1914). Representative Madden expressed the same concern, but in stronger language: "[T]he invisible Government which has controlled the visible government in this Nation for many years has been unscrupulous big business. . . . If this Nation is to be a Government of the people by crooked big business, the doom of our free institutions is assured." *Id.* at 9087.

Representative Nelson used equally striking words: "As surely and rapidly as the properties of all the people pass into the hands of a few trust magnates, public sentiment, rapidly forming, when once fully aroused, will multiply the socialistic vote as a protest against monopoly privilege. And the day when the people must choose between public ownership of trusts for the benefit of all and the private ownership of the trusts for the privileges of the few, will witness the final triumph of socialism in this country. Therefore, we should act in our days of grace, while we are yet masters of our national destiny." *Id.* at 9167.

because they "divide our people into classes, breed discontent and hatred, and in the end riot, bloodshed, and French revolutions."[245] This brief examination of the Clayton Act's legislative history suggests that its substantive goals were identical to those of the Sherman and FTC Acts; the desire to prevent transfers of wealth from consumers to producers caused by monopoly pricing was Congress' paramount, but not exclusive, goal. A more detailed analysis of the Clayton Act's primary amendment and restatement, the Celler-Kefauver Antimerger Act, reveals similar concerns.

The Celler-Kefauver Antimerger Act

Section 7 of the original Clayton Act prevented companies from purchasing the *stock* of rival companies if the acquisition of that stock might lessen competition.[246] A large number of companies evaded the prohibitions of the Act, however, by accomplishing mergers through *asset* acquisition.[247]

A 1948 study by the FTC describing the post-World War II merger movement[248] concluded that corporate acquisitions from 1940 to 1947 had caused the disappearance of almost 2,500 firms with total assets of more than five billion dollars, representing approximately 5.5% of all manufacturing assets in the United States at the time.[249] The report warned:

> [N]o great stretch of the imagination is required to foresee that if nothing is done to check the growth in concentration, either the giant corporations will ultimately take over the country, or the Government will be impelled to step in and impose some form of direct regulation in the public interest.[250]

In recognition of this increased concentration,[251] the Celler-Kefauver

245. *Id.* at 15,955 (remarks of Sen. Borah).

246. 15 U.S.C. § 18 (1914).

247. *See* Arrow-Hart Hegeman Elec. Co. v. Federal Trade Comm'n, 291 U.S. 587 (1934); Federal Trade Comm'n v. Western Meat Co., 272 U.S. 554 (1926).

248. FTC, REPORT ON THE MERGER MOVEMENT: A SUMMARY REPORT V (1948).

249. *Id.* at 17. For a more detailed discussion of the FTC report and other studies of the period on corporate mergers, see Bok, *Section 7 of the Clayton Act and the Merging of Law and Economics*, 74 HARV. L. REV. 226, 230-33 (1961), and the sources cited therein. Many of the citations and references in this section of the paper are from Bok's article. For other discussions of the legislative history, see D. MARTIN, *supra* note 127, ch. 7; Muris, *The Efficiency Defense Under Section 7 of the Clayton Act*, 30 CASE W. RES. L. REV. 381 (1980); Note, *Section 7 of the Clayton Act: A Legislative History*, 52 COLUM. L. REV. 766 (1952).

250. FTC, REPORT ON THE MERGER MOVEMENT: A SUMMARY REPORT V, at 68.

251. *See, e.g.*, S. REP. No. 1775, 81st Cong., 2d Sess. 2 (*quoted in* Brown Shoe v. United States, 370 U.S. 294, 316 (1962)).

Although Congress believed that the nation was experiencing a great increase in industrial concentration, this perception was probably false. One study of the time, and several

Act was enacted to ensure that the antimerger laws applied to acquisition of assets as well as stock.[252]

The most comprehensive judicial expression of the goals of the amendment is the famous statement by Chief Justice Warren in *Brown Shoe Co., Inc. v. United States*:[253]

> The dominant theme pervading congressional consideration of the 1950 amendments was a fear of what was considered to be a rising tide of economic concentration in the American economy. . . . Other considerations cited in support of the bill were the desirability of retaining "local control" over industry and the protection of small businesses. Throughout the recorded discussion may be found examples of Congress' fear not only of accelerated concentration of economic power on economic grounds, but also of the threat to other values a trend toward concentration was thought to pose.[254]

The following section examines the Celler-Kefauver Act's legislative history to find support for the Chief Justice's conclusion. It examines, in turn, the legislators' efficiency, distributive or consumer impact, and other goals.

Improving Economic Efficiency

The quoted passage from *Brown Shoe* did not mention economic efficiency as one of Congress' central objectives. Nor does Professor

subsequent studies, have largely confirmed the conclusion that the merger wave of this period was relatively harmless, and that industrial concentration was not growing during this period. *See* E. MASON, ECONOMIC CONCENTRATION AND THE MONOPOLY PROBLEM 16-43 (1957); Bok, *supra* note 249, at 231-33. Even if Congress' perception was incorrect, however, "Congress relied heavily upon the Commission report in enacting the amended section 7, and no judge can overlook this point in carrying out the task of interpreting the statute in accordance with the intentions and desires of its framers. This is not to say that every legislative misconception must be rigorously applied until it is formally retracted. But even in the foggy world of antitrust, it is no simple thing for a court to overrule a major premise of Congress by appeal to the supervening authority of the *Review of Economics and Statistics*. Thus, if we are to gain an understanding of the outer limits of the court's discretion under section 7, we must turn to the reports and debates which culminated in the passage of the amendment." *Id.* at 234. (footnotes omitted)

252. In most respects the fundamental purposes of the Act were redebated. Representative Celler, for example, stated: "I feel that most of the gentlemen who oppose the bill would like to repeal the Clayton Act in its entirety. That is the import of their argument, it strikes me." 95 CONG. REC. 11,489 (1949). Representative Keating added: "Mr. Speaker, the issue is very clear. Either we should repeal the Clayton Act entirely or we should amend it to make it effective." *Id. See also* Muris, *supra* note 249, at 393 n.47.

253. 370 U.S. 294 (1962).

254. *Id.* at 315. The first sentence was later quoted in United States v. Philadelphia Nat'l Bank, 374 U.S. 321, 363 (1963). The Senate Report stated that a primary purpose of the Act was "to limit future increases in the level of economic concentration resulting from corporate mergers and acquisitions. . . ." S. REP. No. 1775, 81st Cong., 2d Sess. 3 (1950).

Bok find in the legislative record much evidence of a congressional concern for efficiency. He noted that

> none of the justifications for mergers by big companies were accorded any significance by Congress. Efficiency, expansion, and the like were ignored or simply brushed aside in the deliberations. Even opponents of the bill did not seek to argue that the interests of large companies would be infringed unwisely or unfairly by the bill.[255]

He therefore concluded that improved efficiency was not a central goal of the Celler-Kefauver Act.[256] Of course, other commentators believe that, in amending section 7, Congress had significant efficiency goals.[257] These scholars, however, are impeded by their inability to point to a sufficient amount of evidence in the legislative history indicating that economic efficiency figured significantly in the debates leading to the 1950 amendment.[258]

---

255. Bok, *supra* note 249, at 307.

256. Bok's observations imply that Congress did not mean to provide an efficiencies defense in merger cases: "There is little basis for concluding that the achievement of lower costs as such should give rise to favored treatment under Section 7. The possibility of lower costs was brushed aside in the legislative deliberations and there is every reason to believe that Congress preferred the noneconomic advantages of deconcentrated markets to limited reductions in the cost of operations." *Id.* at 318 (citations omitted). *See also id.* at 236-37. The conclusion that Congress was disinclined to permit an efficiencies defense was adopted by the Supreme Court in Federal Trade Comm'n v. Procter & Gamble Co., 386 U.S. 568, 580 (1967) (quoting Brown Shoe Co., Inc. v. United States, 370 U.S. 294, 344 (1962)): "Possible economies cannot be used as a defense to illegality. Congress was aware that some mergers which lessen competition may also result in economies but it struck the balance in favor of protecting competition."

257. *See* 4 P. AREEDA & D. TURNER, *supra* note 4, at subch. 9E; Muris, *supra* note 249, at 393-402. This interpretation opens the door to the assertion that a merger likely to lead to increased efficiency should not be illegal.

258. For the most comprehensive analysis of the legislative history of the Celler-Kefauver Antimerger Act which advocates the conclusion that Congress had strong efficiency goals and did not mean to preclude an efficiencies defense in merger cases, see Muris, *supra* note 249, at 393-402.

Professor Muris provides four categories of direct evidence that Congress indicated that increased efficiency should point towards the legality of mergers:

1. Evidence from the legislative history of prior bills on the same subject which Congress chose not to enact. However, Muris noted that the first serious efforts to amend the Clayton Act began in 1941. *Id.* at 393. Between 1943 and 1949 sixteen bills to amend the Clayton Act were introduced in Congress. *See* D. MARTIN, *supra* note 127, at 221. Thus, quotations from the legislative record of a selected number of these bills, none of which were enacted, provide only very indirect insight into the motivations of the Congress that, years later, passed the Celler-Kefauver Act.

2. Mergers between relatively small firms were permitted. This probably only meant, however, that Congress exempted small mergers because there was little chance that they would lead to a firm with a monopoly power, even if they resulted in a firm that was more efficient and more competitive.

3. The "failing company" exception. The wealth redistribution and efficiency effects of this exception are complex and uncertain. Since the failing company exception can save

Despite the recent vintage of this amendment, a search of its legislative history reveals no evidence of congressional concern with allocative inefficiency. Nor do those scholars advocating a strong efficiency orientation to the Act present such evidence.[259] The record does contain, however, considerable discussion of productive efficiency.

It should come as no surprise that opponents of the bill asserted that it would inhibit the efficiency of both large and small firms.[260]

---

the costs of bankruptcy proceedings, and the management best able to utilize the failing assets will often be a horizontal competitor, the failing company exception could be justified from an efficiency perspective. The exception also, however, has clear distributive effects. It could enable the stockholders and creditors of the acquired company to receive more for their assets. It could also cause a transfer of wealth to the acquiring company if, through the addition of the productive facilities of the failing company, it increased its market power.

The failing company exception could also result in benefits to consumers, for without it there could be a short-term under-supply of the failing company's product. This could result in higher prices to consumers in the short term. Further, if a high level of industry instability increased the cost of capital to businesses in that industry, consumer prices could go up in the long term.

Although Bok recognized that Congress had a number of motivations, he concluded that "Congress's general unconcern with efficiency would indicate that this factor cannot be accorded much importance in accounting for the exception." Bok, *supra* note 249, at 340 (footnote omitted). For a full analysis of the failing company exception, see *id.* at 339-47. Further, the goals of an exception to an Act cannot necessarily be attributed to the rest of the Act.

4. Professor Muris quotes a discussion between Senator Kefauver and Senator O'Connor involving two newspapers that might want to save costs by having "an arrangement by which one plant would print both newspapers, with each one following its own editorial policy." Muris, *supra* note 249, at 400-01 (citing 96 CONG. REC. 16,456 (1950)). The discussion concluded that such a proposal would violate the law only where " 'it would result in a substantial lessening of competition. . . . *It may well be that by effecting a better arrangement for a more profitable undertaking, in the manner described, competition would be stimulated rather than lessened.*' " *Id.* (quoting Sen. O'Connor) (emphasis added by Muris).

Despite his contention that this dialogue evidences an intent to allow efficiency defenses, the venture was to be allowed only if it did not result in a "substantial lessening of competition." Thus, the joint venture was not to be allowed, despite its efficiency-enhancing possibilities, if it might lead to a firm with market power. This exchange probably means that the Act was passed to stop the formulation of firms with market power, and that efficiencies are to be considered only if the merger would not be likely to lead to a significant chance of a lessening of competition or to higher prices for consumers. But, if a merger is not likely to lead to a lessening of competition or to higher prices for consumers, then it should not be prohibited by § 7. Even if the author's and Professor Muris' examinations of the legislative history failed to uncover every reference to a congressional desire for efficiency, it seems fair to conclude that Congress' principal concerns lay elsewhere.

259. *See* discussion of Muris, *supra* note 258.

260. For example, Representative Goodwin stated: "By preventing harmless and reasonable mergers among small and medium-sized concerns, this bill by freezing them to their present status of size will foreclose the chance that they may by consolidation or acquisition ever approximate either the size or efficiency that the big competitors have already achieved. Thus we will hurt small business and help big business." 95 CONG. REC. 11,487 (1949); *see also Hearings before the Subcomm. of the Senate Comm. on the Judiciary*, 81st Cong., 1st &

Even the Act's proponents admitted that efficiency was important.[261] Their view, however, was that the Act would help, not hinder, corporate efficiency. As one Representative stated, "[w]hen three or four producers take the place of 20 or 30 the chances are great that price competition will be crippled—that the big concerns will adopt a live-and-let-live policy towards each other at the sacrifice of their efficiency and their progress."[262] To Representative Celler, "bigness" did not "mean efficiency, a better product, or lower prices."[263] Rather, the "main reason for antitrust laws is that we believe the competitive system is more efficient than monopoly."[264] Moreover, he deprecated "the idea that efficiency and lower prices only come with bigness. We now know that in many lines the middle-sized concerns are either more efficient than the big ones, or else they are of no positive difference. And lower prices do not always accompany bigness."[265]

Thus, Congress' efficiency concerns in passing the Celler-Kefauver Act were substantially identical to its goals in 1914 and in 1890. Allocative efficiency was not a motivating factor, but productive efficiency was a goal of legislators on both sides of the debates. Given the legislators' passion for "competition," it seems clear that they were willing to risk some efficiency losses in order to prevent the possible rise of market power. We can be certain that Congress wanted to err on the side of losing productive efficiency rather than risk the formation of market power. It is, however, unclear how far Congress would have been willing to go. There is no indication that Congress chose to impose large

2d Sess. 140 (1950) (statement of the National Tool & Die Mfg. Ass'n) [hereinafter cited as *Senate Hearings*]; *see also Hearings Before House Subcomm. on the Judiciary*, 81st Cong., 1st Sess. 45 (1949) [hereinafter cited as *House Hearings*] (statement of Gilbert Montague): "[T]hese bills will handicap the small and medium-sized corporation, and will protect the large corporation, and will lay the dead hand of arrested development upon the entire national economy." *Cf. id.* at 83: "[A]n acquisition of this type could be justified in the public interest only if there were some economies resulting, if there was some improvement in efficiency resulting therefrom." (statement of John M. Blair, assistant chief economist, FTC).

261. Senator Donelly, for example, was concerned with the bill's "effect on prices, the effect on productive efficiency." *Senate Hearings, supra* note 260, at 308.

262. 95 Cong. Rec. 11,723 (1949) (remarks of Rep. Yates).

263. *Id.* at 11,717 (1949); *see also id.* at 11,496 (statement of Rep. Boggs).

264. *House Hearings, supra* note 260, at 61.

265. *Id.* at 64. Further, Representative Carroll stated that "[f]ree competition safeguards not only the consuming public; it also encourages small business and the development of new types of business and industry." 95 Cong. Rec. 11,493 (1949). Representative Yates wrote, "When three or four producers take the places of 20 or 30, the chances are great that price competition will be crippled, that declining markets will be dealt with by restriction of output instead of by price reduction, that the big concerns will adopt a live-and-let-live policy towards each other at the sacrifice of their efficiency and their progress . . . ." *Id.*

and certain efficiency losses to gain small and speculative market power benefits. Given Congress' general desire to encourage efficiency in antimerger legislation, categories of mergers likely to result in large and certain efficiency gains should not be prevented short of a substantial risk that the firms might acquire more than an insignificant degree of market power.[266]

Protecting Consumers from Unfair Transfers of Wealth

In enacting the Celler-Kefauver Act, Congress was principally concerned that mergers would create or increase market power leading to supracompetitive pricing which directly harmed consumers. Proponents of the legislation framed the economic issues in terms of protecting consumers from monopolistic exploitation. One Representative predicted that the legislation would help "to preserve the chances of the average man to make a place for himself in business and [protect] the consuming public from unfair exploitation."[267] Another accused certain companies of "maintaining high prices which injure the consumer" and called monopoly prices "outrageous."[268] Quoting with approval from the FTC's report, a Representative perceived that "under competitive capitalism consumers are protected from high prices by the constant rivalry among numerous firms for a greater share of the market."[269] A Senator castigated opponents of the bill:

266. There was apparently no explicit analysis of the possible tradeoffs involved in implementing actions that simultaneously increase efficiency and raise prices to consumers. A very close case was presented when an economist who testified in favor of the legislation stated that mergers should be permitted up until the point where scale economies in that industry were exhausted. *See* testimony of Dr. John D. Clark, member, Council of Economic Advisors, *House Hearings, supra* note 260, at 37: "I am sure that you would find, with respect to any of those companies that you have mentioned, that the actual advantage of cost of production ceased to grow at a point of size far less than that they have now reached. In other words, for example, I do not know the steel industry, but supposing [sic] a $25,000,000 plant exhausted the opportunity for further reduction in unit costs. That gives you a datum point from which to start in determining how far you ought to permit the steel firms to grow in order to attain social advantage." As he stated that this point would come at lower levels of concentration than existed at that time, he did not seem to be advocating increased efficiency as justifying higher prices for consumers. Although Bok does not believe that efficiency was one of Congress' primary goals, *see supra* notes 255-56, he nevertheless wrote, "Perhaps more explicit guidance should be demanded from Congress before adopting an interpretation which could block really important increases in efficiency." Bok, *supra* note 249, at 318.

267. 95 Cong. Rec. 11,506 (1949) (remarks of Rep. Bennett).

268. *Id.* at 11,492 (remarks of Rep. Carroll). Carroll also stated: "We all know that if there is free competition the public will be protected from unduly high prices and artificial scarcities . . . . [C]ompetition keeps prices low and quality high." *Id.* at 11,722.

269. *Id.* at 11,506 (remarks of Rep. Byrne).

> The whole trouble with you folks is, a lot of you forget there is such a thing as the consumer, as the great American buyer, the fellow who keeps these beloved corporations you love so much alive, and makes them profitable and sometimes the Government of the United States has to think about that great group of 140,000,000 consumers, and protect them against unjust exploitation.[270]

One Representative recognized that a prophylactic action was required because, once a company becomes a monopoly, "[t]he protection that surrounds property rights has become attached to the monopoly property."[271]

Even opponents of the legislation framed the issues in terms of harm to consumers, arguing, however, that there was no substantial risk of exploitation of consumers. One opponent stated that the merger bill was not needed because he did "not subscribe to the doctrine that the businessmen of our country are crooks and that those who carry on their business through the instrumentality of corporations are out to fleece and extort higher and higher prices from their customers."[272] Witnesses who testified against the legislation also framed the issues in terms of benefits to consumers.[273] In summary, both supporters and opponents of the amendment wanted to prevent consumers from paying artificially high pricies. The prevailing legislators feared higher prices due to market power so much that they wanted to stop trends towards concentration in their incipiency.[274]

270. *Senate Hearings, supra* note 260, at 180 (remarks of Sen. Kilgore); *see also* 95 Cong. Rec. 8147 (1949) (remarks of Rep. Patman).

271. 95 Cong. Rec. 11,493 (1949) (remarks of Rep. Yates).

272. *Id.* at 11,490-91 (remarks of Rep. Goodwin).

273. James L. Donnelly, former Vice-President of the Illinois Manufacturing Association, referred to "the customers' and consumers' interest which, of course, is paramount in all these considerations . . . ." *Senate Hearings, supra* note 260, at 30. Benjamin C. Marsh, Executive Secretary, People's Lobby, Inc., stated: "The assumption seems to be that competition and absence of monopoly will alone improve the quality of goods and reduce the price, and so benefit consumers . . . . [T]his assumption is not justified . . . ." *Id.* at 251. One opponent of the bill even argued against the amendment on the ground that the existing distribution of wealth in society was fair or, if anything, skewed unduly against the fair and necessary interests of businesspersons. He presented excerpts from works by Professor Slichter of Harvard University at the House Hearings, attempting to demonstrate that a fair distribution of income resulted from technological progress: "[T]he gains of technological progress have not gone in the main to capitalists, as Marx thought they would, or even to consumers, but to employees. . . . Does the economy distribute its product widely and fairly? . . . There is no basis for the oft-expressed fears that incomes are becoming concentrated in the hands of property owners. . . . [S]erious inequities in the distribution of income are inadequate compensation for pioneering and risk taking and inadequate compensation for holders of fixed-income securities." *House Hearings, supra* note 260, at 107-08 (remarks of Mr. Montague); *see also* discussion between Sen. Wiley and Sen. Kefauver, 95 Cong. Rec. 16,490 (1949).

274. As the Court stated in Brown Shoe Co. v. United States, 370 U.S. 294 (1962), "[A]

Additional Goals

An analysis of the legislative history of the Celler-Kefauver Act leads to the conclusion that the implications of rising industrial concentrations in the American economy were Congress' dominant concern.[275] Congress of course was concerned with concentration in particular markets and the amendment was worded to apply to all mergers that might affect competition "in any line of commerce."[276]

It is unlikely, however, that Congress was concerned only with such economic matters as efficiency and the distribution of wealth.[277] Congress also feared that high levels of economic concentration might have disquieting political and social ramifications. Many of the expressed misgivings regarding undue corporate aggrandizement of power were relatively mild and ambiguous.[278] Other warnings, however, were chilling, drawing analogies to the alarming consequences of concentration abroad.[279] Senator Kefauver, one leading sponsor of the

---

keystone in the erection of a barrier to what Congress saw was the rising tide of economic concentration, was its provision of authority for arresting mergers at a time when the trend to a lessening of competition in a line of commerce was still in its incipiency. Congress saw the process of concentration in American business as a dynamic force; it sought to assure the Federal Trade Commission and the courts the power to brake this force at its outset and before it gathered momentum." *Id.* at 317-18 (footnotes omitted).

275. So great was the congressional fear of industrial concentration that it mandated changes in the standards of proof of mergers' anticompetitive consequences. For example, the Supreme Court in United States v. Philadelphia Nat'l Bank, 374 U.S. 321 (1963), held that "[t]his intense congressional concern with the trend toward concentration warrants dispensing, in certain cases, with elaborate proof of market structure, market behavior, or probable anticompetitive effects." *Id.* at 363. The Court went on to state: "Such a test lightens the burden of proving illegality only with respect to mergers whose size makes them inherently suspect in light of Congress' design in § 7 to prevent undue concentration." *Id.* The *Brown Shoe* Court noted "[t]hat § 7 was intended to apply to all mergers—horizontal, vertical or conglomerate. . . ." Brown Shoe Co. v. United States, 370 U.S. 294, 317 n.31 (1962) (citing H.R. REP. No. 1191, 81st Cong., 1st Sess. 11 (1949)). Members of Congress made numerous references to conglomerate mergers. Congressman Boggs, for example, stated that the Act should apply to conglomerate acquisitions because "this is one of the most detrimental movements to a free enterprise economy . . . . This is the type which carries the activities of giant corporations into all sorts of fields, often completely unrelated to their normal operations." 95 CONG. REC. 11,496 (1949).

276. 15 U.S.C. § 18 (1951).

277. *See supra* notes 255-56 & accompanying text.

278. One Representative cautioned that "[t]here has been a growing trend toward economic concentration in the United States . . . which has reached the stage at which it constitutes a vital threat to the American way of life." 95 CONG. REC. 11,497 (1949) (remarks by Rep. Boggs). Equally mild was the observation by Representative Celler that "[b]igness does not mean efficiency, a better product, or lower prices." *Id.* at 11,486 (1949).

279. *Id.* at 11,486 (remarks of Rep. Celler): "I want to point out the danger of this trend toward more and better combines. I read from a report filed with former Secretary of War Royall as to the history of the cartelization and concentration of industry in Germany: 'Ger-

bill, stated:

> I am not an alarmist, but the history of what has taken place in other nations where mergers and concentrations have placed economic control in the hands of very few people is too clear to pass over easily. A point is eventually reached, and we are rapidly reaching that point in this country, where the public steps in to take over when concentration and monopoly gain too much power. The taking over by the public through its government always follows one or two methods and has one or two political results. It either results in a Fascist state or the nationalization of industries and thereafter a Socialist or Communist state.[280]

More than a generation after the end of World War II it is tempting to dismiss these statements as mere rhetoric. The sentiments, however, differ only in degree from those expressed throughout the

---

many under the Nazi set-up built up a great series of industrial monopolies in steel, rubber, coal and other materials. The monopolies soon got control of Germany, brought Hitler to power and forced virtually the whole world into war.' " It should be noted that Representative Celler's interpretation of the historical events which led to Hitler's rise to power is by no means universally shared. *See, e.g.*, A. BULLOCK, HITLER: A STUDY IN TYRANNY (1962).

280. 96 CONG. REC. 16,452 (1950) (remarks of Sen. Kefauver). These strong views were not expressed only by the principal sponsors of the amendment. *See, e.g., id.* at 16,446 (remarks of Sen. O'Mahoney: "Collectivism is moving forward apace throughout the world, and industrial collectivism leads inevitably to political collectivism. That I would like to avoid."), 16,503-04 (remarks of Sen. Aiken: "All of us know too well what has happened in countries where opportunity has been vested in the hands of a few. The result has been that either socialization or a totalitarian form of government has taken over . . . .").

Years earlier, President Franklin D. Roosevelt sent a proposal to Congress entitled Recommendations to the Congress to Curb Monopolies and the Concentration of Economic Power: April 24, 1938, proposing the creation of a Temporary National Economic Committee. *Id.*, *reprinted in* THE PUBLIC PAPERS AND ADDRESSES OF FRANKLIN D. ROOSEVELT 1941 (1938 volume), at 305-32. Roosevelt began his message to Congress with the warning, "[T]he liberty of a democracy is not safe if the people tolerate the growth of private power to a point where it becomes stronger than their democratic state itself. . . . Among us today a concentration of private power without equal in history is growing.

"This concentration is seriously impairing the economic effectiveness of private enterprise as a way of providing employment for labor and capital and as a way of assuring a more equitable distribution of income and earnings among the people of the Nation as a whole." *Id.* at 305-06. Professor Pitofsky, *supra* note 15, at 1064, concluded: "Virtually all proponents of the bill who spoke asserted that the merger trend must be blocked because concentrated economic power would lead to increased government control, because freedom would corrode and totalitarianism prosper, and because absentee ownership by large corporations would diminish local initiative and civic responsibility." (Footnote omitted.) Bok expressed a similar view in his analysis of the legislative history of the amendment. He concluded that "there emerges a common definition of the problem at hand, a common philosophy as to its import, and a common notion, on a very general plane, of what the new act could do about it . . . . This situation was appraised in the same Jeffersonian, egalitarian fashion by almost all who spoke for the bill. . . . In the minds of the Congressmen, the growth of these large economic groups could lead only to increasing government control; freedom would corrode, and the nation would drift into some form of totalitarianism." Bok, *supra* note 249, at 234-36 (footnote omitted).

Sherman,[281] FTC,[282] and Clayton Act[283] debates. The perceived rise in industrial concentration in 1950 merely provided another occasion for congressional repetition of the alarm regarding the increased social and political power of big business.[284]

The debates also show a concern for the welfare of small businesses. In *Brown Shoe*, Chief Justice Warren characterized Congress' desire to protect small businesses as going further than a directive to assist them in borderline cases where so doing would be unlikely to result in higher prices for consumers.[285] Although the debates do evi-

281. *See supra* notes 136-42 & accompanying text.

282. *See supra* notes 206-09 & accompanying text.

283. *See supra* notes 240-45 & accompanying text.

284. Numerous statements in the legislative history display concern for the possible social and political implications of unduly high concentration levels. With the exception of the statements mentioning conglomerate mergers, however, *see supra* note 275, it is unclear whether this manifest anxiety is attributable to concentration within individual markets or to aggregate levels of concentration. For example, Congress' references to "economic concentration," "cartelization and concentration," and "concentration and monopoly" are ambiguous on this point. In light of the fact that Congress worded the final bill in terms of "lines of commerce," Congress possibly was concerned only with concentration levels within markets. Nevertheless, a large conglomerate might possess almost as much social and political power as a similarly sized monopoly, and this country could be taken over by large conglomerates as easily as by large monopolists. In light of the fact that the merger problem facing Congress in 1950 primarily concerned mergers within markets, it is not surprising that Congress paid very little attention to conglomerate mergers. Nevertheless, if Congress had confronted this issue, *see supra* note 61 & accompanying text, it might have been concerned also with aggregate levels of industrial concentration in 1950.

An interesting unanswered question is whether the strong statements that condemned the corporate aggrandizement of social and political power should make any difference in merger cases. What difference would it make, in other words, if, as the Court stated in United States v. Philadelphia Nat'l Bank, 374 U.S. 321, 363 (1963), there are mergers "whose size makes them inherently suspect in light of Congress' design in § 7 to prevent undue concentration"? Should the horizontal merger guidelines be lowered when large mergers are involved?

Even though § 7 was ultimately cast in terms of competition within markets, the amendment was intended to apply to conglomerate mergers. *See supra* text accompanying notes 277-78. Suppose that there were a large conglomerate merger that had no net effect on individual markets. Could the FTC in carrying out its mission to enforce the "policy" or "spirit" of the other antitrust laws, *see supra* note 163, use the congressional fear of increased aggregate concentration levels (expressed in the legislative history of the Sherman Act, the FTC Act, and the original Clayton Act, as well as in that of the Celler-Kefauver amendment) to halt a pure conglomerate merger that was neutral in its economic effects? The question is, for now, unanswered.

285. Chief Justice Warren wrote, "It is competition, not competitors, which the Act protects. But we cannot fail to recognize Congress' desire to promote competition through the protection of viable, small, locally owned businesses. Congress appreciated that occasionally higher costs and prices might result from the maintenance of fragmented industries and markets. It resolved these competing considerations in favor of decentralization." Brown Shoe Co. v. United States, 370 U.S. 294, 344 (1962).

dence a desire to assist small businesses, it is doubtful that Congress meant to do so if this would result in higher prices to consumers.[286]

Summary

The primary goals of the Clayton Act were virtually identical to

---

286. For example, in the Senate Hearings Senator O'Connor asked, "There are some who contend that in instances where a closely held business with a very limited number of principals might by reason of one of a number of causes wish to sell, wish to dispose of its assets, whether they might be prevented from doing so, or be prevented from getting as advantageous a consideration if this enactment is put through, rather than under existing circumstances when they can negotiate possibly with another concern just about of the same size, possibly, nearby, and whether you think it would in the end have any effect." Rep. Patman replied, "I think the public interest is paramount. If this would be injurious to the public I think it should be prevented, even though the owner would probably not get as much. It is the public interest that is involved, and we should not permit these consolidations and mergers to the extent that it will lessen competition or create monopoly, looking at the public interest as No. 1." *Senate Hearings*, *supra* note 260, at 131. In the Senate debates Senator Keon asked: "[A] small-businessman can now sell to a large competitor, whereas, from what the Senator says, if the bill became law, he would be foreclosed from doing so." Senator O'Connor replied: "Not necessarily. It would all depend upon whether or not the sale would have the effect of substantially lessening competition." 96 CONG. REC. 16,441 (1950).

Another goal was to encourage corporate expansion through internal growth rather than through merger. As the Court stated in United States v. Philadelphia Nat'l Bank, 374 U.S. 321, 370 (1963): "[S]urely one premise of an antimerger statute such as § 7 is that corporate growth by internal expansion is socially preferable to growth by acquisition. *See also* United States v. Manufacturers Hanover Trust Co., 240 F. Supp. 867, 947 (S.D.N.Y. 1965): "An underlying premise of the Clayton Act . . . is that internal expansion is more healthy for the economy than expansion by merger."

In Brown Shoe Co. v. United States, 370 U.S. 294 (1962), the Court suggested reasons why Congress preferred internal corporate expansion rather than expansion by merger: "A company's history of expansion through mergers presents a different economic picture than a history of expansion through unilateral growth. Internal expansion is more likely to be the result of increased demand for the company's products and is more likely to provide increased investment in plants, more jobs and greater output. Conversely, expansion through merger is more likely to reduce available consumer choice while providing no increase in industry capacity, jobs or output. It was for these reasons, among others, Congress expressed its disapproval of successive acquisitions." *Id.* at 345 n.72.

The assertion that there are sound economic reasons to prefer corporate growth by internal expansion to growth through merger could be the subject of a lengthy discussion. Regardless, the opinion of Congress should prevail; we must proceed upon the assumption that corporate growth by internal expansion is socially preferable to growth by merger.

Moreover, this judgment may not have reflected any desire to sacrifice significant productive efficiencies. While Congress has condemned the power of large companies, it also encourages the growth of our economy. One way to reconcile these two beliefs is to prefer corporate growth by internal expansion. By making mergers difficult, Congress may have hoped to encourage more of this kind of growth. Perhaps Congress, in expressing this preference, was making the judgment that there were few advantages to consumers that resulted from corporate growth by merger. Congress may have passed the 1950 Amendment in part because it wanted the advantages that came from economic growth but saw few advantages to consumers from mergers and many dangers that might instead result.

those of the Sherman and FTC Acts. The Clayton Act was passed primarily to prevent mergers that might lead to the creation of corporations with sufficient market power to extract wealth unfairly from consumers. The legislative record also evidences a congressional desire to curb the growth of the social and political power of these corporations and to protect small businesses, and suggests that Congress wanted to encourage corporate efficiency. Although the precise role that efficiency was intended to play in Clayton Act analyses is unclear, the debates suggest that this Act, like the Sherman and FTC Acts, is primarily concerned with the efficiency benefits directly passed through to consumers. Congress did not exhibit a desire to forego redistributive goals in order to give nascent monopolists the profits that might flow from increased productive efficiency. Thus, the Clayton Act, together with the Celler-Kefauver Antimerger Act, manifests the same proconsumer, antimonopoly, anti-corporate power and pro-market control bias present in the earlier legislation.

Despite the large number of factors influencing the passage of the antimerger laws, Congress' central purpose deserves emphasis. The antimerger statutes were passed primarily to benefit consumers directly. The overriding economic purpose was the prevention of consumer exploitation through supracompetitive pricing, a likely consequence of merger-created market power. The concept of allocative efficiency does not figure significantly in the legislative record and no significant evidence exists that Congress was willing to forego its market power concerns in order to increase corporate efficiency. Congress hoped to preserve and achieve corporate efficiencies, to be sure, but not at the cost of allowing significant increases in market power. The legislative history suggests that resolution of otherwise doubtful or ambiguous situations should be in favor of a strict antimerger policy. Congress was willing to forego relatively large efficiency gains in order to be very sure that it prevented corporate acquisitions of market power, unless the resulting efficiency gains would be both large and certain and the risk of significant market power slight.

The implications of Congress' noneconomic concerns, however, are less clear. It is extremely difficult to determine how, and to what extent, to implement in an antitrust analysis the fervently expressed congressional goal of preventing corporate aggrandizement of political and social power or the congressional directive to assist small businesses in ways that do not result in artificially high prices for consumers. That determination is beyond the scope of this Article. However, the use of Congress' economic goals—its distributive and efficiency concerns—can be illustrated relatively easily. The next section of this Article briefly analyzes a horizontal merger resulting in a firm with monopoly power. This simplified analysis considers the differences that might arise if redistributive goals, in addition to or instead of efficiency goals, were taken into account in antitrust decisionmaking.

Comparison of Efficiency and Wealth Transfer Goals: Analysis of a Horizontal Merger

Distributive and efficiency goals often work in perfect harmony. Monopoly pricing causes both allocative inefficiency and transfers of wealth from consumers to producers; therefore, firms acquiring monopoly power are viewed negatively from either a distributive or efficiency perspective, at least initially. Similarly, business practices that do not give rise to or take advantage of market power and thus do not harm consumers would not be prohibited under either view of the goals of the antitrust laws.[287] Nevertheless, it often makes a considerable difference whether wealth transfer goals, in addition to or instead of efficiency goals, are ascribed to the antitrust laws.

An illustration of these differences is provided by a brief examination of the economic consequences of a horizontal merger.[288] Suppose the FTC, or a court, is deciding whether to prohibit a horizontal merger, and there is a significant chance that this merger might give the resulting firm substantial, persistent monopoly power. If the new firm were able to restrict output and to charge monopoly prices, both allocative inefficiency and the transfer of wealth from consumers to the mo-

287. This assumes that the practices neither harm consumers as a group nor "unfairly" redistribute property rights among consumers.

288. This analysis omits any explicit consideration of the effects of the merger on small businesses or on the social and political power of trusts or monopolies. The discussion is based upon an analysis first proposed by Professor Williamson in *Economies as an Antitrust Defense: The Welfare Trade-Offs*, 58 AM. ECON. REV. 18 (1968) [hereinafter cited as Williamson, *Economies*]. It is often used by advocates of an efficiency orientation to the antitrust laws as a guide to focus attention on the relevant issues. For example, Judge Bork stated that this form of analysis "can be used to illustrate all antitrust problems, since it shows the relationship of the only two factors involved, allocative inefficiency and productive efficiency. The existence of these two elements and their respective amounts are the real issues in every properly decided antitrust case. They are what we have to estimate—whether the case is about the dissolution of a monopolistic firm, a conglomerate merger, a requirements contract, or a price-fixing agreement." R. BORK, *supra* note 2, at 108. For a more detailed discussion of the maximization of allocative and productive efficiency in a horizontal merger context, see *id.*, ch. 5, and Muris, *supra* note 249, at 384-93. For a cogent analysis of the influence of politics on antitrust enforcement, see Kovacic, *The Federal Trade Commission and Congressional Oversight of Antitrust Enforcement*, 17 TULSA L.J. 587 (1982).

nopolist would result.[289] Further, suppose that the merger would also create significant efficiencies in production. The wealth transfer and efficiency effects of this merger can be illustrated by the following well-known diagram:[290]

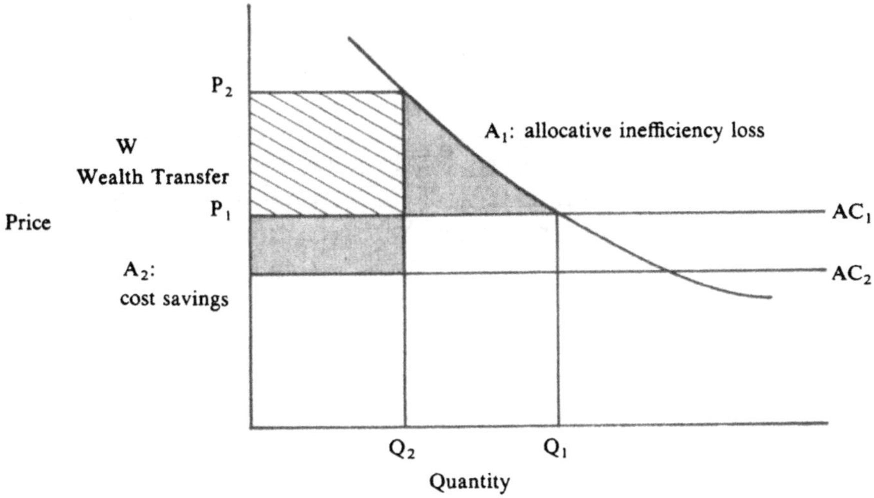

Under the theory that Congress was motivated by efficiency considerations alone, Judge Bork interpreted the diagram, explaining that

> [t]he diagram assumes that the merger reduces the long-run average costs of the two firms from AC_1 to AC_2 but that the increased market power created by the merger results in a restriction of output so that the rate moves from Q_1 to Q_2. We then see that consumers have lost output—for which they would have been willing to pay an amount above cost equal to the area labeled A_1—and have gained in resource savings an amount equal to the area A_2. Obviously, if A_2, the cost savings, is larger than A_1, the dead-weight loss, the merger represents a net gain to all consumers. If A_1 is larger than A_2, a net loss results.[291]

Two additional points concerning this diagram should be explained. First, Judge Bork wrote that the area A_2 represents a gain to consumers. The direct effects of the merger, however, will not produce

289. *See supra* notes 30-36 & accompanying text. This analysis assumes the existence of significant barriers to entry, and ignores, for the sake of simplicity, many topics such as incentives to innovate. For a detailed exposition of these assumptions and other issues involved in the tradeoff, see Fisher & Lande, *supra* note 39, at —.

290. For a more detailed explanation of this diagram, see R. BORK, *supra* note 2, ch. 5 (citing Williamson, *Economies*, *supra* note 288).

291. *Id.* at 108.

this result. Because the monopolist charges the monopoly price P_2, and because A_2 is below this line, all of the cost savings directly accrue to the monopolist. Consumers might, of course, receive some of these benefits indirectly,[292] or in the long run,[293] but it is also possible that part or all of these benefits will be wasted by the monopolist in an effort to obtain or protect its monopoly.[294] The direct effect of the merger, however, is to give the cost savings, shown as A_2, to the monopolist as part of its monopoly profits.

More importantly, Judge Bork's discussion does not consider the wealth that, without the merger, would have been consumer surplus, but was transferred to the monopolist as a result of the merger.[295] In the diagram, the striped rectangle, W, represents the property that, under the theory espoused by this Article, Congress meant to provide

292. The area, A_2, which directly accrues to the monopolist, represents another component of its monopoly profit. This portion of the monopoly profit, however, can be said not to "cost" consumers of the product anything, unlike area W, because it did not exist before the merger. It represents a loss to consumers only if the productivity gains could be realized (perhaps after some period of time) without the merger. Moreover, since area A_2 represents efficiency gains, fewer resources will go into making the product. These resources will be freed for other uses and will accrue to society as a whole. Of course, it is not possible to be sure that all or even most of the A_2 benefits will be passed on to consumers of the product in question, or even to similarly situated consumers. Nevertheless, it would be fair to say that part of the A_2 benefits should indirectly be passed on to some consumers. *See id.* at 107-10.

293. *See infra* note 305. Further, consumers will be directly benefited if the efficiencies are so large that prices decrease.

294. Judge Posner wrote: "[T]he expected profits of the merger will generate an equivalent amount of costs as the firms vie to make such mergers or, after they are made, to engross the profits generated by the high postmerger price through service, competition or whatever." Posner, *supra* note 57, at 821. If this did happen, then the rectangle A_2 should not be counted as a benefit of the merger. See Muris, *supra* note 249, at 392 n.41 for a discussion of Posner's arguments.

295. Judge Posner argues that because firms will compete to obtain monopoly profits, part or all of this monopoly profit could be dissipated by wasteful non-price competition to achieve or protect the monopoly. *See supra* note 54 & accompanying text. If the decisionmaker believed that this were likely to occur, part or all of area W should be counted as an efficiency loss. If, as this paper asserts, "consumers' surplus" was intended by Congress to be the entitlement or property of consumers, and if, as a practical matter, compensating side payments cannot be made, any merger analysis that only considered efficiency would violate Pareto optimality. The consumers will suffer the allocative inefficiency losses, area A_1 and the loss of wealth, area W. The monopolist, and, indirectly, consumers, and still other members of society will obtain the productive efficiency gains. *See* R. BORK, *supra* note 2, at 108. Since these groups are not identical, even if area A_2 exceeded the combined area of A_1 and W, if the decisionmaker were to allow the merger, one result of this welfare tradeoff would be to give wealth to some people and take wealth away from others. Since, as a practical matter, no compensating side payments will ever be made, the tradeoff calculation proposed by this model would violate Pareto optimality. We might still, of course, subjectively wish to allow such a merger despite the fact that it violates Pareto optimality.

to consumers, but that was obtained by the monopolist as a result of the merger.

If a court viewed maximum economic efficiency as the only goal of the antitrust laws, the merger would be prevented if and only if area A_1, the allocative efficiency loss, exceeded area A_2, the productive efficiency gain.[296] Alternatively, if the decisionmaker believed that Congress cared only about preventing "unfair" transfers of wealth from consumers to producers caused by market power, the probable existence of area W would always require prohibiting the merger.

A number of approaches, however, consider both efficiency and redistribution, thus remaining faithful to Congress' design. For example, the total "negative effects" of the merger—the allocative inefficiency (A_1) plus the redistribution of wealth (W)—could be balanced against the "positive" effects of the merger—the productive efficiency gains (A_2). The merger would be prevented only if the negative effects of the merger were likely to outweigh its positive consequences.[297]

Another decisional rule that finds considerable support in the antitrust laws' legislative histories would use the price paid by consumers as the standard and condemn any merger likely to lead to higher prices for consumers. A price standard would probably come closest to faithfully carrying out legislative intent, since Congress' overriding concern was with preventing consumers from paying supracompetitive prices.[298] In cases where price is unlikely to increase there would be no wealth transfer from consumers to firms with market power. This standard would consider only those efficiency gains that accrued directly to consumers. Such gains would occur only when the efficiency gains were so large that they resulted in downward price pressure greater than the upward pressure resulting from increased market power.[299] This rule would not consider any benefits of the merger directly retained by the monopolist. If it were applied in the merger hypothetical,

296. This conclusion ignores Posner's contributions, *supra* notes 54 & 295. If the decisionmakers were persuaded that Posner was correct a high proportion of the time and that the conversion of monopoly profits to costs was significant and long lasting, area A_2 would not be entered into the analysis as a positive factor because both areas A_2 and W would instead be counted as losses to society. The merger would, accordingly, be stopped in any case in which the decisionmaker believed that area A_1, A_2, or R was likely to exist.

297. Moreover, this balancing could be done in a number of ways. If the decisionmaker believed that Congress cared equally about efficiency and redistribution, they should be weighed equally. If, as this Article asserts, it was believed that Congress cared much more about wealth transfers, efficiency concerns could only be counted to break a tie or when the wealth transfer was uncertain.

298. *See supra* notes 80-82, 180-81, 240-41 & 267-72.

299. *See* Fisher & Lande, *supra* note 239, at —.

the resulting increase in productive efficiency, A_2, would not be counted because these benefits accrue directly to the monopolist. Therefore, if either of the negative consequences of the merger, areas A_1 or W, are likely to arise, the merger would be prevented. More concretely, if the product's price is likely to increase, the merger should be prohibited. If the price to consumers is unlikely to increase, however, the merger would be allowed.[300]

These are not the only possible ways to implement efficiency and wealth transfer considerations in merger analysis. The important point is to emphasize that the decision as to which goals are important is crucial, and that the holdings in merger cases and other types of antitrust actions will vary considerably under the different approaches.[301] Professor Williamson, commenting upon the horizontal merger example, points out that "[i]nasmuch as the income distribution which occurs is usually large relative to the size of the dead-weight loss, attaching even a slight weight to income distribution effects can some-

300. This would mean that those mergers creating market power which would result in efficiencies so large that they lead to lower prices for consumers should be permitted. The resulting monopoly profits would be allowed because they were not extracted from consumers, who were made better off by the merger. In these cases the merging firms would be allowed to keep all of their efficiency gains. Adoption of this standard would imply that even though a more complex tradeoff might in some circumstances be warranted, because Congress considered these other circumstances unlikely or too difficult to predict or analyze, for simplicity it used prices-to-consumers as the standard. As a practical matter, of course, this approach is best implemented when merger guidelines are established, not on a case-by-case basis.

One critical determination would be of the proper burden of proof. For example, if one believed that the redistributive concerns of the statute were paramount and that an efficiency defense was appropriate, the very heavy burden of proving efficiency benefits from a merger could be placed upon the defending party. As has been proposed by Areeda and Turner, the decisionmaker could only count efficiency gains when they exceed some threshold level. 4 P. AREEDA & D. TURNER, *supra* note 4, at 148-50. Alternatively, if one believed, contrary to the arguments presented in this Article, that the efficiency goals of the statute were central, redistribution could only be permitted to count, for example, as a "tipping" factor when the competing allocative and productive efficiency considerations were roughly equal.

301. For example, tying arrangements and attempts to monopolize produce obvious redistributive and efficiency effects. Tying arrangements are sometimes used by monopolists as a way to price discriminate and thereby acquire purchasers' surplus. *See* R. POSNER, *supra* note 4, at 176-80. A particularly dramatic monopolization illustration would occur if a firm monopolized the insulin market because this could result in virtually no allocative inefficiency yet create a large wealth transfer. The results of actions in these areas of antitrust concern would change substantially if distributive concerns were included in the decisionmakers' analysis.

More generally, other types of economic regulation might not be in the public interest if only efficiency goals were considered, but would be in society's interest if distributive goals were also a concern.

times influence the overall valuation significantly."[302] Judge Bork also acknowledges that if distributive effects were counted in a horizontal merger analysis, "the results of trade-off calculations would be significantly altered."[303] Indeed, even if the wealth transfer is only assumed to be twice as large as the allocative inefficiency, a very conservative assumption, the inclusion of this factor in antitrust analysis would have a profound effect. A rule that includes only efficiency considerations would permit far more mergers than one considering both efficiency and redistributive effects. Conversely, an approach considering only redistributive effects would prevent far more mergers.

This analysis contains only a summary of the most direct and obvious efficiency and distributive effects of a horizontal merger.[304] A realistic merger enforcement policy must consider severe and potentially overwhelming implementation problems. This is particularly true when enforcers attempt to implement a case-by-case application of theoretical economic concepts to real-world situations that are extremely conjectural. These difficulties include problems in estimating how high the monopoly might be able to raise its prices, how much more efficient the resulting firm might be, what kinds of problems might arise from the uncertainty and unavailability of data,[305] and de-

302. Williamson, *Economies, supra* note 288, at 28. Professor Williamson later wrote that "a product-specific claim that user and producer interests should be weighted unequally . . . does not vitiate the partial equilibrium model. It merely requires that the appropriate weights be specified. To the extent that purchaser interests are given greater weight than supplier interests, the economies burden is increased, *ceteris paribus*." Williamson, *Economies Revisited*, *supra* note 40, at 711. Although Williamson recognizes that his model could certainly incorporate distributive concerns, he states his belief that these concerns should be ignored. *Id.* at 710-11.

303. R. BORK, *supra* note 2, at 110.

304. Indirect, long-run, or dynamic effects also could be examined if the decisionmaker believed that this would further Congress' ultimate goals. Differences in outcomes under the approaches might be particularly pronounced if, in application, only direct effects are considered. Yet, consideration of indirect, long-run or dynamic factors would vastly, and perhaps impossibly, complicate the analysis. For example, if the problem were considered in a dynamic context it would be necessary to compare the present value of resource savings that would occur due to the efficiency gains in a competitive situation with the present value of the net efficiency gain (A_2-A_1) that would occur if the firms merge and produce a monopoly. These savings are affected over time by the rate at which entry occurs or the monopoly power erodes, the expenditure of resources by the monopolist to prevent the erosion of its monopoly power, *see supra* notes 54 & 295, the possibility that the monopoly will, on the average, engage in less than the socially optimal level of research and innovation, *see supra* note 55, and the amount of resources that the monopolist might waste due to X-inefficiency, *see supra* text accompanying note 54. Similarly, the decisionmaker might want to ask why the same efficiencies could not be achieved by means of internal expansion, how soon this might happen, and a large number of other questions.

305. For example, it would seem to be virtually impossible to measure the area of any of

cisions concerning which economic assumptions to apply.[306] These difficulties occur to varying degrees under each of the approaches that explicitly consider efficiency and/or transfers of wealth. At best, they significantly weaken the soundness and predictability of the analyses; at worst, they transform all of these analyses when applied on a case-by-case basis into mere theoretical exercises.

These practical problems support arguments against employing a rule-of-reason analysis to evaluate mergers[307] or many other types of antitrust violations. The better approach is to develop rules that give rise to simplified and predictable antitrust analysis,[308] incorporating

---

the triangles or rectangles presented in the diagram. As one commentator said, "One might assert a *general* theory of the second best as follows: 'If a state of affairs is the product of *n* variables, and you have knowledge of or control over less than *n* variables, if you think you know what's going to happen when you vary "your" variables, you're a booby.' That is, in complex processes (which most social processes are) a move in the right direction is not necessarily the right move. To pick a simple illustration, if I am on a desert island, subsisting solely on cocoanuts and oysters and beginning to hate it a lot, and across the bay from me there is another island, lush and fertile, I do not improve my position in life by swimming half way across." Leff, *Economic Analysis of Law: Some Realism About Nominalism*, 60 VA. L. REV. 451, 476 (1974); *see* R. BORK, *supra* note 2, at 125-27.

306. Conventional microeconomic analysis necessarily rests upon a large number of assumptions. Precise, well-developed prescriptive as well as descriptive models taking these factors into account are a necessity before any analysis can begin, for the violation of any of these assumptions renders the analysis, to some degree, invalid. These assumptions, which are crucial to the competitive operation of the free market, involve the presence or absence of perfect information, the working of the capital market, barriers to entry, economies of scale, immobility of resources, product differentiation, and externalities. The presence of any of these factors complicates economic analysis, and a failure to take them into account can render an economic analysis useless. *See generally* 2 P. AREEDA & D. TURNER, *supra* note 4, at 282-318 for a summary of the debate regarding the theoretical and empirical significance of these and similar factors.

307. These practical considerations do not, however, mean that a direct consumer impact characterization of the goals of the antitrust laws, perhaps with price to consumers as its benchmark, cannot be implemented, or that its implementation would be more difficult than the implementation of an efficiency-based analysis. A rule that considered both efficiency and distribution concerns would be no more complex than a rule that only considered efficiency, since both would require the same prediction concerning market power and economies. Further, an approach that only considered redistributive effects, or an approach that considered efficiency effects only when they were directly passed on to consumers, would be relatively simple. It would not, in the merger example, at least, involve a balancing of competing considerations. If, and only if, the decisionmaker determined that there was a significant chance that the merger might result in a significant transfer of wealth from consumers to a monopolist, *i.e.*, if and only if there were a significant chance that prices to consumers would be raised, would the merger be prevented.

308. Professor Turner concluded in his seminal 1965 article, *Conglomerate Mergers and Section 7 of the Clayton Act*, 78 HARV. L. REV. 1313 (1965): "In theory, the ideal regulatory policy would be one that discriminated carefully on a case-by-case basis between those mergers that threaten substantial anticompetitive consequences and those that do not. In

both efficiency and distributive considerations into the formulation of the merger guidelines.

Despite the critical problem of developing administrative approaches to antitrust analysis, it must be recalled that "when the law-making power speaks upon a particular subject, over which it has constitutional power to legislate, public policy in such a case is what the statute enacts."[309] Congress never promised that the administration of the antitrust laws would be easy.[310] It had definite goals that it wanted to accomplish when it enacted the antitrust laws. The primary obligation of the FTC and the courts is determining Congress' basic objectives. Only then does their task become that of formulating

---

fact, it seems almost impossible to carry out any such policy and still have an effective antimerger statute. . . .

"Taken literally, section 7 asks for a predictive economic judgment, a conclusion as to the probability of various possible economic consequences of a merger, and an assessment of the substantiality of those effects. Except in the most obvious cases, economic theory simply does not permit confident judgments on these issues even when all the economically relevant facts have been duly assembled. Thus, broadening the range of factual inquiry in each case beyond certain limits gives little or no hope of promoting rational decisionmaking. But even if this were not so, the effectiveness of the statute would largely be destroyed if the outcome of cases turned on a review of all the economic facts. With limited enforcement resources, few cases could be brought. With a wide variety of fact situations, the precedential value of particular decisions—their value as guides to the legality of other mergers—would be limited. Inevitably, the number of mergers with substantial anticompetitive effects would tend to increase. Consequently, there is little to be lost and much to be gained by directing the law toward rationally based general rules that are framed in terms of what seem to be particularly significant factual issues, capable of easy resolution." *Id.* at 1318-19 (footnote citing Professor Bok's article, *supra* note 249, omitted).

309. United States v. Trans-Missouri Freight Ass'n, 166 U.S. 290, 340 (1897). The Court also reasoned: "[W]e are asked to read into the act by way of judicial legislation an exception that is not placed there by the lawmaking branch of the Government, and this is to be done upon the theory that the impolicy of such legislation is so clear that it cannot be supposed Congress intended the natural import of the language it used. This we cannot and ought not to do. That impolicy is not so clear, nor are the reasons for the exception so potent as to permit us to interpolate an exception into the language of the act, and to thus materially alter its meaning and effect. It may be that the policy evidenced by the passage of the act itself will, if carried out, result in disaster to the roads and in a failure to secure the advantages sought from such legislation. Whether that will be the result or not we do not know and cannot predict." *Id.; cf.* R. BORK, *supra* note 2, at 69: "There must surely be a canon of statutory construction holding that, other things being equal, courts should attribute to the legislature a policy intent which, because of the scope and nature of a body of law, makes that law *effective in achieving its goals*, renders the law internally consistent, and makes for ease of judicial administration." (Emphasis added.)

310. Senator Cummins, for example, anticipated difficulty in analysis performed under § 5 of the FTC Act: "I have not a bit of doubt of the difficulty of the cases. We have never . . . accomplished anything good yet without great difficulty. If those who passed the antitrust law and those who passed the interstate commerce law had been appalled because they were difficult of administration, we would have yet been without any regulation of interstate commerce." 51 CONG. REC. 11,106 (1914).

implementation approaches that come as close as is practicable to carrying out these goals. Thus, decisionmakers have latitude in deciding precisely how to incorporate both efficiency and distributive considerations in antitrust analysis. To ignore either, however, would contravene congressional desires.

This Article suggests that both distributive and efficiency considerations are meant to play a role in antitrust analysis. Because many antitrust violations cause both economic inefficiency and wealth transfer from consumers to firms with market power, in many antitrust cases no conflict between these goals would arise. Conversely, if the firm or firms in question were unlikely to achieve market power, the activity in question probably would not violate the antitrust laws under any view of the antitrust laws' goals. Nevertheless, the merger example presented in this section illustrates the sort of case in which antitrust results depend greatly upon the goals employed in the analysis.

Conclusion

This examination of the legislative histories of the antitrust laws shows that Congress had a limited number of specific goals. The same small list provides the underpinnings of each of the Acts. The examination of each Act's legislative history in light of the relevant social and economic context has attempted to shed some light on these goals.

Each antitrust law grew in part out of a desire to define and protect consumers' property rights, an antipathy toward corporate aggregations of economic, social, and political power, and a concern for small entrepreneurs. The concern at the end of the nineteenth century focused on the excessive power of trusts and of the industrialists who controlled them, primarily as this power was used to harm consumers. Congress also had efficiency goals and resented trusts because they had the power to determine whether or not individuals had a fair opportunity to compete. Discontent existed over the potential political power resulting from control over thousands of jobs and billions of dollars in assets and over potential disruptions to society that might occur unless these aggregations of power were curbed.

As the United States entered the twentieth century, great increases in industrial concentration occurred, despite the prohibitions of the Sherman Act. The FTC and Clayton Acts were intended to refine and extend the Sherman Act and better implement its basic goals by filling in the gaps in its coverage. In particular, the FTC was given a mandate to prevent "unfair methods of competition." Congress intended this phrase to include such disparate acts as fraud and monopolization primarily because each caused "unfair" transfers of wealth from consumers to producers.

The Celler-Kefauver amendment was born largely in the shadow of World War II. Reminded of the high and rising level of industrial concentration, Congress believed it was necessary to strengthen the Clayton Act. Congress recognized the need for efficient, large-scale economic production, but feared the social unrest, or worse, that could be precipitated by concentrated corporate power. The dramatic statements in the legislative history of the Celler-Kefauver Antimerger Act probably reflect less a fear of imminent fascism than a desire to curb increases in industrial concentration for a large number of social and political reasons.

These congressional value judgments were the motivations underlying the antitrust laws. The effects of market power on allocative efficiency caused little or no concern in even the most recent major antitrust statutes. Of course, in every one of the antitrust laws' legislative histories Congress applauded the productive efficiency of modern corporations. Stressing the benefits resulting from free competition, Congress wanted to provide incentives that would help firms compete vigorously. Congress wanted to encourage economic efficiency and to ensure that the fruits of this efficiency were passed on to consumers, but efficiency was never its primary goal. Congress attempted to accomplish its overriding redistributive aims in such a way that the benefits of modern productivity would still be substantially realized. The evidence does not suggest, however, that Congress wanted the antitrust laws to allow increases in corporate efficiency at the cost of undermining its basic redistributive goals.

The antitrust laws were enacted to become broad and flexible economic mandates to improve "consumer welfare," as Congress defined this term. Recent advances in economic theory provide the methodology that can help determine when market power is likely to harm consumers, as opposed to those times when free market forces that will best ensure consumers' protection are operating. This sophistication should lead to increasingly precise implementations of Congress' commands that all purchasers, whether consumers or businesses, be given the right to purchase products priced at no more than the competitive level and that all sellers be given the right to compete against products priced at no less than that level.

[4]

THE CRITERION OF ECONOMIC PERFORMANCE IN THE ANTI-TRUST POLICIES OF THE UNITED STATES AND THE EUROPEAN ECONOMIC COMMUNITY

by

Alex P. Jacquemin *

> " It is 1978 and by this time every company west of the Mississippi will have merged into one giant corporation known as Samson Securities. Every company east of the Mississippi will have merged under an umbrella corporation known as the Delilah Company.
>
> It is inevitable that one day the chairman of the board of Samson and the president of Delilah would meet and discuss merging their two companies. . . .
>
> . . . The Anti-Trust Division of the Justice Department studied the merger for months. Finally the Attorney General made this ruling. ' While we find some drawbacks to only one company being left in the United States, we feel the advantages to the public far outweigh the disadvantages.
>
> ' Therefore, we're making an exception in this case and allowing Samson and Delilah to merge.' "
>
> Art Buchwald, *Washington Post*, June 2, 1966

In recent years, there has been a growing concern among students of anti-trust policy about the so-called conflict between competition and efficiency. On the one hand, competition is considered as desirable for its economic as well as its social and political values; on the other, efficiency is considered a prime goal of anti-trust law.

In cases where business conduct has the sole effect of lessening competition without producing economies, or of increasing efficiency without harming competition, there is no conflict. In some cases, however, conflict inevitably arises. The object of this article is to analyse the situation where efficiency and market power consequences co-exist, and to consider possible solutions by comparison between the American anti-trust conception and the principles inherent in the Rome Treaty of the European Economic Community.

* The author is Director of the Centre for Interdisciplinary Research in Law and Economics at the University of Louvain (Belgium) and Visiting Assistant Professor of Business, Government and Society at the University of Washington. He is much indebted to S. Marcus, J. McGee, F. Edwards, R. Joliet and W. van Gerven, for helpful comments on earlier drafts of this paper. He wishes also to acknowledge a special debt to D. Hermann, P. Graham, H. de Jong and H. H. Maas.

I. The Two Approaches

In this perspective, it is generally supposed that there is a substantial difference between the two approaches, in that the American tradition condemns *a priori* any combination or agreement increasing market power, regardless of any possible beneficial effects, whereas the Common Market distinguishes between that which is beneficial to the public interest and that which is detrimental.

> " The difference lies not so much in what is being restricted, but in why there is a need to restrict. Though this distinction is theoretical in nature, it should cause court decisions in the respective systems to vary. Whereas a United States court must look solely at the facts in a given case, the E.E.C. Commission must look solely to the effects; and while the former need only determine that a monopoly exists for public policy to be violated, the latter must determine that the public has been harmed by the existence of a monopoly." [1]

In contrast to the Common Market philosophy, which is to encourage cartels or monopolies beneficial to the economy, the American National Committee studying the American anti-trust laws said that indeed

> " these laws are concerned with undue restraints of competition, with monopolization or attempts to monopolize, and with certain practices deemed essentially injurious to competition. Such conduct cannot be excused by proof it represents progressive managerial policy or, if defendant is a monopoly, it has been a good one, has performed acceptable social service, or even benefited the consuming public ".[2]

The judicial application of the American statutes conforms to such principles. According to recent decisions of the United States Supreme Court, " a merger the effect of which may be substantially to lessen competition is not saved because, on some ultimate reckoning of social or economic debits and credits, it may be deemed beneficial. . . . Such is beyond the ordinary limits of judicial competence." [3]

Some cases seem to indicate not only that economies cannot be used as a defence, but that those efficiencies could be used affirmatively in attacking the merger, because they are a threat to " the protection of viable, small, locally-owned business ". The Supreme Court's *Brown Shoe* and *Procter & Gamble* decisions [4] seem indeed to base a finding of illegality upon the existence of new efficiencies.

[1] M. Rishe, " Antitrust Philosophy of the Common Market—Restraint on Prohibition," *DePaul Law Review*, Autumn 1967, No. 1. See also R. Joliet, *The Rule of Reason in Antitrust Law, American, German and Common Market Laws in Comparative Perspectives* (Faculte de Droit de Liege, 1967), 113; and C. Edwards, *Control of Cartels and Monopolies, an International Comparison* (Oceana, 1967), 152.

[2] Report, p. 338.

[3] *U.S.* v. *Philadelphia National Bank*, 374 U.S. 312 (1963).

[4] See *Brown Shoe* v. *U.S.*, 370 U.S. 294 (1962); *Procter & Gamble-Clorox* v. *U.S.* (1967).

Concerning restraints of trade, the development of *per se* rules [5] and a narrow interpretation of the rule of reason [6] have resulted in the rejection of any distinction between " good and bad cartels ".

On the other hand, the differing European concept is explicitly formulated in Articles 85 and 86 of the EEC Treaty. Article 85, para. 3 formulates four tests according to which a restrictive agreement may be justified:

1. The agreement must contribute to improvement of production or distribution, or to technological or economic progress.
2. The public must share in the benefits of the improvement.
3. The restriction must be indispensable for the achievement of these results.
4. The restriction may not be such as to afford the enterprise involved the possibility of eliminating competition with respect to a substantial proportion of the commodity concerned.

The Commission has applied such an exemption chiefly in the cases of exclusive dealing agreements, especially exclusive distribution of foreign goods.[7]

Mergers are in no way prohibited. One explanation of this attitude is that, in a market which is not yet integrated, a merger is considered *a priori* favourable to the public interest.[8] The only limit would come from Article 86 which condemns abuses of a dominant position.[9] But neither the existence nor the attempt to build dominant positions is forbidden. Monopolization as such is not outlawed, whether by internal growth or by mergers, but only the abuse of a monopoly position. " To what extent the acquisition of other enterprises by an enterprise in a dominant position

[5] See, *e.g.*, *United States* v. *Socony Vacuum Oil Company*, 310 U.S. 150 (1940). But see *Appalachian Coals Inc.* v. *U.S.* 288 U.S. 344 (1933) (where cartels were justified on an efficiency basis).

[6] The standard adopted in the *Standard Oil of New Jersey* case (1911) " permits the courts to decide whether conduct is significantly and unreasonably anti-competitive in character or effect; it makes obsolete once prevalent arguments, such as, whether monopoly arrangements would be socially preferable to competition in a particular industry, because, for example, of high fixed cost, or the risks of 'cutthroat' competition or other similar unusual conditions ". *Report of the Attorney General's National Committee to Study the Antitrust Laws*, 11 (1955).

[7] *Blondel*, decision of July 8, 1965, J.O., p. 2194/1965; *Hummel-Isbecque*, decision of September 17, 1965, J.O., p. 2581/1965; *Jallate*, decision of December 17, 1965, J.O., p. 37/1966; *Transocean Marine Paint Association*, decision of June 27, 1967, J.O. 1967, 163/10, and *CECIMO*, decision of March 13, 1969, J.O. 1969, L 69/13.

[8] See H. von der Groeben, " Competition Policy as Part of Economic Policy in the Common Market ", address to the European Parliament, June 16, 1965.

[9] It is generally admitted that Article 85 does not apply to mergers; but see Dabin and Joliet, " Les concentration d'entreprises et le droit de la concurrence ", *Rapport Belge au quatrième colloque de droit européen*, Roma, October 1967, and P. Verloren van Themaat, " Grensoverschrijdende fusies binnen de EEG ", 16 S.E.W. 1968, 162–186.

constitutes abuse of its position within the meaning of Article 86 depends on the market situation in each individual case. But the more an enterprise in a dominant position approaches *monopoly* by merging with another enterprise . . . the more probability there is that such a merger will constitute an abuse." [10]

II. Proposals for Change

Proposals have regularly been made to relax the principles of the American anti-trust policy and to concede that a substantial restraint of competition through mergers and perhaps even through restrictive agreements, could be justified if it is shown that they bring about economic benefits for the public.[11]

Recently, some economists and lawyers have again advocated a more extensive use of the efficiency standard as a defence of mergers.[12] This standard might also be applied to restrictive agreements.

Such a suggestion has found an expression in the 1966 Bank Merger Act providing a public interest exception which may give legality to mergers, which would be illegal if judged solely by Clayton Act standards.[13] Congress now seems willing to allow a court or agency to make economic value judgments in weighing the "public interest benefits" of a merger.[14]

Such a prospect should be closer to the European anti-trust theory which holds that it is sometimes better to sacrifice the competitive process in order to obtain better public performance. In the light of a comparative approach, we propose then to examine the meaning of the efficiency

[10] H. von der Groeben, *op. cit.*, 17–18.

[11] Although the maintenance of competition is an essential policy of the United States, it is well known that there are some departures from that policy. Measures requiring the moderation of competition have been adopted to prevent waste in the exploitation of natural resources, to protect workers, farmers, and small businessmen, to exclude outsiders from state, local or national markets. So, in a sense, the idea that competition may not be the best tool to serve the public interest has never been absent from the American tradition. See Clair Wilcox, *Public Policies Toward Business* (Irwin, 1966), Part VI.

[12] O. E. Williamson, "Economies as an Antitrust Defense—the Welfare Tradeoffs", *American Economic Review*, March 1968; Bork and Bowman, "The Crisis in Antitrust", *Columbia Law Review*, March 1965.

[13] S. 5 of the 1966 Merger Act states that: "The responsible agency shall not approve: (1) any proposed merger which would result in a monopoly, or which would be in furtherance of any combination or conspiracy to monopolize the business of banking in any part of the United States, or (2) any other proposed merger transaction whose effect in any section of the country may be substantially to lessen competition, or tend to create a monopoly, or which in any other manner would be in restraint of trade, *unless it finds that the anticompetitive effects of the proposed transaction are clearly weighed in the public interest by the probable effect of the transaction in meeting the convenience and needs of the community to be served.*

"In every case, the responsible agency shall take into consideration the financial and managerial resources and future prospects of the existing and proposed institutions and the convenience and needs of the community to be served."

[14] But as banking is a regulated industry, the legislative intent is probably limited.

defence and to see whether it may have real importance for the anti-trust policies of the United States and the Common Market. To begin with, we shall analyse the legal and judicial approach to the efficiency defence and see how strictly it has been applied in the U.S. and the EEC. Afterwards, we shall examine what such a defence implies, from an economic point of view.

III. The Legal Constraint

In its first application of the new Bank Merger Act, the United States Supreme Court has attempted to give meaning to the public interest concept by indicating the requirements of the defence.[15]

First, the burden of proof is on the party seeking to invoke the exception.

Secondly, several requirements must be met:

(a) The beneficial consequences of the merger must be specifically described by the merging banks. "It is, for example, not enough merely to show that a merger will result in a greater lending capacity. Defendants must establish what beneficial consequences a higher lending capacity will have as well as what value their benefits will have to the community." [16] Such specifications may be very hard to satisfy.

(b) The beneficial consequences must clearly outweigh any adverse competitive effects.[17] For defendants to prove that this is the case, "they must show that the economic benefits to the community are greater than the harmful consequences of a possible misallocation of resources, of a possible rise in bank charges, and of a possible curtailment of bank services. But exactly how are defendants to measure these harmful consequences of less competition, and if they cannot measure them, how are they to prove that the economic benefits of the merger clearly outweigh them? " [18]

(c) The benefits must be obtainable only through mergers. "If the gains in better service outweighed the anti-competitive detriment and *if the merger was essential to secure this net gain to the public interest*, the merger should be approved." [19] Again, proving that those benefits are not obtainable by any other feasible alternative to merger is a very heavy burden, especially in regard to the alternative possibility of internal expansion.

[15] *U.S.* v. *Provident National Bank*, and *U.S.* v. *First City National Bank of Houston*, 386 U.S. 361 (1967), and *U.S.* v. *Third National Bank*, 88 S.Ct. 882 (1968).

[16] 88 S.Ct. 882 (1968), at 892, and F. Edwards, "Bank Mergers and the Public Interest: A Legal and Economic Analysis of the 1966 Bank Merger Act", working paper, Columbia University, Graduate School of Business, 1968.

[17] 88 S.Ct. 882 (1968), at 893.

[18] F. Edwards, *op. cit.* 45.

[19] 88 S.Ct. 882 (1968), at 893. Emphasis added.

In brief, the actual application of the Bank Merger Act indicates that, if the public interest defence for mergers were extended to every industry, and if section 7 of the Clayton Act were modified to include such a provision, the judicial interpretation would be probably so restrictive that no substantial change would occur.

In fact, such an interpretation adopted by the United States Supreme Court for mergers reflects a policy substantially similar to that embodied in the EEC Treaty for cartels. And it seems that if one accepts the efficiency defence, it is necessary to require more or less the same conditions, independent of the conduct concerned. With respect to Article 85, para. 3, four tests are indeed required to exempt agreements in restraint of competition.[20] The first two conditions state that the arrangement has to contribute towards improving the production or distribution of goods, or promoting technical or economic progress, and to reserve to users a " fair share " in the resulting benefits. There is an analogy with that part of the Bank Merger Act requiring that " the merger is so beneficial to the convenience and needs of the community to be served that it would be in the public interest to permit it ".[21]

A third test is that the agreement must not enable the enterprise to eliminate competition with respect to a substantial portion of the goods. In other words the probable realization of a dominating position shall prevent the exemption of a cartel enforcement under Article 85, para. 3. This requirement is close to the proof demanded by the United States Court, that possible public interest benefits of a bank merger outweigh an adverse competitive effect.[22]

A final test of Article 85 is that the restriction is indispensable to an improvement; this is identical to the U.S. test that the proposed merger be " essential to secure this net gain to the public interest ".

Without pushing the analogy too far, the general perspective seems pretty much the same in both systems,[23] and it appears that the exemption under Article 85, para. 3, is theoretically as hard to obtain as the exception

[20] But here the burden of proof is not on the sole-party seeking to invoke the exception: the Commission may not limit itself to require from the enterprises the proof that the conditions for the exemption are fulfilled but should contribute on its own initiative to establish the relevant facts and circumstances, *Consten-Grundig*, decision of July 13, 1966.

[21] House Banking and Currency Committee, Report No. 1221, 89th Congress, 2d Session, January 24, 1966.

[22] It may be stricter in the sense that a very substantial reduction of competition may not be admitted even if important benefits result. It is less strict in the sense that it does not require a clear outweighing of benefit as compared to loss of competition.

[23] Article 86 which forbids abuses of a dominant position in the Common Market or any substantial part thereof, makes no provision for exemption in the case of activities that promote technical or economic progress or improve production or distribution. But if there is a possibility that an agreement might qualify for exemption under Article 85, yet be subject to prohibition under Article 86, the precedent type of activities are not likely to be often considered abusive.

in the case of a bank merger in the U.S. A commentator of the EEC decision in the *Grundig-Consten* Case [24] has indeed noted that "dispensations under Article 85, para. 3, will be very difficult if not impossible to obtain ".[25]

Nevertheless the EEC Commission has granted the exemption in many cases. It has been possible only because, in doing so, it has avoided a real confrontation between competitive effects and public benefits: the Commission has granted or denied exemptions solely on the basis of the language of the contract provisions and has not required a strict proof of the four tests. If, prima facie, certain causes do appear while others do not, the agreement may be saved. It is even possible that by amending the terms after a first rejection, approval can be obtained.[26] The only evidences used are some vague presumptions.[27] A general expression of such a conception is Regulation No. 19/65 which empowers the Commission to grant exceptions to classes of bilateral exclusive dealing arrangements and licensing agreements, on the basis of Article 85, para. 3, but without the necessity of examining specifically whether the required tests

[24] Decision of September 23, 1964, *CCH Common Market Reporter,* § 2743; 4 C.M.L.Rev. 1966–67, 209–220.

[25] Nerves, "The European Commission's First Major Antitrust Decision", 20 *Business Law* 1965, 431, 436.

[26] Of a total of 31,550 agreements that have been notified, some 1,170 have been disposed of because they have been amended to comply with the Regulation. See Press Release from the Commission of the European Communities, July 1968. *CCH Common Market Reporter,* § 9248.

[27] For the conditions requiring an improvement, see *Blondel,* (July 8, 1965), *Hummel-Isbecque* (September 17, 1965), *Jallate* (December 17, 1965), *Transocean Marine Paint Association* (June 27, 1967), *CECIMO* (March 13, 1969). In those cases the Commission has considered that such agreements reduced difficulties arising from distance, language barriers and differences of law; facilitated service after sale, maintenance of inventories of spare parts, adaptation of goods to local peculiarities; made the goods available more regularly and easily. . . . In fact we think that the sole existence of an importer, without exclusive rights, may be sufficient to overcome these difficulties arising from distance, language questions, juridical differences. . . . For the requirement of an equitable share for users, see *A.C.E.C.-Berliet,* decision of July 17, 1968, J.O. 1968, L 201/9; *CCH Common Market Reporter,* § 9251. "An evaluation of the share of the profit reserved for consumers can only be based on probabilities in the case of agreements that have not yet produced their effects. However, there is sufficient probability that the expected results will be achieved more quickly because of the joint research and it is not likely that unfair sales prices or other unfair conditions will be imposed on [the Consumer]. Thus it may be assumed that the condition set forth in Article 85, para. 3, under which a fair share of the profit resulting from the agreement must be reserved for the consumers, is at present fulfilled." See also the *Transocean case* (June 27, 1967) where no real distinction is drawn between improvement in the product (or in the production process) and the advantages accruing to users. For the criterion of indispensability, see the *Hummel* and *Jallate* decisions where it is simply concluded that the restriction in question was *likewise* indispensable or that " the improvement in distribution would *not be better served* by another sales system ". (Emphasis added.) See also M. R. Mok, " The Cartel Policy of the EEC Commission, 1962–1967 ", 6 C.M.L.Rev. 1968–69, 69–103.

are satisfied. Acordingly, Regulation No. 67/67 of the Commission has granted a group exemption to some exclusive dealing agreements.[28]

The impression gained from comparing the actual legal and judicial approach to the "efficiency defence" in the EEC and the U.S. is, then, that in both countries few anti-competition practices would be sustained by such a defence when rigorously examined. We may wonder whether that conclusion depends upon the degree of the legal constraint or is a reflection of the actual state of economic science. In other words, is it theoretically possible to prove that in some cases a substantial restriction of competition is necessary to improve the market performance?

IV. The Economic Constraint

1. *Efficiency and Competition*

The need to sacrifice some competition in order to obtain more efficiency implies that such a benefit cannot result from existing competition or from an increase in competition. But the principle is that competition provides society with the maximum output that can be obtained, given the actual resources, or more precisely, reduces prices to marginal costs, *i.e.*, makes prices equal to the worth of resources necessary to do the job. It is thus necessary to find cases where this principle does not apply; we have the classical list of "market failures": important economies of scale, external effects, public goods, natural resources.

Usually, those problems are solved by excluding the corresponding activities from the market system and by using devices other than anti-trust, such as public regulation and policies of subsidy and taxation. But in the unregulated area, the value of competition is supposedly intact. Indeed, it is difficult to prove that in this unregulated sector, a decrease in competition is often required for better performance.

Concerning *mergers*, it is generally recognized that in the U.S. the actual level of concentration is high enough to realize the economies of scale, and that the risk of serious economic loss by opposing a merger is very low.[29] This statement is reinforced when we recall that an increase

[28] J.O. of March 6, 1965 and March 25, 1967. See C. Champaud, "The Group Exemptions of E.E.C. Regulation 67/67", 5 C.M.L.Rev. 1967/68, 23.

[29] For a general analysis see J. Bain, "Advantages of the Large Firm: Production, Distribution, and Sales Promotion", *Journal of Marketing, October* 1955. In *Statistical Cost Analysis* (McGraw-Hill, 1960), J. Johnston concludes that the long-run average cost curve is generally flat; beyond a certain minimum scale, a plant cannot produce significant economies of scale. This minimum scale is the most often already reached. See also T. Saving, "Estimation of Optimum Size of Plant by the Survivor Technique", *Quarterly Journal of Economics*, November 1961. Concerning the existence of multiplant economies, Blair states that the evidence tends to be negative, in "Economic Concentration", *Hearings before the Subcommittee on Antitrust and Monopoly of the Committee on the Judiciary*, United States Senate, Part 4, "Concentration and Efficiency", 1965, 1555. See also W. Mueller, "Planning, Regulation and Competition", *Hearings before Subcommittees of the Select Committee on Small Business*, 1967, 18.

in a firm's absolute size is compatible with a constant or decreased degree of concentration if the industry itself is growing, and that a merger is not the only way to increase the firm's absolute size.[30]

In the EEC the problem is different because European enterprises have to adjust to the dimensions of the Common Market and to face increasingly the competition from large-scale foreign business. Nevertheless, it does not necessarily mean that a substantial reduction of competition is then required to achieve economies of scale.

First, the size of European business cannot simply be compared to the dimensions of American enterprise because U.S. business is generally oversized; what we need is to determine the dimension required to achieve economies of scale. Such a size is not *a priori* incompatible with a sufficient degree of competition at the level of the EEC. Secondly, in some sectors the dimension already achieved seems sufficient to achieve these economies.[31] In the rare cases where the size required to achieve economies of scale, is nearly close to monopoly, the best solution is not to accept a substantial " private " reduction of competition but to adopt some kind of state ownership or control beyond the scope of the antitrust policy. The problem of *restrictive practices* may be considered in the light of two complementary arguments.

First, many of these practices, especially the restrictive agreements, are not necessary to obtain the desired beneficial results, such as specialization of output or exclusion of the incompetent. Competition would more effectively provide these results. This has to be understood in Europe where " price-fixing, allocation of goods, quota systems, and joint purchase or sale may all be accepted either as direct aid to good performance, or as inducements to participate in other programmes that are believed to provide such aid ".[32]

Secondly, even if some of these " restrictive " practices might be permitted on the basis of public benefits, it does not mean that they will really harm competition because they may only seem to be restrictive and may in fact express competitive behaviour. This is especially true for the so-called " abusive trade practices ".

As L. Telser states, " few trade practices are abusive under all circumstances. Sometimes a given practice is not only compatible with competition but may actually enhance it ".[33] And he concludes: " Blanket

[30] A statistical study by S. Reid concludes that the " profit-related variables " strongly favour the " internal growth group of firms " when compared with " the merger type group ", in *Mergers, Managers, and the Economy* (*McGraw-Hill*, 1968), 193.

[31] See C. Layton, *Trans-Atlantic Investments*, (The Atlantic Institute, 1966), who refers to the chemical, the motor vehicle, and electrical industries.

[32] C. Edwards, *Control of Cartels and Monopolies* (Oceana, 1967), 152.

[33] L. Telser, " Abusive Trade Practices: An Economic Analysis ", *Law and Contemporary Problems*, No. 3, Summer 1965, 504.

A similar conclusion is reached by J. McGee in his analysis of the Robinson-Patman Act, in " Some Economic Issues of Robinson-Patman Land ", *Law and Contemporary Problems*, Summer 1965, 530.

prohibitions against such practices might harm competition more than would monopoly ".

A consequence of this observation is that the *per se* rule is sometimes very dangerous. Therefore, it would be better to consider the possibility of recognizing that in certain cases certain practices do not substantially restrain competition.

2. *Efficiency and Consumer Welfare*

Efficiency may be defined as the satisfaction of consumer's desires at minimum cost. If this definition is accepted, its fulfilment requires two conditions.

(a) To justify a restriction of competition by an increase in efficiency, it is required that the efficiency effect be translated into a sufficient increase in quantity and/or quality of goods in the economy so that society enjoys a net benefit from the new situation. It must then be proved that, even though they will face a degree of reduced competition as a result of their conduct, the firms in question will offer lower prices, better quality or services, than in the more competitive situation. And this effect cannot be limited to a moment in time; it must be guaranteed that it will be maintained over years. The probable duration of the increased market power must be compared with the probable duration of the beneficial effects.

(b) The effect on the satisfaction of the consumer must be computed on the basis of a broad conception of efficiency. If a restriction of competition does not result in lower prices, it does not mean that the restriction has no effect on the consumer welfare. It is necessary to examine whether the new situation does or does not produce better or new services, better or new products, a higher rate of innovation or technological progress, and a better quality of advertising and sales promotion.[34]

In other words, the range of public performance is very broad and it is impossible to reduce consumer welfare to the price-quantity relationship.[35] It would be too easy to say that other aspects are " deviations from consumer welfare ", for example, that " progress will occur even without special consideration by the law ".[36] On the contrary, such aspects are an important part of consumer welfare and may sometimes be better realized

[34] The sole efficiency concept includes not only the allocation of resources among industries, but also the degree of internal use of actual resources and the amount expended by the firm on alternative uses.

[35] Especially a comparison in static, partial equilibrium, two-dimensional terms, between the " dead-weight " loss from monopoly power and the " cost-savings " from better efficiency, cannot express the net welfare effect for the consumer.

[36] R. Bork, " The Goals of Antitrust Policy ", *Papers and Proceedings of the A.E.A.*, May 1967, 251.

through a merger or even a restraint of trade.[37] Once it is recognized that in a case where consumer welfare and market power consequences co-exist, the balance may be in favour of the consumer welfare effect, it is difficult to understand why, in theory, such a justification would be rejected if the beneficial effect takes the specific form of a better quality of the product, but accepted when it takes the form of a lower price. It even seems that the first form may be much more important for the consumer.

We conclude that an efficiency defence, to have meaning, must correspond to the concept of the consumer welfare defence (or the market performance defence).[38]

But once the multidimensional character of the consumer welfare is admitted, it appears that its estimation cannot rely on scientific judgment.

First, the evidence obtainable would generally be ambiguous. " Predatory price-cutting is not readily to be distinguished from vigorous competition, monopolistic overcapacity from prudent anticipation of demand, deliberate suppression of technology from a wise decision to reject an inferior process, an unpromising product, or an improvement whose immediate adoption would be premature ".[39]

Secondly, even if the evidence were clear, its welfare implications are obscure. The recent *Procter & Gamble* case is an example. If it is true that advantages afforded by a merger which reflect simply greater efficiency " ought not to be a basis for holding the merger illegal ", it is still not obvious that advantages in the form of increased advertising should be permited as a defence. We agree that " to the degree that *Proter & Gamblo* rests on suspicion of advertising, as it clearly did at the Commission level, we seem faced with an incipient policy of governmental intervention in an economic and social process " [40]; but it would also be true that in accepting an increase in advertising as a defence, the Court would be equally engaged in the same incipient policy.

Generally, the value system of the society determines whether, on balance, allocating a larger percentage of resources to activities which result in technological change, production variation, and changing consumer taste, than would be the case under less " imperfect " competition, contributes more to consumer welfare than the losses resulting from the

[37] An illustration is the application of the public interest defence in the merger of the First City National Bank of Houston. The Comptroller of the Currency refers to the following benefits for the Houston community: " The resulting bank will be able to offer more comprehensive automative services; . . . the development of a substantial international department; the creation of a new department to handle equipment leasing financing . . . Cited by C. Edwards, *op. cit.*, 30. This " broader banking services " defence is as plausible a public interest defence as the defence based on price behaviour of actual services.

[38] Market performance is considered as including efficiency in production and marketing units, equity in price to cost relations, and technical progress.

[39] Clair Wilcox, *op. cit.*, 323.

[40] R. Bork, " The Supreme Court *v.* Corporate Efficiency ", *Fortune*, August 1967, 156.

static inefficiencies of the reduced competition.[41] A valuable theoretical standard of consumer welfare which is applicable to the real world simply does not exist.

Thirdly, if there is no clear economic evidence on determinants of market performance, the only available presumptions concerning the relationship between an industry's structure and its performance indicate that the conflict between inefficiencies due to reduced competition, and some other positive market performances, is not the general case,

Indeed, the rate of profit and the discretionary pricing power of firms seem positively related to the degree of concentration,[42] the level of barriers to entry,[43] and the degree of product differentiation.[44] Besides, we have seen that it is doubtful that costs can be lowered by grouping plants together under a unique management. On the contrary, in many concentrated U.S. industries, the largest firms probably would not lose much efficiency if public policy should ever see fit to divide them up.[45]

In the same way, the internal inefficiency of the firm and the probability of an organizational slack seem to increase when the competitve pressure is relaxed and the size raised.[46]

Concerning the effect of market structure on progress, research, and innovation, it is recognized that, at least in the U.S., most firms in principal oligopolistic industries are large enough to be outside the range of obvious

[41] See for example K. Cohen and R. Cyert, *Theory of the Firm* (Prentice-Hall, 1965), Chap. 18; R. Bishop, Monopolistic Competition and Welfare Economics, in *Monopolistic Competition Theory: Studies in Impact*, edited by R. Kuenne (Wiley, 1967), 263. Bishop shows that to bring into a Pareto-optimal relationship a single monopolistically competitive industry with the rest of the economy (considered as universally purely competitive without externalities), requires the Utopian assumption that an omniscient administrator can levy, costlessly, just the appropriate, nondistorting lump-sum taxes. But this implies in turn that the administrator, in restricting product variety, does not respect the consumers' demand-expressed preferences.

[42] See J. Bain, "Relation of Profit Rate to Industry Concentration", *Quarterly Journal of Economics*, August 1951; V. Fuchs, "Integration, Concentration and Profits Manufacturing", *Quarterly Journal of Economics*, May 1961; Kasuo Sato, "Price-Cost Margins and Behavior for Profit Margins", *Yale Economic Essay*, Fall, 1961. One of the rare challenges of that conclusion has been made by G. Stigler, in *Capital and Rates of Return in Manufacturing Industries* (Princeton, 1963), but has been refuted by R. Kilpatrick, "Stigler on the Relationship between Industry Profit Rates and Market Concentration", *Journal of Political Economy*, September 1968.

[43] See, for example, H. Mann, "Seller Concentration, Barriers to Entry, and Rates of Return in Thirty Industries, 1950–1960", *Review of Economics and Statistics*, August 1966; Kamerschen, "Ownership and Control and Profit Rates", *American Economic Review*, June 1968.

[44] W. Comanor and T. Wilson, "Advertising Market Structure and Performance", *Review of Economics and Statistics*, November 1967.

[45] R. Caves, *American Industry: Structure, Conduct, Performance* (Prentice-Hall, 1967), 110.

[46] See O. Williamson, "Managerial Discretion and Business Behavior", *American Economic Review*, December 1963, Part II; and O. Williamson, "Hierarchical Control and Optimum Firm Size", Journal of Polit. Econ., April 1967.

disadvantage from small-scale research,[47] and, more important, that there is no systematic relationship between the degree of market power and inventive success.[48]

The consequence of this state of economic science is that "what we know about the determinants of market performance represents a few islands of knowledge protruding from a sea of ignorance".[49] It seems then unreasonable to favour the market power of a firm on economic grounds, when we ignore so much of the overall impact[50] and when what we know is favourable to competition.

A confirmation is the recent article of O. Williamson who presents an "appropriately qualified trade-off test" between extended economies and market power yielded by a merger. His analysis gives the impression that he is offering a conceptual device which is more or less an empty box. If all his "qualifications" are seriously taken into account, it appears indeed that the device cannot be usefully applied, except as a result of a drastic change in the role of anti-trust laws, and that more research is required from the economists, not from the Court.[51]

47 R. Caves, *op. cit.*, 104.

48 See F. Scherer, "Firm Size, Market Structure, Opportunity and the Output of Patented Inventions", *American Economic Review*, December 1965; E. Mansfield, *Industrial Research and Technological Innovation* (Norton, 1968), 198.

49 R. Caves, *op. cit.*, 113.

50 It is unnecessary to recall the "second best" problem: the results obtained by a partial equilibrium model may differ strongly from those yielded by a general equilibrium model. In a study by Ferguson, the proposed solution is to define a "macroeconomic" conception of the workable competition: the objective is no more to increase the degree of competition in a specific industry, but to judge this degree of competition according to some general public goals such as growth, stability of prices, full employment. That approach is very close to the EEC conception and its effort to integrate planning and competition. See C. Ferguson, *A Macroeconomic Theory of Workable Competition* (Duke University Press, 1968). In the same way, once the consumer welfare is placed in a dynamic context, "the inadequacy of the necessary conditions for an optimum position is apparent". E. Mishan, "A Survey of Welfare Economics", *The Economic Journal*, No. 278, 1960.

51 Among his qualifications for a cost-benefit analysis of a merger, Williamson points out the necessity to take into account: *the inference and enforcement expense needed to prove the existence of economies.* This will be especially costly for many dimensions, such as the technological progress argument which is of a "highly conjectural nature" but which is "nevertheless, potentially of such significance that to dismiss them may run the risk of serious error" (*op. cit.*, 29), or such as the managerial discretion argument for which "the dispute concerns not so much the direction of the effect as its quantitative significance" (*op. cit.*, 31). It is hard to argue that the net benefit of accepting the efficiency defence, which is the present value of the stream of its total gain minus its total cost, will exceed the net benefit which could be obtained by employing elsewhere the resources absorbed by such a defence. *The shape of the time stream of benefits and costs that a merger produces.* But Williamson adds: "It is an easy step from the suggestion that a proposed merger should be delayed until maximum net gains are realized to the proposition that the enforcement agencies should 'arrange' optimal firm pairing" (*op. cit.*, 26). *The income distribution effects.* He notes that "the transfer involved could be regarded unfavourably not merely because it redistributes income in an undesirable

V. Implications for the Policy-Making Process

Commenting upon the opposition between the goals of consumer welfare and small business welfare, R. Bork argues persuasively that "a court is not the proper institution, either by equipment, responsiveness to the electorate, or specialization of function, to write *ab initio* detailed specifications of political compromise between conflicting and incommensurable values. I am at a loss why anyone thinks courts should dictate the terms of a compromise in antitrust. . . ."[52] And he refers to Judge Taft's statement that "a reasonable price test forces judges to 'set sail on a sea of doubt' with no guide 'except the vague and varying opinion of judges as to how much, on principles of political economy, men ought to be allowed to restrain competition'."[53] His conclusion is then that consumer welfare should be the only goal.

But we may wonder why Bork does not apply this argument to the trade-off between restriction of competition and increase of consumer welfare. Once we question the general principle that the competitive process is the best tool to achieve high performance, it has indeed been shown that we cannot escape the use of vague public interest defences which the Court has no intelligent way of applying. The ultimate consequence would be to recognize that the Court must make political choices. Not only would it be admitted that efficiency in supplying consumer welfare should be a *defence*, but, through a logical corollary, the *test of legality* should itself be based on efficiency.

As a result, "a government could take corrective action against inflexible prices, high prices, functionless product differentiation, planned obsolescence, extravagant fancification of products, wasteful packaging, wasteful advertising, or any other type of business behaviour it thought detrimental to an efficient economy".[54] Such an approach would give full effect to "the underlying belief, which, according to S. Marcus, many economists hold, that antitrust should be an instrument of economic planning and not a policeman".[55]

As it has been said, if the qualifications proposed by Williamson in his trade-off solution are closely examined, it appears indeed that they would require a continued and detailed supervision of business, a far cry from the automatic safeguards of competition.

way (increases the degree of inequality in the size distribution of income) but also because it produces social discontent. . . . Distinguishing social from private costs in this respect may be the most fundamental reason for treating claims of private efficiency gains sceptically" (*op. cit.*, 28). *The political significance of control over wealth.* He admits that "the necessary political judgment, ideally, is one for Congress". Through his analysis, it appears that to know and to evaluate such requirements would imply some kind of state ownership or control, beyond the scope of the anti-trust policy.

52 R. Bork, *American Economic Review, loc. cit.*, 246.

53 *loc. cit.*, 247.

54 C. Edwards, "Control of the Single Firm: Its Place in Antitrust Policy", *Law and Contemporary Problems*, Summer 1965, No. 3, 470.

55 S. Marcus, *Competition and the Law* (Wadsworth, 1967), 150.

At this point, a comparison with the EEC system is again useful. Superficially, it may seem that the European legislation is less strict than the American in making provision for exemption in the case of activities that promote technical or economic progress or improve production or distribution (Article 85, para. 3), and in containing no provision that explicitly challenges the power of enterprises. The abuse of dominant position, not its existence *per se*, is forbidden (Article 86). The limitation of production, marketing, or technical development to the prejudice of consumers is especially prohibited.

Our interpretation to the contrary is that such vague and general exemptions and prohibitions will entail judgments involving substantial administrative discretion [56] and will, at least potentially, require the detailed evaluation of total conduct. On the one hand, the European Commission will need information on the organization of production and distribution, the policy of diversification, advertising, the research and development budgets, the description of financial participation and the fluctuations in the assets and the relative profit from the various operations and plants of the firm. Such requirements already appear in cases where exemptions have been granted on the basis of Article 85, para. 3. The Commission has often adopted a system of "provisional validity" (three to five years) and has required detailed reporting during and at the end of the period [57]: those data are not concerned with calculating from outside the real impact of the given conduct on market conditions or on consumer welfare, but with controlling closely the policy of the firm.[58]

On the other hand, the decision whether users get a "fair share of the benefit", whether the agreement does contribute to technical progress, and whether the restrictions are indeed indispensable cannot be purely objective.

Such discretionary requirements seem to be readily accepted in Europe where the economic organization has never been considered as a self-adjusting competitive process. To cope with defects in performance by rational programmes of control has seemed easier than to do so by

[56] A. Jacquemin, *L'entreprise et son pouvoir de marché* (P.U.F., 1967), 216.

[57] For the juridical meaning of that "provisional validity", see the judgment of the Court in Case 10/69, published elsewhere in this issue.

[58] See, *e.g.*, *Transocean Marine Paint Association*, decision of July 27, 1967, J.O. 1967, 163/10; *CCH Common Market Reporter*, § 9188. "It appears advisable to tie in obligations with the decision, in accordance with Article 8, para. 1, of Regulation No. 17. These obligations should make it easier for the Commission to determine whether or not there is reason for it, as provided for in Article 8, para. 3, to revoke or amend this exemption or to prohibit certain practices by the enterprises concerned." The members of the association must then "reveal any changes that might occur in the membership of the association . . . all decisions of the administrative board and all arbitration rulings . . . in so far as they concern the application or interpretation of the provisions of the agreement . . . make an annual report to the Commission on the activities of the association and of its present members, and of any new members, showing separate information on the production and sale of Transocean and other marine paints manufactured by the members . . . indicate the volume of deliveries for which they are mutually bound to pay commissions . . .".

competition. In fact it has been suggested that the European Commission, which according to the Treaty is at one time a legislature, at another time a governmental or an enforcement agency, could become the Planning Agency of the Common Market, in establishing a European order of priorities for important investments and ensuring that the necessary capital would be available to carry them out at the required speed.[59]

The anti-trust policy thus becomes integrated into public policy with respect to investment, credit, taxation, and the great corporations become co-ordinated by some form of permissive planning.[60] Such a conception is made easier by the fact that, in the EEC, the performance-criterion, and more generally the anti-trust laws, are mostly applied by the executive—the Commission—while in the U.S. the emphasis is on judicial enforcement. There is a consequent danger of an increasing transfer of policy-making authority to such an anti-trust agency.[61]

It has been specifically noted that "the grant of exemptions [under Article 85, para. 3] could be co-ordinated with Common Market programming. Thus, if the Community were especially in need of rationalization agreements in certain areas, an exemption for co-operative arrangements in those areas might be more easily obtainable." [62]

In the same perspective, it has been recognized that the focus on abuses of dominant position in Article 86 "does not mean that the Treaty is necessarily more lenient with respect to concentrated economic power. Experience in Holland and elsewhere indicates that an abuse provision permits price control and other direct regulatory measures which in the United States are rarely invoked, even against regulated utilities." [63]

VI. A Tentative Policy Recommendation

A tentative recommendation concerning the use of a performance criterion in American and EEC anti-trust policies can be inferred from the preceding analysis.

[59] R. Marjolin, Vice President of the European Commission, in SEDEIS Bulletin, No. 839, suppl. 1, cited by A. Shonfield, *Modern Capitalism* (Oxford University Press, 1965), 147.

[60] This view is expressed by the "Medium-Term Economic Policy" Committee, set-up by the EEC Council on April 15, 1964.

[61] See B. van der Esch, *Pouvoir discrétionnaire de l'Exécutif européen et contrôle juridictionnel* (Deventer, 1968).

[62] *Antitrust Developments in the European Common Market*, Report of the Subcommittee on Antitrust and Monopoly of the Committee on the Judiciary United States Senate, 88th Cong., 2d Sess., 1964, 18.

[63] *Ibid.*, 19. According to the Dutch Economic Competition Act of 1956, direct measures expressly authorized are orders to the person or persons holding the economically "dominant position" (1) proscribing activities tending to compel others to pursue specific market practices; (2) requiring supply of specified goods or services to designated persons for cash at customary prices and terms; (3) stipulating provisions regarding price; (4) directing terms of delivery, service, and payment . . . .

A. The U.S. Policy

There is no real problem of choice when proposed business conduct tends only to lessen competition, will only result in efficiencies, or has virtually nothing to do with one of these effects. This is recognized as the general case.[64] But once the conduct is a mixed case producing both efficiencies and market power consequences, we may conclude that the Court should not accept economies as a defence to illegality.[65]

First, it has been shown how heavy and costly would be the burden of proof imposed by the alternative approach.

Secondly, cases in which any harmful effects of a decrease in competition are offset by the favourable effects of the conduct are considered as exceptions, not the rule. Maintaining the general principle underlines a strong presumption that the eventual economic losses will not be important.

Thirdly, the enforcement agencies will generally select those cases which should be prosecuted, taking into account, at least implicitly, some of the possible economies,[66] even if such selection may imply political choices.

Fourthly, we may refer to what Professor Reich calls a central myth according to which " the decision makers combine expert knowledge and professionalism with judicial bearing. The tools they use for decisions are science and reason. At the core of the myth is its cardinal point: decisions are not primarily choices between values." [67]

Indeed, those who ask for a more tolerant application of anti-trust laws, in the name of efficiency, do not seem to realize that if a substantial restriction of competition is accepted on such a basis, another device, necessarily more interventionist than competition, will be required to regulate the

[64] D. Dewey, " Mergers and Cartels: Some Reservations about Policy ", *A.E.R.* Proceedings, May 1961, 257; O. Williamson, *op. cit.*, 33, admits: " Most mergers produce neither significant price nor efficiency consequences, and where this is true the analysis of this paper has limited relevance ". For restraints of trade, see 14.

[65] On the other hand, conduct resulting in greater efficiency should not be held illegal on that basis alone. Efficiency *per se* is not under attack.

[66] The recent merger guidelines of the Department of Justice (May 1968) state that " unless there are exceptional circumstances, the Department will not accept as a justification for an acquisition normally subject to challenge under its horizontal merger standards the claim that the merger will produce economies (*i.e.*, improvements in efficiency) because among other reasons, (i) *the Department's adherence to the standards will usually result in no challenge being made to mergers of the kind most likely to involve companies operating significantly below the size necessary to achieve significant economies of scale*; (ii) where substantial economies are potentially available to a firm, they can normally be realized through internal expansion; and (iii) there usually are severe difficulties in accurately establishing the existence and magnitude of economies claimed for a merger ". A similar attitude is adopted for vertical and conglomerate mergers, but stressing the argument that the economies can normally be realized through other means.

[67] Reich, " The Law of the Planned Society ", *Yale Law Journal*, July 8, 1966.

American business world. Thus, the defenders of a loosely applied anti-trust policy may turn out to be the best allies of those who, with Galbraith, consider that competition will be replaced by planning, and anti-trust law by direct regulation with regard to the requirements of large-scale production, invention, and innovation.[68]

This leads to a fifth argument against the use of a market performance defence. Competition is justified not only on the basis that it is the best tool to achieve an optimum allocation of resources, but also because of its broad political implications. It is generally argued that competition disperses economic private power, decision-making, responsibility, and initiative—which is desirable from the standpoint of the viability of democratic institutions. Competition increases popular loyalty to the image and credibility of the free-enterprise system. It reduces the danger of governmental regulation of business that is not only inefficient but also inconsistent with some economic freedoms. From this point of view, Machlup states:

> " While I accept that certain anti-oligopoly policies curtail certain economic freedoms, I believe that these policies also restore or strengthen some economic freedoms, and, on balance, *may* be working for, rather than against a free society. This implies that I accept also . . . that the exercise of oligopoly positions may be economically harmful and may reduce the scope and the degree of freedom, as both valid and significant." [69]

Actually, the American society still accepts the notion that values such as efficiency, welfare, equality, freedom, progress, are built into competition. Trying to present a decrease of competition as something required to reach those values may have deep unforeseen effects on the social attitudes. Such a transformation would be at the level of a political judgment, beyond the limits of judicial competence.

This does not solve the problem of the limits of the competitive process. Our point of view is that if a real mutation is wanted in the domain of competitive policy, it cannot be realized at the judicial level but through some *ad hoc* " planning agency " expressing the will of the Congress. The search for new laws to make the best possible accommodation of planning and liberty is to be preferred to making such choices surreptitiously.[70] Still,

68 *The New Industrial State* (Hamilton, London, 1967), 184–197.

69 F. Machlup, " Oligopoly and the Free Society ", *Antitrust Law and Economics Review*, July–August 1967, 14. See also the classical study of M. Friedman, *Capitalism and Freedom* (University Press of Chicago, 1962).

70 " Once we recognize that the antitrust laws and the competition are not going to provide us with this system of wage and price restraints, then economists . . . are going to bring their energies to bear on how this system of restraint can be administered by the Government with a minimum of damage to the economy, with a minimum of damage to incentives, with a minimum of bureaucratic apparatus, but with a maximum of efficiency." J. K. Galbraith, in " Planning, Regulation and Competition ", *Hearings before Subcommittee of the Select Committee on Small Business*, United States Senate, June 29, 1967.

one may wonder whether the U.S. will find it necessary to change its policies so drastically as to declare such principles openly.

B. The EEC Policy

A first recommendation for the EEC anti-trust policy is the necessity to rely more on the use of a reasonable test in applying Article 85, para. 1, than on the exemption provided by Article 85, para. 3.

In fact, a move in that sense is perceptible. Originally, the Commission had concentrated on exclusive dealing agreements, and had based its decisions on the use of restrictive terms in the contract. These types of restraints on trade have been considered as *per se* violations of Article 85, para. 1. But, as it has been shown, many apparent restrictive practices have no substantial anticompetitive effect, and may even promote competition. The *per se* approach based on administrative regulation and subject only to the exemption provision of Article 85, para. 3, has then resulted in a deluge of registrations of agreements which are often harmless.[71] To avoid the heavy burden of examining closely those individual agreements to see whether they qualify for the complex exemption under Article 85, para. 3, we have already indicated that the EEC Commission, in some specific cases, has declared inapplicable the provision of Article 85, para. 1, under paragraph 3, but without requiring a real proof of the four tests, and also on the basis of Article 85, para. 3, has granted general exemptions to classes of agreements responding to certain criteria, without examining at all if the tests are satisfied.[72]

A recent evolution seems nevertheless more promising. After the European Court of Justice has disapproved the underlying theory that every restraint of trade in the technical sense is prohibited by Article 85, para. 1,[73] the Commission itself has adopted a " rule of reason ". It has promulgated a notice which indicates that in the view of the Commission, some specific groups of agreements do not restrict competition and are not prohibited by Article 85, para. 1.[74] This notice tells us that " the Commission holds the view that co-operation among enterprises does not come under Article 85 of the EEC Treaty . . . in the case where the market position of enterprises co-operating with each other is in the aggregate too weak to lead, through the agreement between them, to an appreciable restraint of competition in the Common Market and . . . impair trade between the Member States ".[75] A recent application of such an interpretation of Article 85,

[71] Regulation No. 17 provides the mechanisms for application for exemptions under Article 85, para. 3.

[72] See *supra*, Chapter III, *in fine*.

[73] See *Société Technique Minière* v. *Maschinenbau Ulm GmbH*, June 30, 1966, *CCH Common Market Reporter*, § 8047; 4 C.M.L.Rev. 1966–67. 197–202, and R. Joliet, *op. cit.*

[74] Notice of the Commission of the European Communities, July 27, 1968, *CCH Common Market Reporter*, § 9248.

[75] *CCH Common Market Reporter*, § 9248.

para. 1, is the *SOCEMAS* case where an important argument of justification was that the activity of *SOCEMAS* in the EEC countries (other than France) was not on a sufficiently large scale to entail appreciable restraints of competition.[76]

By originally relying on the public benefits exemption which required a complex judgment of a political nature, and by refusing to take into account the anti-competitive significance of the agreement, the Commission has been forced into bureaucratic paralysis. Rather than trying then to give a very biased form to the "efficiency defence" offered by Article 85, para. 3, we may hope that the Commission will pursue the policy of a more "reasonable" interpretation of Article 85, para. 1.[77] Once the preservation of a "reasonable" or a "workable" competition is recognized as the goal of the EEC anti-trust policy, the necessity to apply the anti-trust policy to every type of restraint of competition appears clearly. More than exclusive dealing agreements, horizontal agreements and mergers are indeed very important for the future of the Common Market.[78] The idea that those combinations are beneficial to market performance involves the danger of developing strong oligopolistic markets which, once created, are very hard to transform. It is what has happened with the American anti-trust policy which did not develop a strong anti-merger policy until after World War II. "It is necessary to remember that it is easier to prevent the constitution of monopoly positions than to remedy their behaviour and to shackle their growth." [79]

Finally the nature of the exemption provided by Article 85, para. 3, as well as the nature of Article 86, discussed before,[80] leads to the necessity to distinguish the anti-trust policy of the Common Market authorities from their general economic policy, so that the first one could be limited to its specific role.

In conclusion, the role of anti-trust law, in the EEC as well as in the U.S., must be limited to attacks upon those structures and conduct which induce market power. In doing so, it rightly fulfils its mission.

In trying to judge cases on the basis of their contribution to market

[76] *SOCEMAS*, Commission Decision of July 17, 1968, *CCH Common Market Reporter*, § 9250; see also *Alliance des constructeurs français de machines-outils*, J.O. 1966, L201/1.

[77] In that sense, Advocate General K. Roemer has considered that it would be artificial to apply Article 85, para. 1, on the basis of purely theoretical considerations, and then to grant an exemption pursuant to Article 85, para. 3, if a more detailed analysis would have revealed in the first place that the agreement under attack did not substantially restrain competition. See the submissions of Advocate General K. Roemer, cited by Joliet, *op. cit.*, 161.

[78] The Eighth General Report of the EEC Commission (March 1965) indicates that out of the 37,542 cases notified up to March 31, 1965, only 395, or about 1 per cent. involved horizonal restrictions. Until now, no merger has been attacked.

[79] J. Houssiaux, Preface to A. Jacquemin, *L'entreprise et son pouvoir de marché*, *op. cit.*, IX.

[80] See footnotes 26 and 27.

performance, courts take a serious risk of becoming involved in planning policy. The acceptance of such a perspective probably would be quite different in the U.S. than in the EEC, because of the substantial contrast between the anti-trust philosophies of each.

On the one hand, the proposition of an " economic performance " defence in the U.S. does not express in principle a distrust of the competitive process: it has been proposed to liberalize the anti-trust policy and to allow a freer functioning of the market forces, but not to pave the road towards planning.

On the other hand, such a defence is, in the Common Market, closely related to a distrust towards the competitive process as being capable of realizing the best performance. By accepting it, the European Authorities claim at the same time the right of detailed and continuous evaluation of any total conduct pattern of the firms and in so doing, to introduce some kind of Common Market programming.

Our own view is that anti-trust policy is not the right tool for such an objective. The anti-trust authorities must simply analyse combinations or agreements on the basis that, to escape the prohibition of the law, the consequent reduction of competition must not be significant. The premise of this policy thus remains that competition is the best way to serve the public interest, and that the legality of conduct depends on the degree of its anti-competitive effect. To question such a premise requires a different level of governmental policy.

This conclusion does not completely avoid the problem of evaluating some performance criteria which are implicit in the standards of market power. In examining the extent of anti-competitive effects, a performance approach may appear. However, this aspect will be used not to determine whether it serves or disserves the public good, but to calculate indirectly the competitive conditions and the underlying structures and conduct.

Judicial decisions will thus have a greater opportunity to avoid political compromise between " conflicting and incommensurable values ".

The Political Concerns of Competition Law

[5]

THE POLITICAL CONTENT OF ANTITRUST

ROBERT PITOFSKY †

Although the political forces that produced the major antitrust statutes—in 1890, 1914, 1936, and 1950—varied widely, those statutes once enacted have almost always been enforced and interpreted so that economic considerations were paramount. The issue among most serious people has never been whether non-economic considerations should outweigh significant long-term economies of scale, but rather whether they had any role to play at all, and if so, how they should be defined and measured.[1]

There probably has never been a period comparable to the last decade, however, when antitrust economists and lawyers have had such success in persuading the courts to adopt an *exclusively* economic approach to antitrust questions. In this paper, I will urge a different view. It is bad history, bad policy, and bad law to exclude certain political values in interpreting the antitrust laws. By "political values," I mean, first, a fear that excessive concentration of economic power will breed antidemocratic political pressures, and second, a desire to enhance individual and business freedom by reducing the range within which private discretion by a few in the economic sphere controls the welfare of all. A third and overriding political concern is that if the free-market sector of the economy is allowed to develop under antitrust rules that are blind to all but economic concerns, the likely result will be an economy so dominated by a few corporate giants that it will be impossible for the state not to play a more intrusive role in economic affairs.

This view is not at odds with the central beliefs of both the "Chicago" and "Harvard" schools that the major goals of antitrust relate to economic efficiency—to avoid the allocative inefficiencies of monopoly power, encourage efficiency and progressiveness in the use of resources, and perhaps, on fairness grounds, to maintain price close to cost in order to minimize unnecessary and undesirable accumulations of private wealth.[2] Because interpretations that ex-

† Professor of Law, Georgetown University. Subsequent to the preparation and submission of this paper, the author was appointed a commissioner of the Federal Trade Commission.

[1] *See, e.g.*, Blake & Jones, *The Goals of Antitrust: A Dialogue on Policy*, 65 COLUM. L. REV. 377-400, 422-66 (1965); Elzinga, *The Goals of Antitrust: Other Than Competition and Efficiency, What Else Counts?*, 125 U. PA. L. REV. 1191 (1977).

[2] For a summary of the central attitudes, principles, and spokesmen of the "Chicago" and "Harvard" schools, see Sullivan, *Book Review*, 75 COLUM. L. REV.

clude all but economic concerns have lately become so influential, however, it is important to explain why economic concerns, although properly of paramount importance, should not control exclusively.

It can be argued that the political considerations discussed here are ill-defined and incapable of exact or even meaningful definition. Also, it will be difficult to balance vague concepts such as a fear of economic conditions conducive to totalitarianism against the efficiency loss of an industry structure that is disassembled or a series of business transactions that are disallowed. Finally, it may be that when such vague and controversial factors are introduced into antitrust considerations, some enforcement officials and judges will lose sight of the secondary role of these political factors and will distort and misinterpret antitrust policy. There is merit to each of these concerns. But despite the inconvenience, lack of predictability, and general mess introduced into the economists' allegedly cohesive and tidy world of exclusively micro-economic analysis, an antitrust policy that failed to take political concerns into account would be unresponsive to the will of Congress and out of touch with the rough political consensus that has supported antitrust enforcement for almost a century.[8]

I. Political Values

Those advocating a non-economic dimension to antitrust should be as specific as possible about those concerns that they would include in an enforcement equation. The considerations I believe must be taken into account are described below; with respect to each, examples will indicate those enforcement areas or cases in which such considerations appear to have played a role. Also mentioned briefly are some non-economic considerations that do not have a proper role in antitrust enforcement, although they un-

1214 (1974) (reviewing M. Handler, H. Blake, R. Pitofsky & H. Goldschmid, Trade Regulation: Cases and Materials (1974)).

[8] *See* Brodley, *Potential Competition Mergers: A Structural Synthesis*, 87 Yale L.J. 1, 34 n.131 (1977). Brodley accumulates a list of scholars who have emphasized the point about the consensus that supports antitrust enforcement. *See particularly* Hofstadter, *What Happened to the Antitrust Movement*, in The Business Establishment 113, 149 (E. Cheit ed. 1964):

> What makes it possible to institutionalize antitrust activities . . . is not a consensus among economists as to its utility in enhancing economic efficiency, but a rough consensus in society at large as to its value in curbing the dangers of excessive market power. As in the beginning, it is based on a political and moral judgment rather than the outcome of economic measurement or even distinctively economic criteria.

doubtedly have influenced and will continue to influence many courts.

A. *Fear of Concentrated Economic Power*

If the choice were posed solely between monopoly power achieved individually, solely as a result of efficiencies, and government intervention to prevent concentration, the legislative history of the Sherman Act[4] and the overwhelming weight of subsequent judicial interpretation would opt for monopoly power.[5] The most famous judicial statement of the case for a political dimension to antitrust—Judge Learned Hand's explanation in *United States v. Aluminum Co. of America [Alcoa]*[6] that "great industrial consolidations are inherently undesirable" for political as well as economic reasons[7]—granted as much by accepting as an absolute defense the explanation that such a market position was brought about solely through superior skill, foresight, and industry.[8]

The issue is rarely posed that way, however. Instead, there is characteristically a legal challenge to business behavior that produced or maintained monopoly power, or to mergers or cartel arrangements that tend to concentrate or coordinate market power, and a defense that the behavior or arrangements are efficient and therefore tend to contribute to consumer welfare.

As will be developed in a subsequent section of this paper,[9] Congress has in its antitrust enactments—most clearly when it

---

[4] 15 U.S.C. §§ 1-7 (1976).

[5] *See* 21 Cong. Rec. 3152 (1890) (remarks of Sen. Hoar, speaking on § 2):

> [A] man who merely by superior skill and intelligence . . . got the whole business because nobody could do it as well as he could was not a monopolist, but that it [monopoly] involved something like the use of means which made it impossible for other persons to engage in fair competition, like the engrossing, the buying up of all other persons engaged in the same business.

See also United States v. E.I. duPont de Nemours & Co., 351 U.S. 377, 390-91 (1956).

[6] 148 F.2d 416 (2d Cir. 1945).

[7] *Id.* 428. In a frequently quoted passage, Judge Hand suggested the following congressional motive for the enactment of the Sherman Act:

> It is possible, because of its indirect social or moral effect, to prefer a system of small producers, each dependent for his success upon his own skill and character, to one in which the great mass of those engaged must accept the discretion of a few. These considerations, which we have suggested only as possible purposes of the Act, we think the decisions prove to have been in fact its purposes.

Id. 427.

[8] *Id.*

[9] *See* text accompanying notes 29-39 *infra.*

amended section 7 of the Clayton Act in 1950[10]—exhibited a clear concern that an economic order dominated by a few corporate giants could, during a time of domestic stress or disorder, facilitate the overthrow of democratic institutions and the installation of a totalitarian regime. That concern about economic power and the desire that it be dispersed complements the general American governmental preference for a system of checks and balances and distribution of authority to prevent abusive actions by the state. The result is a "tilt" in antitrust, usually evidenced by the design of rules limiting the behavior of monopolists or candidates for monopoly power, and limiting concentration by merger in ways that occasionally incur costs in terms of lost efficiencies.

Perhaps a few examples will help make the point more concrete. If General Motors were to announce a merger with IBM or United States Steel with Xerox, and if those mergers were part of a growing merger trend among the top *Fortune* 200, it seems unlikely that the legality of those transactions would be fully explored from an antitrust point of view solely by an investigation of the extent to which one company bought products from the other or was a potential entrant into the other's product line. Alternatively, suppose that a single wealthy family were to acquire the leading newspaper in each of the twenty largest cities in the United States. One possible response would be enactment of special legislation to head off that development. If a bill were to become bottled up in committee, however, the Sherman Act should be sufficiently flexible to take into account that threat to political values. Finally, the bedrock antitrust rule that efficient, profit-maximizing conduct that would be legal if engaged in by a small company becomes illegal if part of an unreasonably exclusionary program to maintain monopoly power—for example, acquisition and aggressive enforcement of patents[11] or a sales policy that encourages leasing over purchases[12]—can only be understood in light of an antagonism to monopoly power because of political concerns and "in spite of possible costs."[13]

10 Ch. 1184, § 7, 64 Stat. 1125 (1950) (current version at 15 U.S.C. § 18 (1976)).

11 *See, e.g.,* Kobe, Inc. v. Dempsey Pump Co., 198 F.2d 416 (10th Cir.), *cert. denied,* 344 U.S. 837 (1952).

12 *See, e.g.,* Greyhound Computer Corp. v. IBM, 559 F.2d 488 (9th Cir. 1977), *cert. denied,* 434 U.S. 1040 (1978); United States v. United Shoe Machinery Corp., 110 F. Supp. 295 (D. Mass. 1953), *aff'd per curiam,* 347 U.S. 521 (1954).

13 United States v. Aluminum Co. of America, 148 F.2d 416, 429 (2d Cir. 1945).

It is impossible, of course, to prove that massively concentrated economic power, or state intervention induced by that level of concentration, is incompatible with liberal, constitutional democracy. Nevertheless, it is remarkable that historical and contemporaneous democracies are almost invariably associated with market systems, while totalitarian regimes (fascist and communist) almost always are not. Professor Lindblom has noted, as a matter of experience if not logic, that there appears to be an underlying common basis for democracy and a market economy, and common characteristics between democracy and a deconcentrated economic system:

> [Democracies] are systems of rules for constraining rather than mobilizing authority. They grow out of a struggle to control authority rather than to create it or make it more effective. They are therefore political systems that are, again, like markets. They practice decentralization, diffusion of influence and power, and mutual adjustments so that individuals in small groups rather than national collectivities can strive for whatever they wish.[14]

It is sometimes argued that it is pointless to deconcentrate industries or to prevent increases in firm size in the name of protecting the political process because associations of small firms with a common interest are as effective (perhaps more effective because of the appearance of numbers) as larger business units pressing for particular political goals. A striking initial point about this argument is that there are little or no relevant data one way or another on the question. However, the contention that groups of firms are the equivalent of a single firm in organizing to achieve political goals does fly in the face of what we know about firm behavior in the analogous area of cartel organization. We know that, given a large number of participants, different levels of efficiency and capacity, and different outlooks about the rewards of vigorous competition or cautious cooperation, cartels are notoriously difficult to organize and maintain.[15] In the absence of contrary evidence, one might reasonably expect that the kind of uniform commitment to a single set of political goals that might constitute some threat to political stability should be much easier to organize, coordinate, and maintain when relatively few different political and economic interests need to be consulted.

---

14 C. Lindblom, Politics and Markets 165 (1977).

15 *See generally* L. Sullivan, Handbook of the Law of Antitrust 162-63 (1977).

B. *Reduction in the Range of Private Discretion*

Professors Blake and Jones have written:

> Another political objective of antitrust is the enlargement of individual liberty. Not only are we interested in material well-being and distrustful of political power, but we also have a strong libertarian streak. In the absence of strong countervailing considerations, we favor freedom of action and the wide range of choice that freedom implies . . . . [T]he individual who wants to be an entrepreneur rather than an employee ought not to have his opportunities restricted by unnecessary barriers to entry, or by trade practices designed specifically to eliminate him from the field.[16]

Part of the reason we prefer a free-market system over authoritarian alternatives is because important economic decisions that have wide public consequences—which products to make, which technologies to use, where and how much to sell—become subject to the discipline of the market. Every firm is relieved to some extent from the unrelenting demands of a market model, but as markets become concentrated, firms larger, barriers to entry formidable, and prospects of takeover or failure remote, existing sellers are more and more removed from that discipline and would-be challengers find themselves excluded from a fair opportunity to compete.[17]

Some of the bank merger cases,[18] which preserve the opportunity for businessmen to seek alternative sources of capital for investment plans, can be defended on efficiency grounds, but also evidence this concern to disperse decisionmaking authority. Boycott cases in which the Supreme Court has refused to permit groups of sellers to assume an "extra-governmental" role and displace the market mechanism, regardless of the economic justification, are more comprehensible if this set of values is taken into account.[19] Sim-

[16] Blake & Jones, *supra* note 1, at 383-84.

[17] This political concern has been described as more capable of explicit statement as a result of recent advances in the theory of managerial behavior. *See* Brodley, *supra* note 3, at 35-36. There is an echo of that concern in the legislative history of the Sherman Act, where Senator Hoar described the law's concern as "the sole engrossing to a man's self by means which prevent other men from engaging in fair competition with him." 21 CONG. REC. 3152 (1890), *quoted in* United States v. E.I. duPont de Nemours & Co., 351 U.S. 377, 391 n.15 (1956).

[18] *See* United States v. Phillipsburg Nat'l Bank & Trust Co., 399 U.S. 350 (1970); United States v. Philadelphia Nat'l Bank, 374 U.S. 321 (1963). For a discussion of *Philadelphia National Bank*, see text following note 67 *infra*.

[19] *See, e.g.*, Fashion Originators' Guild of America v. FTC, 312 U.S. 457 (1941), *discussed in* Blake & Jones, *supra* note 1, at 429-30.

ilarly, if several leading oil companies not currently in the coal business were to attempt to acquire several leading coal companies, any future decision to develop alternative energy sources, clearly of crucial significance to the national welfare, would be significantly immunized against the discipline of the market. Even if there were some efficiencies to the combination and absolutely no possibility that either company would expand into the product market of the other, an antitrust challenge should incorporate some concern that the welfare of the country is being placed in the hands of a few economically powerful firms and individuals. This is not to imply that non-economic concerns should be dispositive, but only that they are relevant and should be taken into account.

C. *Avoidance of Political Interference*

The Sherman Act was enacted after a decade of unusual labor violence and agrarian unrest culminating in widespread strikes and anarchist agitation.[20] It was a period during which there was wide discussion of alternative economic systems. Thorelli's study of Sherman Act legislative history reports that at least one major theme of legislative purpose was the desire to improve the free market system in order to head off direct regulation or Marxist solutions.[21]

Similar notions were even more pronounced in the legislative history leading to the enactment of revised section 7 of the Clayton Act in 1950[22] and should continue to be influential today. If a few companies were to grow to dominate most of the major product markets in the United States, it is inconceivable that those companies would be left free of political accountability. At a minimum they would be required to report the details of their operations far more extensively than companies do today, and they would be the subject of constant legislative investigation and oversight. Eventually such companies surely would come under direct governmental

[20] *See generally* T. Brooks, Toil and Trouble 38-71 (1964). For a summary of the historical context of the antitrust statutes, see L. Sullivan, *supra* note 15, at 1218-23.

[21] H. Thorelli, The Federal Antitrust Policy (1955). In a frequently quoted debate speech, Senator Sherman said: "You must heed their [the voters'] appeal or be ready for the socialist, the communist, and the nihilist. Society is now disturbed by forces never felt before. . . . These combinations already defy or control powerful transportation corporations and reach State authorities." 21 Cong. Rec. 2460 (1890), *cited in* H. Thorelli, *supra*, at 180. *See also* Blake, *Conglomerate Mergers and the Antitrust Laws*, 73 Colum. L. Rev. 555, 575-76 (1973).

[22] Ch. 1184, § 7, 64 Stat. 1125 (1950) (current version at 15 U.S.C. § 18 (1976)). *See* text accompanying notes 30-34 *infra*.

control. An antitrust system that occasionally disregards claims of efficiency, as in the imposition of per se rules against certain kinds of horizontal cartels [23] or unwillingness to take dubious evidence of efficiencies into account in judging the legality of mergers,[24] reflects these political concerns.

A level of industrial concentration that would raise a serious threat of provoking state nationalization probably is not present in the economy today. It is debatable whether there has been any significant recent increase in concentration among the top 200 American corporations; even if there were some increase in concentration, foreign competition and the improved ability of firms to market their products at greater distances from their home plants probably means that most markets are at least as deconcentrated today as they were twenty or thirty years ago. As a result, there are relatively few situations today in which a political dimension must be incorporated to explain a result. That need not always be the case, however. Technological developments or changes in world trade patterns may generate fierce pressures toward concentration. It would be unfortunate if the antitrust laws were interpreted so that they would be impotent in future times of stress to play their role as a defense against undue concentration of economic power.

D. *Non-Economic Concerns That Should Be Disregarded*

There are a number of non-economic concerns that can play no useful role in antitrust enforcement. These include (1) protection for small businessmen against the rigors of competition, (2) special rights for franchisees and other distributors to continuing access to a supplier's products or services regardless of the efficiency of their distribution operation and the will of the supplier (a kind of civil rights statute for distributors), and (3) income redistribution to achieve social goals.

In terms of legislative history, these different goals stand on very different bases. There was legislative history leading to the enactment of the Sherman Act and to the amendment of section 7 of

[23] *See* United States v. Trenton Potteries Co., 273 U.S. 392 (1927), in which evidence of reasonable price in defense of a price-fixing cartel was rejected precisely because constant government intervention would be necessary to determine whether prices were indeed reasonable.

[24] *See* FTC v. Procter & Gamble Co., 386 U.S. 568, 580 (1967) ("Possible economies cannot be used as a defense to illegality. Congress was aware that some mergers that lessen competition may also result in economies but it struck the balance in favor of protecting competition.").

the Clayton Act in 1950 showing that Congress was concerned with the disappearance of small independent entrepreneurs and their displacement by massive corporations.[25] In 1936 this was of course a dominant concern of the legislature in enacting the Robinson-Patman Act.[26] On the other hand, there are many other indications in the legislative history of the Sherman and Clayton Acts, and in the law as interpreted, that the antitrust laws were designed to preserve competition. These twin goals are impossible to reconcile in circumstances in which small business is disadvantaged by true efficiencies of scale.[27]

After decades of agonizing interpretation, a sort of working compromise has been reached, so that the goal of antitrust is to preserve a competitive process even at the cost at times of the disappearance of less efficient small businesses. That solution is defensible in part because policies that would discriminate in favor of small business in pursuit of mythic virtues of smallness would themselves be inconsistent with another set of political values: maintenance of conditions of equality of opportunity for all businessmen through limitations on the range of private discretion. Moreover, preservation of a competitive system, in part through vigorous antitrust enforcement, will protect small business against the use of unfair tactics by larger companies to gain advantages unrelated to superior skill or efficiency of those larger units.

By contrast, there is no obvious theme in the legislative history of any of the antitrust laws that Congress' purpose was to create procedural protection for distributors or, even more farfetched, to achieve income redistribution. Looking beyond legislative history, these non-economic concerns play no useful role because it is not possible to achieve those goals to any significant extent through antitrust interpretation.[28] Inefficient small businesses will suffer losses regardless of how the antitrust laws are interpreted, and the

---

[25] *See* note 34 *infra.*

[26] 15 U.S.C. §§ 13-13b, 21a (1976).

[27] On the promotion of small business enterprises, see Elzinga, *supra* note 1, at 1196-1200.

[28] On using the antitrust laws to achieve income redistribution one author has written:

> The problem of poverty is attributed more often to the low level of education and job skills of the poor, insufficient aggregate demand, the distorted incentives of current welfare policies, drug addiction and alcoholism, racial discrimination, and a cognitive present orientation among the poor that cuts against exchanging present for future satisfaction. Thus, the pursuit of egalitarian income distribution through antitrust enforcement is likely to have limited results.

Id. 1195-96 (footnote omitted).

income redistribution that can be achieved through antitrust channels is trivial. Moreover, even if Congress were viewed as truly committed to some or all of those goals, they could be achieved more efficiently and with fewer adverse effects through direct subsidy, taxation, and welfare programs.

II. Justification for Inclusion of Non-Economic Concerns

Factors other than strictly economic concerns should be taken into account because the legislative history of the antitrust statutes, in its own right and as interpreted authoritatively in the courts, so requires, because an exclusively economic approach reflects an unrealistically optimistic view of the certainty introduced by that kind of analysis, and because the introduction of non-economic factors does not result in an undue interference with effective enforcement.

A. *Legislative History*

The Sherman Act and most of its amendments do not address specific issues of antitrust enforcement. The key terms "restraint of trade" in section 1 of the Sherman Act and "monopolize" in section 2 were not defined, and the legislative history does not reflect consideration of the possibility that unrelieved pursuit of a free-market competitive system might lead to adverse non-economic effects.[29]

This failure to address the efficiency/political-effects trade-off is not hard to understand. Comprehensive antitrust regulation was a new concept to all legislators, and the most authoritative and exhaustive reviews of the legislative history have detected a series of vague and not always consistent strands of legislative intent.[30] As many have observed, Congress elected generally to leave specific enforcement decisions to the judiciary.

But putting aside the Sherman Act and its admittedly obscure legislative history, can we discern anything with respect to legislative intent from subsequent antitrust statutes? If we can, it seems clear that those subsequent statutes must be interpreted to incor-

---

29 *See* 15 U.S.C. §§ 1-2 (1976).

30 One of these strands involved the desire to avoid the enhancement of prices. *See* H. Thorelli, *supra* note 21, at 180. There was also a broader concern that concentrated economic power would undermine the opportunities of individuals and small businessmen. W. Letwin, Law and Economic Policy in America 59 (1965); H. Thorelli, *supra* note 21, at 180. It was believed that these effects would eventually undermine a private enterprise system. *Id.* 227. *See generally* Blake, *supra* note 21, at 575-76.

porate political concerns, and it appears arguable that these subsequent expressions define Congress' vague intentions in earlier enactments.[31] Specifically, can fair-minded commentators read the legislative history of amended section 7—the most recent major substantive revision of general antitrust policy—and conclude that Congress intended to regulate mergers and joint ventures without taking into account the political consequences of what it perceived to be an ongoing merger movement?

Section 7 outlaws only those mergers the effect of which "may be substantially to lessen competition, or tend to create a monopoly," [32] and thereby fairly establishes the primacy of economic concerns. There is no record that any legislator has suggested that a merger be challenged solely or principally because of an adverse effect on small business, employment opportunities, equitable distribution of wealth, or long-term threats to the stability of the country's democratic process. The question remains, however, whether such factors can be taken into account at all in deciding at what level to draw the line describing unacceptable reductions in competition.

Some of the key passages of section 7's legislative history reveal strong congressional concern with the political implications of mergers; in this era of augmented influence by economists and economically sophisticated lawyers, we seem to have lost sight of

---

[31] Using subsequent legislative history to illuminate the intent of an earlier Congress seems particularly appropriate when we deal with "a comprehensive charter of economic liberty," Northern Pac. Ry. v. United States, 356 U.S. 1, 4 (1958), written with a "generality and adaptability comparable to that found to be desirable in constitutional provisions." Appalachian Coals, Inc. v. United States, 288 U.S. 344, 360 (1933). It also seems particularly appropriate because we deal with the "antitrust laws"—an interrelated network of statutes that supplements and amends earlier versions—designed in toto to govern marketplace competition. *Cf.* United States v. Hutcheson, 312 U.S. 219, 232 (1941) (describing and interpreting the Sherman, Clayton, and Norris-LaGuardia Acts as "interlacing statutes").

A similar situation was presented in Cantor v. Detroit Edison Co., 428 U.S. 579 (1976) in which Mr. Justice Blackmun, concurring in the judgment, found that the Sherman Act's framers never directly faced the question of the extent to which the Sherman Act preempted inconsistent state law. His separate opinion cited a series of subsequent congressional enactments exempting particular kinds of state regulation—fair trade, insurance regulations, and agricultural marketing arrangements—to indicate Congress' earlier "intent" that, absent these special exemptions, these state arrangements would have been superseded by the Sherman Act. 428 U.S. at 607-09 (Blackmun, J., concurring in the judgment). *See also* Steffel v. Thompson, 415 U.S. 452, 463-68 (1974) (interpreting the Civil Rights Act of 1871, 42 U.S.C. § 1983, in part by reading a series of subsequent statutes as part of a historical process through which Congress defined the roles of federal and state courts); United States v. Freeman, 44 U.S. (3 How.) 556, 564-65 (1845) ("[I]f it can be gathered from a subsequent statute *in pari materia*, what meaning the legislature attached to the words of a former statute, they will amount to a legislative declaration of its meaning, and will govern the construction of the first statute.").

[32] 15 U.S.C. § 18 (1976).

these attitudes. Consider the statement by Representative Celler, one of the co-sponsors of the amendment, at the time the bill that eventually became section 7 was originally introduced:

> I want to point out the danger of this trend toward more and better combines. I read from a report filed with former Secretary of War Royall as to the history of the cartelization and concentration of industry in Germany:
>
>> Germany under the Nazi set-up built up a great series of industrial monopolies in steel, rubber, coal and other materials. The monopolies soon got control of Germany, brought Hitler to power and forced virtually the whole world into war.
>
> The report continues:
>
>> A high degree of concentration throughout industry fosters the formation of cartels and readily enables a war-minded government to mobilize for hostilities. Such was the history of war preparations in Germany in both World War I and World War II.
>>
>> . . . .
>
> Mr. Walter Lippmann, writing in *Fortune* magazine several years ago, stated correctly:
>
>> The development of combinations in business, which are able to dominate markets in which they sell their goods, and in which they buy their labor and materials, must lead irresistibly to some form of state collectivism. So much power will never for long be allowed to rest in private hands, and those who do not wish to take the road to the politically administered economy of socialism, must be prepared to take the steps back toward the restoration of the market economy of private competitive enterprise.
>
> All these warnings must make us pause.[33]

Now consider the following characteristic statement by Senator Kefauver, the other leading sponsor of the bill:

> I think we must decide very quickly what sort of country we want to live in. . . . The present trend of great

[33] 95 CONG. REC. 11,486 (1949).

> corporations to increase their economic power is the antithesis of meritorious competitive development. It is no accident that we now have a big Government, big labor unions, and big business. The concentration of great economic power in a few corporations necessarily leads to the formation of large Nation-wide unions. The development of the two necessarily lends [*sic*] to big bureaus in the Government to deal with them. Local economic independence cannot be preserved in the face of consolidations such as we have had during the past few years. The control of American business is steadily being transferred, I am sorry to have to say, from local communities to a few large cities in which central managers decide the policies and the fate of the far-flung enterprises they control. Millions of people depend helplessly on their judgment. Through monopolistic mergers the people are losing power to direct their own economic welfare. When they lose the power to direct their economic welfare they also lose the means to direct their political future.
>
> I am not an alarmist, but the history of what has taken place in other nations where mergers and concentrations have placed economic control in the hands of a very few people is too clear to pass over easily. A point is eventually reached, and we are rapidly reaching that point in this country, where the public steps in to take over when concentration and monopoly gain too much power. The taking over by the public through its government always follows one or two methods and has one or two political results. It either results in a Fascist state or the nationalization of industries and thereafter a Socialist or Communist state. Most businessmen realize this inevitable result. Certain monopolistic interests are being very short-sighted in not appreciating the plight to which they are forcing their Government.[84]

To some extent, preservation of a competitive *process* would achieve the goals that were of concern to these spokesmen; hence it is arguable that the statute is responsibly enforced if exclusively economic considerations, including the dispersal of monopoly power achieved other than by patents or economies of scale, are applied. Legislative history focusing on the protection of competition, not

[84] 96 Cong. Rec. 16,452 (1950). A concern that corporate concentration will inevitably diminish individual freedom is hardly an exclusive preoccupation of "populist" legislators. *See* Elzinga, *supra* note 1, at 1200 (citing warnings to that effect by Friedrick Hayek and Milton Friedman).

competitors, supports that view.[85] But we know that conflicts between political and economic goals do arise—for example, when a merger generating efficiencies contributes significantly to economic concentration in a given market. Is it conceivable that the sponsors of this bill would accept the notion that preservation of efficiencies ought to be treated as paramount?[86]

One might argue that these are the special views of Senators Celler and Kefauver—political hawks on the question of antitrust enforcement—and are not representative of the views of a broad segment of the majority voting in favor of the bill. That is simply not true. A striking feature of the legislative history of amended section 7 was the widely-shared perception of danger to the political well-being of the country and its citizens stemming from the merger movement.[87] As Professor Bok has reported, "there emerges a common definition of the problem at hand, a common philosophy as to its import, and a common notion, on a very general plane, of what the new act could do about it."[88]

Virtually all proponents of the bill who spoke asserted that the merger trend must be blocked because concentrated economic power would lead to increased government control, because freedom would corrode and totalitarianism prosper, and because absentee ownership by large corporations would diminish local initiative and civic responsibility.[89] Of course, that kind of language is not helpful in deciding whether a merger between two companies of given size in specific markets is legal. Congress in 1950 left those questions to the courts much as it did in 1890. But to proceed from that start-

---

85 *See* Brown Shoe Co. v. United States, 370 U.S. 294, 320 (1962).

86 An alternate way of presenting the same argument is to point out that the Senate and House reports do not expressly indicate an intention to interpret the statute in light of political goals. *See* S. REP. No. 1775, 81st Cong., 2d Sess. (1950); H.R. REP. No. 1191, 81st Cong., 1st Sess. (1949). Hence, the legislative rhetoric can be passed off as talk about "aims," and the absence of an express commitment to political values in the reports, an expression of Congress' wish to achieve those aims by exclusive pursuit of economic goals.

Silence in the reports on political issues, however, does not necessarily support that view. In fact, the reports were devoted almost entirely to an explication of the technical aspects of the statute—for example, the reason for the deletion of any reference to the effect on competition between the acquiring and acquired firms—and did not refer to problems generated by the occasional trade-off between efficiency considerations and political values. Accordingly, it seems fair to look beyond the Senate and House reports to the debates and focus upon the reiteration in those debates of the pervasive theme of concern for the protection of political values.

87 Bok, *Section 7 of the Clayton Act and the Merging of Law and Economics*, 74 HARV. L. REV. 226, 234-37 (1960).

88 *Id.* 234.

89 *Id.* 235-36. The Supreme Court has ratified the view that Congress was intent on stemming a rising tide of concentration because of a threat to non-economic values. *See* Brown Shoe Co. v. United States, 370 U.S. 294 (1962).

ing point to the conclusion that Congress in 1950 would be satisfied with a judicial interpretation that excluded all non-economic concerns—a position advocated largely by scholars who would not themselves regard the merger movement as a serious threat to political values—reflects a striking disregard for the political process.

B. *Feasibility of Incorporating Non-Economic Concerns*

Suppose a political component were to be included in an antitrust enforcement equation. Would that introduce chaos into what otherwise would be an orderly, reliable, and predictable regulatory process? Such a result is unlikely. Those opposed to the inclusion of political factors exaggerate the precision of an enforcement approach that incorporates solely economic concerns, and overstate the administrative difficulties and enforcement costs of taking non-economic concerns into account.

1. Illusion of Certainty

Economists and schools of economists disagree on a theoretical level with respect to many crucial antitrust policy issues: Is a vigorous policy of merger prevention justified because cartels are easier to organize and police in a concentrated market? Does vertical integration lead to significant anticompetitive effects? Do massive advertising expenditures diminish or improve opportunities for entry by new firms? Different advocates of the economic approach would answer these and many other policy questions in entirely different ways.

Even if economic theory were clear and consistent, economics provides no system for reliably determining economic effect. We know that a market served by fifteen or twenty firms that is converted by merger to a monopoly or duopoly will produce a different level of price and perhaps efficiency. In contrast, a merger in a ten-firm market between the sixth and eighth firms reduces the total number to nine but allows the combined enterprise to challenge the leaders more effectively. There is no reliable way to determine either the pro- or anti-competitive effect of that merger with anything approaching scientific reliability. As a result, antitrust enforcement along economic lines already incorporates large doses of hunch, faith, and intuition.[40]

---

[40] *See* Sullivan, *supra* note 15, at 6-7.

Another reason that antitrust is something less than a precise science is that so many antitrust questions are factually indeterminate, a condition exacerbated by unavoidable limitations on the judicial process. The recent controversy over the proposed rule that a monopolist does not engage in exclusionary pricing if prices charged are in excess of average variable costs provides an apt example.[41] Among the reasons advanced for such a rule is that a single bright-line formula will contribute to increased reliability and predictability in enforcement. Many courts, persuaded by those arguments, appear to be adopting the average variable cost formula.[42]

It is of course desirable, all things being equal, to adopt prospective rules that are workable. Nevertheless, few if any experienced litigators believe that proof of average variable cost—with accounting records in the hands of defendants and the inevitable slippage of the discovery process—would be anything but a rough approximation. If the evidence relates to a multi-plant firm and involves complicated problems of allocation of general overhead, it is uncertain that even a rough approximation is achievable. Again, the argument that inclusion of political factors will introduce an element of unpredictability into an otherwise reliable enforcement system seems unrealistic.

2. Compatibility of Political and Economic Considerations

Vigorous antitrust enforcement usually serves both economic and political goals, at least as political goals have been defined here. Elimination or containment of monopoly and elimination of unnecessary barriers to entry and unreasonable business practices not only promote economic efficiency but tend to avoid undue concentrations of economic power, to reduce the range of private discretion in the business field, and to minimize the risks of state interference. But unavoidable inconsistencies occasionally do arise, and the question at that point is whether inclusion of political values, reasonably defined and weighted, leads to unacceptable administra-

[41] *Compare* Areeda & Turner, *Predatory Pricing and Related Practices Under Section 2 of the Sherman Act*, 88 Harv. L. Rev. 697, 716-18 (1975) *with* Scherer, *Predatory Pricing and the Sherman Act: A Comment*, 89 Harv. L. Rev. 869, 873-75 (1976) *and* Williamson, *Predatory Pricing: A Strategic and Welfare Analysis*, 87 Yale L.J. 284, 286-306 (1977).

[42] *See, e.g.*, International Air Indus., Inc. v. American Excelsior Co., 517 F.2d 714 (5th Cir. 1975).

tive or anti-efficiency costs. That depends on how political values are introduced into the antitrust equation.

III. Political Factors Applied

A. *Some General Limits*

It has been argued that if political concerns are to be satisfied, there is no clear stopping place short of atomistic competition.[43] That position overstates the difficulties of introducing political values to leaven what would otherwise be an exclusively economic analysis of antitrust problems.

Political concerns ought to be treated as limited factors that influence the way in which prospective rules are designed to accomplish antitrust objectives. If the rules themselves are clear, introduction of a political dimension will not generate undue uncertainty in enforcement. Moreover, because these political concerns are clearly and expressly secondary, major dislocations in competitive policy will be avoided.[44]

The following sections will indicate how political considerations have properly influenced the development of prospective rules with respect to horizontal mergers, an area of major significance in antitrust enforcement.

B. *Political Factors in Horizontal Merger Enforcement*

There is a consensus among economists and antitrust lawyers that mergers among competitors should be prohibited when they lead to concentration, because explicit collusion is more difficult to detect and tacit collusion more likely to occur in concentrated

---

[43] *See* Bork, *The Rule of Reason and the Per Se Concept: Price Fixing and Market Division*, 74 Yale L.J. 775, 831-32 (1965).

[44] Perhaps political concerns also can legitimately serve as a tie-breaker in individual cases. For example, they may contribute to a finding of illegality with respect to a merger of two very large companies when there are neither significant anticompetitive effects nor significant efficiencies as a result of the merger. It is hard to believe the Supreme Court decision in United States v. E.I. duPont de Nemours & Co., 353 U.S. 586 (1957) [duPont-GM], in which the Court ruled that duPont's competitors in the automotive finishes and fabrics market were foreclosed from that market because of the close relationship between duPont and GM (which could have been the reason for GM's purchasing most of its requirements from duPont), is not explained in part by the idea that those two companies were regarded as "too big" and "too influential" from a political point of view.

A problem with that kind of enforcement approach is that it is ad hoc with respect to specific transactions and may be unfair to the parties. Unfairness is particularly pronounced if private treble damage exposure must be taken into account.

markets.[45] There is also general agreement that cartels are inherently unstable, but that stability can be increased (and the costs of cartel administration decreased) if the number of sellers of competing products, and hence the number of potential defectors from the cartel, is reduced.[46]

Against that policy background, several crucial policy issues relating to horizontal mergers arise: First, what is the minimum level at which a lessening of competition or a tendency toward monopoly will occur as a result of mergers? Second, assuming a merger produces significant anticompetitive effects, should countervailing competitive effects in another market be taken into account in measuring the net competitive effect of a merger? Third, to what extent and in which circumstances will merger rules be modified to take into account efficiencies resulting from the merger?

Although the law on these questions may be in a state of flux, it is likely that the minimum levels at which mergers can be challenged successfully remain in the five-to-ten-percent range, at least when markets are moderately or highly concentrated.[47] The courts will not consider evidence of redeeming competitive effects in another market.[48] Efficiencies resulting from a merger are taken into account as a preliminary matter in that horizontal mergers, despite their inevitable price and market allocation effects, are not judged under a per se standard, but evidence of efficiency is probably irrelevant under present law as a defense to any specific merger.[49] This analysis assumes that the misstep in the earlier *Brown Shoe*[50] opinion suggesting that efficiencies of integration might be a reason for striking down a merger,[51] is no longer good law.[52]

---

[45] *See, e.g.,* G. STIGLER, *A Theory of Oligopoly,* in THE ORGANIZATION OF INDUSTRY 39 (1968); *Hearings on Economic Concentration Before the Subcomm. on Antitrust and Monopoly of the Senate Comm. on the Judiciary,* 89th Cong., 1st Sess. 540-51 (1965) (statement of Professor Carl Kaysen).

[46] *See* Weiss, *The Concentration-Profits Relationship and Antitrust,* in INDUSTRIAL CONCENTRATION: THE NEW LEARNING 189-93, 231 (Goldschmid, Mann & Weston eds. 1974) (summarizing relevant economic literature on the subject).

[47] *See* United States v. Von's Grocery Co., 384 U.S. 270, 272 (1966) (combined market share of 7.5% outlawed); Brown Shoe Co. v. United States, 370 U.S. 294, 343-44 (1962) (combined market shares of 5% outlawed on ground that it would require the courts to approve future mergers of similar market shares, thus leading to the oligopoly Congress sought to avoid); Merger Guidelines of Dep't of Justice, 1 TRADE REG. REP. (CCH) ¶ 4510, §§ 5-6 (1968).

[48] United States v. Philadelphia Nat'l Bank, 374 U.S. 321, 370 (1963).

[49] *See* Ford Motor Co. v. United States, 405 U.S. 562, 569-71 (1972); Merger Guidelines of Dep't of Justice, 1 TRADE REG. REP. (CCH) ¶ 4510, § 10 (1968). *See also* FTC v. Procter & Gamble Co., 386 U.S. 568, 580 (1966). *But see* Sullivan, *supra* note 15, at 631.

[50] Brown Shoe Co. v. United States, 370 U.S. 294 (1962).

[51] *Id.* 344.

[52] *See* Blake & Jones, *supra* note 1, at 455-57.

When scholars who advocate antitrust enforcement aimed exclusively at serving economic goals contemplate these rules, they understandably are driven to conclude that the rules are wrong, the policies misguided, and the legislators and judges who impose them unsophisticated or ill-informed.[53] A merger producing a combined market share of five percent could occur in a market with scores of other sellers. Even taking the "incipiency" dimension of section 7 into account, it is doubtful as a matter of economic analysis that one could predict that a reduction in sellers from twenty to nineteen or even from fifteen to fourteen—except in special and unusual circumstances—would *substantially* increase the likelihood of tacit or overt collusion. It is also difficult for those who demand antitrust enforcement solely to achieve allocative efficiency and optimum levels of firm size to comprehend an enforcement policy that refuses to permit as a defense lines of evidence that show directly that these very effects are likely to be achieved by a particular merger. On the other hand, those who support incorporation of non-economic considerations in antitrust enforcement may have some reservations about specific cases and rules, but can generally support the current lines of authority described above.[54] The reasons for that support differ and are illuminating in indicating the ways in which the "political" thinkers part company with *homo economicus.*

1. Threshold Level of Illegality

Measured solely by economic concerns, formidable arguments can be advanced that no merger ought to be prevented unless it produces market concentration in which the top four firms account for more than sixty percent of the market.[55] Advocates claim that this rule would leave ample opportunity to achieve by merger optimum levels of scale, and would not introduce any serious likelihood of tacit collusion.[56]

---

53 BORK, THE ANTITRUST PARADOX 200-04 (1978); Bowman, *Contrasts in Antitrust Theory II*, 65 COLUM. L. REV. 417, 418 (1965) ("Application of oligopoly analyses to market situations such as existed in the *Brown Shoe* case is grotesque.") (citation omitted); Posner, *Antitrust Policy and the Supreme Court: An Analysis of the Restricted Distribution, Horizontal Merger and Potential Competition Decisions*, 75 COLUM. L. REV. 282, 299-313 (1975).

54 *See* notes 45-52 *supra* & accompanying text.

55 BORK, *supra* note 53, at 205-06 (arguing that mergers up to 60% or 70% of a market *should* be permitted, but interpreting Congress' wish to prevent 30%-40% combinations); Posner, *supra* note 53, at 312-13 (advocating that position and citing economic and legal literature in its support).

56 The theoretical justification for that view appears to be that in less concentrated markets, non-conspiratorial uniform behavior either will not occur or, if it does, can be challenged by a more imaginative application of cartel theory in actions

The four-firm/sixty-percent line seems roughly equivalent to the standard governing merger enforcement under the Sherman Act or under section 7 of the Clayton Act prior to its amendment.[57] Given Congress' clear intention in amending the Clayton Act to reach far beyond Sherman Act limits as interpreted in *United States v. Columbia Steel Co.*,[58] other commentators defend an anti-merger rule at a lower threshold level. If the "incipiency" dimension of section 7 is taken into account, and if it is recognized that it is virtually impossible as a matter of economics to describe precisely at what point concentration produces conditions that facilitate collusion, one can persuasively argue that the threshold level ought to be well below the four-firm/sixty-percent level.[59] Even so, it is extremely difficult to defend, strictly on economic grounds, outlawing the kind of five-to-ten-percent horizontal mergers in *Brown Shoe v. United States*,[60] *United States v. Von's Grocery*,[61] and *United States v. Pabst Brewing Co.*[62]

The Supreme Court's position in those cases is comprehensible only if one recalls Congress' concern about the political consequences of what it believed was a rising tide of concentration. Obviously, no particular merger will threaten to produce a nondemocratic political order or generate an unacceptable level of private corporate discretion; it was the general trend that Congress perceived and that it regarded as a threat to political values. Moreover, it does not seem an adequate answer to say that if solely political concerns were at issue it would be enough to outlaw mergers among companies accounting for large market shares—not five-percent mergers in the retail trade. Whether right or wrong on the underlying facts, Congress was concerned with a trend—a

---

for conspiracy under section 1 of the Sherman Act. *See* Posner, *Oligopoly and the Antitrust Laws: A Suggested Approach*, 21 STAN. L. REV. 562 (1969).

57 *See* United States v. First Nat'l Bank & Trust Co., 376 U.S. 665 (1964) (violation of the Sherman Act was found with respect to a merger of the first and fourth largest commercial banks in a city, with a combined share of about 50%, and with the top four firms accounting for about 80% of assets, deposits, and loans); United States v. Columbia Steel Co., 334 U.S. 495 (1948) (no violation of the Sherman Act when combined market share in the horizontal line was 24%).

58 334 U.S. 495 (1948). *See* H.R. REP. No. 1191, 81st Cong., 1st Sess. 8-9 (1949). The Senate committee expressly stated that "the bill is not intended to revert to the Sherman Act test. The intent here . . . is to cope with monopolistic tendencies in their incipiency and well before they have attained such effects as would justify a Sherman Act proceeding." S. REP. No. 1775, 81st Cong., 2d Sess. 4-5 (1950).

59 *See, e.g.*, Sullivan, *supra* note 15, at 620-21.

60 370 U.S. 294 (1962).

61 384 U.S. 270 (1966).

62 384 U.S. 546 (1966).

dynamic process—that it believed had to be checked early, before it developed irresistible political momentum, to preserve fundamental democratic values. Although some of these cases push to the extreme the goal of stopping trends toward concentration, Congress was aware that much concentration in the country had occurred as a result of prior failures to deal with merger trends and apparently was prepared to pay a price to ensure that those failures would not continue.

Antitrusters who emphasize a political dimension in antitrust need not agree with the result in individual cases, including those that expressly cite political factors. In *Von's Grocery,*[63] a merger between the third and sixth-ranked retail food sellers in Los Angeles, with a combined market share of 7.5%, was struck down even though entry was easy and the market only moderately concentrated, on grounds that (1) there was a pronounced trend toward concentration underway, and (2) to protect small dealers ("worthy men") from being driven out of business.[64] Even political antitrusters can regard that result as dubious. During the same period in which the number of single store outlets had fallen sharply, the number of chains increased from ninety-six to 150, and the market share of the top two chains declined from twenty-one percent to fourteen percent.[65] Thus, the trend among those companies that might have been induced to engage in cartels or drift into patterns of tacit collusion—that is, the top firms in the market—was toward deconcentration rather than concentration. Also, entry barriers were low and existing concentration moderate. Finally, the political values that the Court espoused—protection of small businessmen against the rigors of competition from larger, more efficient rivals—would not be served by preventing mergers among relatively small firms near the top of a loosely concentrated market.[66]

2. Treatment of a Defense Based on Redeeming Competitive Values

When merging firms are relatively large in the markets in which they sell and the merger contributes significantly to market

[63] 384 U.S. 270 (1966).

[64] The concentration that concerned the Court arose from the fact that the number of single store retail grocery outlets in Los Angeles had decreased from 5,365 in 1950 to 3,818 in 1961. *Id.* 273.

[65] *Id.* 281, 290-91 (Stewart, J., dissenting).

[66] *Id.* 298 (Stewart, J., dissenting) (noting that the small businessman's "plight" in this market was that he was strong and secure and, indeed, was often the most aggressive competitor against larger chains).

concentration, it is relatively easy to predict significant anticompetitive effects on the basis of non-political values. Those mergers facilitate the organization of explicit cartels and increase the likelihood of inter-firm patterns of coordinated competitive behavior. Nevertheless, defense counsel will frequently argue that despite the reduction in competition in some narrow product or geographic market, the merger allows the combined firm to compete effectively in a different and usually more significant product or geographic market.

United States v. Philadelphia National Bank [*PNB*] [67] presents a classic example of that kind of issue. The merging firms there were the second and third largest commercial banks in the four-county Philadelphia metropolitan area; their combined market share after the merger would have been about thirty percent, and the two-firm concentration ratio in the market would have increased from forty-five to sixty percent.[68] Defendants argued that the increased lending limit of the resulting bank would have enabled it to compete with the large New York banks for national loans, and the injection of additional competition in that national market more than compensated for any reduction of competition in the Philadelphia area.[69]

The argument in defense of the merger certainly does not appear frivolous. In terms of national economic policy, and taking account the ability of banks, by control of credit, to influence competitive initiatives, it may very well be in the long run that additional competition for loans to nationally significant companies would be a major pro-competitive development. And even if the defendants were incorrect on the facts in *Philadelphia National Bank,* there are bound to be many cases in which a lessening of competition in some narrow market is counterbalanced by increases in competition in a different larger market. Nevertheless, the Court refused to consider the contention, noting simply that an exception for redeeming competitive effects in another market would create a loophole in section 7 enforcement that could lead to unacceptable industrial concentration.[70]

---

[67] 374 U.S. 321 (1963).

[68] *Id.* 364-65.

[69] *Id.* 370-71.

[70] "If anticompetitive effects in one market could be justified by pro-competitive consequences in another, the logical upshot would be that every firm in an industry could, without violating § 7, embark on a series of mergers that would make it in the end as large as the industry leader." *Id.* 370.

This issue of the relevance of compensating competitive effects is a difficult, close, vexing question of antitrust policy. The result in *Philadelphia National Bank* can be defended on grounds that do not implicate political considerations—specifically, that competitive advantages and disadvantages are difficult enough to measure, but that it is virtually impossible to incorporate any such measurements into a formula that will permit a conclusion with respect to the net effect on the economy. But it is questionable whether that calculation is really any more difficult than the measurement of tradeoffs that are characteristic of rule of reason areas, such as balancing business reasons for an exclusive dealing contract against the anti-competitive consequences of market foreclosure,[71] or weighing the immediate pro-competitive effect of introducing by joint venture a new competitor into a product area against the loss to the competitive process of a "sidelines pro-competitive effect" because one of the parents, but for the joint venture, might have remained at the edge of the market contemplating independent entry.[72] Calculation of pro- and anti-competitive effects would be no more difficult with respect to the *PNB* "redeeming competitive effects issue" than in these other areas. The difference is that the *PNB* rule, as much as any rule in merger enforcement, has contributed to the success of a policy aimed at preventing loose oligopolies from being converted by merger into tight oligopolies, and that policy of containment is central to the legislative purpose of revised section 7.[73]

3. Admissibility of Evidence of Efficiencies

Advocates of differing views of the appropriate treatment of evidence of efficiency in merger litigation do not fall neatly into schools. Some commentators who have criticized the narrow economic approach would take clear evidence of efficiencies into account in close cases; [74] others who criticize "social theories" of antitrust enforcement would exclude evidence of economies of scale or managerial efficiencies because they are "intractable subjects for litigation." [75]

[71] *See* Tampa Elec. Co. v. Nashville Coal Co., 365 U.S. 320 (1961); Standard Oil Co. v. United States [Standard Stations], 337 U.S. 293 (1949).

[72] *See* United States v. Penn-Olin Chem. Co., 378 U.S. 158 (1964).

[73] *See* note 58 *supra.*

[74] *See, e.g.,* Blake & Jones, *supra* note 1, at 456-57; Sullivan, *supra* note 15, at 631.

[75] Posner, *supra* note 53, at 313. *See also* Turner, *Conglomerate Mergers and Section 7 of the Clayton Act,* 78 HARV. L. REV. 1313, 1339 (1965) (advocating exclusion of evidence of efficiencies on a case-by-case basis but taking such evidence into account in fashioning general merger rules—an approach similar to the one taken here).

The case for exclusion of specific evidence of economies in defense of a merger can be expanded beyond consideration of the difficulties of handling such evidence in trial. First, there is the question whether any such efficiencies, assuming they do result from a consolidation of firms, could be achieved between firms by contract or by some sort of joint venture limited in scope and duration. Either alternative would leave the acquired firm free to pursue independent competitive policies unrelated to achievement of efficiencies. Second, if efficiencies are significant, it is likely that firms will expand or modify their operational techniques in order to achieve them internally. Viewed in this light, mergers may accelerate the achievement of certain kinds of economies, but the mergers are not essential to achieving those economies. Finally, it seems fair to inquire whether the efficiencies will be taken out in the form of increased profits for shareholders, or will be used by the company to compete more aggressively and place pressure on rivals to adopt and implement equivalent efficiencies. Assuming litigation occurs fairly promptly after the merger is inaugurated, it seems unlikely in most instances that there will be reliable evidence of what use will be made of savings introduced as a result of the merger.

When each of those factors is added to considerations of complexity, expense, and delay in litigation caused by the introduction of efficiency questions, a persuasive case begins to emerge either for excluding efficiencies entirely—which seems to be the present view of the law—or accepting such evidence only in close, exceptional cases.

Does a rule excluding evidence of efficiencies in merger litigation reflect "political" considerations? As noted, exclusion can be justified on other grounds, but it can also reflect an essential notion of the political goals of antitrust—that the matter of efficiencies is not dispositive, and that an occasional loss of efficiency as a result of antitrust enforcement can be tolerated and is to be expected if antitrust is to serve other legitimate values. As Justice Brandeis wrote:

> The only argument that has been seriously advanced in favor of private monopoly is that competition involves waste . . . .
>
> Undoubtedly competition involves waste. What human activity does not? The wastes of democracy are among the greatest obvious wastes, but we have com-

> pensations in democracy which far outweigh that waste and make it more efficient than absolutism.[76]

Clearly, the Supreme Court in the 1950's and 1960's believed that Congress preferred less concentrated market structures, including situations in which there could be an efficiency loss and the likelihood of cartelizing tendencies was remote. Even if a narrow exception for evidence of efficiencies were permitted—when the likelihood of competitive injuries was slight, the predicted efficiencies were capable of clear demonstration in court, and there was some likelihood that the efficiencies would be converted into significant competitive effects—that would still reflect an essentially "political" determination to pay an economic price to serve non-economic goals. That position seems to be a valid interpretation of Congress' will.

CONCLUSION

This paper has argued that the trend toward use of an exclusively economic approach to antitrust analysis excludes important political considerations that have in the past been seen as relevant by Congress and the courts. Such considerations as the fear that excessive concentration of economic power will foster antidemocratic political pressures, the desire to reduce the range of private discretion by a few in order to enhance individual freedom, and the fear that increased governmental intrusion will become necessary if the economy is dominated by the few, can and should be feasibly incorporated into the antitrust equation. Although economic concerns would remain paramount, to ignore these non-economic factors would be to ignore the bases of antitrust legislation and the political consensus by which antitrust has been supported.

---

[76] L. BRANDEIS, THE CURSE OF BIGNESS 105 (1934), *quoted in* United States v. Columbia Steel Co., 334 U.S. 495, 534-35 n.1 (Douglas, J., dissenting).

[Vol. 127:1076

"JUSTICE" AND OTHER NON-ECONOMIC GOALS OF ANTITRUST

LOUIS B. SCHWARTZ †

(Comments on Pitofsky, *The Political Content of Antitrust*)

Commissioner Pitofsky's admirable delineation and defense of the role of political considerations in antitrust law exhibits a moderation not required of an academic like me. I would invoke a broader range of congressional history to demonstrate the will of Congress that putative economic gains should not be the exclusive or decisive factor in resolving antitrust controversies. I would not yield as freely as he does to the dogma that the antitrust laws protect "competition not competitors," because the goals of justice and the antitrust laws sometimes demand protection of competitors. I find, as he does not, clear evidence of congressional purpose to "create procedural protection for distributors." Far from dismissing such concerns as "playing no useful role" in antitrust interpretation, I see them serving the very useful role of preventing abuse of power when the growth of power cannot be checked. Further, I see the role of non-economic considerations not merely as a "tie-breaker," but as calling for a definite shift in burden of proof or persuasion, so that practices and structures with anti-competitive potential can be justified only on clear and convincing evidence of economic gain to be passed on to the public. Finally, I miss in the Pitofsky analysis any reference to that venerable non-economic goal of government, namely justice. Never, despite repeated demonstrations by economic modelists that price discrimination may optimize allocation of resources, has Congress wavered from its adherence to the view that it is "unjust discrimination" to charge different customers different prices for identical services.[1]

Regarding the range of congressional manifestations of Congress' willingness to pursue its deconcentration goals if need be at some economic cost, Professor Pitofsky points out that the non-economic goals are clear in the legislative history of antitrust enactments supplementing the Sherman Act, and that "arguably . . . these subsequent expressions define Congress' vague intentions in

† Benjamin Franklin Professor of Law, University of Pennsylvania. B.S. 1932, J.D. 1935, University of Pennsylvania.

[1] *See* Interstate Commerce Act, 49 U.S.C. § 2 (1970).

earlier enactments." In this connection, his footnote 31 reminds us that the antitrust laws constitute an "interrelated network," "interlacing statutes."

There are more elements in this network than he mentions or than is generally appreciated. The Reclamation Act of 1902 limited the sale of water from federal irrigation projects so that no single owner might benefit for more than 160 acres.[2] In section 11 of the Public Utility Holding Company Act of 1935,[3] Congress declared its tolerance for giant utility combines if they effected "substantial economies," [4] but only if they were "not so large . . . as to impair the advantages of localized management." [5] The Small Business Act of 1942 [6] declared congressional policy to assure "small-business concerns [a] fair proportion" of government procurement contracts under arrangements that even permitted the payment of higher prices to small-business suppliers.[7] The Surplus Property Act of 1944 [8] directed the federal government to dispose of war production facilities under standards that included preference for smaller purchasers and "strengthen[ing] and preserv[ing] the competitive position of small business concerns." [9] Our banking regulation clearly subordinates "efficiency" considerations to considerations of excessive concentration of power when it seeks to prevent banks and bank holding companies from extending their operations into "non-banking" business.[10] A judge or administrator who wishes to be responsive to the will of Congress can hardly fail to catch the drift of these legislative enactments. Collectively they portray a view of the public interest that must pervade the interpretation of the antitrust laws, whether or not one approves of all these "preferences" for small business.

The non-economic component of American antitrust policy stands out even more strikingly if one broadens the perspective

---

[2] 43 U.S.C. § 431 (1976). *See* Ivanhoe Irrigation Dist. v. McCracken, 357 U.S. 275, 294-97 (1958).

[3] 15 U.S.C. § 79k (1976).

[4] *Id.* § 79k(b)(1)(A).

[5] *Id.* § 79k(b)(1)(C). *Cf.* SEC v. New England Elec. Sys., 384 U.S. 176 (1966).

[6] 15 U.S.C. §§ 631-647 (1976).

[7] 15 U.S.C. § 631(a) (1976).

[8] Pub. L. No. 457, 58 Stat. 765 (1944) (current version at 40 U.S.C. § 484 and 50 U.S.C. § 1622(d) (1970)).

[9] *Id.* § 2(d). Similar provisions were incorporated into § 207 of the Federal Property and Administrative Services Act of 1949, 40 U.S.C. § 488 (1976).

[10] *See, e.g.*, Bankamerica Corp. v. Board of Governors of the Fed. Reserve Sys., 491 F.2d 985 (9th Cir. 1974); Arnold Tours, Inc. v. Camp, 472 F.2d 427 (1st Cir. 1972).

beyond congressional legislation to consider that major historic event, American imposition of antitrust measures upon conquered Germany and Japan after World War II. No one then suggested that our zeal for industrial deconcentration there was an attempt to impose diseconomies on the defeated. Some believed that the rapid reconstruction of those devastated economies called for decartelization and decentralization. But clearly the dominant motivation was political: a desire to create alternative centers of power that could not readily be marshalled behind authoritarian regimes. I have elsewhere explored "Authoritarian Aspects of Bigness" as a political theme in the antitrust symphony.[11] Finally, it is well known that one goal of the antitrust laws is to avert the need for massive and ongoing government regulation or nationalization—precisely the political goal that has brought even sophisticated businessmen to join in the American consensus supporting the antitrust principle, however avidly each businessman may seek exemption for his own business.

The dogma that "antitrust laws protect competition not competitors" overstates the case and ignores considerations of justice. One must amend that declaration by adding at least the following qualification: "unless individual competitors must be protected in the interests of preserving competition." A conspiracy to put a single small competitor out of business violates the Sherman Act even if there is no showing of significant impact on competition generally.[12] In the Robinson-Patman Act,[13] Congress explicitly extended the anti-discrimination ban to attempts to eliminate "a competitor" as well as to cases of impairment of competition.[14] These may be regarded as instances of Congress' concern with "incipient" impairment of competition or desire to prevent transactions, trivial in themselves, which might "trigger" a series of similar transactions. But they also may be seen as a congressional concern for a non-economic goal: "justice," in the sense of fair and equal treatment of persons in like situations.

That the purpose of the antitrust laws includes "procedural protection for distributors" seems clear from the Automobile Dealer

---

[11] Schwartz, *Institutional Size and Individual Liberty: Authoritarian Aspects of Bigness*, 55 Nw. U.L. Rev. 4 (1960); Schwartz, *American Antitrust Laws and Free Enterprise* in 2 Swiss Review of International Antitrust Law 3 (January 1978).

[12] *See, e.g.*, Klors, Inc. v. Broadway-Hale Stores, Inc., 359 U.S. 207 (1959). *But see* Oreck Corp. v. Whirlpool Corp., 579 F.2d 126 (2d Cir.), *cert. denied*, 99 S. Ct. 340 (1978) (three Justices dissenting).

[13] 15 U.S.C. §§ 13-13g, 21a (1976).

[14] *See* FTC v. Morton Salt Co., 334 U.S. 37 (1948).

Franchise Act of 1956,[15] which undertakes to require auto manufacturers to "act in a fair and equitable manner" in terminating or failing to renew dealer franchises.[16] This legislation was entitled "An Act to supplement the antitrust laws of the United States, in order to balance the power now heavily weighted in favor of automobile manufacturers."[17] Some, including myself, may see the Auto Dealer Franchise Act as misguided or as setting a dangerous precedent for unwarranted "status" protection of dealers generally, but it can hardly be denied that Congress here purported to exercise, as part of its antitrust concerns, a supervision over fair procedure and justice in economic relationships. Moreover, cases such as *Radiant Burners, Inc. v. Peoples Gas Light Co.*,[18] and *Silver v. New York Stock Exchange*,[19] show that the Sherman Act itself can be invoked to guarantee procedural fairness when an industry is engaged in self-regulation. Radiant Burners was given an opportunity to prove that its ceramic burner qualified for the "seal of approval" by the trade association. Silver was guaranteed notice and opportunity for hearing before his private wire connections with an exchange member could be cut off. It is hardly surprising that the antitrust laws, which the Supreme Court has compared to the "Magna Carta" and the "Bill of Rights,"[20] should incorporate a strain of fourteenth amendment due process, procedural as well as substantive.[21] Similarly, it is easy to detect the fourteenth amendment theme of "equal protection of the laws" (the private commercial laws enacted by dominant firms and oligopolists) in the legislation against price and service discrimination.[22] Others have noted as relevant to the debate over concentration that there is evidence that monopolistic enterprises discriminate against blacks more frequently than competitive enterprises.[23]

---

15 15 U.S.C. §§ 1221-1225 (1976).

16 *Id.* §§ 1221(e), 1222.

17 Automobile Dealer Franchise Act, ch. 1078, 70 Stat. 1125 (1956) (current version at 15 U.S.C. §§ 1221-1225 (1976)).

18 364 U.S. 656 (1961).

19 373 U.S. 341 (1963).

20 United States v. Topco Associates, 405 U.S. 596, 610 (1972).

21 *Cf.* A. BERLE, POWER 373-81 (1967) ("Corporate Regulations as 'Laws' under the Fourteenth Amendment").

22 *Cf.* FTC v. Sun Oil Co., 371 U.S. 505, 520 (1963) (citing the House Committee's view that the "'guiding idea'" of the Robinson-Patman Act was "'the preservation of equality of opportunity as far as possible to all who are usefully employed in the service of distribution and production . . . .' H.R. REP. No. 2287, 74th Cong., 2d Sess. 6.").

23 *See* Shepard, *Market Power and Racial Discrimination in White Collar Employment*, 14 ANTITRUST BULL. 141 (1969).

The difficult question is not *whether* non-economic considerations are a proper, indeed conventional, component of the antitrust calculus, but how to take them into account. Pitofsky answered at the conference that political concerns may serve as "tie-breaker in individual cases," and as "limited factors that influence the way in which prospective rules are designed to accomplish antitrust objectives." I would go further:

(1) Except in criminal prosecutions, the weight of the non-economic and non-quantitative goals of antitrust should shift to anyone seeking to justify a monopoly or a "suspect" anti-competitive practice the burden of persuading the tribunal that the justification is established by clear and convincing evidence.[24] Such a rule would operate not merely in cases in which the judge may be left undecided by the economic evidence (a "tie"), but also when he believes that the balance of evidence slightly favors the justification.

(2) A proper deference to the non-economic goals of antitrust and to the uncertainties of many economic measurements would affect the way certain economic testimony is handled. For example, where there is an issue as to defendant's market share and, as usual, conflicting market boundaries are supported by evidence, the tribunal might be guided by the rule that the narrowest reasonable geographic and product boundaries would be accepted.[25] Similarly, when "effect on competition" is the criterion of legality, an adverse effect in one market should suffice to condemn the transaction without exploring the possible pro-competitive impact in another market.[26] So also a court giving proper deference to the political elements of the anti-merger laws would "tilt" towards rather than away from a reasonable administrative judgment that the acquiring company was a potential entrant.[27] Note that these pro-

[24] *See* United States v. Grinnell Corp., 236 F. Supp. 244 (D.R.I. 1964) (Wyzanski, J.), *aff'd with modification of decree*, 384 U.S. 563 (1966).

[25] *See, e.g.*, United States v. E.I. duPont de Nemours & Co., 353 U.S. 586 (1957); United States v. International Boxing Club, 348 U.S. 236 (1955); Reynolds Metal Co. v. FTC, 309 F.2d 223 (D.C. Cir. 1962).

[26] *See* United States v. Topco Associates, Inc., 405 U.S. 596 (1972); United States v. Philadelphia National Bank, 374 U.S. 321 (1963).

Among recent examples of the undermining of prophylactic rules, reflecting inadequate deference to non-economic goals of antitrust, are Continental T.V., Inc. v. GTE Sylvania Inc., 433 U.S. 36 (1977) (repeal of per se prohibition of vertical territorial restraints; balancing of putative interbrand competitive gains against obvious loss of intrabrand competition); United States v. Marine Bancorporation, 418 U.S. 602 (1974) (retreating from the rule that mergers would be judged almost entirely on the basis of market shares and concentration); United States v. General Dynamics Corp., 415 U.S. 486 (1974).

[27] *But see* British Oxygen Corp. v. FTC, 529 F.2d 196 (2d Cir. 1976).

posals are not confined to "prospective" rule-making, as Pitofsky suggests, but apply in cases in which existing rules of law are interpreted in application to past transactions.

(3) A proper deference to the non-economic goals of antitrust and to the unreliability of official discrimination between "good" and "bad" performance by enterprises would lead to a greater receptivity to per se and other prophylactic antitrust rules. Such rules concededly bar some transactions for which plausible economic justifications can be made out. They embody a judgment that the economic gain infrequently sacrificed in such transactions is more than counterbalanced by more effective administration in the majority of cases in which both economic and non-economic goals will be served by strict enforcement.

(4) Recognition of the non-economic goals of antitrust warrants a pro-antitrust resolution of controversies over the bane or benefit of vertical and conglomerate mergers, the desirability of a "shared monopoly" approach to oligopoly, and the desirability of breaking up persistent monopolies even if no "predatory" actions can be proved.

[6]

Bastiaan van der Esch LL.D.*

E.E.C. COMPETITION RULES: BASIC PRINCIPLES AND POLICY AIMS[1]

I. THE ROLE ATTRIBUTED BY THE EEC TREATY TO COMPETITION[2]

This role is directly linked to the main political objective of the Community.

The Community is the embodiment of a policy of progressive unification of Western Europe. The ultimate shape of a united Europe is undefined and rather vague. Only the first step on the road to unity is a certainty and that is the Community as it stands today. This first step aims at the transformation of originally rather isolated national markets into one single common market, similar to every other internal market in the world.

This transformation process implies a reallocation of production factors and it is this reallocation of production factors which the Community has entrusted to the normal working of market forces. This is why the free deployment of these market forces is protected not only by the fundamental rules of the Treaty concerning free circulation of goods, workers and capital, which create obligations for the Member States, but also by the competition rules, which address themselves to all market participants. In other words, the Treaty objective of a system of undistorted competition as contained in article 3 f EEC is complementary to the abolition of internal barriers to trade and the resulting opening up of national markets. Together these provisions organize and protect market unity as a basis of ultimate political unity. Simultaneously, these provisions serve as a stimulus to a more rational, community-wide allocation of production factors, so as to combine unity with social and economic strength.

To avoid misunderstanding, it must always be stressed that the interdictions of restrictive agreements and of abuse of dominant positions contained in article 85 § 1 resp. art. 86 of EEC Treaty protect competition as an instrument of market integration and not as a commitment to a certain social order. Articles 90 and 222 EEC make clear that Member States remain free to determine the size and composition of the public sector. It is not so therefore

* B. van der Esch LL.D. (Leyde), Senior Legal Councillor for Competition, Commission of the European Communities.

1. This article is based upon a lecture for the Japanese Institute of International business law, in Tokio on 13 November 1979.
2. To remain whithin the time available no reference is made to the ECSC competition rules (art. 65 and 66 ECSC). The same applies to art. 92 and 93 EEC dealing with State Aids. It should also be remembered that most Member States have national competition rules which firms must also respect.

that the Treaty enshrines the liberal economy as such. There is room within the Community for those who put their faith in a guided economy, provided the unity of the market is respected.

The two main characteristics of the competition rules are:

- a comprehensive character
- a potential for flexibility

I will deal with each of these characteristics separately.

II. *THE COMPREHENSIVE CHARACTER OF THE COMPETITION RULES*

This comprehensive character signifies that the competition rules do not contain any loop holes nor what one might call blind angles. Let me illustrate this by a few examples:

- the same basic rules apply to industry, commerce, agriculture, banking, insurance and transport, subject to possible adaptations to the particular characteristics of a given sector provided for in art. 87 and 42 EEC;
- public enterprises are apprehended on the same basis as private firms, subject to the proviso of art. 90 § 2 EEC;
- vertical restrictions are treated in the same way as horizontal agreements;
- the interdiction of 85(1) covers both formal agreements and socalled concerted practices. The latter concept covers reciprocal or complementary behaviour producing anti-competitive effects similar to those attached to restrictive agreements;
- where the very basis for competition is lacking, that is to say in the absence of a plurality of operators of matching strength, art. 86 ensures that even the fundamental objectives of the Treaty can be achieved;
- the interdiction both of restrictive practices and of abuses of dominant position are interdictions of effects. The intentions of operators are not determining. What counts are the substantive effects on competitive structures and on the degree of competition within these structures. Economic analysis of whatever industry proposes or practices therefore forms an essential prerequisite to the proper application of the competition rules.

Everyone of these examples of the comprehensiveness of the competition rules provides material for a separate article. All I will do in this article is to elaborate on one or two points, beginning with the fact that all forms of economic, industrial or commercial activity on the Common Market must respect the competition rules.

The Commission's administrative practice provides ample illustrations of this point. Sometimes the economic impact of these examples is modest, but this does not diminish their policy value. So, for instance, for the application of art. 85 § 1 to a restrictive clause accepted by an independent research chemist who marketed the resulting knowledge and practical applications[3]. Idem for a decision by which the Commission exercised its investigatory

3. See *6th Report on Competition*, Brussels, 1977, p. 74 ff. The subsequent appeal against the decision prohibiting a certain restriction was withdrawn.

powers in respect of a firm of accountants which had accepted a role in the implementation of a cartel[4].

Economically more important is the Commission's recent reliance on article 85 to put an end to agreements between the combined London banks and an association of currency brokers. The admission of new market participants is now no longer in the hands of existing operators, but is decided upon by the competent public authorities[5].

The application of article 85 to joint ventures is equally firmly established. A number of extensively reasoned exemptions have been given[6]. Not so long ago, however, an exemption was refused. In that case, the *Wano/Schwarzpulver* decision[7], the joint venture had a rather curious function. Normally such ventures are set up in order to undertake, in combination with a real or potential competitor, a new activity. Here the purpose of the joint venture was different. ICI had decided to cease a certain production in the U.K. but did not want to accept the normal consequence of this which is to leave the U.K. market to other producers. The joint venture served to reserve the British market for one particular competitor in which ICI took an interest. The anti-competitive effects of such an arrangement are obvious and of such magnitude that no exemption could be given.

As a last example of the comprehensiveness of the competition rules, a few words about the fate of restrictive clauses in or of restrictive concerted practices connected with licensing contracts.

In this area two principles are at stake:

1. on the one hand licensing contracts are an indispensable vehicle for the dissemination of technology
2. on the other hand the degree and intensity of free circulation of goods should be the same for patented or branded goods as it is for unpatented or unbranded goods.

The detailed reconciliation of these two principles is a subject in itself. One thing is certain, however, and that is that in the view of the Commission, intellectual or commercial property rights do not include the right to compartmentilise the common market any way one wishes. Last year's *Maize Seed* decision[8] illustrates this. A German licensee of a French plant breeders right systematically used his German exclusive right to hinder imports from France of seeds sold in France by the licensor.

The Commission's decision establishes that in so doing the German licensee violated article 85 § 1 and orders him to cease and desist. The case is presently pending before the Court. The judgment which is expected in the first half of 1980 will be particularly interesting as it will almost certainly clarify some of the controversy still surrounding the application of the competition rules to licensing contracts.

4. Commission decision of 31.1.1979 against *Fides*, Milan, Official Journal L 57 of 8 March 1979 p. 33.
5. The so-called *Sarabex case* has not yet been fully reported upon. See Commission Press release IP (78) 262 of 18 December, 1978. See also Marc Dassesse and Stuart Isaacs, *Banking and the competition law of the EEC*, London 1978.
6. *7th Competition Report* p. 115 ff.
7. Official Journal L 322 of 16 November 1978 and *8th Competition Report* p. 98.
8. Official Journal L 286 of 12 October 1978 p. 23 ff.

Another aspect of the comprehensiveness of the competition rules which deserves more ample explanations concerns the emphasis on effects. A number of comments should be made on this point. As a legal technique, emphasis on effects is not limited to the competition sector. The Member States are subject to it also. Both the interdiction of internal custom duties and the interdiction of quantitative restrictions extend to measures of equivalent effect. Of course, a legal notion of the kind leads to complex questions of fact and of legal qualification.

However, such problems are the inevitable price to pay in a legal order which aims at permanency in ever changing economic and social circumstances. Human inventiveness is such that Treaty rules which would only apprehend formally defined obstacles to trade would quickly be circumvented and rendered inapplicable in fact.

The Court of Justice, in its jurisprudence, has never lost sight of this. It has had the forethought to embrace the useful effect principle of interpretation early in its jurisprudence[9]. The case law on competition matters also reflects this approach.

As a result no single clause of art. 85 and 86 should be interpreted without due regard to their nature as interdictions of effects. Here again a few practical examples may illustrate this point.

The concept of a concerted practice in art. 85 § 1 has given rise to considerable differences of opinion.

The Court said in the *Sugar Case*[10] that the concept of a concerted practice refers to a form of coordination between undertakings which, without having been taken to the stage where an agreement properly so-called has been concluded, knowingly substitutes for the risks of competition, practical cooperation between them which leads to conditions of competition which do not correspond to the normal conditions of the relevant market.

An important element of such normal conditions of competition is that each economic operator determines independently the policy which he intends to adopt in the market (ibidem p. 1952 para 173). This necessary independence in turn strictly precludes any direct or indirect contact between operators capable of influencing market conduct. This may include disclosure of conduct (p. 1942 para 174).

In simpler language this means that signals which aim at influencing the competitive conduct of other operators or which disclose ones own conduct in the market are an indubitable beginning of proof of a concerted practice. Sufficient proof emerges when the nature and the contents of these signals are such that operators remove in advance the uncertainly as to their future conduct which is inhaerent to normal market conditions.

A second example of how the focus on effects reflects itself in the interpretation of many of the terms of art. 85 and 86 is provided by the notion of abuse of a dominant position. Here again the contents is determined in the last analysis by the effect on the competitive conditions prevailing in the

9. Case 8-55, *Fédération Charbonnière Belgique vs. High Authority*, Reports of Cases before the Court 1954-1956 p. 299. For a more recent application see Case 21-78, *K.O. Delkvist vs. Anklagemyndigheden* (1778) EC 1978 recital 21.
10. Judgment of 16 December 1975 Joined Cases 40 etc/73 (1975) EcR p. 1916 par. 26.

market of a specific behaviour of a firm in a dominant position. In the time available all I can do is to draw your attention to the two most recent judgments of the European Court of Justice i.e. the *Banana* [11] and the *Vitamin Case* [12]. These judgments not only confirm the abusive character of certain specific types of behaviour by United Brands resp. Hoffmann-La Roche but also contain pointers as to the parameter within which a dominant firm can be reasonably certain *not* to abuse its position. That will be so whenever it is wise enough to choose a general price level for its product(s) which reflects the economies of scale it is achieving. The same applies to the possible economies resulting from a technological primacy or from any other type of advantage it may have over its competitors.

The risk of abuse begins when the dominant firm does not pass the fruits of its advantages on to the generality of its customers, when it starts to use its economic, industrial or commercial strength to keep these fruits to itself. The nature of such conduct almost inevitably distorts, impairs, contains, neutralises or paralyses competition; its result, more often than not, will be unfair or discriminatory pricing.

In more practical terms it may be said that strict economic and industrial performance in respect of a given product may always be legitimately expressed in the market. The resulting 'muscle' of a dominant firm however must be kept under strict self-control. This muscle should not be used to block or limit access to the market of competitors, actual or potential. The freedom of choice of users and consumers should not be limited. For all these reasons art. 86 EEC imposes on firms in a dominant position a stricter regime than art. 85 EEC on firms operating in competitive conditions. A number of restrictive practices which either would not be apprehended by art. 85 § 1 or which could possibly be exempted under art. 85 § 3 EEC, meet with an outright prohibition if dominant firms would try and resort to the same practice. The fidelity rebate is a case in point.

The repercussions of the focus on effects do not stop on the level of interpretation. This particular legal technique also has important jurisdictional consequences.

Regularly, restrictive or abusive action taken outside the Community produces its prohibited effects within it. Such action is fully apprehended. The Community limits itself to a purely intraterritorial reaction to prohibited intra-territorial effects, even if the ultimate cause is technically extra-territorial. In our opinion, communication with extra-territorial agents of these causes is no exercise of jurisdiction. As to the exercise of our powers of investigation, this remains purely intra-territorial and so do the sanctions on substantive violations of the rules.

There have been a few instances in which Japanese firms have violated the EEC rules either together with common market competitors or alone. Sometimes the motive has been to dampen competition from Japan. To that effect, Japanese imports into the Community were either limited in quantity or regulated as to their price or quality. Covered by the euphemism of orderly

11. Judgment of the Court of 14 February 1978, Case 27/76, *UBC/Commission*, (1978) EcR p. 207.
12. Judgment of 13 February 1979, Case 85/76 HLR/Commission, (1979) EcR 461.

marketing, agreements of the kind are obviously restrictive and apprehended by article 85 § 1, null and void by virtue of article 85 § 2 and rarely exemptable. Two cases in point are *the agreement between French and Japanese manufacturers of ballbearings* [13] and *the agreement between French and Korean producers of mushrooms* [14]

In both cases the public authorities concerned knew and even approved of these agreements. However, such governmental involvement does not provide an alibi for the firms. In the mushroom case fines were imposed.

The Commission's policy in these matters is clear. Regulating the currents of trade into the Community is a public responsibility, part of the common commercial policy, and which can only be legitimately exercised in accordance with the relevant rules of the Treaty, in particular art. 113 EEC. Private enterprise has no right to usurp this responsability.

A different example of violations of the competition rules by Japanese firms is found in the *Kawasaki motor cycles* [15] and *Pioneer Hi-fi equipment* [16] cases. These are straight forward cases of compartmentilisation of the Common Market by the creation of obstacles, such as export prohibitions, to the export of products from one Member State to another.

In these last cases, some of the addressees of the decisions have been, inter alia, Japanese subsidiaries inside the Community.

Another case is presently in the administrative phase. It concerns the buying up by Western and Japanese aluminium producers of all quantities of aluminium which a number of Eastern European Countries made available for export. Instead of competing for a market share, these countries sold their surplusses to their competitors, grouped together. It is another example of so called orderly marketing but pushed to great length and difficult to reconcile with the proper functioning of the common market.

A final illustration of the comprehensiveness of the competition rules may be found in the system of sanctions on violations of the rules. Those who do so, expose themselves to three risks.

The Treaty, in art. 85 § 2, bases itself first of all on the natural preemince of the law over private contracts and declares all restrictive agreements or concerted practices null and void. As a result, such agreements cannot be enforced in law.

Moreover, art. 87 § 2 litt. a provides a legal basis for administrative fines and penalty payments to be imposed on firms which intentionally or negligently infringe the rules. It is on this basis that article 15 of Regulation 17, which implements art. 85 and 86, has set a maximum of 10% of turnover in the preceding year to the fines which can be imposed.

Imposition of fines is not conditional upon proof that the operator concerned knew that he violated the rules.

The third risk is not a sanction but rather a discouragement. Third parties whose interests are damaged by an infringement may have a claim for dam-

13. OJ L 343 of 12 December 1974 p. 19; *Fourth Report on Competition Policy* p. 50-51.
14. OJ L 29 of 3 February 1975 p. 26; *Fifth Report* p. 34-35. See also *Notice of the Commission on imports of Japanese products* OJ C 111 p. 13 of 21 October 1972.
15. OJ L 16 of 23 January 1979 p. 9.
16. Commission decision of 14 December 1979, not yet published.

ages. Tort actions of this kind lie in all Member States. The rarety with which this remedy is used stems from the difficulty inhaerent to proving injury and should not hide its potential effectiveness.

III. A POTENTIAL FOR FLEXIBILITY

What I have said sofar will convey the impression that the competition rules of the Treaty are basically severe and this is undeniably so. Fortunately the Community as an experiment in innovation, always searches for a proper balance between its very ambitious objectives and what one might call the facts of life. In the domain of competition room for this balance is provided mainly by the power of exemption of art. 85 § 3 which introduces a considerable potential for flexibility in the application of the competition rules. The power of exemption thus moderates the basic severity of the rules themselves[17].

The main idea behind art. 85 § 3 is that certain positive effects of a restrictive agreement may off-set the negative effects which are inhaerent to its nature. Logically, the two sides of the balance are situated on the same level, that of the public interest. This is reflected in the four conditions for exemption:

- there must either be an objectively demonstrable improvement of production or distribution or the agreement must promote technical or economic progress;
- the consumer must obtain a fair share of the resulting benefit;
- the restrictions may not go beyond what is strictly necessary for the attainment of the objective invoked;
- competition must not be eliminated for a substantial part of the products concerned.

Once again, books have been written on the significance of these various conditions. I limit myself here to a few comments.

Beyond the technical characteristics of art. 85 § 3, the first point to stress is that normally it must be interpreted strictly, as otherwise the number of exceptions would smother the interdiction. At the same time, the power of exemption undoubtedly constitutes a policy instrument of the first order. This derives not only from its nature and its context, but also from art. 87 EEC litt. c which clearly shows that for the authors of the Treaty the impact and scope of the competition rules may vary from sector to sector, that is to

17. Other methods of modulating the impact of art. 85 § 1 are:

– the definition of quantitative thresholds below which the interdiction does not operate. See *notice of 27 May 1970 concerning agreements of minor importance.* Agreements which remain below these thresholds need not be notified and qualify, on request, for a negative clearance.

– the definition of criteria for types of cooperation between enterprises which may be presumed to be non restrictive. See notice of 29 July 1968, concerning cooperation between enterprises. In this area also there is no need to notify and a negative clearance may be obtained.

– negative clearances based on art. 2 of regulation 17 for other agreements not coming within the ambit of art. 85 § 1.

– sectorial rules based on art. 87 § 2 litt. 2 or, for agriculture, on art. 42 EEC.

say, may relate the degree of competition within the common market to the particular characteristics of a given sector.

In its practice the Commission has never lost sight of these considerations. The Court also recognises that the maintaining of workable competition is but one of the fundamental objectives of art. 3 EEC [18] which constantly has to be reconciled with the other objectives. As a result, the Commission is not only entitled but even positively obliged to give due consideration to the social and conjunctural circumstances in which it operates its competition policy.

Article 85 § 3 thus understood contains a considerable potential for flexibility. In view of the essential function of competition it is clear however that this flexibility can only be used to accommodate considerations of public policy and not the economic and financial comfort of those who request an exemption. The concepts of 'improvement' and 'progress' used in art. 85 § 3 have an objective content, which cannot be detached from the function of the interdiction of art. 85 § 1. Because of this link restrictive practices as a means of freezing existing – usually national – market positions must be considered as incompatible per se. The permanent protection of inefficient producers is hardly ever compatible with the fundamental objectives of art. 2 of the Treaty. Where such protection becomes a temporary necessity for social or regional reasons, this is a matter for the public authorities and not for the interested firms who are unable to assess correctly the general interest involved. Appropriate time limits, conditions and obligations may serve to adapt the required degree of competition to the conjunctural and structural context in which restrictions are proposed. Industrial and commercial efficiency are important but must be reconciled with the requirements of social justice and social progress in and between all regions of the Community. The complexity of this task is increased by the need, both obvious and continuing, to respect the principles of equal treatment and proportionality.

Interesting illustrations of this approach can be found in most decisions granting or refusing an exemption. Areas in which the chances for an exemption are good are cooperation between small or medium sized operators or cooperation even between big firms in high risk sectors. An example of the latter is the recent exemption [19] of an *agreement between Beecham and Parke Davis* on research and development concerning a novel pharmaceutical product. Such cooperation obviously restricts competition in matters of research and development, which in the pharmaceutical, as in the chemical sector, is particularly competitive. However, in the case under consideration, the chances of a more rapid technical and economic progress, through a combined effort were such that they outweighed the restriction of competion resulting from the agreement. As there were few ancillary and no unnecessary restrictions – the parties remain free to produce and market the product if and when they succeed in developing it – an exemption could be given.

Interesting refusals to exempt can be found in the *Distillers decision* [20] and the *Fedetab decision* [21]. Time is lacking to go into details.

18 Case 26/76 *Metro/Commission*, Cases 1977 p. 1904 para 20 and 21. See also *Hoffman-La Roche* judgment already quoted above.
19. Decision of 17 January 1979, OJ L 70 p. 11 ff of 21 March 1979.
20. Commission decision of 20 December 1977, OJ L 50/16 of 22 February 1978.
21. Commission decision of 20 July 1978, OJ L 224 p. 29 ff of 15 August 1978.

Distillers operated a double pricing system for its whisky and wanted to prevent whisky sold at the lower price in the UK to be exported to the continent, where a higher price was applied.

Fedetab operated a system of agreed wholesale and retail margins for all tobacco products, Belgian, as well as imported. As a result, price competition between producers was strictly limited to the consumer prices. Neither the wholesalers nor retailers could compete between them for market shares. Normally operators in the distribution sector greatly contribute to the openness of a market and constitute an important element of a competitive structure. Here, the competitive impulses from the retail end were blotted out.

Both the Distillers case and the Fedetab case are sub iudice before the European Court in Luxemburg, so I abstain from further comment [22]. It should be clear, however, why the Commission has deemed it impossible to grant exemptions.

Both systems are of course more profitable and more easily manageable for the operators concerned. However, these subjective advantages cannot be assimilated to the objective improvement meant in art. 85 § 3.

Yet another example of the flexibility inhaerent to art. 85 § 3 is provided by the Commission's attitude towards crisis cartels, i.e. cartels designed to remedy crises situations in which a whole sector may find itself. It is well known that a structural overcapacity in an industry may intensify competition to the point where it becomes destructive of basically viable productive forces. In such a situation factory closures are inevitable. Normally the timing and scale of capacity reductions must be decided by each operator individually. Such decisions are at the heart of the competitive potential of each producer and any coordination with other producers in these matters seriously affects competition in the market. Under normal circumstances, industry-wide agreements on the reduction of existing capacities have little chance to obtain an exemption under art. 85 § 3 EEC [23].

However, as you know, the Commission has been faced over the last year and a half with a major case of structural overcapacity namely in the synthetic fibre industry. Structural excess capacity, declining prices and the resulting losses endangered the very existence of many firms and of the employment they provide.

Uncoordinated decisions on closures were clearly going to be irrational, dependent as they would be on the chance elements of financial staying power and purely individual assessment of market prospects. Also, individual closure decisions do not guarantee that the least profitable installations are closed first, which endangers the long term viability of the industry as a whole.

Because of these special circumstances prevailing in the fibre industry, the Commission considered that the need for coordinated decisions on the reduc-

22. The Court has upheld the Commission Decision in *the Distillers Case* by Judgment of 10 July 1980 (case 30/78/).
23. This is of course without prejudice to the much less far reaching agreements on specialisation which two or more firms may conclude and which are more easily accomodated under art. 85 § 3. For examples of such exemptions see *7th Report on Competition Policy*, Brussels 1978 p. 95-97.

tion of the structural excess capacity was such that the requirements of art. 85 § 3 could be met. In other words, in the special circumstances of the fibre industry, the potential for flexibility contained in art. 85 § 3 EEC could be drawn upon.

Nevertheless on another aspect of the agreements concluded by the fibre industry, the Commission refused the exemption. The fibre manufacturers, so as to improve prices, also wanted to regulate competition in the market between them and, to that effect, wanted to regulate intra Community trade. This, the Commission declared to be incompatible with art. 85 § 3, mainly because the very severe limit of litt. b was oversteppened, as nearly all the main producers were involved. The synthetic fibre manufacturers therefore abandoned this part of their agreements and they notified recently an alternative agreement. This is presently being screened.

Particularly in sectors in crisis, competition policy and industrial policy have to be closely coordinated, have to go hand in hand so to speak. The Community, as a very young body politic, has to be particularly careful on this point. An established political entity, such as the Member States individually, such as Japan and the U.S. may even use cartels as a form of industrial policy. For the Community this is a much more delicate operation as the general interest of the Community, centred as it is around the need for unity, relates in much more complex manner to the interests of a particular sector. Therefore, when sectorial crisis arise the Community will normally first try and work out a Community policy, combining considerations of industrial, social, regional and trade policy. This is what the Community did in the steel sector where the ECSC Treaty provided certain specific powers on which a policy of administrative guidance could be based.

Such an approach must be preferred to a policy of leaving the sector concerned, with the help of cartels, to try to solve the difficulties. The assessment of the Community interest is too complex a task to be left to sectoral representatives. The Commission is therefore a little bit sceptical of so-called orderly marketing solutions. This attitude is caused by the Commission's preoccupation with market unity and with the relative fragility of the Communities whole enterprise.

If, for serious reasons, the flow of goods onto the Common Market has to be temporarily regulated, the Commission believes that this is a matter of trade policy to be solved on the governmental level and not by the industry concerned. This point of view the Commission expressed as early as 1972 in its well known notice on the imports of Japanese products.

I like to refer in concluding to the Commission's legislative efforts to give the competition rules the precision and the flexibility they need. Work on a number of group exemptions is in progress, namely

- for certain restrictive clauses contained in licensing contracts
- for certain restrictive agreements in the domaine of maritime transport
- idem in the domain of air transport.

Each of these areas presents its own difficulties but in each of them the Commission tries to strike a realistic balance between the need to preserve the integratory function the Treaty expects from competition and the specific characteristics prevailing in the sectors mentioned.

Admittedly, the competition rules of the EEC do not facilitate the life of the business man. However, especially for outside operators, it is a small price to pay for having such a large market at one's disposal.

Furthermore, the role of competition in our societies is a difficult subject. People's willingness to submit to its sometimes harsh consequences varies from country to country and often reflects a nation's position in the world economy. Thus the role of competition has become a subject of discussion and preoccupation on the world level, as is shown by the results of the Tokyo Round and by the discussions in UNCTAD.

The Commission, in its role as the Community's anti-trust authority, is well aware of this. It therefore constantly tries to combine a proper assessment of the place of competition on the scale of human values with an effective implementation of the Treaty's reliance on competition as an instrument of integration. I think that the Commission's daily administrative practice demonstrates this. If ever one has reason to be in touch with the Commission on the matter, because of a notification and request for exemption, because of a complaint or even because of a suspected infringement, one will see that the Commission deals with these matters in a realistic manner. The Commission always makes a serious attempt to get to the economic heart of the matter and to recognize the political context of our quest for unity. It is this economic and political realism which justifies the understanding with which not only the European Parliament but also industry and commerce concerned looks upon the Commission's efforts.

The Extraterritoriality Application of Competition Law

[7]

Extraterritorial Application of E.C. and U.S. Competition Law

Paul Torremans*

The extraterritorial application of the provisions of competition law on the basis of one or other variant of the effects doctrine is now enshrined in both European Union and United States law. Important differences subsist though.

This phenomenon gives rise to a clash between both legal systems and an agreement has been concluded to smooth the impact of this clash. The agreement did nothing to address the problem at its roots and was on top of that declared illegal by the Court of Justice in its judgment in Case C-327/91. It has now been approved by the Council, but certain problems remain.

A different initiative is required to address the problem. This initiative should operate at the level of both public and private international law.

Introduction

The issue of the extraterritorial application of competition law provisions has given rise to different approaches on both sides of the Atlantic. Extraterritoriality almost became a synonym for conflict in the competition law field. We will analyse both the United States and the Community position in some detail, but this paper will focus on a more theoretical analysis of the problem, its different layers and the different solutions that are required. The U.S.-E.C. co-ordination and co-operation agreement, both before and after the intervention of the Court of Justice in case C-327/91, will be at the centre of this analysis. Can such an attempt to replace the conflict model by a co-operation model be successful?

Extraterritoriality in United States competition law

The early stages

The strictly territorial application of the Sherman Act advocated by Supreme Court Justice Oliver Wendell Holmes in *American Banana Co. v. United Fruit Co.*[1] was abandoned very soon afterwards. It was replaced by the principle that United States Courts had extraterritorial jurisdiction over foreign undertakings when a direct effect on commerce and some conduct within the United States could be shown.[2] The effects doctrine was fully embraced in *United States v. Aluminium Company of America (Alcoa)*[3] when Judge Learned Hand stated that:

> "On the other hand, it is settled law . . . that any state may impose liabilities, even upon persons not within its allegiance, for conduct outside its borders that has consequences within its borders which the state reprehends, and these liabilities other states will ordinarily recognise."[4]

As a result U.S. anti-trust law was to be applied to each anti-competitive agreement concluded with

* Faculty of Law, The University of Leicester.

[1] *American Banana Co. v. United Fruit Co.* (1909) 213 U.S. 347.

[2] *United States v. American Tobacco Co.* (1911) 221 U.S. 106, 31 S. Ct. 632, 55 L. Ed. 663 and *United States v. Sisal Sales Corp.* (1927) 274 U.S. 268.

[3] *United States v. Aluminium Corp. of America* 148 F. 2d 416 (2d Cir. 1945).

[4] *Ibid.*, at 443.

the intention to affect United States commerce if the agreement did effectively have that effect. The fact that the undertakings concerned were situated outside the United States or that the agreement was concluded outside the United States was held to be immaterial.[5]

Timberlane and Mannington Mills

The rather crude Alcoa-test triggered off a series of negative reactions at international level.[6]

The fact that other jurisdiction necessarily have certain interests at stake too when U.S. anti-trust law is applied extraterritorially was acknowledged by the United States Court of Appeals for the Ninth Circuit in the *Timberlane* case[7] when it read a requirement for the judge to consider and balance the interests of the different governments involved into anti-trust law.[8]

Establishing a new test Judge Choy stated:

> "A tripartite analysis seems to be indicated. As acknowledged above, the antitrust laws require in first instance that there be some effect—actual or intended—on American foreign commerce before the federal courts may legitimately exercise subject matter jurisdiction under those statutes.
>
> Secondly, a greater showing of burden of restraint may be necessary to demonstrate that the effect is sufficiently large to present a cognizable injury to the plaintiffs and, therefore, a civil violation of antitrust laws.
>
> Thirdly, there is the additional question which is unique to the international setting of whether the interests of and the links to, the United States—including the magnitude of the effect on American foreign commerce—are sufficiently strong *vis-à-vis* those of other nations, to justify an assertion of extraterritorial authority."[9]

The latter step introduced the consideration of policy variables and the evaluation and the balancing of the relevant considerations in each case.[10] This approach had originally been suggested by Kingman Brewster as "a jurisdictional rule of reason".[11] The list of factors to be weighed in the balancing test was subsequently enlarged in the *Mannington Mills* case,[12] when Judge Weiss set forth a non-exhaustive list.

Hartford Fire Insurance

Recently the Supreme Court clarified the way in which United States anti-trust law applies extraterritorially when in *Hartford Fire Insurance Co. v. California*[13] London based re-insurers were

[5] Stephens, "'Reasonable' approaches to the issue of extraterritorial jurisdiction—the US anti-trust example", in Maitland-Walker (ed.) *International Antitrust Law (Vol. 2)*, (1984), at 103; Rubin, "USA—Commentary—Chapter 5 International Enforcement", in Gijlstra (ed.), *Competition Law in Western Europe and the USA* (1984), at USA.C–114–115, Neale and Goyder, *The Antitrust Laws of the USA*, (1980), 3rd ed., at 349.

[6] See Demaret, "L'extraterritorialité des lois et les relations transatlantiques: une question de droit ou de diplomatie?", 21 RTDE (1985), 1–39, at 12 and Cohen-Tanugi, "Les juridictions américaines face aux lois étrangères interdisant la communication de renseignements économiques", (1983) 72 RCDIP, 9 *et seq.*

[7] *Timberlane Lumber Co. v. Bank of America* 549 F. 2d 597 (9th Cir. 1976).

[8] Stephens, *supra*, n. 5 at 105 and Neale and Goyder, *supra*, n. 5 at 350–351.

[9] *Timberlane*, at 613.

[10] Rubin, *supra*, n. 5 at USA.C–122–123; Neale and Goyder, *supra*, n. 5 at 350–351.

[11] Brewster, *Antitrust and American Business Abroad* (1958); see also Attwood and Brewster, *Antitrust and American Business Abroad* (1981).

[12] *Mannington Mills Inc. v. Congoleum Corp.* 595 F. 1287 (3rd Cir. 1979).

[13] *Hartford Fire Insurance Co. v. California* 113 S. Ct. 2891 (1993).

accused of infringing the Sherman Act. The re-insurers had agreed with a number of United States operators in the insurance business to boycott general liability insurers that used a certain type of forms and the effect of this conduct in the United States was that certain types of insurance coverage became unavailable. Their activity took place outside the United States and it complied with United Kingdom legislation. The majority found that the Sherman Act applied to this foreign conduct, because it was meant to produce and it did in fact produce a substantial effect in the United States.[14] The majority rejected the Mannington Mills approach in as far as it would have suggested that elements of international comity formed part of the rule on the basis of which the court takes jurisdiction.[15] In their view comity could only be taken into account once the court had established its jurisdiction. And even in such a case it would only influence the outcome if there existed a true conflict between United States law and the foreign law. The latter problem can only arise when the foreign law requires the defendant to act in a fashion prohibited by United States law or in any other circumstances where it is impossible for the defendant to comply with both his or her domestic law and with United States law. The fact that a certain action or conduct is lawful or even encouraged in the foreign state will not, in itself, lead to the non-application of the provisions of the Sherman Act.[16]

It could be argued that this judgment signals a return to a rather crude form of the effects doctrine. Such a "true conflict" will indeed not arise in the vast majority of cases and this means that comity will play no role at all in these cases. This is even more worrying as the court based its "true conflict" analysis on sections 403 and 415 of the Restatement (Third).[17] These are general provisions and do not limit the analysis to antitrust law. This "true conflict" analysis seems however to contradict earlier judgments of the Supreme Court on the comity issue[18] and is hard to reconcile with the plain text of the Restatement (third).[19] It also bears a striking resemblance to the approach adopted in foreign sovereign compulsion defence cases,[20] although it should be obvious that the principle of comity is wider in scope than the narrow concept underlying the foreign sovereign compulsion theory and that both principles should not be confused. It is submitted that the approach taken by the majority is wrong,[21] even if one takes the separation of powers between the Executive Branch and the Courts into account. It can be accepted that the Executive Branch, before bringing a suit, has determined "that the interests of the United States supersede the interests of any foreign sovereign and that the challenged conduct is more harmful to the United States than any injury to foreign relations that might result from the antitrust action".[22] But this argument definitely does not cover cases brought by or involving private plaintiffs, such as *Hartford Fire Insurance*.[23] At least in the latter cases the courts should effectively consider the wider comity issue. It is submitted that that should also be done in the

[14] *Ibid.* at 2909.

[15] *Ibid.* at 2910; Justice Scalia dissented strongly on this point and would see international comity as an integral part of the rule on the basis of which jurisdiction is determined; see also Fairley "Extraterritorial Assertions of Intellectual Property Rights", in G. Stewart, M. Tawfik and M. Irish (eds.) *International Trade & Intellectual Property* (1994), 141–153, at 146.

[16] *Hartford Fire Insurance Co. v. California* (1993) 113 S. Ct. 2891, at 2910–2911; see also Robertson and Demetriou, "'But that was in another country. . . ': The extraterritorial application of US antitrust laws in the Supreme Court", (1994) 43 ICLQ, 417–425, at 421.

[17] Restatement (Third) of the Foreign Relations Law of the United States (1987).

[18] See *Société Nationale Industrielle Aérospatiale v. United States District Court* (1987) 482 U.S. 522, 543–544 and *Asahi Metal Indus. Co. v. Superior Court* (1987) 480 U.S. 102, 115.

[19] See *infra* n. 24 and the accompanying section of the text.

[20] Griffin, "US Supreme Court Encourages Extraterritorial Application of US Antitrust Laws", 21 *International Business Lawyer* (1993), 389–393, at 391.

[21] See also Highet, Kahale and Gill, "Note under Hartford Fire Insurance Co. v. California", (1994), 88 A.J.I.L. 109–114, p. 114.

[22] U.S. Department of Justice, *Antitrust Enforcement Guidelines for International Operations* (1988), pp. 31–32.

[23] The guidelines seem to recognise this at p. 33.

former circumstances. The decision reached by the Executive Branch should be no more than a powerful factor in the comity interest balancing exercise. If one accepts with the majority in *Hartford Fire Insurance* that the rules of the Restatement (third) determine the way in which the comity discretion operates once the court has taken jurisdiction, the reasonableness test of section 403(1) and (2) should allow the court to proceed with the case if on the basis of comity the exercise of its jurisdiction would be unreasonable. Sections 403(3) and 415 only come into play in cases where the exercise of jurisdiction is reasonable and are there to allow a way out if compliance with the rules of all the States involved is impossible.

The Hartford Fire Insurance approach will not facilitate matters in international antitrust cases. Foreign countries will have substantial difficulties in accepting the extraterritorial application of United States antitrust laws on this basis, especially if one takes into account that the Supreme Court seems to recognise the need for restraint in its own domestic federal system.[24] Why should foreign countries accept the fact that the rules operating in relation to them and their companies are harsher than those which operate when economic players of different states within the United States are involved.?

Extraterritoriality in European competition law

The Dyestuffs case

The *Dyestuffs* case offered the Court of Justice its first opportunity to rule on the extraterritorial application of competition law.[25]

Advocate General Mayras favoured the acceptance of the effects doctrine and specified the requirements for an effect to trigger the extraterritorial application of Articles 85 and 86. The effect should imply a direct and immediate restriction of competition and it should be foreseeable by the infringing undertaking. He did not require any specific intention in relation to the effect.[26]

The judgment of the Court is based on the economic-entity-doctrine though which justifies the fact that the Commission had taken jurisdiction on the basis of the territoriality principle. The facts of this case offered that escape route and the judgment does not contain any explicit ruling on the existence of an effects doctrine based extraterritoriality principle under European law.

The Wood Pulp case

Sixteen years after the *Dyestuffs* case the *Wood Pulp* case[27] provided the Court with an opportunity to review its position in relation to the extraterritorial application of European competition law.

In its *Wood Pulp* decision[28] the Commission established its jurisdiction to rule on an agreement concluded outside the Community by undertakings that were not situated in the Community by stating broadly that:

[24] *FTC v. Ticor Title Ins. Co.* (1992) 112 S. Ct. 2169; on the basis of which one could argue that the Supreme Court attaches more weight to the jurisdiction of U.S. States than to that of foreign sovereign States; see Robertson and Demetriou, *supra*, n. 16, at 424.

[25] Case 48/69, *Imperial Chemical Industries Ltd v. Commission of the European Communities*, [1972] E.C.R. 619.

[26] Case 48/69, *Imperial Chemical Industries Ltd v. Commission of the European Communities*, [1972] E.C.R. 619, opinion of Advocate General Mayras, at 687–694.

[27] Cases 89, 104, 114, 116–117, 125–129/85, *A. Ahlström OY and Others v. Commission of the European Communities*, [1988] E.C.R. 5193, [1988] 4 C.M.L.R. 901.

[28] [1984], O.J. L27/85.

284 Extraterritorial Application of E.C. and U.S. Competition Law

> "Article 85 of the EEC treaty applies to restrictive practices which may affect trade between Member States even if the undertakings and associations which are parties to the restrictive practices are established or have their headquarters outside the Community, and even if the restrictive practices in question also affect markets outside the EEC".[29]

The arguments on the basis of which the Commission established its jurisdiction were clearly based on the effects-doctrine. The essential element of the whole construction was that if the effects of the agreements and concerted practices in the Community were intended, direct and substantial, Article 85 would apply to undertakings situated outside the Community. The Commission argued that the economic effect was substantial and intended on the basis of the fact that "shipments affected by these agreements and practices amounted to about two-thirds of total shipments of bleached sulphate wood pulp to the EEC and some 60% of EEC consumption" and that "the agreements and practices appear to have applied to at least the vast majority of the sales of the relevant product by the parties during the relevant periods."[30] On the point of the requirement that the effect had to be a direct effect the Commission noted that the producers were "exporting directly or doing business within the Community"[31] and that the concerted conduct "concerned shipments made directly to buyers in the EEC or sales made in the EEC to buyers there".[32]

In the Commission's view the concerted conduct must also be implemented inside the Community. This additional requirement can be seen as an attempt to fashion some territorial link with the Community. Implementation was defined as trading directly into the Community or using sales offices or agents to trade in the Community. The latter element was a clear reference to the *Dyestuffs* case, while the first element has as a result that jurisdiction did not arise from the concerted practice of the pulp companies, which was situated outside the Community, but from their conduct (the direct trading) in the Community in implementing the practice.[33] It is interesting to add to this that the economic-entity-doctrine could not be applied in this case, because depending on the pulp company involved there were either no subsidiaries in the EEC or the control exercised over them was not substantial enough.

Advocate General Darmon expressed strong support for the effects-doctrine.[34] He argued that Article 85 applied whenever an effect on inter-state trade was found, without the imposition of any additional requirements concerning nationality or geographic location of the undertakings. It remained however uncertain whether the "effect" referred to in Article 85 constituted, strictly speaking, a basis of jurisdiction.[35]

He suggested a criterion of qualified effect, because an inflexible territorial approach is no longer suitable in a modern economically interdependent world.[36] Such an effect within the Community should be direct and immediate, reasonably foreseeable and substantial.[37]

[29] *ibid.*
[30] *ibid.*
[31] *ibid.*
[32] *ibid.*
[33] See Lange and Sandage, "The Woodpulp Decision and its implications for the scope of EC competition law", (1989) 26 C.M.L. Rev., 137–159.
[34] Cases 89, 104, 114, 116–117, 125–129/85, *A. Ahlström OY and Others v. Commission of the European Communities*, [1988] E.C.R. 5193, opinion of Advocate General Darmon, 5214 *et seq.*
[35] See Goldman and Lyon-Caen, *Droit commercial européen* (1983), 4th ed., at 872, for an affirmative answer.
[36] The Advocate General refers with approval to Idot, *Le contrôle des pratiques restrictives dans les échanges internationaux* (1981), Dissertation University of Paris II.
[37] Reference is made to the opinion of Advocate General Mayras in the *Dyestuffs* case, *supra*, n. 26.

At first sight the Court's judgment[38] seemed to endorse the effects-doctrine, while dismissing any territorial link as immaterial. But it is extremely important to note that the Court did not use the term effects-doctrine and spelled out an implementation requirement. It is the implementation of an agreement or a concerted practice in the Community that gives jurisdiction to the Commission. Implementation is defined in terms of engaging in a transaction with a Community customer and in this sense an agreement is implemented in the Community when its subject matter involves the price, quantity or quality or a product sold to a Community customer. In the latter point one finds the reason why the Court did not uphold the Commission's decision in so far as it concerned the KEA-association, because the association itself did not engage in a transaction with a Community customer.

On balance the Court did not endorse the unrestricted application of the effects-doctrine. The KEA passage of the judgment indicates that the effect should be direct, and in addition to our earlier comments it must be added that the implementation requirement also seems to imply that the effect is substantial and intended.[39]

The Court's judgment also seems to suggest that Article 85 will only apply to non-EEC undertakings if there is an actual effect in the Community, while for Community undertakings even conduct having the object of restraining competition will infringe Article 85.[40] This means that an agreement that has not (yet) been executed only creates problems for Community undertakings.[41]

In the *Woodpulp* case the Commission conducted extensive consultations with third countries that had an interest in this case. It remains unclear if this forms a legal limitation on the Commission's powers or if this is just a discretionary move by the Commission which does not need to have any influence on the actual proceedings, because the Court did not express any opinion as far as these comity-consultations are concerned.[42]

Some Elements of Public International Law[43]

The fundamental principle of public international law that a State can base its jurisdiction on the nationality-principle or on the territoriality-principle is not disputed.[44] The Permanent Court of International Justice recognized the possibility of extraterritorial jurisdiction in the *Lotus* case.[45]

While the basic rule concerning enforcement jurisdiction limits this kind of jurisdiction to the territory of the state concerns,[46] at least as far as enforcement implies the exercise of coercion,[47] the

[38] Cases 89, 104, 114, 116–117, 125–129/85, *A. Ahlström OY and Others v. Commission of the European Communities*, [1988] E.C.R. 5193, [1988] 4 C.M.L.R. 901.

[39] Compare: Ferry, "Towards Completing the Charm: The Woodpulp Judgment", (1989) E.C.L.R., 58–73; see also R. Whish, *Competition Law* (1993), 3rd ed., at 381–382.

[40] See Case 123/83, *Bureau national interprofessionel du Cognac v. Clair*, [1985] E.C.R. 391 and Case 40/73, *Suiker Unie v. Commission of the European Communities*, [1975] E.C.R. 1663.

[41] Lange and Sandage, *supra*, n. 33.

[42] *Ibid*, at 164–165.

[43] For a more detailed approach see: Demaret, *supra*, n. 6, at 24–36; see also Slot and Grabandt, "Extraterritoriality and Jurisdiction", (1986) 23 C.M.L. Rev.; Slater, "L'application extraterritoriale du droit communautaire", [1986] Cahiers de Droit européen, 309–324, at 312–315; Goldman and Lyon-Caen, *supra*, n. 35, at 872 *et seq*.; Rosenthal and Knighton, *National Laws and International Commerce* (1982); Kegel and Seidl-Hohenveldern, "On the territoriality principle in public international law", (1982) Hastings Int'l & Comp. L. Rev., 245; Meessen, "Antitrust jurisdiction under customary international law", (1984) 78 A.J.I.L., 783.

[44] Whish, *supra*, n. 39, at 370–371.

[45] *The Lotus* P.C.I.J. Ser. A No. 10 Ser. C No. 13–11 September 7, 1927.

[46] Slater, *supra*, n. 43, at 312.

[47] Goldman and Lyon-Caen, *supra*, n. 35, at 882 and 886.

basis for prescriptive jurisdiction is unfortunately less clear. One approach consists of reading the *Lotus* judgment as an authorisation for States to enact extraterritorially applicable prescriptive legislation, unless a prohibitive rule of international law opposes such. This approach is not as liberal as it might appear to be at first glance, as international comity clearly forms part of international law and could be seen as an example of a prohibitive rule. A second approach lays down a limited set of accepted grounds of jurisdiction and defines their limits in a second phase.[48]

A third approach starts from the double assumption that international law does not limit the eventual basis of prescriptive jurisdiction but that it doesn't leave it to each state to define the limits of its prescriptive jurisdiction either. It is essential that a sufficient link is shown between the state and the situation over which it wants to have jurisdiction. If such a link is demonstrated that state's exercise of jurisdiction is legitimate under international law, even if another state demonstrates a more substantial link with the case. The only additional requirement is the unconditional respect of the rule of non-interference in the affairs of any other state.[49] The only argument against this opinion is based on its flexibility. It is indeed arguably the case that this flexibility is too large and that this makes it impossible to apply it as part of a rule of international law. If such turns out to be the case, preference should be given to the first approach, which seems to be closer to the intentions of the international judges in the *Lotus* case.[50]

If one has a closer look at the effects doctrine it appears that one could consider the effects-doctrine as a legitimate basis of jurisdiction under international law if one accepts that international law does in principle not put limits to the prescriptive jurisdiction of a state. When the doctrine is accepted, the effects are generally required to be direct, substantial and reasonably foreseeable.[51] The opposite position is taken by those who only recognise a limited number of grounds of jurisdiction, namely nationality and territoriality.[52] They see no possibility to consider the effects-doctrine as originally laid down in *Alcoa*[53] as an application of the territoriality-principle. This analysis is based on international criminal law, under which the principle of objective territoriality only includes those effects that are effectively a part of the crime. The effects where upon jurisdiction has been based in antitrust cases do not come in the latter category and they are a more indirect type of effect. It should however be observed that, even if the rules of criminal international law are as clear as suggested,[54] they cannot be applied as such to antitrust cases.[55] The economic particularities as well as the aims of competition law should also be considered.[56] A tentative conclusion could be that at least there is no waterproof argument against the effects-doctrine in international law and that a moderate version of it could be accepted.[57] This would grant States prescriptive jurisdiction and allow them to legislate in an extraterritorial way. In practice this means that national rules in areas such as competition law

[48] Demaret, *supra*, n. 6, at 26–27 and Slater, *supra*, n. 43, at 312–315.

[49] Mann "The Doctrine of Jurisdiction in International Law", 111 *Receuil des Cours* (1964), 9 *et seq.*, at 43 and Meessen, *supra*, n. 43, at 800.

[50] Demaret, *supra*, n. 6, at 27–28.

[51] *Ibid.*, at 31–32.

[52] Jennings, "Extraterritorial Jurisdiction in the United States Antitrust Laws", (1957) 33 *British Yearbook of Internatioanl Law*, 146.

[53] *United States v. Aluminium Corp. of America* 148 F. 2d 416 (2d Cir. 1945).

[54] See Akehurst, "Jurisdiction in International Law", 46 *British Yearbook of International Law* (1972–1973), 145.

[55] Demaret, *supra*, n. 6, at 32.

[56] Goldman, "Les champs d'application territoriale des lois sur la concurrence", (1969) *Recueil des Cours*, 637, at 698–706.

[57] See the opinion of Advocate General Darmon in the *Woodpulp* case, Cases 89, 104, 114, 116–117, 125–129/85. *A. Ahlström OY and Others v. Commission of the European Communities* [1988] E.C.R. 5193 and [1988] 4 C.M.L.R. 901.

can also cover cases in which effects are felt within the State even if that State is unable to claim jurisdiction on the basis of nationality or on a territorial basis.

A comparative evaluation

It could be argued that both the European Community and the United States apply some form of effects-doctrine. Such a statement implies that the Community has adopted the qualified effects-doctrine, which was suggested in *Woodpulp* by Advocate General Darmon. I do not think that the *Woodpulp* case can be seen as an unconditional endorsement of that view. It is true that the implementation doctrine closely resembles the effects-doctrine and borrows a great deal from it, but the additional implementation requirement is a crucial one. The Court maintained a, maybe slightly artificial, link with the territoriality principle by requiring implementation in the Community.[58] Implementation in the Community affects without doubt competition within the Community. In this respect trading into the Community is not different from trading on the Common Market. These are indications that the Court built in an element of self-restraint, which is without doubt of assistance in avoiding an open conflict resulting from the extraterritorial application of competition law.[59] Such an additional self-restraining requirement is not found in United States antitrust law.[60]

Could the United States style comity principle be called the equivalent of such an element of self-constraint though? It is submitted that it cannot. *Hartford Fire Insurance* reduced comity almost to non-existence and even if the courts are to apply it the debate will become heated and this application will still seem to be problematic. The courts are seemingly ill-equipped to deal with it. There is the conflict between the Executive Branch, that is maybe in a better position to appreciate all factors,[61] and the courts as to who should decide on the comity point. There is also the difference between these cases and private suit cases which does not seem to be reflected in the rule. Comity as applied by the courts does not seem to be a workable solution and does no longer play a self-constraining role in practice after *Hartford Fire Insurance*. One can on the basis of this analysis only approve the choice made by the Court of Justice not to include comity in the European approach at this level in the light of its application problems which we have highlighted.[62]

It is clear that this difference in approach gives rise to conflicts. And a strictly unilateral inclusion of a form of comity or an additional implementation requirement is clearly not sufficient to avoid or remedy these conflicts.

There are two further layers to this comparison though and these require a more theoretical approach. First, one has to turn to the basis in public international law which is used to justify the extraterritorial scope of the legislative initiatives in the competition law area. Justice Scalia, when writing for the four to five minority in *Hartford Fire Insurance*, seemed to rely on what we described as our first public international law approach. Jurisdiction to legislate extraterritorially does only exist in so far as there is no clash with a prohibitive principle or rule of public international law, such as the international comity principle. This means that the provisions of the Sherman Act are only

[58] Compare: van der Esch, "Some aspects of 'extra-territorial' infringement in EEC competition rules", in Hawk (ed.), *Antitrust and trade policy in the United States and the European Community* (1986), at 287 *et seq*.

[59] See also Robertson and Demetriou, *supra*, n. 16, at 423.

[60] Although it may be hard to imagine a case wherein an effect is shown to be direct and substantial and U.S. law could be applied but where there is no implementation in the United States, it is clear that such a case would be the most offending one and that the addition of the implementation requirement helps to avoid that that situation ever arises.

[61] Roth, "Reasonable Extraterritoriality: Correcting the 'Balance of Interests'", (1992) 41 I.C.L.Q., 245–286, at 278.

[62] See Robertson and Demetriou, *supra*, n. 16, at 423–424; the Commission engages in informal consultations though.

extraterritorial in scope in so far as they do not go against international comity. Both the majority in *Hartford Fire Insurance* and the European legislature relied on our third approach. The majority in *Hartford Fire Insurance* found the substantial link which is required under this approach in the substantial effect of the conduct in the United States,[63] while the Court of Justice seemed to indicate that implementation in the Community met the substantial link requirement.[64] It is submitted that the effect link is not sufficiently strong to qualify as a substantial link which justifies the extraterritorial scope of the legislation concerned. It rather amounts only to a minimal link with the U.S., especially if no other links with that State exist, and they cannot as such justify the exercise of extraterritorial legislative authority. The European approach provides for a stronger link as it requires not only that an effect is found in the Community. The anti-competitive conduct must also have been implemented in the Community.

The second additional layer could be called the private international law layer. One does indeed have to decide which court has jurisdiction and which law will be applied, once one accepts that the legislation exists, because these extraterritoriality cases necessarily involve one or more foreign parties and foreign conduct or activity. The extraterritorial scope of the legislations is reflected in the jurisdiction rules. Jurisdiction is therefore taken on the basis of the existence of effects within the jurisdiction or on the basis of effects and implementation within the jurisdiction respectively. The question whether an international comity discretion to decline jurisdiction does exist is the real issue at this stage. We have argued above that such a discretion should exist under the American Restatement (third), even though the majority in *Hartford Fire Insurance* reduced it to the narrow true conflict rule. It is submitted that this does not only represent an arguably wrong interpretation of U.S. law, but that it is also unworkable in combination with the approach the same judges adopted in relation to the public international law issue. This combined approach does not impose serious restrictions on the cases which can be brought before the courts and it does not allow the courts to throw out those cases that would result in a serious clash with other States, whose substantial interests would be affected.

Under European law the situation is not clear at all. There is no clear rule concerning such a discretion and the Court of Justice did not comment on the Commission initiative to set up a practice of international consultation. The result or legal value of the latter is not clear either. The role of the discretion is less urgent here as the grounds on which jurisdiction is taken are narrower in scope, which should eliminate most of the undesirable cases, but the existence of a discretion may nevertheless still be desirable. When the jurisdiction question has received a positive answer our attention should turn briefly to the applicable law issue. Briefly only though, because the answer is a uniform and easy one. Competition law provisions are the perfect example of mandatory rules, both in Europe and in the U.S. The forum will therefore necessarily apply its own competition law as soon as it takes jurisdiction.[65]

All these differences have their importance when an attempt to resolve the extraterritoriality conflict between the U.S. and Europe is made, even if they may not seem to be terribly important in practice at first sight. We will now turn to the attempted solution, but we will return to these issues when we will analyse the value and the impact of the attempted solution.

[63] *Hartford Fire Insurance Co. v. California* (1993) 113 S. Ct. 2891.

[64] See Cases 89, 104, 114, 116–117, 125–129/85, *A. Ahlström OY and Others v. Commission of the European Communities*, [1988] E.C.R. 5193, [1988] 4 C.M.L.R. 901, discussed *supra*.

[65] See Cheshire and North's, *Private International Law* (1992), 12th ed., at 496–503.

The E.C.-U.S. Agreement

In an attempt to solve the extraterritoriality conflict the European Commission concluded an Agreement Regarding the Application of Competition Laws with the United States on September 23, 1991.[66] The agreement aimed to promote co-operation and co-ordination.[67]

The parties agreed to notify one another whenever their respective competition authorities became aware that their enforcement activities, of which a non-exhaustive list is given in the agreement, could affect important interests of the other party.[68] An exchange of relevant information was also planned and regular meetings between officials were institutionalised.[69] The agreement provided for co-ordination of these activities in cases in which both parties have an interest in pursuing enforcement activities. One party could, *e.g.* gather information for the other party.[70]

Comity played an important role in the agreement. Article 6 provided for the normal negative form of comity. Both parties would take each other's interests into account when pursuing their competition law enforcement activities. More important however, and a novelty in this type of agreements, was Article 5 which provided for active comity. The party affected by anti-competitive behaviour on its territory could request the other party to undertake appropriate enforcement action. Such a request has to be considered and it had to be responded to.[71] It is submitted that the Commission had no authority to agree to the positive comity clause.[72] The Commission's competition law powers are delegated to it by the Council and the limits of Article 3(2) of Regulation 17[73] are not wide enough in scope to include the positive comity clause. The United States is not a Member State, neither do they have a legitimate interest, because such an interest should be both significant and reasonably direct.[74] At most they have an indirect interest. This excludes them from the category of plaintiffs, subject to a modification of Regulation 17 by the Council. All they can do is volunteer information to the Commission, but the agreement clearly went beyond that.[75]

The agreement explicitly provided that its provisions did not affect the existing laws in any way and a confidentiality clause allowed a party not to provide information whose disclosure is prohibited by law or whose disclosure would be inconsistent with important interests of that party.[76] Two conclusions are possible on this basis. One is that on the basis of the existing competition law provisions the Commission would have to refrain from implementing major parts of the agreement and would be restricted severely in the amount of detailed information it could exchange with the United States due to the confidential character attached to it.[77] In this hypothesis the agreement would loose much if not all of its practical importance and value. A second conclusion is that Articles

[66] [1991] 4 C.M.L.R. 823–831 and (1991) 30 I.L.M. 1487.
[67] Article 1(1).
[68] Article 2.
[69] Article 3.
[70] Article 4.
[71] Articles 5 and 6.
[72] Walker, "Extraterritorial Application of U.S. Antitrust Laws: The Effect of the European Community—United States Antitrust Agreement", (1992) 33 *Harvard International Law Journal*, 583–591, at 590.
[73] Regulation 17/1962, [1967] J.O. No. 13/204.
[74] Kerse, *EEC Anti-Trust Procedure* (1988), 2nd ed., at 4.19.
[75] Riley, "Nailing the Jellyfish: The Illegality of the EC/US Government Competition Agreement", [1992] 3 E.C.L.R. 101, at 106.
[76] Articles 9 and 8 respectively.
[77] Riley, *supra*, n. 75, at 108–109 and Ham, "International Cooperation in the Anti-Trust Field and in Particular the Agreement between the United States of America and the Commission of the European Communities", (1993) 30 C.M.L. Rev. 571, at 588.

8 and 9 were nothing more than clauses of style. In that case the Commission contemplated to act *ultra vires*.

All this left the agreement on shaky ground, but the real threat to it was the power of the argument that the Commission was not competent to conclude it in the first place.[78] France asked the Court of Justice to annul the agreement on this ground, while also referring to the positive comity and confidentiality arguments raised above.[79] The main incompetence argument was based on Article 228 of the Treaty. On this basis the Commission negotiates for the Community, while the Council binds the Union by concluding the international agreements, unless the Treaty explicitly derogates from this principle[80] or unless the Council delegates its power to the Commission in a certain area. France argued that no such delegation took place in this area, because Regulation 17, while entrusting the implementation of the Community's competition policy to the Commission, did not contain any delegation of the Council's legislative powers. Advocate General Tesauro accepted the arguments put forward by France[81] and the Court of Justice followed its Advocate General and annulled the Act through which the Commission concluded the agreement. The Court pointed out that Article 228 requires an agreement to produce legal effects. This agreement clearly did produce legal effects,[82] because it could, for example, require the Commission to start an investigation into certain anti-competitive practices or to close an investigation on comity grounds. In such a situation Article 210 of the Treaty leads to the conclusion that only the Community can bind itself in an international agreement, as legal personality was given to the Community as a whole.[83] The Community would indeed incur liability at international level in the event of non-performance of the agreement,[84] because this agreement came within the definition which the Vienna Convention gives of an agreement between a State and an international organisation.[85] Under Article 228 this leads to the conclusion that only the Council was empowered to conclude the agreement. This analysis by the Court did not leave any room for the Commission's argument that this was a strictly administrative agreement and that it was empowered to conclude agreements that come in this less important category. The Court ruled that the Commission had acted *ultra vires* in concluding the agreement. Having annulled the Act through which the Commission concluded the agreement on this ground, the Court found it not necessary to discuss the positive comity and confidentiality issues.[86]

The Commission was not prepared to shelve the agreement however. This lead to the Decision of the Council and the Commission of April 10, 1995[87] which re-introduces the agreement. In order to

[78] Riley, *supra*, n. 75, at 103–105 and Ham, *supra*, n. 77, at 579–580.

[79] Case C–327/91 *French Republic v. Commission of the European Communities*, [1994] E.C.R. I–3641 and [1994] 5 C.M.L.R. 517, the Netherlands and Spain joined France in this case.

[80] The Commission's argument to the contrary which relied on the linguistic difference between the term vested which is found in the Treaty and the term conferred which would have indicated that the Commission's powers were restricted to those found in the Treaty itself, was rejected by the Court, see Case C–327/91 *French Republic v. Commission of the European Communities*, [1994] E.C.R. I–3461 and [1994] 5 C.M.L.R. 517, at 544–545.

[81] Conclusion of Advocate General Tesauro in Case C–327/91 *French Republic v. Commission of the European Communities*, [1994] E.C.R. I–3641 and [1994] 5 C.M.L.R. 517, at 520 *et seq*.

[82] Case C–327/91 *French Republic v. Commission of the European Communities*, [1994] E.C.R. I–3641 and [1994] 5 C.M.L.R. 517, at 542.

[83] *Ibid.*, at 543.

[84] *Ibid.*

[85] Article 2(1)(a)(i) of the Vienna Convention of March 21, 1986 on the Law of Treaties between States and International Organisations or between International Organisations.

[86] Case C–327/91 *French Republic v. Commission of the European Communities*, [1994] E.C.R. I–3641 and [1994] 5 C.M.L.R. 517, at 546.

[87] Decision of the Council and the Commission of April 10, 1995 concerning the conclusion of the Agreement between the European Communities and the Government of the United States of America regarding the application of their competition laws [1995] O.J. L 95/45.

conform with the Court's judgment in case C-327/91 the Council binds the European Community under the Treaty of Rome, while the Commission binds the Community under the Coal and Steel Treaty. This Decision simply rectifies the competence problem which came to light in case C-327/91 and the agreement is retroactively approved. The substantive law clauses of the agreement remain unchanged. This means that while the competence issue may have been addressed the positive comity and confidentiality clauses still give rise to the same problems. In an attempt to address these issues the agreement is now accompanied by an exchange of interpretative letters.[88] We will now turn to these problems and analyse them in more detail.

The confidentiality issue was raised by the French and Spanish Governments and it was discussed by Advocate General Tesauro. Article 20 of Regulation 17 forms the cornerstone of this discussion. It contains the principle of secrecy in relation to all information which the Commission acquires during its competition law enforcement proceedings. The Advocate General saw no possibility for the Commission to fulfill its obligations of notification, provision of information and co-ordination under the provisions of the agreement without disclosing any confidential information. While the Court of Justice, having declared the agreement, *ultra vires*, on other grounds, did not find it necessary to address this point, the new version of the agreement is accompanied by an exchange of interpretative letters in which it is made clear that the Community provisions on secrecy need to be respected and that they take precedence over Articles 2, 3 and 5 of the agreement. In practice the latter will happen in the majority of cases and it is submitted that Advocate General Tesauro was right when he concluded that;

> " . . . [that] would lead to the non-application of the Agreement so far as the major provisions are concerned, ultimately emptying it of the whole of its substance".[89]

The exchange of interpretative letters also allows the Commission to inform the Member-States of its dealings with its United States counterparts.[90] This may not be of fundamental importance for the effectiveness of the agreement, but it brings it in line with normal European practice in this area.

The fact that the agreement obliges the Commission to take action at the request of the United States authorities is rather more important. This gives them the right to apply to the Commission, while Article 3(2) of Regulation 17 restricts the power to apply to the Member States and any natural or legal person with a legitimate interest. One cannot call the United States a Member State and it cannot be accepted that the United States authorities act as agents for the United States natural or legal persons that may have a legitimate interest because the effects of the anti-competitive conduct which is at the basis of the application affected them. The Commission argued that it would take action on the basis of information which had been volunteered by the United States authorities. This argument does not make sense, as it would also apply in relation to the Member States and all other parties with a legitimate interest. In the end it is always the Commission's role to initiate formal proceedings. The provisions of the agreement clearly put the United States authorities in the same category as the Member States and third parties with a legitimate interest. They also provide for certain guarantees to make sure that the application is indeed seriously being considered. This is a clear breach of Article 3(2) of Regulation 17[91] and the fact that the Council approved the agreement

[88] [1995] O.J. L 95/51.

[89] Conclusion of Advocate General Tesauro in Case C-327/91 *French Republic v. Commission of the European Communities*, [1994] E.C.R. I-3641 and [1994] 5 C.M.L.R. 517, at 540.

[90] [1995] O.J. L 95/51.

[91] Conclusion of Advocate General Tesauro in Case C-327/91 *French Republic v. Commission of the European Communities*, [1994] E.C.R. I-3641 and [1994] 5 C.M.L.R. 517, at 539.

292 Extraterritorial Application of E.C. and U.S. Competition Law

cannot be seen as an implicit modification of that Article. One should also not under-estimate the political change and the risk which is involved when the United States authorities become effectively one of the players that determine the direction in which European competition policy is being developed and how it is being applied. All this would give an external party a much bigger influence in European matters than was the case ever before.[92]

This leaves the agreement in a rather weak position. The comity provisions may give rise to a new complaint to the Court of Justice, while the confidence solution empties the agreement of most of its substance. We now turn to the evaluation of the agreement and of alternative approaches as solutions to the extraterritoriality conflict.

Solutions and their value

The agreement does not alter the basis on which extraterritorial jurisdiction is being taken. It does not eradicate the general conflict. In a particular case the exchange of information and the co-ordination which will take place under the provisions of the agreement may pre-empt a conflict from arising.[93] A better knowledge of each others procedures and intentions clearly takes away some of the tension. In practice this may lead to the second partner taking territorial action at the request of the party who would otherwise have needed to resort to the extraterritorial application of its own competition law provisions. If a conflict nevertheless arises, the co-ordination provisions of the agreement may assist in its solution. The restrictions which confidentiality places on the exchange of information and the fact that the right to apply is open to legal challenge do weaken these positive aspects of the agreement though.

If we go back to our previous theoretical analysis we find that the agreement does not address the problem at the public international law level at all. An effective solution should do so though, as this is the only way in which a comprehensive solution might be reached. A common approach in relation to the extent to which States can legislate on an extraterritorial basis should be agreed upon and should be the subject of an international Treaty.[94] The comity principle, as expressed in *Timberlane* and *Mannington Mills*, should be an essential part of this common approach. This would then open the way for a jurisdiction Convention at the private international law level. This second initiative is needed because the existence of a common approach on the public international level will not pre-empt a potentially conflictual situation from arising. The basis on which the authorities should be allowed to take jurisdiction should, it is submitted, be the fact that the anti-competitive agreement is implemented in the jurisdiction and this should be coupled with a discretion on grounds of comity.

The E.C.-U.S. agreement operates at a different level and, as described above, it will still only have a limited value at that level. The advantage of the approach which is being suggested is that it would also address the problem of the private anti-trust suit, while the agreement does not interfere with these private suits at all, because the agreement is not binding for the United States Courts. This aspect of the extraterritoriality issue arises almost exclusively in the United States. The majority of the anti-trust cases before American jurisdictions are now of the private suit type.[95] The United States

92 Riley, "The Jellyfish Nailed? The Annulment of the E.C./U.S. Competition Co-operation Agreement",]1995] 3 E.C.L.R. 185, at 191.

93 Conclusion of Advocate General Tesauro in Case C–327/91 *French Republic v. Commission of the European Communities*, [1994] E.C.R. I–3641 and [1994] 5 C.M.L.R. 517, at 522.

94 See also Robertson and Demetriou, *supra*, n. 16, at 424.

95 Fairley, *supra*, n. 15, at 143.

Courts are involved in this type of action, but the United States anti-trust authorities are not and the latter are the only parties that are bound by the agreement.[96] These private suit cases are the most difficult ones in terms of extraterritoriality, because the authorities have almost no control over them. Only the Courts could take action, but the Supreme Court's *Hartford Fire Insurance* decision reduced comity, their sole tool to do so, almost to non-existence. And the fact that the agreement does not address this private suit problem at all shows its limitations and its weakness. The United States Courts would be bound by the combined public-private international law approach though. This approach would thus provide a more effective solution of the conflict in this area.

Conclusion

It is clear that there is a conflict concerning the extraterritorial application of competition law. Co-operation agreements such as the shaky E.C.-U.S. agreement do not provide an adequate solution. They do not operate at the right level and they do specifically not address the issue of the private suits in the United States courts. Nevertheless, the Commission and the Council, as well as the United States authorities, seem to favour this approach, probably because they do not believe that anything better can be achieved in the present political climate.

We argue for a more courageous alternative approach. Initiatives would need to be taken on the public international law level to harmonise the basis for extraterritorial legislative action and on the private international law level to harmonise the basis for extraterritorial jurisdiction. Comity would play an important role in these initiatives and the latter initiative would also retain the implementation requirement. The existing E.C.-U.S. agreement operates at a different level and some of its provisions are worth keeping even though its importance has been reduced substantially. If the agreement is to remain part of the solution that is given to the extraterritoriality issue the active comity issue needs to be resolved. The agreement cannot survive on its shaky grounds which are bound to give rise to a legal challenge by any party that is affected by the application of the agreement.

[96] Ham, *supra*, n. 77, at 583 and 597.

Part II
The Scope of Competition Law

Vertical Restraints

[8]

VERTICAL ARRANGEMENTS AND THE RULE OF REASON*

Frank H. Easterbrook†

The pro free-market approach of Reagan Administration officials in the area of vertical restraints has provoked considerable academic and political discussion. Proponents of stricter market regulation argue that the administration's relaxed attitude amounts to dereliction of duty, and demand that they "enforce the law." Market freedom advocates counter that the administration and courts are overseeing a trend away from an unsound legacy of oppressive restraint on beneficial business practices.

The author is decidedly in the free market camp. He argues that *no* practice that a manufacturer uses to distribute goods should be illegal. He first suggests that restricted dealing is just a way of competing, and that various forms of restricted dealing only serve to widen consumer choice. In so doing, he deals with some common arguments against resale price maintainance and tying. The author then examines the benefits of vertical practices, showing that restricted dealing may be a way of adding information to the "product package".

Although free market advocates may embrace a rule of reason in lieu of per se formulations, the author believes that rule of reason formulations are "empty" and that "they decide no concrete cases." Instead, they serve as a stimulus for interminable discovery and a facilitator of poor decisions by judges and juries. The author proposes, instead, a five-part filtering test to separate the great number of nonharmful vertical practices from the rare number that evidence harm. The filters declare a practice lawful if *any* one of the following is true:

1) The firm lacks market power

---

* Reprinted from *Antitrust Law Journal*, Volume 53, pp. 135–174, (March 21–23, 1984) by permission from the author and the law journal.

† Professor of Law, University of Chicago Law School.

2) The industry shows no widespread adoption of identical practices
3) The output of goods covered by the practice increases
4) The practice is long-lived
5) The firm's profits do not depend on a reduction in competition

I want to make a point as simple as it is controversial. No practice a manufacturer uses to distribute its products should be a subject of serious antitrust attention. It should make no difference whether the manufacturer prescribes territories, customers, quality standards, or prices for its dealers. It should make no difference whether the manufacturer "ties" products together in a bundle, employs full-line forcing or exclusivity clauses, or uses "reciprocity." It should make no difference whether the restrictions are set by contract or by manufacturers' ownership of the retail outlets, the most "extreme" form of control. They are all the same.

This is not a radical proposal. Most of these practices, which I lump under the term "restricted dealing," are in common use. All of them except the prescription of prices and tying are dealt with under a highly deferential standard of review and are lawful except in the rarest of cases. The treatment of prices and tying is an anomaly that should be brought in line with the treatment of vertical integration and other restrictions on distribution.

If restricted dealing arises out of a cartel among dealers or manufacturers, by all means let us prosecute. Cartels are unlawful per se and should remain so. But restricted dealing is not often used by cartels, and most restricted dealing is just a way by which one manufacturer competes with others. Our economy has many ways of assembling and distributing products. The more routes to market, the broader the consumers' choice. The broader their choice, the better off they are. Cartels restrict rather than increase the range of choice. We should welcome restricted dealing as a benefit to consumers and not lump it with cartels, with which it has nothing in common.

As I discuss below, most forms of restricted dealing could be anticompetitive in one manifestation or another. But so too could the charging of low prices or the opening of new plants. There are limits on the ability of courts to sort the beneficial from the deleterious manifestations of these practices, and most of the time it is better not to try than to try and fail.

I. ANTITRUST IS PART OF THE COMMON LAW

Given the title of Representative Seiberling's paper,[1] I obviously need to say a few words about why the courts and enforcement agencies are free to pursue the program of deregulation I have just sketched. Haven't these things been settled? The answer is no. They have not been settled any more than the proper role of the doctrine of contributory negligence in tort law is settled. Antitrust is a form of common law. The Sherman Act of 1890 told the courts to make up a law on the subject of restraint

[1] Seiberling, *Congress Makes Laws; The Executive Should Enforce Them*, 53 ANTITRUST L.J. 175 (1984).

of trade. Congress no more prescribed the content of this law than it prescribes the content of the law of collective bargaining.[2]

The language of the Sherman Act governs no real cases. It tells the courts that "every contract, combination, or conspiracy in restraint of trade" is unlawful, and that "[e]very person who shall monopolize or attempt to monopolize" commerce has committed a crime. The Supreme Court noted very quickly that this language, taken at its broadest, prohibited ordinary bilateral contracts, partnership agreements, corporations and joint ventures. All of these restrain trade, in the sense that those who agree to do one thing lose their freedom to do otherwise, and those who join together as venturers may not compete at the same time.[3] The Court therefore concluded that it must fashion rules for discriminating between ordinary restraints and anticompetitive ones.

Ever since, the Court has treated antitrust as a common law field. In one recent case, it wrote:

> Congress did not intend the text of the Sherman Act to delineate the full meaning of the statute or its application in concrete situations. The legislative history makes it perfectly clear that it expected the courts to give shape to the statute's broad mandate by drawing on the common law tradition.[4]

In another, the Court said "the intent to allow courts to develop governing principles of law [is] unmistakably clear."[5] And it is. The entire history of the Sherman Act is filled with episodes of evolution in the common law style. The Court created and then overruled a doctrine forbidding manufacturers to impose territorial restraints on manufacturers;[6] it created and overruled a doctrine allowing manufacturers to "fix" resale prices by "consigning" the goods to merchants rather than selling them;[7] it created and then narrowed (almost to oblivion) a doctrine allowing manufacturers to establish resale prices by "unilateral" decisions

[2] Section 301 of the Labor Management Relations Act, 29 U.S.C. § 185, creates federal jurisdiction to enforce collective bargaining agreements and leaves to the courts the creation of the substantive principles. Textile Workers v. Lincoln Mills, 353 U.S. 448 (1957).

[3] "[T]he legality of an agreement or regulation cannot be determined by so simple a test, as whether it restrains competition. Every agreement concerning trade, every regulation of trade, restrains. To bind, to restrain, is of their very essence." Chicago Board of Trade v. United States, 246 U.S. 231, 238 (1918).

[4] National Soc'y of Prof'l Eng'rs v. United States, 435 U.S. 679, 688 (1978). Note 11 to *Engineers* collects some of the history. *See also* W. LETWIN, LAW AND ECONOMIC POLICY IN AMERICA (1965); Bork, *Legislative Intent and the Policy of the Sherman Act*, 9 J.L. & ECON. 7 (1966).

[5] Texas Indus., Inc. v. Radcliff Materials, Inc., 451 U.S. 630, 643 (1981).

[6] White Motor Co. v. United States, 372 U.S. 253 (1963) (rule of reason applies to territorial restraints), overruled by United States v. Arnold, Schwinn & Co., 388 U.S. 365 (1967) (per se condemnation), overruled by Continental T.V., Inc. v. GTE Sylvania Inc., 433 U.S. 36 (1977) (rule of reason applies).

[7] United States v. General Electric Co., 272 U.S. 476 (1926) (approving consignment device), overruled by Simpson v. Union Oil Co., 377 U.S. 13 (1964).

not to sell to those who disregarded suggested resale prices;[8] it adopted, abandoned, adopted again, and then substantially modified, a per se rule against cartels;[9] it abolished for antitrust two centuries-old rules of law, one dealing with suits by those in pari delicto and the other dealing with the effects of settlement.[10] There are many other instances of the common law process at work. Congress has responded by holding the text of the Sherman Act inviolate. This does not suggest widespread legislative displeasure with the common law method of construction.[11]

The legislative history made it clear that the Court would control the content of the substantive rules. It also demonstrated that Congress wanted the judges to fashion their doctrine in order to protect consumers from overcharges and the economy as a whole from harm. As the Court recently put it, quoting Judge Bork, the antitrust laws "are a consumer welfare prescription."[12]

[8] *Compare* United States v. Colgate & Co., 250 U.S. 300 (1919) (refusal to deal because of retailer's pricing decisions is lawful), *with, e.g.,* United States v. Parke, Davis & Co., 362 U.S. 29 (1960) (any attempt to enforce the prices laid down is unlawful). Although *Colgate* has not been overruled, *see* Russell Stover Candies, Inc. v. Federal Trade Comm'n, 718 F.2d 256 (8th Cir. 1983), it applies only to simple refusals to sell, devoid of efforts to learn about or enforce compliance with the restraints—in other words, it applies only when the plaintiff makes a litigation mistake and neglects to put in the sort of proof that is available in any complex system of distribution.

[9] *Compare* United States v. Trans-Missouri Freight Ass'n, 166 U.S. 290 (1897) (cartels are unlawful per se), *with* Standard Oil Co. of N.J. v. United States, 221 U.S. 1 (1911) (rule of reason applies to all horizontal agreements), *with* United States v. Trenton Potteries Co., 273 U.S. 392 (1927) (cartels are unlawful per se notwithstanding *Standard Oil*), *with* Broadcast Music, Inc. v. CBS, 441 U.S. 1 (1979) (the per se rule and the definition of "cartels" are legal conclusions rather than methods of analysis and do not apply to all horizontal agreements).

[10] Perma Life Mufflers, Inc. v. International Parts Corp., 392 U.S. 134 (1968) (pari delicto); Zenith Radio Corp. v. Hazeltine Research, Inc., 401 U.S. 321 (1971) (settlement).

[11] An incautious passage in Arizona v. Maricopa County Medical Soc'y, 457 U.S. 332, 354-55 (1982), appears to say that once the Court establishes a per se rule, only Congress may alter the rule. This passage is inconsistent with many other statements discussed above and with the entire history of the development of antitrust. Justice Stevens, the author of *Maricopa*, also wrote *Engineers*, which contains the strongest assertion to date of the common law character of antitrust rules. Here is Justice Stevens' latest perspective, written one year after *Maricopa:*

> Congress phrased some older statutes in sweeping, general terms, expecting the federal courts to interpret them by developing legal rules on a case-by-case basis in the common law tradition. One clear example of such a statute is the Sherman Act. [Citing *Engineers*, among other cases.] For that reason, in *Continental T.V.*, the doctrine of stare decisis did not preclude the Court from overruling its prior decision in [*Schwinn*], even though Congress had not acted in the intervening decade.

Guardians Ass'n v. Civil Service Comm'n of New York, 103 S. Ct. 3221, 3253 n.12 (1983) (dissenting opinion) (citations omitted).

Although Congress has left the Sherman Act alone, § 3 of the Clayton Act, 15 U.S.C. § 14, has some bearing on tying and exclusive dealing arrangements. The Court has read § 3 as a per se statute, but it need not be. It forbids only conduct that may "substantially lessen competition or tend to create a monopoly," which means that economic scrutiny is in order. Interpretation may change as we learn more about the effects of particular practices.

[12] Reiter v. Sonotone Corp., 442 U.S. 330, 343 (1979).

We need not debate whether the *only* purpose of the antitrust laws is the protection of economic efficiency, though I think they should be treated as if it were.[13] It is enough for now that any political goals of antitrust are second-order concerns, which may control only if the economic arguments are closely balanced.[14] None of my argument depends on the extent to which there are other goals, and neither does Rep. Seiberling's. If antitrust law contains noneconomic as well as economic goals, it is legitimate for the Supreme Court to reassess the relative weights of these objectives, just as it is legitimate for the Court to reassess its application of economic principles. The common law does not stand still. The possibility of change is as much a part of "the law" as today's substantive principles. One who urges "adherence to the law" must take the procedure with the substance.[15]

If the Court may reconsider its answers, the enforcement agencies may ask for such reconsideration. No one thinks it illegitimate for an enforcer to bring a "test case," seeking to expand the reach of the law. Yet there is no ratchet in antitrust. Just as what was once lawful may be proscribed under new approaches, so what was once condemned may be restored to legitimacy as judges reassess their earlier acts. The belated arrival of wisdom is no reason for refusal to learn and change.

One word on the meaning of Congress' repeal (1975) of the Miller-Tydings Act (1937) and the McGuire Act (1952), which had permitted states to authorize manufacturers to adopt resale price maintenance (RPM) schemes. The 1975 statute concerns RPM *alone*. It does not speak to other distribution practices. The Supreme Court therefore was on firm ground in 1977 when it overruled *Schwinn* and brought all distribution practices other than RPM within the rule of reason. It can continue to change the rules as new knowledge directs.

The Court is free to change the rules on RPM, too. Congress could have adopted legislation in 1975 to "freeze" the law. It could have approved the per se rule for resale price maintenance, yet it did not. Similarly, the Rudman Amendment, which forbids the Department of Justice from spending any funds to upset the per se treatment of RPM, is an exercise in procedure rather than substance. Congress always has a choice when it legislates on antitrust, and the Court honors Congress when it respects that choice. The choice made in 1975 was to return

[13] Easterbrook, *Is There a Ratchet in Antitrust Law?*, 60 TEX. L. REV. 705, 713-17 (1982).

[14] *See, e.g*, Fox, *The Modernization of Antitrust: A New Equilibrium*, 66 CORNELL L. REV. 1140 (1981); Pitofsky, *The Political Content of Antitrust*, 127 U. PA. L. REV. 1051 (1979), among the many scholars who conclude that noneconomic principles may properly be used as doubt-resolvers (and as constraints for very large mergers).

[15] *See* Baxter, *Separation of Powers, Prosecutorial Discretion, and the "Common Law" Nature of Antitrust Law*, 60 TEX. L. REV. 661 (1982); Easterbrook, *On Not Enforcing the Law*, REGULATION, Jan/Feb 1983, at 14.

RPM issues to the control of antitrust principles, free of state law, rather than to adopt a legislative rule specifying how to treat RPM. Doubtless, Congress thought in 1975 that the result of the repeal would be application of the per se rule. But whenever Congress repeals a statute, it makes some assumption about the status of the remaining law. It would be quite unfortunate if legislators' *assumptions*, rather than positive legislation, could alter the course of legal development. The President cannot veto an assumption. And the "state of the law in 1975" had two components: one component was per se illegality of RPM; and the other component was the common law nature of antitrust, which allows judges to change the rules when presented with better arguments. If Congress approved one (the per se rule) by silence, it approved the other too.

The history of RPM has been one of constant fluctuation and, as a practical matter, legality. The decision in *Dr. Miles* (1911), which declared RPM unlawful per se, was followed rather quickly by *Colgate* (1919), which told manufacturers how to achieve RPM through "unilateral" demand. *Colgate* ratified existing practice. *General Electric* (1926) approved still another method—the agency or consignment device—for practicing RPM. Even *Schwinn*, which made most territorial allocations among dealers unlawful per se, left open the consignment route to legality. During the 1960s, *Colgate* and *General Electric* were narrowed to the point of overruling, but this makes rather than diminishes my point. Congress knew (or easily could have known) in 1975 that RPM had been lawful—even without resort to the Miller-Tydings and McGuire Acts—for most of the time the Sherman Act had been in effect. It became unlawful in practice only in the 1960s. What the Court decides from 1911 to 1926, and reconsiders in the 1960s, it can review yet again in the 1980s. And everyone should expect it to do so.

II. RESTRICTED DEALING IS A WAY TO COMPETE

The antitrust laws exist to stop trusts or cartels from reducing the output of goods and services. The reduction brings about monopoly prices, the conspirators' goal. It also causes a misallocation of resources, as people shift to things that seem "cheaper" but really cost society more to produce in order to get the same level of satisfaction.

Cartels cooperate to cut output. Yet other forms of cooperation are procompetitive. All large firms entail a great deal of cooperation. Within Ford Motor, the engine and body divisions cooperate, and someone "dictates" a price at which things will be sold. The firm "dictates" that they be sold as a package. Sears tells its store managers what to sell, and at what price. The antitrust laws tolerate, indeed encourage, such agreements. They create the goods and services we value.

Just as there can be cooperation within a firm, there can be beneficial cooperation across firms. Restricted dealing is a form of cooperation. One firm (the retailer) agrees to do things the way a manufacturer specifies, just as an employee does things within an integrated firm. The agreement is not a displacement of the market. Such contracts are the market at work. All contracts restrain in the same sense restricted dealing restrains.

A. VERTICAL RESTRAINTS ON DEALERS

Why, then, would cooperative agreements in the chain of distribution be subject to antitrust scrutiny? The usual argument for prohibition is that restricted dealing is "like" a cartel in the sense that firms agree on price (or quality, or place of distribution). True enough. But one can find such agreements inside every firm too. The fact that two practices have such a feature in common is just the beginning of analysis. This holds, too, for the subsidiary rationale used to attack ties, exclusive distribution and reciprocity: that these "extend" a monopoly from one market to another. Perhaps they do. But they can do this only if there is a monopoly to start with, and even then there will be difficult questions about whether the "extension" is profitable to the firm or harmful to consumers. One must look further.

Before going on, I want to dispatch a line of argument one hears too often in political discourse. It is that restricted dealing, and especially resale price maintenance, is bad because it enables manufacturers to jack up the retail price of its products. So it does. Resale price maintenance is no different in this respect from other restrictions (for example, if there are fewer dealers, each can charge more).

So what? If Russell Stover wants its chocolates to sell for $20 per pound, it can achieve this easily enough. It may raise the wholesale prices. It may improve or change the product's quality or style, so that it tastes better than Godiva. The observation that these things influence retail prices is not even interesting as an antitrust concern. Every manufacturer may sell what it wants and charge what the traffic will bear. Other manufacturers, perhaps using less chocolate per pound or employing more efficient manufacturing, may sell different goods and charge less. This is competition. Consumers will choose. The question is whether restricted dealing affects price in an *anti*competitive way. If manufacturers may affect retail prices by changing wholesale prices or quality, why may they not affect prices through restricted dealing?

The argument must be that restricted dealing can facilitate a real cartel, such as an agreement among manufacturers or dealers to charge an elevated price. One of the cartel arguments might run like this:[16] Dealers—

[16] One example of such an argument may be found in Pitofsky, *In Defense of Discounters: The No-Frills Case for a Per Se Rule Against Vertical Price Fixing*, 71 GEO. L.J. 1487 (1983).

say, druggists—in some city collude to drive up the price of toothpaste. Each dealer is worried that the others will "cheat," that is, that other dealers will reduce the price in order to make additional sales at the expense of those adhering to the fixed price. So the dealers conscript the manufacturers to help them out. The manufacturers set a fixed resale price and penalize dealers that sell at a lower price.

The argument that restricted dealing is a way of enforcing a dealers' cartel conceals substantial problems. First, the industry must be one in which the dealers can form a cartel. But when will this be? Most retail markets have free entry, and retailing is about as close to an atomistic market as you can get. There is a drug store on every other corner. There are so many retailers (and potential retailers) of toothpaste and other consumer goods that the firms could not form or sustain a cartel with or without the aid of manufacturers.

As for the manufacturers: Why go along? What's in it for them? A manufacturer that helps dealers form a cartel is doing itself in. It will sell less, and dealers will get the monopoly profits. Manufacturers could be "paid" in higher wholesale prices for cooperating, but that would increase the incentives of dealers not to join the cartel—to cheat by buying the product at a lower price and selling on a lower margin. If significant numbers of dealers cheat, bye-bye cartel.

It won't do to get just one manufacturer of toothpaste to adopt restricted dealing. All or almost all must do so. If there are holdouts, noncooperating dealers can sell the holdouts' products for less. That would destroy the cartel. Yet why would all manufacturers want to go along? It pays one or more to hold out. Dealers could conscript all manufacturers only when the conditions of a manufacturers' cartel existed.

Things are just as bad if the manufacturers make slightly different products. One manufacturer may hang back by setting the cartel price, but changing what it supplies for the price. It may put more paste in the tube, or use a formula that requires less paste per brushing. Differentiated products spoil the use of restricted dealing to enforce a cartel.

Then there is a problem of verification. Why are manufacturers any better at policing prices than fellow dealers are? The cheating dealer can't attract extra business without advertising its lower prices. Then its fellow conspirators learn in the same way manufacturers do. They could enforce the deal themselves. The extra enforcement from the cutoff by the manufacturer may be too late, or too little.

So the dealers' cartel explanation won't amount to much unless there are (1) few dealers; (2) few manufacturers; (3) homogeneous products; and (4) easy policing. If we see many dealers and many manufacturers, we can exclude the cartel possibility. And if we see some manufacturers using restricted dealing while others do not, or if we see substantially differentiated products, we can exclude the cartel hypothesis no matter how many or few dealers and manufacturers there are.

The conditions for restricted dealing to be a useful part of a dealer's cartel just do not exist very often. (I could show the same for the use of restricted dealing as part of a manufacturers' cartel, but that is unnecessary. The argument proceeds in the same way.) We do not condemn business practices under the antitrust laws unless they are anticompetitive in a given case or are so likely to be anticompetitive that detailed investigation is unnecessary. Because the conditions under which restricted dealing is anticompetitive are so rare, automatic condemnation would pick up far too many procompetitive examples to be worthwhile.

B. Tying and Other Packaging Decisions

Many marketing practices do not require the cooperation of dealers. Tying arrangements, reciprocity, and vertical integration fall in this category. Vertical integration is almost always lawful. Courts today take the sensible position that integration is a method of making and selling one's product, and that competition against other producers supplies the necessary constraint. Indeed, vertical integration is lawful even when the resulting firm is a monopolist at one of the levels.[17] Tying and reciprocity have been treated differently, as unlawful per se when the firms involved possess market power.[18]

The difference is not sustainable. Tying (and reciprocity) involve the same kinds of decisions as vertical integration about how much will be put in one bundle and how much will be sold separately. The vertically integrated firm sells a bundle of design-manufacture-distribution-delivery, things that *could* be, and often are, sold separately. The firm selling a tied package of goods (houses to credit, or salt to salt-injecting machines) also is offering a bundle; reciprocity is a two-way bundle (goods for goods, rather than a straight sale of cash for goods).

Courts frequently say that tying and reciprocity are different because they can be used to "extend" monopoly power from one market to another. This is the "leverage" objection. It has been clear for some time, though, that the leverage objection is naive. It assumes that the firm can get something for nothing. If a firm has market power in, say, salt-injecting machines, it can sell or lease those machines for the monopoly price. It can't get another monopoly price by tying salt to the machine. If the monopoly price of the machine is $50,000, and a lifetime supply of salt at the competitive price is worth $10,000, the monopolist can't

[17] *E.g.*, Paschall v. Kansas City Star Co., 727 F.2d 692 (8th Cir. 1984) (en banc) (newspaper with market power integrates into distribution).

[18] Northern Pacific Ry. v. United States, 356 U.S. 1 (1958) (tying); Betaseed, Inc. v. U&I, Inc., 681 F.2d 1203 (9th Cir. 1982) (reciprocity).

make money by charging more than $60,000 for the two as a package. To get the buyer to pay more than $10,000 for the salt, it must take less than $50,000 for the machine.[19] The seller can take its monopoly profit only once. And although the seller of the machine could "monopolize" the supply of salt *used with the machine*, it could not monopolize salt in general, for there are many additional uses of salt.

It is possible to describe circumstances under which vertical integration, ties, reciprocity and exclusive dealing (a form of short-term vertical integration) are harmful to competition. If undertaken by real monopolists (firms with two-thirds or more of their markets), these practices might slow down the rate of entry. Suppose computer repair is a specialized service. If a computer monopolist ties service to its machines, then entry will take longer, because a potential entrant will need to provide (or arrange for) service as well as the manufacture of machines.[20] The monopolist can collect a monopoly profit for longer, before its position finally erodes. Vertical integration can have the same effect.[21]

In the run of cases, though, this is not likely. Entry-deferral depends on real monopoly of *both* products or stages of production, and most firms do not have such monopolies. Those who bundle products or vertically integrate usually are participants in competitive industries. When they are not, their monopoly usually covers only one product. Again, the salt case is typical. Tying salt to salt-injection machines would not slow down entry into salt-injection; because most salt is used for other purposes and there are plenty of sellers, the would-be salt-injection-machine maker can concentrate on this alone, without starting up salt production. The would-be salt seller can concentrate on that alone, with-

---

[19] The Supreme Court has recognized this; *see* United States Steel Corp. v. Fortner Enters., Inc., 429 U.S. 610, 622 (1977), which suggests that some reconsideration of the doctrine may not be far behind. (The discussion in the text assumes that the products are tied in fixed proportions. The variable-proportions tie may be a method of increasing returns through price discrimination. W. BOWMAN, PATENT AND ANTITRUST LAW (1973). Imperfect price discrimination has ambiguous economic effects. Price discrimination is not generally unlawful, though, and if the objection to tying is its facilitation of price discrimination, the objection goes far beyond ties.)

[20] There may be offsetting benefits of this tie. The repair contract may ensure that the user of the machine does not use "inefficiently much" repair service. The monopoly price of the machine induces customers to hold on to their machinery longer than is socially optimal. (Repair could be excessive in the sense that the least-cost way to produce a given amount of computation entails more units of hardware and fewer units of repair, while the monopoly price of the hardware induces substitution toward repair.) Given a monopoly of machines, it may be desirable for the monopolist to supply repair and to offer the sale of subsequent or additional machines at a lower price, again reducing the incentive to excessive repair. This could be what was going on in United States v. United Shoe Machinery Corp., 110 F. Supp. 295 (D. Mass.), *aff'd mem.*, 347 U.S. 521 (1954). It is unnecessary to pursue the benefit question here.

[21] Part IV of the Antitrust Division's Department of Justice Merger Guidelines explains why and points out that this horizontal, entry-deferring effect, is the principal (if not the only) concern about vertical practices.

out worrying about the tiny fraction of the market "foreclosed" by the salt-machine tie.[22] The conditions under which ties, vertical integration, and related practices protect monopoly by raising rivals' costs are sufficiently rare that they cannot support any presumption against (or even suspicion of) the practices.

C. RATIONALES OF THE VERTICAL PRACTICES

I have opened this discussion by asking whether vertical practices are likely to be anticompetitive. Although this is the appropriate method of analysis, it is not the ordinary one. The customary approach is to ask whether a practice is procompetitive. If the person analyzing the practice finds it has no procompetitive use, the person recommends condemnation (and if the person is a judge, does the condemning). This common approach is inappropriate because it uses ignorance as the basis of condemnation. We live in a world where knowledge is scarce and costly, ignorance rampant. For many practices, even the most careful economists can say no more than that there are possible gains, possible losses. When a demonstration of competitive benefit is the condition of legality, we end up condemning whatever we do not yet understand. Yet the burden in antitrust is on the plaintiff, not the defendant; Congress did not tell courts to proscribe all poorly-understood practices.

Nonetheless, I do not want to sound a completely agnostic theme. Most business practices have some explanation, else they would not have survived. There is great difficulty in knowing what the explanation *is* in a particular case. Often the best anyone can do is offer a menu of possibilities, some pro- and some anti-competitive. When the anticompetitive explanations have been eliminated, the procompetitive explanations are left—although we still do not know which explanations matter.

Again tie-ins offer an example. One simple explanation is that putting things together in a package is a cheaper way of selling them. The "ties" of left to right shoes, shirts to buttons, cars to tires, are examples. There is nothing suspicious or even unusual about package sales. Another explanation is that the "tie" changes the incentives of the people making the products. The *Hyde* case is an illustration.[23] A large acute-care hospital

[22] This does not mean that the tie in International Salt Co. v. United States, 332 U.S. 392 (1947), the subject of the discussion in the text, was harmless. The tie in that case—the user was required to take International's salt unless some other firm's was cheaper—may be seen as a way for International to get access to its rivals' prices. Knowledge of prices may be useful in shoring up a cartel among salt sellers. For such an explanation of the case, *see* Peterman, *The International Salt Case*, 22 J.L. & ECON. 351 (1979). *Cf.* Cummings & Ruhter, *The Northern Pacific Case*, 22 J.L. & ECON. 329 (1979) (related explanations). I omit such anticompetitive possibilities from the discussion not because they are unlikely but because they really have little to do with tying as tying. If this information-gathering is the right way to view *International Salt*, then the appropriate antitrust objection is to the cartel, not to the tie.

[23] Jefferson Parish Hosp. Dist. No. 2 v. Hyde, 104 S. Ct. 1551 (1984). I was the counsel for the petitioner in *Hyde*, so you may discount my description appropriately.

"tied" anesthesiology services to the use of its operating rooms. Anyone who wanted an operation had to use the hospital's anesthesiologists. This bundling made it possible for the anesthesiologists and other professionals to work together as a team and so reduced the cost of making the real product, medical care. The more interesting effect, though, is that the tie made it possible for the M.D. anesthesiologists to make an unbiased choice between supplying their services and those of nurse anesthetists, who can perform many of the routine aspects of care. An "open" hospital is marked by competition among M.D.s to supply their own service, even if the least-cost way to care for the patient is a mix of anesthesiologist and anesthetist service. The tie means that the hospital sells a bundle of service and can make up that service from the most efficient components.

There are as many explanations of ties as there are examples. Ties and reciprocity may be useful in cheating on cartels (one way to cheat is to sell a package in which the implicit price of the "tied" product is less than the competitive one); they may facilitate price discrimination; they may facilitate the introduction of new products by helping firms to capture more of the value of their innovations; they may reduce the costs of business transactions by establishing lines of mutual dependence that serve as "bonds" of good behavior. The extensive literature discusses these and many more possibilities.[24] The task of finding which reason explains which case is stimulating and difficult. Ultimately, though, it cannot be dispositive. In the absence of a strong showing that the arrangement is anticompetitive, it cannot make much difference to antitrust which procompetitive explanation is the right one.

A different set of explanations underlies manufacturers' directives to dealers about location, services and prices. In order to make headway here, we must ask why a (sane) manufacturer ever sets up a system of distribution in which the *dealer* obtains the benefits of higher prices. The

[24] The literature is so large—and contains so many excellent treatments—that to cite any risks slighting others. I therefore give just a few examples. Richard Posner and I have collected and discussed others in R. POSNER & F. EASTERBROOK, ANTITRUST 802-10, 814-17 (tying), 869-76 (vertical integration) (2d ed. 1981). For the examples, *see* W. Bowman, *supra* note 19 (price discrimination); Easterbrook, *Predatory Strategies and Counterstrategies*, 48 U. CHI. L. REV. 263, 307-12 (1981) (tying may increase appropriability of investments in information); Kenney & Klein, *The Economics of Block Booking*, 26 J.L. & ECON. 497 (1983) (tying may reduce the costs of information and avoid over-searching); Klein, Crawford & Alchian, *Vertical Integration, Appropriable Rents, and the Competitive Contracting Process*, 21 J.L. & ECON. 297 (1978) (vertical integration may reduce costs of opportunistic behavior); Marvel, *Exclusive Dealing*, 25 J.L. & ECON. 1 (1982) (exclusive dealing may create efficient rights in customers' patronage); Rubin, *The Theory of the Firm and the Structure of the Franchise Contract*, 21 J.L. & ECON. 223 (1978) ("franchise ties" may improve the incentives of store managers); Williamson, *Credible Commitments: Using Hostages to Support Exchange*, 73 AM. ECON. REV. 519 (1983) (bonding explanation of reciprocity). Courts increasingly accept these and other justifications for ties and related practices. *E.g.*, Principe v. McDonalds Corp., 631 F.2d 303 (4th Cir. 1980), *cert. denied*, 451 U.S. 970 (1981); Krehl v. Baskin-Robbins Ice Cream Co., 664 F.2d 1348 (9th Cir. 1982).

manufacturer wants to get its product from plant to customer. To do this, it "buys distribution." The difference between the wholesale and retail price is the "cost of distribution."

If the manufacturer can create distribution more cheaply than other dealers, it will integrate and save this expense (although it incurs the new expense of operating a retail division). When Sears owns a store, the cost of distribution is the price of land, fuel and staff, the same things an independent retailer must cover. Sears, like the non-integrated firm, wants to hold this cost as low as possible.

The manufacturer's interest is the same as the consumer's. Each wants to keep his cost down. For a given retail price, the manufacturer wants the highest wholesale price. For a given wholesale price, it wants the lowest retail price in order to sell more units. The manufacturer looks out for the consumer here, just as it does in picking the materials out of which to build the product. Few believe that manufacturers pay "too much" for their raw materials or labor, or that, if they did, this would be an antitrust problem. Yet critics of restricted dealing apparently accuse manufacturers of ill-serving their own interests when they buy distribution services. What can be going on?

The essential point about restricted dealing is that these contractual provisions do more than just get "a product" from plant to purchaser. They affect the nature of the product. Some attributes of a product can be installed at a factory. A TV comes with a 19-inch tube or a 25-inch tube built in. Some attributes are added later on. Information is one. How do you use a computer? How do you connect one part to another? The manufacturer can "build in" some information by putting booklets in its boxes, but it can also supply information via trained salesmen. The more ways there are to do this, the more likely it is for each consumer to find some satisfying combination of product attributes.

Look at the market in computers. There are at least four different combinations of hardware and information. One is that the manufacturer puts a machine and a book in a box and sells the combination. The retailer sells the closed box, with minimal additional demonstration. If you don't like it, or find that you can't make it work, you can take it back. That's the end of the service. Commodore, in conjunction with retailers such as K-Mart and Toys-R-Us, has followed this strategy with great success.

The second combination is to do what Radio Shack has done, to own your own stores and franchise others. Then you can furnish special information and display services in your own stores. Radio Shack charges for the service by setting a higher price. The problem: the consumer cannot easily compare one brand against another and so may not appreciate your machine; worse, the costs of single-brand selling may be higher.

IBM has taken a third path, opening product centers that display its machines. A customer can learn all about the IBM's abilities and what products work in what ways with what peripherals. IBM charges for its information through the wholesale price to independent dealers, where consumers can compare different brands. This strategy works, though, only when the manufacturer has a very large volume. Other manufacturers do not sell enough to justify special stores that dispense information.

These are the only combinations that work well in a world without restricted dealing. Restricted dealing adds a fourth option, which Apple and others seem to be pursuing. Apple places its computers in retail stores, requiring dealers to display them and provide extensive information and knowledgeable support. It has no stores of its own. But such a method of distribution is very hard to sustain without restricted dealing. The customer may soak up all that information in the "full service" store and then order the computer from a mail order outlet. It then becomes difficult for a dealer to recover its costs, since it cannot charge by the hour for presale advice. Competition from low-service outlets—"free riders"—slowly undermines the full-service stores. The drain of sales to low-service stores is a kind of tax on presale information. The tax leads to too little being provided, as consumers see things.

Restricted dealing makes it easier for manufacturers and dealers to pursue this fourth option, the option of full-service outlets by sellers too small to justify vertical integration. If all dealers charge the same price, the customer will go to the one with better service, just as the manufacturer intended. Or if the dealers are placed far apart, each must compete for customers (against the products of other manufacturers) by supplying better information and service.

Restricted dealing thus may increase the number of ways manufacturers can compete to provide what some segment of the population wants to buy. The more ways there are to slice up the product-service continuum, the more likely any one customer's wants will be satisfied.

The explanation presented above is a version of the "special services-free riding" explanation first raised by Lester Telser, developed by Robert Bork and Richard Posner, adopted by the Supreme Court in *GTE Sylvania*, and advanced by the Antitrust Division as the basis of still further legal change.[25] It differs from the other presentations by focusing on

[25] Telser, *Why Should Manufacturers Want Free Trade?*, 3 J.L. & Econ. 86 (1960); R. Bork, The Antitrust Paradox 280-98, 429-40 (1978); Bork, *The Rule of Reason and the Per Se Rule: Price Fixing and Market Division* (Pts 1 & 2), 74 Yale L.J. 775 (1965), 75 Yale L.J.

the role of restricted dealing in increasing consumers' choice. "More service," standing alone, may or may not be beneficial. Some careful economists have shown that more is not always better: those who want "more" may end up increasing the price and inflicting needless losses on those who want to get information out of *Consumer Reports.* Those who do not need or like the information or other attributes added by the restricted dealing are made worse off, and their losses may exceed the gains of the consumers who appreciate what restricted dealing does.[26]

I emphasize the role of restricted dealing in expanding choice to point out that it functions just like other forms of product diversification. The *availability* of restricted dealing makes it possible for manufacturers to produce a particular bundle of attributes (some built in, some added by dealers). So long as there is competition among manufacturers to choose methods of distribution, the theoretical possibility of a reduction in welfare will not come to pass.

To see why, consider an example. Suppose each manufacturer may choose only one color for its automobiles (equivalent to the practical need to have a single rule for distribution). Suppose further that about 30 percent of the population has a fanatical desire to own canary yellow cars, and that the other 70 percent prefers basic black and are repulsed by the thought of driving a yellow car. If the desires of the people who want yellow cars are sufficiently intense, a monopolist may find that its profit-maximizing strategy is to choose yellow and raise the price to extract the surplus from the canary-fanciers, while accepting the loss of sales to many who prefer black. A legal rule requiring the use of black paint might be the social optimum. But if there are one or two other auto manufacturers, there is no need for legal intervention. At least one of the rivals will find it profitable to make black cars, satisfying this demand; perhaps someone will compete on yellow cars, too.

The situation is the same in distribution. If Apple caters to those who want one combination of hardware and information, Commodore and others will compete with different strategies. As F.M. Scherer astutely put the matter at an ABA National Institute last fall, quoting from two economists who now sit on the FTC, "The greater the number of price/quality options, the better."[27]

---

373 (1966); R. POSNER, ANTITRUST LAW: AN ECONOMIC PERSPECTIVE 147-67 (1976); Posner, *Antitrust Policy and the Supreme Court: An Analysis of the Restricted Distribution, Horizontal Merger and Potential Competition Decisions,* 75 COLUM. L. REV. 282 (1975); Continental T.V., Inc. v. GTE Sylvania Inc., 433 U.S. 36, 47-57 (1977); Brief for the United States as Amicus Curiae in Monsanto Co. v. Spray-Rite Serv. Corp., 104 S. Ct. 1464 (1984).

[26] Spence, *Monopoly, Quality and Regulation,* 6 BELL J. ECON. 417 (1975); Scherer, *The Economics of Vertical Restraints,* 52 ANTITRUST L.J. 687 (1983).

[27] Scherer, *supra* note 26, at 704, quoting Douglas & Miller, *Quality Competition, Industry Equilibrium, and Efficiency in the Price-Constrained Airline Market,* 64 AM. ECON. REV. 657, 668 (1974).

Although I have offered a version of Lester Telser's explanation of restricted dealing, there are many more. One, which William Baxter has suggested and others have elaborated on, is that restricted dealing is a method of advertising in which retailers lend their reputation to manufacturers.[28] The retailers may be able to signal the high quality, availability, or stylishness of the goods more cheaply than other ways open to manufacturers. Retailers then demand some restricted distribution as their compensation for the service. (Fewer will shop at Neiman Marcus if the goods "certified" by it are available for less at K-Mart.) A number of other interesting, provocative and sometimes even convincing explanations of restricted dealing have appeared recently or are floating in samizdat form among the profession.[29] All of these approaches, like Lester Telser's, show how the costs of organizing a market and conveying information lead to forms of organization that depart from the textbook model of atomistic competition. These departures are not "failures." On the contrary, they are evidence that markets adapt to the costs of organization and information in a way that economizes on all costs, including the costs of the markets themselves.[30]

It really does not matter which explanation is "right." There are fascinating intellectual questions here, and ultimately only good, hard, empirical work can offer answers. Contrary to popular belief, the Chicago School not only welcomes empirical work but also has led the field. The Law School publishes the *Journal of Law & Economics*, which specializes in antitrust, regulatory, and corporate issues. Empirical work appearing in this *Journal* has tested the structure-conduct-performance paradigm underlying the antipathy to concentration and found it wanting; it has

---

[28] Baxter, *Vertical Practices—Half Slave, Half Free*, 52 ANTITRUST L.J. 743 (1983); V. Goldberg, The Free Rider Problem, Imperfect Pricing, and the Economics of Retailing Services (draft of Dec. 1983); H. Marvel, Resale Price Maintenance (draft of Oct. 1982).

[29] *E.g.*, Butler & Baysinger, *Vertical Restraints of Trade as Contractual Integration: A Synthesis of Relational Contracting Theory, Transaction-Cost Economics, and Organization Theory*, 32 EMORY L.J. 1009 (1983); Liebeler, *1983 Economic Review of Antitrust Developments: The Distinction Between Price and Nonprice Distribution Restrictions*, 31 UCLA L. Rev. 384 (1983); M. Schwartz & D. Eisenstadt, Vertical Restraints, U.S. Department of Justice, Antitrust Division, Economic Policy Office Discussion Paper 82-8 (Dec. 1982).

[30] One sometimes reads—even in the pages of this *Journal*, *e.g.*, Spivack, *The Chicago School Approach to Single Firm Exercises of Market Power: A Response*, 52 ANTITRUST L.J. 651, 669-72 (1983)—that discussions of the sort that appear in the text are based on theoretical models of frictionless, costless markets, and that the existence of costs in real markets justifies disregarding these discussions. Such statements rest on misunderstanding of the analysis. Those who oppose restricted dealing and demand that markets resemble the classical model of atomistic competition with continuous double auctions are the ones tied to unrealistic assumptions. The Telser approach to restricted dealing rests on the high costs of information. Restricted dealing may be a beneficial response to the high cost of conveying (and establishing property rights in) information. *See also* Barzel, *Some Fallacies in the Interpretation of Information Costs*, 20 J.L. & ECON. 291 (1977); Telser, *Margins and Futures Contracts*, 1 J. FUTURES MARKETS 225 (1981) (showing why even the markets closest to atomistic competition gain from elements of organization). As for the claim (*e.g.*, Spivack, *supra*) that the Chicago approach to antitrust is theory divorced from evidence, *see* text and note at note 31, *infra*.

explored claims that particular practices are "barriers to entry" and found them unsupported; it has shown many of the claims made about older cases to be empty.[31] At Chicago no economic model is worth much without testing. Theory in the abstract is valuable because it tells you where to look, and also because one logical exercise can expose the flaws in another. Often condemnation in antitrust is based on little more than a flawed logical contention that a practice could be anticompetitive. A logical ("theoretical"?) response may be perfectly adequate.[32]

People at Chicago and elsewhere have carried out a number of sophisticated tests that tend to confirm the proposition that restricted dealing is beneficial to consumers. These matters are outside the scope of this paper, however. For current purposes it does not matter why restricted dealing is used, once we have concluded that there is little likelihood of anticompetitive effect. Unless a firm with market power can enlarge its profits by harming consumers, there is no sound justification for the use of antitrust. No plausible story of restricted dealing shows how it could help manufacturers at the expense of consumers.

D. THE EFFECT OF VERTICAL RESTRAINTS ON SMALL OR DISCOUNT BUSINESSES

One brief word on the relation between restricted dealing and the survival of small dealers and discount houses. This crops up so often—

---

[31] On the relation between structure and performance, *see, e.g.*, Peltzman, *The Gains and Losses from Industrial Concentration*, 20 J.L. & ECON. 229 (1977) (evidence showing that concentration stems from the growth of efficient firms; *see also* the exchange at 22 J.L. & ECON. 183-211 (1979), on the interpretation of the data); Demsetz, *Industry Structure, Market Rivalry, and Public Policy*, 16 J.L. & ECON. 1 (1973) (data showing that only the largest firm in an industry earns abnormal profits, which contradicts a monopoly or collusion interpretation); Leitzinger & Tamor, *Foreign Competition in Antitrust Law*, 26 J.L. & ECON. 87 (1983) (showing that once a product is imported into the United States, domestic concentration ratios have no influence on profits, thus implying that the market is international). On the interpretation of practices as barriers to entry, *see, e.g.*, Benham, *The Effect of Advertising on the Price of Eyeglasses*, 15 J.L. & ECON. 337 (1972) (data showing that advertising, once thought a barrier to entry, is procompetitive); Nagle, *Do Advertising-Profitability Studies Really Show that Advertising Creates a Barrier to Entry?*, 24 J.L. & ECON. 333 (1981) (detailed examination of how advertising relates to profits); Kwoka, *Advertising and the Price and Quality of Optometric Services*, 74 AM. ECON. REV. 211 (1984) (study showing that advertising leads to lower prices and higher average quality); Lynk, *Information, Advertising, and the Structure of the Market*, 54 J. BUS. 271 (1981) (data on competitive benefits of advertising). On the interpretation of particular cases, *see, e.g.*, the studies cited in note 22, *supra*, and McGee, *Predatory Price Cutting: The Standard Oil (N.J.) Case*, 1 J.L. & ECON. 137 (1958) (showing that Standard Oil did not engage in the practices of which it was accused); Peterman, *The Clorox Case and the Television Rate Structures*, 11 J.L. & ECON. 321 (1968) (showing that the foundation of the Court's decision, its supposition about quantity discounts, was false).

[32] It is also appropriate to extrapolate from existing work. If available data show that firms in certain kinds of markets have no power to influence price, it is appropriate to infer that similar markets behave in the same way. We cannot test every proposition about every market.

in judicial opinions as well as the lobbying efforts of some retailers—that it cannot be ignored.[33]

Whatever role political values play in antitrust, surely they do not call for courts to protect these market participants at the expense of consumers. Such protectionism turns antitrust on its head. Antitrust protects competition, not competitors. Protection also does not work. Courts may stop today's contract between a manufacturer and its dealers, but this does the dealers no favors. They get paid, after all, for accepting contractual restraints. They share in the benefits. Eliminate a restraint that is beneficial in competition, and manufacturers stop the payments. (Perhaps they raise the wholesale price.) Judges also cannot stop the world. Firms frustrated in one pursuit may turn to others, such as vertical integration by internal growth that wipes out dealers.

The discount chains' claim that restricted dealing threatens the chains' existence, and their low prices, also has a hollow ring. Just why K-Mart's existence is threatened if it can't sell shirts with little crocodile emblems has never been explained. There are lots of other knit shirts in the world. Perhaps discount stores love to be free riders—they take advantage of the information and other benefits created by rival stores, then increase their own volumes at these retailers' expense. It is more profitable to take a free ride than to provide one's own service, but this is hardly a legitimate concern of the law.

The discount stores' bleats are also simply wrong. Only a small minority of manufacturers used RPM when it was lawful between 1919 and 1975. Only a small minority of manufacturers use any form of restricted dealing today. Most products can be sold without special services or information. S.S. Kresge (the old K-Mart) flourished during the days of manufacturers' greatest freedom. It flourished because discount stores offer a combination of price and service that many customers value. Most manufacturers want to hold the "cost of distribution" (the retailer's mark-up) as low as possible. The K-Marts of the world do this, to everyone's great benefit. Nothing in restricted dealing threatens the ability of consumers to find low prices.

III. THE PATH AHEAD: PRESUMPTIONS REPLACE BOTH PER SE RULE AND RULE OF REASON

If vertical arrangements are procompetitive most of the time, what is the appropriate course for antitrust? Certainly recognition of the com-

[33] *See, e.g.*, Paschall v. Kansas City Star Co., 727 F.2d 692, 706 (8th Cir. 1984) (en banc) (Bright, J., dissenting: "The majority in this case . . . permits a monopolist to destroy hundreds of independent businesses. What a sad day for the American ideal that permits every person on his or her own initiative to own a small business.").

petitive benefits of practices means elimination of per se condemnation, which is reserved for practices that are always, or almost always, anticompetitive. The usual alternative to condemnation per se is evaluation under the rule of reason.

A. THE EMPTINESS OF THE RULE OF REASON

Restricted dealing could reduce economic efficiency. It could be a facilitating device for a dealers' or manufacturers' cartel, although this is unlikely. (The right thing to do when this occurs is to punish the cartel, not to prosecute the symptom.) It could raise the costs of new entrants and protect existing market power, although this also is unlikely. It could reduce welfare if there are peculiar demand conditions (the yellow car example), although this is the most unlikely of all. In principle, a rule of reason inquiry could search for one of these three sources of economic loss, calling on courts to condemn practices whenever the economic losses exceed the competitive benefits.

It is fantastic to suppose that judges (and juries) could carry out the evaluation entailed in such a search. The welfare implications of most forms of business conduct are beyond the ken of almost all economists. If you assembled 12 economists and gave them all available data about a business practice, plus an unlimited computer budget, you would not soon (or ever) get unanimous agreement about whether the practice promoted consumers' welfare or economic efficiency more broadly defined. They would inevitably discover some gaps in the data, some avenues requiring futher exploration. At least one of the economists would construct a new model showing how the practice *could* reduce efficiency if certain things (unknowable from the data) were present. A global inquiry invites no answer; it puts too many things in issue. (This is why macroeconomic predictions are so chancy.) To get an answer to a practical problem, you must start with some assumptions and fixed points of reference.

The economists might be able to reach agreement, but they would not do so on the basis of exhaustive empirical inquiry. They would resort to clues and shortcuts. They would use their economic knowledge of other markets to draw inferences about this one. One inference would be based on survival: if a practice has lasted a long time, despite competitive pressure, the practice is almost certain to be procompetitive. Otherwise the market position of the firm using the practice would have eroded under challenge from rivals. A firm collecting an overcharge ultimately loses sales to firms charging the competitive price. The evidence does not always permit such long run evaluation, though, and the central purpose of antitrust is to speed up the arrival of the long run (so that firms lose market power faster). The economists therefore might look at output changes in the short run. Does the firm using the challenged practice increase sales or reduce them? An increase suggests procompetitive effects, a lower effective price per unit of quality delivered. Does the firm increase its market share or lose it? Again an increase suggests procompetitive effects. These tests require some difficult work—the economists will need to employ regression analysis to hold other variables constant and isolate the effects of the challenged practice—but at least they offer a highly reliable rule of thumb.[34]

If the economist has a way to approach vertical practices, a judge has none. According to the Supreme Court, "the inquiry mandated by the Rule of Reason is whether the challenged agreement is one that promotes competition or one that suppresses competition. . . . [T]he purpose of the analysis is to form a judgment about the competitive significance of the restraint."[35] How does a court tell whether the arrangement promotes or suppresses competition? It must

> [C]onsider the facts peculiar to the business to which the restraint is applied; its condition before and after the restraint was imposed; the nature of the restraint and its effect, actual or probable. The history of the restraint, the evil believed to exist, the reason for adopting the particular remedy, the purpose or end sought to be achieved are all relevant facts.[36]

These formulations are empty. They decide no concrete cases. No wonder judges and justices routinely protest that courts cannot make the judgments called for by such rules. "[C]ourts are of limited utility in examining difficult economic problems. . . . [They are] ill-equipped and ill-suited for such decision-making [and cannot] analyze, interpret, and evaluate the myriad of competing interests and the endless data that would surely be brought to bear on such decisions. . . ."[37]

Of course judges cannot do what such open-ended formulas require. When everything is relevant, nothing is dispositive. Any one factor might or might not outweigh another, or all of the others, in the factfinder's contemplation. The formulation offers no help to businesses planning their conduct. Faced with a list of such imponderables, lawyers must

---

[34] F.M. Scherer points out (*supra* note 26) that the quantity test is not infallible. Under certain conditions it may be misleading. But these conditions are rare. We are searching for usable tests, not perfect ones.

[35] National Soc'y of Prof'l Eng'rs v. United States, 435 U.S. 679, 691-92 (1978).

[36] Chicago Board of Trade v. United States, 246 U.S. 231, 238 (1918), a passage repeatedly cited with approval by the Court. United States v. Penn-Olin Chemical Co., 378 U.S. 158, 176-77(1964), contains an even longer illustrative list, as does Times-Picayune Publishing Co. v. United States, 345 U.S. 594, 614-26 (1953), which applies to the rule of reason in general a list originally given in a merger case, United States v. Columbia Steel Co., 334 U.S. 495, 527-28 (1948).

[37] United States v. Topco Assocs., Inc., 405 U.S. 596, 609-12 (1972). *See also* Standard Oil Co. of California v. United States, 337 U.S. 293, 307-14 (1954). Both of these cases use the incapacity of the courts as a basis of per se condemnation—quite the opposite of the appropriate response to ignorance, but I let that matter pass.

engage in ceaseless discovery (they might find something bearing on a factor, and the factor might be dispositive). The higher the stakes—and stakes are very high in antitrust—the more firms are willing to spend on discovery and litigation. The marginal week of discovery or trial just might mean saving a few million or tens of millions of dollars. Litigation costs are the product of vague rules combined with high stakes, and nowhere is that combination more deadly than in antitrust litigation under the rule of reason.[38] Lawyers engaged in litigating about mergers (which are governed by the rule of reason) have known this for a long time.

From time to time the Court writes as if the rule of reason had content. In the *GTE Sylvania* case,[39] the Court stated that territorial restraints should be evaluated by comparing the increase in interbrand competition created by additional point-of-sale services against the reduction in intrabrand competition created by the territorial restraint. The Court also called on district judges to separate price from nonprice restraints. These are snipe hunts.

No one can sensibly weigh inter- and intrabrand competition against one another; they are not commensurable. The reduction in "intrabrand competition" is the *source* of the competitive benefit that helps one product compete against another. Intrabrand competition as such is worthless; one might as well complain when a corporation does not have internal competition to make the product most cheaply. Vertical integration eliminates this form of "competition," but in so doing it may enable the manufacturer to reduce its delivered price. No manufacturer wants to have less competition among its dealers for the sake of less competition. The reduction in dealers' rivalry in the price dimension is just the tool the manufacturer uses to induce greater competition in the service dimension.[40] As I spelled out above, restricted dealing alters the product's attributes. There is no "less" in one column to "balance against a gain" in the other, any more than the manufacturer's sole prerogative to decide what physical product to make creates a "reduction in intrabrand competition."

The injunction to separate price from nonprice restraints is equally vacuous. *Every* restricted dealing arrangement is designed to influence price. It must be. If territorial limits induce dealers to supply additional

[38] High stakes and vague rules also inhibit settlement. Cases are settled when the parties can agree on the likely outcome of a trial, and that agreement is harder to come by in antitrust. *See* Easterbrook, Landes & Posner, *Contribution Among Antitrust Defendants: A Legal and Economic Analysis*, 23 J.L. & ECON. 331, 353-64 (1980), for an analysis of the settlement process in antitrust.

[39] Continental T.V., Inc. v. GTE Sylvania Inc., 433 U.S. 36 (1977).

[40] Posner, *The Next Step in the Antitrust Treatment of Restricted Distribution: Per Se Legality*, 48 U. CHI. L. REV. 6, 18-22 (1981).

service and information, they do so only because they raise the price and thus call forth competition in the service dimension. If restrictions are a way of compensating retailers for lending their reputations (as a form of advertising), again they must affect price in order to provide that compensation. Every argument about restricted dealing implies that the restrictions influence price. There is no such thing as a free lunch;[41] the manufacturer can't get the dealer to do more without increasing the dealer's margin.

Restrictions influence price, and this also means that price signals are the manufacturer's best way of finding out whether a dealer is adhering to the restraints. The manufacturer's first clue that a dealer is in breach is likely to be a reduction in that dealer's price below that of other dealers. The price-cutting dealer probably is skimping on service. The manufacturer's eyes and ears are likely to be the dealers, the first to know if another dealer is cutting price. Any manufacturer with a system of restricted dealing therefore values complaints by one dealer that another is cutting price, because (a) it is easier to observe price than to observe the services, and (b) the change in price suggests a change in service provision. Under *GTE Sylvania*, though, a manufacturer who attends to these signals is likely to be accused of entering a price-fixing conspiracy with the complaining dealer. The court's focus on price complaints ensures that the systems that produce the greatest service benefits for consumers, and therefore the greatest incentives for some dealers to cut price and take a free ride, will also be the ones most open to challenge on the ground that the manufacturer and dealers that try to enforce the restraints have entered into a "price-fixing agreement." This cannot be a useful or stable approach.

B. SOME FILTERS TO SEPARATE THE BENEFICIAL FROM ANTICOMPETITIVE

With the price vs. nonprice and inter- vs. intrabrand competition "tests" abolished, however, the courts again are at sea in rule of reason cases. They should use the economists' way out. They should adopt some simple presumptions that structure the rule of reason inquiry.[42] Away with the foggy consider-everything approach! The increased use of strong pre-

[41] I assume Milton Friedman's copyright on this phrase has expired.

[42] In National Collegiate Athletic Ass'n v. Univ. of Okla., No. 83-271, argued Mar. 20, 1984, the Solicitor General, as amicus curiae, has asked the Supreme Court to move in this direction. The Solicitor General argues that in most cases courts should take a "quick look" at the nature of the practices involved and condemn or absolve the defendant on the basis of this inquiry, without the usual rule of reason scrutiny. The NCAA has agreed with the Government's approach, although it has proposed some modifications similar to the presumptions that I discuss in the text below. The Court therefore may address the question this term. (As I am counsel for the NCAA in this case, you again should apply the appropriate discount factor to the discussion. *NCAA* has nothing to do with restricted dealing, so the discount ought to be small.)

sumptions would guide businesses in the planning of their affairs by making it possible for counsel to state that some things do not create risks of liability. They would reduce the costs of litigation by drawing attention to particular topics capable of resolution. They would promote settlement. And if sometimes the presumptions let socially undesirable litigation escape, that is a bearable cost. The per se rule condemns whole categories of practices even though courts acknowledge that some practices in these categories are beneficial.[43] The court permits such overbreadth because all *rules* are imprecise. One cannot have the savings of decision by rule without accepting the cost of occasional mistakes.[44] We accept these mistakes because almost all of the practices covered by per se rules are anticompetitive, and an approach favoring case-by-case adjudication (to prevent condemnation of beneficial practices subsumed by the categories) would permit too many deleterious practices to escape condemnation.

The same arguments lead to the conclusion that the rule of reason's application to vertical arrangements should err on the side of tolerance. Most vertical arrangements are procompetitive. The rules of litigation accordingly should be "stacked" so that they do not ensnare many of these beneficial practices just to make sure that the few anticompetitive ones are caught. When almost all examples of a practice are procompetitive or neutral, the rules should have the same structure (although the opposite slant) as those that apply when almost all examples are anticompetitive.

The legal system should be designed to minimize the total costs of (1) anticompetitive practices that escape condemnation; (2) competitive practices that are condemned or deterred; and (3) the system itself. The third is easiest to understand. You do not use a $500,000 pile driver to swat flies. Some practices, although anticompetitive, are not worth deterring. And whenever you act, you want to do so at the least cost. A shift to the use of presumptions addresses (3) directly, and a change in the content of the legal rules influences all three points. Consideration (2) is especially important where, as with vertical arrangements, most examples of the category are beneficial. A legal system that errs even a few percent of the time is likely to "catch" mostly desirable practices. Better to change the presumption than to take the risk. Judge Breyer put it well:

> [W]hile technical economic discussion helps to inform the antitrust laws, those laws cannot precisely replicate the economists' (sometimes conflicting) views. For, unlike economics, law is an administrative system the effects of which depend upon the content of rules and precedents

---

[43] Arizona v. Maricopa County Medical Soc'y, 457 U.S. 332, 342 (1982) (condemning a horizontal arrangement even on the assumption that it saved consumers millions of dollars).

[44] *See* Ehrlich & Posner, *An Economic Analysis of Legal Rulemaking,* 3 J. LEGAL STUD. 257 (1974).

> only as they are applied by judges and juries in courts and by lawyers advising their clients. Rules that seek to embody every economic complexity and qualification may well, through the vagaries of administration, prove counter-productive, undercutting the very economic ends they seek to serve. Thus, despite the theoretical possibility of finding instances in which horizontal price fixing, or vertical price fixing, are economically justified, the courts have held them unlawful per se, concluding that the administrative virtues of simplicity outweigh the occasional "economic" loss. . . . Conversely, we must be concerned lest a rule or precedent that authorizes a search for a particular type of undesirable pricing behavior end up by discouraging legitimate price competition.[45]

The question, then, is what simple rules will filter the category of probably-procompetitive practices out of the legal system, leaving to assessment under the rule of reason only those with significant risks of competitive injury.

I offer five presumptions or filters. Each screens out vertical cases in which the risk of loss to consumers and the economy is sufficiently small that there is no need of extended inquiry (and significant risk that inquiry would lead to wrongful condemnation or to the deterrence of competitive activity as firms try to steer clear of the danger zone). There is nothing special about these presumptions. I mean them as illustrations, not as prescriptions. Some other, similar collection doubtless would do as well. The point of the exercise is to find good screening tools that may be administered at low cost in litigation and in counseling. Many might serve this function.

Vertical arrangements should be deemed lawful, without further inquiry, if any one of the following five things is true: (1) the firm employing the arrangement lacks market power; (2) firms use different methods of distribution; (3) the arrangement in question has led to an increase in output by the defendants; (4) the arrangement in question has been in use longer than five years; or (5) the firm cannot increase its profits by harming consumers. I explain each of these below.

1. *Market Power*

Market power is the ability to raise price significantly without losing so many sales that the increase is unprofitable. Most firms have a little power, because their products are not perfectly interchangeable with the goods of others. But few firms have substantial power over price. Firms that lack power cannot injure competition no matter how hard they try. They may injure a few consumers, or a few rivals, or themselves (see (5) below) by selecting "anticompetitive" tactics. When the firms lack market

[45] Barry Wright Corp. v. ITT Grinnell Corp., 724 F.2d 227, 234 (1st Cir. 1983) (citations omitted).

power, though, they cannot sustain deleterious practices. Rival firms will offer the consumers better deals. The process of rivalry is sufficient insurance. Rivals' better offers will stamp out bad practices faster than the judicial process can. For these and other reasons, many lower courts have held that proof of market power is an indispensable first step in any vertical case under the rule of reason.[46] The Supreme Court has established a market power hurdle in tying cases, despite the nominally per se character of the tying offense, on the same ground offered here: if the defendant lacks market power, other firms can offer the customer a better deal, and there is no need for judicial intervention.[47]

All three of the possibly anticompetitive manifestations of vertical arrangements can occur only if there is market power. The arrangements may facilitate cartels, but first there must be sufficient concentration and market power to make a cartel plausible. They may raise rivals' cost of entry, but this effect occurs only when the rival must enter on multiple levels simultaneously. When there is no market power, many existing firms stand ready to sell and make simultaneous entry unnecessary. Vertical arrangements may lead to inferior outcomes if there are unusual demand conditions, but again this depends on the existence of a monopolized or tightly oligopolistic market.[48]

An inquiry into market power does *not* entail the definintion of a "market," a subject that has bedeviled the law of mergers. Market definition is just a tool in the investigation of market power.[49] The process of identifying a product's substitutes in production and use, and the potential producers of these products, which is all market definition means, helps a court to determine whether a firm has the power to raise price significantly. Sometimes this is a close and difficult question, in which event the inquiry into power is of little use as a ready filter for vertical arrangements. But at other times it is obvious on even the briefest inquiry that a firm has no power. Here the filter offers a quick, painless, and correct end to litigation.

Even a brief recap of some of the central cases in the law of vertical restraints shows that it is easy to knock out many cases at the threshold.

---

[46] *E.g.*, White & White, Inc. v. American Hosp. Supply Corp., 723 F.2d 495 (6th Cir. 1983); Graphic Prods. Distribs., Inc. v. Itek Corp., 717 F.2d 1560, 1568-71 (11th Cir. 1983) (collecting authorities); Valley Liquors, Inc. v. Renfield Importers, Ltd., 678 F.2d 742, 745 (7th Cir. 1982); Products Liability Ins. Co. v. Crum & Forster Ins. Co., 682 F.2d 660, 663-65 (7th Cir. 1982); Muenster Butane, Inc. v. Stewart Co., 651 F.2d 292, 298 (5th Cir. 1981); Cowley v. Braden Indus, Inc., 613 F.2d 751, 755 (9th Cir.), *cert. denied*, 446 U.S. 965 (1980).

[47] United States Steel Corp. v. Fortner Enters., Inc., 429 U.S. 610 (1977).

[48] *See* Spence, and Scherer, *supra* note 26.

[49] *See* Areeda, *Market Definition and Horizontal Restraints*, 52 ANTITRUST L.J. 553 (1983); Landes & Posner, *Market Power in Antitrust Cases*, 94 HARV. L. REV. 937 (1981); and UNITED STATES DEPARTMENT OF JUSTICE MERGER GUIDELINES (June 14, 1982), *reprinted in* 2 TRADE REG. REP. (CCH) ¶¶ 4500-4505.

Fortner, a tying case, was in litigation for more than a decade before the Court finally got rid of it on the ground that a firm that supplies less than one percent of the nation's credit—in an almost atomistic market—lacks market power. That was equally obvious on the day the complaint was filed.[50] *GTE Sylvania*, the dominant territorial restraints case, also lasted more than a decade. In the end, as in the beginning, it was clear that a firm selling about two percent of America's TV sets, in a market with at least 20 strong rivals, had no power.[51] The *Standard Stations* case concerned exclusive dealing contracts signed by a refiner of petroleum with about 16 percent of the retail stations in the west.[52] Standard had six large and more than 70 small rivals. The contracts were for short terms, so that dealers could bolt to rival refiners very quickly (and rivals could bid for dealers). Once more, the absence of market power could have been determined on the pleadings. The list could be extended to *Brown Shoe* (vertical merger affecting less than five percent of an unconcentrated market), *White Motor* (exclusive distribution arrangements of a tiny firm in industry dominated by General Motors and others), and a host of others.

The market power filter is equally useful for the cases now in litigation that have come to public attention. K-Mart's challenge to Lacoste's method of distributing shirts, the FTC's challenge to Russell Stover's method of pricing chocolates, dealers' objection to Apple Computer's restrictions on mail order sales, Fairchild's complaint about Data General's bundling of computer hardware with operating systems, dealers' objection to Mazda's allocation system that links today's allocation of RX-7 cars to yesterday's sales of GLC cars—all of these could be dismissed quickly for lack of power. There are hundreds of brands of knit shirts (and entry is easy); chocolates from scores of chocolatiers across the globe may be found in every drug and department store; the market for small computers is cutthroat competition at work (entry is rampant, exit frequent, and if anyone has power, which is unlikely, it is IBM, not Apple or DG); and even if (again unlikely) Mazda, just about the smallest firm selling autos in the U.S., has some power over those who fancy sports cars, it has none over the dealers, who can switch to other brands or even carry other brands simultaneously. Nonetheless, these cases have dragged on and on.[53] Each should have met a quick demise.

---

[50] United States Steel Corp. v. Fortner Enters, Inc., 429 U.S. 610 (1977).

[51] Not until Continental T.V., Inc. v. GTE Sylvania Inc., 694 F.2d 1132 (9th Cir. 1982) (on remand after the 1977 decision of the Supreme Court), was this litigation, which arose out of a dealer terminated in 1965, finally put to rest.

[52] Standard Oil Co. of Cal. v. United States, 337 U.S. 293 (1949).

[53] *In re* Data General Corp. Antitrust Litig., 529 F. Supp. 801 (N.D. Cal. 1981), appeal pending, has had the longest life. It arose out of events in the early 1970s. The district court dismissed the case (after the jury found for plaintiff) on the ground that no matter how one defines the market, and on the court's definition DG's share was less than 2%, DG had no market power. The Apple cases are in litigation, and the Antitrust Division

2. *Widespread Adoption of Identical Practices*

Unless all or almost all firms in an industry use the same vertical restraints, a case should be dismissed on the pleadings. The rationale for this filter is that every one of the potentially-anticompetitive outcomes of vertical arrangements depends on the uniformity of the practice. For example, RPM or territorial restraints could facilitate or enforce a cartel only if all firms in the industry use identical practices. Recall the toothpaste illustration from Part II.A. If Colgate and Aim use RPM, while Gleem and Ultra-Brite do not, RPM cannot facilitate anyone's cartel. Dealers that want to cheat on a dealers' cartel will sell more Gleem (and more house brands) at reduced prices. And the lack of identical practices in the manufacturing industry means that RPM cannot facilitate a cartel there, either. The whole point of a "facilitating practice" is that when everyone does things the same way, this reduces the number of things the cartel must monitor to control cheating. When everyone does *not* do things the same way, nothing can be "facilitated."

The argument that vertical restraints may impede entry by requiring the new entrant to come in with several products (or at several levels) simultaneously also depends on uniform adherence to the vertical restraint. If a monopoly manufacturer has long-term exclusive dealing contracts with its distributors, its distribution network is "foreclosed" to a would-be entrant. The prospective manufacturer must come in on two levels (making plus distribution) or arrange for coordinated entry. But if there are four manufacturers in the industry, and only one or two use exclusive distribution, the would-be entrant will find a group of distributors anxious to be its agents if it offers a better deal, which it will. (Recall the hypothesis: the lack of entry allows the existing firms to charge a price above the competitive level. The new entrant will find distributors queueing up if it charges a price closer to the competitive one. If the existing firms charge only the competitive price, there is no problem whether or not the new entrant can find distributors.)

Finally, the possibility that unusual demand conditions lead those using restricted dealing to supply a package that is privately profitable but

has appeared as amicus curiae on behalf of Apple. The Mazda cases also are ongoing. One suit filed in 1979 in Oklahoma was decided by a jury in favor of plaintiffs and is on appeal (after an initial remand). Mazda Distributors (Gulf), Inc. v. Fox Motors, Inc., No. 83-2125 (10th Cir.). Again the Division has appeared as amicus to point out both Mazda's lack of market power and the competitive benefit of this "tie": it rewarded Mazda's best-selling dealers and thus encouraged them to sell more cars and take better care of its customers. Another Mazda suit is awaiting trial in Texas. The K-Mart/Lacoste imbroglio was settled. The FTC's quixotic pursuit of Russell Stover, begun in 1978 under Chairman Pertschuk, went through three rounds of litigation before ending in Russell Stover's favor in 1983. The administrative law judge found for Russell Stover, the full FTC reversed (over Chairman Miller's dissent), and the court of appeals then set aside the order on the ground that the FTC had disregarded the remainder of the *Colgate* doctrine. Russell Stover Candies, Inc. v. Federal Trade Comm'n, 718 F.2d 256 (8th Cir. 1983).

socially inferior (the yellow car case) also depends on uniformity of practice, for the reasons already discussed. Even those who think restricted dealing is a serious concern for antitrust concede that, when we see a variety of terms of trade in the market, we can dismiss this possibility as a source of harm.[54]

The uniform-practice filter is exceptionally powerful. It screens out *almost all* challenges to vertical practices. In almost every market the manufacturers employ a staggering variety of selling methods. Some bundle products together and others do not; some use restricted dealing and others do not. I do not survey the cases (even the brief list above was tedious), but you can run through them in your own mind. It is hard to compile a list of ten in the history of antitrust that would proceed past this filter, and some of those (such as the *Standard Stations* case) fail the market power filter. Whatever explains a solitary manufacturer's use of RPM, exclusive contracts, ties or other practices, the practice cannot be anticompetitive.[55] The fact that other sellers use different methods offers consumers a choice. The competing offers of different products and different methods are competition at work.[56]

3. *Effect on Output*

If vertical arrangements are anticompetitive, the output and market share of those using them must fall. This is a simple allocation of the Law of Demand. If a firm raises the effective price of a product of given quality, it will sell less. Similarly, if a firm improves the quality of a product and charges the same price, it will sell more. If it both increases the price and increases the quality, it may sell more or less, depending on whether consumers value the improvement at more than the cost. To take a trivial example, if Commodore puts a new and better instruction manual in the box with its Commodore 64 computer, it may raise its price to cover the extra cost. If its sales increase despite the higher price, we know that

---

[54] *See* text and note at note 27, *supra.*

[55] A favorite argument of those who would condemn vertical restraints runs something like this: "Sure, I see that territorial restrictions will induce the provision of display and information services for computers and other high-tech products, maybe even for new products of other sorts. Once the product becomes established, the rationale for the restraint vanishes. But if you take just a casual look, you will see that manufacturers of dog food and toothpaste used RPM, and manufacturers of blue jeans used territorial and customer limits. How can you explain the *dog food* case, for goodness sake? There must be something anticompetitive going on!" I do not know why a few canners of dog food used RPM, and neither does anyone else. There is no reason to care about this, though, if we do know that the use of the practice could not have been anticompetitive. There are many things we do not understand, but it is not appropriate to use antitrust to condemn the objects of our ignorance.

[56] The Supreme Court recognized this, for all practical purposes, in United States Steel Corp. v. Fortner Enters., Inc., 429 U.S. 610 (1977), when it gave, as one of the reasons for finding that U.S. Steel lacked market power in the credit market, the ability of other firms to elect to match or not match U.S. Steel's terms without interference from any artificial obstruction.

the extra information was worth the higher price, and then some, to consumers.

We can perform exactly the same test in all restricted dealing cases.[57] Look at what happens when the manufacturer adopts the practice. Hold other things, such as demand, constant. (There are statistical tools for doing this, if the data are available.) If the manufacturer's sales rise, the practice confers benefits exceeding its costs. If they fall, that suggests (although it does not prove) that there are no benefits.[58] Unless the practice failed one of the other filters, further inquiry would be in order.

Most vertical arrangements appear to have increased output. In *GTE Sylvania*, the adoption of the territorial restraints coincided with an expansion of Sylvania's sales and market share. In *Monsanto*, the defendant's sales and share tripled at the time it adopted restricted distribution.[59] U.S. Steel's "tie" increased its sales of prefabricated houses and credit. The hospital in *Hyde* adopted its "tie" when it opened its doors; it grew like Topsy and continues to expand at the expense of other hospitals that use different staffing practices.[60] In a number of restricted dealing cases that did not reach the Supreme Court, defendants put into evidence sophisticated economic studies of sales and share. So far as I am aware, in every vertical case in which econometric methods have been used, the economists found that the practices expanded output.

4. *Long-Lived Practices*

Sometimes the challenged practices were adopted so long ago that information about changes in output and share is no longer available. The third filter then is not useful, for it requires knowledge of what happened at the time the practice was adopted. The fourth filter asks the output question from a different perspective: did the practice survive? If a vertical practice is a method of collecting monopoly profits, the firms using this practice ultimately will lose their positions to firms offering consumers a better deal. As they lose market power, they will

---

[57] Richard Posner has elaborated on this filter, and I therefore do not need to go into detail in the text. *See* Posner, *The Rule of Reason and the Economic Approach: Reflections on the Sylvania Decision*, 45 U. CHI. L. REV. 1, 17-19 (1977). F.M. Scherer's demonstration (note 26, *supra*) that the output test *could* be inaccurate in some cases does not affect the point. If these cases are sufficiently rare, as his own analysis suggests they will be, then the output filter still has value.

[58] "Does not prove" because other things in the market may have happened at the same time. A rival's introduction of a popular new product might account for the change in sales, and the practice might still be harmless to competition or even beneficial.

[59] Here, though, the inference is unreliable, and application of this filter is arguably inappropriate. Monsanto introduced a new product at the same time it adopted restricted dealing practices, and it is very difficult to discern which is the cause of Monsanto's growth.

[60] By the time the case reached the Supreme Court, the hospital, which opened in 1971, was the fourth or fifth largest in the New Orleans metropolitan area, with about 6.2 percent of the area's patient-days.

need to abandon the practice in order to avoid being swamped by the competition.

This process may take a long time—and the firms will collect monopoly profits in the interim—but it will happen sooner or later. Even the best device for extracting an overcharge, merger to monopoly, does not last forever. General Motors, U.S. Steel, and other aggregations formed by merger are now but shadows of their former selves (in market share terms, anyway).

When the barriers to entry into the business are low, we would expect the erosion of position to occur reasonably quickly. (Indeed, if there are no entry barriers, there can never be monopoly exploitation no matter what the rest of the market looks like. The threat of entry prevents the exercise of power.)[61] The Antitrust Division's Merger Guidelines suggest that two years is "reasonably quickly" in antitrust; the Division inquires how much new output would be available within two years in response to a five percent increase in price. But for some practices two years is too short. Prospective entrants recognize that a new distribution practice may be abandoned by the firm that adopted it; firms do make mistakes. They may wait before entering. And entry itself may take a while. Thus for current purposes five years may be a better guide than two.

The proposed filter, then, is that if a firm has employed a vertical arrangement continuously for five years, and has not substantially lost its market position, a challenge to the practices should be dismissed.[62] The most reasonable interpretation of a persistent practice is that the practice is persistently beneficial to consumers. Long-term vertical arrangements cannot usefully be explained as cartel-facilitating practices. Cartels themselves rarely (maybe never) last for five years. Although vertical arrangements may slow down entry, they do not interdict it. By the time five years has elapsed, most or all of the anticipated entry will have occurred. If the practice has survived for five years, it is probably beneficial; if it is not, its demise in the market probably will precede its demise at the hands of a court. Business practices customarily predecease the litigation they spawn.

5. *Profits Must Depend on the Reduction in Competition*

The threat of antitrust liability is not the only reason businesses shy

---

[61] W. BAUMOL, J. PANZAR & R. WILLIG, CONTESTABLE MARKETS AND THE THEORY OF INDUSTRY STRUCTURE (1982).

[62] Five years is a number pulled from a hat. The length of time should depend on how difficult it is to enter the business—considering entry barriers (costs borne by the new firms that were not borne by the existing ones), entry hurdles (costs that would not be recoverable if entry were abandoned, an important consideration in any strategic decision about entry), and the entry lag (how long entry takes even if there are low hurdles and no barriers). The lower the barriers, hurdles and lags, the less time should be required before a court deems that new entry would have smothered any anticompetitive practice.

away from certain practices. Entrepreneurs fear business losses as much as—more than—losses in damages. The business losses occur sooner and with greater certainty. Markets impose their judgments automatically.

Antitrust law is useful in making cartels and monopolistic practices unprofitable. The premise of the damages remedy is that the threat of losses deters.[63] The recovery for overcharges brings home to the offender the losses it imposes on others, and the trebling makes up for the likelihood that the offense will escape detection and punishment. The deterrent threat assumes that businesses attend rationally to the risk of loss—if they do not, deterrence fails. If they do pay attention to losses, though, then it is safe to confine antitrust remedies to practices by which businesses obtain profits by harming competition. The market brings home to the offender any losses it imposes on others, and it brings them home more quickly than courts can. Unless there is a link between the antitrust injury and the defendant's profit, there is no need for judges to impose a sanction. The sanction imposed by the business losses will clear up the practice in due course.[64] This is the reason why courts do not impose penalties on firms that introduce unsuccessful products (such as the Lockheed L-1011 jet). These products may waste more of society's resources than antitrust violations do, yet the losses imposed by failure are adequate to induce businesses to take care. And the cost of judicial intervention is high—it includes the risk of mistakenly condemning hard competition.

Two cases show how this filter would work in practice. Grinnell Corp. purchased mechanical snubbers for use in building nuclear reactors. It bought a two-years' supply from Pacific Scientific Co. Barry Wright Corp., which had been Grinnell's supplier, brought suit, contending that the "exclusive" contract for a substantial portion of all snubbers sold in the U.S. reduced competition in the snubber market. If competition were reduced, though, suppliers of snubbers would charge higher prices in the future. Grinnell would be the poorer. It is a buyer of snubbers, not a producer. Why would Grinnell be the instrument of its own harm? If contracts of this nature harm competition, the overcharges they create will induce the purchasers to abandon these arrangements; if the purchasers want them, that is excellent evidence that they are efficient.[65]

---

[63] Illinois Brick Co. v. Illinois, 431 U.S. 720 (1977).

[64] A more complete discussion appears in Easterbrook, *Predatory Strategies and Counterstrategies*, *supra* note 24, at 276-79. *See also* Landes, *Optimal Sanctions for Antitrust Violations*, 50 U. CHI. L. REV. 652, 669-72 (1983); Posner, *supra* note 57, at 16-17.

[65] Judge Breyer made this point, in a magnificent opinion from which I have already quoted a large chunk. As he explained: "Grinnell had every interest in promoting new competition . . . Had Grinnell believed that the long-term nature of the contracts significantly interfered with new entry, or inhibited the development of a new source of supply, it is difficult to understand why it would have sought the agreements." Barry Wright Corp. v. ITT Grinnell Corp., 724 F.2d 227, 238 (1st Cir. 1983).

AM International makes offset duplicators. By some accounts, AM is a dominant firm with more than 50 percent of the market for such machines. (I assume for now that this is a relevant market, which it probably is not in light of the many other methods of duplication.) Buyers often want collators to sort and stack the printed sheets. AM does not make collators but is a distributor of collators made by others. In 1980 it stopped carrying collators made by Norfin, Inc. and started selling another firm's collators exclusively. Norfin maintains that AM is trying to exclude it from the business—not only terminating distribution but also engaging in predatory pricing of collators, trade disparagement of Norfin, and a variety of other underhanded practices to reduce competition.[66] Yet AM has no reason to monopolize the collator business. It does not make the things; the remaining collator makers, not AM, would collect any monopoly profits. AM's interest, on the contrary, is to keep the prices of collators as low as possible. Collators are complements of duplicators. They work together to produce the finished good (printed, sorted sheets). The less collators cost, the more AM can charge for its duplicators. The more collators cost, the less likely consumers are to want AM's machines. AM can be counted on to protect the consumer's interest. If AM has erred, its own interests will lead it to restore competition to the collator market. The antitrust laws should be bystanders in cases such as this.

If courts had perfect information and wisdom, it might be appropriate to damn Grinnell's or AM's practices. The threat of antitrust liability might speed up firms' recognition of their own self-interests. If we are certain enough that practice *X* is harmful and must be snuffed out, no penalty is too high, no retribution too swift. But courts do not have perfect information and the judicial process is both slow and costly. It is a mistake to suppose that because markets correct business errors only slowly, judges must be better. One must compare the costs and risks of the two processes.

The costs of the judicial process—including the costs of errors, which deter beneficial practices—suggest the wisdom of letting the competitive process rather than the courts deal with conduct that does not create profits by reducing competition. If the practice really is anticompetitive and privately unprofitable, it will go away in time. If it persists, the appropriate inference is that it has competitive benefits.[67] We may not

[66] AM International, Inc. v. Norfin, Inc., No. 80 C 6824 (N.D. Ill.).

[67] Phillip Areeda proposed in these pages that antitrust be used to condemn anticompetitive practices whether or not the perpetrator has market power. He gave as an example a boycott that excludes one firm from the market but leaves one hundred more in competition. Areeda, *Introduction to Antitrust Economics*, 52 ANTITRUST L.J. 523, 526 (1983). The boycott should be condemned, he reasoned, because it is "sensible to assume that business people are acting in their own self-interest and to assume that an unambiguously exclusionary purpose tends to indicate an anticompetitive effect." Areeda wants to start

yet understand these benefits, but our understanding is not a condition of legality.

IV. CONCLUSION

I have argued that vertical practices are usually procompetitive, that these practices permit firms to compete on the level of market organization and entire systems of service, as well as on the traditional terms of product design and pricing. The more ways to compete, the better. Vertical arrangements almost never threaten competition.

Judges are free to employ the common law tradition to modify antitrust rules in response to this recognition, and they should do so. They should not just fob the questions off into a rule of reason inquiry, though, because the rule of reason is vacuous. They should instead create a series of simple presumptions that filter out the cases in which anticompetitive effects are unlikely. Once they have concluded, using these presumptions, that given practices are not apt to injure competition, they should leave the practices alone and not demand proof about why the practices are beneficial.

Where does this leave antitrust? The kinds of practices that may get past the filters are those that arise in highly concentrated industries (Herfindahl-Hirschman Index exceeding 1800), the members of which pursue parallel business practices that might help them coordinate a cartel or slow down entry. The *Ethyl* case[68] is one that would be taken seriously under my approach. *International Salt, Dr. Miles* and others also were sufficiently difficult to call for "full" rule of reason scrutiny.[69] By and large, though, the approach sketched above puts an end to litigation about vertical arrangements. Perhaps experience under such an approach ultimately would suggest the wisdom of per se legality, on the

with the obviously-anticompetitive practice and infer the bad effect. Why do this? Is it not equally appropriate to start from the obvious lack of market power and infer that the practice is (a) not anticompetitive at all, or (b) a self-correcting mistake? To assert that *X* is obviously anticompetitive is to avoid one of the most difficult problems of antitrust analysis.

[68] The FTC held that Ethyl, DuPont and two smaller companies had used a number of parallel distribution practices in a very concentrated industry in order to facilitate formation and policing of a cartel. The court of appeals set the order aside on the ground of insufficient evidence (as well as legal disagreement with the FTC's authority to act). E.I. du Pont de Nemours & Co. v. Federal Trade Comm'n, 729 F.2d 128 (2d Cir. 1984). One is tempted to say that if there was not enough evidence in *Ethyl* there will never be enough evidence, but the judgment may be premature. (The *Ethyl* practices, if they were as the FTC described them, would have passed all five filters except #4, longevity. The longevity could have been explained on the ground that tetraethyl lead is a dying industry, not one to attract very expensive entry even if there were a cartel. The "entry barrier" proviso to #4 therefore would have come into play.)

[69] In *International Salt* the tying may have facilitated enforcement of a cartel. *See* note 22, *supra*. There may have been a real cartel in *Dr. Miles*, too.

ground that the results of the extended search have not been worth the candle. No matter. By the time we learn enough from this staged-presumption approach, there will doubtless be new theories and data about vertical arrangements, and it will be time to start the process of evaluation again.

V. SOME THOUGHTS ON *MONSANTO*

The Supreme Court released its opinion in *Monsanto Co. v. Spray-Rite Service Corp.*[70] two days before I addressed the Antitrust Section at its Spring Meeting.[71] The Court announced a new approach to inferring agreements for purposes of the *Dr. Miles* prohibition of resale price maintenance. Under *Monsanto,* it is not enough that dealers complain to manufacturers about prices, or even that dealers and manufacturers are in constant communication about price. An unlawful agreement may not be inferred from termination in response to price complaints. To support an inference of conspiracy, there "must be evidence that tends to exclude the possibility that the manufacturer and nonterminated distributors were acting independently."[72] The evidence must show "a conscious commitment to a common scheme designed to achieve an unlawful objective."[73] Applying this standard, the Court concluded that the evidence was sufficient to support a jury's verdict against Monsanto. I offer some preliminary thoughts about the opinion.

First, the Court unanimously recognized the value of restricted dealing. This is why it held that the prohibited conspiracy may not be inferred from even persistent discussions of price.

> A manufacturer and its distributors have legitimate reasons to exchange information about the prices and the reception of their products in the market. Moreover, it is precisely in cases in which the manufacturer attempts to further a particular marketing strategy by means of agreements on often costly nonprice restrictions that it will have the most interest in the distributors' resale prices. The manufacturer often will want to ensure that its distributors earn sufficient profit to pay for programs such as hiring and training additional salesmen or demonstrating the technical features of the product, and will want to see that "free riders" do not interfere . . .
>
> . . . Permitting an agreement to be inferred merely from the existence of complaints, or even from the fact that termination came about "in response to" complaints, could deter or penalize perfectly legitimate conduct. As Monsanto points out, complaints about price-cutters "are natural—and from the manufacturer's perspective, unavoidable—re-

[70] 104 S. Ct. 1464 (1984).

[71] Because the Antitrust Section requires prepared remarks to be delivered to the editor of this *Journal* in advance of the meeting, the preceding text was written without the benefit of the Court's decision in *Monsanto.*

[72] 104 S. Ct. at 1471.

[73] 104 S. Ct. at 1473.

> actions by distributors to the activities of their rivals." . . . [D]istributors are an important source of information for manufacturers. In order to assure an efficient distribution system, manufacturers and distributors constantly must coordinate their activities to assure that their product will reach the consumer persuasively and efficiently.[74]

The Court rejected Spray-Rite's argument that restrictions on dealers are "suspect" because they depart from the model of atomistic competition. The Court implicitly rejected the common notion that antitrust offers dealers a "right to make independent decisions"; on the contrary, the Court saw the value of coordination between dealer and manufacturer in designing the full package of attributes (product and service) that will be offered to customers. It saw why manufacturers have a "legitimate" interest in dealers' prices—because prices influence dealers' ability and incentive to supply special services. The Court's recognition of the value of restricted dealing supports many of the arguments offered earlier in this paper.

Monsanto thus answered the question whether *Dr. Miles* is the rule or the exception. Its per se approach is an exception to the principle that manufacturers and dealers have a legitimate, joint interest in establishing optimal arrangements for the sale of their product. *Dr. Miles* is the exception because restricted dealing ordinarily is beneficial. The Court not only approved discussions about price but also fortified the *Colgate* rule, which allows manufacturers to demand that retailers charge particular prices. The decision to endorse *Colgate* in strong terms must reflect substantial dissatisfaction with *Dr. Miles*.

Second, the Court recognized more clearly than ever before that all restricted dealing is of a piece, that the legal distinctions are artificial. It wrote: "[T]he economic effect of all of the conduct described above—unilateral and concerted vertical price-setting, agreements on price and nonprice restrictions—is in many, but not all, cases similar or identical."[75] This, too, is consistent with the arguments I have presented.

Third, the Court described the objection to RPM in an economic manner. Instead of saying that RPM is unlawful because it interferes with "the central nervous system of the economy" or some other rhetorical, but empty, formulation, the Court portrayed RPM as a practice that may facilitate cartels.[76] The *Monsanto* opinion largely reads as if the Court has adopted the economic approach to restricted distribution.

---

[74] 104 S. Ct. at 1470.

[75] *Id.* Justice White took the same position in Continental T.V., Inc. v. GTE Sylvania Inc., 433 U.S. 36, 68-70 (1977) (concurring in the judgment).

[76] It did this by indirection, summarizing the position of the Antitrust Division: "They say that the economic objections to resale price maintenance that we discussed in *Sylvania* [citation omitted]—such as that it facilitates horizontal cartels—can be met easily in the context of rule-of-reason analysis." 104 S. Ct. at 1469 n.7.

Fourth, these positions, taken together, call *Dr. Miles* and the per se rule into question. If restricted dealing and price arrangements are ordinarily procompetitive, if there is no real difference between the effects of price and nonprice restraints, and if the objection to RPM is the same as that to other vertical restraints, then it follows that per se condemnation of RPM is anomalous.

The Court did not say so. It was invited by the Solicitor General and several other amici to overrule *Dr. Miles*, but it declined. It replied that the parties had agreed to the per se instructions given to the jury, and that as a result "we have no occasion to consider the merits of this argument" (attacking the per se rule).[77] In declining to speak, though, the Court spoke. The manner of its refusal to speak invited further challenges to *Dr. Miles*.

Spray-Rite and many supporting amici—including the attorneys general of 46 states, the National Mass Retailing Institute, and the Small Business Legal Defense Committee—had urged on the Court the same argument Representative Seiberling makes in his paper. They said that the issue was foreclosed by precedent and by the Consumer Goods Pricing Act of 1975. It would have been simple for the Court to reject the Solicitor General's argument by saying that the issue has been settled, and that it is for Congress to make changes. Justice Brennan filed a brief concurrence to this effect. But the Court took a different path, leaving the issue open and implying that it has the power—perhaps the inclination—to proceed on its own. The days of *Dr. Miles* may be numbered.

I do not want to leave the impression of unreserved joy about this opinion. The Court affirmed the judgment against Monsanto by pointing to some evidence from which the jury could have inferred actual RPM agreements among Monsanto and some nonterminated dealers. The sort of evidence to which the Court pointed is common in complex systems of distribution. Monsanto had more than 100 dealers and many field personnel. It would be surprising indeed if a search of Monsanto's, or any other manufacturer's, files did not turn up some documents that could be read as expressing "agreement" on price. If one or two such documents are enough to go to a jury, then the manufacturer does not have the breathing space the Court intended to provide for the discussions of price and service that the justices recognized as legitimate. The cost of trial, and the risk of erratic judgments, will deter manufacturers from using the practices the Court calls beneficial.

The amicus brief filed by Donald Turner suggests a way of handling this problem: even express price agreements should not be unlawful per se if they are ancillary to a system of distribution with legitimate nonprice

[77] *Id.*

elements.[78] The Court never referred to this suggestion. Perhaps the justices deemed it, like the Solicitor General's argument, foreclosed by Monsanto's failure to object to the jury instructions. If so, then the affirmance in *Monsanto* is a ticket good for this day and train only, and in a future case with identical evidence the defendant still has a legitimate motion for summary judgment.

There is also a question of remedy. Why does the existence of a RPM agreement between Monsanto and Dealer #1 give Spray-Rite (Dealer #101) a right to lost profit damages? The Court treated the case as if every one of Monsanto's dealers acquired tenure when Monsanto struck an illegal agreement with one dealer. The RPM agreement with Dealer #1 might hurt consumers of Monsanto's products, but what concern is this of Spray-Rite? Is it that Spray-Rite has a right not to be fired for attempting to undermine the RPM agreement with Dealer #1? Certainly the terminated dealer should be required to have proof to that effect, but why is it enough? It would be legitimate to fire a dealer for attempting to undermine the sort of tacit understanding with Dealer #1 that *Colgate* supports, so why is firing to protect RPM different? And why is Spray-Rite's lost profit the proper measure of damages, when antitrust is designed to protect competition rather than competitors?

These questions of causation and damages lurk in every dealership termination case. No one briefed these issues in *Monsanto*, and the Court cannot be faulted for passing them by. They await attention by the lower courts, and they offer further opportunities to reduce the scope of the *Dr. Miles* rule in the common law fashion.

---

[78] Brief for National Agricultural Chemicals Ass'n at 12-23, *Monsanto*. *See also* Eastern Scientific Co. v. Wild Heerbrugg Instruments, Inc., 572 F.2d 883 (1st Cir.), *cert. denied*, 439 U.S. 833 (1978).

[9]

The Rule of Reason and the Economic Approach: Reflections on the *Sylvania* Decision

Richard A. Posner†

In the absence of antitrust prohibitions, manufacturers commonly restrict competition among their distributors or dealers. They may forbid the dealer to sell from any location other than that designated in the dealership agreement ("location clause"), set maximum or minimum resale prices, assign exclusive territories to dealers, reserve certain customers to the manufacturer, forbid distributors to sell to other than authorized dealers, or forbid dealers to sell to other dealers. One restriction on competition among dealers, resale price maintenance (placing a floor under the dealer's resale price), was held to be illegal per se under section 1 of the Sherman Act as early as 1911, in the *Dr. Miles* case.[1] But the legality of nonprice restrictions in distribution was not even considered by the Supreme Court until it decided the *White Motor* case in 1963.[2] The Court in *White Motor* reversed a summary judgment entered in favor of the government, holding that it was premature to deem the particular restrictions involved (exclusive dealer territories and reservation of certain customers to the manufacturer) illegal per se. Four years later, the Court in *Schwinn*[3] held that such restrictions were indeed illegal per se when imposed in contracts of sale. On the other hand, if the dealership agreement created an agency relation-

---

† Professor of Law, The University of Chicago. This article is adapted from a talk given on November 2, 1977, to an Antitrust Law Briefing Conference sponsored by the Federal Bar Association. Robert H. Bork and Kenneth W. Dam commented helpfully on a previous draft.

[1] Dr. Miles Medical Co. v. John D. Park & Sons Co., 220 U.S. 373 (1911).

[2] White Motor Co. v. United States, 372 U.S. 253 (1963).

[3] United States v. Arnold, Schwinn & Co., 388 U.S. 365 (1967).

ship between dealer and manufacturer, a nonprice restriction on competition among dealers was not illegal per se. Last term, ten years after *Schwinn*, the Court in *Continental T.V., Inc. v. GTE Sylvania Inc.*[4] repudiated *Schwinn* and held that nonprice restrictions on dealer competition are not illegal per se even if imposed in a sales contract.

The *Sylvania* decision has generated considerable excitement in the antitrust defense bar. The Court seemed to go out of its way to overrule *Schwinn:* it could, as urged by Justice White in his concurring opinion, have adopted the distinction whereby the lower court upheld the legality of Sylvania's location clause without questioning *Schwinn.*[5] Furthermore, the Court's opinion places unusual emphasis on the role of economics in deciding antitrust cases, including "Chicago" economics, which is hostile to many of the traditional rules of antitrust liability.

My interest in *Sylvania* is based not only on the fact that it is one of the most discussed antitrust decisions of recent years. I briefed and argued the *Schwinn* case for the government. Subsequently, my views on the proper treatment of restrictions in distribution under the antitrust laws took a 180-degree turn, and the article expressing my new thinking was heavily cited by the majority in *Sylvania.*[6]

I. From *Schwinn* to *Sylvania*

To understand the possible significance of *Sylvania* for the development of antitrust doctrine, it is necessary to go back to the government's brief in *Schwinn.*[7] The brief did not argue that restricting competition among one's distributors was illegal per se. It argued that the adverse effect of such a restriction on competition

---

[4] 97 S. Ct. 2549 (1977).

[5] The Ninth Circuit and Mr. Justice White thought *Schwinn* distinguishable for two reasons. First, Sylvania's action did not restrict intrabrand competition as severely because Sylvania, unlike Schwinn, did not limit the territories where or the customers to whom its dealers could sell. Second, Sylvania's market share was much smaller than Schwinn's at the time they adopted their respective restricted distribution systems and so the restraints imposed by Sylvania had more potential for increasing interbrand competition. *See* 97 S. Ct. 2563 (White, J., concurring); 537 F.2d 980, 988-92 (9th Cir. 1976) (en banc), *aff'd on other grounds*, 97 S. Ct. 2549 (1977).

[6] Posner, *Antitrust Policy and the Supreme Court: An Analysis of the Restricted Distribution, Horizontal Merger and Potential Competition Decisions*, 75 Colum. L. Rev. 282 (1975); *see* 97 S. Ct. at 2557 n.13, 2559 nn.18-21 & 2561. *See also* 97 S. Ct. at 2568 n.10. (White, J., concurring). A revised version of the relevant portions of that article appears in R. Posner, Antitrust Law: An Economic Perspective 147-66 (1976).

[7] Brief for the United States, United States v. Arnold, Schwinn & Co., 388 U.S. 365 (1967).

at the dealer level created a presumption of illegality that could be rebutted, in principle at least, by showing that the restriction had an offsetting procompetitive effect in enabling the manufacturer to market his product more effectively in competition with other manufacturers. The government brief was profoundly skeptical, however, that this showing could ever be made except possibly by a small and struggling new entrant. Indeed, the government thought that restrictions on competition in distribution imposed by an established manufacturer were likely to reduce competition at the manufacturing level as well as at the dealer level. Specifically, the brief suggested that Schwinn had sought to restrict the distribution of its bicycles in order to reinforce an image of superior quality that would reduce the substitutability of other bicycle brands and thus increase Schwinn's monopoly power in the bicycle market.

This analysis reflected the then prevailing thinking of the economics profession on restricted distribution. The Supreme Court, to its credit, was not convinced, but neither was it persuaded that restricted distribution was sufficiently innocuous (or beneficial) to justify rejection of the per se approach. The Court, in an opinion by Justice Fortas, adopted an arbitrary compromise. It held that restrictions on distribution were illegal per se when imposed in sales contracts but not when imposed in agency contracts, even though it had recently held, in *Simpson v. Union Oil Company,* that resale price maintenance in an agency contract was illegal per se.[8] *Simpson* precluded the Court in *Schwinn* from simply deeming restrictions in distribution outside the reach of section 1 of the Sherman Act when accomplished through agency contracts. So, to distinguish *Simpson,* the Court observed that the "net effect" of Schwinn's restrictive consignment agreements was "to preserve and not to damage competition in the bicycle market."[9] But this statement undermined the Court's blanket condemnation of the identical restrictions when imposed in contracts of sale.

The lower federal courts were plainly unhappy with the per se rule of *Schwinn* and exercised their ingenuity to find exceptions to the rule.[10] Meanwhile, academic opinion was changing. Lester Telser's pioneering article on resale price maintenance,[11] though pub-

[8] 377 U.S. 13 (1964).

[9] 388 U.S. at 382.

[10] The cases are collected in note 14 of the Court's opinion in *Sylvania,* 97 S. Ct. at 2557. For an exhaustive analysis of the evolution of restricted distribution law to the eve of *Sylvania,* see ABA Antitrust Section, Monograph No. 2, Vertical Restrictions Limiting Intrabrand Competition (1977).

[11] Telser, *Why Should Manufacturers Want Fair Trade?* 3 J. Law & Econ. 86 (1960).

lished well before the *Schwinn* case was decided, began winning more adherents among academic economists and lawyers. Telser had argued that manufacturers impose minimum resale prices on their dealers not in order to give the latter monopoly profits, which would be an absurd motivation for a manufacturer, but to induce them to provide the optimal level of presale services.[12] Dealers would compete with each other in offering successively greater services until their marginal cost curve rose to intersect the price fixed by the manufacturer. Therefore, the manufacturer could, simply by altering that price, automatically vary the level of dealer presale services provided. This analysis can easily be extended to nonprice restrictions.[13] The manufacturer gives the dealer an exclusive territory so that the dealer can charge a price that will support the level of services desired by the manufacturer. The dealer will provide that level of services rather than pocket the difference between a high price and the cost of distribution with little service because, if he does not, the manufacturer will reassign the territory to another dealer.

One reason why Telser's analysis was not more influential at the time *Schwinn* was decided is that many economists viewed the presale services encouraged by resale price maintenance and cognate nonprice restrictions as of dubious value to consumers,[14] a view reflected in the government's brief in *Schwinn*. These services were thought to be forms of advertising, and economists in this period regarded advertising as a socially wasteful activity that served only to reduce the elasticity of demand for advertised products. In particular, it was thought that heavy advertising convinced the consuming public, without any basis in real differences among brands of the same product, that less heavily advertised brands were not good substitutes for more heavily advertised ones. Acceptance of this view of advertising has receded in recent years. Economists are more likely now to regard advertising as a source of genuine consumer information, sometimes irrespective of its content.[15] In addition, studies have shown that heavy advertising is associated with unsta-

---

[12] He also argued that in some cases manufacturers might adopt resale price maintenance in order to shore up a manufacturers' cartel. This possibility is discussed in text and notes at notes 21-22 *infra*.

[13] As demonstrated in Bork, *The Rule of Reason and the Per Se Concept: Price Fixing and Market Division*, (pt. 2), 75 YALE L.J. 373 (1966).

[14] For a representative specimen of this thinking, see Comanor, *Vertical Territorial and Customer Restrictions:* White Motor *and Its Aftermath*, 81 HARV. L. REV. 1419, 1429-30 (1968).

[15] *See, e.g.*, Nelson, *Information and Consumer Behavior*, 78 J. POL. ECON. 311 (1970).

ble consumer brand preferences—intensive advertising does not cement consumer loyalty to the advertised brand but, on the contrary, is the recourse of sellers who have difficulty holding on to their customers.[16] It is a weapon of competition rather than of monopoly.

Not all economists and lawyers knowledgeable in economics who write on monopoly questions, perhaps not even most, view restricted distribution so benignly. Nevertheless, the profession now views restricted distribution more favorably than it did when *Schwinn* was decided. Justice Fortas's skepticism concerning the government's economic arguments in *Schwinn* has been, tentatively at least, vindicated.

II. The Scope of *Sylvania*

This article is not centrally concerned with the question whether the Court in *Sylvania* was correct in overruling *Schwinn*. Obviously I think the decision is good economics, and because it is well settled that per se illegality is appropriate only when there are grounds for confidence that a practice is on balance anticompetitive, good antitrust law as well. A more difficult question is whether the Court should have followed the principle of stare decisis and avoided overruling so recent a precedent. I can think of no compelling reason why. No doubt some firms relied on that part of the *Schwinn* decision which allowed manufacturers to restrict distribution by means of consignment agreements, but *Sylvania* did not disturb their reliance. The only people who relied to their detriment on the per se rule laid down in *Schwinn* were the plaintiffs in *Sylvania*-type cases.

More interesting and problematic than the merits of *Sylvania* are the many questions regarding both substance and method in antitrust law that the opinion raises. How many other antitrust precedents must the Court in logic re-examine, having embraced, I believe for the first time, the "free rider" concept?[17] Will the Court's strong endorsement of franchise distribution and, relatedly, of the primacy of interbrand competition lead it to adopt more permissive rules concerning other restrictions on intrabrand competition that sellers impose on their franchised dealers and distributors? How far is the Court prepared to press the suggestion in the *Sylvania* opinion that economic considerations should be dominant in the decision of antitrust cases? And what precisely is the Rule of Reason inquiry

---

[16] *See* Telser, *Advertising and Competition*, 72 J. Pol. Econ. 537 (1964).

[17] *See* 97 S. Ct. at 2561.

envisaged by the Court in restricted distribution cases, now that they have been removed from the per se category? These questions are explored in the remainder of this article.

A. Implications of the Free-Rider Concept

I said earlier that the reason why a manufacturer might want to restrict competition in the distribution of his product is to evoke the optimal level of dealer presale services. As the Court in *Sylvania* noted, the restriction is necessary because in its absence any dealer who offered presale services would be inviting competing dealers to provide no (or fewer) services and thereby underprice him. This "free-riding" danger would deter dealers from offering presale services, at least in the optimum amount.

The territorial system of the soft-drink companies, currently under challenge by the FTC (which is, however, re-examining the case in light of *Sylvania),* nicely illustrates the nature of the free-rider problem.[18] The Coca Cola Company considers it very important that Coke be available to the consuming public in vending machines in bars, game rooms, athletic stadiums, and other locations where a sudden onset of thirst may induce the consumer to try, and it is hoped like, Coke. The cost of distribution through thousands of scattered low-volume outlets is very high, however, and if Cokes sold at these locations were priced to cover the full cost of distribution, the price would be so high that Coca Cola's promotional objective would be defeated. Accordingly, each bottler-franchisee is given an exclusive territory in order to encourage him to maintain a below-cost price (that is, to "advertise" in the manner found to be most effective in the soft-drink industry) in these outlets and recoup his losses by charging a price well above cost in the supermarkets, where the steady customer buys. This system of pricing could not be sustained if there were competition among bottlers, for then some bottlers would do no promotional below-cost selling but would instead cater only to the supermarket trade stimulated by the bottlers who did. Stated otherwise, many bottlers would take a free ride on the taste for the product created by the promotional practices of the bottler who made Coke widely available at low prices.

A more conventional example of the free-riding problem, closer to *Sylvania* itself, is provided by the facts in *United States v. Gen-*

[18] *See* Coca Cola Co., [1973-1976 Transfer Binder] TRADE REG. REP. (CCH) ¶ 21,010 (FTC, initial decision, Oct. 8, 1975).

eral Motors Corp.[19] In the late 1950's, discount houses in Los Angeles were offering new Chevrolets to the public at bargain prices. They usually obtained these cars from Chevrolet dealers located across town. A cooperating dealer, because he offered no presale services in connection with the sale of the cars through discount houses, could offer the discount house an attractive price, and the discount house could get by with a small mark-up over that price because it offered few presale services. Customers of the discount houses probably utilized the presale services provided by other dealers before striking their bargains at the discount house. It is evident that if the discount selling had become sufficiently widespread, Chevrolet dealers would have become much less willing to offer presale services, at least without the awkward expedient of charging the potential customer for the service itself (for example, by levying an entrance fee to the dealer showroom).

All this the Supreme Court in *Sylvania* was well aware of, but it may not have been fully aware of the potential reach of the free-rider concept. The Court must have realized, because Justice White emphasized the point in his concurring opinion,[20] that the concept applies with equal force to resale price maintenance. The Court offered, however, two reasons for distinguishing resale price maintenance from nonprice restrictions in distribution.[21] The first is that resale price maintenance can be used to bolster collusion at the manufacturer level: if colluding manufacturers have fixed the retail as well as the wholesale price, then one of the manufacturers who is cheating his fellows by undercutting the cartel price cannot pretend that his market share is increasing only because the retailers who carry his product have decided, for their own reasons, to accept a lower mark-up over the wholesale price of his product. But this collusion-enhancing effect of resale price maintenance depends on each retailer's handling only one manufacturer's brand of the product in question, which is the exceptional rather than the normal resale price maintenance situation. The retailer who handles the brands of several manufacturers will increase his purchases of, and his sales efforts for, the brand of the manufacturer who offers him the lowest wholesale price—the cartelist who is cheating. The presence of resale price maintenance will not make this type of cheating any easier to detect.

Furthermore, exclusive territories or other nonprice restrictions

---

[19] 384 U.S. 127 (1966).

[20] 97 S. Ct. at 2567-68.

[21] *Id.* at 2558-59 n.18.

on dealer competition are also potential methods of shoring up a manufacturers' cartel. They prevent a cheater from arguing that any increase in his market share above the quota assigned him by the cartel was due not to his price cutting but to competition among his dealers. To be sure, nonprice restrictions would be effective in shoring up cartels only in exclusive dealing situations, but, as we saw, the effectiveness of resale price maintenance in shoring up cartels is similarly limited. In short, the possible role of restricted distribution in facilitating collusion at the manufacturer level does not distinguish price from nonprice restrictions.[22]

There is an even more fundamental objection to the Court's attempted distinction between resale price maintenance and nonprice restrictions on dealer competition. That resale price maintenance might sometimes be used to bolster a cartel at the manufacturer level cannot, under accepted legal standards, justify making the practice per se illegal. For example, under the test of *Northern Pacific*, which the Court in *Sylvania* quoted and endorsed, only arrangements which have a "pernicious effect on competition and lack . . . any redeeming virtue"[23] are per se unlawful. The fact that resale price maintenance might sometimes be used to bolster a cartel does not support the conclusion that it has a "pernicious effect on competition," which implies something more than a mere possibility of abuse. As for the second prong of the *Northern Pacific* test, the free-rider analysis, by which the Court found "redeeming virtue" in nonprice restrictions in distribution, applies equally to resale price maintenance. Telser originally developed the analysis to explain resale price maintenance.

The second basis for distinguishing between price and nonprice restrictions suggested by the Court in *Sylvania* was the recent repeal of the fair-trade exemption to the Sherman and Federal Trade Commission Acts.[24] It is true that the legislative history reflects both a rejection of the justifications that have been offered for resale price maintenance and an awareness that the effect of repealing the exemption would be to throw it into the per se category.[25] However, Congress's repeal of the fair trade exemption, even if motivated by

[22] The approach to restricted distribution cases suggested below, *see* text and notes at notes 50-54 *infra*, is not designed to ascertain when restrictions on distributors are employed as an enforcement device by a manufacturers' cartel.

[23] *Id.* at 2558 (quoting White Motor Co. v. United States, 372 U.S. 253, 263 (1963) (quoting Northern Pac. R. Co. v. United States, 356 U.S. 1, 5 (1958))).

[24] *See* Consumer Goods Pricing Act of 1975, Pub. L. No. 94-145, § 3 (1975), 89 Stat. 801 (amending 15 U.S.C. 45(a) (1970)).

[25] *See* H.R. REP. No. 94-341, 94th Cong., 1st Sess. (1975).

dislike of resale price maintenance, was not a legislative decision to place the per se rule beyond the power of courts to reexamine. That issue was not put to Congress. Moreover, if the important thing is not what Congress did, but the antitrust view that led to this result, then since the policy considerations relative to resale price maintenance and nonprice restrictions are the same, the legislative history argues for preservation of the per se rule of *Schwinn.*

To appreciate the fragility of the distinction between price and nonprice restrictions in distribution, imagine that a few years from now a case involving a manufacturer accused of illegal per se resale price maintenance comes before the Supreme Court. This company is just like Sylvania—a small, faltering competitor whose market share rose after it adopted a restricted distribution system. The only difference is that because of the nature of this company's product (say, a pocket calculator) it is sold through numerous outlets located very close to each other. It would be utterly impracticable for this manufacturer to assign its dealers exclusive territories in order to stimulate the provision of presale services (display or local advertising or whatever): the territories would be only a few blocks in extent and policing adherence to territorial restrictions would therefore be impossible. Suppose the defendant proved that, because of these facts, it adopted resale price maintenance as the only feasible method of procuring dealer presale services that were both necessary and effective in enabling it to remain an effective competitor. How could the Supreme Court condemn this use of resale price maintenance consistently with the analytical foundations of the *Sylvania* opinion?

Dr. Miles is not the only precedent undermined by the free-rider concept employed in *Sylvania.* In *United States v. Sealy, Inc.,*[26] decided the same day as *Schwinn,* the Supreme Court, in an opinion by Justice Fortas, held that an arrangement by which a group of small mattress manufacturers parcelled out exclusive territorial rights to sell under a common trademark was a per se illegal market division. The mattress manufacturers adopted this scheme not in order to charge a monopoly price for mattresses; the aggregate market share of the group, less than twenty percent, was too small to make this a plausible objective and in any event the members remained free to sell mattresses other than under the common trademark. Almost certainly they did it, rather, to overcome the

[26] 388 U.S. 350 (1967). *See also* United States v. Topco Assocs., Inc., 405 U.S. 596 (1972). The Court in *Sylvania* distinguished *Topco* as involving a horizontal restraint. 97 S. Ct. at 2562 nn.27 -28. The significance of this distinction was not elaborated. *Sealy* was not cited.

same kind of free-rider problem involved in restricted distribution cases. Without exclusive territories, one member of the group could take a free ride on the goodwill created by another member who promoted the Sealy name in his territory. The prospect of free-riding would reduce the incentive of each member to promote the Sealy name vigorously.

Another endangered precedent is *Associated Press v. United States*,[27] in which the Court held that the Associated Press could not give its members veto power over the admission of new members. The Associated Press is a joint venture of newspapers. The newspapers belonging to it pool the news and information gathered by each member. In exchange for furnishing news to the pool, a member (before the Supreme Court's decision) obtained the exclusive right to distribute in its own market the news that other members furnished the pool. This system of exchange would be undermined if each member did not possess an exclusive right to AP news in its market—if, in other words, the association had to admit additional members in areas where it already had a member. The incentive to furnish the Associated Press with local news would be reduced if competitors who made any effort to gather news could receive as of right the news procured by industrious members.

B. More Endangered Precedents: Tie-in and Maximum-Resale-Price Cases

So far I have been discussing how the free-rider concept relied on in the *Sylvania* opinion may force a re-examination of precedents outside of the narrow area of nonprice restrictions on distribution. But the Court in *Sylvania* may have been making a broader point when it said:

> Service and repair are vital for many products, such as automobiles and major household appliances. The availability and quality of such services affect a manufacturer's goodwill and the competitiveness of his product. Because of market imperfections such as the so-called "free rider" effect, these services might not be provided by retailers in a purely competitive situation, despite the fact that each retailer's benefit would be greater if all provided the services than if none did.[28]

This language, plus repeated intimations in the opinion that interbrand competition is more important than intrabrand competi-

[27] 326 U.S. 1 (1945).

[28] 97 S. Ct. at 2561.

tion,[29] suggest a possible willingness to consider afresh the legality of restrictions on competition in the distribution process which do not prevent free-riding but which do enhance the manufacturer's competitiveness.

Perhaps the time has come to reconsider the per se tie-in rule as it has been applied to franchise distribution systems. As recently as the second *Fortner* decision[30] the Court held that a seller who requires a buyer to take an unwanted second product as the condition of purchasing a product is guilty of an illegal per se tie-in, so long as the seller has at least some "economic power" over the desired product. The requirement of "economic power" is apparently satisfied by showing even a slight consumer preference for the tying product over competing goods. The lower federal courts have interpreted the tie-in rule as preventing franchisors from requiring their franchisees to buy products as a condition of retaining the franchise. For instance, Chicken Delight cannot require its franchisees to buy chickens from it; nor can Sinclair require its franchised gasoline dealers to buy tires, batteries, and other automobile accessories from it.[31] Yet it is difficult to believe that Chicken Delight or Sinclair have more monopoly power than Schwinn or Sylvania. If the latter are allowed to prevent their dealers from selling outside assigned territories or to nonapproved outlets because they impose these restrictions only in order to enhance their own competitiveness, why should not Chicken Delight or Sinclair be permitted to restrict their dealers' purchasing freedom? These measures, too, enhance the franchisor's ability to compete and hence increase interbrand competition, which according to *Sylvania* is "the primary concern of antitrust law."[32] A per se rule is no more appropriate for this situation than for the particular distribution restrictions imposed by *Schwinn* and *Sylvania.*

Some tie-ins are imposed by monopolists as a method of price discrimination, but tie-ins imposed by franchisors who are in competition with other sellers of the same product, just as Schwinn and Sylvania are in competition with other sellers of bicycles and television sets, are not of this kind. Franchise tie-ins are methods not of

---

[29] *See id.* at 2559 n.19, 2560-61.

[30] United States Steel Corp. v. Fortner Enterprises, Inc., 429 U.S. 610 (1977).

[31] *See* Siegel v. Chicken Delight, Inc., 448 F.2d 43 (9th Cir. 1971), *cert. denied,* 405 U.S. 955 (1972); Osborn v. Sinclair Refining Co., 286 F.2d 832 (4th Cir. 1960), *cert. denied,* 366 U.S. 963 (1961). Presumably, even under the most extreme view of the reach of the tie-in rule, Sinclair may "tie" its gasoline to its franchise—it cannot be required to allow dealers to sell some other gasoline company's gasoline under the Sinclair trademark.

[32] 97 S. Ct. at 2559 n.19.

discriminating or otherwise exploiting or extending monopoly power but of promoting interbrand competition by assuring quality control and product and service uniformity. This redeeming virtue should be enough under the principles of *Sylvania* to remove the franchise tie-in from the category of practices that are illegal per se.

It may be argued that the "goodwill defense" in tie-in law already protects the tie-in that promotes interbrand competition and therefore that *Sylvania* should have no impact on the law of tie-ins. However, the goodwill defense typically fails on the ground that the defendant could have protected his goodwill by other, less restrictive means, such as by promulgating and enforcing detailed product specifications.[33] The basis of this approach—the notion that interbrand competition can be adequately protected by a per se rule subject to a defense judged under the least-restrictive-alternative standard—was, however, explicitly rejected by the *Sylvania* Court. It noted: "The location restriction used by Sylvania was neither the least nor the most restrictive provision that it could have used. But we agree with the implicit judgment in *Schwinn* that a per se rule based on the nature of the restriction is, in general, undesirable."[34]

Still another precedent threatened by *Sylvania* is *Albrecht v. Herald Co.*[35] The Court in *Albrecht* held that it was per se unlawful for a newspaper publisher to place a ceiling on the price at which its retail distributors could sell its newspaper to the consumer. Because the publisher had assigned the distributors exclusive territories, the most likely reason for the price ceiling was to prevent the distributor from using his distribution monopoly for his benefit rather than the publisher's. The logic of *Sylvania* is that restrictions imposed on dealers by manufacturers promote interbrand competition and are therefore not per se illegal, save perhaps if the manufacturer has a monopoly. That logic demolishes *Albrecht*.

C. The New Importance of Economics

Wholly apart from the Court's kind words for franchise restrictions and its adoption of the free-rider concept, certain language in the opinion concerning the use of economics to guide antitrust analysis can be expected to reverberate throughout the lower federal courts. The Court said that "competitive economies have social and

---

[33] *See, e.g.*, International Business Mach. Corp. v. United States, 298 U.S. 131 (1936). Under the per se tie-in rule, the defendant bears the burden of proving that the tie-in was necessary to protect his goodwill. *Id.* at 138-39.

[34] 97 S. Ct. at 2562 n.29.

[35] 390 U.S. 145 (1968).

political as well as economic advantages, but an antitrust policy divorced from market considerations would lack any objective benchmarks,"[36] and that any "departure from the rule of reason standard must be based upon demonstrable economic effect."[37] One must not read a Supreme Court opinion like a bond indenture, but it does appear that the Court is implying that antitrust prohibitions must have an economic rationale and that the aesthetic delights of smallness and the yearning to resurrect a nation of sturdy Jeffersonian yeomen will not be permitted to decide antitrust cases. This impression is reinforced by the frequency of the Court's citations to the writings of members of the "Chicago School," like Bork and me, who argue that economic efficiency is the only goal of antitrust law.[38]

Most of the antitrust rules limiting "vertical" restrictions (a restriction imposed up or down the chain of production and distribution, rather than between competitors) lack an economic basis, or, more precisely, have no stronger economic basis than *Schwinn*'s per se prohibition of nonprice restrictions in distribution.[39] In fact, the Court in *Sylvania* intimated that all per se proscriptions of vertical restraints, mysteriously excepting the rule against resale price maintenance which it tepidly endorsed, are due for reexamination. The Court stated: "[W]e do not foreclose the possibility that particular applications of vertical restrictions might justify *per se* prohibition,"[40] suggesting that it is prepared to reconsider *all* such prohibitions de novo, using the newly accepted economic approach.[41] Tie-ins (not only in franchising), reciprocal buying, exclusive dealing, vertical mergers involving large market shares, boycotts—practices and transactions heretofore regarded as per se illegal or nearly so—may receive a more sympathetic judicial response in the wake of *Sylvania*.

D. The Rule of Reason in Restricted Distribution Cases

1. *What Is the Rule of Reason?* The Court in *Sylvania* did not hold that restrictions on competition at the distribution level are legal; it held only that such restrictions are to be tested under the Rule of Reason rather than automatically condemned. The Court

---

[36] 97 S. Ct. at 2559-60 n.21.

[37] *Id.* at 2562.

[38] *See, e.g., id.* at 2561.

[39] *See* R. Posner, Antitrust Law: An Economic Perspective 171-211 (1976).

[40] 97 S. Ct. at 2562.

[41] Read in context, "vertical restrictions" may refer only to nonprice restrictions in distribution. Or perhaps the Court was momentarily inattentive to the host of other vertical restrictions that the courts have held to be per se violations of the antitrust laws.

did not, however, describe the Rule of Reason test. The opinion speaks as though the Rule of Reason were the normal standard for deciding antitrust cases and the per se concept the exception. The Court called the Rule of Reason the "prevailing standard of analysis"[42] and implied that prior to *Schwinn* the standard was used many times in restricted distribution cases. Were this true, there would be no need to specify the meaning of the Rule of Reason as applied to restricted distribution. It is not true.

The Rule of Reason is rarely used to decide cases. Agreements among competitors are ordinarily condemned outright under the per se rule forbidding price fixing or its equivalents. Mergers are governed by reasonably specific rules evolved in decisions construing section 7 of the Clayton Act. Vertical restrictions other than mergers are governed by per se rules (for example, tie-ins), by rules developed in decisions interpreting section 3 of the Clayton Act (requirements contracts, for instance), or by rules developed in monopolization cases under section 2 of the Sherman Act. The reader is invited to compile a list of cases of which it may fairly be said that the Rule of Reason was the determinative legal standard. The list will be a short one.

The content of the Rule of Reason is largely unknown; in practice, it is little more than a euphemism for nonliability. Before *Schwinn*, restrictions on distribution were tested under the Rule of Reason, meaning: they were lawful. The Court in *Sylvania* may not have intended by its invocation of the Rule of Reason to bless all restrictions in distribution, but it was deceived if it thought it was subjecting those restrictions to scrutiny under a well-understood legal standard.

The Court's only effort to provide some content to the Rule of Reason was to quote from Justice Brandeis's opinion in *Chicago Board of Trade:*

> The true test of legality is whether the restraint imposed is such as merely regulates and perhaps thereby promotes competition or whether it is such as may suppress or even destroy competition. To determine that question the court must ordinarily consider the facts peculiar to the business to which the restraint is applied; its condition before and after the restraint was imposed; the nature of the restraint and its effect, actual or probable. The history of the restraint, the evil believed to exist, the reason for adopting the particular remedy, the purpose or end

[42] 97 S. Ct. at 2557.

> sought to be attained, are all relevant facts. This is not because a good intention will save an otherwise objectionable regulation or the reverse; but because knowledge of intent may help the court to interpret facts and to predict consequences.[43]

This is not a helpful formulation. To be told to look to the history, circumstances, purposes, and effects of a challenged restriction is not to be provided with usable criteria of illegality. If Justice Brandeis had said that the test was whether the restriction was on balance pro- or anti-competitive, this would at least have excluded criteria unrelated to competitiveness. Perhaps that is the meaning of the first sentence quoted above. Yet arguably competition should not be the exclusive determinant of an unreasonable restraint of trade. This formulation would prohibit those restraints that, while reducing competition, on balance increase efficiency. For example, it would bar a merger that gave the acquiring firm a monopoly but, in so doing, reduced the costs of serving the market to such an extent that the monopoly price after the merger was lower than the competitive market price had been before it.

Other formulations of the Rule of Reason are no more instructive. Illustrative is the formulation in *Columbia Steel:*

> In determining what constitutes unreasonable restraint, we do not think the dollar volume is in itself of compelling significance; we look rather to the percentage of business controlled, the strength of the remaining competition, whether the action springs from business requirements or purpose to monopolize, the probable development of the industry, consumer demands, and other characteristics of the market. We do not undertake to prescribe any set of percentage figures. . . . The relative effect of percentage command of a market varies with the setting in which that factor is placed.[44]

Developed to guide the decision of merger cases, the *Columbia Steel* standard was quickly superseded in its original context by enactment of the Celler-Kefauver Antimerger Act in 1950.[45] It was, however, later applied in the *Times-Picayune* case[46] to determine the reasonableness of a newspaper publisher's requirement that advertisers buy space in both the morning and evening editions. But

---

43 Chicago Bd. of Trade v. United States, 246 U.S. 231, 238 (1918), *quoted in* 97 S. Ct. at 2557-58 n.15.

44 United States v. Columbia Steel Co., 334 U.S. 495, 527-28 (1948).

45 Act of Dec. 29, 1950, 64 Stat. 1125 (codified at 15 U.S.C. § 18 (1970)).

46 Times-Picayune Publishing Co. v. United States, 345 U.S. 594, 614-26 (1953).

Times-Picayune is one of the very few Supreme Court cases in modern times in which the Rule of Reason was the rule of decision.

The Rule of Reason in its present state is a poor guide to the decision of restricted distribution cases. Its formlessness is clearly conveyed by the American Bar Association's recent monograph on restricted distribution.[47] This sixteen-page discussion of how the Rule of Reason might be applied to restricted distribution cases invites the courts to consider whether the restraint is ancillary to a legitimate business purpose or anticompetitive in purpose; if the former, whether the restriction is reasonably necessary to accomplish the legitimate business purpose—and to this question "[t]he degree of consumer acceptance of the product, the physical characteristics of the product and any unique marketing problems involved, the duration and scope of the intrabrand restraint, the strength of interbrand competition, and the acceptability of less restrictive alternatives might all be relevant";[48] whether the defendant has market power, as determined by a study of market share, entry, and potential interbrand competition; the degree of product differentiation; a host of potentially exculpatory factors including the defendant's interests in maximizing market penetration, stimulating distributor service and other activity, and obtaining a market presence; and, finally, the effect of the challenged restriction on the survival of small business.

A start toward making the Rule of Reason more manageable is to adopt Professor Bork's position that the essential spirit of the Rule is to condemn only those practices that are, on balance, inefficient in the economic sense.[49] This would exclude some of the factors listed in the standard formulation of the Rule of Reason. But without further particularization Bork's efficiency standard is insufficiently precise to guide the decision of restricted distribution cases.

2. *Making the Rule of Reason Operational.* There are at least two approaches to making the Rule of Reason a usable standard in cases involving restrictions on distribution. The first, loosely suggested by the *Chicago Board of Trade* formulation, is to require the trier of fact to balance the reduction in intrabrand competition against the increase in interbrand competition attributable to the restriction. To illustrate, the judge or jury would try to figure out how much money or welfare Sylvania's customers lost because its

[47] *See* ABA ANTITRUST SECTION, *supra* note 10, at 55-71.

[48] *Id.* at 57.

[49] Bork, *The Rule of Reason and the Per Se Concept: Price Fixing and Market Division*, pt. 1), 74 YALE L.J. 775 (1965).

dealers were not able to compete with each other and how much they gained because the location clause increased the presale services provided by the dealers. Besides requiring a trial of unmanageable complexity to quantify these impacts, this approach calls for an inquiry that is often unnecessary. Since Sylvania is not a monopolist, it would not knowingly impose a restriction on dealer competition that made the consumer of Sylvania products a net loser—that could only reduce Sylvania's sales and profits. Under this kind of balancing approach, the Rule of Reason would be used not only to prevent abuses of market power but to correct the mistakes of the powerless.

The second, and in my opinion vastly superior, approach is to focus on the single question whether the restriction is intended to cartelize distribution or, on the contrary, to promote the manufacturer's own interests. The goal is to isolate, and condemn, restrictions that are imposed nominally by the manufacturer but are in fact desired for monopolistic purposes by dealers using the manufacturer as their enforcement agent.

Under this test, many cases would be dismissed simply on a showing that the dealers' share of the relevant market was too small to give them the power to collude effectively. If American Motors has two percent of the U.S. automobile market and its dealers sell only American Motors cars, it is inconceivable that the purpose of giving American Motors dealers exclusive territories is to cartelize the distribution of automobiles. While it is true that, in principle, some (very few) consumers may so prefer American Motors to competing brands of automobiles that the dealers in those cars face as a group a downward-sloping demand curve, the slope is too close to being horizontal for courts to worry about dealer collusion.[50]

The suggested approach would automatically preclude liability unless the manufacturer had a very large market share or unless all or most of the manufacturers in the market imposed uniform restrictions on their dealers so that (in either case) the dealers had a monopoly position in a genuine economic market. Where these conditions are satisfied, however, it may be quite difficult to determine whether the restriction is evidence of a dealers' cartel or of the manufacturer's wish to stimulate the provision of presale services. If no presale services (local advertising, display, and so forth) are

[50] My suggested emphasis on market shares is consistent with the importance attached to them in the early price-fixing cases, such as United States v. Addyston Pipe & Steel Co., 85 F. 271 (6th Cir. 1898), *aff'd as modified*, 175 U.S. 211 (1899), before the per se rule against price fixing crystallized.

in fact provided, this is strong evidence of cartelization. But even if extensive presale services are provided, that would not be conclusive evidence against cartelization; individual dealers might be stepping up service competition in order to capture as much of the profits generated by their cartel as possible.[51]

Where services are provided by dealers who dominate a relevant market, a possible way to distinguish a dealer cartel from a restriction that serves the manufacturer's interests is suggested by the fact that in the former situation limitations on dealer competition should reduce the output of the product in question while in the latter case output should increase. The object of the dealers' cartel is to raise the price of the good above its previous (competitive) level. If this goal is attained, the amount of the good demanded, and hence supplied, will fall (although sales may later rise as individual dealers add services in order to increase their sales at the higher price and in so doing shift their demand curve to the right). The manufacturer, in contrast, limits competition among his dealers in order to increase the value of and thus the demand for his product; and generally, although not invariably, a higher demand and hence a greater output will result from his effort. In *Sylvania* the defendant's market share increased after the imposition of the restriction (in *Schwinn* it fell), but it would take careful analysis, perhaps utilizing econometric methods, to determine whether the restriction was the cause of Sylvania's gain in sales or whether its sales would have increased even more without it. I would place on the government the burden of overcoming the inference created by Sylvania's sales gain that the location clause was in fact imposed for the manufacturer's benefit.

The Court in *Sylvania* considered Sylvania's increased sales *revenues* to be evidence that the challenged restriction was employed for Sylvania's benefit.[52] The appropriate output measure, however, is physical quantity rather than revenue. Monopoly reduces *physical* output; sales revenues may or may not be greater (profits will of course be greater, at least in the short run). By

[51] The reader may wonder what difference it makes whether dealers engage in service competition because they are trying to maximize their share of a dealer cartel's profits or because the manufacturer restricts price competition; in either case the service competition and the resulting higher level of services provided consumers result from the elimination of price competition. The difference is that the manufacturer, acting voluntarily, will restrict dealer competition only to the extent necessary to evoke the optimal level of presale services. A dealer cartel might restrict dealer price competition much more, resulting in an excessive level of services and a net reduction in consumer welfare; or the dealer cartel might attempt to suppress service as well as price competition.

[52] 97 S. Ct. at 2552.

reducing demand for the product sold by the dealers, a dealer cartel will also reduce the dealers' demand from the manufacturer, causing his output to fall. Probably his revenues will also fall, because he does not benefit from the increase in the retail price brought about by the dealers' cartel. However, his revenues might rise were the dealers compensating him, in the form of a higher wholesale price, for acting as the cartel's policeman.

To summarize, I suggest a three-stage inquiry for determining the legality of restricted distribution, now that the inappropriate per se rule of illegality has been discarded (as should be clear, I would use this inquiry whether the restriction is price or nonprice in character):

1. Does the restriction embrace so large a fraction of the market as to make cartelization a plausible motivation for the restriction? If not, the restriction should be held lawful.

2. If the restriction does embrace a sufficiently large fraction of the market to make cartelization a possible motivation, do dealers in the product in question provide any presale services? If not, the restriction should be deemed unlawful. (An alternative would shift the burden of justification to the defendant at this point).

3. If the answer to both of the previous questions is yes (large market share and presale services provided), did the manufacturer's output increase or decrease after imposing the restriction? If his output increased, the burden would shift to the government of showing that it increased for reasons unrelated to the restriction. If output fell after imposition of the restriction, the restriction would be deemed unlawful, unless perhaps the defendant could prove that he *intended* by adopting the restriction to increase his output.

The suggested guide may appear to overlook a much simpler method of determining the nature of the restriction, namely, by ascertaing whether it was imposed by the manufacturer or by the dealers. But this approach is unsound (and not really simple). Dealers as well as the manufacturer are hurt by free-riding; it is a detail whether the initiative in seeking to prevent free-riding was taken by the dealers or the manufacturer. This point was missed in Justice Fortas's opinion for the Court in the *General Motors* dealers case.[53] The government briefed the case on the assumption that the main issue was the lawfulness of General Motors' location clause. The Court, demonstrating the same obsession with form at the expense of substance evinced in *Schwinn* and *Sealy*, ruled that because com-

[53] United States v. General Motors Corp., 384 U.S. 127 (1966).

peting dealers had collaborated to enlist General Motors' assistance in enforcing the location clause, the case involved an illegal per se horizontal conspiracy, regardless of the reasonableness of the clause. But if the clause was reasonable, the dealers should have been entitled to band together for the innocent purpose of persuading General Motors to carry out mutually beneficial contractual obligations.

Thus I disagree with Professor Bork's contention that detection of a dealer cartel is easy because of the large numbers of dealers who must join the cartel to make it effective.[54] It may be easy to detect cooperative activity among the dealers but it is difficult to determine whether the purpose of the activity is to cartelize retail distribution or to overcome a genuine free-rider problem. The three-stage inquiry outlined above may be the simpler method of deciding this question after all.

Conclusion

The Supreme Court's *Sylvania* decision gives new prominence to the economic approach to antitrust law. Pursued to its logical conclusion, that approach requires the Court to reexamine a variety of other practices besides the nonprice distribution restrictions that were the subject of the opinion. But it must be admitted that economic science is more serviceable for deciding which practices should and which practices should not be classified as per se illegal restraints of trade than for guiding the trial of cases in which per se rules have been held inapplicable. Determining whether a challenged restriction on distribution is really a device for overcoming free-rider problems and hence increasing competition or whether it is a method of dealer cartelization is a formidable task. I have suggested a possible approach to this problem. Many hard questions remain unanswered, such as whether the three-stage approach should be used as the standard for adjudging criminal liability and, if not, how a criminal conspiracy among dealers to restrain trade could ever be proved, consistently with sound economic principles. It remains to be seen whether the law can develop rules for restricted distribution cases that will be at once effective and economically sound.

---

[54] Bork, *Vertical Restraints: Schwinn Overruled*, 1977 Sup. Ct. Rev. 171, 190-91.

Public Undertakings and State Aids

[10]

Article 90, Economic Policy and the Duties of Member States

Christopher Bright

Introduction

EC competition law is often seen as a nexus between Brussels bureaucracy and industry. Articles 85 and 86, the principal instruments of competition policy enforcement, apply to undertakings. They are not concerned with measures imposed by national governments.[1] These governments have a place in the Article 85 and 86 machinery—there is, for example, a duty of close and constant liaison by the Commission with Member States;[2] a duty on the Commission to consult the Advisory Committee on Restrictive Practices and Monopolies composed of representatives of Member States before taking certain decisions;[3] a duty to inform a Member State of investigations on its territory,[4] and a duty on a Member State to undertake investigations on behalf of the Commission,[5] a practice which has begun to develop. There are similar obligations in the Merger Regulation[6] and the Sectoral Regulations.[7] In addition, other institutions of Member States, their courts, have a role to play.[8]

The focus of this article is, however, on the duties that each Member State has under the competition rules. These duties encompass the illegal use of state aid, a subject which has been much in the headlines due to, among other things, the *Rover* case.[9] The elimination of market-distorting state aids was an important aspect of the Commission's 1992 programme[10] and remains a central policy objective.[11] The 1985 White Paper also identified that the single market programme 'must necessarily be accompanied by increased surveillance by the Commission in the field of competition rules to ensure that . . . Member States adhere to these rules'.[12] It stated that:

> . . . Member States have not always withstood the temptation to yield to protectionist measures . . . . There is no reason why Member States, whose Heads of State and Government are committed to the completion of the Internal Market, should not expect and welcome the knowledge that the Commission will carry out its duties of enforcing the rules that make such a completion possible, even if such enforcement is likely sometimes to effect them directly and individually.[13]

These statements heralded the determination of the Commission to tackle not only illicit state aids but also, through the use of its powers under Article 90 of the EEC Treaty, the effect of state ownership and the grant of special or exclusive rights by Member States, usually to indigenous players, where it leads to unwarranted partitioning of the internal market and to impediments to competition. These principles were put into context by the 1987 Green Paper on Telecommunication Services and Equipment[14] which set out specific objectives to be achieved in terms of liberalisation and market structure across the Community as a whole, and identified Article 90 as a means of achieving the objectives. Much has been achieved in this sector under Article 90. Similar sectoral initiatives have been taken in the energy[15] and postal services sectors[16] although progress in these areas using Article 90 is less apparent.

In making the statements in the White Paper the Commission was doing no more than reminding Member States, as the Court has often done,[17] that they are required under Article 5 of the EEC Treaty to:

Christopher Bright, Linklater & Paines, London

1 For example in *Corbeau* (Case C-320/91) the Court stated in relation to Article 86: 'Toutefois l'article 86 ne vise que les comportements anti-concurrentiels qui ont été adaptés par les entreprises de leur propre initiative et non pas les mesures étatiques.'
2 Regulation 17/62, Article 10(2).
3 *Ibid.*, Article 10(3).
4 *Ibid.*, Article 14(2).
5 *Ibid.*, Article 13.
6 Regulation 4064/89.
7 Regulations 1017/68 (transport by rail, road and inland waterway), 405/87 (maritime transport), 3975/87 (air transport).
8 Notice on co-operation between national courts and the Commission in applying Articles 85 and 86, OJ 1993 C39/6.
9 *British Aerospace and Rover v Commission* Case C-294/90.
10 White Paper on Completing the Internal Market COM (85) 310 final, 14 June 1985.
11 The Court (Case C-325/91) recently struck down as invalid a Commission communication expanding Member States' reporting obligations on state aids set out in the Commission's first Article 90(3) Directive, the Transparency Directive (80/723/EEC). The Court said any elaboration of the Transparency Directive should be by way of an amending Article 90(3) Directive. The Commission has stated its intention to adopt such a measure and continue the pressure on state aids.
12 Note 10 above, paragraph 19.
13 *Ibid.*, paragraph 152.
14 COM (87) 290 final.
15 COM (88) 238 final.
16 COM (91) 476 final.
17 For a statement of the Court's approach see Advocate General Van Gerven's opinion in *Dutch PTT's v Commission* Joined Cases C-48/90 and 66/90.

> take all appropriate measures, whether general or particular, to ensure fulfilment of the obligations arising out of this Treaty or resulting from actions taken by the institutions of the Community. They shall facilitate the achievement of the Community's tasks.
> They shall abstain from any measure which could jeopardise the attainment of the objectives of this Treaty.

Alongside the Commission, the European Court of Justice has assisted in the development, in effect, of new instruments by which the Community authorities, and the national courts on application by private litigants, can tackle head-on the impediments to competition and market integration that state intervention in the market-place have in many cases led to. In a country where Community institutions, and the Commission in particular, are often characterised as the last bastions of socialism, the idea of Brussels, and for that matter Luxembourg, standing up and rolling back the frontiers of the state is something of a paradox. Nonetheless, the combined activities of the Commission and the Court under Article 90 amount simply to that: a reversal, in the name of the single market and the consumer, of decades of state involvement in industry.

Any system of government with strong federal or central rules oriented towards a market economy and focused on norms of competition will need to find some means of reconciling these rules with the rights of sovereign states or nations which have subscribed to those rules to arrange their domestic affairs how they choose. This issue has also arisen, for instance, in the United States.[18]

Article 90

Article 90 sits among the rules on competition in the EEC Treaty.

Article 90 states:

> (1) In the case of public undertakings and undertakings to which Member States grant special or exclusive rights, Member States shall neither enact nor maintain in force any measure contrary to the rules contained in this Treaty, in particular to those rules provided for in Article 7 and Articles 85 to 94.
> (2) Undertakings entrusted with the operation of services of general economic interest or having the character of a revenue-producing monopoly shall be subject to the rules contained in this Treaty, in particular to the rules on competition, in so far as the application of such rules does not obstruct the performance, in law or in fact, of the particular tasks assigned to them. The development of trade must not be affected to such an extent as would be contrary to the interests of the Community.
> (3) The Commission shall ensure the application of the provisions of this Article and shall, where necessary, address appropriate directives or decisions to Member States.

As is evident from Article 90(1), the duty on Member States is not to enact or maintain any measure contrary to any rules contained in the Treaty. It is not limited to competition issues. Apart from the competition rules the principal rules which have been in question in Article 90 cases are those on free movement and freedom of establishment, particularly Articles 30 and 59.[19]

Article 90(1) applies to both public undertakings and undertakings, public or private, that have been granted special or exclusive rights. The purpose is to encompass undertakings which Member States have put in a privileged position in the market-place—whether that privilege stems from ownership and control or the grant of rights. The concept of 'special and exclusive rights' is not one that is yet settled. In particular, the idea of special rights remains to be developed.[20]

A breach of Article 90 only occurs where there is a breach of another relevant provision of Treaty rules and there is a causal link to a Member State. For the purposes of the competition rules there needs to be established all the incidents of a breach of Articles 85 and 86 including an effect on trade between Member States and, for Article 86, the existence of a dominant position within the Common Market or a substantial part of it. Some of the Court's more interesting 'substantial part' decisions have taken place in an Article 90 context, including the *Bodson*[21] case where a series of local monopolies dispersed around France in the hands of one group and accounting for 9 per cent of all French communes was considered to qualify, and the *Merci*[22]

18 In *Parker v Brown* 317 US 341 (1943) the Supreme Court acknowledged the ability of the states to displace competition in certain markets by creating regulatory regimes of various kinds.

19 The free movement and the competition rules are inextricably interwoven. In *France v Commission* (Case C-202/88 at paragraph 41) the Court stated: 'it should be borne in mind . . . that, as the Court has consistently held, Articles 2 and 3 of the Treaty set out to establish a market characterised by the free movement of goods where the terms of competition are not distorted . . . Article 30 et seq must therefore be interpreted in the light of that principle, which means that the competition aspect of Article 3(f) of the Treaty has to be taken into account.'

20 In *France v Commission* and the *Telecommunications Services* case (Joined Cases C-271/90, 281/90 and 289/90) the Court has struck out the inclusion of special rights in Article 90(3) directives where the Commission has not adequately defined them. 'Special' probably encompasses exclusivity granted to a limited class (see Advocate General Jacobs' opinion in the *Telecommunications Services* case). The concept is also used in EC procurement rules where it specifically includes rights, for instance, to lay equipment on, over or under the highway.

21 *Bodson v Pompes funèbres des régions libérées* Case 30/87.

22 *Merci Convenzionali Porto di Genova v Siderurgica Gabrielli* Case C-179/90.

case where the port of Genoa was held to qualify due to its importance to Italian trade.

Both the operative provisions of Article 90(1) and (2) and the powers of implementation in Article 90(3) have given rise to considerable controversy. Central and local government have been caught by the rules. The operative provisions have been applied in sectors as diverse as express couriers,[23] operation of ports and stevedoring,[24] funeral services,[25] executive recruitment consultants,[26] television,[27] tobacco,[28] banking,[29] insurance,[30] oil refining and waste collection of oil,[31] loss adjusting[32] and air ticket sales.[33] Much of this spread of cases has originated by way of Article 177 references to the Court arising out of an infringement proceeding in Member States for breach of or non-compliance with statutory monopolies or, in some cases, out of ordinary commercial contract disputes.[34] In many instances the case has involved small and medium-sized businesses rather than large utilities. Another series of cases has arisen in the utilities sector, particularly in relation to telecommunications[35] but also concerning electricity[36] and postal services.[37] These cases have arisen from the Commission's zeal to introduce, through its implementing powers under Article 90(3), the principles and disciplines of the single market into the sheltered world of national utilities.

Together the Court and Commission have begun a pincer movement. Many would see this activism of the Commission, the Court being dependent on cases brought to it, as long overdue.[38]

Are Member States Free to Grant Monopolies?

That such a question needs answering at all is a testament to the potential for Article 90 in the hands of the Commission and the Court. It is trite law to say that Member States may take undertakings into public ownership and give them privileged status in terms of special and exclusive rights. This proposition:

> depends in part upon Article 222 EEC, preserving intact the system of property ownership in the Member States, which are therefore free to determine the extent and internal organisation of their public sectors; and in part from the clear inference to be drawn from Article 90(1) EEC that the conferment of special and exclusive rights upon an undertaking does not, in itself, constitute an infringement of the Treaty.[39]

While such propositions may be a useful analytical starting point they run the risk of being misleading. The very existence of Article 90 is an indication that the rights of Member States with respect to public undertakings and any privileged position they may wish to give to them are limited. Member States may be free to take particular undertakings into public ownership. That is very different from saying only public undertakings may perform particular functions.

The question is to what extent Member States' rights are limited. The jurisprudence of the Court, and the approach of the Commission, show an initial attempt to reconcile the Treaty's apparent acceptance of special and exclusive rights with general principles. Over time this appears to have shifted to a bolder approach to the existence of the rights at all.

The early debate in the Court on Article 90(1) revolved around distinguishing the existence and exercise of the special or exclusive right. In this way it might be said that although special and exclusive rights could exist, care would need to be taken in the way that Member States caused the rights to be exercised by the public or privileged undertaking. An attempt was made to identify a sacrosanct core of privileged status that a Member State could rely on being able to create. This existence/exercise debate is reminiscent of that which has taken place in reconciling Article 222 and Article 36.[40] Such an approach would be consistent with undertakings, public or not, having a defence to state mandated behaviour.[41] A voluntary breach of Article 86 by public or privileged undertakings would not suffice.[42]

This approach, much argued for by Member States, would not, however, necessarily pose a fundamental

23 Commission decision OJ 1990 L10/47.
24 *Merci*, see Note 22 above.
25 *Bodson*, see Note 21 above.
26 *Höfner and Elser v Macrotron* Case C-41/90.
27 *ERT v DEP* Case C-260/89; *Sacchi* Case 155/73.
28 *GB-INNO-BM v KT* Case 13/177.
29 *Zücher v Bayerischie Vereinsbank* Case 172/80.
30 *Commission v Greece* Case 216/87.
31 *Campus Oil v Minister for Industry and Energy* Case 72/83; *Fabricants Raffineurs d'Huile de Graissage v Inter-Huiles* Case 172/82.
32 *Ameyde v UCIAAACI* Case 90/76.
33 *Ministère Public v Lucas Asjes* Case 209/84.
34 *Höfner* concerned a claim for a debt and *Merci* a restriction and damages claim.
35 *France v Commission* Case C-202/88 (Terminal Equipment); *Telecommunication Services*, Note 20 above.
36 *Ijsselcentrale* OJ 1991 L28/32.
37 *RTT v GB-INNO-BM* Case C-18/88; *Dutch PTT's*, Note 17 above.
38 See Pappalardo, 'State Measures and Public Undertakings: Article 90 of the EEC Treaty Revisited' [1991] 1 ECLR 29 for a discussion of the slow awakening of the Commission.

39 Wyatt and Dashwood, *European Community Law*, (3rd edn), Sweet & Maxwell, 1993, at 547.
40 See *ibid.*, 573 to 575.
41 See Commission Decisions (82/896/EEC) *AROW/BNIC* OJ 1982 L379/1 and (85/206/EEC) *Aluminium Imports* OJ 1985 L92/1.
42 See *France v Commission*, Note 19 above.

threat to the scope of the state sector in Member States or the activities of those entities, public or private, with special or exclusive rights. This was the approach taken in *Sacchi* where the grant of monopoly rights was distinguished from abusive behaviour by the undertaking concerned.

Out of this debate, a number of strands in the jurisprudence are apparent.

The Imputation Artifice

One very significant strand in the Court's thinking is the examination of a situation induced by the state as if it were a situation created by an undertaking acting on its own. A veil is drawn over state interference for the purpose of analysing the factual situation and seeing whether the result can be classified as a breach of the competition rules. The imputed behaviour of the undertaking is then linked to the measure involved and responsibility laid at the door of the Member State.

In the words of Advocate General Van Gerven in the *Dutch PTT's* case:

> Cette jurisprudence s'articule autour de l'idée centrale que de telles mesures étatiques, combinée avec l'une ou l'autre forme de comportement d'enterprise, ont, pour la structure de la concurrence sur le marché communautaire, *les mêmes conséquences* qu'un comportement d'enterprise qui n'est pas lié à une intervention des pouvoirs publics.

Many of these cases concern the extension by a Member State of a privileged position of an undertaking in one activity to an activity in a neighbouring but distinct market.

In *RTT v GB-INNO-BM*[43] the Court stated:

> c'est l'extension du monopole de l'establissement et de l'exploitation du réseau téléphonique au marché des appareils téléphoniques, sans justification objective, qui est prohibée . . . lorsque cette extension est le fait d'une mesure étatique.

The same reasoning was used in *Telecommunications Services*.

It is well established that where a dominant undertaking (without state conferred privileged status) uses its dominant position to reserve an ancillary or related market to itself without objective justification and risking eliminating all competition that this will be regarded as an abuse of Article 86.[44] In these cases the extension of the privileged position by the state from one market to a related market is regarded as equivalent.

Other cases involve issues such as excessive pricing. In *Bodson* the issue was whether the prices of external services at funerals were excessive. These prices were set by the state in concessions granted to undertakings. In *Ahmed Saeed*[45] the issue was the approval of fares which were in any event contrary to Article 85(1) and Article 86.

In cases such as *Bodson* and *Saeed* the finding of incompatibility does not necessarily threaten the grant of the privileged status. If pricing abuses exist they can be modified. The 'extension' cases do, however, have a direct impact on the scope of the privilege conferred by distinguishing a core and ancillary privilege, the latter being regarded as incompatible with the Treaty principles. This has been taken further by the idea of inherent abuse.

The Expanding Category of Inherent Abuse

Another tack taken by the Court is the idea of the actual or potential abuse being inherent in the privileged position. In *ERT v DEP*, exclusive rights granted by Greece to ERT in respect of television broadcasting were challenged. ERT produced and broadcast its own programmes and was also responsible for re-transmitting broadcasts from other Member States. DEP, a municipal information office, which itself began to broadcast television programmes, was prosecuted for infringement of the ERT monopoly. The Court stated that:

> Article 90(1) of the Treaty prohibits the granting of an exclusive right to re-transmit television broadcasts to an undertaking which has an exclusive right to transmit broadcasts, where those rights are liable to create a situation in which that undertaking is led to infringe Article 86 of the Treaty by virtue of a discriminatory broadcasting policy which favours its own programmes.

The Court believed that under such a system of cumulation of rights, equality of opportunity between its own and foreign programmes would be liable to be seriously compromised.

This theme was picked up again in *RTT v GB-INNO-BM* and in *France v Commission*. Both these cases concerned the rights of public telecommunications operators with regard to the supply or approval for supply of equipment. In both cases the Court regarded the conferring of specification and type approval powers on to a service provider also in the business of supplying equipment as having the potential for abuse. It gives one competitor an advantage over others in that the privileged one can decide on whether or not competitor

43 Case C-18/88.
44 *Telemarketing v CLT* Case 311/84.
45 *Ahmed Saeed Flugreisen and Silver Line Reisebüro v Zentrale zur Bekämpfung Unlauteren Wettbewerbs* Case 99/86.

products should have market access.[46] Type approval should in these circumstances, if effective competition is to be maintained and transparency guaranteed, be performed by an entity independent of those supplying goods or services in the telecommunications market.

These cases deal with conflicts of interest inherent in the state measure which may distort competition. Another group of cases takes the idea of a problem inherent in the right conferred a step further.

In *Höfner & Elser v Macrotron* a German law on the promotion of employment conferred an exclusive right on the Federal Employment Office to provide recruitment agency and job placement functions. Notwithstanding this, for a number of years private recruitment consultants had been in operation and had been tolerated by the authorities. The private agencies had found a role due to the inability of the authorities to meet demand. In an action to enforce payment of a contract debt the issue of the invalidity of the contract as a result of the German law was raised.

The Court decided that the exclusive right to carry on the activity of a public employment agency is in breach of Article 90(1) where the privileged agency cannot avoid infringing Article 86. This would be the case where the agency is 'manifestly incapable of satisfying demand on the market for such services' and the actual pursuit of those activities by private consultants is rendered impossible by a law under which such activities are illegal and contracts relating to them void. The undertaking would be limiting production, markets or technical development as identified in Article 86(b).

Advocate General Jacobs seeks to draw a broader principle to the effect that where national law confers an exclusive right on someone—whether in the form of a patent, registered design or monopoly in the provision of services—and he fails to produce the goods or services covered by the exclusive right, that failure may amount to an abuse of a dominant position with the effect that the exclusive right can no longer be enforced. He draws on *Volvo v Veng*,[47] concerning the registered design for a car part, and the circumstances of *Höfner* into one category.

In *Merci Convenzionali Porto di Genova v Siderurgica Gabrielli* the Court considered an Italian law requiring port undertakings to ensure that certain stevedoring companies are used to unload ships. These companies are required to employ Italians only. Gabrielli sought to import a shipload of steel through Genoa. The unloading of the ship was slow and delayed and Gabrielli sued the port authority. The Court affirmed the doctrine that if the mere exercise of the rights leads to an abuse, that is, it is inherent, or if the rights are likely to lead to an abuse, then they are inconsistent with Article 90(1). The abuses in question in this case were payment for unsolicited services, charging disproportionate fees and imposing unfair prices and trading conditions, refusing the use of modern technology thereby increasing costs and causing delay and discriminatory pricing. The Genoa monopoly is before the Court again in *Corsica Fermes Italia v Corporation Piloti del Porto di Genova*[48] in relation to use Port of Genoa pilots.

In both *Höfner* and *Merci* it was open to the Court to take the more limited approach of saying that the particular exploitation of the exclusive right was delinquent, along the lines of *Bodson*, rather than saying that the delinquency was inherent in the right. Conspicuously the Court chose to challenge the right itself.

The Overall Rule

These doctrines give an idea of the approach of the Court in individual cases. In many senses the approach is a pragmatic one with each case being assessed individually. Much of the attention of the cases is on the perceived delinquency of the undertaking concerned (whether in terms of monopoly extension, conflict of interest, pricing or service levels) and the connection between this and a Member State.[49] The question is where the boundary of the rule lies.

It is clear that the process under way is one of separate sovereigns with separate legal systems and goals attempting to settle conflicts. The process is one of seeking to identify the major values which are relevant and to attribute to each an appropriate sphere of influence. The primacy of EC law over Member State law, combined with the decisions being in the hands of EC institutions, is likely at this stage of development of the Community, where many of its core goals—particularly the internal market—remain to be achieved, to lead to a result which emphasises Community norms over those of Member States.

In *France v Commission*, according to some commentators,[50] the Court significantly shifted its position towards the Community norm. It firmly rejected the idea that the Commission could only act in relation to the abusive exercise of rights granted. The Court

46 See also *Van Eycke* Case 267/86 for another example of an undertaking being given a regulatory role.
47 Case 238/87.
48 Case C-18/93.
49 See Advocate General Van Gerven's attempt to rationalise the cases in the *Dutch PTT's* case.
50 Leigh Honcher, 'Regulated Industries and Competition in Community Law', paper given at Institute of European Law, University of Birmingham, 13 May 1993.

decided that the Commission's power of surveillance under Article 90(3) entitled it to spell out the obligations of Member States under the Treaty. The ambit of that power therefore depends only on the scope of the rules that the Commission was seeking to enforce.

So far as Article 86 is concerned the scope is as wide as the existing case law and its unfulfilled potential will allow. The case law appears to have gone as far as saying that dominance together with special rights may itself be an issue, particularly as the limitation of production inherent in a public monopoly may be an abuse.[51]

Article 85 is as yet an undeveloped field in Article 90 terms. In *Bodson* it was decided that Article 85 does not in any event apply to contracts for concessions concluded between French communes acting in their capacity as public authorities and undertakings entrusted with the operation of a public service. Article 85 only applies to agreements between undertakings. This considerably reduces the scope of Article 85 and Article 90 in combination since the award of exclusive rights by public authority will not be caught. Similarly where the public authority is acting in the capacity of an undertaking, Article 85 will apply to appropriate agreements but Article 90 is unlikely to, unless the Member State has some causal link with the agreement.

The situation is different where a Member State endorses, condones or reinforces an anti-competitive agreement which is in any event in breach of Article 85.[52] Article 5 of the Treaty requires Member States not to adopt or maintain in force any measures which would deprive the competition rules of their effectiveness. They would be in breach of this if they were to require or favour the adoption of agreements within Article 85 or to reinforce their effects.[53] To the extent that the undertakings involved were privileged this would be within Article 90(1).[54]

Both the situation with regard to public undertakings and that with regard to the encouragement, condoning or reinforcement of agreements that are within Article 85 and involve enterprises with privileged status could have far-reaching effects.[55]

When regard is had to other rules of the Treaty, in particular Article 30 on free movement of goods and Article 59 on freedom to provide services, it appears increasingly likely that opportunities will be found to impugn special and exclusive rights. Take for example The Telecommunications Terminal Equipment Directive[56] and The Telecommunications Services Directive. These are both cases where the monopoly 'extension' was not the abuse of Article 86 relied on by the Commission. Instead the Commission identified the restriction of market access by competitors and the obligation to take unwanted services as the abuses in the Telecommunications Services Directive and the restriction of users to renting equipment and the limiting of outlets which may impede technical progress in the Terminal Equipment Directive. In addition the Commission raised Article 59 arguments and Article 30 arguments respectively.

General Economic Interest: the Escape Mechanism?

On this view Article 90(1) subjects Member States to onerous duties in respect of undertakings to which they have granted special or exclusive rights and which are of an economic or commercial nature.[57] The only mitigation of the duty then lies in Article 90(2) which allows a relaxation of the competition rules where a service in the general economic interest has been entrusted to an undertaking, but only so far as the application of those rules does not obstruct the performance of the tasks entrusted and to the extent that it is not contrary to the interests of the Community.

There are indications of this approach emerging in the cases. In *RTT v GB-INNO* the Court indicated that the extension of an existing dominant position through a state measure is contrary to Article 90. The Court took one step further, however, in saying:

> En effet, l'exclusion ou la restriction de la concurrence sur le marché des appareils téléphoniques ne peut être regardée comme justifée par une mission de service public d'intéret économique générale

51 In *Höfner* Advocate General Jacobs specifically refutes this idea. He says 'The plaintiffs are, in my view, stretching the wording of Article 86 to breaking point when they assert that the mere fact that a monopoly extends further than is necessary in the public interest constitutes an abuse of a dominant position. If that view were accepted it would mean that . . . nationalisation could take place only so far as it were justified in the public interest.' He goes on to say that Community law does not provide this.

52 *Ministère Public v Lucas Asjes* Joined Cases 209 to 213/84; *Ahmed Saeed*, Note 45 above.

53 The attribution artifice has begun to encroach into this area as well. In *Asjes* the approval of the authority for the air fares was necessary for them to be effective. Nonetheless the fares were regarded as affected by 85(1) issues.

54 Even where there is no privileged status there may be a breach of the Treaty when Articles 3(f), 5 and 85 are read together. See *Asjes* and *Vilaamse Reisbureaus v Sociale Dienst*.

55 Gyselen, 'State Action and the Effectiveness of the EEC Treaty's Competition Provisions', [1989] CML Rev. 33.

56 Directive 88/301/EEC OJ 1988 L131/73.

57 Where the tasks are non-economic the rules do not apply; see *Poucet v Calmurac* Case C-159/91 and *Pistre v Concava* Case C-160/91; and see *Höfner* (Note 26 above) for the classification of tasks. In *Höfner* the services of a state employment bureau were regarded as economic even though they were provided free and were connected with social policy objectives.

> .... La production et la vente de terminaux notamment d'appareils téléphoniques est une activité qui doit pouvoir être exercée par toute entreprise.

The Court went on to say that it was sufficient for standards and approval processes to be set to meet system security concerns.

This is one illustration of a trend to the second guessing of the merits of the award of special or exclusive rights by Member States. It is no longer enough for the Member States to assert that the service is of general economic interest. Again in *Merci v Gabrielli* the Court, in the absence of convincing evidence, refused to consider that the stevedoring activities concerned constituted a service in the general economic interest. Without defining the concept, the Court indicates that stevedoring does not possess specific characteristics different from those vested in other activities of economic life.

This is the beginning of a trend to an objective judgment about what constitutes a service in the general economic interest and the limitation of the ability to grant special and exclusive rights. Three further developments fit into this trend.

In its most recent Article 90 judgment *Procureur du Roi v Corbeau* the Court has made it clear that, even where a task in the general economic interest has been entrusted (in this case a postal service) for the purposes of Article 90(2), the nature of the entrusted service must be circumscribed. M Corbeau was offering an enhanced mail delivery service with additional benefits not available from the conventional postal service, such as collection from the sender's premises, distribution with greater speed and reliability and the option of changing the delivery address during the course of distribution. It decided that:

> It is contrary to Article 90 of the EEC Treaty for legislation of a Member State which confers on an entity such as the Régis des Postes the exclusive right to collect, carry and distribute mail to prohibit, under threat of criminal sanctions, an economic operator established in that State from offering certain specific services dissociable from a service operated in the public interest which fulfil economic operators' specific needs and call for certain additional benefits not available from the conventional postal service, in so far as those services do not jeopardise the economic stability of the service operated in the general economic interest by the holder of the exclusive right. It is for the national court to consider whether the services in question in the main proceedings satisfy those criteria.

This process of reasoning is also apparent in the Commission's proposal on voice telephony. In its Green Paper on Telecommunications Services and Equipment the Commission indicated that it would move to liberalise terminal equipment sales and services other than voice telephony. The question arises as to how one aspect of a telecommunications operator's business can be distinguished from another. The Commission, in Recital 18 of the Telecommunications Services Directive,[58] picks out voice telephony as a service capable of special treatment under Article 90(2) on the basis that opening it up to competition could threaten the financial viability of telecommunication organisations providing a universal network. Other services than voice telephony were regarded as suitable for liberalisation. The Commission has since conducted a review which concludes that full liberalisation, including for voice telephony, is possible in the medium term. The concerns about financial viability, it appears, are considered surmountable through payment of access charges to new competitors and a rebalancing of overall charges. This indicates that the Commission regards Article 90(2) as a dynamic and not a static concept, with the Commission working with Member States, using powers under other parts of the Treaty, to overcome obstacles to the removal of privileged positions.

Lastly, in relation to postal services, the Commission has issued a Communication to the Council setting out guidelines on the balance between liberalisation of the sector and safeguard of a universal service. The Commission accepts that a universal, basic postal service accessible everywhere at uniform prices and adequate quality requires the operation to have some exclusive rights. These are necessary to balance the accounts. Otherwise competitors would pick off the profitable services and leave the operator with less profitable ones. This demonstrates a very narrow concept of what is in the general economic interest. It is however consistent with Articles 5 and 104 of the EEC Treaty. Article 5 requires the Community institutions to take care not to prejudice the internal and external financial viability of the Member States. Article 104 allows Member States to pursue economic policies needed to ensure balance of payments equilibrium and confidence in its currency. This duty and right sit counterbalanced with the concept in Article 2 of the progressive approximation of economic policies of Member States, a concept that is strengthened in the Maastricht Treaty.

Concentrating increasingly on the concept of 'general economic interest' means that the Community institutions need to rely less on arguments about whether or not the competition rules would obstruct the performance of the tasks entrusted[59] or whether or not relaxation of the rules is against the Community interest.

58 Directive 90/388/EEC 1990 OJ 192/10.

59 See *British Telecommunications* Commission Decision (82/861/EEC) OJ 1982 L360/36; *Radio Telefis Eirain v Commission* Case T-69/89.

These concepts do, however, increase the ability of the Community institutions to deny the availability of Article 90(2).

The effect of the Court and Commission's approach appears to be the creation of a prohibition and approval mechanism for special and exclusive rights or privileges granted to public undertakings. The imputation principle, the expanding category of inherent abuse and the increasingly objective approach to defining 'general economic interest' has severely constrained Member States' freedom under Article 222. The challenge for the future for Member States is to attempt to develop the approval mechanism. In time, some balancing mechanism along the lines of Articles 85(1) and 85(3) may emerge, with the approval mechanism focusing on essential interests (akin to 'mandatory requirements' in Article 30 terms) that Member States can protect. Member States will, in addition, need to refine the consequences of an adverse decision and take a more sophisticated approach to the nature and incidents of privileged positions.

The Effect of Adverse Decisions

The majority of cases have arisen by way of Article 177 reference where the final effect of the Court's decision in the rights concerned is left open for the national court to resolve. However, the assumption in these cases appears to be that Member States will withdraw the privileged status once an infringement finding has been made. This, indeed, is the practice of the Commission.[60]

It is clear that Article 90 has direct effect, at least where it is effective in combination with a breach of directly effective provisions of the Treaty such as Articles 30, 59, 85 and 86.[61] This applies equally to Article 90(1) and 90(2).[62] Parties can consequently claim the benefit of the provision in national proceedings. In the 'inherent abuse' cases this may well mean that the parties will be entitled to the annulment of the legal provision in question. In other cases it may not be necessary to annul the whole privileged status but merely the offensive element of it, for example, prices imposed that are unfair or discriminatory. Whatever the approach the results achieved may substantially affect the nature of the privileged status and its operation granted by the State.

In all cases the question of whether damages may be available where parties have been excluded from the market or have suffered loss as a result of the state measure remains open.

The Commission's Notice on co-operation with the national courts fails to deal with Article 90 actions. To the extent that issues relating to Articles 85 and 86 arise in national proceedings, however, there is no reason in principle why the co-operation and assistance from the Commission should not be forthcoming. So far as Commission action is concerned this may take the form of a directive or a decision.

Mitigating Action

A further question must be whether Member States can confer privileged status in a manner which avoids the breaches of Treaty rules. Take for instance arguments about excessive pricing in *Bodson* and *Merci*. It may be possible for a Member State to test the prices set to ensure they are not excessive. In *Bodson* a portion of the market was in private hands and charges could have been set in monopoly regions to reflect those in regions with competition. Indeed the Court suggested that this comparison be done to see if the pricing was in fact excessive. In *Merci* the pricing and practices of the port and stevedores could have been regulated to achieve a different result. Similarly in cases such as *Höfner* the privileged agency could be put in a position to meet demand.

There is a hint in *ERT* that such an approach may be acceptable. In that case the Court noted that 'in the absence of any guarantee concerning the retransmission of programmes from another Member State' the exclusive right to broadcast its own and foreign programmes might lead to discriminatory treatment. No indication is given of the nature of the 'guarantee' that may be acceptable.

Again in *RTT v GB-INNO-BM*, in relation to Article 30, the Court found that telecommunication apparatus standard setting by a public undertaking without an appropriate appeals mechanism would be an infringement of the free movement rules. This presupposes that access to an appeal mechanism would correct the infringement.

The issue of mitigation is particularly important in the United Kingdom. Although a large number of public sector monopolies have been privatised they have not all been opened as yet to full competition. In the context of public procurement the Utilities Directive[63] and the Utilities Supply and Works Contracts Regulations 1992[64] contain a lengthy list of UK undertakings, public and

60 Telecom Service Equipment Directive, *Dutch PTT's*.
61 *ERT*; Advocate General Jacobs in *Höfner*.
62 Case T-16/91.
63 Directive 90/531/EEC OJ 1990 L297/1.
64 SI 1992 3279.

private, subject to the procurement rules on the basis of their possessing 'special or exclusive' rights. Many of these are subject to regulatory regimes under the supervision of a regulatory office. The purpose of the regulator is to control any abuse of monopoly power that may accrue from the special or exclusive rights and to compensate for the lack of competition.

There are clear complications between the application of Article 90 and the role of the regulator. There may well be cases where the Regulator has not done enough to control the advantages emanating from special and exclusive rights.

In such cases, Article 90 may give rise to possibilities, particularly for those undertakings prepared to rely on their directly effective rights rather than Commission action. In many cases, however, the potential for infringements of Articles 85 and 86 will have been removed through devices such as the RPI-X formula, obligations on separation of function and transparency of accounting and regulatory approval of access agreements. The question, particularly in the light of *Höfner, Merci* and *Corbeau*, will be whether this is enough. If more than lip service is to be paid to the notion of Article 222 it should be. Certainly the public sector undertakings appear to have alighted on this idea with the proposal by the CEEP of a European Charter of Public Service. This would define the role of public undertakings in the provision of utility services and may provide some defence against Article 90 claims.

In the United States the doctrine of immunity due to state action embraces this concept of mitigation. The 'state action' doctrine allows an exemption from the Sherman Act where one of the states, recognised in US law as quasi-sovereign bodies, requires action to be carried out.

This exemption appears to apply only where the state has put in place a system of regulation at the same time. Action which substitutes public regulation for private competition can be exempt. But action which merely seeks to free an industry from the structures of anti-trust law will not be.[65]

Undoubtedly the concept of proportionality inherent in Article 90(2), and in the nascent exemption mechanism postulated earlier, will enable, and may require, a similar result in the Community.

Article 90: Ebb or Flow?

Since the mid 1980s there has been not just an incoming tide but a tidal wave of legislative and administrative action under Article 90. The extent of judicial activism has already been described.

Commission activism is evident from the Commission's Annual Reports on Competition Policy. There has been a steady flow of action by the Commission since its first measure under Article 90(3), the Transparency Directive.[66] This has encompassed preliminary proceedings and decisions addressed to specific infringements such as Greek legislation reserving access to the public property insurance market to Greek public sector insurance companies and requiring staff of state banks to recommend these companies.[67] In this case at least, the Commission has faced a lack of co-operation from the Member State in ending the infringement, resulting in the Commission taking Article 169 proceedings against Greece which, in turn and after an adverse decision by the Court,[68] were not complied with until further infringement proceedings by the Commission. Greater enthusiasm for compliance by Member States may be shown when, and if, the Maastricht Treaty comes into force, when the Commission will have the power to propose to the Court a fine on Member States for failure to comply.[69]

In addition to dealing with specific infringements the Commission has established a firm base for broader measures aimed at sectoral liberalisation. Its success in *France v Commission* and the *Telecommunications* Case clearly set out the potential that the Commission has. The Commission has been able to use this success to its advantage in moving forward liberalisation talks in other sectors such as energy. A combination of broad sectoral proposals and specific infringement procedures in the postal, telecommunications, transport and energy fields has enabled the Commission to establish a platform on which it can build, if necessary through the use of measures adopted under different powers to Article 90.

This activity does however now seem to be on an ebb. In part, the Commission appears for the time being to have backed away from confrontation with Member States on these issues while the Maastricht debate remained unsolved and as the subsidiarity principle takes root and is developed in Community practice. Concerns about Community unemployment levels may have also taken some of the energy out of Commission activism, since liberalisation of these sectors may lead, in the absence of Community-wide programmes to deal with the problem, to significant rationalisation. The

65 Sullivan, *Antitrust*, West, 4th reprint, 1990, at 731.

66 Directive 80/723/EEC, OJ 1980 L195/35.
67 Decision 85/276/EEC, OJ 1985 L152/25.
68 *Commission v Greece* Case 226/87.
69 Article 171(2) EEC Treaty as amended at Maastricht.

Commission has, in any event, brought Member States to the negotiating table in many of these areas and progress will no doubt be made. In time the Commission will return to its agenda.

When it does, the degree of erosion of Member State independence in the area of privileged undertakings will become apparent. As the current process marches forward, the Community will increasingly assume the mantle of policy direction in economic policy. The usefulness of privileged undertakings to the fulfilment of that policy may well become apparent to the Commission. If so, Member States will gain some ground in this area, albeit within the confines of a Community framework programme.

Article 59 of the EEA Agreement contains provisions identical to Article 90. The EFTA Surveillance Authority will be responsible for enforcing this in EFTA countries (including Sweden, Austria, Norway, Finland, Iceland and Liechtenstein). This may well prove to be a new area of Commission activism as it seeks, with the EFTA SA, to ensure a common approach throughout the EEA.

In the meantime the power-house to drive the development of Article 90 must be the national courts and the European Court of Justice acting on Article 177 references.

[11]

The Velvet Revolution: Article 90 and the Triumph of the Free Market in Europe's Regulated Sectors

Anthony Gardner

Introduction

Article 90 of the Treaty of Rome contains a delicate balance between what may be considered to be a presumption that public monopolies and privileged undertakings are legal, on the one hand, and the recognition that they may be illegal if they fall foul of the rules enshrined in the Treaty, particularly those on competition.[1]

Article 90(1) provides that Member States may only grant special or exclusive rights to public undertakings if they respect the Treaty rules.[2] Article 90(2), addressed to the undertakings themselves, provides that they are subject to the Treaty as long as the application of those rules does not prevent them from carrying out their assigned tasks in the 'general economic interest' (the so-called 'public mission' exception).[3] Finally, Article 90(3) enables the Commission to address appropriate directives or decisions to Member States in order to ensure that public undertakings act in conformity with the Treaty, especially with Article 90(1).[4]

The delicate balance within Article 90 between opposing models of economic organisation—the free market versus state planning—is reflected in the text of the Treaty as a whole. Article 222 states that 'This Treaty shall in no way prejudice the rules in Member States governing the system of property ownership.' Although Article 37 calls on Member States to adjust their state monopolies so as to eliminate discrimination between nationals of Member States regarding the conditions under which goods are procured and marketed, it implicitly recognises the valid existence of such monopolies.[5] On the other hand, Article 3(f) states that one of the key activities of the Community is 'the institution of a system ensuring that competition in the common market is not distorted'. Article 5, finally, calls on the Member States to abstain from any measure which might jeopardise the attainment of the Treaty's objectives, including those enshrined in Articles 85 and 86.

These Articles indicate that the framers of the Treaty of Rome wished to adopt a neutral position in the debate between state planning and free competition and that they preferred to leave to the Member States the liberty, within certain limits, to choose the appropriate model of economic organisation. Indeed, until the mid-1970s the Court of Justice and the Commission considered that Member States were free to confer exclusive rights on undertakings for considerations of public interest of a non-economic nature and that the grant of such rights could not of itself violate Article 90(1). Moreover, the rules contained in Article 37, regarding the adjustment of state trading monopolies, and in Article 30, regarding the free movement of goods, were interpreted restrictively such that public monopolies and privileged undertakings were found to be compatible with them. From the mid-1970s to the mid-1980s, the Court of Justice and the Commission began to apply these Treaty Articles to remove barriers to trade, most notably in the form of national import monopolies. It was only following the mid-1980s, however, that Article 90(1) in conjunction with Article 86, supplemented by the general obligation contained in Article 5, began to be applied against public

Anthony Gardner, Director for European Affairs in the National Security Council of the White House, is on leave from Coudert Brothers, Brussels. The opinions expressed in this article are purely personal.

1 Readers wishing to have a good historical overview of pre-1990 jurisprudence on Article 90 are referred to Aurelio Pappalardo, 'State Measures and Public Undertakings: Article 90 and the EEC Treaty Revisited', [1991] 1 ECLR 29; Richard Wainwright, 'Public Undertakings under Article 90', [1990] *Fordham Corporate Law Institute* 239; and Giuliano Marenco, 'Legal Monopolies in the Case Law of the Court of Justice of the European Communities', [1991] *Fordham Corporate Law Institute* 147.

2 Article 90(1) reads as follows: 'In the case of public undertakings and undertakings to which Member States grant special or exclusive rights, Member States shall neither enact nor maintain in force any measure contrary to the rules contained in this Treaty, in particular to those rules provided for in Article 7 and Articles 85 to 94.'

3 Article 90(2) reads as follows: 'Undertakings entrusted with the operation of services of general economic interest or having the character of a revenue-producing monopoly shall be subject to the rules contained in this Treaty, in particular to the rules on competition, in so far as the application of such rules does not obstruct the performance, in law or in fact, of the particular tasks assigned to them. The development of trade must not be affected to such an extent as would be contrary to the interests of the Community.'

4 Article 90(3) reads as follows: 'The Commission shall ensure the application of the provisions of this Article and shall, where necessary, address appropriate directives or decisions to Member States.'

5 The scope of application of Article 37 is much narrower than that of Article 90 because the former deals exclusively with goods, rather than with services, and because it requires proof of an effect on interstate trade and discrimination between nationals of Member States.

monopolies and privileged undertakings. Until recently, however, these Articles have only been applied when undertakings *exercise* their special or exclusive rights in an abusive manner. As described below, the recent extension in the application of these Articles to attack the *existence* of such rights is of considerable importance to the structure of the European economy.

The dramatic shift in the terms of the debate between state planning and free competition during the 35 years following the Treaty of Rome may be seen in the text of Article 3a of the Treaty of European Union signed at Maastricht: 'the activities of the Member States and the Community shall include ... the adoption of an economic policy ... *conducted in accordance with the principle of an open market economy with free competition*' (*emphasis added*). In other words, the neutrality towards public and privileged enterprises in the text of the Treaty of Rome as signed in 1957 has now been supplanted by a presumption of illegality. The Treaty now contains a policy statement that the Community shall be guided by free market principles—consumer welfare and efficiency in particular—in its search to perfect the single market and to implement an economic and monetary union.

This development is not only to be explained in terms of the growing public realisation that growth and prosperity are more likely to be achieved in the long term through free competition than state intervention; it is to be explained by an activist policy on the part of the Commission, supported by the Court of Justice, to eliminate the significant barriers placed in the way of the single market by the existence of monopolies and public and privileged undertakings. Rather than merely subjecting these undertakings to the competition rules, the Commission has singled them out for stricter treatment under the rules.

Article 90 has been frequently used in conjunction with other Articles of the Treaty of Rome, such as Article 7 (non-discrimination on grounds of nationality), Articles 30 to 36 (free movement of goods), Article 48 (free movement of workers), Articles 52 and 53 (freedom of establishment), Article 59 (freedom to provide services), Article 85 (restrictive practices) and Article 86 (abuse of dominant position). Monopolies or privileged undertakings which have an effect on the cross-border supply of goods or services may be found in certain circumstances to be incompatible with Articles 30 or 59, without any need to refer to Articles 90 and 86. However, the liberalisation of Europe's regulated sectors has been most dramatically achieved by means of the combined application of Articles 90 and 86. The triumph of the free market in Europe's regulated sectors is due in large part to three jurisprudential innovations of the Court of Justice regarding the combined application of these two Articles, as well as to the Court's support for the Commission's use of quasi-legislative powers under Article 90(3).

First, the Court has practically erased the distinction under Article 86 jurisprudence between the concept of the *existence* of a dominant position on the relevant market and the *exercise* of that dominance in an abusive manner. Several recent cases have suggested that the mere existence of a dominant position of a public or privileged undertaking on the relevant market may, in certain circumstances, be abusive *per se* and that the mere grant by a Member State of special or exclusive rights to such an undertaking might constitute a 'measure', within the meaning of Article 90(1), contrary to the Treaty of Rome.

Second, the Court has recently sought to define the minimum sphere of exclusive rights compatible with the financial viability of public monopolies and privileged undertakings, rather than seeking to define—as it once did in the past—the maximum sphere of exclusive rights which these undertakings may enjoy without infringing the competition rules.

Third, the Court has narrowly interpreted the 'public mission' exception in Article 90(2) such that it now affords little protection from the Commission's efforts to pry open the remaining regulated sectors—such as voice telephony, postal services and energy—to free competition.

Fourth, by establishing for itself exceptional powers under Article 90(3) to issue sweeping legislation concerning public monopolies and privileged undertakings without the need for approval by the Council of Ministers or the European Parliament, the Commission has galvanised the Member States to take action within the Council of Ministers to liberalise the remaining regulated sectors under the traditional harmonisation powers found in Article 100A of the EC Treaty.

The Structural Abuse of a Dominant Position

Article 86 cases have traditionally focused on the issue of whether a dominant position has been exercised in an abusive manner. This line of inquiry leads to an examination of the behaviour of the dominant undertaking in question. In several recent cases involving Article 86 in conjunction with Article 90, however, the emphasis appears to be shifting from proving abusive behaviour to identifying the existence of exclusive or special rights conferring on an undertaking a dominant position whose structure is likely to result in an abuse.

The *Port of Genoa*[6] case involved the question

6 *Merci Convenzionali Porto di Genova SpA v Siderurgica Gabrielli*, Case C-179/90, [1991] ECR I-5889.

whether the Treaty of Rome permits a Member State to reserve certain exclusive rights, such as loading and unloading operations, to a national port, at compulsory rates, when shipping companies can effect such operations themselves at lower cost. Under Italian legislation unloading operations were reserved to dock-work companies whose workers were required to be Italian nationals in violation of the non-discrimination provision in Article 7 of the Treaty of Rome. The case against the company managing the Port of Genoa (Merci Convenzionali) was brought by an Italian company (Siderurgica Gabrielli) which had imported steel by ship from Hamburg. Although the ship was equipped to unload the cargo itself, Siderurgica Gabrielli was obliged to use the services of Merci. Under Italian legislation Merci was, in turn, obliged to assign the work to the dockers' company which enjoyed a monopoly over loading and unloading operations. Due to a dockers' strike, however, the steel was unloaded three months late and Siderurgica Gabrielli suffered considerable financial loss.

The Court of Justice held that although the grant of exclusive rights to an undertaking is not incompatible with the Treaty *per se*, a Member State infringes Article 90, in conjunction with Article 86, when that undertaking is led by the simple exercise of its rights to abuse its dominance or when those rights are capable of creating a situation in which the undertaking is led to commit such an abuse.

One possible interpretation of the Court's judgment is that the *existence* of rights granted by a Member State to an undertaking may *inevitably* lead that undertaking to abuse its dominance in certain circumstances. Merely by observing the terms of the grant of exclusive rights, in other words, the undertaking may have no choice but to act in an abusive manner. The difficulty with this interpretation is that it does not square with the facts of the case: neither Merci Convenzionali nor the dockers' company was inevitably led by its exclusive rights to resist implementing modern unloading techniques. They simply chose to do so because there was no competition in the market for their services.

Alternatively, the judgment may be read more restrictively to mean that the *existence* of monopoly or special rights may be *likely* to lead a public or privileged undertaking to abuse its dominant position in certain circumstances. Indeed, it is perfectly plausible that the existence of the exclusive rights enjoyed by Merci Convenzionali and the dockers' company were likely to lead them to use their dominance in an abusive manner: an undertaking whose business, and profits, are guaranteed by the absence of competition is unlikely to exert itself in providing high quality and low cost service. Even if this interpretation of the judgment is correct, it would amount to a silent revolution whereby monopoly or special rights are presumed to be illegal unless the undertakings concerned can show that these rights have been exercised legally.

In the *Port of Genoa* case, however, the Court appears to have required proof of *abusive behaviour*. Had it wished to do so, the Court could have explicitly found that Merci Convenzionali and the dock workers' company had *actively* abused their exclusive rights by requiring payment for services not requested, charging prices which were disproportionate to the value of the services rendered, and offsetting price reductions to some customers with higher prices to other customers.[7] However, the Court appears to have put forward a more far-reaching proposition: a public or privileged undertaking may *passively exercise* its special or exclusive rights in an abusive manner merely by 'enjoying the quiet life', that is by being inefficient and thereby unable to satisfy market demand for its services. Indeed, Merci Convenzionali and the dockers' company failed to install modern technology which would have reduced the cost and increased the speed of unloading operations.

If this interpretation is correct, the judgment has far-reaching implications. By finding that inefficient public monopolies may abuse their exclusive rights by exercising them passively, the Court set a stricter standard than the one applying to private monopolies whose exclusive rights have never been found abusive on the ground of efficiency. Moreover, the Court overlooked the possibility that an inefficient public or privileged undertaking may choose to change management or implement new techniques in order to become more efficient in the future. As few public undertakings enjoying exclusive or special rights in Europe today perform their functions in a manner which consumers consider to be satisfactory, few would be safe from legal challenge.

In the *Greek Television Monopoly*[8] case, the Court took one step closer to finding that the mere *existence* of a dominant position of a public monopoly or privileged undertaking may be abusive, without regard to the actual behaviour of the undertaking in question. In that case a municipal information company and the mayor of Thessaloniki were sued for establishing a local television company. The Court declared that

7 In *Corsica Ferries v Corpo dei Piloti del Porto di Genova*, Case C-19/93, judgment delivered 17 May 1994, not yet reported, the Court of Justice also found that the Republic of Italy had infringed Article 90(1), in conjunction with Article 86, by investing the authorities of the Port of Genoa with the right to charge higher tariffs for compulsory services supplied to maritime transport companies which sail between Member State ports than to those which conduct activities between Italian ports.

8 *ERT v Dimotiki*, Case C-260/89, [1991] ECR I-2925.

the competition rules do not prohibit Member States from granting to an undertaking an exclusive right to transmit radio and television images in order to promote a non-economic public interest. This declaration was in perfect harmony with the Court's prior jurisprudence.[9] However, the Court noted that the creation of an exclusive television right is contrary to Article 90(1) when it is liable to create a situation in which the undertaking benefiting from that right is led to infringe Article 86. This situation would arise, for example, if the undertaking were to implement discriminatory policies favouring its own programmes. The cumulation of monopoly rights over both normal transmission and retransmission rights would constitute such discrimination.

What is striking about this case is that, according to the Court, discrimination need only be *likely* rather than *proven*. It was not necessary to show that the Greek television monopoly actively discriminated against foreign programmes; it was sufficient that the cumulation of monopoly rights would *probably* lead to this result. In another case decided the same year, the Court similarly found that since the Belgian Telephone and Telegraph Authority competed in the telephone equipment market, its power to set technical specifications for telephones and terminal equipment, as well as to approve telephones for connection to the public network, would *probably* lead it to discriminate against other suppliers.[10] This approach contrasts with that taken in cases under Article 59, in which discrimination in favour of national services must be *proven* by demonstrating the absence of non-protectionist justifications.

The boundaries of traditional Article 86 jurisprudence have been stretched farthest in the *Höfner*[11] case involving the German Federal Employment Office. According to the Law on the Promotion of Employment, the Office had the exclusive right to offer job placement services. Accordingly, the activities of private recruitment agencies were considered to be void under the German Civil Code. The case involved a dispute between a private recruitment agency and a company in need of an executive. According to the contract entered into between the parties, the agency presented the company with an allegedly suitable candidate for the post. When the company decided not to hire the candidate nor to honour the fee stipulated in the contract, the agency brought suit. The recruitment agency countered the argument about the invalidity of the contract under German law with the claim that the grant to the Federal Employment Office of exclusive rights to conduct job placement services violated Article 90(1).

In this case the Court appeared to suggest that the existence of a dominant position need not necessarily be distinguished from its abusive exercise in cases involving public monopolies. Simply by reason of its government-imposed monopoly in the market for job placement, the Federal Employment Office was found to be abusing a dominant position. The very fact of its dominance led to a conclusion of abuse, notwithstanding the absence of any *active conduct* on its part to hinder the maintenance or growth of competition. The mere *grant* by the German Government to the Federal Employment Office of an exclusive right to conduct job placement was held to infringe Article 86 because the Office was manifestly unable to satisfy market demand for its services and because of the legal prohibition on private companies from providing similar services.

If this interpretation is correct, it would amount to a silent revolution. In the *Port of Genoa* case there was sufficient evidence that Merci Convenzionali and the dock workers' company were exercising their dominant position in an abusive manner, even though the Court preferred to devote more attention to the passive abuse which may result from inefficiency. Similarly, in the *Greek Television Monopoly* case it appears that the Greek television monopoly had actually implemented discriminatory policies favouring its own programmes, even though the Court emphasised that the likelihood of such discrimination was sufficient to demonstrate abuse. In *Höfner*, however, the Court finally appears to have crossed the Rubicon: a Member State may infringe Article 90, in conjunction with Article 86, merely by granting monopoly rights to an undertaking even if that undertaking does not engage in abusive behaviour.

The judgment in *Höfner* is all the more striking because the Federal Employment Office sought to exercise its monopoly rights in a responsible manner. Although it was not compelled by German law to allow the activities of private recruitment agencies, it chose to tolerate them. It appears that the Court considered this tolerance as further evidence that the Federal Employment Office was manifestly incapable of satisfying market demand.

9 In *Sacchi*, Case 155/73, [1974] ECR 409, the Court declared: 'nothing in the Treaty prevents Member States, for considerations of public interest, of non-economic nature, from removing radio and television transmissions, from the field of competition by conferring on one or more establishments an exclusive right to conduct them.'

10 The Court also found that the Belgian Telephone and Telegraph Authority had committed an abuse by extending its dominant position in the provision of telephone communication to the non-ancillary equipment market. *RTT v GB-Inno-BM*, [1991] I ECR 5941. In *Kingdom of the Netherlands & Others v Commission* [1992] ECR 565, the Commission found that the Dutch Postal Service had committed an abuse by extending its dominant position in the supply of basic postal services to the non-ancillary market for express courier services. Such services have since been liberalised throughout the Community.

11 *Höfner and Elser v Macrotron*, Case C–41/90, [1991] ECR-I 1979.

The Minimum Sphere of Public Monopoly Compatible with its Financial Viability

In the *Corbeau*[12] case the Court of Justice answered several questions posed by the Criminal Court in Liège regarding the compatibility of the Belgian postal monopoly with the EC Treaty. Mr Corbeau conducted a courier business which consisted of the home collection and distribution of mail before noon the next day in or around Liège. The postal monopoly brought criminal proceedings against Mr Corbeau for breaching the 1956 Law on Postal Service which granted it exclusive rights over mailing activities in Belgium.

The Court affirmed that Article 90(2) permits Member States to grant exclusive rights to undertakings charged with the provision of a universal service to the extent that the resulting restrictions of competition are necessary to achieve the public mission in question. The Court went on to hold that an undertaking enjoying these rights may restrict or eliminate competition only insofar as this is necessary to ensure its existence on economically acceptable terms. In other words, the scope of the exclusive rights must be defined as narrowly as possible, while ensuring the financial viability of the undertaking in question. This jurisprudence may have been inspired by the ancillary restraints doctrine in competition law according to which restrictive provisions in agreements which would otherwise be contrary to Article 85(1) are permissible if they are directly related to and reasonably necessary for the implementation of a pro-competitive transaction.

According to the Court, the financial viability of public monopolies and privileged undertakings can only be ensured if they have the right to prevent competitors from undermining their ability to use profitable activities to cross-subsidise loss-making activities required under universal service obligations: if competitors were permitted to engage in 'cream skimming' by targeting profitable activities without assuming any universal service obligations, the economic viability of the undertakings would be undermined.

Public monopolies and privileged undertakings may not assert rights of monopoly, however, when competitors seek to offer specific activities which do not fall within the sphere of universal service obligations and which both respond to particular needs of certain consumers (for example, businesses) and involve certain services not traditionally offered by the undertakings themselves. The Court concluded that it is up to national courts to decide which are the minimum exclusive rights compatible with the economic viability of undertakings providing universal services.

In the postal sector the universal service obligation consists of the collection and delivery of mail to everyone in the national territory on equal terms, regardless of the remoteness and unprofitability of certain areas. While the Court left it up to the Liège Criminal Court to determine the proper scope of the Belgian postal monopoly's exclusive rights, it indicated that the collection of mail at home and rapid delivery within a restricted geographic area is a service not traditionally offered by the postal monopoly and is not of such a nature as to jeopardise the monopoly's 'core' areas of profitable activity. The Court therefore appears to have found that a service is distinct from a service of general economic interest when it is a value-added service rather than a basic service.

Although the judgment is fully in line with the Court's prior jurisprudence on the need to protect telecommunications operators' exclusive rights in certain profitable areas in order to finance loss-making activities required under their universal service obligations, it is innovative in several important respects.

First, the judgment reflects a change in the Court's approach towards the issue of the compatibility between the EC competition rules and the activities of public monopolies and privileged undertakings. Whereas it once sought to define the maximum sphere of exclusive rights which these undertakings may enjoy without infringing the competition rules, it now seeks to define the minimum sphere of exclusive rights compatible with these undertakings' financial viability. This new approach encourages a far more restrictive policy toward public monopolies and privileged undertakings.

Second, following its approach in *Höfner*, the Court did not address the issue of when an undertaking enjoying exclusive rights exercises those rights in an abusive manner. By proceeding directly to an analysis of the 'public mission' exception in Article 90(2) without first discussing Article 90(1), the Court appears, once again, to have endorsed the view that the mere *existence* of monopoly rights may, in certain circumstances, infringe Article 86. A less radical interpretation is, however, possible: the Court may have considered that the Belgian state infringed Article 90(1), in conjunction with Article 86, by failing to respond to new market developments—such as high quality and rapid value-added services—by modifying the original monopoly right over postal services granted to the Belgian postal monopoly 40 years previously. Such an interpretation would be consistent with the jurisprudence of the *Port of Genoa* case that a public monopoly may exercise its dominant position in an abusive manner by leading the 'quiet life'.

The Court's emphasis on defining exclusive rights in such a manner as to create an equilibrium between

12 *Régie des Postes v Paul Corbeau* [1993] ECR I 2533.

profitable and loss-making activities raises practical difficulties: it is not always simple to identify the sectors which will generate profits and those which will generate losses, especially in high technology industries where the market-place changes rapidly.[13] If these sectors cannot be properly identified, it will be difficult to determine which exclusive rights may or may not be open to free competition and what access charges, if any, should be paid to the holder of such rights. Moreover, it is often difficult to determine the degree of cross-subsidisation of a loss-making service by a profitable one which is necessary to enable a public monopoly to continue to provide the former. This determination requires a complex assessment of the market price for each type of service and the methods of apportioning gains and losses.[14] Finally, the Court's approach apparently overlooks the advantages of direct subsidies in comparison with cross-subsidies: the former are generally considered easier to calculate and monitor.

By leaving national courts with the task of defining the proper sphere of exclusive rights, the Court may have opened a Pandora's box: in the light of the very uneven familiarity of national court judges with EC competition rules, or with the economics of cross-subsidisation, it may be expected that exclusive rights which will be prohibited in some Member States will be protected in others. In particular, public monopolies or monopolies enjoying exclusive rights in countries which have a *dirigiste* tradition will find it easier to survive than those in countries which have greater confidence in free competition. Concerned by this prospect, Advocate General Tesauro stressed in his conclusions to the Court that business activities subjected to free competition and to public monopoly 'must be defined in identical terms throughout the Community'.

The Vanishing 'Public Mission' Exception

The combined impact of the *Höfner* and *Port of Genoa* jurisprudence under Article 90(1) would have been less dramatic had public monopolies and privileged undertakings been able to claim protection from the chill winds of free competition by invoking the 'public mission' exception under Article 90(2). Indeed, until recently it had been generally accepted that this exception could be invoked readily (and successfully) by a public monopoly or privileged undertaking in the event that proceedings were brought against it under either Article 85 or Article 86. The exception has been particularly significant in the case of proceedings under Article 86, which does not contain an equivalent to the exemption provision in Article 85(3).[15] The Court's recent judgments involving public monopolies and privileged undertakings, however, have exposed how narrowly the 'public mission' exception is to be interpreted.

This narrow interpretation has resulted from the meaning given to the words 'entrusted', 'general economic interest' and 'obstruct' in the text of Article 90(2). Undertakings 'entrusted' with the operation of services of a 'general economic interest' are subject to the Treaty rules, particularly those relating to competition, only insofar as these rules do not 'obstruct' the performance of the tasks assigned to them.

In order for there to be entrustment, there must be an act of public authority granting certain rights to a specific undertaking. There is no entrustment if a legal approval is granted to or an obligation imposed on *all* undertakings. Moreover, the entrustment must be for a specific task. Public and privileged undertakings will not be permitted to restrict competition, for example, in areas which extend beyond the core activity with which they have been entrusted.[16]

Services may be classified as being of a general economic interest if they are made available to the general public rather than to private interests. In practice, the Commission and the Court have rarely found public service monopolies to have general economic interest. In *Corbeau*, the Court indicated that services are of a general economic interest only if they benefit all users on the entire territory of the Member State in question and if they are supplied at uniform tariffs and similar quality without regard to specific situations and the degree of profitability of each individual activity. According to the Commission, a general economic interest must be national rather than Community-wide in scope since public monopolies exist within the boundaries of

13 For example, coin-operated telephone booths were long considered to be a loss-making activity because they were frequently vandalised. With the introduction of phone cards, however, they have become very profitable.

14 Nonetheless, the prohibition of cross-subsidisation of non-reserved services by monopoly profits gained in reserved services has become a key principle in the Commission's telecommunications policy. See the Commission's Guidelines on the Application of the EEC Competition Rules in the Telecommunications Sector, OJ 1991 C233/2. Indeed, the Commission regularly requests telecommunications operators involved in co-operation agreements to issue a guarantee of non cross-subsidisation as a condition for exemption under Article 85(3).

15 Unlike Article 85(3), whose application is regulated by Council Regulation 17/62, OJ 1962 L204/62, Article 90(2) is regulated by the interpretation given to it by national courts and the Commission rather than by secondary legislation.

16 For example, in *RTE v Commission* [1991] ECR 485, *BBC v Commission* [1991] ECR 535, *ITP v Commission* [1991] ECR 575 ('*Magill*'), the Court of First Instance held that the restrictive conduct of the undertakings concerned should have been limited to their core business of broadcasting rather than extended to a neighbouring market for weekly television programmes.

individual Member States.[17] This view would appear to contradict the purpose of the single market programme to ensure the provision of services within the Community on a transnational basis.

The application of the Treaty rules obstructs the performance of tasks assigned to public monopolies and privileged undertakings only when their performance is rendered impossible, rather than merely problematic. For example, the Commission has rejected the argument that the monopolisation over imports and exports of electricity is necessary in order to fulfil the public mission of electricity generating firms to ensure the security of electricity supplies.[18] Although this mission was quite clearly rendered more problematic, the application of the rules of free competition did not render it impossible. A monopoly would be able to invoke the Article 90(2) exception only if there were no less stringent measures restrictive of competition which could guarantee the provision of the public mission.[19]

Ultimately, the issue of whether the performance of a public mission is rendered impossible or merely problematic by the application of the Treaty rules will have to be determined by national courts.[20] As mentioned above, the *Corbeau* case requires national courts to make this determination by defining the minimum sphere of monopoly rights compatible with the financial viability of public monopolies. Even though the opening up of specific value-added sectors in 'non-core' areas of activity to free competition certainly complicates the life of public monopolies, the Court appears to have considered that their public mission (for example, of assuring universal service) is not necessarily endangered thereby.

Whether or not the 'public mission' exception has been defined out of existence will therefore be determined by the views of national courts in the Member States. It is possible that a national court will be more sympathetic to parties invoking this exception than the Commission, the Court of Justice or the Court of First Instance. When seeking to determine whether an undertaking has been entrusted with monopoly or special rights, whether the operation of a particular activity is of general economic interest or whether the application of the Treaty rules would obstruct the performance of tasks assigned to an undertaking, however, it is possible that a national court would suspend proceedings and ask the Commission for an opinion, according to the procedure set forth in the Commission's Notice on co-operation with national courts.[21]

The Powers of the Commission under Article 90(3)

At the same time as the special or exclusive rights granted by Member States to monopolies or privileged undertakings have come to be viewed as almost automatically infringing Article 90(1) and the ability of public or privileged undertakings to invoke the 'public mission' exception under Article 90(2) has been practically eliminated, the power of the Commission to issue directives or decisions under Article 90(3) to break apart or restructure regulated sectors of Member States' economies has been considerably strengthened.[22] This power has enabled it to act more rapidly and effectively than would otherwise be the case if it had to undertake infringement proceedings against Member States pursuant to Article 169[23] or if it had to wait for the Council to take action under Article 100A or Article 87 in co-operation with the European Parliament.[24]

With the blessing of the Court of Justice, the Commission has gained quasi-legislative powers as an exception to the Council's legislative monopoly in this area. The Court, however, has placed limits on these powers. It suggested that the Commission should use Article 90(3) only when swift action is required or when the proposed legislation does not require considerable consultation or debate. Moreover, the Court has stated that these powers should not be used to micro-manage the means by which the Member States liberalise their regulated sectors. For example, the Court held that the inclusion in the Commission Directive on Telecommunications Services of an obligation on telecommunications authorities to terminate leasing or maintenance contracts on no more than one year's notice fell outside the powers of the Commission. The Court considered that individual decisions taken under Articles 85 and/or

17 *Screensport/EBU*, OJ 1991 L63/32. The Commission rejected the argument made by the members of the European Broadcasting Union that they needed to establish a European television sports station in order to fulfil their 'public mission' of bringing less popular sports to the attention of the European public.

18 *Ijsselcentrale and Others*, OJ 1991 L28/32. Long-term contracts with lengthy notice periods between suppliers and consumers were found to be perfectly well suited to preserving security of supplies.

19 This is, in effect, an application of the fundamental principle of proportionality in EC law.

20 *Commune d'Almelo v NV Energiebedrijf IJsselmij*, Case C-393/92, judgment of the Court of Justice delivered on 27 April 1994 (not yet reported).

21 OJ 1993 C39/6.

22 This power was confirmed by the Court of Justice in *French Republic v Commission* [1991] ECR 1223.

23 Under Article 169 the Commission may bring Member States before the Court of Justice to put an end to specific infringements.

24 Under Article 100A the Council, acting on a proposal from the Commission and in co-operation with the European Parliament, adopts measures for the approximation of Member State laws in order to bring about the establishment and proper functioning of a single market. Under Article 87 the Council, acting on a proposal from the Commission and after consulting with the European Parliament, may issue regulations or directives defining the application of Articles 85 and 86 to various sectors of the economy.

Article 86 were the appropriate means under the Treaty for dealing with any anti-competitive aspects of such contracts.[25]

Paradoxically, the Commission's successful recourse to Article 90(3) as a quasi-legislative tool may have reduced its usefulness in the effort to carry out further liberalisation: the use of Article 90(3) in the sectors of telecommunications terminal equipment[26] and non-voice telephony telecommunications services[27] has galvanised the Member States to take action within the Council to open up other regulated sectors to free competition.

For example, the Council has decided to liberalise telex, mobile telephony, paging, satellite services and, most important, voice telephony by 1998. Moreover, a recent judgment of the Court of Justice confirming that the EC competition rules apply to the electricity sector,[28] coupled with the Commission's intention to file Article 169 infringement actions with the Court of Justice[29] against Member States which have failed to terminate their import and export monopolies, and the Commission's threat to adopt Article 90(3) directives against specific Member States in the absence of satisfactory progress to liberalise the transport and distribution of gas and electricity sectors have prompted the Council to give priority attention to several Commission proposals based on Article 100A.[30] As the Commission released its Green Paper on postal services in 1992[31] and a Communication to the Council and the European Parliament on the Development of EC Postal Services,[32] it is unlikely to have recourse to its powers under Article 90(3), unless the Council refuses to take action. Finally, the Commission may be hesitant to force faster liberalisation in remaining regulated sectors—such as utilities, transport, broadcasting and certain telecommunications services—on its own at a time when its activities are being increasingly scrutinised for their compatibility with the principles of subsidiarity and proportionality, and with the efforts of the Community to correct the democratic deficit by increasing the powers of the European Parliament.[33]

25 *French Republic v Commission* [1991] ECR 1223.
26 Commission Directive 88/301, OJ 1988 L131/73.
27 Commission Directive 90/388, OJ 1990 L192/10.
28 *Commune d'Almelo v NV Energiebedrijf IJsselmij*, Case C-393/92, judgment of the Court of Justice delivered on 27 April 1994 (not yet reported).
29 The Commission has introduced Article 169 actions against several Member States for their failure to terminate their import and export monopolies over energy supplies.
30 OJ 1992 C65/4 and 14. The proposals, amended by the European Parliament in order to bring about a gradual transition to an internal market in the energy sector, do not presently require unbundling of production, transport and distribution functions in the gas and electricity sectors or third party access; they will, however, require transparency in the financial accounts of public utilities. OJ 1994 C123/1. The Council has already adopted directives on price transparency, the transit of gas through transmission grids and the transmission of electricity through grids.
31 Green Paper on the Development of the Single Market for Postal Services, COM(91) 476 final (released on 11 June 1992).
32 COM(93) 247 final (2 June 1993). The Commission has proposed maintaining a universal postal service in the core area of standard letters but opening up to competition value-added services such as express mail, direct mail and the delivery of publications and parcels.

Conclusion

The recent jurisprudence of the Court of Justice regarding the combined application of Articles 90 and 86 amounts to a 'velvet revolution' in which Europe's regulated sectors are exposed, one after another, to the forces of free competition in a manner compatible with their universal service obligations. This jurisprudence is revolutionary because it has reversed the decades-old presumption—reflected in the very text of Article 90—that public monopolies and privileged undertakings are compatible with the EC Treaty and that Member States are free in principle to determine their preferred system of property ownership. Whereas the jurisprudence of the Court had previously suggested that public monopolies were permitted unless prohibited in specific circumstances, it now appears to suggest that they are prohibited unless permitted in specific circumstances.

Public monopolies and privileged undertakings are now *presumed* to be incompatible such that Article 90(1) has been practically subsumed into the inquiry under Article 90(2) of whether the 'public mission' exception applies. This presumption results from a recent line of cases indicating that the Court is prepared to find that the mere existence of a public monopoly's dominant position may *ipso facto* eliminate the 'effet utile' of Article 86, regardless of whether the public monopoly has engaged in abusive behaviour or whether there is any causal link between the existence of the exclusive rights and the abuse in question. Moreover, the Court continues to limit the scope of the interests which may qualify for the Article 90(2) exception; even when this exception applies, the Court has instructed Member State courts to define the sphere of the monopoly rights in the narrowest way compatible with their financial viability.

Under the weight of the Court's jurisprudence, the success of the Commission's use of its powers under Article 90(3) and the growing consensus in the

33 However, it must be noted that in December 1994 the Council gave its approval in principle to the Commission's proposal in its green paper on the liberalisation of telecommunications infrastructure and cable TV networks to adopt a new Article 90(3) Directive, which would extend the scope of the Telecommunications Services Directive to include the leasing of capacity by cable companies.

Community, including in Member States with a tradition of economic *dirigisme*, that market liberalisation and privatisation are the best guarantees of consumer welfare and economic growth, it may be expected that Europe's remaining monopolies and regulated sectors will be opened to freer competition. The trend towards greater liberalisation—which has taken place principally in the telecommunications, post and air transport sectors—will therefore become the rule rather than the exception.

Part III
Selected Legal Concepts and Challenges in Competition Law

The Rule of Reason and Per Se Rules

[12]

The "Rule of Reason" in Antitrust Law: Property Logic in Restraint of Competition

by
RUDOLPH J. PERITZ*

Though modern antitrust scholars, policy makers, and judges agree on very little, they do concur on two fundamental propositions. First, they agree that "courts should refuse to validate any private arrangement restricting competition on the basis of a claim that the arrangement advances other social ends."[1] In short, "competition" constitutes the only legitimate policy basis for antitrust doctrine. Second, they agree that the Supreme Court's adoption of the "rule of reason" in 1911 represents the emergence of modern antitrust law.[2] That is, the "rule of reason" affords

---

* Associate Professor of Law, New York Law School. Some of the research for this Essay was done while a Langdell Fellow at Harvard Law School. I would like to express my appreciation to the Law School, as well as to friends and colleagues who gave helpful comments on earlier drafts, especially Michael Botein, David Gray Carlson, John Flynn, Janice Haney-Peritz, Duncan Kennedy, David Schoenbrod, Katherine van Wezel Stone, and G. Edward White. Speeches based on versions of this Article were presented to the Conference on Systems Science and Jurisprudence at Harvard Law School on June 26, 1987, and to the Critical Legal Studies Conference at American University, Washington College of Law, on October 1, 1988.

This Article constitutes the historical and theoretical foundation for a series of studies of modern antitrust law. The first, entitled *A Genealogy of Vertical Restraints Doctrine*, is forthcoming in 40 HASTINGS L.J. (1989) (March issue).

1. L. SULLIVAN, HANDBOOK OF THE LAW OF ANTITRUST 182 (1977); *see* P. AREEDA, ANTITRUST ANALYSIS: PROBLEMS, TEXT, CASES 5, 8, 7-43, 49-50 (3d ed 1981); C. KAYSEN & D. TURNER, ANTITRUST LAW: AN ECONOMIC AND LEGAL ANALYSIS 44 (1959); R. POSNER, ANTITRUST LAW: AN ECONOMIC PERSPECTIVE ix (1976). At the same time, there is little agreement concerning the substance of the term "competition." *See, e.g.*, 1 P. AREEDA & D. TURNER, ANTITRUST LAW: AN ANALYSIS OF ANTITRUST PRINCIPLES AND THEIR APPLICATION 5-44, 49-50 (3d ed. 1981); McNulty, *Economic Theory and the Meaning of Competition*, 82 Q.J. ECON. 639, 639-50 (1968); Peritz, *The Predicament of Antitrust Jurisprudence: Economics and the Monopolization of Price Discrimination Argument.* 1984 DUKE L.J. 1205, 1209-13.

2. Standard Oil Co. v. United States, 221 U.S. 1 (1911). For an early and well-respected rendition of this view of modern antitrust law, see REPORT OF THE ATTORNEY GENERAL'S NATIONAL COMMITTEE TO STUDY ANTITRUST LAWS 5 (1955) [hereinafter ATTORNEY GENERAL'S REPORT]. *Cf.* United States v. Aluminum Co. of Am., 148 F.2d 416, 429-33 (2d Cir. 1945) ("the old dispensation . . . ended with Standard Oil Co. v. United States"); R. BORK,

the analytical tool for making judgments about the competitive effects of market conduct and in turn for identifying "unreasonable restraints of trade."

An orthodox history of early antitrust law provides the common ground for this consensus about the normative and analytical basis of modern antitrust doctrine. This standard account usually proceeds as follows. In the late nineteenth century, growing public concern about the consolidation of American industry was chronicled in the popular press, in political party platforms, and on state court dockets.[3] Whether to attack the trusts or merely to defuse civil unrest, Congress passed the Sherman Act of 1890.[4] Unfortunately, neither the Act's language nor the legislative history "is very illuminating about what specifically is allowed or prohibited."[5] As a result, some modern commentators accord the "legislative history of the antitrust laws . . . relatively little weight."[6] The language of the statute itself, which follows the general language of the common law, is viewed as "singularly opaque" and vague, particularly its first section.[7] Section one of the Act provides that "[e]very contract, combination in the form of trust or otherwise, or conspiracy, in restraint of trade or commerce . . . is declared to be illegal."[8] The

THE ANTITRUST PARADOX: A POLICY AT WAR WITH ITSELF 18-19 (1978) (rule of reason cases began modern antitrust law).

3. *See infra* notes 25-132 and accompanying text. Thoughtful treatments of the early history of antitrust law include R. HOFSTADTER, *What Happened to the Antitrust Movement?*, in THE PARANOID STYLE IN AMERICAN POLITICS AND OTHER ESSAYS 188 (1965); J.W. HURST, LAW AND SOCIAL ORDER IN THE UNITED STATES 245-66 (1977); W. LETWIN, LAW AND ECONOMIC POLICY IN AMERICA: THE EVOLUTION OF THE SHERMAN ANTITRUST ACT (1965); H. THORELLI, THE FEDERAL ANTITRUST POLICY: ORIGINATION OF AN AMERICAN TRADITION (1955); Flynn, *Rethinking Sherman Act Section I Analysis: Three Proposals for Reducing the Chaos*, 49 ANTITRUST L.J. 1593 (1980) [hereinafter *Rethinking Sherman Act*]; Flynn, *Antitrust Jurisprudence: A Symposium on the Economic, Political and Social Goals of Antitrust Policy—Introduction*, 125 U. PA. L. REV. 1182 (1977) [hereinafter *Antitrust Jurisprudence*]; Fox, *The Modernization of Antitrust: A New Equilibrium*, 66 CORNELL L. REV. 1140 (1981); Lande, *Wealth Transfers as the Original and Primary Concern of Antitrust: The Efficiency Interpretation Challenged*, 34 HASTINGS L.J. 65 (1982). For an insightful analysis of the state antitrust law of this period, see May, *Antitrust Practice and Procedure in the Formative Era: The Constitutional and Conceptual Reach of State Antitrust Law, 1880-1918*, 135 U. PA. L. REV. 495 (1987).

4. S. 3445, 50th Cong., 2d Sess., 20 CONG. REC. 1120 (1889) (as amended) (codified at 15 U.S.C. § 1-7 (1985)); *see also* Senator Reagan's earlier Bill, S. 3440, 50th Cong., 1st Sess., 19 CONG. REC. 7512 (1888).

5. P. AREEDA & D. TURNER, *supra* note 1, at 14-15; *see also* J. AUERBACH, *President Roosevelt and the Trusts*, 175 N. AM. REV. 877, 891 (1902) (describing the legislation as "crudely drawn, imperfectly considered, hastily enacted . . . .")

6. P. AREEDA & D. TURNER, *supra* note 1, at 15.

7. *Id.* at 14; R. BORK, *supra* note 2, at 19-20.

8. Sherman Act, 15 U.S.C. § 1 (1982).

Supreme Court struggled with the statute for twenty-one years, the familiar story continues, until they finally got it right by announcing the "rule of reason" in *Standard Oil v. United States.* [9] The "literalist" opinions that preceded *Standard Oil* "reveal some early confusion about the relationship of § 1's prohibition to common law notions of 'restraint of trade.' "[10] Indeed, a "literalist" strategy for interpreting the Sherman Act appears naive or stupid. How can *every* contract in restraint of trade be illegal? Such literalism would outlaw not only price fixing agreements, but also partnership agreements and even simple contracts for the sale of goods—certainly an unreasonable view of the statute.[11] In short, the "literalist" opinions marked a series of failed attempts to make sense of enigmatic statutory language.[12]

Is that what the "rule of reason" left behind? Did the old "literalist" majority on the Court really take such naive positions on statutory interpretation? This Article will show that they did not. Rather, their conflict with the new "rule of reason" majority centered on fundamental differences over whether competition should constitute antitrust's only normative ground. Consequently, the well-settled history of antitrust's formative years, by focusing primarily on competition, tells only half of the story.

A strikingly different history emerges from this Article's reformulation of legislative and judicial history. First, the legislative debates chronicle a conflict between commitments to fostering competition and commitments to protecting property rights, a tension that produced the Sherman Act of 1890. From the earliest moments of federal antitrust history, assuring competitive markets never constituted the sole concern of legislators or judges.[13] Second, it was this tension between competi-

9. 221 U.S. 1 (1911); L. Schwartz, & J. Flynn, Antitrust and Regulatory Alternatives 14-15 (5th ed. 1977). For an argument that the "literalists" were proto-price theorists, see R. Bork, *supra* note 2, at 22-23. For critiques of that claim, see *infra* note 22 and sources cited therein.

10. P. Areeda, *supra* note 1, at 314.

11. United States v. Trans-Missouri Freight Ass'n, 166 U.S. 290, 351-56 (1897) (White, J., dissenting).

12. R. Bork, *supra* note 2, at 19-20.

13. Of course, numerous historical actors have participated in these struggles. The analysis that follows, however, is not interested in finding the authorial intent of particular opinion writers or opinions, legislators or legislatures, committees or lobbyists. What Senator Sherman had in mind or how Justice Holmes' antitrust jurisprudence developed is not this Article's concern. Instead, this Article looks at a series of statements that constituted the discourse of early antitrust law. This archive houses not only familiar articulations, but also forgotten statements about antitrust. Neither evolutionary nor chaotic legal doctrine emerges from this archival study. Rather, the documents put under this new light, the unremarkable debate transcripts in the *Congressional Record*, and the court opinions reinvigorated and so recovered

tion and property, this struggle between two logics,[14] that motivated the well-known jurisprudential disagreement between the "literalist" and "rule of reason" factions on the Court. The literalists were not naive; they developed a scheme based on the familiar categories of direct and ancillary restraints, a scheme that we continue to use today.[15] Compromise with the proponents of the rule of reason was not possible, however, because the literalists' competition-driven views were profoundly incompatible with their colleagues' property-directed commitments. Third and most surprisingly, the emergence of the rule of reason represented the triumph of a property-driven logic, not the competition-directed analysis universally associated with the rule today.[16] Thus, when Justice Oliver Wendell Holmes wrote that the Sherman Act "says nothing about competition,"[17] he represented the rule of reason's position in the early battle over the foundations of antitrust law.

This Article's fundamental revision of early antitrust history is important for several reasons. First, the conventional learning, embedded in a competition paradigm, excludes half the legislative and doctrinal history of antitrust's formative years. Redefining the framework to reflect a tension between competition and property logics brings to light the other half of this history. Second, the so-called literalist opinions and their rule of reason successors make more sense reinterpreted within this new his-

---

report a series of confrontations between opposing logics that have shaped modern antitrust law. By opening this archive of forgotten struggles and reconstructing the conflicts that produced early antitrust doctrine, we get a sense of their conditions of possibility. We are able to define what is unspoken in modern antitrust law, and why.

14. In describing the tension or conflict between "competition" and "property," this Article refers to those concepts as logics, rhetorics, or rhetorical modes. The three labels are treated as synonymous, each identifying a set of assumptions and beliefs about competition and property, as well as a system of logical relations among the assumptions and beliefs. They have been called competition and property paradigms or models as well.

15. R. BORK, *supra* note 2, at 22-23. For a recent opinion applying a distinction between direct and ancillary restraints, see Business Elec. Corp. v. Sharp Elec. Corp., 108 S. Ct. 1515, 1522 (1988).

16. The tension between competition and property insinuates a second tension—between commitments to liberty and equality. *See infra* notes 51, 255-61 and accompanying text. Until the early 20th century, competition seemed to allow for the illusion of equality.

> Why do so many [courts] force upon legislation an academic theory of equality in the face of practical conditions of inequality? Why do we find a great and learned court in 1908 taking the long step into the past of dealing with the relation between employer and employee in railway transportation, as if the parties were individuals—as if they were farmers haggling over the sale of a horse?

Pound, *Liberty of Contract,* 18 YALE L.J. 454, 454 (1909); *see also* J. BENTHAM, THE THEORY OF LEGISLATION 119-22 (Ogden ed. 1931) (tension between equality and security should be resolved in favor of security because perfect equality cannot be attained or maintained).

17. Northern Sec. Co. v. United States, 193 U.S. 197, 403 (1904).

torical framework.[18] Third, and perhaps most importantly, the new framework allows us to understand modern antitrust law and its relationship to both the Sherman Act and the early cases.[19] Finally, in destabilizing the previously unquestioned link between antitrust and competition, and in authenticating the importance of property logic to antitrust law, this Article also raises a new set of questions about the relationship between competition and the efficiency norm. A full explication of these questions is beyond the scope of this Article. For now, there is only the caution that a deep understanding of modern antitrust doctrine and scholarship must include consideration of how the tension between competition and property logics produces the efficiency norm in its various forms.[20]

This Article takes as its point of departure the references to policy conflict articulated in the early legislative debates about the relationship between competition and combination[21] and discussed in Robert Bork's more recent rendition of an antitrust paradox—between free competition and protection of small business.[22] These two portrayals of competition's

18. This Article's methodology is informed by the work of Michel Foucault, a French philosopher. *See, e.g.*, M. FOUCAULT, POWER/KNOWLEDGE: SELECTED INTERVIEWS AND OTHER WRITINGS BY MICHEL FOUCAULT 1972-1977 (C. Gordon ed. 1980); M. FOUCAULT, DISCIPLINE AND PUNISH: THE BIRTH OF THE PRISON (A. Sheridan trans. 1979); M. FOUCAULT, *Nietzsche, Genealogy, History*, in MICHEL FOUCAULT: LANGUAGE, COUNTER-MEMORY, PRACTICE: SELECTED ESSAYS AND INTERVIEWS (Bouchard ed. 1977); M. FOUCAULT, MADNESS AND CIVILIZATION: A HISTORY OF INSANITY IN THE AGE OF REASON (R. Howard trans. 1973). M. FOUCAULT, THE ORDER OF THINGS: AN ARCHAEOLOGY OF THE HUMAN SCIENCES (1973). One important implication of Foucault's work is that historians and other scholars must avoid placing responsibility either simply in the individual or in the economic. *See, e.g.*, C.C. LEMERT & G. GILLAN, MICHEL FOUCAULT, SOCIAL THEORY AS TRANSGRESSION 4-20 (1982).

19. *See* Peritz, *A Genealogy of Vertical Restraints Doctrine*, 40 HASTINGS L.J. (1989) (forthcoming) (examining doctrine of vertical restraints as exemplary case of modern antitrust law).

20. *See, e.g.*, Coleman, *Efficiency, Utility, and Wealth Maximization*, 8 HOFSTRA L. REV. 509, 512-26 (1980) (observing that the nexus between competition and efficiency is unclear); *cf.* Peritz, *supra* note 1, at 1280 (arguing that price theorists have promoted efficiency by inverting the traditional view that competition implies a constellation of values, one of which is efficiency).

21. *See infra* notes 25-132 and accompanying text.

22. This tension between the logics of competition and private property should not be confused with Robert Bork's claim of an antitrust paradox. His view is that efficiency (a proxy for *laissez-faire*) and protectionism are values that constitute a policy at war with itself. R. BORK, *supra* note 2, at 6-7.

First, persuasive historical analysis has already shown that Mr. Bork is mistaken about an impossibly early appearance of the efficiency norm. *See, e.g.*, Fox, *supra* note 3, at 1154 n.76; Hovenkamp, *Antitrust Policy After Chicago*, 84 MICH. L. REV. 213, 249-55 (1985); Lande, *supra* note 3, at 82-106; May, *supra* note 3, at 553-93; Peritz, *supra* note 1, at 1249 n.252.

Moreover, Mr. Bork's paradox makes no sense analytically. In current vertical restraints

antagonists—large combinations of capital and "small dealers and worthy men"[23]—seem to contradict one another. This Article develops a concept of property that unravels the contradiction. It shows how seemingly antipodal commitments to large accumulations of capital and to Jeffersonian entrepreneurialism constitute two modes of a coherent property logic.

This new framework—the conflict between competition and property—also describes a significantly different mechanism at work in the production of antitrust doctrine. The position that there have always been two logics or rhetorics in productive conflict disputes the orthodox view that competition represents the only positive norm for antitrust and that combination, small business, or other "anticompetitive" commitments constitute negative values that can or must be subordinated.

This Article proceeds in the following manner. Section I returns to a recognized but unexplored gap in the Sherman Act's legislative history—the reticence accompanying the eleventh-hour redrafting of Senator Sherman's bill and quick passage of what amounted to an entirely

---

doctrine, for example, efficiency and protectionism seem to be allied values rather than adversaries. The "free rider" rationale that Mr. Bork espouses and that the Supreme Court has embraced in Continental T.V., Inc. v. GTE Sylvania, Inc., 433 U.S. 36, 54-57 (1977) (citing, *inter alia,* Bork, *The Rule of Reason and the Per Se Concept: Price Fixing and Market Division,* 75 YALE L.J. 373, 403 (1966)), purports to legitimate a manufacturer's imposition of nonprice restraints on dealers or distributors. Such restraints on intrabrand competition are reasonable when they increase distributional efficiencies, thereby allowing the manufacturer to compete more effectively against other manufacturers. The restraints purport to serve distributional efficiency by encouraging dealers or distributors to promote the manufacturer's products. Restraints such as customer and territorial limitations encourage dealers or distributors to promote a product by protecting their customer base from other dealers. That is, they preclude dealers from appropriating the value of others' promotional activities. In short, they deter "free riders." Thus, distributional *efficiency* is effected by the court's *protectionist* attitude toward manufacturer's restraints. Though Mr. Bork defines them as antithetical, efficiency and protectionism go hand in glove down the path of Mr. Bork's "free rider" analysis. For excellent critiques of the "free rider" rationale within the context of resale price maintenance, see Flynn, *The "Is" and "Ought" of Vertical Restraints After* Monsanto v. Spray-Rite Service Corp., 71 CORNELL L. REV. 1095, 1131-42 (1986); Levmore, *Rescuing Some Antitrust Law: An Essay on Vertical Restrictions and Consumer Information,* 67 IOWA L. REV. 981, 984-86 (1982); Pitofsky, *In Defense of Discounters: The No-Frills Case for a* Per Se *Rule Against Vertical Price Fixing,* 71 GEO. L.J. 1487, 1492-94 (1983).

Not only does Mr. Bork's paradox make no sense, but the traditional antitrust value of Jeffersonian entrepreneurialism, or protectionism according to Mr. Bork, is produced by the interplay of competition and property logics, not by anti-efficiency sentiments. *See* Peritz, *supra* note 19.

Finally, the norm of efficiency as it has appeared in antitrust doctrine is a product of the fundamental conflict between the logics of property and competition. For a discussion of efficiency within the context of the "free rider" rationale for vertical restraints on distribution, see *id.* For a full analysis of the efficiency norm's production, see *id.*

23. United States v. Trans-Missouri Freight Ass'n, 166 U.S. 290, 338 (1897).

new piece of legislation. This gap in the *Congressional Record* is emblematic of the tension between competition and property. Next, section II explains how the Court's literalist majority in the early antitrust cases applied a logic of competition to interpret the Sherman Act. Section III shows how the Court's shift to a "rule of reason" in *Standard Oil v. United States*[24] represented victory for the new majority's property logic. Finally, section IV maps the structure and dynamics of early antitrust history.

I. The Legislative Debates: Industrial Liberty and Fair Price

To set the context for the narrative that follows, a brief account of what happened in the congressional debates is appropriate. For more than two years, the Senate and the House debated a bill, originally introduced in 1888 with the following operative language: "*Be it enacted* . . . that all arrangements, contracts, agreements, trusts, or combinations . . . made with a view, or which tend, to prevent full and free competition . . . or which tend, to advance the cost to the consumer . . . are hereby declared to be against public policy, unlawful, and void. . . ."[25] While a number of amendments were offered and discussed, most of the congressional debate centered on three issues: the proper constitutional reach of congressional authority under the commerce clause, an explicit labor exemption, and the desirability of state court jurisdiction.[26] Eventually, the 1888 bill was referred to the Committee on the Judiciary for revision. Six days after the 1888 bill's referral, Committee Chairman Edmunds introduced an amended bill that was quite different from its predecessor. In place of the 1888 language of "full and free competition" and "cost to the consumer," the 1890 Bill substituted "contract . . . in restraint of trade or commerce," and "monopolize, or attempt to monopolize . . . trade or commerce."[27] The 1890 Bill was passed in a matter of days. Despite these changes, however, we now take for granted that there are, or should be, no significant differences between the two versions. We assume that proper antitrust policy is based on free competition and its connection to consumer prices, even though the language referring to these policies was jettisoned in the final bill. Neither logic nor history,

---

24. 221 U.S. 1 (1911).

25. S. 3445, 50th Cong., 2d Sess., 20 CONG. REC. 1120 (1889) (as amended); S. 3440, 50th Cong., 2d Sess.,19 CONG. REC. 7512 (1888) (as amended).

26. Hans Thorelli agrees with this assessment. *See* H. THORELLI, *supra* note 3, at 177-210.

27. S. 1, 51st Cong., 1st Sess., 21 CONG. REC. 2901 (1890); *see* S. 3445, 50th Cong., 2d Sess., 20 CONG. REC. 1120 (1889); *see also*, S.3440, 50th Cong., 1st Sess., 19 CONG. REC. 7512 (1888) (predecessor bill).

however, compels this conclusion. This section explains why the Sherman Act cannot be viewed simply as a mandate for free competition and consumer sovereignty.[28]

A. The Competition Logic of Industrial Liberty

Given the nexus of modern antitrust doctrine with competition and given the wealth of scholarship on the Act's legislative history corroborating that nexus, we would expect to find numerous statements concerning competition in the floor debates about Senator Sherman's Bill. Following is a sampling of references to competition in the *Congressional Record.* Senator Sherman himself stated:

> This bill, as I would have it, has for its single object to invoke the aid of the courts of the United States . . . in dealing with combinations that affect injuriously the industrial liberty of the citizens. . . . It is the right of every man to work, labor, and produce in any lawful vocation. . . . This is industrial liberty and lies at the foundation of the equality of all rights and privileges. . . .
>
> The sole object of . . . [a trust] is to make competition impossible. It can control the market, raise or lower prices, as will best promote its selfish interests, reduce prices in a particular locality and break down competition and advance prices at will where competition does not exist. Its governing motive is to increase the profits of the parties composing it. The law of selfishness, uncontrolled by competition, compels it to disregard the interest of the consumer.[29]

Although Senator Sherman's references to competition sound familiar, his use of the term depended on a set of assumptions and beliefs that have grown unfamiliar to us in recent years. In talking about "full and free competition," Senator Sherman and others made frequent reference to something called "industrial liberty."[30] Although modern readers might understand this term to mean freedom from governmental regulation or other market intervention, Senator Sherman and his contemporaries were concerned with another kind of power. Their attentions focused on "combinations of capital" that "make competition impossible."[31] Such market power "advance[d] the cost to the consumer"[32] by

28. The clearest example of an attempt to connect free competition and consumer welfare is R. BORK, *supra* note 2, at 66.

29. 21 CONG. REC. 2457 (1890) (statement of Sen. Sherman).

30. *Id.*

31. *Id.*; 21 CONG. REC. 1768 (1890) (Sen. George: extorted wealth); 21 CONG. REC. 2572 (1890) (Sen. Teller: predatory pricing).

The term "combination" was used to represent a wide range of agreements, trusts, corporate holding companies, and secret understandings. There were "loose" combinations, such as agreements to agree on price, and "tight" combinations, such as the Standard Oil Trust. Although today we tend to use the term less inclusively, this Article's use of the term will follow the more relaxed usage of the congressional debates. "Combination" will mean any

the "ultimate fixing of a price."[33] The interest of the public was safe only so long as competition remained free of such market power.[34] In our terms, the primary strategy of Sherman and others was to limit market power and thereby to prevent monopoly pricing; their ultimate goal was to enhance the consumer's well-being.

While "full and free competition" may have been seen as the best way to protect consumers, the related notion of "industrial liberty" signified a broader set of assumptions and beliefs, which captured the congressional imagination. As Senator Sherman's statement above indicates, industrial liberty was valued not only for its potential downward push on prices. Senator Teller expressed as much when he said, "I do not believe that the great object in life is to make everything cheap."[35] Industrial liberty also embodied a sense of the public as competitors and employees of the new large combinations of capital, whose power rendered "the boasted liberty of the citizen . . . a myth."[36] Thus, in the House debate, Representative Mason pointed out that even if "trusts have made products cheaper, . . . [they] have destroyed legitimate competition."[37]

Senator Reagan first introduced his own antitrust bill[38] and later offered several amendments to Sherman's bill[39] to assure a cause of action for the small competitors injured by large combinations of capital—a realistic "remedy for the great mass of people."[40] Industrial liberty (whether enjoyed by capital or labor) was thought to require rivalrous marketplace participants, and perhaps some supervision and control of industries characterized by firms with large cumulations of assets. In sum, the idea of industrial liberty demanded conditions of rough compet-

---

private agreement producing a cartel, pooling arrangement, trust, or merger. In contrast, "cartel," "pooling arrangement," "trust," and "merger" are used in their narrow senses.

32. S. 3445, 50th Cong., 1st Sess., 19 CONG. REC. 8483 (1888) (Sen. Sherman's original bill).

33. 21 CONG REC. 137 (1889) (statement of Sen. Turpie); *cf.* Kennedy, *The Role of Law in Economic Thought,* 34 AM. U.L. REV. 944 (1985) (describing the relationship between classical economic and legal thought).

34. 21 CONG. REC. 2458 (1890) (remarks of Sen. Sherman, quoting from Craft v. McConoughy, 79 Ill. 346, 350 (1875)); *see also* 20 CONG. REC. 1458 (1889) (statement of Sen. Jones) (these combinations of capital could "plunder the public").

35. 20 CONG. REC. 1457 (1889) (statement of Sen. Teller); 21 CONG. REC. 2726 (1890) (statement of Sen. Edmunds) (the "great monopolies . . . command everybody, laborer, consumer, producer, and everybody else.").

36. 21 CONG. REC. 2561 (1890) (statement of Sen. Teller).

37. 21 CONG. REC. 4100 (1890) (statement of Rep. Mason).

38. S. 3440, 50th Cong., 1st Sess., 19 CONG. REC. 7512 (1888).

39. *See, e.g.,* 21 CONG. REC. 2597 (1890).

40. *Id.* at 3146.

itive equality.[41]

In congressional debates, a distinction was drawn between industrial liberty and unrestrained competition, the belief being that some competition impinges on industrial liberty. For example, in the heated debate just prior to the 1888 bill's referral to committee and radical redrafting, Senator Platt articulated a tension between industrial liberty and that bill's language of free competition; he noted that the "bill proceeds upon the false assumption that all competition is beneficent to the country . . . ."[42] Later, in House debate over the Conference Report on the 1890 bill as enacted, Representative Stewart stated his understanding of the new language: "It is just as necessary to restrict competition as it is to restrict combination . . . ."[43] Thus, the congressmen shared the belief that "unrestrained competition" is not free competition because it diminishes industrial liberty. Rather, "free and fair competition" was seen as the victim of both unrestricted competition and unrestricted combination. The trusts were seen as embodying the forces of both unrestricted extremes.

The concern for consumer and producer liberty also implicated political liberty. For example, Senator Jones argued that if the trusts were allowed to continue, "the boasted liberty of the citizen is a myth . . . and our Government is a farce and a fraud."[44] Senator Sherman echoed these sentiments in stating that industrial liberty is "the foundation of the equality of all rights and privileges."[45] He believed that rough competitive equality was important not only for economic or vocational liberty, but for political liberty in a democratic society as well.

> They had monopolies and mortmains of old, but never before such giants as in our day. You must heed their appeal or be ready for the socialist, the communist, and the nihilist. Society is now disturbed by forces never felt before.
>
> The popular mind is agitated with problems that may disturb social order, and among them all none is more threatening than the ine-

41. *See, e.g., id.* at 2457 (statement of Sen. Sherman, arguing that a "corporation . . . [is] an artificial person without fear of death, without a soul to save or body to punish; but if other corporations can be formed on equal terms a monopoly is impossible."). For a discussion of the impulse toward equality, see *infra* notes 251-61 and accompanying text.

42. 21 CONG. REC. 2729 (1890) (statement of Sen. Platt).

43. *Id.* at 5956 (statement of Rep. Stewart).

44. 21 CONG. REC. 2457 (1890); *see, e.g.,* R. ELY, PROBLEMS OF TODAY: A DISCUSSION OF PROTECTIVE TARIFFS, TAXATION, AND MONOPOLIES 126 (2d ed. 1890) (asserting that honest government and monopoly were not compatible); *infra* text accompanying note 100.

45. 21 CONG. REC. 1457 (1890); *cf.* F. HAYEK, THE ROAD TO SERFDOM 25 (1944) (arguing that political freedom is dependent upon economic freedom); Stigler, *Wealth, and Possibly Liberty,* 7 J. LEGAL STUD. 213, 214-15 (1978) (analyzing personal liberty in terms of economic endowment).

quality of condition, of wealth, and opportunity that has grown within a single generation out of the concentration of capital into vast combinations to control production and trade and to break down competition.[46]

Given the commitment to industrial liberty and the identification of trusts as the threat to it, the solution seemed simple enough. Whether by forfeiture of assets to the government[47] or by private treble damage actions, political power in the form of antitrust legislation could protect the natural process of competition from the market power of unnatural combinations of capital.[48] This seemingly rational and natural alignment of legislation and competition, however, remained problematic even after the 1890 Bill's passage,[49] not because of concern over governmental intervention into some sacred arena called "the competitive market,"[50] but because of deep convictions about something else. The alliance between political power and competition was undercut by the imaginative force and normative appeal of something called "fair price."

The desire to assure fair prices was not the only source of tension in the relationship between industrial liberty and private agreements such as trusts and price fixing cartels. Another area of conflict was over the role of government in ensuring industrial liberty. On the one hand, industrial liberty was taken to mean rough competitive equality. In this sense, it called for the restraint of trusts and other powerful combinations. Thus, governmental action to dissolve private agreements in restraint of competition was a legitimate way to achieve industrial liberty. This impulse to equalize market power constituted a movement toward the ideal of perfect competition. At the same time, this impulse generated the ideal's demise. Under this view industrial liberty could suggest that private agreements were a means of achieving countervailing power

---

46. 21 CONG. REC. 2460 (1890) (remarks of Sen. Sherman).

47. Section six of the 1890 Bill, as enacted, afforded a brutal weapon for equalizing competition by seizing the offending firms' property upon finding a section one violation. S. 1, 51st Cong., 1st Sess., § 6, 21 CONG. REC. 2901 (1890). It stated that any property

> owned . . . by any combination . . . and being in the course of transportation from one State to another . . . shall be forfeited to the United States, and may be seized and condemned by like proceedings as those provided by law for the forfeiture, seizure, and condemnation of property imported into the United States contrary to law.

Id.; see 15 U.S.C. §§ 1-7 (Supp. IV 1986); *see also* 21 CONG. REC. 125 (1889) (Sen. Turpie offering resolution calling for seizure of trust goods).

48. Compare the ascendent 19th century view of corporations as natural organic groups. Horwitz, Santa Clara *Revisited: The Development of Corporate Theory*, 88 W. VA. L. REV. 173, 178-83 (1985).

49. 21 CONG. REC. 6208 (1890) (Senate concurring in the SECOND CONFERENCE REPORT); 21 CONG. REC. 6314 (1890) (House adopting SECOND CONFERENCE REPORT).

50. Indeed, markets were seen as uniformly uncompetitive. *See* 21 CONG. REC. 2726-27 (1890).

against trusts or cartels.[51] Thus, this impulse toward competitive equality could not provide an indisputable basis for deciding whether a private agreement in restraint of competition was a social evil.

On the other hand, industrial liberty was also taken to mean the freedom to enter into contracts to further one's own interests. This *laissez-faire* view of market conduct, unspoken in the debates, was founded in the social value of liberty. In this sense, industrial liberty involved freedom from political power and therefore, freedom from government dissolution of private agreements. Thus, industrial liberty could also mean enforcing private agreements, whether or not they restrained competition.

This tension in the notion of industrial liberty can be understood in two ways. First, "liberty" can mean either freedom from governmental power or freedom from market power. These views, with their radically different concerns, employed conflicting strategies to achieve their goals. The freedom from government power view required the government to enforce private agreements, whether or not they restrained competition. In contrast, where the goal was freedom from market power, the government was to intervene to enjoin private agreements that restrained competition. Second, the tension in industrial liberty can be understood in terms of two impulses—one toward equality and perfect competition and the other toward liberty and free competition (or *laissez-faire* competition). This tension between equality and liberty is developed more fully in the course of this study and is introduced at this juncture for the limited purpose of unpacking the notion of industrial liberty.

In spite of the tension, these two sides of industrial liberty did share one important tenet. For entirely different reasons, both views held that one benefit of industrial liberty was "fair price." Those who argued for equalization of market power called for governmental intervention to dissolve private agreements, such as trusts or price fixing cartels, in order to reinstate the "full and free competition" necessary to produce fair prices.[52] Those who claimed the liberty to enter into private agreements in restraint of competition characterized their combinations as contracts

51. A modern analogue of "industrial liberty" and its impulse toward equality is the notion of "workable competition," described as a pragmatic tool for judging whether a market is competitive. *See, e.g.,* Clark, *Toward a Concept of Workable Competition,* 30 AM. ECON. REV. 241, 253-56 (1940); Stocking, *The Rule of Reason, Workable Competition, and Monopoly,* 64 YALE L.J. 1107, 1108-12 (1955). Whereas the ideals of perfect competition and perfect monopoly are purely analytic tools rather than desirable and attainable market conditions, "workable competition" rather than "workable monopoly" is the appropriate antitrust goal. ATTORNEY GENERAL'S REPORT, *supra* note 2, at 320-39; P. AREEDA, *supra* note 1, at 40.

52. *See, e.g., infra* text at note 54.

to charge fair prices in the face of ruinous competition.[53] Thus, each side of the industrial liberty tension claimed fair price as its own product.

B. The Property Logic of Fair Price

Both views of industrial liberty—freedom from market power and freedom from government power—had many proponents at the time. Yet, the congressional speeches employing the rhetoric of industrial liberty championed only the freedom from market power view. These speeches called for governmental intervention to dissolve trusts and other private agreements in restraint of competition. But other speeches by freedom from market power advocates deployed a very different form of argument. For example, Senator George stated:

> These trusts and combinations are great wrongs to the people . . . . They increase beyond reason the cost of the necessaries of life and business and they decrease the cost of the raw material, the farm products of the country. They regulate prices at their will . . . . They aggregate to themselves great, enormous wealth by extortion. . . . Then making this extorted wealth the means of further extortion from their unfortunate victims . . . they are fast producing that condition in our people in which the great mass of them are the servitors of those who have this aggregated wealth at their command.[54]

Senator Jones reiterated the negative impact of trusts on the public: "These commercial monsters called trusts . . . [are] preying upon every industry, and by their unholy combinations robbing their victims, the general public . . . ."[55] Senator Turpie agreed: "The conspirators of the trust . . . are hunting the prey, dividing the spoil in every market. . . . [If they] pirate upon the earnings of the people, justice may . . . strike down the offense and the offenders."[56]

Moreover, those speeches seeking enforcement of private agreements advanced the very same logic, founded in the notions of "fair profit" or "fair return." The following excerpts are examples of speeches using this logic. Senator Platt stated:

> The true theory of this matter is that prices should be just and reasonable and fair, that prices . . . should be such as will render a fair return to all persons engaged in its production, a fair profit on capital, on labor, and on everything else that enters into its production. . . . [E]very man in business . . . has a right, a legal and a moral right, to obtain a fair profit upon his business and his work; and if he is driven by fierce competition to a spot where his business is unremunerative, I believe it is his right to combine for the purpose of raising prices until

53. *See, e.g., infra* text at note 57.
54. 21 Cong. Rec. 1768 (1890) (statement of Sen. George).
55. 20 Cong. Rec. 1457 (1889) (statement of Sen. Jones).
56. 21 Cong. Rec. 137 (1889) (statement of Sen. Turpie).

> they shall be fair and remunerative.[57]

Representative Stewart also emphasized a notion of fair return on investment:

> A rate war between railroads is absolutely injurious to the community. Why, it cannot be otherwise. In the first place the doctrine of fair play requires, and everybody concedes, that the railroads should have a just compensation for their services. We ought not to ask them to do anything for less than will pay the interest on the investment and the running expenses. That is only reasonable and fair.[58]

Representative Morse echoed these concerns for a fair price:

> [If this Bill] proposes to deny to manufacturers and merchants the right to control the price at which their goods shall be sold, the right to say they shall not enter into ruinous competition, the right to exact a fair and living profit on the sale of their goods by the merchant who handles them, it will be unwise legislation and injurious to the manufacturer, to the merchant, to the consumer, and the whole people, and strike a blow at the business interests of the country, because it will violate a sound business principle, to "live and let live."[59]

These speeches representing the freedom from government view illustrate the workings of a logic very different from the competition rhetoric of industrial liberty. They describe the contours of a property rhetoric whose foundation is the notion of a "fair profit" or "fair return." Briefly, the argument is as follows: It is an independent social good that those who work, those who put their labor or capital into the market, should get a fair return on their input. This social good benefits both producers and consumers. "Fair profit" or "fair return" is a social good that the government should enforce, whether the evil be competition or combination and whether the harm be low profits or high prices. It is a social good to be enforced in much the same way that one's possession of property is protected from theft or extortion.

Like the competition rhetoric of industrial liberty, the property rhetoric of fair price embodied a tension. Fair price could be characterized as the consequence of competition as well as the consequence of combination. The following analysis of fair price focuses on two excerpts from the *Congressional Record* to develop the implications of this property logic seeking to argue the benefits of private agreements in restraint of competition: first, Representative Stewart's description of the grand struggle between competition and combination;[60] second, the concerns of

---

57. *Id.* at 2720-30 (1890) (statement of Sen. Platt).

58. *Id.* at 5957 (statement of Rep. Stewart).

59. *Id.* at 5954 (statement of Rep. Morse).

60. 21 CONG. REC. 5956 (1890) (FIRST CONFERENCE REPORT); *see also id.* at 5954 (statement of Rep. Morse).

Representative Morse and Senator Platt that the new antitrust law not deny the legal and moral (property) right to obtain a fair profit.[61]

Representative Stewart described competition and combination as "two great forces . . . contending for . . . mastery."[62] They "are correctives of each other, and both ought to exist. Both ought to be under restraint."[63] Although competition was the acknowledged social good to be protected by restraining combinations of capital, Representative Stewart believed that "[i]t is just as necessary to restrict competition as it is to restrict combination . . . ."[64]

Representative Stewart continued his speech about these "two great forces" by offering two diverse examples of the need to allow some combination. First, he observed that there was "hardly a class in the country today that . . . is not in some form of combination."[65] "[W]here competition is excessive and becoming destructive . . . the laborer is justified in entering into combinations for self-protection."[66] In other words, when market conditions have destroyed the value of labor, and when market price has fallen below fair return, a combination can legitimately restore the fair and natural price to commodities or services.[67]

---

61. *Id.* at 5954; *id.* at 2730 (Statement of Sen. Platt).

62. *Id.* at 5956 (FIRST CONFERENCE REPORT).

63. *Id.*

64. *Id.* Nonetheless, the image of combinations as a second force contending against the natural force of competition was seen as a problematic representation of nature, markets or society. There were at least two reasons for this. First, combinations were thought to effect great changes in established social and economic relationships. Second, the very presence of combinations suggested that there was a second natural tendency in addition to the natural tendency to compete. Were trusts "monsters" endangering the natural competitive state of markets, or were they evidence of a natural tendency to combine? Were they unnatural and to be restrained, or natural and perhaps beneficial? Both views of combination were articulated in the popular press and in scholarly writing of the times. Some opponents of trusts argued for governmental regulation and even public ownership, while proponents expressed faith in the notion of potential competition. *See generally* H. THORELLI, *supra* note 3, at 109-32. These responses to the problem of how to characterize the appearance of large combination are described in detail *infra*, text accompanying notes 103-32, in the context of classical economic and legal theory. For now, the tension between these tendencies to compete and to combine are presented as a context for describing the following excerpts about combinations as statements about the property logic of fair return or fair price.

65. 21 CONG. REC. 5956 (1890) (statement of Rep. Stewart).

66. *Id.*

67. There is a striking similarity to modern predatory pricing doctrine, founded in the cost accounting comparison of price to some measure of cost—whether marginal, average variable, or just average. The 19th century baseline of labor value has been expanded into a labor-and-capital based minimum for exchange value. *See* Cargill, Inc. v. Monfort of Colo., Inc., 479 U.S. 104, 113-19 (1986); Brodley, *The Goals of Antitrust—Pre-Trial Hearing No. 1: A Verbatim Account of an Imagined Proceeding*, 28 ANTITRUST BULL. 823, 826, 835-38 (1983) (setting out variants of cost-based predatory pricing doctrine); Brodley & Hay, *Predatory Pricing: Competing Economic Theories and the Evolution of Legal Standards*, 66 CORNELL L. REV.

Representative Stewart's second example of the need to allow some combination appears somewhat later in the debates, when the focus had shifted to the relationship between the 1890 Antitrust Bill and the recently enacted Interstate Commerce Act (ICA). The ICA saved the railroads from self-inflicted ruinous competition, by permitting them to form rate associations.[68] The ICA called for just and reasonable charges, proscribed territorial discrimination, and prohibited pooling. In response to Representative Bland's skepticism about the Antitrust Bill's effectiveness in controlling railroad combinations and rate agreements,[69] Representative Stewart argued that, whichever statute applied, "the doctrine of fair play requires . . . just compensation."[70] "What is the objection, if the rate is just and reasonable?"[71] In other words, both the ICA and the proposed Antitrust Bill should be interpreted to permit railroads to agree on rates that would stop rate wars and allow them to "pay the interest on the investment and the running expenses."[72]

Representative Stewart's references to "just compensation" and to covering interest and expenses echoed the rationale in earlier rate regulation cases, such as *Munn v. Illinois.*[73] Thirteen years earlier, *Munn* had addressed the fourteenth amendment due process question of "taking" private property in the public interest. The Illinois statute under scrutiny was one of the numerous "Granger laws" passed in the agricultural states of the Midwest and West to regulate the warehousing and transportation of grain.[74] The particular statute in *Munn* defined grain elevators as public warehouses and established maximum rates for storing grain. The crucial issue in the case involved the power of state government to regulate the owners' return on their business, thereby trumping private agreements regarding price and limiting the investment return on private property.[75] *Munn* and similar rate regulation cases stand for the proposition that constitutional protection of property demands only that

738, 741-42 (1981) (describing economic theories and judicial applications of predatory pricing).

68. Interstate Commerce Act of 1887, ch. 104, 24 Stat. 379 (1887); 21 CONG. REC. 5957 (1890).

69. 21 CONG. REC. 5953, 5957 (1890); *cf.* Stigler, *The Theory of Economic Regulation,* 2 BELL J. ECON. 3 (1971) (modeling firms as buyers in a market for government regulation).

70. 21 CONG. REC. 5957 (1890).

71. *Id.* at 5951.

72. *Id.* at 5957.

73. 94 U.S. 113 (1877).

74. *See, e.g.,* S. BUCK, THE GRANGER MOVEMENT: A STUDY OF AGRICULTURAL ORGANIZATION AND ITS POLITICAL, ECONOMIC AND SOCIAL RAMIFICATIONS, 1870-1880, at 123, 159, 166, 179, 194 (1913). All the "Granger" cases are in volume 94 of the United States Reports.

75. 94 U.S. at 114.

an investor be able to receive a certain *minimum* fair profit and not the *maximum* profit possible through private agreement.[76]

The rationale of Representative Stewart's comments parallels the reasoning in these rate cases: just compensation to railroads and to labor requires some *minimum* rate of return. In all of these cases, some minimum protection of property rights "is only reasonable and fair."[77] Stewart's statements emphasize the value of combinations insofar as they could secure for the producer a fair profit or fair return on property, whether that return derives from capital or labor.[78] Moreover, it is clear that a fair return to the producer entails a fair price to the consumer—no more and no less.

In the same debate, Representative Morse recapitulated the view that combination is a legitimate means for assuring a fair return on property. He asserted that the Bill would destroy the " 'contract system' of selling goods, the intention of which is to fix a fair and living profit to the merchant . . . ."[79] The reference here is to resale price maintenance (a manufacturer's setting of retail prices).[80] Whatever our own view of a

76. Regarding state regulation of rates and the issue of just compensation, see, for example, Bluefield Water Works & Improvement Co. v. Public Serv. Comm'n, 262 U.S. 679, 692-93 (1923) (stating that there is no constitutional right to profits such as are realized or anticipated in highly profitable enterprises); Missouri *ex rel.* Southwestern Bell Tel. Co. v. Public Serv. Comm'n, 262 U.S. 276, 291 (1923) (Brandeis, J., concurring) (describing methodology for determining a fair return on investment); Smyth v. Ames, 169 U.S. 466, 546 (1898) (stating that a company is entitled to no more than a fair return upon the value of that which it employs for the public convenience).

77. 21 CONG. REC. 5957 (1890).

78. For a recent analysis of constitutional law doctrine regarding fair price, see Siegel, *Understanding the Nineteenth Century Contract Clause: The Role of the Property-Privilege Distinction and "Takings" Clause Jurisprudence,* 60 S. CAL. L. REV. 1 (1986).

79. 21 CONG. REC. 5954 (1890).

80. In 1937, Congress passed the Miller-Tydings Resale Price Maintenance Act, which granted state fair trade statutes an exemption from the federal antitrust laws. Act of Aug. 17, 1937, ch. 690, 50 Stat. 693 (codified as amended at 15 U.S.C. § 1 (1985)). In 1952, the McGuire Act was passed to strengthen the fair trade statutes, by allowing state sanctioned resale price maintenance, whether or not retailers agreed with the manufacturer. These provisions were repealed by the Consumer Goods Pricing Act of 1975, Pub. L. No. 94-145, § 2, 89 Stat. 801. The position of Chicago School adherents is that vertical price restraints should not be illegal per se. Monsanto v. Spray-Rite Co., 465 U.S. 752, 761 (1984) (holding nevertheless that vertical price restraints remain illegal per se). They would apply a "rule of reason." *See, e.g.,* Baxter, *Vertical Restraints and Resale Price Maintenance: A "Rule of Reason" Approach,* 14 ANTITRUST L. & ECON. REV. 13, 13 (1982) (arguing that vertical price restraints should not be illegal per se); Posner, *The Next Step in the Antitrust Treatment of Restricted Distribution: Per Se Legality,* 48 U. CHI. L. REV. 6, 31-32 (1981). For some reactions in trade journals against arguments to loosen the per se illegality of resale price maintenance, see, for example, Pertschuk & Correia, *Resale Price Maintenance—Why the* Per Se *Rule Should be Enforced,* 15 NAT. J. 1201, 1201-02 (1983); Taylor, *Congress Objects as Administration Seeks Relaxing of "Vertical Price-Fixing" Ban,* Wall St. J., May 16, 1983, at 12, col. 1. For scholarly critiques,

price-fixing manufacturer's intent,[81] the value articulated is consistent with Representative Stewart's argument for allowing some combination—that is, protecting the value of one's property from competition, whether that property takes the form of labor, rolling stock, manufacturer's goods, or retailer's goodwill.

Senator Platt and some of his colleagues expressed a fear that the Bill would make all agreements between competitors illegal and would result in the "brutal warfare" of "unrestricted competition."[82] In an earlier Senate debate over the 1888 Bill, Senator Platt stated that:

> every man in business . . . has a right, a legal and moral right, to obtain a fair profit upon his business and his work; and if he is driven by fierce competition to a spot where his business is unremunerative, I believe it is his right to combine for the purpose of raising prices until they shall be fair and remunerative.[83]

Although no speaker argued against "breaking up the great monopolies which get hold of the whole of a particular business or production in the country and are enabled, therefore, to command everybody, laborer, consumer, producer, and everybody else,"[84] a number of congressmen agreed that unrestrained competition was the culprit. Senator Platt, for example, declared that "the great monopolies of this country are every one of them built upon the graves of weaker competitors that have been forced to their death by remorseless competition."[85] In the animated debate just prior to the introduction of the 1890 Bill, Senator Platt summarized this position:

> The true theory of this matter is that prices should be just and reasonable and fair, that prices, no matter who is the producer or what the article, should be such as will render a fair return to all persons engaged in its production, a fair profit on capital, on labor, and on everything else that enters into its production.[86]

These notions of fair return or fair profit appear alien in statements

---

see Comanor, *Vertical Price-Fixing, Vertical Market Restrictions, and the New Antitrust Policy,* 98 HARV. L. REV. 983, 990-1002 (1985); *supra* note 22 and sources cited therein.

81. Ever since the 1911 Supreme Court decision in Dr. Miles Medical Co. v. John D. Park & Sons, 220 U.S. 373, 384-85 (1911), there had been little question that vertical price fixing was illegal per se. That is, the plaintiff need not show purpose, power, or competitive effects. Then, in 1977, the Court's decision in Continental T.V., Inc. v. GTE Sylvania Inc., 433 U.S. 36, 57-59 (1977), raised some questions regarding the continuing viability of a per se standard for vertical price fixing, though the case involved nonprice restraints, all of which were adjudicated under the "rule of reason." It was Monsanto v. Spray-Rite Co., 465 U.S. 752 (1984), that put those questions to rest.

82. 21 CONG. REC. 2729 (1890).

83. *Id.* at 2730.

84. *Id.* at 2726 (statement of Sen. Edmunds).

85. *Id.* at 2729 (statement of Sen. Platt).

86. *Id.* Underlying this theory is a problematic image of "natural" markets populated by

about competition. In contrast, they comfortably inhabit statements about protecting the value of one's property—whether labor, rolling stock, manufacturer's goods, or retailer's goodwill. With this rehearsal of the tension between competition and property as an epilogue, debate on the 1888 Bill ended.

C. Property Logic and the Language of the Common Law

Six days after the debate's closure, Senator Edmunds introduced a new bill. The 1890 Bill replaced the previous Bill's language of "free competition" and "cost to the consumer" with language of the common law—"restraint of trade or commerce" and "monopolize."[87] One week after the new Bill's introduction, after only a few hours of floor debate, both Houses quickly passed the new Sherman Act.[88] Aside from Congress' well-known concerns about the earlier Bill's constitutionality,[89] what other significance can be attributed to the radical change in language?

There is much evidence to suggest that Congress intended to codify the common-law meaning of the terms used in the new Bill. For example, Senator Hoar, who first asked that the new Bill be taken up by the full Senate, immediately expressed hope for an early vote. His reason for anticipating such expedited treatment of an entirely new Bill was that the Bill was already "well understood."[90] The obvious implication of this assertion is that much off-the-record negotiation and compromise had accompanied the new Bill and had already familiarized everyone with the Bill's content. Beyond this familiarity with the Bill's language, however, there was also a common ground for the Senators' understanding of the new Bill's language. Apparently, it was taken for granted that there was a common law that would provide the groundwork for the development of a federal common law of monopoly and restraints of trade.[91] This assumption is suggested in Senator Hoar's statement in the *Congressional*

individuals—by equally powerful laborers and capitalists. *See, e.g., id.* at 2727 (statement of Sen. Edmunds).

87. *Id.* at 2901 (1890) (Chief Clerk reading substitute bill reported by the Committee on the Judiciary); *id.* at 3146, 3148, 3152 (monopoly "a technical term known to the common law").

88. *Id.* at 3153 (Senate passage, April 8, 1890); *id.* at 6314 (House passage, June 20, 1890). The delay in House action was due to an eleventh-hour attempt to include a specific reference in section one to transportation, in order to assure the Bill's priority over the Interstate Commerce Act. *Id.* at 4088-104, 5950-61, 5981-83, 6312-14.

89. *Id.* at 3148 (statement of Sen. Edmunds); H. R. REP. NO. 1707, 51st cong., 1st Sess. 1 (1890) (report of the House Judiciary Committee).

90. 21 CONG. REC. 3145 (1890).

91. *See id.* at 3152 (statement of Sen. Hoar) ("I do not mean to say that [the committee]

Record: "We have affirmed the old doctrine of the common law . . . and have clothed the United States courts with authority to enforce that doctrine . . . ."[92] Senator Edmunds later added that the Committee took the new Bill's language—"monopolize," for example—"out of terms that were well known to the law already."[93] In response to a question about an ingenious rancher's monopoly of short-horn cattle trade with Mexico, Senator Edmunds stated, "Anybody who knows the meaning of the word 'monopoly,' as the courts apply it, would not apply it to such a person at all . . . ."[94] He continued:

> "[M]onopoly" is a technical term known to the common law . . . . [A] man who merely by superior skill and intelligence . . . got the whole business because nobody could do it as well as he could was not a monopolist . . . . [Monopoly] involved something like the use of means which made it impossible for other persons to engage in fair competition . . . .[95]

This common-law "meaning" upon which Congress seemed to rely came from the states[96] or from sources outside the United States, as there was no federal common law of monopoly or restraints of trade prior to the Sherman Act.[97] Under the common law developed in the several states, price fixing agreements were generally void and unenforceable, though there were a few notable exceptions.[98] State governments attacked some of the more visible trusts, typically arguing that their corporate charters did not permit the formation of such trusts.[99] In one common-law case, the chief justice of the Michigan Supreme Court ventured even farther: "Monopoly in trade or in any kind of business in this country is odious to our form of government . . . . Its tendency is . . .

---

stated what the signification was, but I became satisfied that they were right and that the word 'monopoly' is a merely technical term which has a clear and legal signification.").

92. *Id.* at 3146, 3152.

93. *Id.* at 3148.

94. *Id.* at 3151 (statement of Sen. Edmunds). It is interesting to note that this floor debate seemed to recognize a distinction between monopoly and monopolize—something that has been central to section two doctrine. The distinction has been made between a condition of monopoly and acts of monopolization. That is, the courts have called for some conduct evidencing predatory intent. *See, e.g.,* United States v. Griffith, 334 U.S. 100, 105-06 (1948); Standard Oil Co. v. United States, 221 U.S. 1, 61-62 (1911); United States v. Aluminum Co. of Am., 148 F.2d 416, 429-30 (2d Cir. 1945) (L. Hand, J.); United States v. Grinnell Corp., 236 F. Supp. 244, 248 (D.R.I. 1964) (Wyzanski, J.), *aff'd except as to decree,* 384 U.S. 563 (1966).

95. 21 CONG. REC. 3152 (1890). The example given of unfair means is merger—"the buying up of all other persons engaged in the same business." *Id.*

96. For thoughtful treatments of the state antitrust law context, see H. THORELLI, *supra* note 3, at 155-63; May, *supra* note 3.

97. *See, e.g.,* H. THORELLI, *supra* note 3, at 36-37.

98. *See, e.g.,* Central Shade-Roller Co. v. Cushman, 143 Mass. 353, 364, 9 N.E. 629, 631 (1887).

99. *Id.*, 9 N.E. at 630.

destructive of free institutions, and repugnant to the instincts of a free people, and contrary to the whole scope and spirit of the federal Constitution."[100]

In contrast to the states' treatment of private agreements in restraint of competition, the most recent and best known case under the British common law espoused a radically different view. In *Mogul Steamship Co. v. McGregor, Gow & Co.*, a "shipping conference" or cartel was not dissolved, even though it financed a "fighting ship" to carry cargo at prices that "would not repay a shipowner for his adventure."[101] Although Lord Bowen declared that "intentionally to do that which is calculated . . . to damage, and which does, in fact, damage another in that other person's property or trade, is actionable," this agreement was not a common-law restraint of trade because it did "nothing more . . . than pursue to the bitter end a war of competition . . . ."[102] Thus, the British court protected the freedom to enter into private agreements in restraint of competition, characterizing the agreement as an acceptable form of competition.

Though there is no record of how these and other statements formulating restraints of trade doctrine engaged the imaginations of individual congressmen, a great deal can be said about what they took for granted concerning classical legal doctrine and economics. From a sketch of the contours of classical economics and then classical contracts and property doctrine, a good likeness (for our limited purposes) of the shared cultural context of the Fifty-First Congress emerges. That cultural context included some sense[103] of monopolies and restraints of trade. Perhaps

100. Richardson v. Buhl & Alger, 77 Mich. 632, 658, 43 N.W. 1102, 1110 (1889).

101. 23 Q.B.D. 598, 612 (1889), *aff'd*, 1892 A.C. 25.

102. *Id.* at 614-19. Taking a middle ground of sorts, the opinion later confided that a party to the agreement could challenge it. *Id.* at 620. The court deemed the agreement not void, but rather unenforceable. *Id.* at 632.

103. The classical economists were the strongest supporters of the view that the tendency to compete was natural and that competitive markets were inevitable. *See, e.g.*, A. WALKER, THE SCIENCE OF WEALTH: A MANUAL OF POLITICAL ECONOMY. EMBRACING THE LAWS OF TRADE, CURRENCY, AND FINANCE (1875); F. WAYLAND, THE ELEMENTS OF POLITICAL ECONOMY (1837); *cf.* 3 J. DORFMAN, THE ECONOMIC MIND IN AMERICAN CIVILIZATION 1865-1918 359-89 (1949) (demonstrating that there was a substantial relationship between the classical economists' work and the public perceptions of the times); R. HOFSTADTER, SOCIAL DARWINISM IN AMERICAN THOUGHT, 1860-1915, at 145 (1949) (observing that Francis Wayland's book was the most popular college textbook in political economy during the period).

The neoclassicists asserted that, although markets were not competitive, there was always potential competition lurking in the wings. Andrew Carnegie articulated this view most sublimely. *See* Carnegie, *The Bugaboo of Trusts*, 148 N. AM. REV. 141, 150 (1889). Scholarly renditions of the neoclassical position include J.B. CLARK, ESSENTIALS OF ECONOMIC THEORY viii (1907); Giddings, *The Persistence of Competition*, 2 POL. SCI. Q. 62, 65 (1887); Gunton, *The Economic and Social Aspects of Trusts*, 3 POL. SCI. Q. 385, 385-408 (1888). For a

most salient here, it also included an account of the unnatural appearance of monopolies and restraints of trade in an otherwise lawfully and naturally competitive marketplace.

A naturalistic sense of lawfulness and rationality constituted the foundation of nineteenth century discourse, whether scientific, economic, or legal. Hence, when Representative Stewart spoke of "two great forces working in human society,"[104] he imagined competition and combination as two lawful and rational agencies contending with one another. This claim that there might be *two* natural tendencies—one to compete and the other to combine—rather than an unrivaled tendency to compete, was a recent development prompted by the changing face of American industry and labor.[105] The nineteenth century belief in natural law and its rationality animated a desire to characterize the tendency to combine as natural and rational, because the alternative—asserting the unnaturalness of the widespread practice of combination—would call into question the very belief in natural law and its rationality. At the same time, a profound ambivalence gripped the nineteenth century attitude toward combinations. The success of such combinations was at odds with classical legal and economic doctrines, which espoused the inevitability of competition.[106] Under these doctrines, if only the tendency to compete

direct critique of this view, see Bullock, *The Trusts and Public Policy,* 87 ATLANTIC MONTHLY 737, 742 (1901) ("There can be no *potential* competition when *actual* competition is hopeless.").

The New School of Economics was an American response to the foregoing views of markets as inevitably competitive. Although the adherents to this school had differing solutions, they all agreed that the problem was the inevitability of combination. *See, e.g.,* A. HADLEY, RAILROAD TRANSPORTATION—ITS HISTORY AND ITS LAWS 124 (1885); Andrews, *Trusts According to Official Investigations,* 3 Q.J. ECON. 117 (1889); Clark, *The Limits of Competition,* 2 POL. SCI. Q. 45 (1887). Ultimately, the most influential New Schoolers asserted that competition and combination were both possible and that some industries tended toward combination, based on their characteristic of high fixed costs and low marginal costs. Adams, *The Relationship of the State to Industrial Action,* in 1 PUBLICATIONS OF THE AMERICAN ECONOMIC ASSOCIATION 471 (1887); *cf.* R. ELY, PROBLEMS OF TODAY, *supra* note 44.

104. 21 CONG. REC. 5956 (1890). For examples of contemporaneous views of concentration as the result of a natural evolutionary process, see Andrews, *The Economic Law of Monopoly,* 26 J. SOC. SCI. 1, 11-12 (1890); Jenks, *Capitalistic Monopolies and Their Relation to the State,* 9 POL. SCI. Q. 486, 503-09 (1894). For a recent analysis, see Horwitz, *supra* note 48, at 191 (portraying the development of the "inevitability of concentration" position).

105. This claim was prompted as well by the specter of European politics. 21 CONG. REC. 2460 (1890) ("be ready for the socialist, the communist, and the nihilist"). Regarding the influence of European schools of political economy and the emergence of a separate "American" economics, see Adams, *supra* note 103, at 471 (1887).

106. *See, e.g.,* F. WAYLAND, *supra* note 103, at 4; H. WOOD, THE POLITICAL ECONOMY OF NATURAL LAW 16-17 (1894). For recent surveys, see H. COMMAGER, THE AMERICAN MIND: AN INTERPRETATION OF AMERICAN THOUGHT AND CHARACTER SINCE THE 1880'S (1950); R. HOFSTADTER, SOCIAL DARWINISM IN AMERICAN THOUGHT (rev. ed. 1959); E.

was natural, then competitive markets were inevitable, making governmental intervention unnecessary. In other words, the natural tendency to compete would overcome the current wave of combinations. In contrast, if Representative Stewart was correct, if there had evolved two natural tendencies and forces (competition and combination) then the prospects for competitive markets were indeterminable.

Representative Stewart's view was also tough to swallow because it challenged the classical view that a fair price derived from free exchanges between roughly equal individuals.[107] Under this labor theory of value, since commodities embody a worker's labor, it is labor that imparts market value.[108] Free exchanges among numerous independent trading partners produce "natural" or "market" prices.[109] Moreover, since each party to such idealized transactions was imagined as getting something in return that was proportional to his contribution, the prices and the process were seen as not only natural and free, but also fair and just.[110] Insofar as combinations charged prices higher or lower than the natural market price, classical economics considered them unnatural, and perhaps unjust, interlopers in the process of competitive markets.

Although classical economics permitted regulation of combinations, it required such governmental intervention to conform with the classical view of property law. Under this view, the state could interfere with an individual's property rights only in a very limited set of circumstances and through a very limited set of processes. This notion of property derived from the strongly held sentiment, still powerful today, that a person has a right to the product of her labor.[111] An example of the problem raised by these sentiments is presented by the hypothetical question already recounted about a short-horn cattle monopoly.[112] The issue

---

PURCELL, THE CRISIS OF DEMOCRATIC THEORY: SCIENTIFIC NATURALISM & THE PROBLEM OF VALUE (1973).

107. *See supra* note 103 and sources cited therein.

108. If capital were expended, then, of course, the price naturally would reflect both kinds of input units. *See, e.g.*, J.B. CLARK, *supra* note 103, at 14-17; F. WAYLAND, *supra* note 103, at 4-5.

109. As Arthur T. Hadley observed in his well-known study of the railroad industry, "We accept almost without reserve the theory of Ricardo, that, under open competition in a free market, the value of different goods will tend to be proportional to their cost of production." A. HADLEY, *supra* note 103, at 69.

110. *See, e.g.*, J.B. CLARK, *supra* note 103, at 77; M. HORWITZ, THE TRANSFORMATION OF AMERICAN LAW, 1780-1860, at 109-39, 160-88, 253-66 (1977); Kennedy, *supra* note 33, at 943-45, 956.

111. See *supra* notes 76-78 and accompanying text for a discussion of the constitutional limits imposed on state regulation of that property right. For an exhaustive treatment of state antitrust regulation during this period, see May, *supra* note 3.

112. *See supra* notes 94-95 and accompanying text.

was under what circumstances the state can rightfully interfere with the accumulation of property that would result from this cattle rancher's hard work and ingenuity (his labor). The response was given that the state can interfere only when the rancher has acted improperly by creating unnatural or "fictitious" prices.[113] This response, however, did not address the real problem. Even if nothing improper was done, a gap would appear between fair price and market price. That is, a monopoly price would be charged. Should the law characterize the monopoly profit as a property right or as a "fictitious" price?

This battle had already been fought on constitutional grounds. As discussed above, *Munn v. Illinois* (and other "Granger" cases) recognized a state's right to regulate profit when there was a public interest in the industry.[114] In that case, the Supreme Court upheld an Illinois statute that set maximum prices farmers could be charged for wheat storage in Chicago's grain elevators.[115] But what about all those industries that were not clothed in something called the "public interest"? What about short-horn cattle?[116] It was not clear that government could preserve or impose competitive conditions—that is, indirectly control monopoly pricing in those industries not clothed in the public interest.

Such controls would have to overcome strong commitments to the sanctity of property. In particular, any governmental intervention, even indirect price regulation by imposition of competition, would have to confront a justification for monopoly profit couched in clearly classical terms. This justification held that a monopoly price for short-horn cattle was a competitive reward fairly won by "superior skill and intelligence."[117] Rather than confront the hard case of monopoly earned in the meritocracy of the competitive process, Senator Edmunds hedged his response: "He has not bought off his adversaries. He has not got the possession of all the horned cattle in the United States."[118] Thus, Senator Edmunds failed to address what would happen if this gentleman rancher *had* gotten hold of all the horned cattle in the United States, using only his ingenuity, thus "prevent[ing] other men from engaging in fair competition with him."[119]

113. 21 CONG. REC. 4102 (1890) (statement of Rep. Fitnian).

114. 94 U.S. 113, 126 (1877).

115. *Id.* at 135-36.

116. *See* Williams v. Standard Oil Co., 278 U.S. 235, 240 (1929) (finding that the petroleum industry is not clothed with the public interest).

117. For an explication of the relationship between property and liberty, see *infra* text accompanying note 234.

118. 21 CONG. REC. 3151-52 (1890).

119. *Id.* at 3152 (statement of Sen. Hoar).

The question was a difficult one, not only because of the problem of earned monopoly, but also because the reality of a national economy filled with combinations such as trusts and cartels called into question the classical economics founded in an unrivaled tendency to compete. This experience suggested that after the rancher dominated the market, his rivals might decide to cooperate rather than compete. They might choose, and even agree, to charge the price set by the dominant rancher. Given that the dominant rancher was interested in the monopoly profits his efforts allowed, he would not compete to the death. He would simply charge his monopoly price, knowing that his rivals would rather follow his lead than compete with his ingenuity and superior intelligence. The resulting market would not tend toward competition, but rather toward loose combination. Today, we might call this loose combination the price leadership of oligopoly. For those who believed in the natural tendency to compete embodied in classical economic theory, price leadership was irrational conduct.[120] The economic facts, however, did not seem to fit the classical theory.

The most ardent believer in the classical view had to concede that the tendency to compete would take time to emerge. Until it did, the ingenious rancher's rivals would enjoy unearned monopoly profits. Could the state legitimately restructure or otherwise regulate the entire industry, in the service of free exchange or fair profits? If the industry were regulated, all could be reassured that "they could safely embody their labor in commodities and freely exchange them."[121] In other words, the property value of their labor (and other input factors), embodied in commodities, would be protected by the contract law principle of free exchange. Everyone would get no more than a fair return—everyone, that is, except perhaps the ingenious and skilled gentleman rancher no longer receiving his hard-earned monopoly profits.[122]

120. Scholarly responses included the work of neoclassicists like John Bates Clark, who argued that "To regulate combinations is possible and, in some directions, desirable; to permanently suppress them is impossible; to temporarily repress them is either to force them into illegal forms, or to restore the internecine war from which a natural evolution has delivered us." Clark, *supra* note 103, at 61; *see* Northern Sec. Co. v. United States, 193 U.S. 197, 400-10 (1904) (Holmes, J., dissenting) (expressing similar fears).

121. Kennedy, *supra* note 33, at 956; F. WAYLAND, *supra* note 103, at 4-5 (describing four fundamental laws that create and protect the right to the fruits of one's labor).

122. These problems of reconciling monopoly profit with the idea of free exchange and with a labor theory of value become even more complex when viewed in the context of the new 19th century property right or entitlement to incorporate for general purposes (and thus to form trusts). One way to understand the evolution of corporations from the privileged products of special legislation, to corporations as creatures of the state, and then to corporations as "persons" for constitutional purposes is to think of each movement as a step in conceiving of the corporation as an entity rather than a combination. *See generally* Horwitz, *supra* note 48,

It is easy to see why monopolies or combinations in restraint of trade were so problematic. Their very existence called into question one of the basic tenets of classical economics and legal doctrine—the fairness of market price as derived from free exchanges between roughly equal individuals. Because actual market prices could mean monopoly price, predatory price, or competitive price, actual market transactions no longer seemed constrained by the competitive ideal of the market. Given the ubiquity of trusts and other sorts of combinations, countless trades could not be characterized as free exchanges between roughly equal individuals.

This dissonance between combinations and the competitive ideal did not go entirely unnoticed. In a scholarly critique of the classical view, influential economist Henry Carter Adams wrote that combinations, and corporations in particular, were destroying the "strategic equality" among classically conceived competitors.[123] Making the imbalance even more pronounced, he wrote: "[T]hese corporations assert for themselves most of the rights conferred on individuals by the law of private property, and apply to themselves a social philosophy true only of a society composed of individuals who are industrial competitors."[124] Motivated by similar concerns, other scholars, the popular "literature of protest," farmer and labor groups, as well as both the Democratic and the Republican Parties' platforms called for some antitrust action.[125] Still, as Roscoe Pound has written, the classical economic vision continued to direct the production of legal doctrine:

> When in the last quarter of the nineteenth Century our courts were called upon with increasing frequency to pass on the validity of social legislation, in the transition from pioneer, rural, agricultural America

at 176-86 (discussing development of corporate personality). By then applying a labor theory of value to this entity, now treated as a private person, an argument can be made to limit the state's power over what could then be seen as vested property rights. The doctrinal watershed was the decision in Charles River Bridge v. Warren Bridge, 24 Mass. (7 Pick.) 344 (1829). The Sherman Act introduced the daunting task of distinguishing between groups that were "properly" entitled to treatment as entities from those that were combinations, whether by agreement or by merger, in restraint of trade. *See, e.g.*, 21 CONG. REC. 2457 (1890) (statement of Sen. Sherman, describing corporations as creatures of law and portraying combinations as devices to prevent competition); *id.* at 2567 (statement of Sen. Hoar, commenting on the unconstitutionality of congressional legislation that would deprive a state corporation of its state charter and function); *id.* at 2570 (statement of Sen. George, asking: "As a combination, who else is to combine with it except its own stockholders in the corporation?"). The problem was particularly difficult, given the staying power of the classical economic and legal images of laboring and trading individuals.

123. Adams, *Publicity and Corporate Abuses*, in 1 PUBLICATIONS OF THE MICH. POL. SCI. ASS'N 109, 116 (1894), *reprinted in* H. THORELLI, *supra* note 3, at 320.

124. *Id.*

125. For an excellent overview, see H. THORELLI, *supra* note 3, at 108-52.

> to the urban, industrial America of today, they turned to an idealized picture of the economic order with which they were familiar, the principles of which had been set forth by the classical political economists. They pictured an ideal society in which there was a maximum of abstract individual self-assertion. This was "liberty" as secured in the Fourteenth Amendment.[126]

This repression of the impulse toward equalizing market power and its effects on liberty were reinforced by unquestioned belief in the principle that greater size always entails greater efficiency.[127] Thus, the wave of industrial combination, whether trusts, cartels, or pools, raised deeply troubling questions about the classical view that combinations would dissipate because competition was inevitable.

The impulse toward equality could also be repressed by invoking the classical view of competition as free exchange. Supporters of monopoly and combinations in restraint of trade could call upon the powerful idea of liberty.[128] In much the same way that the individualist notion of liberty as "abstract individual self-assertion"[129] suppressed the tension within industrial liberty, it forged a connection between combinations and competition. In both instances, the impulse toward liberty overpowered a complementary commitment to equality. In both instances, this idealized notion of liberty legitimated private agreements, whether or not they restrained competition, by supporting the counterfactual image of typical market transactions as free exchanges between roughly equal parties. In this way, the impulse toward liberty constituted the foundation for a freedom of contract regime that relied on an ideal of equal competition and viewed social and economic reality as momentary aberrations from the ideal. Thus, the impulse toward liberty provided a powerful normative ground not only for the classical view of competition as free trade, but also for the freedom to enter into private agreements, without regard for their effects on competition. This idealized notion of liberty and its insinuation of equality within the classical view of competition as free trade was seen as justifying both competition and its restraint, both industrial liberty and fair price. It provided common ground for explaining and defending contradictory market conduct and conflicting social values.

---

126. Pound, *The Theory of Judicial Decision*, 36 HARV. L. REV. 641, 653 (1923).

127. *See, e.g.*, D. WELLS, RECENT ECONOMIC CHANGES AND THEIR EFFECT ON THE PRODUCTION AND DISTRIBUTION OF WEALTH AND THE WELL-BEING OF SOCIETY 73-75 (1896); Carnegie, *Popular Illusions About Trusts*, in THE GOSPEL OF WEALTH, AND OTHER TIMELY ESSAYS 81-82 (2d ed. 1933); *cf.* Clark, *supra* note 103, at 46 (all social classes benefit from increased efficiency achieved through industrialization).

128. *See infra* note 234 and accompanying text.

129. Pound, *supra* note 126, at 654.

These tensions produced profound economic and political implications. They encouraged the belief that monopolization and combinations in restraint of trade were justifiable. Not only could ingenious *individuals* win short-horn cattle monopolies in the free exchanges of competitive markets, but the freedom to contract (and the liberty interest associated with a fair return on one's property) was seen as legitimating agreements to *combine* one's capital or labor with another. In sharp contrast, perceptions of social and economic reality unconstrained by the classical images exploded popular and scholarly beliefs in naturally competitive markets and in natural connections between liberty and equality. Eventually, the loss of liberty itself became an issue:

> The power of groups of men organized by incorporation as joint-stock companies, or of small knots of rich men acting in combination, has developed with unexpected strength in unexpected ways, overshadowing individuals and even communities, and showing that the very freedom of association which men sought to secure by law when they were threatened by the violence of the potentates may, under the shelter of the law, ripen into a new form of tyranny.[130]

The Sherman Act passed through a Congress struggling with tensions between the political and economic mythology of artisans and local markets, and the reality of a new economic order of large scale enterprise and national markets.[131] Despite the classical image of competition as free trade and the underlying view of human nature as embodying an irresistible tendency to compete, unregulated markets in reality seemed to produce combinations of capital without bounds. Industrial liberty, characterized in the debates as freedom from private (market) power, authorized governmental intervention to reestablish the competitive markets overrun by powerful combinations of capital. But a return to the classical image of perfect competition was not seen as an unalloyed good. A contrasting rhetoric of fair price as well as a contrasting sense of human nature as embodying a tendency to combine provided the logic for arguments that some combination was a social good.

Congress' eleventh-hour turn to the common-law language of monopolization and restraints of trade represents a retreat from the 1888 Bill's explicit and unmediated imposition of competition as the only natural and legitimate form of commerce. The 1890 Bill's common-law language of monopolization and restraint of trade carried with it familiar and stable images drawn from classical economic and legal thought—

130. 2 J. BRYCE, THE AMERICAN COMMONWEALTH 407-08 (1889).

131. The balance between state and corporate power shifted noticeably with the passage of the 1889 New Jersey general incorporation statute, followed by the Delaware legislation. *See, e.g.*, E. JONES, THE TRUST PROBLEM IN THE UNITED STATES 30-31 (1923).

powerful though counterfactual images of mythic proportion.[132] The classical views of economics and the common law proceeded on the assumption that competition was the natural state of society and markets. These classical ideals mediated the deeply felt fears engendered by the widespread experience of disruption in traditional social and economic patterns. The revised language proclaimed that trusts and restraints of trade, not competition, were the problem. Although criticism of the classical view of economics and departures from the common-law regime of freedom of contract began to appear, congressional repose in the traditional language of the common law suggests a retreat to the traditional doctrine and classical view. Moreover, economic and political impulses toward both liberty and equality were seen as best served by permitting this natural state to flourish. Finally, the idealized portrayal of commercial markets as free exchanges between roughly equal individuals also satisfied the social demand for a fair return on one's property or labor.

In the social and political turmoil of the new economic order, the Sherman Act's language of the common law sought shelter from, but only shifted the battleground for, the tension between the logics of competition and private property. As this Article brings to light, confrontations between the rhetorics of industrial liberty and fair price, as well as their relationships to the social values of liberty and equality, characterize both the Sherman Act and the 1888 Bill, as well as the arguments favoring and opposing each version and its amendments. The next section examines the antitrust doctrine that emerged from the Supreme Court as a result of these tensions embodied in the Sherman Act. It also discusses what positions the Court took in this conflict between the logics of competition and private property.

II. The "Literalists": Competition Logic and Equality

The Court's early antitrust opinions[133] interpreting the Sherman Act have been characterized as "literalist" constructions of the statute.[134] But as William Letwin warned more than twenty years ago, we should not allow the "literalist" label to obscure each succeeding opinion's drift away from the proposition that *all* restraints of trade violated the Sher-

132. The standard reference for the cultural apparatus of mythology is C. LEVI-STRAUSS, THE ELEMENTARY STRUCTURES OF KINSHIP (R. Needham ed., J. Bell & J. von Sturmer trans., rev. ed. 1969) (published first in France under the title LES STRUCTURES ELEMENTAIRES DE LA PARENTE (1949)).

133. Northern Sec. Co. v. United States, 193 U.S. 197 (1904); United States v. Addyston Pipe & Steel Co., 175 U.S. 211 (1899); United States v. Joint Traffic Ass'n, 171 U.S. 505 (1898); United States v. Trans-Missouri Freight Ass'n, 166 U.S. 290 (1897).

134. W. LETWIN, *supra* note 3, at 172-76.

man Act.[135] Rather, the doctrinal movement evident in these early opinions marks successive approximations of the "rule of reason" developed in Justice White's early dissents and later adopted in his *Standard Oil v. United States* majority opinion.[136] Despite this apparently converging doctrine, *Standard Oil*'s New Majority thought the remaining distance important enough to shift to Justice White's rhetorical banner of reason. Indeed, some Justices and commentators portrayed the move as a radical shift.[137] Within a few weeks of the adoption of the "rule of reason," Congress reacted by holding private meetings and public hearings, which ultimately resulted in two major pieces of antitrust legislation—the Clayton and Federal Trade Commission Acts of 1914.[138]

This section explores the conditions that prompted the Court to shift to a "rule of reason." Three important observations emerge from considering the cases leading up to the decision in *Standard Oil.* First, the opinions reflect and often articulate a conflict between the logics of competition and property; despite what we might think today, competition policy was not the unrivaled major premise for early antitrust doctrine. Second, the lines were clearly drawn. The "literalist" or Old Majority took competition as its first principle, while the "rule of reason" minority and lower courts asserted the axiomatic nature of property protection. Third, those Justices who later constituted the "rule of reason" or New Majority saw the shift as significant precisely because, as Justice Holmes stated in his dissenting opinion in *Northern Securities Co. v. United States,* "[t]he act says nothing about competition."[139] As described in the last part of this Article, Holmes' statement and the property logic accompanying it signaled impending victory for the New Majority under the "rule of reason."

A. *United States v. Trans-Missouri Freight Association*

The Old Majority first formulated its "literalist" interpretation of the Sherman Act in *United States v. Trans-Missouri Freight Association*

135. *Id.*

136. Standard Oil Co. v. United States, 221 U.S. 1, 60 (1911).

137. *See, e.g., id.* at 100-03 (Harlan, J., dissenting); A.H. WALKER, THE "UNREASONABLE" OBITER DICTA OF CHIEF JUSTICE WHITE IN THE *Standard Oil* CASE 1-13 (1911) [hereinafter A.H. WALKER, OBITER DICTA]. Albert H. Walker also wrote the first account of the Sherman Act's legislative debates and early case law. A.H. WALKER, HISTORY OF THE SHERMAN LAW OF THE UNITED STATES (1910).

138. Clayton Act, ch. 323, 38 Stat. 730 (1914) (current version at 15 U.S.C. §§ 12-44 (1982)); Federal Trade Commission Act, ch. 311, 38 Stat. 717 (1914) (current version at 15 U.S.C. §§ 41-77 (1982)).

139. 193 U.S. 197, 403 (1904).

tion.[140] In *Trans-Missouri,* the Freight Association was accused of fixing uniform rates and terms in violation of the Sherman Act. The defendants convinced the trial and appellate courts that their agreement "regulated" rather than "suppressed" competition.[141] In particular, the trial court found that the Association had fixed "reasonable prices" to prevent "unhealthy competition" and "to avert personal ruin."[142] The court stated, "The public is not entitled to free and unrestricted competition, but what it is entitled to is fair and healthy competition . . . ."[143]

In the Supreme Court, the railroads claimed that "competition . . . simply leads in railroad business to financial ruin and insolvency . . . [and] to the destruction of innocent stockholders . . . ."[144] In short, the defendants' arguments and lower court opinions, couched in the common-law language of reasonable restraint, restated prior congressional speeches extolling the virtue of combination, the need to restrain competition, and the property right to a fair return on capital committed to the marketplace.[145]

The Supreme Court reversed the lower courts' holding that the Freight Association's fixing of uniform rates and terms was reasonable under the Act. Writing for the majority, Justice Peckham made it clear that all price fixing agreements were illegal, regardless of the reasonableness of prices fixed: "Competition . . . is a necessity for . . . securing in the end just and proper rates."[146] "Competition, free and unrestricted, is the general rule."[147] In response, Justice White wrote a dissenting opinion built upon the idea of reasonableness.[148] He argued that Congress intended to institutionalize the common law, which distinguished between reasonable and unreasonable restraints of trade.[149] Justice White concluded that whether sanctioned by the Interstate Commerce Act's mandate for just and reasonable rates or the Sherman Act's common-law ground for permitting reasonable restraints of competition, the railroads'

140. 166 U.S. 290 (1897).

141. 58 F. 58, 73 (8th Cir. 1893), *rev'd,* 166 U.S. 290 (1897); *see also* Chicago Bd. of Trade v. United States, 246 U.S. 231, 238 (1918) (true test of legality is whether the restraint merely regulates rather than suppresses competition).

142. 53 F. 440, 451 (C.C.D. Kan. 1892), *aff'd,* 58 F. 58 (8th Cir. 1893), *rev'd,* 166 U.S. 290 (1897); *cf. In re* Greene, 52 F. 104, 112-13 (C.C.S.D. Ohio 1892) (holding that constitutionally, the federal government cannot regulate the property of a corporation created by a state).

143. 53 F. at 453.

144. 166 U.S. at 330.

145. *See supra* notes 47-67 and accompanying text.

146. *Trans-Missouri,* 166 U.S. at 333.

147. *Id.* at 337.

148. *Id.* at 343.

149. *Id.* at 346.

ratemaking association was unobjectionable.[150] Either the majority's position outlawing a reasonable restraint was unreasonable, or the legislation itself was unreasonable. The consequence of this unreasonable interpretation or legislation, Justice White maintained, was a subjection of liberty of contract and freedom of trade "to the mere caprice of judicial authority."[151]

Although *Trans-Missouri* and the other early cases have been recognized as attempts to grapple with the proper relationship between the common law and the Sherman Act,[152] attention to the opinions' underlying logics permits an understanding of precisely what was at issue. To begin, it is useful to remember that the *Trans-Missouri* majority and dissenting opinions were arguing about the reasonableness of an agreement to fix prices, a debate already reported in the legislative record. The issue of reasonable price again precipitated a confrontation between the conflicting rhetorics of competition and property. On one side, the majority was quick to attribute to Congress an intent to prohibit all price agreements because it was impossible to determine whether any agreed price was reasonable.[153] Underlying the majority's position was a commitment to the sovereignty of competition—that is, to the belief that only competition can produce a reasonable price. Neither parties to an agreement nor judges are permitted to displace the pricing mechanism of competition.

On the other side, Justice White's four-man dissent believed that "[t]he plain intention of the [common] law was to protect the liberty of contract and the freedom of trade."[154] If the government intervened to stop private parties from entering into a reasonable contract, then unreasonable prices would be the consequence. Moreover, such judicial injunction interfered with the freedom to enjoy one's property in two ways. First, a contract between willing parties was voided; the impulse toward liberty was thwarted. Second, the value of the property involved was (unreasonably) diminished by virtue of (unreasonably) lower profits. As a result, unhealthy competition and unreasonable prices would prevail due to the illegitimate exercise of judicial authority.[155] Like the congressional speeches about fair price and the constitutional overtones of unrea-

150. *Id.*

151. *Id.*

152. *See, e.g.*, P. AREEDA, *supra* note 1, at 31; W. LETWIN, *supra* note 3, at 144-81.

153. *Trans-Missouri*, 166 U.S. at 331-32.

154. *Id.* at 355.

155. *Id.*

sonable price, Justice White's dissent exhibited concern for the right to fix fair prices in order to assure a fair return on one's property.

Both Justices Peckham and White took the debate over competition beyond a concern for pricing effects. Consistent with the congressional debates about competition and combination, each argued that not only the economic effects, but also the social and political effects of the other's prescription would harm rather than help the peace and prosperity of American society. Justice Peckham saw the problem as "motives of individual or corporate aggrandizement as against the public interest."[156] Even if consumers benefit from lower prices, he wrote, private agreements in restraint of trade would drive "out of business the small dealers and worthy men whose lives have been spent therein . . . . Mere reduction in the price of the commodity dealt in might be dearly paid for by the ruin of such a class . . . of small but independent dealers."[157] It is clear that Justice Peckham's view of industrial liberty required roughly equal firms of relatively small size

> because it is not for the real prosperity of any country that such changes should occur which result in transferring an independent business man, the head of his establishment, small though it might be, into a mere servant or agent of a corporation for selling the commodities which he once manufactured or dealt in, having no voice in shaping the business policy of the company and bound to obey orders issued by others.[158]

In this scenario, the problem was "combinations of capital [that] drive out of business all the small dealers in the commodity, and . . . render the public subject to the decision of the combination."[159] The solution to maintaining this important middle class of independent entrepreneurs was "competition, free and unrestricted."[160]

In contrast to this vision of industrial liberty practiced by numerous independent entrepreneurs, Justice White saw a different problem and, not surprisingly, a different solution. The problem for Justice White was "the danger of contract or combination by the few against the interest of the many and to the detriment of freedom."[161] For Justice White, the majority's commitment to free competition "strikes down the interest of the many to the advantage and benefit of the few."[162] To illustrate his

156. *Id.* at 322-23.
157. *Id.* at 323.
158. *Id.* at 324.
159. *Id.* at 323-24.
160. *Id.* at 337.
161. *Id.* at 355-56.
162. *Id.*

point, Justice White referred to *In re Debs,*[163] in which the trial court's interpretation of the Sherman Act in issuing an injunction against the striking union in the infamous Pullman Company case "makes [the Act] embrace every peaceable organization or combination of the laborer to benefit his condition either by obtaining an increase of wages or diminution of the hours of labor."[164] In short, a prohibition of reasonable agreements to create the countervailing power necessary to bargain for fair wages—a fair return on labor—threatened industrial warfare. In much the same fashion, wrote Justice White, the "utmost liberty of contracting" was necessary to forestall the ruin that free competition between railroads would entail.[165] "Undue restraint of the liberties of the citizen," proscribing agreements in reasonable restraint of competition, would bring on a state of industrial warfare.[166]

As *Trans-Missouri* illustrates, the disagreement between the "literalist" and "rule of reason" factions involved much more than a lawyerly argument over proper techniques of statutory interpretation. Rather, the underlying conflict was normative and involved a choice between two competing visions of society. On the one hand, the literalists argued that the policy directing the antitrust laws should rest upon free and unrestricted competition between roughly equal market participants, whether or not the consequence in any particular transaction is fair or reasonable. On the other hand, the advocates of a rule of reason urged that antitrust policy should tolerate large consolidations of capital and allow private agreements that restrain trade when the agreements protect a fair return from property or some other reasonable exercise of freedom of contract. Supreme Court opinions in antitrust's formative period can be understood as a series of struggles to win this conflict between competing visions of society.

B. *United States v. Joint Traffic Association*

Justice Peckham's opinions in the two terms following *Trans-Missouri* showed movement toward the "rule of reason" position. Evidence of such movement is found in the *United States v. Joint Traffic Associa-*

163. 64 F. 724, 745-55 (C.C.N.D. Ill. 1894), *aff'd as to decree,* 158 U.S. 564 (1895).

164. *Trans-Missouri,* 166 U.S. at 356.

165. *Id.* at 355. It is important to keep in mind that Justice White attempted to justify accumulations of capital by reference to combinations of labor. *Cf.* 21 CONG. REC. 2728 (1890) (statement of Sen. Hoar, distinguishing combinations of labor from combinations of capital).

166. *Trans-Missouri,* 166 U.S. at 354.

tion[167] concession that the Antitrust Act required a "reasonable construction." Moreover, the literalists shifted from the position that every contract in restraint of trade was illegal, to the position that only those contracts "whose direct and immediate effect" was to restrain interstate commerce were illegal.[168] Contracts with only an indirect effect on commerce did not violate the Act. While this new doctrine sounded very much like Justice White's formulation of an unreasonable restraint of trade, there remained an important difference. For Justice White, even a contract with a direct restraint on interstate commerce could still be deemed reasonable under certain circumstances.[169]

Although there was some convergence of the literalist and rule of reason views in *Joint Traffic Association,* there was no doctrinal movement on two critical points. First, the defendants claimed that the statute as interpreted would destroy fifth amendment rights of liberty and property by limiting their right to make contracts:

> A just freedom of contract . . . is one of the most important rights . . . of "liberty," for all human industry depends upon such freedom for its fair reward.
>
> The use of property is an essential part of it . . . . Its use is abridged when the owner is precluded from any contract that is necessary . . . to secure to him a just compensation for its employment.[170]

In response to this constitutional claim of fair return, Justice Peckham wrote that an argument "that private property shall not be taken for public use without just compensation . . . is, we think, plainly irrelevant," because Congress has the power to regulate private contracts that restrain interstate commerce.[171] Despite "general liberty of contract . . . there are many kinds of contracts which . . . may yet be prohibited."[172] The takings issue, however, was plainly relevant to the railroads, to Justice White and his colleagues, and to some members of the fifty-first Congress, all of whom produced statements making property-

167. 171 U.S. 505, 568 (1898) (quoting Hopkins v. United States, 171 U.S. 578, 600 (1898)).

168. *Id.* These statements also can be characterized as concessions to the dissenting Justices' property logic.

169. *Trans-Missouri,* 166 U.S. at 350.

170. *Joint Traffic Ass'n,* 171 U.S. at 533.

171. *Id.* at 571. Justice Peckham also refused to adopt the government's argument that the railroad industry was clothed with the public interest and was subject to government regulation as were the warehouses in Munn v. Illinois, 94 U.S. 113 (1877). *See supra* note 73-75 and accompanying text. Thus, the statement that the "taking" argument was irrelevant represents a refusal to acknowledge the legitimacy of a property logic, whatever its permissible conclusions about the price fixing conspiracy.

172. *Joint Traffic Ass'n,* 171 U.S. at 572.

based arguments. The takings issue was irrelevant to Justice Peckham because his statements were competition-based.

The second point in *Joint Traffic Association* on which there was no doctrinal movement was the majority's position that competition is the only legitimate arbiter of what constitutes a reasonable price. Justice Peckham conceived of the Sherman Act as a congressional enactment of the natural laws of competition. "We do not think . . . that ordinary freedom of contract in the use and management of their property requires the right to combine . . . for the purpose of stifling competition among themselves, and of thus keeping their rates higher than they might otherwise be under the laws of competition."[173] Moreover, in sharp contrast to the defendants' constitutional claim that the statute destroys property, Justice Peckham wrote that the agreement "destroys competition" between the parties.[174] Thus, although the *Joint Traffic Association* majority's doctrine moved away from a literalist position and toward a rule of reason standard, an impasse remained. Both the majority and the dissent were committed to incompatible normative positions staked in competition and property logics.

C. *United States v. Addyston Pipe & Steel Co.*

In the Court's following term, Justice White actually joined Justice Peckham's majority opinion in *United States v. Addyston Pipe & Steel Co.*[175] The common ground for this apparent resolution of the conflict between Justices Peckham and White was the Sixth Circuit's reconstruction of the common law: it held that all reasonable and ancillary restraints were considered valid, because they promoted "the free purchase and sale of property."[176] Thus, the Sherman Act could be read as simply restating the common law in its proscription of all direct restraints.[177] Circuit Judge Taft's legerdemain seemed to bridge the gap between the positions of Justices Peckham and White. The relationship between the common law and the statute was presented in a new and acceptable way that promoted property interests. Moreover, in holding that the defendants' price agreement was direct and thus illegal, Judge Taft's opinion rested on a common law that served competition as well. To allow such agreements would entail the judicial "power to say . . . how much restraint of competition is in the public interest" and thus would require

173. *Id.* at 570-71.
174. *Id.* at 564-65.
175. 175 U.S. 211, 244 (1899), *aff'g* 85 F. 271 (6th Cir. 1898).
176. 85 F. 271, 281 (1899) (Taft, J.).
177. *Id.*

courts to "set sail on a sea of doubt."[178] In short, competition remained for Judge Taft the final arbiter of what constitutes a reasonable price.

Despite the doctrinal confluence of Justice White's common-law position and Justice Peckham's statutory-law position in *Addyston Pipe,* the mediation between property and competition logics was illusory. Simply put, Judge Taft's assertion that competition was the only legitimate pricing mechanism precluded anything more than a momentary relaxation of tensions. The fact remained that a property logic, with its emphasis on freedom of contract and a fair return from property, recognized the legitimacy and reasonableness of some direct restraints of trade, including some agreements about price. Nonetheless, in Justice Peckham's opinion for a unanimous Court, a conflict between these two positions was averted because the prices were found to be unreasonable.[179] All participating Justices agreed that when "private contracts . . . result in the regulation of interstate commerce," Congress has the power to legislate, because the "liberty of the citizen . . . is limited by the commerce clause."[180] The uncontroversial logic was that given congressional power to trump state legislation that affects interstate commerce, there can be no question of the power to trump private regulation of interstate commerce.

D. *Northern Securities Co. v. United States*

Before long, the illusory coalition in *Addyston Pipe* evaporated in the heat of the notorious *Northern Securities Co. v. United States.*[181] *Addyston Pipe*'s fallout, however, created a new alliance, which found Justice Harlan writing a majority opinion that followed the interpretive practices of Justice Peckham's earlier opinions, but Justice Peckham joining in two dissenting opinions—one by Justice White and the other by Justice Holmes.[182] Moreover, Justice Brewer, while concurring in the Court's

178. *Id.* at 284.

179. 175 U.S. at 238.

180. *Id.* at 229.

181. 193 U.S. 197 (1904). The defendants included buccaneering financiers and captains of industry, J.P. Morgan, John S. Kennedy, and James J. Hill. President Theodore Roosevelt provided the government's trustbusting animus.

182. *Northern Securities* involved a "tight" combination, rather than the "loose" combinations or cartels attacked in the preceding government prosecutions. It seems appropriate to say something about the problem of a slippery slope between contracts among entities and contracts fusing multiple entities into one. First, "loose" combinations, such as price fixing cartels or profit pooling agreements were under attack, both in the state and federal courts. Though a few states prosecuted "tight" combinations, both United States v. E.C. Knight Co., 156 U.S. 1 (1895), which confined the Sherman Act to a narrow view of interstate commerce, and the Justice Department's prosecutorial neglect of the trusts, gave confidence to promoters

holding, also announced his shift to a "rule of reason" analysis, a shift premised on "the inalienable right[ ] of every citizen" "to manage his own property and determine the place and manner of its investment."[183] In short, *Northern Securities* saw the Old Majority's literalist rhetoric of competition go up in smoke.

Still, Justice Harlan wrote for the Court in *Northern Securities;* Justice Brewer's defection to a rule of reason analysis did not impel him to disagree, as it did Justice Peckham, with the plurality holding that the Northern Securities Company's formation was an illegal combination.[184] Nonetheless, it was clear that a majority of the Court no longer agreed with the old Peckham-Harlan reliance on a competition-founded Sherman Act. The Old Majority disintegrated under the pressure of this paradigm case of an ancillary and thus reasonable restraint under the traditional common law. The defendants argued, with plausible support in the congressional debates, that the common-law meaning of restraint of trade was the basis for interpreting the Sherman Act. Thus, they contended, it is highly relevant that, under the common law, "[i]t has been held repeatedly that such restraints as result from the sale or the purchase of property are not within the provisions of [the] anti-trust statutes."[185] The common "law does not require competition. The business of a rival may be purchased for the purpose of being rid of his competition."[186] The defendants argued at great length that the common law authorized citizens or state corporations to dispose of their property and invest their money in any way they chose.[187] Characterizing this right in

and business owners who engaged in trustbuilding and other sorts of interstate merger activity. To the extent that trusts seemed less risky than cartels, the tendency to combine tended toward trustbuilding. Second, "loose" combinations were unstable and difficult to enforce. They were unstable for many reasons. Simply agreeing on a price was difficult, given the differing costs faced by different parties. An acceptable price for a more efficient firm might not be an adequate price for a less efficient one. In some sense, no one was entirely pleased with the agreed upon price. It is not surprising that some parties to such compromise agreements would give secret discounts or cheat in other ways. If the agreements were to have any value, they would require policing mechanisms. Even with such provisions, however, simple identification of noncomplying parties was of little value, because state courts typically refused to enforce the agreements. The greater the number of participating entities, the greater the transaction costs associated with reaching and privately enforcing an agreement to restrain competition. Thus, "tight" combinations or fusion of many entities into one entity can be understood as a rational response to the instability and high transaction costs associated with contracts between entities. *See, e.g.,* H. THORELLI, *supra* note 3, at 72-77; Washburn, *History of a Statute: The Sherman Antitrust Act of July 2, 1890,* 8 B.U.L. REV. 95, 97-98 (1928).

183. *Northern Sec.*, 193 U.S. at 361.

184. *Id.* at 360-64.

185. *Id.* at 293.

186. *Id.* at 275.

187. *Id.* at 237, 241, 245-46, 254, 264, 272, 275, 287, 290, 293-97.

the fifth amendment terms that had already been rejected in earlier cases, the defendants concluded: "This constitutional provision protects the right to acquire property—equally with the right—to hold the same after it has been acquired."[188]

In the last battle won before losing the war, Justice Harlan took up the rhetoric of competition in the name of stare decisis. First, he posed the question directly: "[Does the Sherman Act forbid] every combination or conspiracy in restraint of trade . . . ? Or . . . only such restraints as are unreasonable . . . ? . . . Does the act of Congress prescribe . . . that the operation of the natural laws of competition . . . not be restricted or interfered with by any contract, combination or conspiracy? "[189] Justice Harlan answered the question straightforwardly, taking "certain propositions . . . plainly deducible" from the early literalist opinions, as well as the common law of the several states.[190] The major premise of the Court's earlier opinions was that "the act is not limited to restraints . . . that are unreasonable in their nature, but embraces *all* direct *restraints.*"[191] In sum, he rejected a rule of reason analysis because "Congress has, in effect, recognized the rule of free competition by declaring illegal every combination or conspiracy in restraint of interstate and international commerce."[192]

Justice Harlan also addressed the constitutional challenge raised by the defendants. He wrote that "the constitutional guarantee of liberty of contract does not prevent Congress from prescribing the rule of free competition," because the "natural effect of competition is to increase commerce, and an agreement whose direct effect is to prevent this play of competition restrains . . . trade and commerce."[193] Justice Harlan noted that it was not necessary to deal directly with defendants' due process claim regarding property because the questions raised were too abstract and general.[194] This cavalier treatment of the property argument, however, was unconvincing, especially because the questions posed were neither abstract nor general. They dealt with material consequences of specific positions taken regarding the constitutional scope of congressional power. In concrete terms, the defendants were arguing that the government's interference with their reasonable strategy to limit the ru-

188. *Id.* at 295.

189. *Id.* at 328-29.

190. *Id.* at 331 (citing Hopkins v. United States, 171 U.S. 578 (1898); United States v. Joint Traffic Ass'n, 171 U.S. 505 (1898)).

191. *Id.* (emphasis in original).

192. *Id.* at 337.

193. *Id.* at 331-32.

194. *Id.* at 333-34.

inous effects of competition was an unconstitutional taking of their property. The government was preventing them from entering into agreements to preserve the reasonable value of their assets. The real problem for Justice Harlan was that he could not resolve questions about property rights with statements produced by a commitment to competition. He could only repeat that the rule of competition was paramount—not much of a response to arguments that the rule of property should prevail.

Little more could have been said to resolve this impasse between two logics in conflict. For Justice Harlan, whose thinking was inscribed with the logic of competition, and for his colleagues and the circuit court judge, it was enough to write, "If such combination be not destroyed, all the advantages that would naturally come to the public under the operation of the general laws of competition . . . will be lost."[195] For the defendants and the dissenting Justices, who were committed to a property logic, the issues took on a different character. For them, the majority's view would "deprive the individual of his freedom to acquire, own and enjoy property by descent, contract or otherwise, because railroads or other property might become the subject of interstate commerce."[196] In those words, and in Justice Holmes' dissent as well, we hear the sound of not-so-distant trumpets. The Old Majority's entrenchment in competition would soon be overrun. A New Majority, with recruits won under the banner of reason, would soon shift the balance in favor of the property logics of fair return on property and freedom of contract. Few memories of the long struggle would survive the last battle.

III. The "Rule of Reason": Property Logic and Liberty

Indeed, *Northern Securities* was the last great battle between the two factions. It is easy to see why this case splintered the Court, impelling Justices Peckham and Brewer to abandon their competition logics in favor of the rule of reason. Unlike the earlier cartel cases, this merger or trust presented two familiar themes. On one side, a trust was restraining competition and extracting unfair prices from consumers. On the other side, a merger appeared to be a sale of property whose effects on competition were tolerated at common law because they were seen as ancillary.

The circumstances under which the Northern Securities Company trust was formed offer a new perspective on the opening aphorism in Justice Holmes' *Northern Securities* dissent: "Great cases like hard cases

195. *Id.* at 327.
196. *Id.* at 377.

make bad law."[197] This was a great case because "of some accident of immediate overwhelming interest which appeals to the feelings and distorts the judgment"[198]—the involvement of men with (in)famous public personae, such as financier J.P. Morgan and, in the background, President Theodore Roosevelt. It was also a "hard case" because of the attendant economic problems, problems mentioned only in passing and only in Justice Harlan's opinion for the Court.

Justice Harlan dedicated several pages to recounting in minute detail the large sums of money involved in the consolidations and the huge expanses of competing railway roads, now merged, from the Great Lakes to the Pacific Ocean. "The Great Northern Railway Company and the Northern Pacific Railway Company owned . . . two lines, main and branches, about 9,000 miles in length, [which] were and are parallel and competing lines across the continent . . . and . . . were engaged in active competition for freight and passenger traffic . . . ."[199] In addition, the two companies purchased over 200 million dollars in capital stock of the Chicago, Burlington, and Quincy Railway Company, whose lines aggregated about 8000 miles. Following that, the principals filed articles of incorporation in New Jersey for the Northern Securities Company and authorized capital stock of 400 million dollars. Stock in this new corporation was exchanged for railroad company stock, which was held and voted by the Northern Securities Company board of directors. Thus, a holding company or trust had been formed to control over 17,000 miles of track (as well as rolling stock and other assets) covering the Western United States and to consolidate three railroads, two of which had parallel and competing lines. This series of transactions was easily portrayed as a combination in restraint of trade or a monopolization of the railroad transportation business in a substantial part of the country. These facts clearly supported the Court's finding of a Sherman Act violation.

There was, however, another side to these economic circumstances. Justice Harlan's opinion made brief mention of Northern Pacific's economic distress:

> Prior to 1893 the Northern Pacific system was owned . . . by the Northern Pacific Railroad Company . . . . That company becoming insolvent, its road and property passed into the hands of receivers appointed by the courts of the United States. In advance of foreclosure and sale a majority of its bondholders made an arrangement with the Great Northern Railway Company for a virtual consolidation of the

197. *Id.* at 400.

198. *Id.*

199. *Id.* at 320.

two systems . . . .[200]

Only one further allusion was made to this agreement made in advance of foreclosure,[201] an agreement designed to save the value of the Northern Pacific shareholders' property from ruinous competition. Justice Harlan concluded that the decree ordering the trust's dissolution would "destroy, not the property interests of the original stockholders of the constituent companies, but the power of the holding corporation."[202] Perhaps he felt that another willing buyer could have been found. It was unlikely, however, that anyone other than Northern Pacific's parallel and overlapping rival would have found the 9000 miles of parallel and overlapping track attractive, especially given the recent history of fierce competition and the claims of overcapitalization.[203] Justice Harlan also might have believed that the overcapitalization claims were well-founded or that the Northern Pacific shareholders' alternative—selling assets for salvage value at a foreclosure sale—represented the natural and just workings of the laws of competition on private property put at risk in commerce. Indeed, there were those "who believe that [the rule of competition] is more necessary in these days of enormous wealth than it ever was in any former period of our history."[204] At the very least, Justice Harlan was persuaded to apply a rule of competition because, "as Congress has embodied that rule in a statute, that must be, for all, the end of the matter, if this is to remain a government of laws, and not of men."[205]

While Justice Harlan's opinion discussed all the issues raised in the case, the opinions of the two dissenting Justices, Justice White and Justice Holmes, divided the issues. Justice White's dissent addressed the fifth amendment question of congressional power to regulate or control ownership of state chartered railroads. He repeated the apocalyptic vi-

200. *Id.* at 320-21.

201. For doctrinal articulations of the modern failing company defense to antimerger actions, see United States v. General Dynamics Corp., 415 U.S. 486, 506-07 (1974); United States v. International Harvester Co., 564 F.2d 769, 773-74 (7th Cir. 1977).

202. *Northern Sec.,* 193 U.S. at 357-58.

203. For introductions to the natural monopoly cost structure that can provide the point of departure for a loss-minimizing logic of ruinous competition between railroads, see T. MORGAN, J. HARRISON, & P.R. VERKUIL, ECONOMIC REGULATION OF BUSINESS: CASES AND MATERIALS, at 15-17 (2d ed. 1985); R. POSNER & F. EASTERBROOK, ANTITRUST 4-11 (2d ed. 1984).

But there is another account of the railroads' financial plight: overcapitalization. In other words, the promoters raised much more capital than the firms required, either in anticipation of monopoly profits or in funding outrageously high promoters' fees. H. THORELLI, *supra* note 3, at 280-81, 315, 417, 422, 522, 540, 575. Justice White seemed to discount this claim. *Northern Sec.,* 193 U.S. at 366-67 (White, J., dissenting).

204. *Northern Sec.,* 193 U.S. at 337.

205. *Id.* at 338.

sion of a literalist Court's "disregard [of] the great guaranty of life, liberty and property and every other safeguard upon which organized civil society depends."[206] Justice White also raised one argument that distinguishes *Northern Securities* from the earlier cartel cases. He asserted that governmental prohibition of mergers or "tight" combinations constitutes regulation of property ownership. "[T]he power of Congress to regulate commerce," he argued, does not entail the power "to regulate the ownership of stock in railroads, which is not commerce at all."[207] In separating the status of ownership from the conduct of commerce, Justice White's argument was the fifth amendment analogue of the familiar common law doctrine that restraints ancillary to the sale of a business were reasonable. Indeed, several defendants characterized the formation of the trust as the sale of a business to a competitor.[208]

Justice Holmes' dissent focused on the common-law notion of "combination." The Old Majority's refusal to recognize the Act's common-law foundation led Justice Holmes to conclude with a Hobbesian, literalist vision of the Sherman Act as keeper of the natural laws of competition: Justice Harlan's position "would make eternal the *bellum omnium contra omnes.*"[209] In Justice Holmes' view, Congress did not mean to enact as positive law Herbert Spencer's social darwinism. Rather, Congress was concerned with restraints of trade because of "their intended effect upon strangers to the firm."[210] That is, Congress feared "trusts, the objection to which, as every one knows, was not the union of former competitors, but the sinister power exercised . . . by the combination in keeping rivals out of the business and ruining those who already were in."[211] Clearly, Justice Holmes was taking up the "combination" and "fair price" side of the congressional debates—statements produced by the logic of property. "It was the ferocious extreme of competition with others, not the cessation of competition among the partners, that was the evil feared,"[212] he concluded. In short, the feared evil was the maintenance of market conditions destructive of the right to a fair price.

According to Justice Holmes, while predatory pricing and other such conduct should be enjoined under the Act, the Act does not require dissolution of combinations. The Act does not "require all existing competitions to be kept on foot, and . . . invalidate the continuance of old

206. *Id.* at 397.
207. *Id.* at 368.
208. *See, e.g., id.* at 275, 287, 293.
209. *Id.* at 411 (war of all against all).
210. *Id.* at 404.
211. *Id.* at 405.
212. *Id.*

contracts by which former competitors united in the past."[213] Dissolution or disintegration introduced dangers even more threatening than governmental redistribution of property. For Justice Holmes, the Old Majority's competition-based rhetoric entailed "the universal disintegration of society into single men, each at war with all the rest, or even the prevention of all further combinations for a common end."[214] "If that were its intent I should regard calling such a law a regulation of commerce as a mere pretense. It would be an attempt to reconstruct society."[215]

Justice Holmes' turn to hyperbole suggests that he too was caught up in the heated struggle between property and competition logics. For example, Justice Holmes characterized the majority's commitment to competition as entailing a "universal disintegration of society" or a literal ban on combination.[216] Yet, the direct-indirect effects doctrine carried forward in Justice Harlan's opinion for the Court both evidenced compromise and allowed for the creation of some combinations. Nonetheless, Justice Holmes and the new rule of reason majority required more. They subordinated competition rhetoric to its property-based counterpart.[217] Most telling was his statement that "the Act says nothing about competition."[218] The ironic implication was that the old literalist majority should take seriously the *literal* language of the statute. In analyzing the common-law doctrine of "restraints of trade," rather than the meaning of "competition," Justice Holmes quipped, "I stick to the exact words used."[219] As if to emphasize the uncompromising nature of this

213. *Id.* at 410.

214. *Id.* at 407.

215. *Id.* at 411.

216. *Id.* at 407.

217. Although much has been made of the "great case" or interpersonal dimension of Justice Holmes' dissent, its language of hyperbole is more usefully understood as emerging from a commitment to the primary importance of property rights. W. LETWIN, *supra* note 3, at 229-37.

218. *Northern Sec.*, 193 U.S. at 403. Some commentators have trivialized this statement as disingenuous. That interpretation is based on the assumption that Justice Holmes' subjective intent was to jab at Theodore Roosevelt, who had appointed him and who, according to that view, expected his appointee to toe the line. *See, e.g.*, W. LETWIN, *supra* note 3, at 229-37. Whether or not this subjective intent was working, it (as Justice Holmes himself might have said) is not relevant here. What is relevant is the manner in which Justice Holmes articulated his intent, whatever it was. In other words, I take his statement seriously at an objective level: that he chose to make his statement in anti-"competition" terms is itself significant because of the force relations that produced it, and because of what it announces about the relative strength of those forces. For a brief analysis of Justice Holmes' freedom of contract view in a state antitrust law case, see May, *supra* note 3, at 536-37 (describing Justice Holmes' view of an overbroad state antitrust statute as an unconstitutional taking of property).

219. *Northern Sec.*, 193 U.S. at 403.

demand, Justice Holmes characterized the railroad combination's effect on competition as immaterial:

> If such a remote result of the exercise of an ordinary incident of property and personal freedom is enough to make that exercise unlawful, there is hardly any transaction concerning commerce between the States that may not be made a crime by the finding of a jury or a court.[220]

Certainly the novelty, size, and complexity of this series of transactions and the resulting trust made them anything but ordinary. Moreover, the competitive effects of the three-way consolidation were immediate, rather than remote. But for Justice Holmes, it was the exercise of a property right that appeared proximate. In the process of portraying the Act's legislative history as a rehearsal of common-law property rights, he ignored precisely the statements serving competition upon which Justice Harlan relied.[221]

In tandem, the Harlan and Holmes opinions in *Northern Securities* carried forward the conflict between competition and property logics evident in congressional debates over the Sherman Act. Along with Justice Brewer's brief concurring opinion, the four dissenting Justices effected a shift of power on the Court. The formal announcement of doctrinal victory for the new rule of reason majority and its property logic was made several years later in the companion cases of *United States v. American Tobacco Co.*[222] and *Standard Oil v. United States.*[223] The remainder of this section examines the Court's new property logic as explicated in Justice White's opinions in *American Tobacco* and *Standard Oil.*

In *American Tobacco,* Justice White grounded the rule of reason not in its salutary effect on trade and commerce, but rather in a purpose "to prevent that act from destroying all liberty of contract and all substantial right to trade, and thus causing the act to be at war with itself by annihilating the fundamental right of freedom to trade . . . ."[224] In his *Northern Securities* dissent, Justice White had already expressed concern about the

220. *Id.*

221. *See supra* notes 204-05 and accompanying text.

222. 221 U.S. 106 (1911).

223. 221 U.S. 1 (1911). *Standard Oil* also met Justice Holmes' definition of a great case. Like *Northern Securities, Standard Oil* was filed during Theodore Roosevelt's trustbusting administrations, in the same federal court in Minnesota, with virtually the same pleadings. *See* W. LETWIN, *supra* note 3, at 253. Though in *Standard Oil* a New Majority formed behind Justice White's "rule of reason," the results were the same as in *Northern Securities*: the Court affirmed a decree breaking up the trust.

224. *American Tobacco,* 221 U.S. at 180. For claims that policy conflict only arose at the time of the Clayton Act, see F. ROWE, PRICE DISCRIMINATION UNDER ROBINSON-PATMAN ACT xi (1962 & Supp. 1964) ("paradox of antitrust at war with itself"); Bork, *The Place of Antitrust Among National Goals,* in BASIC ANTITRUST QUESTIONS IN THE MIDDLE SIXTIES:

consequences of governmental regulation of this fundamental right: "The principle that the ownership of property is embraced within the power of Congress to regulate commerce, whenever that body deems that a particular character of ownership . . . may restrain commerce, . . . is in my opinion in conflict with the most elementary conceptions of rights of property."[225] Justice White believed that the rule of reason would forestall the Sherman Act's unreasonable intrusion into the citizen's liberty to buy and sell property. His belief arose from the following jurisprudential context. In the cases preceding *Standard Oil,* the battle on the Court was waged at two levels of discourse. First, it was expressed in terms of the relationship between the Sherman Act and common-law restraints of trade. The "literalists" maintained that the Sherman Act prohibited every agreement in restraint of competition. The "rule of reason" faction argued that the common-law notion of liberty to contract sanctions such agreements to the extent that they fix prices that allow a fair return on property or labor put into the market. Second, the conflict in the Court was also expressed in terms of the relationship between congressional power to regulate interstate commerce and fifth amendment rights of liberty and property. For example, the literalists argued that the Constitution's commerce clause trumps an individual's right to buy railroad company stock when the transaction "directly" restrains interstate commerce. In contrast, the "rule of reason" faction insisted that the fifth amendment protects an individual's right to purchase railroad company stock, even if it eliminates competition between railroads in interstate commerce.

These common-law and constitutional arguments in the cases preceding *Standard Oil* set the terms of an ongoing conflict between those committed to "full and free competition" and those committed to individual rights of property. It is important to recognize, however, that the fifth amendment rhetoric of liberty introduced a new element into the conflict. The property logic of "fair price," heard in the congressional debates, was now joined by an aligned but independent rhetoric of liberty to contract. This new rhetoric made explicit a tension within the notion of industrial liberty. As shown in the earlier discussion of the legislative debates, references to industrial liberty were taken to mean markets characterized by rough competitive equality.[226] This image of freedom from (private) market power reappeared in the literalist jurisprudence of full

---

FIFTH CONFERENCE ON THE IMPACT OF ANTITRUST ON ECONOMIC GROWTH 12 (Nat'l Indus. Conf. Bd. 1966); for a critique, see Peritz, *supra* note 1, at 1231-61.

225. *Northern Sec.,* 193 U.S. at 370.

226. *See supra* notes 29-46 and accompanying text.

and free competition. The legislative debates, however, made no reference to the other aspect of industrial liberty—freedom from governmental intrusion into private agreements. This unspoken side of industrial liberty found voice in Justice White's constitutional rhetoric of liberty to contract. Thus, Justice White grounded the rule of reason in a constitutional rhetoric not heard in the congressional debates.[227]

Justice White's rule of reason separated the language of industrial liberty from its rhetorical moorings. Under the banner of reason, the *Standard Oil* opinion replaced the competition logic of "liberty to pursue any livelihood or vocation" with the property logic of "freedom to acquire, own, and enjoy property." For the literalists, the problem in merger cases such as *Standard Oil* was the accumulation of property to consolidate market power. Their Sherman Act solution entailed regulation of property rights when they restrained competition. For the rule of reason faction, the problem was a "literalist" Sherman Act with government intruding upon individual liberty and property rights. The rule of reason solution invited private regulation of competition to protect those individual rights. The clearest statement of this concern is found in Justice White's earlier *Northern Securities* dissent:

> For it would follow that if Congress deemed [that] the acquisition by one or more individuals engaged in interstate commerce of more than a certain amount of property would be prejudicial to interstate commerce, the amount of property held or the amount which could be employed in interstate commerce could be regulated.[228]

If Congress could regulate an individual's right to exchange or use property, Justice White believed, liberty of contract would be destroyed.

In the rule of reason opinions for the New Majority, Justice White abandoned explicit fifth amendment references. Instead, he returned to common-law discourse for a parallel property-liberty argument: "Monopolies were unlawful because of their restriction upon individual freedom of contract."[229] At common law as well, the argument's axiomatic point of departure was "freedom to contract [which] was the essence of freedom from undue restraint on the right to contract."[230] The rule of reason's deployment of this common-law rhetoric of liberty effected two important changes in antitrust jurisprudence. First, the New Majority was willing to allow some private agreements that restrain competition.

227. Justice White believed, of course, that there were numerous antecedents in legislative references to the common law of restraints of trade. *Standard Oil,* 221 U.S. at 50, 61.

228. *Northern Sec.,* 193 U.S. at 370 (White, J., dissenting).

229. It was this restriction on freedom of contract that caused "injury to the public." *Standard Oil,* 221 U.S. at 54.

230. *Id.* at 62.

Second, it was an impulse toward liberty that animated that willingness. The rule of reason represented a diminished interest in equalizing (private) market power and a heightened concern for curbing governmental power. Although limiting governmental intrusion can be portrayed as expanding the domain of everyone's personal autonomy, inattention to market power would benefit the status quo of those already in positions to acquire or maintain market power.

Despite the New Majority's distaste for equalizing market power, liberty itself imposed some limitations on dominant firms. That is, under the rule of reason an exercise of the fundamental right to freedom of trade could sometimes amount to an unreasonable restraint of trade. In particular, the rule of reason allowed that market power could be exercised in some "unnatural" way, beyond the making of normal and usual contracts. Thus, "unusual and wrongful" acts, such as predatory pricing followed by purchases of rival firms, overstepped the bounds of freedom and properly called for governmental intervention.[231] In general, however, sovereign involvement was unreasonable since the "centrifugal and centripetal forces resulting from the right to freely contract was the means by which monopoly would be inevitably prevented if no extraneous or sovereign power imposed it and no right to make unlawful contracts having a monopolistic tendency were permitted."[232] Evidence of predatory pricing and other kinds of "fierce competition" provided the specific foundation for the New Majority's affirmances of decrees breaking up the Standard Oil and American Tobacco Companies. That instantiated the rule of reason's proscription of "unlawful contracts having a monopolistic tendency." Further, monopoly by sovereign grant was both familiar and unpopular. But what did Justice White mean by his reference to "extraneous power" imposing monopoly?

Examining Justice White's reference to "extraneous or sovereign power" imposing monopoly can elucidate the rule of reason's liberty-property logic and its relationship to the congressional debates' property logic of fair price. One way to approach the question is to think about the image of centrifugal and centripetal forces swirling around a nuclear "right to freely contract." The metaphor of two countervailing forces parallels Representative Stewart's image of two great natural forces in society—combination and competition—tempering one another.[233] Nonetheless, there are two significant differences between the views of Representative Stewart and Justice White. First, Representative Stew-

231. *Id.* at 181.
232. *Id.* at 62.
233. *See supra* notes 60-62 and accompanying text.

art's central or meta-principle of fair price or fair return on property placed in the market represents a property logic committed to the principle of equality. In sharp contrast, Justice White's opinion deploys a property logic committed to the principle of liberty. It places freedom of contract at the nucleus of these natural forces: one pulls inward to consolidate or combine, while the other force pushes outward to disperse or atomize. These opposing energies "result[ ] from the right to freely contract."[234] Second, Representative Stewart's model of two contending forces calls for an occasional third force—governmental intervention to restrain extreme forms of competition or combination. Again in sharp contrast, Justice White's view entails only two natural forces resulting from liberty of contract. Moreover, should a third or extraneous force enter his equation, its presence could (or would) destroy the delicate balance of natural forces and thereby impose monopoly. In Justice White's allegory of natural reason, the literalists were an extraneous force foreign to this natural system. Their unreasonable imposition of competition would annihilate freedom of contract, the center of Justice White's imaginary system. Thus, under the rule of reason, government intervention was proper only when proscribing "unlawful contracts having a monopolistic tendency."[235] Hence, liberty of contract did not require equalization of market power, as did industrial liberty. Nor did it demand fair profits or fair return on property put into the market. Rather, liberty of contract meant freedom from governmental intervention, except to regulate unreasonable restraints of trade.

This category of monopolistic contracts was ambiguous, whether or not it was circumscribed by the traditional doctrines of common-law restraints. Still, both the Standard Oil and American Tobacco Companies were found to have made "unlawful contracts having a monopolistic tendency."[236] The Court upheld the decrees calling for dissolution in both cases. Given these harsh consequences, the Court's imaginative shift to the rule of reason should have had an immediate deterrent effect on trustbuilding. Despite ongoing factionalism on the Court, the *Standard Oil* and *American Tobacco Co.* cases stood as examples of a unified will to engage in trustbusting. The splintered Court in *Northern Securities* could no longer be relied on for the view that mergers were safe alternatives to price fixing cartels. Yet, no one took the new jurisprudence to be a threat to corporate mergers, particularly not those in the business community who were intent on merging with competitors. Indeed, by 1914, Senator

234. *Standard Oil*, 221 U.S. at 62.
235. *Id.*
236. *Id.*

Thompson could read into the *Congressional Record* a list of 445 active trusts.[237]

Despite the fact that the 1911 opinions used the rule of reason to break up the great oil and tobacco trusts, this new rationale was widely perceived to be pro-big business. Why the public outrage? Though most Supreme Court opinions do not attain cultural significance, a few do become public currency. Like *Brown v. Board of Education*[238] and *Roe v. Wade*,[239] *Standard Oil* resolved an issue embedded in (ideo)logical controversy. Just as the two more recent opinions confronted questions of race and gender relations, *Standard Oil* can be understood as raising questions of class relations. The public's identification with Justice Peckham's image of a middle class of "small dealers and worthy men"[240] at the mercy of the powerful trusts provides the context for understanding how the "rule of reason" quickly became the protrust symbol that stirred public sentiment and congressional action, despite the apparently severe antitrust consequences of corporate dissolution (the antitrust version of capital punishment).[241] While it is unlikely that the lawyerly niceties of the shift to a "rule of reason" were widely known, it was easy to understand the difference between prohibiting every restraint of competition and prohibiting only *unreasonable* ones. Consumers, grangers, small businessmen, union members, muckrakers, politicians, financiers, and industrialists all could decide, in their own terms, who might benefit and who might lose from this shift. Indeed, no one has ever doubted that the 1914 antitrust legislation was passed in reaction to the rule of reason. What has not been clear before, however, is the significance for antitrust jurisprudence, of the 1914 statutes' explicit language of "competition," which is quite different from the Sherman Act's common-law language of restraint of trade and monopolization.[242] What becomes clear is the connection between Congress' legislation in reaction to the rule of reason and the literalist rhetoric of "full and free competition."

Reaction against the Court's rule of reason was widespread. Some in the legal community immediately expressed concern over a perceived weakening of the Sherman Act. Later reactions, including those in the

237. 51 CONG. REC. 14218-21 (1914) (statement of Sen. Thompson).

238. 349 U.S. 294 (1955).

239. 410 U.S. 113 (1973).

240. United States v. Trans-Missouri Freight Ass'n, 166 U.S. 240, 323 (1897).

241. The image of individual entrepreneurism appeared in the labor union movement as well, particularly in their credo of equality of opportunity. *See* H. THORELLI, *supra* note 3, at 147.

242. For a discussion of Sherman Act legislative history and its references to competition, see *supra* notes 29-53 and accompanying text.

business community, complained of the practical effects of the rule of reason—namely dissolution and its effect on competition.[243]

In particular, the practical effects of the *Standard Oil* case were distressing. Senator Reed reported during the Clayton Act debates that the so-called rivals created in the oil industry produced even more wealth for their shareholders in fragmented form than they did as the Standard Oil Company of New Jersey.[244] Moreover, both the oil and tobacco trusts' offspring were still engaging in predatory pricing and other forms of unfair competition against independents.[245] Much like the regional operating companies that have provided local telephone service since the 1982 agreement between AT&T and the Reagan Administration, Standard Oil's offspring enjoyed (unregulated) regional monopolies and were owned by a common pool of shareholders. In material terms, the dissolution was consistent with Justice White's dissenting opinion in *Northern Securities,* which argued against federal regulation of an individual's purchases of property, regardless of the effects on competition. Here, property ownership—holding shares of the Standard Oil Company—was not disturbed. Even more troubling was the fact that the 1911 Standard Oil miniatures were run by common management.[246] Thus, despite the dissolutions, there was no effective change in market power. Continued market domination protected the value of shareholders' property. Despite decrees requiring formalistic changes, there was no redistribution of wealth or market power from the miniatures to their trading partners and rivals. Given the continued predatory practices of the miniatures, the rule of reason had fostered no practical improvements in the quantity or quality of competition. In sum, the rule of reason decisions had no equalizing effects on market power or distribution of wealth. In practical terms, the *status quo ante* survived the dissolutions.

Legislative reaction to the Court's rule of reason appeared at both the state and federal levels. Between 1911 and 1913 twenty states quickly passed new antitrust laws.[247] Then in 1914 Congress passed two

243. 51 CONG. REC. 15864, 15866 (1914) (statement of Sen. Reed); *id.* at 14211-12 (1914) (statement of Sen. Shield); *id.* at 14520 (1914) (letter of J.T. Suter); *see* A.H. WALKER, *supra* note 137. For an interesting analysis of the Supreme Court's 19th century contract clause cases and the jurisprudence of "reason," see Siegel, *supra* note 78.

244. 51 CONG. REC. 9267, 14211-12, 14520, 15864, 15866 (1914).

245. *Id.; see also* E. JONES, *supra* note 131, at 46-87. *But see* McGee, *Predatory Price Cutting: The Standard Oil (N.J.) Case,* 1 J.L. & ECON. 137, 143 (1958) (arguing that the trial records contain no evidence of predatory pricing activities).

246. 51 CONG. REC. 14520 (1914).

247. A few state statutes actually preceded 1911. Moreover, the figure of 20 statutes is the arithmetic mean of two different figures that appear in the debates. *See* 51 CONG. REC. 15857 (1914) (Senate figure, 19 states); 51 CONG. REC. 9157 (1914) (House figure, 21 states).

statutes. Though radically different in regulatory philosophy,[248] both statutes deployed the language of "competition" abandoned by the New Majority. The Clayton Act proscribed a set of specific practices whose effect "may be to substantially lessen competition,"[249] while the Federal Trade Commission Act called for a regulatory agency to determine and enjoin "unfair methods of competition."[250] Perhaps the requirements of substantiality and unfairness were in some sense concessions to the property position. Nonetheless, congressional choice of the term "competition" in reaction to the New Majority's rhetorics of "liberty" and "property" reintroduced the logic of competition as a powerful force in the production of antitrust law.

Justice White's rule of reason opinions elaborated upon Justice Holmes' stark statement in *Northern Securities* that the Sherman Anti-Trust Act says nothing about competition. Yet, by 1914 legislative activity in Congress and in the several states had produced explicit connections between antitrust and competition. At the very least, the tension between property and competition was recharged.

IV. The Logical Structure of Early Antitrust Law

The preceding history of early antitrust law chronicles a confrontation between property and competition logics. The tension between these two logics produced Senator Sherman's 1888 Anti-Trust Bill and its concern for the consumer, the debates over its provisions, and the break to the 1890 Bill's language of "restraint of trade." This same tension also was responsible for the Court's literalist period and the rule of reason that displaced it. While competition logic and an associated impulse toward equality were factors in the production of early antitrust discourse, deep commitments to liberty and property rights produced an opposing logic that later dominated competition logic.

In the course of describing the competition rhetorics of industrial liberty and full and free competition, a second tension emerged. Impulses toward liberty and equality were seen as forces animating a tension within the notion of industrial liberty. Later, these same impulses were shown to be working in the property rhetorics of fair return on property and liberty of contract. It is clear that commitments to liberty and equality participated in the very conflict between competition and property logics. While these tensions, and the interplay between them,

---

248. 51 CONG. REC. 16144 (1914).

249. Clayton Act, ch. 323, 38 Stat. 730 (1914) (current version at 15 U.S.C. § 18 (1982)).

250. Federal Trade Commission Act of 1914, ch. 311, 38 Stat. 717 (current version at 15 U.S.C. § 41 (1982)).

are not necessarily stable over time, a structural analysis of the logic of early antitrust law can serve a clarifying function at this juncture. The following section presents such a stop-action description—a schematic mapping—of the structure and dynamics of early antitrust history.

While modern antitrust jurisprudence is the product of a history that does not stop in 1914, these fundamental tensions can help make sense of that history. Take for example the notion of industrial liberty and its conflicting impulses toward liberty and equality. The very same tension is evident in the modern idiom of "free competition." On the one hand, free competition can represent the belief that private restraints of competition are good because they are rational responses to market conditions. In this sense, governmental restraints are bad because they impinge upon individual liberty of contract, without which markets cannot function. The implication is that free competition and price fixing cartels are perfectly compatible. We have seen this logic at work in the *Mogul Steamship Co. v. McGregor, Gow & Co.*[251] opinion's view of competition as survival of the fittest, and in that court's refusal to enjoin a price fixing cartel from using predatory prices to protect its monopoly power. On the other hand, free competition or industrial liberty can also reflect the belief that private restraints are bad because they produce or apply monopoly power. In this sense, government restraints are good when they tend to dissolve monopoly power. The implication here is that free competition and price fixing cartels are incompatible. The literalists applied this logic in the railroad ratemaking association cases to break up price fixing cartels, thereby imposing "full and free competition," to benefit not only independent producers, but also consumers.[252]

Impulses toward liberty and equality have been seen in the workings of property logic as well. On the one hand, the property logic appearing in the congressional debates over the Sherman Act called for passage of a statute that would protect the fair profit of independent entrepreneurs from the extremes of competition and combination. This impulse toward equalizing market power to equalize wealth, not taken up in the early cases, seemed to authorize the courts to develop a common law of competitive torts to protect both consumers and independent entrepreneurs

251. 23 Q.B.D. 598, 614-15 (1889), *aff'd,* 1892 A.C. 25, 58-60; *see supra* notes 101-02 and accompanying text.

252. *See supra* notes 133-96 and accompanying text; Flynn, *Rethinking Sherman Act, supra* note 3, at 1608-19; Fox, *supra* note 3, at 1146-55; Kauper, *The "Warren Court" and the Antitrust Laws: Of Economics, Populism and Cynicism,* 67 MICH. L. REV. 325, 332 (1968); Note, *The Logic of Foreclosure: Tie-In Doctrine after* Fortner v. U.S. Steel, 79 YALE L.J. 86, 92-93 (1969) (authored by John C. Ladd).

from cartels and trusts.[253] On the other hand, the property logic driving the rule of reason called for government protection of monopoly power and profit, unless acquired by unreasonable means. Criticized in Justice Harlan's *Northern Securities* opinion, this impulse toward liberty sometimes took the form of fundamental rights of contract, property, or liberty.[254]

To give a fuller view of the implications of these logics as they appeared in antitrust's formative years, these logics are reorganized below according to their relationships to equality and liberty. "Equality," as it is used here, means the following: Having many competitors with roughly equal market power is, in and of itself, a social good because it makes the process of competition more fair or just. In addition, regulating the extremes of competition and combination produces a more equitable distribution of wealth. Market participants can expect a fair return on capital or labor put into the market, and consumers can expect to pay a fair price for goods and services. Finally, as Justice Peckham wrote in *Joint Traffic Association,* having many competitors and an equitable distribution of wealth encourages civic virtue.[255] That is, a vibrant middle class of "small dealers and worthy men" is crucial to the workings of democratic government because their economic freedom allows them better opportunity to act independently in social and political matters.[256]

In contrast, the following is an abstraction of the notion of liberty as it appeared in antitrust's formative years: Liberty of contract and freedom in the use of one's property are, in and of themselves, fundamental rights in a democratic society.[257] Further, these fundamental rights allow individuals to combine in commercial ventures. Consequently, individuals are able to shelter from the ravages of ruinous competition a reasonable return from property or labor put into the market. Protecting these fundamental rights as well as the expectation of reasonable profits is necessary for the maintenance of some competitive markets.

Employing these logics of competition and property, as well as impulses toward equality and liberty, a snapshot of the logical structure of early antitrust law might look like this:

253. *Cf.* Lande, *supra* note 3, at 93-106; *supra* notes 51-86 and accompanying text.

254. Northern Sec. Co. v. United States, 193 U.S. 197, 333-34 (1904).

255. United States v. Joint Traffic Ass'n, 171 U.S. 505, 577 (1898).

256. *See, e.g.,* Kaysen, *The Corporation: How Much Power? What Scope?,* in THE CORPORATION IN MODERN SOCIETY 85-105 (E. Mason ed. 1959).

257. *Northern Sec.,* 193 U.S. at 239-95 (defendants' arguments); *id.* at 364-72, 397 (White, J., dissenting).

P R O P E R T Y

L I B E R T Y			E Q U A L I T Y
	government protection of monopoly power & profit	government protection of fair profit to the independent entrepreneur	
	government sanction of survival of the fittest	government imposition of full & free competition	

C O M P E T I T I O N

The field diagram represents relationships developed from the legislative debates, court opinions, and other textual materials from the early years of antitrust law. The top half of the diagram represents the domain of property and the bottom half represents the domain of competition. The line separating them, running across the diagram, can be thought of as the border, or battle line, between their incommensurate assumptions and beliefs. Whereas property logic evaluates market transactions according to their impact on individual ownership and exchange rights, competition logic judges market transactions based on their effects on the market process. The right half of the diagram reflects the impulse toward equality; the left half, the impulse toward liberty. The vertical line between them can be imagined as a barrier that both connects them and anchors their opposing impulses.

It is clear that *both* relationships—between property and competition, and between equality and liberty—are tensions, not simple oppositions. In other words, though property and competition logics have produced conflicting antitrust doctrine, they also support one another. For example, the rule of reason faction believed that protection of property rights drives competitive markets. The notions of liberty and equality share a similar relationship of tension, rather than simple opposition. For example, the literalists believed that a large class of individual entrepreneurs is better than a large class of middle managers because the rough equality associated with this large middle class of independent businesspeople tends to disperse the power required to enjoy liberty. The inequality inherent in answering to one's superiors in large corporate hierarchies tends to limit the ways in which those with less power can exercise liberty. Freedom to make a choice requires freedom from the imposition of another's choice. In sum, the idea of a tension suggests that there is both conflict and mutual support in the two relationships.

The field diagram is also divided into four quadrants, each of which grounds the early antitrust policy produced by an interaction between the two tensions. The upper left quadrant, where the commitment to liberty influences property logic, represents the policy of government protection of monopoly power and profit. The rule of reason and its concern for freedom of contract were products of the interaction of these two forces in this area. The lower left quadrant, where liberty influences competition logic, represents the policy of government sanction of survival of the fittest. The clearest example of this policy position is the British common-law case of *Mogul Steamship Co.*[258] The lower right quadrant, where competition logic acts instead on the impulse toward equality, represents the policy of government imposition of workable competition. Although Justice Holmes characterized this policy as atomization of rivals to impose perfect competition, the literalists countenanced some restraints, making their view closer to what we today might call workable competition.[259] Finally, the upper right quadrant, where equality sentiments shape property logic, represents the policy of government protection of fair profit to independent entrepreneurs. The congressional debates included numerous calls for fair return on capital or labor put in the market.[260]

While this field diagram was developed from antitrust's early years, it also represents the logical structure that supports modern antitrust law. As described in a forthcoming study on vertical restraints doctrine, the field diagram depicts a logical structure that makes sense of the seem-

258. 23 Q.B.D. 598 (1889), *aff'd,* 1892 A.C. 25.

259. Regarding the notion of "workable competition," see *supra* note 51 and sources cited therein.

260. A few words should be said about the diagram itself, which is a snapshot of a dynamic process. First, the boundaries between quadrants are porous. If the operators (competition, property, liberty, equality) were simple oppositions, there would be no seepage. But because the tensions between them include an element of mutual support as well as conflict, there may be doctrinal flow across lines. For example, liberty needs equality, competition needs property, and so on. Second, the quadrants need not be the same size, though the diagram shows them as equal. In other words, at any given moment in history, the productive capacities of all four quadrants need not remain equal. There are numerous ways to describe this phenomenon. Here are three variations: (1) One of the two intersecting lines (or axes) could rotate. For example, if the vertical line connecting PROPERTY and COMPETITION rotated in a clockwise direction, the P/C line could cut a 45 degree angle through the upper right and lower left quadrants. This rotation would extend the influence of liberty in the upper PROPERTY half of the field and constrict its influence in the lower COMPETITION section. (2) One axis could migrate, while remaining perpendicular to the other axis. For example, if the horizontal line connecting LIBERTY and EQUALITY moved up the page toward the PROPERTY operator, the upper PROPERTY half of the structure would decrease in size, and the lower COMPETITION section would grow larger. (3) Finally, one axis could levitate. The P/C line could rise from the page. With this movement, interactions between tensions might decrease in intensity. Each of these possibilities—rotation, migration, and levitation—carries the same implication: that the field diagram as presented is a snapshot of a dynamic historical process.

ingly haphazard movements of current case law, as well as its misunderstood connections to doctrinal antecedents.[261] There may be other grounds for the production of antitrust law and for the production of other law or simply other discourse. Most likely, however, a statement located on another field diagram simply does not appear to us to be a statement about antitrust law, unless it also occupies a position on the diagram appearing above.

One thing this map does not tell us is *where* any particular statement is positioned. Nonetheless, we can identify *likely* locations, just as lawyers and scholars have always done, by making informed judgments about the relative strengths of particular legal arguments in local settings. What is clear now, however, are the logics supporting antitrust argument. Thus, modern antitrust law, whether court opinion, journal article, jury instruction, or legislative conference report, can be understood in terms of the interplay of these two tensions. Do the texts indicate strong commitments to liberty or equality? Do they deploy the logic of competition or property? What doctrinal changes tend to accompany shifts in commitments? Considering such questions not only helps to explain seemingly haphazard shifts in doctrine, but also reveals how modern antitrust law still embodies the same tension between competition and property, and the same impulses toward equality and liberty.

Conclusion

In antitrust's formative years, shifting balances of power between rhetorical modes were evident from the earliest moments of the Sherman Act's legislative history, through the history of struggle between the "literalist" and "rule of reason" factions, to passage of the twin 1914 statutes. But those battles settled nothing. Nor could they prove that one logic was somehow better or stronger. Rather, those confrontations represented the very conditions of possibility for early antitrust law.

As we approach the centennial of the Sherman Act's passage, policy issues and the doctrinal alternatives in antitrust can now be analyzed in terms that not only include competition, but also recognize the fundamental conflict with the common-law logic of property rights. Whether we imagine them as mutually constituted, or whether we imagine competition policy as embedded in a pre-existing common-law property regime, or whether we imagine common-law property rights as subject to competition policy, we can no longer ignore the property logic that produced

261. Peritz, *A Genealogy of Vertical Restraints Doctrine*, 40 HASTINGS L.J. (1989) (forthcoming).

early antitrust doctrine. The right to a "fair profit," the liberty to combine, and the freedom to dispose of one's assets are all historical instances of property logic in restraint of competition.

Competition logic exhibits an internal tension as well, animated by commitments to liberty and equality. That tension continues to operate in the modern idiom of "free competition," which can be understood as freedom from private market power or from government intervention. Thus, competition free from private market power implies that governmental intervention is good when it equalizes market power. But competition free of sovereign power means that governmental intervention is bad because it impinges on individual liberty. The context for analyzing antitrust law is completed with the recognition that the same commitments to liberty and equality produced tensions in the logic of property rights as well.

Finally, it is important to make explicit an important implication regarding the relationship between competition and efficiency. This study introduces an analytical structure for understanding how the tension between the competition policy and property rights has produced the efficiency norm in its various forms. In short, it shows a different mechanism at work in the production of antitrust doctrine, sharply different from the orthodox view that competition represents the only positive norm for antitrust and contrary to today's neoclassical view that efficiency is a proxy for competition. Placing competition into its logical and historical context allows us to recapture the positive values associated with combinations, small businesses, fair profit, and other doctrinal formulations that we currently associate with negative values such as "anticompetitive" practices or "anti-efficiency" policies. With an analytical structure that recognizes antitrust doctrine as a series of sociopolitical choices, we can start the Sherman Act's second century by making better informed judgments about antitrust doctrine and policy.

[13]

Article 85 and the Rule of Reason*

Richard Whish and Brenda Sufrin

I. Introduction

Many commentators on EEC competition law have given consideration to the question of whether a 'rule of reason' ought to be read into Article 85(1) of the Rome Treaty.[1] This is the issue which will be examined in this essay. It will involve a consideration of the function of the rule of reason in US antitrust law and a comparison of antitrust law in the United States and in the Community. Thereafter the authors will consider, with particular reference to recent pronouncements of the European Court of Justice and the Commission of the European Communities, whether a rule of reason already exists under Article 85(1) or is in the process of emerging. Lastly, they will ask how desirable it is that a rule-of-reason analysis be employed under Article 85(1), and whether it is desirable that this particular terminology should be imported from the US into EEC competition law.

The background to the discussion is familiar: Article 85(1) prohibits agreements whose object or effect is the prevention, restriction or distortion of competition. However, even an agreement which comes within the scope of Article 85(1) may be authorised by the Commission where it satisfies the criteria of Article 85(3). To do so, the agreement must contribute to an improvement in the production or distribution of goods or to technical or economic progress, and must yield a fair share of the resulting benefit to consumers; at the same time, it must not contain indispensable restrictions of competition and must not substantially eliminate competition. The tendency of the Commission over many years has been to hold that various types of agreement—for example exclusive dealing, exclusive purchasing, licences of intellectual property rights, joint ventures for research and development—infringe Article 85(1), but then to authorise them under the provisions of Article 85(3). Protagonists of the rule of reason would argue that many of these agreements do not in any real sense prevent, restrict or

Lecturers in Law at Bristol University.

[1] The literature in English is fairly extensive. See for example René Joliet, *The Rule of Reason in Antitrust Law* (Martinus Nijhoff 1967); Valentine Korah, 'The Rise and Fall of Provisional Validity—the Need for a Rule of Reason in EEC Antitrust' *Northwestern Journal of International Law and Business* (1981) 320; Mark Schechter, 'The Rule of Reason in European Competition Law' *LIEI* (1982/2) 1; Stephen Kon, 'Article 85(3): a Case for Application by National Courts' 19 *CML Rev* 541 (1982); Ian Forrester and Christopher Norall, 'The Laicization of Community Law: Self-help and the Rule of Reason: How Competition Law is and could be Applied' 21 *CML Rev* 11 (1984); Korah, 'EEC Competition Policy—Legal Form or Economic Efficiency' 39 *CLP* 85 (1986); Angus Maciver, 'EEC Competition Policy in High Technology Industries' *Fordham Corporate Law Institute* (1985) Chap 25; James Venit, 'Pronuptia: ancillary restraints or unholy alliances' 11 *EL Rev* 213 (1986).

2 *Richard Whish and Brenda Sufrin*

distort competition, so that they ought not to require vindication under Article 85(3). The attractions of this type of analysis are said to be that it would get the Commission off the backs of business people trying to conduct their affairs in the most efficient way possible, and that it would have immense procedural advantages.

Agreements which fall within Article 85(1) are void and unenforceable unless they are exempted under Article 85(3), either individually or under one of the six block exemptions.[2] If one takes the example of two companies anxious to develop jointly a new and technically advanced product, one must ask whether it is reasonable to subject them to the delay involved in seeking an exemption for their agreement, and to the risk that the commercial balance of their relationship will be altered through the intervention of the Commission. It is also arguable that it is inappropriate that an agreement such as this, if unnotified (and not within Regulation 418/85 on research and development agreements[3]), should be void and unenforceable. The parties could theoretically even be fined for entering into an agreement of a type encouraged by the Commission,[4] anxious to foster new technology. The rule-of-reason argument would say that the agreement, far from restricting competition, may introduce a new product on to the market, thus increasing competition overall.

In the case of patent licences, a licensee may be so uncertain about the risks involved in going into production of a newly patented product that he will only take the licence at all if given an exclusive territory. The argument can then unfold perfectly logically: without the exclusivity, the licensee will not enter the market. The licensor may be unable to produce in the licensee's territory (for example, because he lacks the resources—that is why he is looking for a licensee). So, the licence with territorial exclusivity creates rather than destroys competition, and should not come within Article 85(1). The same reasoning can be used for exclusive dealing,[5] franchising and other types of agreement.

Advocates of the rule of reason point out that this approach to Article 85(1) would have procedural advantages. Only the Commission has power to grant individual exemptions.[6] Obtaining an individual exemption is a lengthy process, which may involve negotiations whereby the Commission will grant an exemption if certain clauses in the agreement are amended. The Competition Directorate of the Commission (DG IV) is notoriously short-staffed and cannot deal fully with every case notified to it. As a result, the Commission issues each year only a small number of individual

[2] Implementation of the draft exemptions on know-how licensing (OJ 1987 C214/2) and franchising (OJ 1987 C229/3) will bring the number to eight.

[3] OJ 1985 L53/5.

[4] See e.g. Programme of the Commission for 1985, (EC) *Bulletin* Supp 4/85, 10–12. It is important to point out that it is not just the Competition Directorate that is keen to encourage new technology; other Directorates are also involved e.g. DG XII (Research and Development) and DG XIII (Telecommunications, Information Industries and Innovation).

[5] See e.g. the note by Korah on the Commission's decision in *Polistil/Arbois* in 5 *ECLR* 203 (1984).

[6] Art 9(1) Regulation 17/62, OJ 1959–62 Spec Ed 87.

decisions granting or refusing exemptions, and some of these are selected for such treatment on policy grounds.[7] Other cases, amounting to over 90 per cent of those notified, are dealt with on an informal basis.[8] This may be by a so-called 'comfort letter' to the parties which indicates either that the agreement is not within Article 85(1) at all or that the Commission considers that it qualifies for exemption. The difficulties caused to third parties by this practice have partly been overcome by the Commission's decision to publish in the Official Journal notice of its intention to issue one of these letters.[9] However, comfort letters are problematic for the parties too, as was confirmed in the *Perfumes* cases,[10] for such an administrative letter is not the same as a formal decision and binds neither national courts, third parties nor national competition authorities, but can terminate the provisional validity of an old agreement. The Commission also informally settles some cases after it has commenced proceedings and issued a Statement of Objections if the parties have amended or terminated the agreement or behaviour which was allegedly contrary to the competition rules. Again, the legal significance of such a settlement is uncertain.[11]

Faced with these difficulties, the attractions of a mode of reasoning whereby fewer agreements fall within Article 85(1) in the first place is obvious. It is questionable, however, whether these procedural problems justify a major reanalysis of Article 85(1): this would rather seem like the tail wagging the dog.

The supporters of the rule of reason would argue that many restrictions *on conduct* are not restrictions *of competition*. They would draw upon US experience in antitrust matters and show that, in applying the Sherman Act 1890, the Supreme Court has in recent years become much more sensitive about deciding what is meant in that Act by a 'restraint of trade'. Practices which at one time were consistently condemned under the antitrust laws are now subject to rule-of-reason analysis and upheld. In particular, the 'Chicago School' has had a profound impact upon the development of antitrust in the last twenty years and has influenced the partial retreat from antitrust enforcement in the United States.[12] The argument is that, if a US-style rule of reason were to be adopted, and particularly if it were based upon the economic thinking of the Chicago School, there would be a radical

[7] In 1986 it reached 21 final decisions and 2 decisions rejecting complaints under Arts 85 and 86: 16th Annual Report on Competition Policy, pt 44. The number of individual exemptions granted was 6 in 1984, 5 in 1985 and 9 in 1986.

[8] See generally Nicholas Green, *Commercial Agreements and Competition Law* (Graham and Trotman 1987) 304–15.

[9] See OJ 1982 C343/4 and OJ 1983 C295/7. The Commission does not in practice usually publish notices. In 1986 it settled 74 cases by administrative letter, but only one following publication of a notice in the Official Journal: see 16th Annual Report pt 44 and p 259.

[10] Cases 253/78 and 1–3/79 *Procureur de la République* v *Giry & Guerlain* [1980] ECR 2327 and Case 99/79 *Lancôme SA* v *Etos BV* [1980] ECR 2511.

[11] See Case 71/74 *Frubo* v *Commission* [1975] ECR 563 in which the Commission was held not to be bound by assurances, in a letter signed by an official, as to the attitude it would take to amendments to an agreement.

[12] The contributions of the Chicago School will be explained further below.

shift in EEC competition law and practice, and the problems for business caused by the existing rules would, if not evaporate, at any rate diminish. The main emphasis would be on analysis of agreements under Article 85(1), and the main enforcement of the rules could take place in national courts.[13]

II. The rule of reason in US antitrust law

It is not possible here to analyse in depth the growth of the rule of reason in the United States, but a brief discussion of the origins of US antitrust law and the development of the rule of reason is necessary for what follows. The Sherman Act 1890 was passed against a background of widespread ill-feeling against railroad companies, which were in a position to exploit their monopolies to the disadvantage of farmers, shippers and other traders. Also, many industries were in the hands of the 'trusts', combinations of powerful firms which perfected techniques for driving competitors out of the market and indulged in practices widely regarded as exploitative and unfair. Both major parties had by 1888 accepted the need to control the problem of monopoly, although it was unclear how this could best be done. What emerged was a piece of legislation which harnessed the common-law notion of restraint of trade. Section 1 of the Sherman Act provided that 'Every contract, combination in the form of trust or otherwise, or conspiracy, in restraint of trade . . . is hereby declared to be illegal.' Section 2 made it an offence to monopolise or to attempt to monopolise a market. These provisions are still the foundations of US antitrust, and many millions of words have been spilled on their meaning. What did Congress mean by these apparently simple words? Did they express a single philosophy of competition? If so, what philosophy of competition? How were the courts supposed to proceed? By what standards were they to be guided? What has followed has been complex, but two particular issues stand out as far as the authors are concerned. First, we shall consider briefly how the courts set about deciding what is and what is not a restraint of trade and, secondly, we shall look at the broader debate about the function and role of antitrust in the United States.

A. THE US COURTS AND THE RULE OF REASON

Congress left it to the courts to make sense of the Sherman Act and in the early days the Supreme Court struggled to do so. Clearly, it could not be the case that *every* restraint of trade came within the Act. The well-known

[13] National courts are able to apply Article 85(1): indeed the Commission is eager that more enforcement should take place in domestic courts as this would relieve it of some of the burden it now carries. See e.g. 13th Annual Report on Competition Policy pts 217–18; 15th Annual Report pts 38–43; 16th Annual Report pts 41–2. However, there is a difference between national courts assuming some of the policing of what one might call blatant anti-competitive behaviour and asking them to undertake more complex economic analysis under a rule of reason.

quote in *Chicago Board of Trade* v *US*[14] is one of the best statements of the essential problem:

> But the legality of an agreement or regulation cannot be determined by so simple a test, as whether it restrains competition. Every agreement concerning trade, every regulation of trade, restrains. To bind, to restrain, is of their very essence.

Thus, the courts had to begin the process of distinguishing between those restraints which were within and those which were outside the mischief of the Act. This process is still continuing, but at least there is now some sort of conceptual framework within which the issue can be argued. This was not so at the time that the courts first set about interpreting the bald words of the Sherman Act.

In *United States* v *Transmissouri Freight Associations*,[15] eighteen railroad companies had fixed their freight rates in order, they claimed, to avoid ruinous price wars. Was there a restraint of trade? One way of deciding this would be to ask whether the rates fixed were themselves 'reasonable'. 'Reasonableness' is a great friend of the common law—the law of tort and contract rely heavily upon it. Justice White, speaking for the minority, was apparently prepared to go along this path, although in later judgments he was to alter his position. The majority took a different line: reading the Act literally, it condemned *every* restraint of trade. This agreement restrained the participants' pricing behaviour and so was caught. The problem with this approach is that it seems to embrace as much as Justice White's would have excluded. Neither seems to offer a sensible way of distinguishing acceptable and unacceptable restraints. The White approach is unsatisfactory, for who could assess the reasonableness of the freight rates? One function of competition is that the market, and not judges, should determine the level of prices.[16]

In *US* v *Addystone Pipe and Steel Co*,[17] Judge Taft, sitting as a circuit judge, suggested that the rules of the common law might be invoked in order to make sense of the Sherman Act. At common law, a restraint which was 'merely ancillary to the main purpose of a lawful contract, and necessary to protect the covenantee in the enjoyment of the legitimate fruits of the contract, or to protect him from the unjust use of those fruits by the other party' would be upheld. However, restraints whose sole object was the restriction of competition would not be permitted. The Supreme Court, in the same case, did not pursue this idea, but in due course the doctrine of 'ancillarity' became an important tool in antitrust analysis. It still has vitality in US antitrust, although it is not the only mechanism whereby good and bad restraints of trade are distinguished. As we shall argue later, a limited doctrine of 'ancillarity' or, as we would prefer, 'objective necessity' has been read into Article 85(1) of the Treaty. What we wish to question is

14 246 US 231 (1918).
15 166 US 290 (1897).
16 This was later accepted emphatically in *US* v *Trenton Potteries* 273 US 392 (1927).
17 85 Fed 271 (6th Cir 1898).

whether a more ample 'rule of reason', as that term is used in the United States, exists or should exist under EEC law.

In *Standard Oil* v *US*,[18] Chief Justice White said that the way of deciding whether a restraint was within the Sherman Act or not was to apply a 'standard of reason' and that only *undue* or *unreasonable* ones should be condemned. At several points in his speech, he referred to the 'rule of reason', a term used in earlier cases but now brought into the centre of antitrust analysis. In fact, the judgment was not especially helpful at a practical level, and it took many more cases to establish what was meant by the rule of reason. In the *Chicago Board of Trade* case,[19] Justice Brandeis remarked:

> [t]he true test of legality is whether the restraint imposed is such as merely regulates and perhaps thereby promotes competition or whether it is such as may suppress or even destroy competition.

What emerges from this is that the rule of reason is applied to decide whether a restraint is caught by the Sherman Act, except in those cases where an agreement is illegal 'per se' (see below). In applying the rule of reason, the doctrine of ancillarity is not the only way in which the courts distinguish good and bad restraints. As experience of antitrust problems has grown, and as economic analysis has become more sophisticated, the US courts have been prepared to take a much wider view of the impact an agreement might have upon competition. The doctrine of ancillarity is sometimes adequate to enable the courts to uphold a restraint. This is particularly so where a property right—for example, the goodwill associated with a business—is transferred from a vendor to a purchaser. However, the doctrine of ancillarity is not so useful when considering, for example, whether restraints in a distribution agreement or a research and development project are in restraint of trade. A wider doctrine is needed to analyse such agreements, and the approach now taken by the US courts is to ask whether the restrictive provisions of the agreement decrease or increase competition on the market as a whole. For these purposes it is necessary to conduct a wide-ranging inquiry, which includes analysis of the product market in question and sensitivity to economic theory. The pro- and anti-competitive effects of an agreement are weighed against one another and, if the former outweigh the latter, there is no infringement of the Sherman Act. The Supreme Court recently explained the point well:

> [T]he inquiry mandated by the Rule of Reason is whether the challenged agreement is one that promotes competition or one that suppresses competition ... [T]he purpose of the analysis is to form a judgment about the competitive significance of the restraint.[20]

The rule of reason has given the courts a tool for distinguishing legal and

[18] 221 US 1 (1911).

[19] See n 14 supra.

[20] *National Society of Professional Engineers* v *US* 435 US 679, 691–2 (1978).

illegal restraints of trade. Most enforcement of antitrust laws in the United States takes place in the courts, the most common situation being that of an injured individual suing for treble damages, for example, where he has been the victim of price-fixing or bid-rigging. This contrasts with the position in the EEC (and indeed the UK), where private law litigation is much less common in competition law.

The US position imposes a great burden on the judiciary. Not surprisingly, in the course of time the courts began to identify certain types of agreement which, because of their 'pernicious effect on competition and lack of any redeeming virtue are conclusively presumed to be unreasonable and therefore illegal without elaborate inquiry as to the precise harm they have caused or the business excuse for their use.'[21] Such agreements were said to fall per se within the Sherman Act. Price-fixing, both horizontal[22] and vertical,[23] was an example. Eventually, market-sharing was also subjected to a per se rule.[24] In other words, in these cases it was only for the plaintiff to show that the agreement actually existed: thereafter, there was no room for further argument under the rule of reason. The 'per se' approach relieved the courts of the need to analyse the effect of the agreement in its market context. Thus, one ends up with the situation in which some types of agreement come within the Sherman Act per se, whereas others have to be subjected to the rule of reason before this can be established. This does not fully reflect the subtlety of the situation. It is not always possible to tell with certainty whether the courts are applying per se or rule-of-reason analysis in any particular case. Furthermore, it becomes increasingly clear that there are intermediate positions between per se and rule-of-reason analysis and that there is an increased blurring of the formalistic dichotomy between the two.[25] Again, as antitrust theories and opinions change, so the courts sometimes alter existing categories. At the moment, there is an important drift away from per se illegality, and the rule of reason is playing an ever larger part in US antitrust analysis. For example, in *National Collegiate Athletic Association* v *Board of Regents of the University of Oklahoma*,[26] the Supreme Court subjected the rules of the NCAA to rule-of-reason rather than per se analysis, even though they had the effect, among other things, of inhibiting price competition. In the end, the rules were condemned, but the significance of the case is the shift away from per se treatment. A similar decision was *GTE* v *Sylvania*,[27] which will be considered further below. On the other hand, in *Jefferson Parish Hospital District No. 2* v *Hyde*,[28] the Supreme Court declined the oppor-

21 *Northern Pacific Railway* v *US* 356 US 1, 5 (1958).
22 See *US* v *Trenton Potteries Co* 273 US 392 (1927).
23 *Dr Miles Medical Co* v *John D. Park and Sons Co* 220 US 373 (1911).
24 *US* v *Topco Associates* 405 US 596 (1972).
25 See Ernest Gellhorn, *Antitrust Law and Economics* 3rd ed (West 1986) 186 et seq.
26 468 US 85 (1984).
27 433 US 36 (1977).
28 466 US 2 (1984).

tunity to relax the per se standard in relation to tie-in transactions in favour of the rule of reason, as the law on the matter was too well-established for such a change.[29] In *US* v *Columbia Picture Industries*,[30] it was suggested that there might be some *tertium quid* between per se illegality and rule-of-reason analysis, a hybrid standard combining elements of each. These cases reveal something of the changing currents in US antitrust law. When he was responsible for antitrust matters at the Department of Justice, William Baxter, an enthusiast of the Chicago School, went so far as to say that he would favour abolishing the term 'per se' from US antitrust law altogether.

Within the context of US antitrust, the move towards rule-of-reason analysis and away from per se illegality has much to commend it. Per se rules exclude economic analysis. Indeed, they are intended to do so, in order to simplify the task of the court. As understanding of the economics of competition improves, among lawyers as well as economists, it is appropriate that the courts should find some way to give expression to this fact. In the United States, given the structure of the legislation, the simple words 'restraint of trade' in section 1 of the Sherman Act have to bear most of the intellectual strain of the subject. The drafting of Article 85 does not contain the same tension; because of its shape, it is not necessary for the words 'restriction of competition' to carry the same weight as the similar words in the Sherman Act. This is not to deny the importance and desirability of economic analysis. What we wish to question is whether economic analysis as expansive as that undertaken by the US courts under the rule of reason should take place under Article 85(1): it is arguable that the existence of Article 85(3) suggests that more complex cases are best dealt with under the exemption procedure. US law has no provision which matches Article 85(3); the only expression enabling the merits of the agreement to be evaluated is found in the 'restraint of trade' formula. In EEC law, even if an agreement is within Article 85(1), it is possible to go on and explore it in greater detail under Article 85(3).

B. THE US ANTITRUST DEBATE

It would have been hard enough for the courts to decide what was meant by a restraint of trade if there existed a single conception of the function of competition, or (which is not necessarily the same thing) of competition law. The reality of the matter is different. There are different views on the function of competition, and opinions change about competition just as they do about politics. There have by now been several generations of US antitrust law and there is a tendency for one generation of antitrust theoreticians to try to show that the previous one misconstrued what Congress intended when passing the Sherman Act.[31] The Chicago writers

[29] However the Supreme Court was split 5:4 on this issue; and the majority in favour of the retention of per se illegality for tie-ins went out of its way not to apply this standard in the case before it.

[30] 1980–1 Trade Cases 63,698.

[31] See Herbert Hovenkamp, 'Antitrust Policy after Chicago' 84 *Michigan Law Review (Mich L Rev)* 213 (1984–5).

have been immensely influential in recent years.[32] Robert Bork is perhaps the best known of the Chicago School, although many of its basic features are attributable to Aaron Director's work in the 1950s. Many other influential writers such as Telser,[33] Bowman[34] and Easterbrook[35] have been associated with it. The claim of the Chicago School is that the sole function of competition law should be the maximisation of economic efficiency; Congress never intended that any other issues should be relevant. The antitrust authorities should only intervene when firms act in a way which suppresses output with the consequence that price rises. Intervention is only rarely called for, as generally the market itself will discipline monopolists and the process of competition will drive out inefficient producers. Antitrust enforcement is itself wasteful of resources and frequently inefficient. The economic model of the Chicago School reveals that many practices such as tie-ins, resale price maintenance and 'predatory' pricing, habitually thought to be anti-competitive, have no adverse effect on consumer welfare. Indeed, the tolerance of the Chicago School extends beyond these individual practices: at one point in his book, Bork declares that 'every vertical restraint should be legal'.[36] This economic model reveals 'truths' about particular types of economic behaviour and is supposedly neutral in terms of values: antitrust problems, viewed through the lens of price theory alone, are more easily solved than when other issues of a socio-political nature are brought into the equation. Therefore, it is wrong to apply competition law with 'uncritical sentimentality', so as to protect the 'small guy' against powerful competitors or to ensure a reasonable dispersal of power throughout the community; social and political criteria should be left out of the account before the relentless logic of the economic theory.

This is a powerful brew of theories, and there is no doubt that the Chicago School has had a significant effect on US antitrust.[37] The shift away from per se illegality already noted, and the more expansive inquiry conducted under the rule of reason, have both been influenced by the Chicago commentators. A landmark decision was *GTE* v *Sylvania*.[38] Sylvania, a manufacturer of television sets, had seen its market share fall to less than 2 per cent by 1962. A new distribution policy was introduced, which was intended to attract more competitive and aggressive retailers.

[32] See e.g. Robert Bork, 'The Rule of Reason and the Per Se Concept: Price Fixing and Market Division (part 2)' 75 *Yale Law Journal (Yale LJ)* 373 (1966); Richard Posner, 'The Chicago School of Antitrust' 127 *University of Pennsylvania Law Review (U Penn LR)* 925 (1979) and Bork, *The Antitrust Paradox: a Policy at War with itself* (Basic Books 1978).

[33] See e.g. Lester Telser 'Why Should Manufacturers Want Fair Trade?' 3 *Journal of Law and Economy* 86 (1960).

[34] See e.g. Ward Bowman 'Tying Arrangements and the Leverage Problem' 67 *Yale LJ* 19 (1957).

[35] See e.g. Frank Easterbrook, 'The Limits of Antitrust' 63 *Texas Law Review* 1, 24 (1984).

[36] *The Antitrust Paradox* (n32 supra) 297.

[37] See Eleanor Fox, 'The New American Competition Policy—From Anti-trust to Pro-efficiency' 2 *ECLR* 439 (1981).

[38] 433 US 36 (1977).

This was to be achieved, inter alia, by giving each dealer a certain amount of immunity from 'intra-brand competition' (i.e. Sylvania products sold by other retailers). This would act as a spur to investment in, and proper promotion of, these goods. Each dealer was restricted to selling its goods from specified premises (a location clause). By 1965, Sylvania's market share had risen to 5 per cent—an apparent vindication of its new distribution policy. The Supreme Court accepted that a location clause in a distribution agreement should no longer be subjected to a per se rule, but rather should be analysed under the rule of reason. This involved weighing up the agreement in its market context in order to decide on balance whether it had the effect of limiting or enhancing competition. The judgment of the court delivered by Justice Powell went out of its way to discuss the advantages and disadvantages of vertical restraints, citing a wealth of academic literature and specifically overruling an earlier decision of the Court, *US* v *Arnold Schwinn*,[39] which had adopted a highly formalistic approach towards vertical restraints.[40] This undoubtedly was a change of approach by the Court. To the extent that it marked a move away from purely mechanical jurisprudence to a more sophisticated analysis of antitrust matters, in which the influence of economics is properly recognised, it is an important step forward. The increased role of economic analysis in US antitrust is also revealed by the Department of Justice's merger guidelines of 1982 (as revised in 1984)[41] and by its vertical restraints guidelines of 1985.[42] If Article 85(1) were to be read subject to a US-style rule of reason, and if it were to embody the economic ideas of the Chicago School, then EEC competition law would be radically different. However, quite apart from the issue of whether US and EEC competition law are sufficiently similar to merit such an identity of approach, which we shall consider below, we would make three points about the antitrust debate in the US itself.

First, it is not the case that the whole edifice of antitrust law has crumbled under the influence of the Chicago School. Many of the old rules still stand and some have been reaffirmed by the Supreme Court against the tide of Chicago reasoning. Having accepted, in *Sylvania*, that non-price vertical restraints should be subject to the rule of reason, an obvious question was whether the Supreme Court would apply the same type of analysis to vertical price restraints. Even if there are reasons for treating price restraints more suspiciously than non-price restraints, logic would suggest that each should be tested under the rule of reason, rather than that a purely formalistic line should be drawn between the two. In *Monsanto Co* v *Spray-Rite Service Corp*,[43] the Supreme Court had an opportunity to comment on this. The Department of Justice argued in its Amicus Curiae brief that the

39 388 US 365 (1977).

40 A formidable list of critical articles is appended to Justice Powell's judgment, 48.

41 49 Fed Reg 26,283 (1984).

42 48 BNA Antitrust & Trade Reg Rep 193; see also 6 *ECLR* 46 et seq (1985).

43 465 US 752 (1984).

per se standard was no longer appropriate for resale price maintenance. The Supreme Court declined to comment on the issue, since neither of the actual litigants had taken the point; had it been enthusiastic to unleash the full logic of Chicago economics, it could have used this opportunity more creatively.[44]

Secondly, the reasoning of the Chicago School on the function of competition law has increasingly been subjected to criticism. Many commentators do not agree that the sole function of the Sherman Act is (or was ever) the promotion of economic efficiency. Other goals—the dispersal of power, the protection of the small business, the decentralisation of the economy, the preservation of an open market with opportunities for all—are also important.[45] The Sherman Act itself was prompted by complaints from small business people rather than from consumers. In the 1930s, mergers came high on the antitrust agenda at a time when the increasing concentration of wealth and power was viewed with suspicion in a democracy committed to the ideal of equal opportunities for all. This worry culminated eventually in the passing of the Celler-Kefauver Act 1950. Whatever Bork might say, the health and vitality of the 'small guy' is an important part of the American dream.

Thirdly, the economic analysis of the Chicago School has been criticised, in particular on the grounds that it relies on a static economic model which fails to take into account strategic behaviour in the real world, and that it ignores important short-term market phenomena.[46] The problem with excessive reliance on economic theory is that there tend to be many simplifying assumptions in economics which fail to reflect what truly happens in the market place.[47] Also, it is difficult to balance the social costs of economic behaviour against the 'pure' issue of economic efficiency. In the end, however, it is not the sophistication of the economics or the reading of history that lead to these disputes: 'the main gap between Chicago and its critics is social and political philosophy'.[48]

What we hope emerges from this discussion is that competition policy does not exist in a vacuum; it is not timeless or free from the political and social environment in which it is developed and where it produces its effects. Competition policy cannot be value-free. It is as much a tool of economic and political policy as manipulating the exchange rate or chang-

[44] See also the *Jefferson Hospital* case, n 28 supra.

[45] See for example Robert Pitofsky, 'The Political Content of Antitrust' 127 *U Penn LR* 1051 (1979); Louis Schwarz, '"Justice" and Other Non-economic goals of Antitrust' ibid 1076; Eleanor Fox, 'The Modernization of Antitrust: a New Equilibrium' 66 *Cornell L Rev* 1140 (1981); Irwin Stelzer 'Economic Defences in Antitrust Litigation' 4 *ECLR* 253 (1983).

[46] See for example Oliver Williamson, 'Predatory Pricing: A Strategic and Welfare Analysis' 87 *Yale LJ* 284 (1977); F. M. Scherer, 'The Economics of Vertical Restraints' 52 *Antitrust Journal* 687 (1983); William Comanor, 'Vertical Price-fixing, Vertical Market Restrictions and the New Antitrust Policy' 98 *Harvard L Rev* 983 (1985).

[47] See Eleanor Fox, 'The Politics of Law and Economics' 61 *New York Univ L Rev* 554 at 581–5 (1986).

[48] Eleanor Fox, 'Consumer Beware Chicago' 84 *Mich L Rev* 1714 (1984–5).

ing regional policy. Even if the Chicago view in its most purified form were to come to dominate the world of antitrust law in the US, this would not mean that at last the essence of the Sherman Act had been discovered. It would mean instead that in the United States of the 1980s, anxious about its economic role in a rapidly changing world and disillusioned with the regulatory years of the post-war era, a particular confluence of political and economic forces had produced a particular brand of antitrust. 'If one hundred years of federal antitrust policy have taught us anything, it is that antitrust is both political and cyclical'.[49] There will always be shifting standards in antitrust law, as there will be in politics and economics. What we must consider is whether the similarities between the United States and the European Community—economically, politically and socially—are so great that it would be appropriate to adopt US reasoning and, in particular, the type of analysis advocated by the Chicago School, when interpreting Article 85(1) of the Rome Treaty. It can be dangerous to import legal standards from a system whose social and political context is substantially different.[50]

III. Comparison of antitrust law in the US and EEC

There are six matters which we wish to explore.[51]

A. THE FUNCTION OF COMPETITION

We have already mentioned the context in which the Sherman Act was passed and the way that antitrust law in the US has had to evolve to meet the requirements of any particular time. In the case of the EEC, the most important point is that the competition rules must be read in the context of the Treaty as a whole. Teleological interpretation of the Treaty has resulted in some remarkable case-law in the Court of Justice, not least in the area of competition law. The Preamble of the Treaty includes a reference to the need for 'balanced trade and fair competition'. This term in itself is value-laden. The aims of the Treaty are expressed in Article 2: the promotion of a harmonious development of economic activities, a continuous and balanced expansion, an increase in stability, an accelerated raising of the standard of living and closer relations between the States belonging to the Community. These goals are to be achieved through the establishment of a common market and the approximation of the economic policies of Member States. Article 3(f) provides that the Community shall include in its activities 'the institution of a system ensuring that competition in the common market is not distorted'. These early provisions of the Treaty are pregnant with meaning, and provide a backdrop against which the com-

[49] Hovenkamp, op cit 213.
[50] See Otto Kahn-Freund, 'On Uses and Abuses of Comparative Law' 37 *Mod L Rev* 1 (1974).
[51] See Joan Bodoff, 'Competition Policies of the US and EEC: an Overview' 5 *ECLR* 51 (1984).

petition rules have been, and will continue to be, developed.[52] On a teleological reading, it would be hard to conclude that the competition rules should solely be applied in order to maximise economic efficiency in a narrow, technical, sense.

In practice, the EEC competition rules have been applied for a variety of purposes—to ensure that markets are kept reasonably open, to protect the consumer, to deal with industries in decline, to protect the process of competition itself and, above all, to assist in the process of integrating the common market. The Commissioner currently responsible for competition has spoken of the need to adopt a positive competition policy, not determined in isolation but integrated with the economic, industrial and social policy of the Community.[53] What other functions Articles 85 and 86 might fulfil remains to be seen. Sometimes the issue of unemployment has arisen in competition cases,[54] and the Commission has referred to it in its Annual Reports.[55] It is not obvious at first that this is an issue that can be considered under Article 85. However, it might be possible to argue that the idea of 'economic progress' in Article 85(3) could be interpreted subject to the aim expressed in Article 2 of promoting an 'accelerated raising of the standard of living'. Regional policy is also an issue of concern to the Commission. We do not mean to suggest that 'anything goes' when it comes to applying competition law; however, it is important to emphasise that the Treaty itself envisages an expansive role for the competition rules, and that there is potential for growth in several directions. The Commission will want to hold on to the powers it has under Article 85(3) in order that it can participate fully in the development of competition policy.[56]

B. MARKET INTEGRATION

Following on from the last point, it is particularly important in the case of the EEC to bear in mind that the Treaty states in Article 2 that the means of achieving its aims include the establishment of a common market. When the Sherman Act was passed in 1890, the United States already had an integrated market.[57] The position in Europe is quite different. After thirty years of the EEC, there is still not a truly common market, and one object of the Single European Act 1986 is to make it more of a reality. The goal for the completion of the internal market is now 1992, although that looks increasingly over-optimistic. It is almost impossible to overstate the importance that is accorded to integration of the market. It has been said,[58] with

[52] See Case 6/72 *Europemballage & Continental Can Co* v *Commission* [1972] ECR 157 and Cases 6–7/73 *ICI and Commercial Solvents* v *Commission* [1974] ECR 223.

[53] See e.g. Peter Sutherland, 'Towards a Positive Competition Policy' 6 *ECLR* 283 (1985).

[54] See e.g. Case 26/76 *Metro SB-Grossmarkte GmbH and Co KG* v *Commission* [1977] ECR 1875, para 43.

[55] See e.g. 14th Annual Report, 12.

[56] See Stephen Hornsby, 'Competition Policy in the 1980's: More Policy Less Competition' 12 *EL Rev* 79 (1987).

[57] The US Constitution itself forbids taxes or duties on trade between states in Art 1.

[58] See Korah, 'EEC Competition Policy—Legal Form or Economic Efficiency' 39 *CLP* 85, 91 (1986).

some justification, that it has been elevated to a goal in itself rather than being the means to an end, as Article 2 clearly states.

One of the reasons that competition law has such a large part to play in the integration of the market is that agreements between undertakings can be very effective in partitioning the market. There are many different ways in which this can occur. Horizontal agreements may involve market-sharing on national lines; a dominant firm may try to prevent inter-state trade in its products; distribution agreements can isolate national markets from one another in numerous ways; agreements involving intellectual property rights are particularly likely to have a geographical dimension, for the rights themselves emanate from purely national systems of law. The integration of the market is promoted through the application of other parts of the Treaty, particularly the provisions on the free movement of goods and services, but the Commission uses the competition rules as an important part of its strategy.

It is necessary to consider what implications this has in institutional and procedural terms. If the sole function of competition law were to be the promotion of economic efficiency, it might be possible to leave the institutions of individual Member States to deal with enforcement, although even this is questionable: different Member States have widely varying experiences of competition law, so that one might expect uneven treatment of economic behaviour from one Member State to another.[59] However, EEC law is not solely concerned with economic efficiency, which makes the issue of enforcement more complex. A domestic court is not in a good position, when dealing with Articles 85 and 86, to weigh up different policy considerations, and it is hard to see how the Community interest of market integration would be expressed in domestic litigation. There is no guarantee that all courts throughout the Community would be prepared to give the same weight to the need to bring about an integrated market. It might be possible for the Commission to be represented in some sort of *amicus curiae* role to assist the domestic court, but different courts might give different weight to its views.

Involvement in domestic litigation would lead back to the problem that the Commission is under-resourced: appearances in the courts of twelve Member States could only exacerbate this. It would also require a careful consideration of the procedural law of Member States to ensure that rules of court allowed for appropriate representation.[60] The most appropriate guardian of the Community interest would appear at this stage to be the Commission, acting under the reviewing eye of the Court of Justice. Certainly this is not an issue that could be left to the 'magic' of the market in which the Chicago economists place so much faith. It may be the case that

[59] See generally Ernst Steindorff, 'Common Market Antitrust Law in Civil Proceedings before National Courts and Arbitrators' *Fordham Corporate Law Institute* (1985) 409.

[60] It is not entirely clear what the Commission's position was in *Hasselblad GB Ltd* v *Orbinson* [1984] 3 CMLR 679 (CA).

the market knows best what level a price should be or whether a firm is being so badly managed that it is ripe for a take-over, although this is contentious,[61] but it cannot give expression to the ideal of a common market. That cannot be measured using pricing theory. Furthermore, it would be difficult for the European Court of Justice to protect the Community interest simply in Article 177 references from national courts. This is particularly true since, except in the case of a final court, reference to the European Court of Justice is not obligatory; one need look no further than the enforcement of EEC competition rules in the UK courts to see that the lower courts can go somewhat awry in this area.[62] One of the most effective ways in which the Commission can keep control is through the medium of Article 85(3).

A further complication is the periodic enlargement of the Community. Spain and Portugal are relative newcomers; Norway may join the Community in the near future; and there is at least a possibility of further accessions. This being the case, one can expect that the issue of market integration will continue to be a dominant feature in competition law decisions, and that the Commission will remain the most significant watchdog. A related point is that there are particular markets, such as banking and insurance, where the competition rules are applied as one part of the overall strategy of breaking down national barriers to trade.[63]

The pursuit of single-market integration does tend to produce some hard cases, where the injustice to an individual undertaking is the price paid for furthering the Community's goals. The question then is whether there is a convincing way of trading one policy off against the other, or whether this is a clash of competing goals that can only be resolved by unashamedly subordinating one issue to the other.

One famous example of the conundrum is the *Distillers* affair. The company's dual pricing system, underpinned by export disincentives, was condemned by the Commission,[64] despite the convincing arguments of commercial necessity put forward by the company. The Commission could not tolerate such a strategy of dividing markets, whatever the reasons. Because of the procedural complications of the case, the Court of Justice never gave a judgment on the merits[65] and one can only surmise whether it would have been more sympathetic to Distillers' predicament. In the event, Distillers reacted by withdrawing certain brands from different markets, and so the consumer was deprived of choice while inter-State trade and

[61] See e.g. Brian Chiplin and Mike Wright, *The Logic of Mergers* (Hobart Paper 107, 1987).

[62] See e.g. *Argyll* v *Distillers* [1986] 1 CMLR 764 (Outer House, Court of Sessions) and *Cutsforth* v *Mansfield Inns Ltd* [1986] 1 CMLR 1.

[63] On insurance, there have been important recent cases both under Art 169 (Cases 220 and 252/83 and 205 and 206/84 *Commission* v *Germany etc* [1987] 2 CMLR 69) and under Article 85 (Case 45/85 *Verband der Sachversicherer eV* v *Commission)* (not yet reported).

[64] [1978] 1 CMLR 400.

[65] Case 30/78 *Distillers* v *Commission* [1980] ECR 2229.

competition were advanced not one jot.[66] After the hearing in the Court of Justice, Distillers attempted to reach an accommodation with the Commission. In the end, however, the Commission stuck to its original position, that it could not allow division of markets on national lines.[67] This outcome may upset many commentators, but it cannot be described as 'wrong' in a legal or economic sense. Instead it means that the Commission has decided, in a hard case, that the broader issue of market integration should prevail over the particular predicament of Distillers.

C. INSTITUTIONS

There is a considerable difference in the political systems of the United States and the European Community. As far as competition policy is concerned, it has been very much left to the courts in the US to breathe life into and apply the antitrust rules. However, in the EEC, it was decided at an early stage that the central role should be performed by the Commission. Council Regulation 17/62 gave effect to this decision. The other important body has, of course, been the Court of Justice and, in this area as in many others, it has been responsible for major developments. However, it is not an appropriate body to deal with the mass of complexities involved in competition issues, although it can give important leads, as, for example, in *Pronuptia*[68] and *Nutricia*.[69] There needs to be a body such as the Commission to convert these leads into workable and sufficiently detailed rules. One effect of rule-of-reason analysis would be that much more responsibility would be given to national courts, and there would be fewer cases in which Article 85(3) would have to be invoked. Whether or not national courts could or should be given this added responsibility has been discussed above.

D. TIME—THE MATURITY OF THE SYSTEMS

The EEC system of competition law is not yet mature. It has developed remarkably quickly in many ways, and in recent years, particularly since Peter Sutherland became the Commissioner responsible for competition, the pace of change has accelerated. But the position has not yet been reached, as Forrester and Norall have suggested,[70] at which it would be reasonable to hand over more analysis to the national courts under Article 85(1). The central involvement of the Commission, which is promoted by its current application of Article 85, will remain important for some time. Three points in particular should be made.

[66] See Korah, '"Goodbye Red Label": Condemnation of Dual Pricing by Distillers' 3 *EL Rev* 62 (1978) and Charles Baden Fuller, 'Economic Issues Relating to Property Rights in Trade Marks: Export Bans, Differential Pricing, Restrictions on Resale and Repackaging' 6 *EL Rev* 162 (1981). Red Label is now available again in the UK.

[67] (EC) *Bull* 9/1987 pt 2.1.67.

[68] Case 161/84 *Pronuptia de Paris* v *Schillgalis* [1986] 1 CMLR 414.

[69] Case 42/84 *Remia BV & Verenidge Bedrijven Nutricia* v *Commission* [1987] 1 CMLR 1.

[70] Op cit n 1.

First, the competition law system would not have developed in the way it has without the Commission's decisive involvement. The Commission has developed its policy on such matters as franchise agreements, specialisation and research and development by looking at the agreements notified to it.[71] It is precisely because of the incentive to notify produced by the orthodox analysis under Article 85(1) that the Commission has gained the know-how to be able to publish its block exemptions. The standard pattern is that the Commission grants a few individual exemptions in respect of a particular type of agreement, then distils the principles from them into a draft block exemption. This is as true of the two drafts now being circulated (on know-how and franchising[72]) as it was of the earlier block exemptions.

The second point is that there are important matters that have yet to be sorted out. It is possible that in due course the Commission will want to look into the possibility of producing further block exemptions, for example on trade mark and copyright licences. It is still hoping to produce guidelines on the applicability of Article 85 to joint ventures, although this is a complex issue because of one of the other 'immature' aspects of EEC competition law, merger control.[73] The Commission is also directing its attention to parts of the economy which, historically, have enjoyed a kind of de facto immunity from the competition rules.[74]

The third point, already made, is that continuing accessions to the Community retard the process of maturation.

E. PROCEDURE AND ENFORCEMENT

There are many differences between the US and EEC approaches to enforcement. The Commission is at the heart of the system for reasons already referred to. A particular point is the one about notification. To some commentators it is this, combined with the nullity of contract, which is the most irksome aspect of EEC competition law. There is an intimate relationship between the substance of the competition rules and the procedural framework within which they are operated, and much of the criticism of EEC law is really about procedure. However, while considerable attention has been given to the negative aspects of the Commission's procedures, little has been said on the other side of the equation.

The Commission is itself acutely aware of the procedural problems that firms experience in competition law matters. It is a trite but important point that many of these problems would at least recede if the resources of DG IV were to be increased. It is not surprising that it has had some problems in devising and implementing a competition policy for twelve such hetero-

[71] In the case of franchise agreements, it also had the benefit of the Court of Justice's judgment in *Pronuptia* (n 68 supra).

[72] The first draft of the franchising block exemption in the Official Journal (OJ 1987 C229/3) followed three Commission decisions: *Pronuptia* OJ 1987 L13/39, *Yves Rocher* OJ 1987 L8/49, and *Computerland* OJ 1987 L222/12.

[73] See the 16th Annual Report on Competition Policy pts 38 and 39.

[74] See for example the recent spate of decisions on the insurance, banking and commodities markets.

geneous States as make up the Community. However, it has taken various steps in recent years in order to try to accelerate the decision-making process and to introduce more certainty into the system. It is important to bear in mind that the Commission is subject to the general principles of administrative law when reaching formal decisions and that this means that it must give all interested parties—not just the parties to a particular agreement—a chance to be heard. Speedy decisions and the requirements of procedural fairness are not easily compatible.

The use of comfort letters and the problems associated with them have already been referred to. However, the reality of the matter is that many firms are willing to accept a comfort letter as a way of disposing of their case. The Commission's decision not to publish notices prior to a comfort letter, as it suggested it would do in 1983, is unfortunate; it is desirable that decision-making, whether of a formal or informal kind, should be as public as possible, if not from the perspective of the actual parties to an agreement, at any rate in the public interest.[75] It is particularly regrettable that the Commission seems to have decided not to make public the fact that it has changed its policy in this respect.

A further important change has been the introduction into three of the block exemptions[76] of an opposition procedure. Again this procedure does have its legal difficulties,[77] but there are signs already that it is being used, and there must be a reasonable likelihood that it will be more so in the future.[78] Form A/B invites those notifying agreements to consider whether the agreement in question might qualify for the opposition procedure. It may transpire that the opposition procedure will be used more or less according to the block exemption in question.[79]

The Commission is in the process of increasing the numbers of block exemptions. There should shortly be new ones on franchising and know-how licensing, although early comment has suggested that the latter may not be of much assistance, at least to industry in the UK.[80]

One further important change has been the internal reorganisation of DG IV, so that specialist teams in particular sectors now see a case through from beginning to end. This should lead to quicker decisions than before. It is certainly the case that, in the last couple of years, the output of DG IV has increased.[81]

[75] See Ivo van Bael, 'The Antitrust Settlement Practice of the EEC Commission' 23 *CML Rev* 61 (1986).

[76] Regulation 2349/84 on patent licensing, Reg 417/85 on specialisation agreements and Reg 418/85 on research and development agreements; the drafts on franchising and know-how licensing also provide for an opposition procedure.

[77] See Denis Waelbroeck, 'New Forms of Settlement of Antitrust Cases' 11 *ELR* 268 (1986) 272 et seq.

[78] According to the Commission's 16th Annual Report, in 1986 one notification invoking the opposition procedure was received under Regulation 417/85, two under 418/85 and thirty-two under 2349/84.

[79] See previous footnote.

[80] See Korah, 'Commission's Draft for a Regulation Exempting Knowhow Licensing' 8 *Business Law Rev* 198 (1987).

[81] We do not mean by this that the work of DG IV should be measured by so crude a yardstick as the number of decisions it reaches in a year.

It is unfortunate, in the light of the comments just made, that the backlog of cases in the last few years has actually increased. From 1985 to 1986 it increased by 209; 153 of the new notifications came from Spain and Portugal, but the underlying trend is also up. As the Commission remarks, this problem will continue 'given the numbers of staff as compared with the volume of work'.[82]

The procedures involved in competition law in the United States are very different, not least because of the importance there of enforcement through private law actions. But also, quite apart from disparities in the substantive law and in the political and economic circumstances of the United States and the European Community, it is an important point that in the US there is no body which has a role quite like that of the European Commission. The Federal Trade Commission and the Department of Justice have important roles in US antitrust law, but they are not involved in the process of achieving a common market of twelve independent States with widely varying cultures, economies, languages and legal systems. To the European Commission, the competition rules are a part, but only a part, of the various powers available to it to integrate the market in order to advance the objectives of the Treaty.

A different point on procedure is that the Commission has more power under Articles 85 and 86 than it does under other parts of the Treaty. Not surprisingly, this means that it is unenthusiastic about adopting a type of analysis under Article 85(1) which would weaken its influence in competition matters. As pointed out above, the operation of Articles 85 and 86 was delegated by the Council to the Commission at a very early stage; as a result of this, the Commission has both formulated and enforced competition policy, largely independently of the Council and the Member States.[83] Of course, it is subject to political pressures and considerations and to review by the Court of Justice. However, its position is very different in competition matters from the situation in relation to the free movement of goods, for example. In that area, the Commission can cajole national governments, make proposals as to how restrictions on imports and exports might be eliminated and, where necessary, use Article 169 proceedings; however, it is dependent upon the Court of Justice, the Council of Ministers and Member States for real progress. Under the competition rules, it has important powers of its own.

In the United States, enforcement is quite different. Private actions are numerous and are encouraged by a system in which a successful plaintiff is awarded treble damages and a successful attorney takes a considerable contingency fee. There is no notification system comparable with that in the Community. However, it is illuminating to ask whether the system in the

[82] 16th Annual Report pt 44.

[83] The Advisory Committee on Monopolies and Restrictive Practices is a forum in which Member States may express their opinions, but its position is relatively remote.

United States produces more certainty than is afforded by EEC law, since certainty is one of the most important considerations for businessmen. Rule-of-reason analysis is not simple: the weighing of pro- and anti-competitive effects and the balancing of inter- and intra-brand restrictions of competition that US courts are prepared to engage in is complex. It will be suggested below that EEC law may be more certain in its operation than US law.

F. THE UNIQUENESS OF THE EEC

Above all, it is necessary to bear in mind the highly unusual nature of the Community. It is a supra-national organisation but not yet a federation, and it is engaged in a unique experiment in economic, and even political, integration between sovereign States. Transplanting the devices which have been employed to control business behaviour in a mature federal State of a particular ideological complexion into this different context is not necessarily useful.

IV. EEC law, with particular reference to recent judgments and decisions

We should now turn to the judgments of the Court of Justice and the decisions of the Commission in order to see to what extent rule-of-reason analysis is used in interpreting Article 85(1). In particular, we shall consider whether there has been any discernible shift in this direction in recent years.

A. EARLY CASE-LAW OF THE COURT OF JUSTICE

In *La Technique Minière* v *Maschinenbau Ulm GmbH*,[84] the Court of Justice, in one of its earliest judgments on the competition rules, appeared to apply the rule of reason to Article 85(1). This was a reference under Article 177 from the Court of Appeal in Paris. The Court of Justice was asked to consider the compatibility with Article 85(1) of exclusive sales rights granted by a German producer of leveller machines to a French dealer. The Commission argued that any exclusive right infringed Article 85(1) and could only be permitted, if at all, under Article 85(3). The Court of Justice declined to accept such a mechanical standard. Rather, it emphasised the importance of undertaking a careful analysis of the market before deciding that Article 85(1) applied:

> [A]n agreement whereby a producer entrusts the sale of his products in a given area to a sole distributor cannot automatically fall under the prohibition in Article 85(1). But such an agreement may contain the elements set out in that provision by reason of a particular factual situation or of the severity of the clauses protecting the exclusive dealership.[85]

[84] Case 56/65 [1966] ECR 235.
[85] Ibid 248.

The Court then proceeded to say that in any given case it was necessary to consider the economic context within which the agreement would operate: the nature of the products, the position of the parties on the market, the clauses in the contract and so on. This judgment therefore rejects a mechanical or per se approach to deciding whether there is a restriction of competition and is suggestive of rule-of-reason analysis. One particularly important statement of the Court was as follows:

In particular it may be doubted whether there is an interference with competition if the said agreement seems really necessary for the penetration of a new area by an undertaking.[86]

It is significant, however, that the contract referred to the Court in *LTM* contained an obligation not to appoint anyone else in the dealer's area and an exclusive purchase term. It did *not* attempt to confer absolute territorial protection on the dealer,[87] and the Court did not comment on the exclusive purchasing term. In the operative part of the judgment, the Court, while repeating that contracts granting an exclusive right of sale are not necessarily incompatible with Article 85(1), said that special attention should be given to whether the agreement was capable of partitioning the market in certain products between Member States.[88]

Just a fortnight after its judgment in *LTM* came the Court's decision in *Consten and Grundig* v *Commission*.[89] Grundig of Germany had given Consten an exclusive right to sell its goods in France. The agreement authorised Consten to use the Grundig name and emblem in France and Consten became the registered owner in France of the Grundig trade mark 'Gint'. The object of all this was to give Consten complete territorial protection against parallel imports of Grundig products, which, as Grundig's prices were much higher in France than in Germany, were an attractive proposition to third parties. As tariff barriers were coming down, here were private undertakings erecting new barriers to inter-State trade. The Commission held that the agreement came within Article 85(1) and that it was impossible to grant an exemption under Article 85(3). On a rule-of-reason analysis, one could say that the agreement only infringed Article 85(1) if, judged in its economic context, it was likely to diminish rather than increase competition. If Consten would not have entered the market at all but for the territorial protection, it could be said that the agreement did not restrict competition in Grundig products. In fact, it was likely to stimulate competition between Grundig and other brands, and lead to an increase in trade between Member States because of the greater promotion of Grundig products in France. On the other hand, this would be to sanction an agreement which sealed off one national market from another. Here we

86 Ibid 250.

87 At least in legal terms: it might of course be that the value of the goods in relation to transport costs etc would be so low as to prevent parallel importing on economic grounds.

88 [1966] ECR 235, 251.

89 Cases 56 & 58/64 [1966] ECR 299.

have a crisis in EEC competition law: which policy objective should take priority? The answer was, of course, the integration of the market. Thus the Court said:

> Since the agreement thus aims at isolating the French market for Grundig products and maintaining artificially for products of a very well-known brand separate national markets within the Community, it is therefore such as to distort competition within the Common Market.[90]

So, where an agreement confers absolute territorial protection on the dealer, it comes within Article 85(1) *notwithstanding the economic circumstances*. If there is a rule of reason in EEC law, it is of limited application, for it is displaced where an agreement has the effect of retarding the integration of the common market; and anything to be found in *LTM* must be read subject to *Consten and Grundig*. Many judgments since have reflected the Court's commitment to market integration.[91]

It was also argued in *Consten and Grundig* that the Commission should have balanced the restrictions of intra-brand competition against the enhancement of inter-brand competition when deciding whether there was an infringement of Article 85(1). The Court pronounced that:

> Although competition between producers is generally more noticeable than that between distributors of the same make, it does not thereby follow that an agreement tending to restrict the latter kind of competition should escape the prohibition of Article 85(1) merely because it might increase the former.[92]

This again seems to eschew the type of rule-of-reason analysis undertaken by US courts today, which involves balancing the restrictive and the pro-competitive aspects of an agreement.

B. LATER CASES OF THE COURT OF JUSTICE

As already mentioned, market integration continues to be an important issue in the Court's case-law. However, the important question for our purposes is whether recent case-law has indicated that the seed sown in *LTM*, albeit subject to the *Consten and Grundig* principle, has led to the growth of the rule of reason. Many decisions of the Commission criticised by commentators for mechanically applying Article 85(1) to agreements which do not in reality distort competition are inherently unlikely to be considered by the Court of Justice because of their subject-matter. The parties to a research and development agreement, having received a nod of approval from the Commission in the form of a comfort letter or a formal decision, are unlikely to take the matter to the Court of Justice in order to satisfy their scruples as to the most appropriate form of analysis under Article 85.

[90] Ibid 343.

[91] See e.g. Case 28/77 *Tepea BV* v *Commission* [1978] ECR 1391 and the severe penalties imposed in Cases 100–103/80 etc *MDA SA* v *Commission* (Pioneer) [1983] ECR 1825.

[92] [1966] ECR 299, 342.

The Court has, however, had opportunities to consider the compatibility with Article 85(1) of other types of agreement such as licensing arrangements, franchises and selective distribution networks. In *Metro SB-Grossmarkte* v *Commission*,[93] it confirmed the Commission's view that so-called 'qualitative' conditions of selective distribution networks may in some cases fall outside Article 85(1) because competition is not distorted by a condition that goods may only be sold at a certain standard of premises, as long as anyone with premises meeting those standards can sell the goods if they wish. This shows that price competition is not the only form of competition recognised by the authorities—competition may manifest itself in various ways, and is not necessarily distorted by allowing the development of distribution channels with different characteristics and priorities. But this is not the same as rule-of-reason analysis in the American sense; rather, this is a separate branch of EEC competition law, which has been carefully developed by the Court of Justice and Commission in a series of cases and decisions.[94] The position on selective distribution systems had become relatively clear until the judgment in *Metro 2*[95] which, as we shall suggest below, seems to create worrying uncertainty precisely by introducing more economic analysis into the application of Article 85(1).

It was *Maize Seeds*[96] in 1982 that was celebrated in some quarters as heralding a new era of rule-of-reason analysis in Community law. Since then, there have been a number of important judgments in which arguably the same trend can be discerned—*Coditel 2*,[97] *Pronuptia*,[98] *Nutricia*[99] and the second *Metro* judgment.[100]

Of the cases before the Court of Justice, it is significant that two, *Maize Seeds* and *Coditel 2*, concerned intellectual property rights.[101] The continuing existence in the Community of intellectual property rights which operate on a national basis is difficult to reconcile with the integration of the market. The Court has developed a jurisprudence based on the dichotomy between the existence and the exercise, the specific object and the essential function of such rights.[102] The licensing of such rights, necessarily involving an agreement between undertakings, has been the province of the Commission which, in the face of continual criticism, invariably held that any licence of intellectual property containing elements of exclusivity infringed Article 85(1). Licensing is peculiarly suited to rule-of-reason analysis: the

93 Case 26/76 [1977] ECR 1875.

94 See *Green*, op cit 518–26; Richard Whish, *Competition Law* (Butterworths 1985) 443–8.

95 Case 75/84 *Metro-SB-Grossmarkte GmbH* v *Commission* [1987] 1 CMLR 118.

96 Case 258/78 *Nungesser KG (LC) and Kurt Eisele* v *Commission* [1982] ECR 2015.

97 Case 262/81 *Coditel SA* v *Ciné Vog Films SA No. 2* [1982] ECR 3381.

98 Case 161/84 *Pronuptia de Paris* v *Schillgallis* [1986] 1 CMLR 414.

99 Case 42/84 *Remia BV & Verenidge Bedrijven Nutricia* v *Commission* [1987] 1 CMLR 1.

100 See n 95.

101 *Pronuptia* did as well, but in the context of a distribution franchise.

102 See case 78/70 *Deutsche Grammophon Gesellschaft mbH* v *Metro-SB-Grossmarkte and Co* [1971] ECR 487; Case 15/74 *Centrafarm BV* v *Sterling BV* [1974] ECR 1147; Case 16/74 *Centrafarm BV* v *Winthrop BV* [1974] ECR 1183 and Case 102/77 *Hoffman-La Roche* v *Centrafarm* [1978] ECR 1139.

licensor of a patent, for example, need not grant a licence at all; without his consent no one else can produce the patented products or use the patented process; how, then, can conditions inserted in the licence distort competition, when without the licence there would be no competition at all? The Commission, however, always refused to accede to this reasoning, or to accept the argument that if a licensee will not tool up without exclusivity, that exclusivity cannot distort competition. Instead, it held that exclusive licences were caught, but was then generous with exemptions under Article 85(3). In *Maize Seeds*, the Court gave a judgment which at least partially checked this formalistic approach. It held that an open exclusive licence of plant breeders' rights, whereby the licensor undertakes not to grant other licences in respect of the same territory and not to compete there himself with the licensee, did not necessarily fall within Article 85(1). It would not do so if, as here, the territorial exclusivity was necessary to enable the licensee to enter a difficult market or where new technology was being disseminated. This pronouncement has much in common with the earlier judgment in *LTM*; there would be little reason in logic to limit the reasoning to plant breeders' rights. Indeed, the Commission, while unenthusiastic about this method of analysis, conceded in the block exemption on patent licensing that the reasoning in *Maize Seeds* was equally applicable to patents. However, the Court also held that, to the extent that the licence conferred absolute territorial protection on the licensee, it fell within Article 85(1) and could not be granted an exemption.

Two points need to be made about *Maize Seeds*. First, if Article 85(1) was really read subject to the US-type rule of reason, absolute territorial protection would not be automatically caught by Article 85(1): it would all depend on the market circumstances. In some cases, the 'anti-competitive' effect of absolute exclusivity might be more than offset by the pro-competitive effect of the agreement at the level of inter-brand competition. The Court of Justice, however, refused to adopt such an analysis of the licences. Secondly, to the extent that in *Maize Seeds* (as in *LTM*) the Court held that in some cases open exclusive licences (or dealerships) might not come within Article 85(1) at all, who really benefits from this analysis? Even if these cases are symptomatic of partial rule-of-reason analysis under Article 85(1), it is an approach which gives little certainty to businessmen. One can identify with some certainty an attempt to confer absolute territorial protection, and the legal consequences of this. However it is altogether more difficult to decide when the newness of the technology or the problems of penetrating a new market are so pronounced as to render Article 85(1) inapplicable. Furthermore, there can be no guarantee that the parties' own appreciation of these matters will match that of the Commission or the Court of Justice. It is clear from Recital 11 of Regulation 2349/84 that the Commission intends to apply the *Maize Seeds* doctrine narrowly. This was also shown in *Velcro/Aplix*[103] where the condemned

[103] OJ 1985 L 233/22.

licences did not, according to the Commission, involve new technology so as to immunise them from Article 85(1). Even if the Commission were to be more indulgent than this, the problem would remain of deciding whether any *particular* case was within the spirit of the 'partial rule of reason'. It might be possible to say, for example, that, after *Maize Seeds*, a certain percentage of agreements formerly caught by Article 85(1) (but which quite possibly benefited from block exemption under Regulation 2349/84) no longer are caught by the competition rules at all. But would it be possible to state with any conviction whether any *particular* agreement fell within this fortunate class? With such subjective judgments to be made, lawyers may still have to advise their clients to notify the licence or take the easier route and comply with the terms of the block exemption. Even if a patent licence is outside Article 85(1) under the *Maize Seeds* doctrine in its early days (i.e. while the technology is new and the risk of production great), Article 85(1) would begin to bite later on when this was no longer the case. The very success of the licensing arrangement could undermine the rationale that provided the immunity from Article 85(1) in the first place. At that point, the issue of exemption under Article 85(3) would arise. This being the case, there is much to be said for negotiating the agreement in the context of the provisions of the block exemption anyway, particularly in view of the possibility of invoking the opposition procedure.

Coditel 2 involved a licence of a copyright. The notion of copyright covers different things in different Member States,[104] and the Court of Justice has, significantly, failed to define its 'specific purpose' as it has done with other forms of intellectual property. In *Coditel 1*,[105] it did not apply its usual 'exhaustion of rights' formula to the copyright in a film, but recognised that the essence of the right was the ability to levy a charge each time the film was shown. This performing right type of copyright was recognised as distinct from the copyright in works of which copies are made and then sold to the public, such as books, tapes and records. This same appreciation of the realities of the cinema market was demonstrated in *Coditel 2*. Both Coditel cases concerned Chabrol's film '*Le Boucher*'. The production company which owned the rights in the film gave exclusive distribution rights in Belgium to Ciné Vog. Coditel, a group of three Belgian cable TV companies, picked up a German transmission of the film and retransmitted it in Belgium. In the first case, the issue before the Court related to Articles 59 and 60 of the Treaty, but the second one involved a claim that the distribution licences were incompatible with Article 85. In the light of 'the characteristics of the cinematographic industry', the Court rejected the idea that a licence for the exclusive right to exhibit a film in a territory of a Member State necessarily fell within Article 85(1). However,

104 See the Adolf Dietz Report *Copyright Law in the European Community* (Brussels 1978) and Gillian Davies and Hans Hugo von Rauscher auf Weeg, *Challenges to Copyright and Related Rights in the European Communities* (ESC Publishing 1983).

105 Cases 52 & 62/79 [1981] ECR 833.

it might do so in a particular case 'where there are economic or legal circumstances the effect of which is to restrict film distribution to an appreciable degree or to distort competition on the cinematographic market, regard being had to the specific characteristics of that market'.[106]

This does reflect a kind of rule-of-reason approach: the Court accepted that the licensee had to be given an exclusive right to exhibit, for the distribution of a film is quite different from the distribution of a book or a washing-machine or maize seeds. However, in *Coditel 2* the nature of the product was crucial, and the national territorial restriction, most unusually held not to infringe Article 85(1), has to be seen in the context of a copyright system which still gives rights that are nationally delineated. This being the case, we would suggest that *Coditel 2* is of limited value as a precedent.

The *Nutricia* case[107] concerned agreements entered into on the transfer of two businesses. The agreements contained no-competition clauses whereby the vendor undertook not to compete with the purchasers in the same market for ten years. The geographical market concerned was the Netherlands. The Commission held[108] that these restrictions were caught by Article 85(1) and refused an exemption, holding that four years was a sufficient period. The Court, on the appeal from this decision, adopted what, again, could be described as a rule-of-reason approach, holding that without a no-competition clause the transfer of the undertaking could not be given effect. If the vendor could remain in the market and win back his former customers, then the new undertaking would go out of business. The Court might well have added that no businessman would take such a transfer in the first place on such terms. So long as the duration and scope of these clauses were limited, the Court conceded that they were outside Article 85(1): if they were so limited, then they had the required 'beneficial effect' on competition.

This is an interesting idea: the Court seems to be asking not that the clauses do not have the negative effect of restricting, distorting or preventing competition, but that they have a positively beneficial effect if they are to escape Article 85(1). This seems to resemble the requirements under Article 85(3) rather than Article 85(1). In the event, the Court upheld the Commission's decision that a ten-year clause was not only too long to escape Article 85(1), but could not be exempted. The Court was satisfied that the Commission had appraised the 'complex economic matters' in a proper way and did not itself go into the merits of the case.

It is doubtful that this judgment is indicative of a rule-of-reason approach. Rather, it is consistent with the more limited 'ancillary restraint' approach used in the United States and referred to earlier. We do not think, however, that it is helpful to use the same terminology under Article 85 that is used in analysing the Sherman Act where 'ancillary restraint' (like 'per se

[106] [1983] ECR 3381, 3402.
[107] Case 42/84 *Remia BV Verenigde Bedrijven Nutricia NV* v *Commission* [1987] 1 CMLR 1.
[108] *Nutricia/Zuid Hollandse Conservenfabriek* [1984] 2 CMLR 165.

illegality' and the 'rule of reason') has a particular meaning developed over many years; indeed, we would argue that the importing of the language of US antitrust law, sometimes in a rather indiscriminate way, has done more to obscure than to clarify these difficult issues, and that EEC law requires its own vocabulary, adapted to its own particular needs. We would suggest that *Nutricia* is an example of a few limited situations in which restrictions may be held to fall outside Article 85(1) because of their 'objective necessity':[109] without a restrictive covenant (suitably limited in time, space and subject-matter) the business could not have been sold *at all* and so it was objectively necessary to the agreement. This term was used by Advocate General Lenz in *Nutricia* itself. Furthermore, it would be wrong to suggest that the reasoning in *Nutricia* is particularly novel or symptomatic of some new departure in EEC competition law. It is entirely consistent with the Commission's own decision in *Reuter/BASF*,[110] now more than ten years old. The issue dealt with in these cases—the validity of a restrictive covenant taken on the sale of a business—is one of the standard problems of competition law, and the decision to exclude objectively necessary restraints from Article 85(1) is in line with their treatment in US and UK law.[111]

In *Pronuptia*, the Court was concerned, for the first time, with a particular type of commercial activity: franchising. Franchising has become of major importance in the EEC only relatively recently and was unknown when Article 85 was written; now it is ubiquitous. *Pronuptia* concerned a franchise for the supply of wedding dresses and associated accessories. Mrs Schillgallis, the franchisee for Hamburg, Oldenburg and Hanover, was in dispute with Pronuptia, the franchisor, over her royalty payments and in the course of the litigation pleaded that the agreement was void for contravening Article 85(1). Like the *Coditel* cases, therefore, *Pronuptia* came to the Court as a reference under Article 177.

The Court identified the crux of a franchising agreement: that it enables the franchisee to operate as an independent business while using the name and know-how of the established franchisor. Franchise systems involve the application of uniform commercial methods: they also depend on the franchisee keeping up to the mark and maintaining proper standards of quality. The falling off of one franchisee will ultimately affect the reputation of the others, since the consumer sees only the homogeneous face of the system as a whole. The Court held that Article 85(1) would not apply to franchise agreements unless they involved restrictions which went beyond those demanded by the nature of a franchise system. Thus, the provisions which prevent the know-how and assistance provided by the franchisor to

[109] See similarly *Halsbury's Laws of England* Vol 52 para 19.43 headed 'Restrictions Necessary for the Promotion of Competition' and Derrick Wyatt and Alan Dashwood, *The Substantive Law of the EEC* 2nd ed (Sweet and Maxwell 1987) 367–72.

[110] [1976] CMLR D44.

[111] See further J. Heydon, *The Restraint of Trade Doctrine* (Butterworths 1971).

the franchisee from benefiting competitors escape Article 85(1),[112] as do the clauses which preserve the identity and reputation of the franchise organisation.

Pronuptia has been hailed as the most important illustration of the 'rule of reason' approach to vertical distribution.[113] This is an oversimplification. Most of the restrictions permitted were allowed under what we have called the doctrine of objective necessity, and the case is consistent with *Nutricia.* A franchisor would not supply secret know-how to a franchisee if the latter could pass it on to a competitor. On the issue of the commercial risk to the franchisee, the approach of the Court was orthodox. The *Pronuptia* agreement contained a prohibition on the franchisee opening a second shop and an obligation on the franchisor not to grant more franchises in a certain territory (which was thus reserved to the first franchisee), nor itself to compete in these territories. The combination of these clauses was seen as giving territorial protection to the franchisee. The Court admitted that 'it is certainly possible' that a franchisee would not be prepared to take the franchise without such protection, but said that this was a matter for exemption under Article 85(3). Such territorial protection would certainly be crucial to many franchisees, who would be ill-advised to go ahead without it. Its importance may vary with the type of goods or services being franchised: wedding dress purveyors have a limited potential clientele at any one time and the franchisee would be unlikely to see territorial protection as any less 'indispensable' than the know-how and assistance provisions. A real rule-of-reason approach would have taken this on board, but *Pronuptia* again shows that such an approach falters before the anathema of territorial restrictions—even if not on a national basis. Admittedly, there is a slight suggestion of the partial rule-of-reason approach as seen in *LTM* and *Maize Seeds:*[114] the Court says that Article 85(1) catches the territorial restraint 'since it concerns a mark that is already widely known',[115] the inference being that in some circumstances it would not have been applicable. But, as in the cases of *Maize Seeds* and *LTM*, we wonder how helpful this hint of a partial rule of reason would be. It may be that, in a few rare cases, the territorial restrictions in a franchise would be outside Article 85(1) because of the novelty of the mark or the problem of penetrating a particular market. But it would be extremely difficult to predict whether the relevant authorities would think this of any particular franchise system; and the successful operation of a franchise network might have the very effect of bringing it within Article 85(1).

The final judgment that must be considered is *Metro (2).*[116] VerLoren van Themaat AG described the Court's approach to 'simple' selective distribu-

[112] Including the clause by which the franchisee agrees not to open a competing business even for a short time after the agreement has expired.

[113] Roger Goebel, 23 *CML Rev* 683, 691 (1986).

[114] See James Venit, 'Pronuptia: Ancillary Restraints or Unholy Alliances' 11 *EL Rev* 213 (1986).

[115] [1986] 1 CMLR 414, 444.

[116] [1987] 1 CMLR 118.

tion systems in the first *Metro* case as being 'rule of reason'.[117] In the second *Metro* case, the Court had to reconsider the issue of selective distribution agreements under Article 85(1). It did not say that simple systems are always outside Article 85(1), but confirmed that they may be. The Court spelt out the type of situation in which they would be caught as being when so much of the market is tied up in such systems that there is rigidity of pricing and no workable competition left. The Court refused to take the line that a large number of systems on a market necessarily has those effects: they must be proved. This judgment suggests that more economic analysis should be undertaken when deciding whether Article 85(1) applies to selective distribution systems. What had been relatively clear earlier is therefore rendered less certain. If this is rule-of-reason analysis, the paradox will have been noted that its employment may render agreements currently outside Article 85 subject to its provisions. Economic analysis here is used to the detriment of the parties to the agreement. We do not suggest that there is anything illogical in itself about this, but emphasise the point since protagonists of the rule of reason usually vaunt it as a way of enabling agreements to escape from the application of Article 85(1). Also, whether the approach in *Metro 2* is 'rule of reason' or not, it does not give businessmen and their advisers any certainty. In order to say whether their selective distribution system is outside Article 85(1), they will have to appreciate the effects which systems already in operation on the market have on the level of prices and the competitive process; this requires extensive market analysis, and in many cases it is possible that the relevant data are all but unobtainable. It is also difficult to understand how a new system can be said to fall within Article 85(1) because the market is *already* rigid and structured through the prior existence of so many selective distribution networks: the systems whose establishment on the market led to these conditions must surely have been caught themselves in the first place. On the other hand, the Court may mean that it is necessary to prevent the situation of workable competition becoming unworkable, rather than stopping a new system from making a bad situation worse. If this is so, then one is asking the businessman to judge whether his network will be the one to tip the market from one state to another—an almost impossible assessment for him to make.

Our conclusion, therefore, is that the case-law of the Court of Justice contains little to suggest that it is moving towards the adoption of a US-style rule of reason. Some cases can be explained on the basis of the doctrine of objective necessity, and even here the Court has proceeded cautiously. The case-law on objective necessity can be expected to grow as experience of business phenomena increases, but in a gradual way. Some cases contain a hint of a partial rule of reason, but subject to the overriding issue of market integration (except in *Coditel 2*), and really seem to offer little of any use to

[117] It is interesting to note that the Court itself has never used the term 'rule of reason' when considering Article 85(1) in its judgments, including those given since the arrival of Judge Joliet in 1985.

the lawyer and his business client. In the area of selective distribution systems, the injection of more economic analysis into Article 85(1) seems to have done more to subvert business arrangements than to have advanced the cause of certainty.

D. RECENT DECISIONS OF THE COMMISSION

There has been criticism of the Commission that it has failed to follow the lead of the Court of Justice in *LTM*, *Maize Seeds* and *Pronuptia*: that somehow it is out of tune with the spirit of the Court's pronouncements. We have already indicated that we do not consider the Court to have adopted an approach to Article 85(1) in its recent judgments which is either particularly novel or helpful. However, the criticism is there: with regard to *Maize Seeds*, it can be said that the Commission simply paid lip-service to this judgment in preamble 11 of the block exemption on patent licensing.[118] The Commission's decision in *Velcro/Aplix*[119] has been criticised in a similar vein. We must therefore look at the Commission's recent decisions to see the extent to which there is a disparity between its approach and that of the Court of Justice.

(i) *The position on research and development agreements*

Much of the criticism of the Commission has focused on its attitude to agreements on research and development, an area in which it is inherently unlikely that the Court will become involved.[120] Research and development is vital to the welfare of the EEC economy generally. In an era of rapidly changing technology and increasing world competition, it is necessary that EEC firms should be in the vanguard. It would be a nonsense if the competition rules were applied in such a clumsy and unsophisticated way that they acted as a serious deterrent to research and development and frustrated Community moves to encourage small businesses by making life easier for them.[121] At this point, it is the procedural issue that is particularly significant. If it is going to take several years to get an individual exemption (if at all), and given that there is the chance that the Commission will refuse to grant one (in which case the agreement may be void) or might impose new terms on the parties (in which case the commercial balance of the agreement may be significantly altered), the competition rules may be a serious obstacle. Until recently, the Commission's tendency was to hold that joint ventures for research and development were caught by Article 85(1); even if the venturers were not *actual* competitors, the Commission would justify its intervention on the basis that they were at least *potential*

[118] Regulation 2349/84.

[119] OJ 1985 L233/22. See Korah, 10 *EIPR 296 (1985)*.

[120] It is only likely to do so if and when the venturers litigate and a national court refers. This is in itself unlikely. If the parties have negotiated something suitable with the Commission they are unlikely then to want to go to Luxembourg.

[121] See the Report from the Belmont European Community Law Office 'The European Community; 1986 review and 1987 prospects—competition/antitrust overview'.

competitors. This would be done despite assertions that the venturers could not or would not have separately developed the venture product, and it left the Commission open to the criticism that it did not look sufficiently at the economic realities of the situation. One famous victim of the Commission's approach was the *Vacuum Interrupters* agreement.[122] Another example was the decision in *Rockwell/Iveco*,[123] where the Commission held that an agreement for the production of rear-drive axles was within Article 85(1), even though Iveco, the truck manufacturing division of Fiat, had hitherto made axles for itself and did not have the technology which Rockwell had developed in the United States. The joint venture was to use an Iveco plant to bring on to the market a new, specialised axle producer which would supply other manufacturers as well as Iveco. Without the agreement, Iveco could not have obtained the new technology and would not have produced the axles for other manufacturers and Rockwell would not have entered the European market where 95 per cent of truck axles were still made by vehicle manufacturers themselves. The Commission recognised the merits of this arrangement, but dealt with the matter by granting an exemption under Article 85(3) rather than negative clearance under Article 85(1).

Critics would argue that this type of case should be dealt with by invoking the rule of reason;[124] the effect of the agreement was to increase competition on the market so that Article 85(1) should not have been applied at all. The writers doubt, however, that it is desirable or necessary to invoke the US rule of reason for these purposes. What is called for is a more realistic appraisal of what is meant by 'potential competition' in cases such as this. The Commission has expressed sympathy for the idea of careful analysis of such joint ventures under Article 85(1), but increased sophistication in dealing with them can be achieved otherwise than by invoking the rule of reason. In its 13th Annual Report, the Commission indicated the issues it would bear in mind in deciding whether joint ventures fall within the competition rules in the first place, apparently on more generous grounds than before.[125] It may be correct to say that, until this Report, the Commission had taken an unduly cautious approach towards agreements on research and development, at a time when it was still gaining experience of them. As a result of its increased knowledge of such projects (obtained in large part through the process of notification which rule-of-reason analysis would render unnecessary) its position has altered to some extent.

Further evidence of a change in the Commission's attitude is discernible

[122] [1977] 1 CMLR D67.

[123] [1983] 3 CMLR 709.

[124] See in particular Korah's views on this matter, widely expressed and well-known, put with particular clarity in *R and D and the EEC Competition Rules Regulation 418/85* (ESC Publishing 1986) Chap 1.

[125] See pts 53–5.

in the *Optical Fibres* decision.[126] There, agreements for the production and sale of optical fibres were entered into between producers of complementary, not competing, technology. The Commission held the basic agreements to be outside Article 85(1) although all the joint ventures taken together created a network which was within Article 85(1) as there would be a distortion of competition between the joint venture companies themselves. So, although the Commission did intervene in the arrangements and amendments had to be made before an individual exemption could be granted, the decision was significant for admitting that the basic agreements between the non-competitors were outside Article 85(1). This contrasts with the treatment of *Rockwell/Iveco* and suggests that the latter agreement might be treated differently if the decision were to be made today. There is more evidence of the Commission's new approach in *Mitchell Cotts/Sofiltra.*[127] These firms entered into a joint venture for the manufacture of glass-fibre filters. As Mitchell Cotts was not a producer of these products, the collaboration at the production level of the market was held to fall outside Article 85(1). The marketing joint venture required exemption, however, since both firms were involved in the distribution of these products.

It would, in the writers' view, be an exaggeration to suggest that these recent decisions indicate a switch to rule-of-reason analysis under Article 85(1) by the Commission, in the sense in which that term is used in the United States. It may well be that the Commission, chastened by the criticism of its decisions, is now rather more careful in its analysis of agreements. In particular, it is now more sensitive to the issue of potential competition and it spells out with greater care than hitherto why any given clause is dealt with under Article 85(1) or Article 85(3). It may also be that, as it acquires greater experience in dealing with research and development agreements, it will adopt a slightly less interventionist approach than in the past. This, however, is not to say that it has embraced or will embrace the rule of reason.

Furthermore, it is worth recalling the various procedural changes which arguably have diminished the force of the rule-of-reason argument. Thus, for example, a comfort letter was sent in *United Reprocessors*,[128] enabling co-operation between three European companies involved in nuclear oxide fuel reprocessing services to go ahead. In *Bayer/BP*,[129] a notice was issued, less than a year after the parties notified their rationalisation agreement, indicating the Commission's intention to grant an exemption. The Commission was able relatively quickly to indicate its willingness to renew the exemption granted to the *de Laval/Stork* joint venture.[130] In these cases,

[126] OJ 1986 L236/30. See on this (and on BP/Kellogg [1986] 2 CMLR 619) Korah, 'Critical Comments on the Commission's Recent Decisions' 12 *EL Rev* 18 (1987).
[127] [1988] 4CMLR 111.
[128] 16th Annual Report pt 69.
[129] OJ 1987 C253/5.
[130] OJ 1987 C255/3.

beneficial projects have been given as green a light as possible pretty quickly. However, we would not suggest that the Commission's procedures are always immune from criticism. For example, the notice in the Official Journal in the matter of *Elopak/Metal Box—Odin*[131] would seem to be a perfect example of how not to proceed: it does not say why the opposition procedure in Regulation 418/85 does not apply, it does not say why the agreement comes within Article 85(1), and it concludes with the ambiguous remark that the Commission does propose 'to adopt a favourable attitude for (sic) the notified agreements'. Similarly unhelpful is the notice in *Rich Products/Jus-rol.*[132] This case concerns a know-how licence granted to an English company. It is exclusive, but there is no question of absolute territorial protection. It is impossible to tell whether the Commission considers that it comes within Article 85(1) or not, a matter of importance to would-be opponents of the agreement. As pointed out earlier, decision-making ought, in the public interest, to be as transparent as possible, and this requires that as much information as possible be vouchsafed to the public at large about the Commission's reasoning.

On a different point, in the case of research and development, it must again be asked how helpful the rule of reason would be in practice. Is it possible to predict with certainty when an agreement can be said to be going to increase rather than decrease competition on the market, which is the analysis that would be required under a full-scale rule of reason? How can you prove in a case like *Vacuum Interrupters*[133] that the parties would not have entered into the agreement without the restrictive provisions contained in it? The parties would say that, but the Commission would be inclined to say the opposite. The problem is the same one that arises under the partial rule-of-reason approach in *LTM*, *Maize Seeds* and *Pronuptia*. It is hard to see that there would be any more certainty for the individual parties to research and development agreements. Also, many joint venture restrictions fall short of those that could come within the category of objective necessity mentioned above. There is a difference between a restriction which is objectively necessary, in the sense that the thing transferred could not be transferred without it, and a restriction which diminishes a commercial risk without actually being necessary.

This may be a good point at which to mention a conundrum thrown up by the 'objective necessity' approach we have identified. Article 85(3) provides that exemption can only be given to clauses which, inter alia, are *indispensable* to the agreement concerned. One might wonder how this can be squared with the idea that some restrictions in commercial agreements do not fall within Article 85(1) because they are objectively necessary. If the clause in question is objectively necessary, one might argue that the agreement should never require analysis under Article 85(3) at all; alter-

[131] OJ 1987 C 215/3.
[132] OJ 1987 C209/3.
[133] OJ 1977 L48/32, [1977] 1 CMLR D67.

natively, one could argue that whenever the Commission decides to grant an exemption under Article 85(3), its finding as to indispensability must mean that the agreement should never have come within Article 85(1) in the first place. If the logic of this is correct, the objective necessity doctrine under Article 85(1) would mean that Article 85(3) is redundant! One answer to this is to say that, when looking at Article 85(1), the Commission (and Court) ask themselves whether the restrictive provisions are of the very essence of the agreement, whereas under Article 85(3) they ask whether the parties could have accepted restrictions less extensive than those contained in the agreement.[134] Another is to say that the restrictions permitted under the doctrine of objective necessity under Article 85(1) are sui generis, limited in number and scope, and placed into a special category only after careful consideration of their nature and effect by the Court of Justice. Either way, there is no match between objective necessity under Article 85(1) and indispensability under Article 85(3).

We have suggested that the rule of reason would do little to advance certainty in EEC competition law. It is worth mentioning that in the United States there can be considerable uncertainty about the application of the antitrust laws to joint ventures. There are joint venture guidelines,[135] and the National Co-operative Research Act 1984 took some cases outside the per se standard. This, however, still leaves the parties with the problem of deciding whether their agreement enhances or reduces competition on the market as a whole. In the case of *Toyota/General Motors*,[136] it took a considerable period to establish whether the joint venture between those two companies infringed the antitrust laws.

(ii) *The position on franchising*

With regard to distribution franchising, the Commission has followed and built upon the lead given by the Court of Justice in *Pronuptia*. The franchising issue presented a novel situation in EEC competition law, for the Commission had not hitherto issued any decisions in that area, nor issued notices or press releases about it, nor dealt with it in its Annual Reports. The Court in *Pronuptia* was therefore given the first bite at the cherry. The contrast with the patent licensing saga could not be more stark. The Commission's response has been swift. It issued a decision on the standard form *Pronuptia* agreement[137] in which the territorial protection clauses held within Article 85(1) in the *Pronuptia* judgment were granted exemption. But it is now clear that many standard clauses in a distribution franchising agreement do not come within Article 85(1). In the 16th Annual Report, commenting on its decisions in *Pronuptia* and *Yves Rocher*[138], both of which followed the same pattern, the Commission said:

[134] See Jonathan Faull, 'Joint Ventures under EEC Competition Rules' 5 *ECLR* 358 (1984).
[135] 1984 Trade Reg Rep CCH 22,139.
[136] 5 *ECLR* 49 (1984).
[137] OJ 1987 L13/39.
[138] OJ 1986 C95/3; a favourable decision was later reached: OJ 1987 L8/49.

Several obligations imposed on the franchisees did not restrict competition since they were a necessary prerequisite for the proper functioning of the networks: they were designed either to safeguard their uniformity and reputation or to prevent the use by competitors of the know-how and commercial knowledge transferred by the franchisor to the franchisee under the terms of the contract.[139]

This, of course, is an echo of the Court's reasoning in the *Pronuptia* judgment, but the term 'indispensable' with its suggestion of Article 85(3) is replaced by 'necessary prerequisite'. The Commission also issued a decision exempting the *Computerland* standard form agreement.[140] Like *Yves Rocher*, this agreement did contain an exclusive territory clause, albeit a fairly modest one.[141]

In August 1987, the Commission published a draft of a block exemption for distribution and servicing franchises.[142] This draft generally follows the pattern of the *Pronuptia* judgment and the subsequent Commission decision. Recital 6 says: 'Franchising agreements can fall under Article 85(1) when they include territorial protection of the franchisee'; but Recital 9 admits: 'the limited territorial protection granted to the franchisees is indispensable to protect their investment and to guarantee that they will concentrate their activity on the contract territory'.

As far as the basic provisions of the franchise agreement are concerned, the communication and protection of the know-how, the maintenance of the identity and reputation and so on, these are listed in Article 3 of the Regulation as permissible. Recital 11 makes it clear, however, that normally, in the absence of 'particular economic and legal circumstances', they will not be within Article 85(1) at all. The only matter which the Recitals actually specify as bringing the agreement within Article 85(1) but meriting exemption is that of territorial restrictions,[143] although other permissible restrictions are listed in Article 2 (the white list). These include an obligation on the franchisee not to deal with competing goods. This is one of those restrictions which are not covered by the doctrine of objective necessity, although it may be important to the commercial success of the franchisor's business.

The draft Regulation would give exemption to franchise agreements including exclusive territorial terms, unless they go so far as to oblige the

[139] 16th Annual Report 53 para 4.

[140] OJ 1987 L222/12.

[141] After the first year of the agreement, an area with a radius of less than 1km from the location of the franchise outlet.

[142] OJ 1987 C229/3. The Commission says in Recital 4 of the draft that industrial (i.e. manufacturing) franchises raise quite different considerations. The Commission's franchising experience has not yet been in this area, and the draft does not cover them. For comment on the draft see Korah, 'Franchising and the Draft Group Exemption' 8 *ECLR* 124 (1987).

[143] The recitals do not mention the suggestion of the Court in *Pronuptia* that in rare cases territorial restrictions might fall outside Art 85(1) (see above, p 28); to this extent the Commission has taken a narrower view than the Court.

parties to refuse to serve customers from outside the allotted territory.[144]

The same comments apply to this Regulation as are made above about the *Pronuptia* judgment itself. It is difficult to describe the Commission's approach as the application of the rule of reason, for territorial restrictions are automatically seen as coming within Article 85(1) and requiring exemption, no matter how 'indispensable' they might be. The answer must be that they are 'indispensable' to the commercial viability of the franchising arrangement for the franchisee: they do not form part of the very nature of the agreement. The separation of those two issues is what the Commission is doing when dividing what is outside Article 85(1) from what is exempted by Article 85(3). This approach, however, is in line with the reasoning of the Court of Justice; it is hard to see that it has failed to follow its lead.

Our conclusion, therefore, is that the Commission is not noticeably out of step with the Court of Justice; in truth, neither has embraced the US rule of reason in its most ample form and the indications of a partial rule of reason that have occasionally erupted are unhelpful. But both the Court and the Commission are continually refining their attitudes to different business phenomena.

V. Conclusions

In the light of the foregoing considerations, the call for the adoption of a US-style rule of reason should be resisted and, indeed, there is much to be said for dropping this term (and the terms 'ancillary restraint' and 'per se illegality') from EEC antitrust law altogether, on the basis that they do more to confuse than to clarify. EEC competition law requires its own vocabulary, carefully honed to express its own particular tensions.

One ground for jettisoning the term 'rule of reason' from the vocabulary of EEC competition law is that it is now used in other areas of the law, for example, in the provisions on free movement of goods. Under the *Cassis de Dijon* doctrine,[145] indistinctly applicable measures which, prima facie, have an equivalent effect to quantitative restrictions according to the *Dassonville* formula[146] are none the less not caught by Article 30 if they are necessary to the 'imperative requirements' of the Member State concerned. This principle has begun to be termed the rule of reason by some Advocates General and commentators.[147] There, however, one is not saying that the 'restrictions' are not in reality restrictions at all, but that Article 30 is not applicable to them. It is more an Article 85(3) exercise than a rule-of-reason one in the competition sense. With the terminology so hijacked (albeit in a

[144] The other 'black clauses' cover such things as reciprocal franchising between competing manufacturers, resale price maintenance and no-challenge clauses.

[145] Case 120/78 *Rewe-Central* v *Bundesmonopolverwaltung für Branntwein* [1979] ECR 649.

[146] Case 8/74 *Procureur du Roi* v *Dassonville* [1974] ECR 837.

[147] See Verloren van Themaat AG in Case 231/83 *Cullet* v *Le Clerc* [1985] ECR 305, 311–12.

good cause), there is even more incentive to find different expressions to reflect the difficulties experienced in the area of competition law.

A different reason for abandoning this terminology in EEC competition law is that it invites misleading comparison with antitrust law analysis in the United States. We have suggested above that the context of US antitrust law is so dissimilar from that of the EEC that comparative analysis should be undertaken with great caution.

Quite apart from the issue of terminology, the writers have other doubts about the wisdom of analysing Article 85(1) in a way that relies on an approach similar to that in the Sherman Act. It would not help the cause of certainty. As Joliet himself said:[148]

> Generally business groups in Europe, just as in America, complain about the lack of certainty in Antitrust law. At the same time, they are inclined to demand more flexibility. Such demands are irreconcilable. *A rule of reason under Article 85(1) would bring about more uncertainty for business men.* [Emphasis added].

The matter of certainty is, of course, important. It is in no one's interest to retard beneficial collaboration between firms striving to compete in a competitive international market. However, the best answer to this problem is for the Commission to continue to improve its procedures, to publish block exemptions where this is possible, and to develop such notions as objective necessity and potential competition. We also expect its sophistication in dealing with economics to continue to improve, but do not consider that this goes hand in hand with rule-of-reason analysis. This would stifle the proper application of Article 85 which, precisely because of its more ample wording, does not bear the same intellectual burden that the words 'restraint of trade' do in the Sherman Act. We doubt, too, that it would be helpful to draw the national courts further into the application of Article 85 by asking them to undertake extensive economic analysis under Article 85(1). We are happy for them to enforce the competition rules against blatant cartels and abuses of a dominant position. We do not consider them to be appropriate fora for deciding upon complex economic issues.

We are also of the opinion that protagonists of the rule of reason fail to give due consideration to the significance of single market integration. Even if this is not a goal approved by all observers, to call for the application of the competition rules in a way which ignores it is fundamentally to misconstrue the context in which EEC law is applied. Also, there is a certain disingenuousness in complaining about EEC competition law when it (with other provisions of the Treaty) has done so much to open up markets which until relatively recently were difficult to penetrate. Competition law in one sense benefits everyone on the market—even those who object to some of the particular ways in which it is applied.

Our conclusion, therefore, is that there are sound reasons for resisting the call for a rule of reason under Article 85(1). It may be that there is a second

148 Op cit 189–90.

generation of competition lawyers in the Commission who take a less dogmatic view of competition law than their predecessors, and that there is an increased awareness of the significance of economics in competition law. These things are to be welcomed. But we do not see that increased sophistication necessarily requires rule-of-reason analysis. Rather, there is much to say for the current approach of the Court and the Commission, albeit that it is important to keep an eye on the existing procedural problems. In particular, we think that it would be helpful to cease to use the terms 'rule of reason' and 'per se illegality', as they confuse more than they clarify, and that there are sound reasons for the Court and Commission maintaining close control over commercial agreements as the common market matures.

Dominance, Concerted Practices and Joint Dominance

[14]

CONCEPT OF A DOMINANT POSITION WITHIN THE MEANING OF ARTICLE 86

by

Valentine Korah*

I. INDEPENDENT BEHAVIOUR AND FREEDOM FROM RISK

The objection to market power expressed by classical economists is the ability of the monopolist to pursue goals other than production and distribution of goods and services that customers are prepared to pay for with a minimum of resources. Their emphasis was on efficiency, both in the use of existing resources[1] and in increasing output with existing or new investment when and where demand is buoyant and more than a normal return on capital may be expected.[2]

The functions of prices in competitive markets include matching supply and demand in the short and long terms. Prices act as signals. If demand exceeds supply, prices rise and in the short term ration the use of scarce resources through high prices that deter those whose demand is least strong. In the longer term, prices that yield high profits encourage new suppliers to enter a market or existing firms to expand production, thereby increasing supply to the benefit of customers. Where supply exceeds demand, prices that yield low profits have the opposite effects. If competitive pressures from existing or new firms are allowed to operate freely, this ensures that those firms that use existing resources inefficiently, or enter markets where demand is insufficient should earn lower profits and be unable to expand as much as those making products for which customers are prepared to pay a price yielding higher profits. Where markets

---

* Reader in English Law, University College London; Barrister.

Temple Lang of the Commission's Legal Service analysed the meaning of "abuse" in the light primarily of the *Vitamins* judgment: "Monopolisation and the Definition of 'Abuse' of a Dominant Position under Article 86 EEC Treaty", 16 C.M.L. Rev. 1979, 345. I should like to analyse the concept of "dominant position" primarily in the light of *United Brands* and *Vitamins*, although other cases will be cited.

I have derived considerable assistance from many discussions with Baden Fuller and from his piece, "Article 86 EEC: Economic Analysis of the Existence of a Dominant Position", 4 E.L. Rev. 1979, 423. For a descriptive analysis, see Temple Lang, "Some Aspects of Abuse of Dominant Positions in European Antitrust Law", 3 *Fordham International Law Forum* 1979/80, 1.

1. Sometimes called "X efficiency".

2. Sometimes called "allocative efficiency".

are less competitive, however, existing firms have greater freedom of action in their pricing and other marketing strategies and the risk of new competition materialising is less. Existing firms may be able to survive and expand even if they operate inefficiently. Like their predecessors, modern economists focus their interest on the discretionary power of the monopolist both in marketing and production, unconstrained towards efficiency judged in terms of customer demand rather than profits for shareholders or employees.

Monopoly may be defined either in terms of freedom of action for the monopolist or absence of risk. Many firms have enough market power to adopt a marketing strategy—most well-advertised brands sell at higher prices than unbranded substitutes and trade mark holders can choose whether to advertise more or cut prices. In a competitive market, however, price differences maintained by advertising become eroded by retailers' house brands and monopoly pricing of manufacturers' brands becomes eroded by competition from other brands. Only a monopolist can exercise a marketing strategy without exposing himself to considerable risks if he makes the wrong decision.

There is no sharp division between monopoly and competition: market power is a matter of degree. Considerable market power over a period of time presupposes the absence of substitutes to which customers could turn at lower prices and the existence of barriers to entry preventing new competition from materialising, even when supply is profitable. The absence of new competition does not demonstrate market power. Even a sole supplier may be constrained by fear of entry and charge only competitive prices where barriers to entry are not high; in which case, the market is already operating competitively. There will be market power only if entry is not attracted when prices and other market policies are such that an efficient existing firm can earn abnormal profits on the capital invested therein. It is, however, difficult to judge whether the existing firm is earning high profits.[3]

Economists may not agree as to what should be done about market power where it is based on economies of scale rather than anticompetitive conduct, but there is considerable unanimity as to the indications of its existence.

In *Hoffmann-La Roche* v. *Commission*,[4] which I shall call "*Vitamins*",

3. Allowance must be made for unusual efficiency or risk. Company accounts are likely to demonstrate historical costs, not opportunity costs. Economists and management are interested not in what assets originally cost, reduced by depreciation, but in their value in the next best use. This is rarely reflected in accounts.

4. Case 85/76, (1979) E.C.R. 461; (1979) 3 C.M.L.R. 211.

the Commission had condemned[5] requirements contracts and loyalty rebates which encouraged Roche's 22 largest customers to buy a large percentage of their requirements from it, even though they might prefer to buy some vitamins from other producers. In confirming the finding that Roche was in a dominant position over all but one of the vitamin groups, the Court of Justice repeated the definition it had given in *United Brands* v. *Commission*:[6]

> "38 . . . The dominant position thus referred to [by Article 86] relates to a position of economic strength enjoyed by an undertaking which enables it to prevent effective competition being maintained on the relevant market by affording it the power to behave to an appreciable extent independently of its competitors."

In *Continental Can* v. *Commission*,[7] the Court impliedly accepted the Commission's definition which was based on independence from suppliers, customers and competitors. Reference to suppliers has been dropped since the *A.B.G.*[8] decision. BP was squeezed between the OPEC price increases for crude oil and the maximum legal price at the Dutch petrol pump, which left it unable to sell at any price that would enable it to cover its costs, including the replacement of crude. Although it was dependent on a cartel between its suppliers, the Commission found that it was dominant, dropping the idea of independence from suppliers from its definition. Nevertheless, it is thought that this change in the definition is not very significant. Competition from competitors normally prevents one exploiting either suppliers or customers. It may be that the Court will return to the idea of independence from suppliers in a case where the firm uses its market power to exploit its suppliers.

The other change in the formulation since *Continental Can* is the reference to the power to prevent effective competition from being maintained.[9] It seems to refer to the ability to exclude competitors, rather than

---

5. O.J. 1976, L 223/27; (1976) 2 C.M.L.R. D25.

6. Case 27/76, (1978) E.C.R. 207; (1978) 1 C.M.L.R. 429, at para. 65.

7. Case 6/72, *Europemballage and Continental Can* v. *Commission* (1973) E.C.R. 215; (1973) C.M.L.R. 199. The Commission's decision was reported in J.O. 1972, L 7/25; (1972) C.M.L.R. D11. Advocate General Roemer expressly approved the Commission's view at p. 257.

8. *A.B.G.*, O.J. 1977, L 117/1; (1977) 2 C.M.L.R. D1. On appeal: Case 77/77, *BP* v. *Commission* (1978) E.C.R. 1513; (1978) 3 C.M.L.R. 174. The Court did not decide the question of dominance since it held there was no abuse.

9. Used in Case 78/70, *Deutsche Grammophon* v. *Metro* (1971) E.C.R. 487, para. 17 and in *United Brands*, derived from E.C.S.C. Treaty, Article 66(7) which refers to "a dominant position shielding [an undertaking] against effective competition in a substantial part of the common market"—not quite the same concept.

to competitive pressures, but in this context the Court does not seem to treat the test as separate,[10] in which case the new definition does no harm. Provided substitutes are not available, ability to exclude competitors, if exercised, may lead to an absence of competitive pressures.

In *United Brands* the Court held (at paras. 113-119) that a dominant position could exist despite lively competition and price wars. The price wars did not occur in all areas at once and United Brands was not squeezed out of the market, though one might comment that its market share had fallen. The Court observed at para. 111 that its market share at 40-45% of bananas sold in six Member States was several times as large as that of its largest rival and the Court had pointed to some possible barriers to entry. To these we will return.

In *Vitamins*, after confirming that dominance need not be absolute, provided the firm has at least an appreciable influence on the conditions under which competition will develop, and is able largely to disregard competition, the Court distinguished parallel behaviour:[11]

> "39 . . . A dominant position must also be distinguished from parallel courses of conduct which are peculiar to oligopolies in that in an oligopoly the courses of conduct interact, while in the case of an undertaking occupying a dominant position the conduct of the undertaking which derives profits from that position is to a great extent determined unilaterally."

In its enquiry into the oil industry[12] the Commission alleged that the oil suppliers were jointly dominant, though no collusion was found. So did the Dutch cartel authorities in relation to the oil shortage in the Netherlands.[13] This is a difficult concept, and seems to have been rejected firmly by the Court in *Vitamins*. If none of the suppliers is charging competitive prices, then each may be able to reap some monopoly profit. But in the absence of collusion such market power is not joint:[14] each firm enjoys it, so long as in fact the others choose not to compete in certain ways.

---

10. See Temple Lang, *Fordham*, cited at the beginning of this article, at pp. 4 and 10.

11. But see vitamin A, at paras. 51 and 52 of the judgment, where the leading firm in a tight oligopoly was held to be dominant.

12. Commission of the European Communities, *Report by the Commission on the behaviour of the oil companies in the Community during the period from October 1973 to March 1974*, Competition—Approximation of Legislation Series—1976 no. 26 at pp. 8 and 154-5.

13. Baardman, in *Regulating the Behaviour of Monopolies and Dominant Undertakings in Community Law* (Bruges Week 1977), General Ed. the late J. Van Damme, p. 277 at 284-6. The concept has been invoked in the EEC decision in *A.G.B.*, cited in n. 8 above.

14. In the *Sugar Cartel* (O.J. 1973, L 140/17; (1973) C.M.L.R. D 65, 104), the Commission treated as jointly dominant two producers in the Netherlands who concerted their marketing

Roche's share of the vitamin A group was 47% and that of its competitors, 27%, 18%, 7% and 1%. The Court said:

> "51. Since the relevant market thus has the particular features of a narrow oligopolistic market in which the degree of competition by its very nature has already been weakened, Roche's share, which is equal to the aggregate of the shares of its two next largest competitors, proves that it is entirely free to decide what attitude to adopt when confronted by competition."

The Court referred also to Roche's technical lead and to overcapacity which would deter new entrants,[15] and confirmed the finding that Roche enjoyed a dominant position. Had Roche's share been some 25 or 30%, it might be argued, despite paragraph 39, that each of the large firms might have enjoyed some market power, so long as none of them competed actively in price, and that none should be allowed to adopt conduct likely to keep out of the market equally efficient firms. This question, however, has not yet arisen and there is no sign that the Court will so decide.

II. MULTIPLE INDICATIONS OF MARKET POWER

In both *United Brands* and *Vitamins*, the Court stressed that many factors, no one of them sufficient on its own, may indicate market power. After stressing the significance of other factors, the Court stated in *Vitamins*:

> "41. Furthermore although the importance of the market shares may vary from one market to another the view may legitimately be taken that very large shares are in themselves, and save in exceptional circumstances, evidence of the existence of a dominant position.
>
> An undertaking which has a very large market share and holds it for some time, by means of the volume of production and the scale of the supply which it stands for—without those having much smaller market shares being able to meet rapidly the demand from those who would like to break away from the undertaking which has the largest market share—is by virtue of that share in a position of strength which makes it an unavoidable trading partner and which, already because of this secures for it, at the very least during relatively long periods, that freedom of action which is the special feature of a dominant position."

---

strategies. This decision was quashed by the Court ((1975) E.C.R. 1663; (1976), C.M.L.R. 295, para. 420) on the ground that it did not consider that the concerted practices were adequately established, so it did not consider the concept of joint dominance.

15. See p. 410 below.

Of course, where barriers to entry are low, even the sole supplier will not long be able to exploit customers or suppliers, and may act as if the market were already competitive for fear of attracting entry, so the writer is not happy with the first part of the first sentence. It is, however, modified.[16] The Court admits that there may be exceptions to the significance of large market shares and it refers in the second paragraph to market shares that endure[17] and this is unlikely to happen unless there are entry and expansion barriers. It does refer to the inability of suppliers to expand. Sometimes this may be cheaper than new entry and may be a more powerful constraint on the behaviour of the firm with the large market share. In this carefully qualified form, the writer has little objection to the stress placed on very large market shares.[18]

III. RELEVANT MARKET—SUBSTITUTES IN SUPPLY AND DEMAND

1. *Product market*

To calculate market shares, one must define the relevant market. In *Vitamins*, there was only one difficulty in doing so. No group of vitamins could be made in plant built for the production of other groups, and the demand was also specific: no group of vitamins performed the function of others. Each was clearly a separate market as was agreed by the parties. To this, there was one exception. For bio-nutritive uses vitamins C and E were, indeed, made in separate plants and performed different functions, but each could also be used as an antioxidant, for which purpose they competed with each other and with other substitutes. Roche argued that all

16. The two formulations may represent a difference of view between the Judges.

17. Most economists assess dominance over a period of time long enough for new plant to be erected, but some are concerned with market power that endures less long. See Baden Fuller, *op. cit.* at the beginning of this article, at p. 436.

18. In earlier cases, the Court seemed to confirm that market shares alone might be determinative. In Cases 40 *etc.*/73, *Suiker Unie* (1975) E.C.R. 1663, the Sugar Cartel appeal, it confirmed that Raffinerie Tirlemontoise was dominant solely on the basis of an 85% market share. If this had been maintained for many years, one might assume that there was some barrier to entry. See below, vitamin B6, *etc.* Contrast Advocate General Roemer in *Continental Can* at p. 260, where he said that market shares rarely yield conclusive findings as to market power, and the Commission's Memorandum on "Le problème de la concentrations dans le Marché Commun" (1966).

At this point, I have assumed that there are no substitutes, since, if there were, these might form part of the market within which shares are being considered. In practice, however, markets have been defined so as to exclude quite close substitutes.

three uses constituted a single market. Economists would say that there were three markets from the demand side, but that competitive pressures from one might affect the others.

In answer to a question from the Court, the parties disagreed on the percentage of these vitamins used as antioxidants. Roche stated that it was 30% for vitamin C[19] and 60% for E. The Commission stated that it was far less.[20] If, however, the antioxidant market for vitamins C and E was substantial, and Roche could not discriminate in price between those using the vitamin for bio-nutritive purposes and those using them as antioxidants, it might lose a large part of its turnover were it to raise the price of the vitamins without considering how far customers needing antioxidants might switch to other products. If the third market is important, pressures from substitutes there may affect the bio-nutritive markets. Another mechanism described by Baden Fuller[21] might make the antioxidant market relevant to the bio-nutritive one. If one of the barriers to entry was the large size of plant needed in relation to demand on the bio-nutritive market, a new entrant might be able to get established by selling part of its output as antioxidants. The writer has long regretted[22] the emphasis placed on market definition both in the EEC and the U.S.A.[23] Markets often do not have precise limits. A narrow definition of the market on which attention should be focussed, however, does not matter provided that competitive pressures from outside that market are taken into account.[24]

Since its judgment in *Continental Can*,[25] the Court has insisted that the

---

19. At p. 569, Advocate General Reischl states that this was the proportion of total sales by Roche and the other manufacturers.

20. Herr Reischl explains some of the difficulties of calculation at p. 569. Since Roche did not know for what purpose its customers used their supplies, estimates could not be accurate.

21. *Op. cit.* at the beginning of this article, at p. 425.

22. "Abuse of a Dominant Position", 53 Notre Dame Lawyer 1978, 768, 780. See also Baden Fuller, *op. cit.* at the beginning of this article, at pp. 434 and 425.

23. In the famous *Alcoa* case: *U.S.* v. *Aluminum Co. of America* 148 F 2d 416 (2d Cir. 1945) whether Alcoa monopolised seems to have depended on whether the relevant market was virgin ingot of which it supplied 91%, or whether it included both virgin and secondary (scrap) aluminium of which it supplied 64%, or whether the market included both these but excluded aluminium used by Alcoa for fabricating other products. One would have thought that all these percentages were relevant to its market power. Each statement is true but qualified by the other two. See Areeda, *Antitrust Analysis: Problems, Text, Cases* (2nd. ed. 1974), paras 242 *et seq.*

24. See Advocate General Roemer in *Continental Can*, cited in n. 7 above, at pp. 259 and 262, where he considered that the relevant market for closures might include England, not then part of the Community.

25. Cited at n. 7 above, para. 32. For critical comment, see Korah, "The Control of Mergers under Article 86 of the Rome Treaty: Continental Can", (1973) *Current Legal Problems*, 82, 104 *et seq.*

Commission should define the relevant market and give reasons for its decision. It went so far as to quash the decision based on a finding of Continental Can's dominance over the cans used for meat and fish, and metal closures, on the ground that the Commission had failed to state why those making cylindrical cans could not switch to making the more complex shapes. It is thought that the Court was right to insist on such an analysis: Continental Can would enjoy little discretion in its market decisions, were the makers of cylindrical cans able to switch easily should it raise prices, or if canners who made their own cans were likely to start selling some. The Commission had dealt fairly shortly with the competition from other kinds of container such as glass or plastic but, contrary to the advice of Advocate General Roemer at p. 259, the Court considered this sufficient. The Commission had pointed out that food in glass or plastic could not be cooked, that glass was heavy and breakable, and plastic not rigid, but had made no studies of the extent to which a relative change in price would have caused customers of one kind of packaging to switch to another.

Sometimes, the Commission has selected very small markets. In *General Motors Continental*,[26] it confirmed that General Motors enjoyed a dominant position in relation to the certification of newish Opel cars bought abroad by Belgian residents, as fit to be driven on Belgian highways. Of course, when deciding where to buy what kind of car, a motorist would consider a wider market, such as family saloons, minis or sports cars, and the cost of certifying the car on import to Belgium would be a minor consideration, but once the car had been bought abroad, the owner would indeed be dependent on the only firm allowed by law to issue the necessary certificates. This dominance would affect only those who had already bought an Opel car abroad; but it may be that control under Article 86 was especially needed, in that the abuse alleged consisted of overcharging those buying cars abroad and so interfering with the integration of the market.

It may be that the definition of the relevant market depends on the nature of the abuse being alleged.[27] In *Hugin* v. *Commission*[28] the Court confirmed that Hugin enjoyed a dominant position over the spare parts

26. Case 26/75, (1975) E.C.R. 1367.

27. As Professor Waelbroeck suggested in a conference organised by European Studies Conferences in Brussels in September 1978.

28. Case 22/78, (1979) E.C.R. 1869; (1979) 3 C.M.L.R. 345, para. 5 of the judgment. The Court quashed the decision, as it was not satisfied that the abuse had generated perceptible effects on trade between Member States. It, therefore, did not consider whether cutting off supplies was abusive.

for the cash registers it produced, since these were not interchangeable with those for other machines and could not be efficiently manufactured in small quantities. It stated that to decide whether Hugin was dominant:

> "5. . . . it is necessary, first, to determine the relevant market. In this respect account must be taken of the fact that the conduct alleged against Hugin consists of the refusal to supply spare parts to Liptons and, generally, to any independent undertaking outside its distribution network."

Is it enough to show that a customer refused supplies is dependent on the firm alleged to be dominant, while that might not constitute dominance in relation to an anticompetitive abuse? It might be argued that the examples of abuse set out in Article 86 are based on the idea that a dominant firm should not exploit its customers, in which case any firm in a position to do so should be held to be dominant. On the other hand, when conduct alleged to restrict competition is in question, then a wider market in which competition can be judged should be considered relevant. The difficulty with this distinction is that refusals to supply may be anticompetitive, for instance when supplies are refused to dealers selling on low margins, as well as harming the firm wishing to buy. In both *General Motors Continental* and *Hugin*, the alleged abuse did harm to the dominant firm's customers directly, but no market analysis was made to see whether it also harmed the public indirectly through the reduction of competition, so customer dependence may have been the test used.

One further distinction may be important since the *Hugin* judgment. The Court pointed out that owners of cash registers do not buy spare parts, they acquire them as part of a servicing arrangement. The Court held, therefore, that the relevant market was supply to independent undertakings which specialise in the maintenance and repair of cash registers. One wonders what the position would have been had there been no undertakings, such as Liptons, which currently performed such servicing, but only one which wanted to start such a business, perhaps a distributor who had been liable for the guaranteed aftersales service, who wanted to start his own business of repairing machines that had fallen out of guarantee. Of course the justifications for refusing to supply a new customer must be more extensive than those for cutting off an existing one, but that relates to "abuse". I am questioning only whether the definition of the relevant market should be different. Baden Fuller (at p. 426) goes further and points out that for a firm employing engineers to service Hugin machines, there were substitutes. They could use their skills to service other machines. The limitation of the demand side of the market to those who were currently buying spares, bypasses those who were most dependent on Hugin for spares: the shops that had bought its machines.

United Brands[29] raised many difficulties in establishing dominance, and must be considered at some length. United Brands was condemned by the Commission for making exports of bananas between Member States difficult, for cutting off a former distributor when he started to promote a rival brand, and for charging high and discriminatory prices. It supplied some 40-45% of the bananas consumed in six Member States, and the Court had to decide whether bananas were the correct product market and whether three Member States has properly been excluded from the relevant geographic market. The Court started with a dubious statement of principle:

> "22. For the banana to be regarded as forming a new market which is sufficiently differentiated from other fruit markets it must be possible for it to be singled out by such special features distinguishing it from other fruits that it is only to a limited extent interchangeable with them and is only exposed to their competition in a way that is hardly perceptible."

Economists would not look to physical differences between products to see whether they are in the same market, but to the extent that relative price changes result in a switch in demand—to the cross elasticity of demand. (When considering what other firms compete with the firm alleged to be dominant, they would also look to the cross elasticity of supply.) Economists are less concerned with the physical nature of the product than with customers' preferences expressed in the market, though these may be affected by the physical characteristics of the product. The Court seems to have adopted a criterion for a wide market definition, excluding products where the cross elasticity of demand is small.

Yet it does not seem to have applied this criterion. The Court looked to a study by the F.A.O. and considered that the cross elasticity of demand was low, although the price of bananas had to be reduced by up to 20% in the summer months, when other fruit are available. We are not told the extent to which demand for bananas was lower in the summer than in the winter.[30] The Court is hardly to be blamed for having difficulty with the economists' concept of cross elasticity.[31]

---

29. Cited at n. 6 above.

30. Baden Fuller, *op. cit.* at the beginning of this article, at p. 426, suggests that bananas in summer may have been a by-product of winter ones. The Court ignored the temporal dimension of the market definition.

31. The Commission, which has access to economists for advice, had defined price elasticity of demand in Germany of -0.74% as meaning that were prices doubled, demand would be reduced by 74%. Economists, however, think at the margin. No sane seller doubles his price lightly. Elasticities are relevant at the margin, and a businessman might be interested in a 1

The Commission had been concerned by the needs of the young and old for bananas, but it is thought that their interests needed no protection. Unless those buying for such people could be charged more than the rest of the population, so many sales to the others would have been lost if prices had been raised to the maximum price the old or young would pay, that such price rises were highly improbable.

2. *Geographic market*

In *United Brands*, the Commission had excluded from consideration three countries where bananas from certain areas were protected: the U.K., where Commonwealth preference gave Caribbean bananas an advantage over the Chiquita ones brought by United Brands from Southern and Central America, France, which gave preference to its own overseas territories, and Italy, where there was a quota scheme. The Court stated:

> "44. The conditions for the application of Article 86 to an undertaking in a dominant position presuppose the clear delimitation of the substantial part of the common market in which it may be able to engage in abuses which hinder effective competition and this is an area where the objective conditions of competition applying to the product in question must be the same for all traders."

One difficulty with this statement is that geographic, like product, markets may not have clear boundaries. Others are that there may be no area without discrimination, or the discrimination may favour the firm whose dominance is being assessed. Moreover, even if United Brands suffered from discrimination in the three countries, it might have had other advantages which enabled it to overcome it and still be dominant. A firm with strong patent protection may be able to overcome adverse discrimination. The writer, however, does not object to the exclusion of part of the geographic market. Were United Brands dominant there too, its dominance in the other six countries would probably be more regrettable than otherwise. What is important is that these areas considered not to be part of the relevant market should, nevertheless, be analysed. If it be easy for another firm to import bananas, whether from outside the common market, of from the excluded Member States, then United Brands might

---

or 2% rise in real prices, not a doubling. Demand curves are often drawn as straight lines for ease of explanation of some concept, but they are rarely straight outside the abstract world of the teacher. Prices are often inelastic over a range, until they become so high that another substitute becomes relevant, near that point they may be quite elastic, then continue inelastic until another substitute becomes relevant. It is unlikely that the slope of the demand curve will be constant over a range that includes doubling the price.

have little market power even were it to supply all the bananas in the six States. It may well have been right to exclude the three States where, evidently, United Brands supplied a smaller part of the market, but we are told too little by Court or Commission to know.

3. *Conclusion on relevant market*

It is submitted that the Court has rightly been concerned to analyse the relevant market, but unfortunately its attention has been focussed on the need for a definition and the reasons therefor, rather than on analysis. It may be just as true to say that United Brands supplied over 40% of the bananas sold in the six-State market as to say that it supplied a far lower proportion of the fresh fruit sold there. Each statement is a half truth, qualified by the other. There is no unique way the relevant market can be correctly described. Competition is a question of degree. United Brands met close competition from other branded bananas, less close competition from unbranded bananas and, at some times of the year, substantial competition from summer fruits, as well as competition at all times from apples and oranges. Where the market ends is a question of degree not of definition. It may be sensible to define an area for investigation and call that the relevant market, but competitive pressures from outside are important.

IV. BARRIERS TO ENTRY

These have been stressed in virtually all the cases by both Commission and Court. Usually economies of scale and advanced technology have been said to be barriers to entry, and in *General Motors* the legal exclusive right was quite rightly stressed. Some economists say that the only entry barriers that matter are exclusive rights conferred by law and a minimum economic scale of operations that is large in relation to the demand and its likely increase.

1. *Exclusive rights conferred by law*

Patents and other exclusive rights often restrain entry effectively, but not necessarily. In the cases best known for the aspect relating to the free movement of goods,[32] the Court has repeatedly stressed that whether a

32. *E.g.* Case 24/67, *Parke Davis* v. *Probel* (1968) E.C.R. 55, (1968) C.M.L.R. 47; Case 78/70, *Deutsche Grammophon* v. *Metro* (1971) E.C.R. 487, (1971) C.M.L.R. 631, *etc.* Con-

patentee enjoys a dominant position depends on the absence of close substitutes.

2. *Economies of scale*

Baden Fuller[33] has elegantly demonstrated why economies of scale are not necessarily barriers to entry. If the market is expanding and can already absorb the production of some 10 plants of the minimum efficient scale, the market will soon be able to absorb the output of a new plant. If it can take only one, and is expanding but slowly, a prospective new entrant would realise that once his plant came on stream, there would be substantial idle capacity, and the owners of the two plants might compete in price until they were only covering their variable costs, allowing nothing for the capital costs. Such an investment is unlikely to be profitable. It is the probable lack of profits, rather than the size of the investment, that is the entry barrier. Many banks and other institutions will lend money for a profitable investment and large firms are often able to enter a new and profitable market. Only if the economies of scale continue to be large until a plant size is reached that can supply most of the existing market and expected increase, is there an entry barrier. This does not appear from the Community decisions.

As regards *United Brands*, I am told that a firm had to be able to bring a ship to Rotterdam or Bremerhaven at least once a week to catch the weekend trade in ripe bananas to be viable, although, presumably, two firms might arrange to bring one in a fortnight in alternate weeks, using the same ripeners. It does seem that the minimum size of operation was fairly large, about 10% of the demand in the six States.[34] This, however, does not appear from the decision. Economies must have continued beyond that point. A firm with ships only two days apart would probably be better able to cope with a temporary shortage, in a market where supplies are fixed for the period of the voyage, and the produce highly perishable, even when still green. Changes in the speed of ripening, which necessarily took between 5 and 8 days, would be easier to arrange when the consequent glut or shortage could be spread over frequent cargoes.

---

trast *General Motors*, cited at n. 26 above, where the legal exclusive right to issue certificates did confer a dominant position.

33. *Op. cit.* at p. 429.

34. It may be, however, that the relevant market was larger and the percentage less if those two ports also supplied France. See my argument about vitamins C and E, in text to n. 18 above.

3. *Vertical integration*

In *United Brands* the Court devoted several paragraphs to describing the degree of vertical integration enjoyed by U.B.C. It is not clear, however, whether it considered that this contributed to its dominant position.[35] United Brands owned banana plantations, although it bought in half its supplies; it had developed a new more prolific variety, resistant to disease, but seems to have enjoyed no plant breeders' rights; it owned two thirds of the refrigerated vessels on which its bananas travelled to Europe, although there was a freight market on which these could be hired by others; it had contractual arrangements with ripener/distributors in Europe, though these were not exclusive; its Chiquita brand, backed by careful quality control at all stages, was favoured by customers over other brands and attracted a premium. As Baden Fuller states (p. 440), vertical integration is not usually considered by economists to be a barrier to entry: barriers to entry at each level may be added up, but not multiplied.

4. *Technological lead*

Such an advantage[36] has been mentioned in several decisions and judgments, even when any patents have expired. The Court continues to mention such a lead in *United Brands* and *Vitamins.* Of course, the market leader's technological advantages may give it a margin of profit which a new entrant cannot obtain; but usually it has been paid for by investment in research and development. Where the technology can be copied at no greater cost by competitors, should it be treated any differently from the erection of a factory or any other investment? I shall return to this when considering the *Vitamins* judgment.

V. THE VITAMINS JUDGMENT

Apart from *Hugin*, when the only issue on dominance was the definition of the relevant market, the Court's latest views are set out in *Vitamins.* After stating that many factors might be relevant, but that large and continuing market shares were strong and even sufficient evidence of dominance,[37] the Court looked to various factors considered relevant by

35. The factors indicating lack of dominance were not stressed in the appraisal of either Commission or Court, but added by the author.

36. See Baden Fuller at p. 437—also text to n. 37 below.

37. See text to n. 15 above.

the Commission. At paragraphs 44-47 it listed some factors that it considered irrelevant.

1. *Factors that were not relevant*

The fact that Roche had maintained high market shares could be due to its effective competition. Nevertheless, the Court added that if a dominant position could be established from evidence, the maintenance of a high market share might indicate conduct amounting to an abuse (para. 44). The Court was not treating the maintenance of market share as an indication of dominance, and it is strange that the loyalty discounts that were held to amount to an abuse, partly because they made it more difficult for Roche's competitors to expand sales, were not considered by the Court at this point. Since the Court decided (para. 123) that conduct which reduces the enfeebled competition that remains to the dominant firm amounts to an abuse even if its effects are not perceptible, it did not state the extent of the foreclosure, but if it were substantial, it must have increased the barriers to entry and expansion.[38]

Despite the contrary opinion of Advocate General Reischl (p. 574), the Court held that Roche's wide range of vitamins was also irrelevant (para. 45). It had been conceded that each group of vitamins constituted a separate market, and some of Roche's competitors, such as the chemical producers, also enjoyed any cost savings in transport as they too supplied other products to the customers for vitamins.[39] Yet again, the Court condemned the tying effect of loyalty discounts that were aggregated across the various groups of vitamins, making it difficult for competitors who did not supply all those needed by a particular customer to obtain custom on the basis of efficiency. Surely, these effects, if they were substantial, must also have raised barriers to entry and expansion. This is another example of the relevance of factors outside the market defined as relevant.

The Court also refused to consider Roche's position as the largest vitamin producer in the world as relevant. Since each group of vitamins was made in a separate plant, there would be no economies of scale in production. The Commission had argued that Roche's strong world posi-

38. See Reischl at p. 580 in relation to Vitamin H. Of course, Roche could not use its market power twice over. To the extent that it encouraged customers to place additional orders with it, it had to give discounts, which must have reduced its profits. The Chicago School of economists would say, therefore, that it did not foreclose competition from equally efficient firms.

39. Is this an example where the Court would have looked to a factor outside the market defined as relevant, had it not found a compensating element?

tion enabled it to adopt regional strategies, but this was not thought conclusive. Despite this inconclusive argument, the Court held irrelevant Roche's position as the largest producer in the world. It added that some of its competitors were also large.

2. *Factors that were relevant*

The Court went on to list four factors that it did consider relevant: 1) the relationship between Roche's market shares with those of the next largest producers;[40] 2) its technical lead; 3) its highly developed sales network; and 4) the absence of potential competition;

> "the first because it enables the competitive strength of the undertakings to be assessed, the second and third because they represent in themselves technical and commercial advantages and the fourth because it is the consequence of the existence of obstacles preventing competitors from having access to the market."

One might think that the fact that viable competitors were smaller demonstrates that substantial economies of scale do not continue beyond the competitors' level of turnover, but it is possible that inefficiently small competitors might survive if the dominant firm were making monopoly profits. If they are much smaller than the dominant firm, they may be less willing to challenge its price leadership. Advocate General Reischl (at p. 565) pointed out the importance attributed to market shares in French, German and United States law.

The technical lead and developed sales network may well have conferred advantages on Roche;[41] but although efficiency may deter new or expanding firms, it is not usually listed by economists as a barrier to entry. It keeps out only less efficient firms, and those only as long as the dominant firm remains more efficient. Moreover, Roche must have invested money to gain its technical lead and marketing facility. Only if a newcomer would have to pay more would it be at a relative disadvantage. Of course, if Roche's advantages resulted from economies of scale they might have constituted an entry barrier.

The lack of potential competition seems to have been due to idle capacity which made further investment unprofitable.[42] The Court con-

40. See also *Continental Can*, cited at n. 7 above, at para. 30, where the Court stressed the much smaller shares of Schmalbach's competitors. Ditto in *United Brands*.

41. See text to n. 33 above.

42. It was not alleged that Roche had deliberately built excess capacity to deter competitors. For a general discussion of the distinction between idle and excess capacity, and why the former is not treated by economists as an entry barrier see Baden Fuller at p. 439.

sidered that Roche's position was privileged, because it could itself meet the total world demand. One might add that this privilege was bought at a price. Where there is excess capacity it is unlikely that the industry is currently profitable. Existing suppliers may try to increase their turnover by price cutting until only variable costs are covered.

The writer doubts whether these factors protected Roche from firms operating with equal efficiency. Article 86, however, and the preliminary articles of the Treaty do not mention efficiency specifically, although it can be read into Article 2—the higher standard of living that might be achieved by more efficient production and distribution of goods and services.

3. *Analysis of the vitamin markets*

In the light of these considerations, the Court analysed the markets for each group of vitamins separately. It placed considerable stress on market shares, but did not decide whether these should be judged by value or volume. Roche's tended to be higher by value. Advocate General Reischl pointed out that assessment by value was misleading when the value or part of the turnover was found at a different level of trade from the rest. The Commission had objected to assessment by tonnage, since some sales were at higher concentrations than others. Herr Reischl pointed out that allowance could be made for this and thought that comparisons by quantity were more reliable. Economists tend to agree since economies of scale are an engineering concept based on physical quantities.

The Advocate General rightly stressed (p. 580) that large market shares are less important when demand is expanding as it is for vitamins. Nevertheless, one might add that with substantial idle capacity in the industry, expansion in demand would not encourage new entry or expansion for some time.

In the case of vitamin B3, the Commission had found dominance solely on the basis of market shares, which by volume had increased from 18.9% in 1972 to 41.2% in 1974. The Court considered that in the absence of other indications, this was not sufficient to establish a dominant position. In 1973 a Japanese exporter had a larger share of the Community market.

At the other extreme, in considering vitamin B6[43] the Court seems to have accepted market shares in the eighties as sufficient evidence of a dominant position, especially as none of the four competitors reached as much as 10%. Roche may well have enjoyed freedom from competitive

43. See also B, C, and H. For vitamin C the share may have been as low as 64%.

constraints, there were no substitutes and we are told of some general entry barriers. Earlier[44] the Court had referred to market shares that endure, but here we are told of the shares over only three years. It is regretted that the qualifications made in paragraph 41 of the judgment seem to be neglected at this point.

Between these extremes came the A group,[45] of which Roche supplied 47% in all three years by value and volume. Other producers supplied 27, 18, 7 and 1% respectively. The Court characterised this as a narrow oligopolistic market, but did not refer to paragraph 39, where it had stated that oligopoly should be distinguished from monopoly. It looked also to Roche's technical advantage over its competitors and to the deterrent to new entrants caused by excess capacity.

4. *Roche's market behaviour*

Having established a *prima facie* case of dominance, the Court was, nevertheless, prepared to consider whether Roche's conduct demonstrated competitive pressures. The Court stated (para. 71) that having to lower prices under the pressure of price cuts from competitors would be incompatible with the independence of behaviour that is the hallmark of monopoly. Roche had produced statistics to show that world prices had dropped in real terms. Without admitting that world markets were representative of the common market, the Court pointed out that they indicated a correlation between prices on the one hand and the volume of production and costs on the other, rather than between prices and the pressures of competition. But what are the pressure of competition if not based on the volume of production and costs? Nevertheless, the writer agrees that falling world prices do not indicate a lack of dominance. In some industries technology improves rapidly and the costs of normally efficient firms diminish. Even a monopolist finds that it pays to reduce prices if marginal costs decline.

Roche had substantially reduced the price of Biotin, *i.e.*, vitamin H, of which it used to supply 100% but now only 93% in the common market, when it first expected imports from Japan. In the light of various manage-

44. See text to n. 16 above.

45. See also Group E, where Roche enjoyed shares in the fifties and lower sixties, other producers shares of 16%, 6%, 1% and an importer 19% by value. Since Roche alleged that some 60% of vitamin E may have been used in the antioxidant market in competition with other substitutes, and price discrimination was not possible between that and the bionutritive market, the writer is not convinced that Roche was dominant over vitamin E.

ment documents which seemed to show strategic pricing policies,[46] the Court treated this as a deliberately and freely chosen pricing policy rather than submission to competitive pressure. This indicates a limited view of competition. Most firms have some room for price strategy, to spend on promotion rather than cut prices, yet surely they cannot all be subject to the *ex post facto* control under Article 86, if they have substantial market shares.

In the light of various circumstances, the raising of prices, as well as their reduction, management documents indicating a choice of pricing policy and Roche's initiative in reducing prices before entry from Japan, the Court found no circumstances to rebut the initial and tentative finding that Roche enjoyed a dominant position over all vitamins listed by the Commission save B3.

In *United Brands* the Court refused to take into account the fact that the dominant firm had been making losses for four of the last five years. This may have been justified, since there had been a series of accidents—oil prices had risen, export taxes had been imposed on the countries where its bananas were grown, and there had been a serious hurricane. Five years is not very long to judge a monopolist's profit. Moreover, the figures were probably based on historic cost less depreciation, rather than on opportunity costs, the cost measured by alternative uses of the assets, which is the measure used by economists and sophisticated managements.

VI. CONCLUSION

Since its judgment in *United Brands*, the Court has confirmed findings of dominance when the firm involved seems to have been subject to lively competition and even when it was making losses while losing market share, as in that case. It still treats market shares in the eighties as a sufficient prima facie indication of dominance, although in *Vitamins* it had found the existence of entry barriers to the production of vitamins generally and there were no substitutes in the bio-nutritive market. Both Commission and Court tend to treat the cost of capital investment and the existence of knowhow as serious entry barriers, even when the minimum economic scale is not shown to be large in relation to the market, and without enquiring

46. At p. 425, Baden Fuller criticises the Court's excessive reliance on management documents on the ground that managers often like to believe that they have more market power than in fact they have.

Moreover, if the test of market power be the absence of risk, such a price cut to avoid the loss of market share does seem to indicate the lack of market power.

whether competitors could acquire technical help at no higher price than the firm alleged to be dominant. Nevertheless, in *Vitamins*, the Court has shown a far greater depth of understanding than in its earlier judgments.

The writer is, however, concerned that after defining the relevant market, often narrowly, neither Court nor Commission seem to consider competitive pressures that come from outside. They define a dominant position in terms of market power, but do not consider limitations to the power of a firm alleged to be dominant that come from outside the market defined as relevant. The United Kingdom Monopolies and Mergers Commission habitually considers competitive pressures exerted by suppliers of products outside the scope of its investigation: the extent to which sellers of tinned pet foods meet competition from scraps; that the makers of mineral insulated cable are subject to competition from other heat resistant cables. Of course, an analysis that requires officials to take into account more than the products supplied in the relevant market would be more complex and will not permit the simple use of market share criteria, but the Court has recognised that market shares are not the sole criterion of a dominant position, and a fuller analysis would result in the choice of the relevant market, which can only be arbitrary when there is no clear break in the chain of substitution on both the demand and supply sides of the market, from determining the matter. Arbitrary discretion would be limited by the relevance of other factors.

A further cause for concern is the apparent irrelevancy of efficiency. Some officials in the Commission appear to be concerned that there should be as many firms as possible in the market—that large firms should decline and smaller firms flourish. Like the classical economists, the writer is concerned that efficient firms, whether large or small, should flourish at the expense of those less good at providing what customers are prepared to buy. Barriers to entry consisting of earlier investment, for instance in technology or a good distribution network, do not keep out equally efficient firms, unless the first into the market has an advantage over those who enter later. This may have been the case for the Chiquita trade mark —other firms had to promote their brands after the Chiquita mark had won consumer acceptance and may have had to spend more on promotion—but it seems unlikely in the case of technology, which is usually acquired more easily at a later date unless there is patent protection, or a distribution network where other distributors can be encouraged to become equally efficient.

[15]

An Analysis of the Principles of Concerted Practice and Collective Dominance: A Distinction without a Difference?[1]

Trevor Soames

The concept of concerted practice is now, through a substantial amount of case law developed by the European Commission, the European Court of Justice ('ECJ') and more recently the Court of First Instance ('CFI'), well established and reasonably well defined. However, that of joint dominance is still at its earliest stages of development and inevitably lacks clarity: indeed, it would appear that two distinct forms of joint dominance analysis are developing, one which applies to the abusive exploitation of a dominant position under Article 86 of the EC Treaty (and, for that matter, Article 54 EEA[2]) and the other to the control of concentrations under the EC Merger Regulation ('ECMR').

The purpose of this article is to review the jurisprudence of both concepts, in their various forms, and analyse what behaviour they are capable of controlling: in particular the extent, if at all, they enable the European Commission to apply the competition rules and thereby control non-collusive parallel behaviour, particularly in oligopolistic markets. The importance of this question was underlined in the Commission's decision in the *Cartonboard*[3] case, in which substantial fines were levied on members of an alleged cartel which the Commission held had engaged in a variety of severe infringements of the competition rules (in particular, price fixing and market sharing). In its decision, the Commission expressed great concern at the 'considerable lengths' taken by the participants in the cartel 'to conceal their unlawful conduct'.[4] The reasons why the Commission considered that the attempts to disguise the existence of the cartel were a 'particularly grave aspect of the infringement'[5] were directly related to its concern that, as things stand, the application of the competition rules of the EC Treaty to control non-collusive parallel behaviour is circumscribed.

The nature of the problem, as perceived by the Commission, is apparent from the analysis in the *Cartonboard* decision of a number of arrangements which the Commission considered demonstrated that the major producers of cartonboard had agreed in advance on so-called 'price initiatives', which one of them would 'lead' the increase (and when) and the dates on which each of the others would 'follow' by sending out their letters to customers announcing price increases. The Commission stated:

> Had they been challenged, the producers could as a result of this elaborate scheme of deception have attributed the series of uniform, regular and industry-wide price increases in the cartonboard sector to the phenomenon of 'oligopoly behaviour'. They could argue that it made sense for all the producers to decide of their own volition to copy an increase initiated by one or other of the market leaders as soon as it became publicly known; unlawful collusion as such would not necessarily be indicated. Customers might well suspect and even accuse them of operating a cartel; and given the relatively large number of producers, economic theory would be stretched to its limits and beyond, but unless direct proof of collusion were forthcoming – and they went to some lengths to ensure that it was not – the producers must have had hopes of defeating an investigation into their pricing conduct by the competition authorities by invoking the defence of oligopolistic interdependence.[6]

Trevor Soames, Norton Rose, Brussels

1 This article was prepared for the 13th Annual Antitrust Conference held in Cambridge in September 1994 by European Study Conferences. It has since been updated to reflect recent developments.

2 For convenience, this article will make no distinction between the principles of concerted practice or joint dominance as between the EC Treaty and the Agreement establishing the EEA, as the substance of Articles 85 and 86 EC and that of Articles 53 and 54 EEA are, for our purposes, the same. Therefore, this article will make reference to Article 85 or Article 86 as appropriate, and not the equivalent provisions of the EEA Agreement. The same treatment is given to other legislative instruments, such as the EC Merger Regulation (Council Regulation (EC) 4064/89 of 21 December 1989 on the control of concentrations between undertakings, OJ 1989 L395/1, as reprinted in OJ 1990 L257/14).

3 *Cartonboard*, OJ 1994 L243/1. This decision is being challenged before the Court of First Instance in Cases T–295/94 etc., *Buchmann and Others v Commission*. These cases are pending hearing.

4 *Ibid.*, see Recitals 165 and 167 in particular.

5 *Ibid.*, Recital 167.

6 *Ibid.*, Recital 73.

This article will argue that because of the limitations placed on the application of the principle of concerted practice under Article 85 to oligopolistic parallel behaviour, the Commission is left with little opportunity to control such behaviour except in circumstances in which it can prove that it was a result of collusion, or in extreme cases that the existence of collusive behaviour (that is, concertation) was the only plausible explanation for the parallel conduct in question.

It has been suggested that the principle of joint dominance under Article 86 may fill the gap in regulatory control but that very much depends on the true meaning and effect of the developing and still unclear jurisprudence that defines its application. Can the Commission apply Article 86 to behaviour which can be considered as abusive, and therefore prohibited, because undertakings who individually would not have been considered dominant can be regarded as enjoying a joint dominant position? If so, what conditions have to be satisfied for it to apply and, in particular, does its scope extend to non-collusive oligopolistic behaviour? It is perhaps because of the difficulty of applying the competition rules to non-collusive oligopolistic behaviour that the Commission has developed a somewhat self-standing concept of joint dominance in the context of concentration control under the ECMR as a means of controlling the development of market structures which are considered likely to enhance the feasibility of collusive or non-collusive parallel behaviour.

Concerted Practice

Article 85(1) of the EC Treaty provides that:

> The following shall be prohibited as incompatible with the common market: all agreements between undertakings, decisions by associations of undertakings and *concerted practices* which may affect trade between Member States and which have as their object or effect the prevention, restriction or distortion of competition within the common market . . . (*emphasis added*)

The reference to 'concerted practices' in Article 85(1) brings under its control forms of collusive behaviour that do not qualify as agreements or decisions by associations of undertakings.[7] The main effect of the concept of concerted practice is to ensure that undertakings cannot avoid the application of the prohibition on anti-competitive practices contained in Article 85(1) by ensuring that the collusive behaviour is characterised by a lesser degree of formality than is inherent in either 'agreements' or 'decisions', however expansively interpreted.

The essential elements of the concept of concerted practice have been defined in a number of leading cases, only the most important of which are referred to in the following paragraphs. In *Dyestuffs*[8] the ECJ held that the purpose of including 'concerted practice' in Article 85(1) was to:

> bring within the prohibition of that article a form of coordination between undertakings which, without having reached the stage where an agreement properly so-called has been concluded, knowingly substitutes practical cooperation between them for the risks of competition.[9]

The ECJ stated that it was unnecessary for a concerted practice to have all the elements of a contract but it could arise out of co-ordination which becomes apparent from the behaviour of the participating undertakings.[10] Although parallel behaviour of itself could not be identified with a concerted practice, the ECJ considered that it could amount to strong evidence of such behaviour if it could be shown to have led to conditions of competition which did not correspond to those which would normally have been expected to apply in the particular market under review.[11] The ECJ stated that the existence or otherwise of concerted behaviour could only be determined by a detailed review of the operations of the market. In the event, the review which the ECJ then proceeded to carry out was not particularly thorough[12] and it came to the conclusion that it was unlikely that the similar price increases which had occurred on all the national markets were the result of parallel but independent action (that is, non-collusive parallelism).[13] In particular,

7 For an evaluation of the general principles of Article 85, reference can be made to a wide variety of texts including *Butterworths Competition Law* (Division I by Professor Richard Whish and Peter Freeman), 1991 and updated thereafter, and Bellamy & Child, *Common Market Law of Competition*, (ed. Vivien Rose), Sweet & Maxwell, 4th edn 1992, at Chapter 2.

8 Case 48/69, *ICI v Commission* [1972] ECR 619.
9 *Ibid.*, paragraph 64.
10 *Ibid.*, paragraph 65.
11 *Ibid.*, paragraph 66.
12 Among the critical analyses of the judgment of the ECJ in *Dyestuffs* was that of the late Professor Joliet (later to be the judge rapporteur in the *Woodpulp II* case) who condemned the Court's willingness to conclude that there had been collusive behaviour falling within the prohibition of Article 85(1) on the basis of a series of advance price announcements without clear evidence of concertation – although there was some, see paragraphs 96 and 97 and the *rapport d'audience* – and without undertaking a thorough examination of the market conditions: 'La notion de pratique concertée et l'arrêt ICI dans une perspective coopérative', 15 Cahiers Dr. Eur. (1974).
13 Note 8 above, paragraphs 101 to 113 in particular.

the ECJ identified the making of advance announcements of price changes by the undertakings operating in the market as having:

> eliminated in advance any uncertainties concerning their reciprocal behaviour on the different markets and thereby also eliminated a large part of the risk inherent in any independent change of conduct on those markets.[14]

After reaching the conclusion that the implementation of general and uniform increases in prices on the different markets could only be explained by 'a common intention' on the part of the undertakings concerned to adjust price levels (and discounts) – as well as to minimise the risk of 'changing the conditions of competition' inherent in increasing prices[15] – the ECJ made the following vital statement of principle:

> Although every producer is free to change his prices, taking into account in so doing the present or foreseeable conduct of his competitors, nevertheless it is contrary to the rules on competition contained in the Treaty for a producer *to cooperate with his competitors, in any way whatsoever*, in order to determine *a coordinated course of action* relating to a price increase and to ensure its success by prior elimination of all uncertainty as to each other's conduct regarding the essential elements of that action, such as the amount, subject-matter, date and place of the increases. (*emphases added*)

In the *Sugar*[16] case, the ECJ built on the definition of concerted practice expounded in *Dyestuffs* by explaining that the criteria of 'co-ordination' and 'co-operation' in that case did 'not require the working out of an actual plan'. The Court defined a concerted practice as being:

> a form of cooperation between undertakings, which, without having been taken to the stage where an agreement properly so-called has been concluded, knowingly substitutes for the risks of competition, practical cooperation between them which leads to conditions of competition which do not correspond to the normal conditions of the market . . . Such practical cooperation amounts to a concerted practice, particularly if it enables the persons concerned to consolidate established positions to the detriment of effective freedom of movement of the products in the common market and of the freedom of consumers to choose their suppliers.[17]

The insertion of the word 'knowingly' in the extract cited above makes it clear that the Court considered that unconscious parallel behaviour could not constitute a concerted practice, but left the door somewhat ajar for conscious, although non-collusive, parallel behaviour to be so considered. In a further statement of principle the Court held that concerted practice had to be:

> understood in the light of the concept inherent in the provisions of the Treaty relating to competition that each economic operator must determine independently the policy which he intends to adopt on the common market including the choice of the persons or undertakings to which he makes offers or sells.
>
> Although it is correct to say that this requirement of independence does not deprive economic operators of the right to adapt themselves intelligently to the existing and anticipated conduct of their competitors, it does however strictly preclude any direct or indirect contact between such operators, the object and effect whereof is either to influence the conduct on the market of an actual or potential competitor or to disclose to such a competitor the course of conduct which they themselves have decided to adopt or contemplate adopting on the market.[18]

On the facts of the case, the Court concluded that the documentary evidence demonstrated that Suiker Unie, Centrale Suiker Maatschappij and Raffinerie Tirlemontoise had contacted each other and that 'they in fact pursued the aim of removing in advance any uncertainty as to the future conduct of their competitors'[19] and that the activities under consideration:

> did not in any way result from independent decisions by the producers concerned but were concerted between them because they knowingly substituted for the risks of competition practical cooperation between them, which culminated in a situation which did not correspond to the normal conditions of the market, even taking account of its special nature, and allowed Netherlands producers to maintain positions which they had established to the detriment of effective freedom of movement of the products in the common market and of the freedom of consumers to choose their suppliers.[20]

In *Zuchner*,[21] the ECJ expanded on its previous jurisprudence by indicating that the existence of an information exchange might be sufficient to enable the national court to conclude that there had been a concerted practice within the meaning of Article 85(1) even if there were no 'contacts'.[22] The Court went on to say that the referring national court could conclude that the parallel conduct constituted a concerted practice 'if it is established . . . that such parallel conduct exhibits the features of coordination

14 *Ibid.*, paragraph 112.
15 *Ibid.*, paragraphs 104 to 114.
16 Cases 40/73 etc., *Suiker Unie v Commission* [1975] ECR 1663.
17 *Ibid.*, paragraph 26.
18 *Ibid.*, paragraphs 173 and 174.
19 *Ibid.*, paragraph 175.
20 *Ibid.*, paragraph 191.
21 Case 172/80, *Zuchner v Bayerische Vereinsbank* [1981] ECR 2021.
22 *Ibid.*, paragraph 21.

and cooperation characteristic of such a practice and if that practice is capable of significantly affecting conditions of competition in the market.'[23]

The principles established by the ECJ in *Dyestuffs* and *Sugar* have been followed in a large number of subsequent Commission decisions and judgments of both the ECJ and CFI. In particular, in a series of 13 separate judgments on applications for annulment brought by addressees of the Commission's decision in the *Polypropylene* case[24] the CFI held that the existence of a concerted practice had been established. Although the wording varied somewhat between the judgments, the following statement from *Shell v Commission*[25] is representative:

> In the present case, [Shell] was in contact with other producers and took part in meetings of the 'big four', and its operating companies took part in local meetings concerning the fixing of price and sales volume targets, during which information was exchanged between competitors about the prices they wished to see charged on the market, the prices they intended to charge, their profitability thresholds, the sales volume restrictions they judged to be necessary, their sales figures or the identity of their customers. Through those contacts and its participation in those meetings, it took part, together with its competitors, in concerted action the purpose of which was to influence their conduct on the market and to disclose to each other the course of conduct which each of the producers itself contemplated adopting on the market.
>
> Thus, not only did [Shell] pursue the aim of eliminating in advance uncertainty about the future conduct of its competitors but also, in determining the policy which it intended to follow on the market, it could not fail to take account, directly or indirectly, of the information obtained through those contacts or during those meetings. Similarly, in determining the policy which they intended to follow, its competitors were bound to take into account, directly or indirectly, the information disclosed to them by [Shell] about the course of conduct which [Shell] itself had decided upon or which it contemplated adopting on the market.[26]

In summary, therefore, for a concerted practice within the meaning of Article 85(1) to be deemed to exist, the following criteria have to be satisfied:

- there must be co-ordinated behaviour;
- the co-ordination must be as a result of direct or indirect contact;
- the purpose of such contact was to affect market behaviour.

Obviously, and to the understandable irritation of the competition authorities, those engaged in collusive cartel behaviour that risks being seen as falling within the prohibition of Article 85(1) – whether it be by way of agreement, decision or concerted practice – generally take great pains to 'cover their tracks' by, for example, ensuring that no written record exists of their contacts or those that did exist were not retained: this is clearly evidenced by a review of many of the major cartel cases of recent years. As a result, it can be very difficult for the Commission to obtain sufficient evidence to prove that parallel behaviour was a result of prohibited collusion.[27]

It is unfortunate that the very real difficulties faced by the Commission in establishing the existence of collusive cartel behaviour have sometimes led some of the dedicated but perhaps overenthusiastic officials in DGIV to construct statements of objections and, ultimately, final decisions on the basis of evidence, part of which has been dealt with in a rather imaginative and unsatisfactory manner. Practitioners are unfortunately faced, with disconcerting frequency, with a variety of techniques which may be intended to assist the Commission in proving the existence of prohibited behaviour, but which are somewhat dubious; for example, the reliance sometimes placed by the Commission on purported evidence such as documents (or parts of documents) which have been taken out of their true context, or selectively quoted or badly translated. The detailed analysis conducted by the CFI in *Flat Glass*[28] revealed the unsatisfactory nature of some of the Commission's analysis in that case, but unfortunately the investigative techniques that were exposed in the CFI's judgment were not, and are not, unique to that case.[29]

23 *Ibid.*, paragraph 22.
24 OJ 1986 L230/1.
25 Case T–11/89, *Shell International Chemical Company Limited v Commission* [1992] ECR II 757.
26 *Ibid.*, paragraphs 301 and 302.

27 A taste of the frustration felt by the Commission can be gleaned from *Cartels: Proof and Procedural Issues* by two officials of DGIV/C, Maurice Guerrin and Georgios Kyriazis, Fordham, 1992. For example, the authors expressed concern that there is 'an obvious imbalance in the power play which opposes on one side the authors of a secret cartel, who are in possession of the evidence concerning the infringement of competition rules and deploy all necessary efforts to dissimulate it by using all available means, and on the other side the officials of the antitrust authority who, whatever the extent of their powers to carry out investigations and their determination to implement them, are very often helpless against the sophisticated methods of dissimulation and destruction of evidence employed by those responsible for the organisation of the cartel.' See also the Commission's decision in the *Cartonboard* case at Recitals 73 and 167: 1994 OJ L243/1.
28 Cases T–68/89 etc., *Società Italiano Vetro v Commission* [1992] 5 CMLR 302.
29 For the uninitiated, a reading of the CFI's judgment in *Flat Glass* can be rather disconcerting. For those who are not tempted to wade through the whole judgment a flavour of the

Crucial to a complete understanding of the concept of concerted practice and the evidence that has to be adduced by the Commission to prove its existence is the *Woodpulp II* case.[30] In the contested decision which was appealed to the ECJ,[31] the Commission found that 40 wood pulp producers and three of their trade associations had infringed Article 85(1) by concerting on prices for the supply of bleached sulphate wood pulp announced for deliveries within the EC. The Commission imposed fines of between ECU50,000 and 500,000 on 36 of the 43 addressees of the decision. The main body of the case revolved around the Court's analysis of whether the system of quarterly price announcements was, in itself, an infringement of Article 85(1) and/or was evidence of prior concertation.

The Court held that the making of quarterly price announcements on the wood pulp market could not be regarded as constituting in itself an infringement of Article 85(1).[32] The Court rejected the Commission's argument that the price announcement system was deliberately introduced by the pulp producers in order to enable them to ascertain the prices that would be charged by their competitors in the following months. It was alleged that the disclosure of the prices that would be charged well before their application at the beginning of a new quarterly period gave sufficient time for producers to align their prices at similar levels. Furthermore, the Court did not accept the additional argument put forward by the Commission that the implementation of the price announcement mechanism had the effect of making the market artificially transparent by enabling producers to obtain a rapid and accurate picture of the prices quoted by their competitors. In coming to its conclusion, the Court referred to its previous judgment in *Sugar*[33] that a concerted practice comprises a form of co-ordination between undertakings which, without having been taken to the stage where an agreement properly so-called had been concluded, knowingly substitutes practical co-operation for the risks of competition. The Court held that the communications condemned by the Commission arose from announcements made to third parties, namely users, and constituted market behaviour which did not lessen each undertaking's uncertainty as to the future actions that may be taken by the other undertakings.[34]

The Court did not accept the alternative proposition put forward by the Commission, namely that the system of price announcements constituted evidence of concertation at an earlier stage. To prove the alleged concerted practice the Commission relied on:

- the parallel conduct of the pulp producers in making quarterly price announcements, in the simultaneity or near simultaneity of the announcements and the fact that the announced prices were identical;
- the direct and indirect exchange of information on prices through meetings and contacts between certain pulp producers.

In the event, the Court ruled as inadmissible the documentary evidence relied on by the Commission to prove the existence of meetings and contacts between the producers.[35] Therefore, the only remaining evidence on which the Commission could base its case of an Article 85(1) infringement was the system of quarterly price announcements, the simultaneity or near simultaneity of the price announcements and the parallelism of the price announcements in the period of time under consideration. The Court took as its task to undertake a detailed study of whether such circumstances constituted 'a firm, precise and consistent body of

29 continued
case can be derived from paragraphs such as 92, 93, 94, 142, 205, 215, 218, 219, 224, 226 and 273.

The discomfort felt by the Commission with the *Flat Glass* judgment was made clear in the study of the types of evidence used by the Commission in establishing the existence, or otherwise, of collusive behaviour (whether by way of agreement, decision or concerted practice) contained in Guerrin and Kyriazis, Note 27 above. The authors, whose unit was primarily responsible for the *Flat Glass* decision, found the attitude of the CFI to be 'alarming' because it tended to 'examine findings of fact and evidence individually, examining if each of them alone is sufficient to prove the alleged cooperation, contrary to the consistent case law of the ECJ which evaluates the various elements of evidence in relation to each other as well as the behaviour of the companies'. No doubt the ECJ will, at some point, resolve this dispute but until then the Commission is on notice that its decisions in competition cases will be annulled in whole or in part if it fails to heed what the CFI has clearly indicated.

30 Cases C–89/85 etc., *A Ahlstrom Oy v Commission* [1993] ECR I 1307, as amended by an order of the Court of 20 January 1994.

31 *Woodpulp* OJ 1984 L85/1.

32 *Ibid.*, paragraph 65.

33 Note 16 above, at paragraphs 26 and 173.

34 Note 31 above, paragraphs 59 to 65.

35 The documents were ruled inadmissible because the Commission was unable to specify between which producers the concertation established by each telex or document took place and over what period. As a result, the Court considered that it was not possible to rely on the documents as evidence of infringement because of the Commission's inability to specify, to the satisfaction of the Court, what their probative value was: *ibid.*, paragraphs 68 and 69.

evidence of prior concertation'.[36] The Court held that parallel conduct could not of itself be regarded as furnishing proof of concertation unless that was the 'only' plausible explanation for that conduct. Relying on *Sugar*,[37] the Court reasserted that Article 85 did not deprive undertakings of the right to adapt themselves intelligently to the existing and anticipated conduct of their competitors.

The evaluation undertaken by the Court to establish whether the parallel conduct could be explained by something other than concertation involved the appointment of economic experts to examine the market for bleached sulphate pulp and to report on whether the natural operation of the wood pulp market would lead to a differential price structure or to the observed uniform price structure: this was a far cry from the rather less rigorous analysis conducted by the Court in *Dyestuffs* and which Professor Joliet, the judge rapporteur in *Woodpulp II*, had trenchantly criticised at the time.[38] The experts concluded, as the appellant undertakings had argued, that the simultaneity or near simultaneity of the price announcements was a direct result of the very high degree of transparency of the market and that such transparency could be explained by the nature and structure of the market.[39] Furthermore, the experts concluded that the normal operation of the market was a more plausible explanation for the uniformity of prices than collusive behaviour.[40]

In the result, the Court held that concertation was not the only plausible explanation for the parallel conduct because:

> To begin with, the system of price announcements may be regarded as constituting a rational response to the fact that the pulp market constituted a long-term market and to the need felt by both buyers and sellers to limit commercial risks. Further, the similarity in the dates of price announcements may be regarded as a direct result of the high degree of market transparency, which does not have to be described as artificial. Finally, the parallelism of prices and the price trends may be satisfactorily explained by the oligopolistic tendencies of the market and by the specific circumstances prevailing in certain periods. Accordingly, the parallel conduct established by the Commission does not constitute evidence of concertation.
>
> In the absence of a firm, precise and consistent body of evidence, it must be held that concertation regarding announced prices has not been established by the Commission.[41]

The judgment of the ECJ in *Woodpulp II* confirmed that Article 85 cannot be applied to non-collusive parallel behaviour and that it is not sufficient for the Commission to rely on parallel behaviour as proving, of itself, the existence of concertation contrary to Article 85(1) unless, after detailed economic analysis, that is the only plausible explanation.

The effect of *Woodpulp II* is clear from the Commission's decision in the *Cartonboard* case in which it recognised that in the absence of direct proof of collusion it would have been difficult to have demonstrated that the parallel behaviour was a result of prohibited concertation. Nevertheless, the decision indicated that the Commission had some confidence that even had there been no direct evidence it may have been able to conclude that the parallel behaviour was collusive:

> Even without the documentary evidence of collusion and Stora's detailed statements, the uniformity of the price increases announced by the cartonboard producers and the simultaneity of their introduction in each west European national market over a period of several years are so striking that on this basis alone the inference of prior collusion would have been almost inescapable.[42]

In the event, the Commission felt able to conclude that the observed parallel behaviour, 'coupled with the incriminating documents . . . leaves no doubt whatever that the price increases were planned, organized and monitored by a European cartel of producers.'[43] Some producers argued that the industry price initiatives subject to Commission investigation were not the result of collusion but a result of market forces and the legitimate acquisition of information from the press or customers. The Commission accepted that price increase letters originating from competitors were found at a number of producers in the course of on-the-spot inspections, but set against 'the direct evidence of collusion' this did not provide an innocent explanation for the close parallelism in pricing behaviour.[44]

In conclusion, the concept of concerted practice is well defined but does not extend to non-collusive parallel behaviour. Furthermore, a concerted practice cannot be presumed to have taken place merely

36 *Ibid.*, paragraph 70.
37 See paragraph 174 of the judgment, cited at Note 16 above.
38 Professor Joliet, Note 12 above. See also Gerwin van Gerven and Edurne Navarro Varona, 'The Wood Pulp Case and the Future of Concerted Practices', (1994) 31 CML Rev. 575 to 608.
39 Note 31 above, paragraphs 81 and 82.
40 *Ibid.*, paragraph 101.

41 *Ibid.*, paragraphs 126 and 127.
42 Note 3 above, Recital 113.
43 *Ibid.*
44 *Ibid.*, Recital 114.

on the basis of observed parallel behaviour unless it is found, after detailed economic evaluation, that the only plausible explanation is concertation (that is, collusion). Some commentators have considered that because Article 85(1) does not provide a system capable of controlling non-collusive parallel behaviour in oligopolistic markets, the concept of joint or collective dominance under Article 86 has become of greater importance since 'it could provide such a means of regulation.'[45] The following section of this article will review the jurisprudence relating to joint dominance and consider whether it does, or could, apply to such behaviour.

Joint Dominance

Compared to the concept of concerted practice under Article 85(1) the application of that of joint dominance under Article 86 is at its earliest stage of development with a limited number of Commission decisions applying its principles, and three somewhat obscure judgments of the CFI and the ECJ. The use of a somewhat different version of joint dominance by the Commission, as part of its appraisal of concentrations under the ECMR and thereby to exercise some control over the development of market structures that could facilitate either collusive or non-collusive oligopolistic behaviour, is rather more advanced, with a number of extant Commission decisions but, to date, no judgments of either the CFI or ECJ.

Application of joint dominance in Article 86 procedures

Article 86 prohibits the abusive exploitation 'by one or more undertakings' of a dominant position within the Common Market or in a substantial part of it. Despite the reference within the text of Article 86 of it applying to the behaviour of more than one undertaking, the number of cases on joint or collective dominance is extremely limited and there have only been sporadic efforts by the Commission to develop its principles.

In its *European Sugar Industry* decision[46] the Commission found that there had been infringements of Articles 85 and 86 on the part of Raffinerie Tirlemontoise ('RT'), Suiker Unie ('SU') and Centrale Suiker Maatschappij ('CSM'). The Commission stated that some of the measures taken by the three companies towards their clients and dealers which it had condemned as concerted practices contrary to Article 85 also comprised infringements of Article 86.[47] The Commission concluded that RT had abused its individually held dominant position and that certain behaviour of the two Dutch sugar producers, SU and CSM, comprised an abuse of jointly held dominant position:

> SU and CSM have a dominant position on the Dutch market which constitutes a substantial part of the Common Market. These two producers cooperate closely in almost all their activities, that is to say the joint purchase of raw materials, rationing of production, collaboration in the use of intermediate products, pooling of research, cooperation on market research, advertising and sales promotions and the harmonization of ex-factory prices and conditions of sale. Towards other undertakings and particularly towards the three dealers mentioned above, these two producers have acted in a uniform manner and always appear as a single entity.
>
> The dominant position of these two producers is due to the fact that they produced all Dutch sugar and their sales represent more than 85 per cent of the Dutch market, and that they are able to behave independently which permits them to act without taking any particular account of their competitors. This dominant position is strengthened further by the fact that they control by various direct or indirect means almost all the sugar imported into the Netherlands.[48]

The Commission then set out the various grounds on which it considered that SU and CSM had exploited their dominant position.

Subsequent judicial developments restricted the potential scope of application of a concept of joint dominance, particularly the combined effects of the judgments of the ECJ in a number of cases in which it sought to maintain a distinction between the application of Articles 85 and 86 such as *Sugar*,[49] *Hoffmann-La Roche*[50] and *Zuchner*.[51] It is perhaps for this reason that joint dominance did not rear its head again until the late 1980s when it became expedient for the Commission to revive it with a view to its use as an additional method of concentration control if the Council of Ministers failed to adopt what was ultimately to become the ECMR.

In its 1975 judgment in the *Sugar* case, the ECJ did not have to come to a conclusion on the finding of joint dominance in the Commission's prior *European Sugar Industry* decision.[52] However, in its

45 See, for example, Alison Jones, 'Woodpulp: Concerted Practice and/or Conscious Parallelism', [1993] 6 ECLR 273.
46 *European Sugar Industry* OJ 1973 L140/17.

47 *Ibid.*, section E, first paragraph.
48 *Ibid.*, section E(1).
49 Note 16 above.
50 Case 85/76, *Hoffmann-La Roche v Commission* [1979] ECR 461.
51 Note 21 above.
52 Note 46 above.

discussion of the application of Article 85, the Court emphasised that although each economic operator must determine independently the policy which it intended to adopt on the Common Market, that requirement of independence did 'not deprive economic operators of the right to adapt themselves intelligently to the existing and anticipated conduct of their competitors.'[53] In 1979, the Court held in *Hoffmann-La Roche*[54] that oligopolistic but non-collusive parallel behaviour fell outside the scope of Article 86:

> A dominant position must also be distinguished from parallel courses of conduct which are peculiar to oligopolies in that in an oligopoly the courses of conduct interact, while in the case of an undertaking occupying a dominant position the conduct of the undertaking which deprives profits from that position is to a great extent determined unilaterally.[55]

Finally, in the *Zuchner* judgment of 1981[56] the Advocate General, Sir Gordon Slynn, drew a distinction between the concept of concerted practice under Article 85 and the control of abusive dominant behaviour under Article 86:

> A concerted practice, while lacking the consensual nature of an agreement or decision, implies a series of independent acts which between them substitute cooperation for competition. In contrast, one of the hallmarks of a dominant position covered by Article 86 is its unilateral nature. As a result . . . it is right to point out that only the former applies if the facts establish the existence of a concerted practice. Nevertheless, it may be that, when making its findings of fact, the Amtsgericht [the referring national court] may also wish to consider whether there is evidence of an abuse of a dominant position, rather than a concerted practice.[57]

For its part, the ECJ stated that 'Article 86 deals with the abuse of a dominant position and does not cover the existence of concerted practices, to which solely the provisions of Article 85 apply'.[58]

It was not until 1987, during the period of time when the Commission was asserting its competence over mergers[59] (and other transactions that the Commission felt convenient to portray as mergers) under both Articles 85 and 86, that the Commission raised the joint dominance issue in a direct and substantive way. It is likely that this was done in an effort to increase the level of uncertainty in the field of merger control (so as to persuade recalcitrant Member States that it would be better for them to accede to the Commission's pressure and adopt the much-delayed merger regulation than continue the unwelcome level of uncertainty). Furthermore, the principle of joint dominance, if developed successfully, could have been a useful addition to the somewhat limited arsenal of weapons available to the Commission should the Council fail to adopt the proposed merger regulation in an acceptable form.

In 1988 the ECJ delivered its judgment in the *Alsatel v Novasam*[60] case on an Article 177 reference. During the course of the written procedure, the Commission submitted observations in December 1986 and April 1987 and raised the issue of joint dominance. The Commission pointed out that although Alsatel (with approximately one-third of the Alsatian market) did not enjoy a dominant position at regional, let alone national, level, the concept of joint dominance under Article 86 may have been of relevance. The *rapport d'audience*[61] states that the Commission observed that:

> the case should be considered from the point of view of a dominant position occupied by undertakings collectively. Until now the Court has expressly acknowledged that undertakings are collectively in a dominant position where several undertakings belonging to the same group of undertakings, or adopting an agreement, decision or concerted practice amongst themselves, together have the power to impede competition in a substantial part of the relevant market.

After citing *Deutsche Grammophon v Metro*[62] and the *Sugar* case in purported support of that proposition the Commission is then reported to have argued that:

> a dominant position occupied by undertakings collectively may also arise from parallel behaviour on the part of several undertakings . . . If, therefore, it is established the [the contracts under consideration] reflect a standard trading practice, they must be regarded as an abuse of a dominant position occupied by undertakings collectively.

The attempt to apply the concept of joint dominance to parallel non-collusive oligopolistic behaviour did not get very far. The Court considered that it was

53 Note 16 above, paragraphs 173 and 174.
54 Note 50 above.
55 *Ibid.*, paragraph 39.
56 Note 21 above. See the comment of Professor Valentine Korah in EL Rev. [1982] at 226 to 229.
57 Note 21 above, at 2039.
58 *Ibid.*, paragraph 10.
59 The impetus for the Commission's pressure came from the variety of interpretations that could be accorded to the sometimes hazy reasoning of the ECJ in the *Philip Morris* case, Cases 142 and 156/84, *BAT and R.J. Reynolds v Commission* [1986] ECR 1899.

60 Case 247/86, *Alsatel v Novasam* [1988] ECR 5987.
61 *Ibid.*, at 5993 and 5994.
62 Case 78/70, *Deutsche Grammophon v Metro* [1971] ECR 487.

unable to consider the application of joint dominance as it was unconnected with the facts before the national court which made the Article 177 reference and was based solely on the somewhat imprecise information in the Commission's possession. If it wished, the Commission could investigate the matter further under the powers conferred on it but it was not a matter which the Court had any need to decide on.[63]

In December 1988, the Commission adopted the controversial *Italian Flat Glass*[64] decision. The Commission held that three Italian producers of flat glass had infringed both Articles 85 and 86. As regards Article 86, the Commission considered that the three producers enjoyed a collective dominant position, operating in a so-called 'tight oligopoly' and thereby enjoying a degree of independence from competitive pressures that enabled them to impede the maintenance of effective competition, notably by not having to take account of the behaviour of other market participants.[65] The basis for the Commission's conclusion that the flat glass producers were jointly dominant was set out as follows:

> The undertakings present themselves on the market as a single entity and not as individuals.
>
> As may be seen from what was said in paragraphs 35 to 42, the three producers jointly maintain special links with a group of wholesalers who are the main glass distributors in Italy, they instigate the meetings, and they do everything possible to get them to accept price list changes and to ensure that the changes are passed on downstream in a consistent manner, so as to prevent any individual decisions by the wholesalers from creating commercial pressures on each producer leading to changes in market equilibria.
>
> The business decisions taken by the three producers display a marked degree of interdependence with regard to prices and terms of sale, relations with customers and business strategies.
>
> The three undertakings have in addition established among themselves structural links relating to production through the systematic exchange of products, as described under heading 6. The exchanges are, firstly, the result of some undertakings' lack of primary products or certain processed products and, secondly, the expression and instrument of their desire to prevent this situation from resulting in changes in their relative positions on the market and in existing relations between them.[66]

The application for annulment of the Commission's decision was one of the first cases to come before the CFI. The detailed investigation conducted by the judge rapporteur and the Court, as well as the eventual judgment, concentrated on the finding that there had been an infringement of Article 85(1). Indeed, it was only in respect of the infringements of Article 85(1) that the Commission had imposed fines because, first, it considered that they should not be imposed cumulatively in respect of the same set of facts and, second, because it was the first time that the concept of collective dominance had been applied by the Commission.[67] The failure of the Commission to substantiate its central allegation, made at Recital 79 of the decision, that the three flat glass manufacturers presented themselves on the market 'as a single entity and not as individuals' meant that it was unnecessary for the Court to deal with the issue of joint dominance in any detail.[68] As regards Recital 79, the central plank of the Commission's case regarding the application of Article 86 to the facts of the case, the Court held that:

> It is evident from all the foregoing that the Commission has far from substantiated that statement.
>
> It follows that, even supposing that the circumstances of the present case lend themselves to application of the concept of 'collective dominant position' (in the sense of a position of dominance held by a number of independent undertakings), the Commission has not adduced the necessary proof. The Commission has not even attempted to gather the information necessary to weigh up the economic power of the three producers against that of Fiat, which could cancel each other out.[69]

As a result, the Court confined itself to some broad statements of principle which, by their nature, were not necessary to its determination of the case and can be regarded very much as *obiter dicta*. It would be a grave mistake to regard the oft-cited statement at paragraph 358 of the judgment[70] as being the CFI's last word on this subject and it is highly likely that, as and when the application of joint dominance comes before the CFI for decision, a more detailed and enlightening analysis may be forthcoming.[71] In *Flat Glass* the CFI had to decide

63 See Josephine Shaw, 'Collective Dominance or Concerted Practices', EL Rev. [1989], at 96 to 99.
64 *Italian Flat Glass* OJ 1989 L33/44.
65 *Ibid.*, Recitals 78 and 79.
66 *Ibid.*, Recital 79.

67 *Ibid.*, Recital 84(a).
68 Note 28 above, paragraph 365.
69 *Ibid.*, paragraphs 365 and 366.
70 See below.
71 The Commission's decision in *Cewal* OJ 1993 L34/20 is under appeal to the CFI in Cases T-24/93 *Compagnie Maritime Belge*, T-25/93 *Dafra Lines*, T-26/93 *Deutsche Afrika-Linien* and T-28/93 *Nedlloyd Linien*. The summary of the applications (contained in OJ 1993 C122/8) states that the pleadings raise the question of whether Article 86 'covers the abuse of a collective dominant position and whether Article 86 can be applied simultaneously with Article 85(1) of the EC

on a number of highly controversial matters primarily relating to whether the Commission's reasoning, which established an infringement of Article 85(1), was soundly based. The Article 86 joint dominance issue was of subsidiary importance (particularly in the light of the fact that no fines had been imposed by the Commission for the alleged Article 86 infringement). The Court noted that the very first words of the first paragraph of Article 86 provide that 'one or more undertakings' may abuse a dominant position and concluded that the word 'undertakings' had the same meaning in Article 86 as it did under Article 85, namely that it refers to 'two or more economic entities which are capable of competing with each other'.[72]

The Court's statement of principle at paragraph 358 of the *Flat Glass* judgment reads as follows:

> There is nothing, in principle, to prevent two or more independent economic entities[73] from being, on a specific market, united by such economic links that, by virtue of that fact, together they hold a dominant position vis-à-vis the other operators on the same market. This would be the case, for example, where two or more independent undertakings jointly have, through agreements or licences, a technological lead affording them the power to behave to an appreciable extent independently of their competitors, their customers and ultimately of their consumers . . .

The precise meaning of 'economic links' is unclear: does it refer to arrangements which would be capable of falling within the scope of Article 85 (such as an agreement or concerted practice) or does it refer to some other type of 'link'; for example, a purely 'economic' link as opposed to a consensual one? The reference in paragraph 358 to agreements or licences, when taken together with the cryptic reference in paragraph 359 of the judgment to Article 8(2) of Council Regulation 4056/86[74] (which refers to the Commission's power to withdraw the benefit of the block exemption where the conduct of a liner conference[75] has effects which are incompatible with Article 86), indicates that the CFI contemplated that joint dominance could be of relevance to abusive behaviour where the 'economic links' are consensual (and thereby also capable of falling within the scope of Article 85). However, in addition, there may be other forms of economic linkage not involving any form of consensual arrangement or collusive behaviour between two or more independent undertakings but which, nevertheless, may fall within the scope of the principles set out by the Court. For example, if undertaking A and undertaking B are, separately, the licensees of undertaking C in the manufacture and distribution of a new product and between them they occupy a dominant position in a discrete market and they operate (independently) in a similar but abusive manner, for example by engaging in excessive pricing, then perhaps they may be considered as jointly dominant for the purposes of Article 86. Recent ECJ case law on the issue has only further confused the definition of collective dominant position.[76] The ECJ judgment pronounced in April 1994 in the *Almelo* case[77] suggests that independent licensees could be considered as being jointly dominant. The *Almelo* case is one of a number of recent

71 *continued*
Treaty to a given conduct'. No date for the oral hearing has yet been set for these cases.

72 Note 28 above, paragraph 357.

73 Therefore, two or more separate undertakings, as distinguished from the situation considered in Case 30/87, *Bodson v SA Pompes Funebres* [1988] ECR 2479.

74 OJ 1986 L378/4.

75 A liner conference is a group of two or more vessel-operating carriers which provide international liner services for the carriage of cargo and which, most importantly for the purposes of this analysis, 'has an agreement or arrangement, whatever its nature, within the framework of which they operate under uniform or common freight rates and any other agreed conditions with respect to the provision of liner services': see Article 1(3)(b) of Regulation 4056/86.

76 Please note that in Case 66/86, *Ahmed Saeed Flugreisen v Zentrale zur Bekämpfung Unlauteren Wettbewerbs* [1989] ECR 803, the ECJ considered the application of Article 86 to an air carrier with a dominant position on the relevant market and which 'has succeeded in imposing on other carriers the application of excessively high or excessively low tariffs or the exclusive application of only one tariff on a given route' (see paragraphs 42 and 46). The Commission argued (see page 810 of the *rapport d'audience*) that airlines authorised to serve a route which constitutes a substantial part of the common market, occupy on that route a joint dominant position, since price competition is eliminated by the concerted action with regard to tariffs and other sorts of competition, for example with regard to capacity. A careful reading of the Court's phraseology demonstrates that the issue of joint dominance did not however form part of the relevant part of its judgment, which related solely to the behaviour of a single undertaking, dominant in its own right, and which acted in a manner that resulted in forcing other competing carriers to follow a particular pricing policy (in the context of air services which are operated on the basis of bilateral or multilateral air service agreements). The opinion of Advocate General Lenz suggested at paragraph 34 that where, for example, only two air carriers operate on an air route this 'enables them jointly to dominate the relevant market' and, at paragraph 35, that Article 86 can be applied to situations where a dominant undertaking or dominant undertakings acting together behave in an abusive manner. It does not seem to this author that the Advocate General was contemplating a situation where Article 86 is applied to two or more undertakings, none of which are dominant individually, but if looked at collectively could be regarded as dominant. As a result, the relevance of this case to joint dominance jurisprudence is limited: *per contra* Julian Currall, *Article 86 EEC Treaty (Abuse of a Dominant Position)*, Fordham University, Spring 1993, at note 16.

77 Case C-393/92 *Almelo* [1994] ECR I-1477.

Article 90 cases which have come before the Court on Article 177 references. *Almelo* concerned *inter alia* the question whether the regional electricity distributors in the Netherlands occupied a collective dominant position on the market for the public supply of electricity in the Netherlands to local distributors. These regional distributors were each entitled to impose an exclusive purchasing obligation on their local distributors pursuant to the model general conditions of supply drawn up by the Association of Operators of Electricity Undertakings in the Netherlands. The Court held that this obligation was contrary to Article 85(1).

As regards Article 86 and having cited paragraph 358 of the *Flat Glass* judgment, Advocate General Darmon considered that (*emphasis added*) 'No dominant position can exist . . . without a *minimum* of links enabling the undertakings in question collectively to dominate the market',[78] and that therefore the national court had to assess whether the regional distributors were united by 'sufficiently close economic links' that they collectively held such a position. In this respect the Advocate General noted that the regional electricity distributors were already bound to their local distributors by the same type of contract, and by implication indicated that the regional electricity distributors could be considered to be occupying a collective dominant position. The ECJ in its judgment, which did not make any reference to paragraph 358 of *Flat Glass*, went even further and defined the concept of collective dominant position for the national court as the following:

> In order for such a collective dominant position to exist, the undertakings in the group must be linked in such a way that they adopt the same conduct on the market. It is for the national court to consider whether there exist between the regional electricity distributors in the Netherlands links which are sufficiently strong for there to be a collective dominant position in a substantial part of the common market.[78a]

Thus, in the Court's view a number of undertakings could occupy a collective dominant position where they are bound together by sufficiently strong links – whether economic or otherwise – provided that these links lead them to adopt the same conduct on the market.

The implications of such an approach are profound because it may bring under the control of Article 86 (with all the attendant consequences of invalidity, liability to damages and possible fines) parallel behaviour which is not collusive but where the affected undertakings have some common link over and above the fact that they operate in the same oligopolistic market but short of collusive behaviour.

This view is further supported by the later case of *La Crespelle*[79] decided by the ECJ in September 1994, which like the case of *Almelo* raised Article 90 issues. The case related to whether the insemination centres of France, in the independent exercise of their exclusive right to store semen and carry out insemination in their own territories, had abused their dominant position by charging additional costs to users who requested them to supply semen from production centres in other Member States. The Court considered that by establishing these monopolies, which were territorially limited but together covered the entire territory of France, a dominant position had been created. The Court did not however discuss whether this dominant position could be considered to be a collective dominant position as defined by the Court in *Almelo*, nor whether such behaviour could fall within Article 85(1).

The issue of collective dominant position has recently been considered in two further cases. First, in Joined Cases C–140/94 to C–142/94 *DIP SpA v Comune di Bassano del Grappa and Others*, where the question was raised whether the Italian law at issue, which subjected the opening of a shop for retail sales to the grant of a trading licence issued by the mayor of the commune in question, acting on the advice of a municipal committee on which members of Traders' organisations sat, facilitated either a concerted practice or the creation of a collective dominant position between existing retailers and whether it permits them to abuse that position by enabling them to impose selling prices which they could not have imposed had there been more effective competition on the market. In its judgment of 17 October 1995, the ECJ held that the Italian law was contrary to neither Article 85 nor Article 86. So far as Article 85 is concerned, the Commission had argued that even if the Italian law had the effect of protecting the entire national market from effective competition (which the Commission doubted) Article 85 not be applied to the individual retailers without evidence of any agreement or concerted action on their part designed to avail themselves of the position of influence afforded to them by the operation at communal level of the Italian law, in order to further the protection of their own

78 *Ibid.*, paragraph 117 of the Opinion.
78a *Ibid.*, paragraphs 42 and 43.

79 Case C–323/93 *La Crespelle* [1994] ECR I-5077.

commercial positions on the relevant retail markets. Advocate General Fennelly in his Opinion of 6 July 1995 stated at paragraph 53 that the Court may not presuppose the existence of such agreements and that:

> While it is true that the Court has never required proof of the existence of a perfect or fully-elaborated agreement, attributable to a State measure, when applying Article 5 in conjunction with Articles 85 and 86 of the Treaty, it is equally clear that a presumed predisposition on the part of the retailers to act in a certain manner, without any direct or indirect evidence of concerted contact or coordination of behaviour, cannot in itself justify the conclusion that the Law allowed those retailers to develop or extend in a concerted fashion their mutual efforts across Italy.

The ECJ, in considering whether an agreement, decision or concerted practice within the meaning of Article 85 could be inferred from the rules in question, held that the opinions adopted by the municipal committee could not be regarded as agreements between traders which the public authorities had required, favoured, or reinforced the effects of. This was because the representatives of the traders' organisations were in a minority on the municipal committee, sitting side by side with representatives of workers and public authorities and they were present as experts on distribution problems rather than to represent their own business interests, and because municipal committees were obliged to observe the public interest.[79a]

In its argument presented before the Court on Article 86 and the concept of a collective dominant position, the Commission argued that there was no collective dominant position in this case because such a position could only exist among the retailers which held trading licences if there was already no or limited competition among those undertakings. By imposing limits on the total number of shops, the Italian law did not in fact restrict competition between those shops which were already in existence. Moreover, none of the cases could involve the shops occupying a dominant position in a substantial part of the Common Market since the application of the relevant Italian law is always at a local level. Advocate General Fennelly agreed with the Commission on this point and stated at paragraph 64 of his Opinion that:

> The concept of collective dominance cannot be used to substitute for the lack of any direct evidence of the existence, and still less of any abuse, of a dominant position (namely by an individual undertaking already present in some or all of the 8000 affected communes).

Having cited paragraph 358 of the *Flat Glass* judgment Advocate General Fennelly then went on to say that:

> leaving aside the dispersed nature of the markets at issue in these cases, there is nothing in the orders for reference or the submissions before the Court which suggests that some or all of the existing traders act, or possess distinctive commercial features, on their respective markets which in any way, with respect to their suppliers, competitors or customers, enable them effectively to behave as a single economic unit.

Advocate General Fennelly thus referred back once again to the CFI's definition of collective dominant position as being one based on ***economic*** links whether consensual or not. However, he made no reference to the Court's judgments in ***Almelo*** or in *La Crespelle* nor to the test mentioned in those judgments regarding 'sufficiently strong links'.

In its judgment, the ECJ held that the national rules in question could not be considered to put individual traders in dominant positions or all the traders established in a municipality in a collective dominant position, a salient feature of which would have been that traders did not compete against each other. But although the Court did, unlike the Advocate General, refer to the judgment in *Almelo*, it went no further than citing paragraph 42 of that judgment – that for a collective dominant position to exist, the undertakings in question must be limited in such a way that they adopt the same conduct on the market.[79b]

The second case further considering the issue of collective dominance, ***Bosman***,[80] is still pending before the ECJ. Advocate General Lenz delivered his well publicised Opinion in this case on 20 September 1995. This case raises important issues on the application of Articles 48, 85 and 86 of the Treaty to the rules on foreign football players and the rules on transfers of football players to other Member States. The Advocate General considered that these rules were not compatible with either Articles 48 or 85. At point 283 of the Opinion he considered whether the professional clubs of the individual associations (as regards rules on foreign players) and the professional clubs of the entire Community (as regards the rules on transfers of football players to other

79a Paragraphs 16 to 19.

79b Paragraphs 26 and 27.

80 Case C–415/93 *Bosman* pending.

Member States) together occupied a dominant position. In assessing this question the Advocate General did not refer to the 'sufficiently strong links' test in *Almelo* and confined himself to an analysis of *La Crespelle* and paragraph 358 of *Flat Glass*. He concluded that the clubs in a professional league could be 'united by such economic links' that together they are to be regarded as having a dominant position. Advocate General Lenz noted that the football clubs are dependent on each other if they wish to be successful and added that such a national community of interests can probably be found scarcely in any other sector. But the Advocate General concluded that since there was no evidence of abuse, he did not need to consider the question further.

It will be interesting to see what approach the Court takes in *Bosman* above on the question of collective dominant position and in particular as regards the joint application of Articles 85 and 86. In *Almelo* the Court considered that the regional electricity distributors could be abusing their collective dominant position and that this conduct could fall foul of Article 85(1). It is worth taking another look at the context of *Flat Glass* where the Commission assessed the conduct of the undertakings under both Articles 85 and 86. As has been pointed out by Julian Currall, who represented the Commission before the Court:

> In the *Flat Glass* cases, the CFI held that collective dominance was indeed possible, not only in narrow situations previously considered [citing *Ahmed Saeed* in particular] by the Court of Justice but also where the undertakings concerned entered into an *agreement or concerted practice*, as a result of which they adopted identical or virtually identical behaviour towards customers. (*emphasis added*)[81]

The conditions under which the concept of joint dominance applies to circumstances where the link between the undertakings concerned is something other than an agreement or concerted practice remains unclear. Nevertheless, there remains some controversy about the extent to which it is proper for Article 86 to be applied to a factual situation that may also fall within the scope of Article 85(1). To the extent that an agreement or concerted practice between undertakings, which can properly be regarded as jointly dominant, has adverse effects on competition then it could fall under both provisions simultaneously. There is some jurisprudence that indicates that this may not be permissible and that the application of Article 85(1) excludes that of Article 86: for example, the Court observed in *Zuchner*[82] that 'Article 86 deals with the abuse of a dominant position and does not cover the existence of concerted practices, to which solely the provisions of Article 85 apply.'[83] However, the cases of *Hoffmann-La Roche*,[84] *Ahmed Saeed*,[85] *Tetra Pak I*,[86] *Flat Glass*[87] and *Almelo*[88] all related to the simultaneous application of Articles 85 and 86 to the same factual context and indicate that such is not the case. In *Tetra Pak I* the Court recognised that the application of Article 85 to an agreement may not preclude the alternative application of Article 86 and cited *Ahmed Saeed* as authority for the proposition that Articles 85 and 86 may be applicable simultaneously.[89] In the appeal against the Commission's decision in the *Cewal*[90] case this issue is specifically raised.

If Article 86 can be applied to the behaviour of undertakings deemed to occupy a joint dominant position at the same time as Article 85 is being applied to the same behaviour, then the CFI made clear at paragraph 360 of the *Flat Glass* judgment that for the purposes of establishing an infringement of Article 86 of the Treaty, it is not sufficient to 'recycle' the facts constituting an infringement of Article 85. The Court held that it is not possible to deduce from facts that have merely been recycled a finding that the parties to an agreement or concerted practice which jointly hold a substantial share of the market, and by virtue of that fact alone hold a collective dominant position, have abused that collective dominant position. A cursory review of the Commission's decision reveals that no detailed analysis had been conducted specific to the application of Article 86 and that the factual circumstances and reasoning relating to the Article 86 infringement was merely incorporated by reference. This was inadequate. This approach was approved by Advocate General Fennelly in his Opinion of 6 July 1995 in the *DIP SpA* case discussed above.

Since the *Flat Glass* judgment the Commission has adopted three decisions that apply the concept of

81 Note 76 See also Schodermeier, 'Collective Dominance Revisited: An Analysis of the EC Commission's New Concepts of Oligopoly Control', [1990] 1 ECLR 28.

82 See text at Note 58 above.
83 Note 21 above, paragraph 10.
84 Note 50 above.
85 Note 76 above.
86 Case T-51/89, *Tetra Pak Rausing v Commission* [1990] ECR II 347.
87 Note 28 above.
88 Note 77 above.
89 Note 86 above, paragraph 21.
90 Cases T-24/93 *Compagnie Maritime Belge*, T-25/93 *Dafra Lines*, T-26/93 *Deutsche Afrika Linien* and T-28/93 *Nedlloyd Linien*. See *Cewal* OJ 1993 L34/20.

joint dominance. In the *French-West African Shipowners' Committees*[91] decision, the Commission concluded that there had been infringements of both Articles 85 and 86 and imposed substantial fines.[92] The finding of joint dominance was based on the fact that a number of the addressees of the decision were linked by cross-shareholdings or ran 'co-ordinated services' with each other. The Commission went on to say that the effect of the cargo sharing system was to eliminate all effective competition[93] and as most members of the shipowners' committees were members of the Cowac and Mewac liner conferences they presented a 'united front to shippers at their regular consultations, concerning, in particular, the fixing of freight rates.'[94] As a result, the Commission concluded that the market position of the shipping companies that were members of the committees had to be assessed collectively.[95] Whether the Commission was correct to assess the members of the shipowners' committees as being jointly dominant, despite the fact that the decision does little more than 'recycle' the analysis used in respect of the Article 85(1) infringement, was never tested by the CFI because, as part of an arrangement whereby lower fines were imposed, it was apparently agreed between the Commission and the main parties fined that no appeal would be made to Luxembourg.

In its 1993 decision in the *Cewal*[96] case, the Commission applied Article 86 to the activities of a liner conference which benefited from a block exemption under Article 3 of Council Regulation 4056/86. In a rather imaginative interpretation of what the CFI had said at paragraph 359 of its judgment in the *Flat Glass* case regarding Article 8 of that Regulation, the Commission held that liner conferences are an example of agreements between economically independent entities which enable economic links to be formed that can confer on such entities a joint dominant position, and that the agreement between the members of the Cewal liner conference constituted such an agreement.[97]

91 *French-West African Shipowners' Committees* OJ 1992 L134/1.

92 Unlike in the *Flat Glass* decision, the Commission imposed fines in respect of the infringements of both Articles 85(1) and 86, in circumstances where the infringement of the latter Article was found to have taken place as a result of the undertakings concerned being found to have abused a joint dominant position: see *ibid.*, Recitals 71 and 72.

93 *Ibid.*, Recital 56.

94 *Ibid.*, Recital 57.

95 *Ibid.*, Recital 58.

96 Note 71 above.

97 *Ibid.*, Recital 49.

Furthermore, the Commission, citing *Tetra Pak I*, stated that the fact that some of Cewal's activities had been authorised by a block exemption did not prevent Article 86 from being applied to the activities of the conference.[98] In a more detailed and self-standing analysis than the one that Commission had conducted in the *French-West African Shipowners' Committees* case, it came to the conclusion that Cewal held a dominant position on the group of shipping routes that it operated between northern Europe and Zaire and that dominant position was 'held jointly by the members of Cewal given that they are linked to each other by the conference agreement, which creates very close economic links between them, as evidenced, for example, by the existence of a common scale of freight rates.'[99] In concluding that the members of Cewal had abused that joint dominant position the Commission made a greater effort than in the *French-West African Shipowners' Committees* decision to demonstrate a self-standing case of abusive behaviour: whether it was sufficient will be decided on by the CFI in Cases T–24/93 etc.

The most recent application of the principle of joint dominance, other than under the ECMR, was the Commission's decision in the *Rødby*[100] case which related to the application of Article 90(1) of the EC Treaty. The Commission held that the market position of Deutsche Bundesbahn and DSB (which owned and managed the port of Rødby as well as operating ferry services) was to be assessed collectively on the basis that they operated a joint service on the route between Rødby and Puttgarden and it was the question of access to the port of Rødby (and that route) that formed the substance of the case. The Commission considered that the joint operation of the Rødby-Puttgarden service was sufficient to constitute the requisite economic link for the purposes of a joint dominance analysis.[101]

Application of joint dominance in ECMR procedures

The ECMR enables the Commission to assess the compatibility with the Common Market of those concentrations which have a Community dimension, as defined in Article 1(2).[102] In undertaking this

98 *Ibid.*, Recital 50.

99 *Ibid.*, Recital 61.

100 Commission decision concerning a refusal to grant access to the facilities of the port of Rødby [Denmark] OJ 1994 L55/52.

101 *Ibid.*, Recitals 11 and 12.

102 See Note 2 above.

appraisal the ECMR sets out, at Article 2, those matters which the Commission must take into account and states that concentrations with a Community dimension must be declared either compatible or incompatible with the Common Market depending on whether or not they create or strengthen a dominant position as a result of which effective competition would be significantly impeded in the Common Market or in a substantial part of it. There is no reference to the creation or strengthening of a joint dominant position.

Faced with its natural concern to ensure that it had some form of effective control over concentrations that would create or exacerbate market structures that would, on the basis of generally accepted economic theory, have a tendency to oligopolistic parallel behaviour, the Commission produced an inventive response. In *Nestlé/Perrier*,[103] and in a number of subsequent decisions which refined the analysis contained in that decision, the Commission held that a concept of joint dominance was included in the ECMR in the absence of its explicit exclusion.[104]

It is suggested that, from a reading of the Commission's decisions applying a joint dominance analysis in the ECMR cases to date, its application in the ECMR context is not the same as that contemplated by the CFI in *Flat Glass* and in respect of which the Commission has had to struggle in a number of subsequent Article 86 cases. As was pointed out by a minority of the Advisory Committee on Concentrations, the *Flat Glass* judgment limited the application of collective dominance to those cases where there are proven economic links between the undertakings and that minority was of the view that joint dominance under the ECMR could not be applied unless there were such links.[105] Until decided otherwise by the CFI, and ultimately the ECJ, the Commission will continue to apply a concept of joint dominance in the course of its appraisal of concentrations under the ECMR, which is designed to control the creation of joint dominant positions that may be expected significantly to impede competition in the Common Market. That joint dominance will be deemed to exist where the concentration would create a duopoly or oligopoly whose members were in a position to behave to an appreciable extent independently of actual and potential competitors, customers and ultimately consumers. For such a conclusion to be reached, it is not necessary for the Commission to conclude that the oligopolistic market structure would result in collusive parallel behaviour, only that it might (and a history of prior cartelisation will be of relevance in such an analysis) or that it might result in non-collusive parallel behaviour.

Because of its narrow field of application (that is, the control of concentrations falling within the scope of the ECMR) and its divergent nature, the concept of joint dominance developed by the Commission in the *Nestlé/Perrier* case is of limited relevance to the scope of this article, namely, the interrelationship of the concept of joint dominance under Article 86 and that of concerted practice under Article 85. Hence, a more detailed discussion of the ECMR and joint dominance must be left to one side.

Conclusions

The concept of concerted practice under Article 85 is well defined with a substantial body of case law and decisions. Its application is wide and will encompass anti-competitive behaviour between undertakings where there has been any form of contact between them but it will not, as things currently stand, apply to non-collusive behaviour. Concertation cannot be deemed to have taken place merely on the basis of observed parallel behaviour unless, exceptionally, there is simply no other explanation. Finally, for a concerted practice to be found to have taken place it is not necessary for the participating undertakings to be individually or collectively market dominant.

As a result, in circumstances in which the Commission is able to prove an infringement of Article 85(1) (either by way of agreement, decision or concerted practice) there is little incentive for the Commission to seek to use a joint dominance analysis under Article 86. This is particularly so when it is insufficient for the Commission merely to 'recycle' arguments and analyses that have been used to prove the Article 85(1) infringement and it has to undertake the task of defining the market and estab-

103 *Nestlé/Perrier* OJ 1992 L356/1.

104 *Ibid.*, Recitals 110 to 115. For a detailed discussion of the Commission's interpretation of Article 2 of the ECMR in respect of joint dominance and the application of that principle generally to concentrations falling within the scope of the Commission's control under the ECMR, see Jones and Gonzalez-Diaz, *The EEC Merger Regulation*, Sweet & Maxwell, 1992 and articles such as: Winckler and Hansen, 'Collective Dominance under the EC Merger Control Regulation', (1993) CML Rev., at 787 to 828; Chris Bright, 'Nestlé/Perrier: New Issues in EC Merger Control', IFLR (September 1992); and Briones Alonso, 'Economic Assessment of Oligopolies under the Community Merger Control Regulation', [1993] 3 ECLR 118.

105 OJ 1992 C319/3.

lishing market dominance in a way that is unnecessary for an Article 85 case, unless there is a specific reason for so doing. Examples of such reasons include the Commission's desire: to get round the application of an Article 85(3) block exemption; to impose fines for the infringement of Article 86 in circumstances when the arrangement had been notified for an Article 85(3) individual exemption and, therefore, the Commission was unable to impose fines for the continued operation of the arrangement contrary to Article 85(1); to get around evidential problems that may make it difficult for the Commission to prove an infringement of Article 85(1), particularly when there is limited evidence of direct or indirect contact.

It may be that the Commission will try to use the concept of joint dominance to control non-collusive oligopolistic behaviour where the undertakings concerned have purely 'economic links' or 'sufficiently strong links' that would not fall within the definition of agreement, decision or concerted practice within the meaning of Article 85(1): that is, non-collusive links. It is not possible to be certain whether the scope of joint dominance extends to cover such non-collusive oligopolistic behaviour as it is unclear whether the CFI's requirement in *Flat Glass* for there to be 'economic links' and the ECJ's requirement in *Almelo* for there to be 'sufficiently strong links' contemplate links that would not be covered by Article 85(1). The Court's judgment awaited in *Bosman* may cast light on this question.

The concepts of joint dominance and concerted practice are distinct and different, but in many circumstances their application may overlap. In practice, however, the usefulness of joint dominance under Article 86 (as opposed to the different concept employed under the ECMR) is likely to be limited to cases where the Commission has a specific reason for using it as an adjunct to an Article 85(1) case. Its application to the independent and non-collusive behaviour of undertakings which are linked whether economically or otherwise is uncertain, but will undoubtedly be a fruitful source of future argument, and without argument what would competition lawyers do with their time?

[16]

The Herchel Smith Lecture 1998: Article 86 of the E.C. Treaty and Intellectual Property Rights

ROSA GREAVES

Rosa Greaves, Allen & Overy Professor of European Law, Durham European Law Institute, University of Durham

The impact of intellectual property rights[1] on competition and thus on the internal market created by the Member States should not be underestimated. At its most basic level, the owner of the intellectual property has the right to exclude certain acts by potential competitors such as manufacturing and importing infringing products, as well as to impose certain obligations on contracting parties, such as a limitation on the field of use. Thus the enforcement of these rights has an effect both on the free movement of goods within the Community and on the application of the E.C. competition rules.

The purpose of this article is to consider to what extent and under what circumstances does Article 86 of the E.C. Treaty, which prohibits the abuse of a dominant position in a substantial part of the Common Market, apply to the market behaviour of owners of intellectual property rights.

By way of introduction, the article will set out first the purpose and essential elements of Article 86. This will be followed by an evaluation of how the European Commission and the European Court of Justice have interpreted and applied Article 86 to the market behaviour of owners of intellectual property rights. The article will conclude with a brief and non-exhaustive review of how English courts have so far dealt with Article 86.

The Purpose and Essential Elements of Article 86

Before briefly describing the elements of Article 86 there are some general matters which need to be underlined. First, the E.C. competition rules enshrined in Articles 85 and 86 of the E.C. Treaty cannot be considered in isolation. This is particularly so within the context of intellectual property rights which are exclusive rights, territorial in nature, conferred by a Member State with the possibility of parallel protection being obtained in other Member States. Many of the early cases where a conflict between intellectual property rights and Community law had to be resolved concerned the free movement of goods provisions, Articles 30 to 36 of the E.C. Treaty.[2] In *Consten & Grundig v. Commission*,[3] the first case involving intellectual property rights heard by the European Court of Justice, both sets of Treaty provisions were pleaded. The E.C. competition rules seek to ensure that the removal of obstacles posed by national laws to the freedom of movement of goods, persons and capital within the European Community (in other words obstacles to intra-Community trade), which are governed by Articles 30 to 36 of the E.C. Treaty, are not reintroduced by anti-competitive behaviour of undertakings. Thus Article 85 is concerned with anti-competitive agreements while Article 86 focuses on the anti-competitive behaviour of undertakings. Consequently, the competition rules may apply if it is the intellectual property owner who uses his exclusive right to distort competition within the internal market or abuses a dominant market position he holds.

Secondly, in the absence of harmonisation, the relationship between intellectual property rights and the E.C. Treaty has been determined primarily by the case law of the European Court of Justice.[4] Under the Community's legal order, the Court of Justice has the exclusive competence to determine the meaning and scope of Community law, including these Treaty provisions. Thus it is the Court which over the years has elaborated on the extent to which Community law impinges on the rights of intellectual property owners in order to ensure that a competitive integrated market, a key objective of the E.C. Treaty, is achieved.

Thirdly, the E.C. competition rules are primarily enforced by the European Commission according to the substantial and procedural rules set out in Council Regulation 17/62.[5] The Commission, after lengthy investigations, may decide to issue a Decision addressed to the appropriate undertakings. Such Decisions may be appealed to the Court of First Instance under Article 173 of the E.C. Treaty by those to whom decisions are addressed or by those who are directly and individually concerned with the decision (*e.g.* the complainant). A further appeal on law may be made to the European Court of Justice from the judgment of the Court of First Instance. The judgment of the Court of Justice is final.

Fourthly, the European Court of Justice ruled in *BRT v. SABAM*[6] that Articles 85 (1) and 86 are directly

The author would like to thank Emily Reid and Francis Pritchard for their comments on earlier drafts.

1 The expression "intellectual property rights" will be used to include patents, trade marks, copyrights, registered and unregistered design and analogous rights such as patent breeders' rights.

2 Art. 36 contains an express derogation from the basic freedom of movement of goods where the impediment to this freedom is a protection of intellectual property rights. Although Art. 36 mentions only the protection of "industrial and commercial property", the European Court of Justice ruled in Case 78/70 *Deutsche Grammophon Gesellschaft* [1971] E.C.R. 487; [1971] C.M.L.R. 631 that the protection extended to copyright.

3 Cases 56 & 58/64 [1966] E.C.R. 299; [1966] C.M.L.R. 428.

4 See for example the *Phil Collins* case, Joined Cases C–92 and C–326/92 [1993] E.C.R. II–5154; [1993] 3 C.M.L.R. 773 at para. 22, where the Court ruled that the principle of non-discrimination on the grounds of nationality enshrined in Art. 6 of the E.C. Treaty applied to national laws conferring rights on intellectual property owners.

5 O.J. 204/62 (Spec. ed. 1959–1962), p. 87.

6 Case 127/73 [1974] E.C.R. 51; [1974] 2 C.M.L.R. 238.

applicable with direct effect in the national legal orders. Direct effect means that these Articles apply to relationships between individuals and create rights directly in respect of the individuals concerned which national courts must safeguard. Articles 85 (1) and 86 are therefore part of the national legal order and can be pleaded before a national court either as a cause of action and/or as a defence.

The elements of Article 86

Article 86 of the EC Treaty states that

> Any abuse by one or more undertakings of a dominant position within the common market or in a substantial part of it shall be prohibited as incompatible with the common market in so far as it may affect trade between Member States.

The first thing to note about Article 86 is that it applies only to anti-competitive behaviour which has a European dimension, and therefore the undertaking's conduct which is under scrutiny must "affect trade between Member States". This requirement, however, has been interpreted very widely and to date there has been only one case, *Hugin*,[7] where this condition was not met. Thus it is fair to state that, if all the other conditions of Article 86 are met, it will be extremely rare for a case to be dismissed owing to the fact that the abusive behaviour did not affect trade between Member States. In view of the territorial nature of intellectual property rights, it is extremely unlikely that a situation could be envisaged often where an argument could be sustained that the behaviour of the owner of the right did not affect trade between Member States.

In addition, in order for Article 86 to apply to a given situation, two requirements have to be proven. First, it is necessary to establish that the undertaking concerned is dominant in a substantial part of the Common Market and, secondly, that the behaviour of the undertaking is abusive within the meaning of the Article.

In order to satisfy the first requirement, it is necessary to determine the relevant market and then to assess the economic power the undertaking has within that defined relevant market. The relevant market is established by identifying the relevant product, geographical and temporal markets. Although the European Court has not laid down a definitive test of what constitutes the relevant product market, interchangeability of goods or services is the preferred test.[8] Interchangeability is established by looking primarily at the demand side substitutability (*e.g.* physical characteristics; price; intended use) but the supply substitutability should also be considered.

The geographical market, which in most cases is obvious, must also be defined in each case. In some cases the geographical market has been drawn very narrowly. This has been particularly so in the transport sector where an air route between two airports[9] and a sea route between two ports[10] was established by the European Commission as the geographical market.

The Commission investigating an alleged breach of Article 86 will aim to define the product market narrowly as this will facilitate a finding of dominance. Once the relevant market has been defined then an analysis of the economic power the undertaking concerned has in the defined relevant market is carried out.

Dominance has been defined by the European Court of Justice in this often-quoted passage from the judgment in *United Brands v. Commission*:

> a position of economic strength enjoyed by an undertaking which enables it to prevent effective competition being maintained on the relevant market by affording it the power to behave to an appreciable extent independently of its competitors, customers and ultimately of its consumers.[11]

The approach taken by the Commission to measure market power is well documented, since many of the appeals to the Court of Justice are on the issue of dominance. Although no single factor is taken as the definitive test, market shares are very important in providing evidence of market power. Other factors indicating market power are barriers to entry (a controversial issue among economists) and the conduct or performance of the undertaking. Examples of barriers to entry include intellectual property rights,[12] superior technology[13] and access to financial resources.[14]

One last question needs to be asked before proceeding to the issue of abuse. According to Article 86, a dominant position must exist in the whole or a substantial part of the Common Market. There must be a Community dimension also in the dominance itself. This is a different test from that establishing the geographical market, since that test is part of the formula for establishing whether the undertaking concerned has dominance in the first place.

It is quite clear that each Member State would be regarded as being a substantial part of the Common Market. In *Hugin*, London, owing to the concentration of a large number of people, was considered to be a substantial part of the Common Market. It is more difficult to accept the Commission's finding in *B&I v. Sealink Harbours Ltd*[15] that the port of Holyhead is a substantial part of the Common Market.

As far as abuse is concerned, Article 86 offers a non-exhaustive list, concerned with pricing policies (excessive, discriminatory and unfair), discriminatory or unfair conditions of trading and control of markets to the detriment of consumers. However, the abuse which has triggered several investigations leading to important rulings from the European Court of Justice, has been

7 Case 22/78 [1979] E.C.R. 1869; [1979] 3 C.M.L.R. 345.
8 See, for example, Case 6/72 *Continental Can* [1973] E.C.R. 215; [1973] C.M.L.R. 199 at para. 32.
9 *London-Sabena* [1988] O.J. L317/47; [1989] 4 C.M.L.R. 662.
10 *Sealink/B&I-Holyhead* [1992] 5 C.M.L.R. 255.
11 Case 27/76 [1978] E.C.R. 207; [1978] 1 C.M.L.R. 429 at paras 65 and 66 of the judgment.
12 Case 22/78, *Hugin v. Commission* [1979] E.C.R. 1869; [1979] 3 C.M.L.R. 345; Case T-30/89, *Hilti v. Commission* [1992] 4 C.M.L.R. 16; Case T-69/89, *RTE v. Commission* [1991] 4 C.M.L.R. 586.
13 Case 27/76, *United Brands v. Commission* [1978] E.C.R. 207; [1978] 1 C.M.L.R. 429 at paras 82–84; Case 85/76, *Hoffmann-La Roche v. Commission* [1979] E.C.R. 461; [1979] 3 C.M.L.R. 211 at para. 48.
14 *United Brands, ibid.*, at para. 122.
15 See n. 10 above.

refusal to deal, such as the well-known case of *Magill*,[16] which is considered below.

Application of Article 86 by the European Commission and the European Court of Justice to Intellectual Property Rights

Establishing dominance

The Court of Justice has made it absolutely clear that an undertaking is not in a dominant position merely because it is the owner of an intellectual property right.[17] They may be in a privileged position because intellectual property rights do confer market power, but they are not automatically dominant within the meaning of Article 86. The mere fact the owner can prohibit importation of infringing goods[18] or exercise the right to distribute the protected product does not in itself constitute a dominant position.[19] The existence and normal use of intellectual property rights, protected by the E.C. Treaty under Articles 222 and 36, do not necessarily equate to a dominant position. Thus regard must be taken of the existence or possible entry of competing products into the market which could substitute for the protected product.[20] This market analysis, outlined above, is usually undertaken by the Commission, which has to define the relevant market convincingly and examine the economic power that the undertaking holds in that relevant market. The intellectual property owner must be shown to be able to impede the maintenance of effective competition in a substantial part of the Common Market. However, the danger for the intellectual property owner is that the Commission's practice is to define the relevant product market very narrowly, and the Court does not often disagree with the Commission. A prime example of this is the well-known case of *United Brands*, where the Commission defined the product market as bananas. Other possible relevant product markets had been suggested, such as fresh fruit. The Court, however, applying the rules on interchangeability, agreed with the Commission's assessment and ruled that the characteristics of the product (bananas), namely the softness, seedlessness, taste and handling quality, was such that for a distinct group of consumers (the young, old and ill) there was no substitute. The narrowness of the product market can be further illustrated by cases such as *Hilti*,[21] where a separate product market was ruled to exist for nails for use with nail-guns, and *Tetra Pak II*,[22] where cartons for use with filling machines were also held to be a separate market from the product with which they are used.

Although it may be highly unlikely that a patented product will have no substitutes, the same cannot be said for products protected by trade marks, copyright and design rights if the test of substitutability is dependent on the characteristics of the user. It was commented at the time that the product market in *United Brands* could have been narrowed even further, to "Chiquita" bananas themselves (the branded product). Such a narrow determination of the product market is particularly worrying for owners of intellectual property rights since the ownership of the intellectual property becomes a particularly significant factor in assessing dominance in the defined relevant market.

In addition, the huge importance given to the characteristics of the user of a product in determining the relevant product market in *United Brands* may cause problems for certain industries where users are particularly dependent on the protected product.[23] For example, are office users of a particular computer operational system a distinct market?

The judgments of the Court in several cases involving a copyright-type of right, such as *Hugin* (cash registers), *Volvo*[24] and *Renault*[25] (spare parts) establish that spare parts can form a market separate from that of the product for which they are needed. Thus the owners of the copyright on the drawings of the product and its spares are automatically in a dominant position in the defined relevant market.

In *Magill* the relevant market was defined as advance television weekly programme listings. In upholding the Commission and the Court of First Instance's finding that the undertaking concerned was dominant in the market for weekly television programme listings, the Court did its utmost to distance itself from the controversial issue of reconciling national copyright law with the Community's competition rules. The Court confirmed that the undertakings enjoyed a "factual monopoly" over basic information not available from any other source. The fact that it was not available from another source, mainly because of the copyright, was conveniently ignored. The Court preferred to conclude that the economic power of the owners of that information lay in the fact that, since they were the sole source, they had total control over information about the programmes' titles, times and dates. This information was the raw material for the production of weekly television guides which constituted a secondary market. So the undertakings had the economic power in the relevant market to act independently of any other party.

16 Joined Cases C-241-242/91P, *Radio Telefis Eireann v. Commission* [1995] 4 C.M.L.R. 718 (ECJ); appeal from the judgment of the Court of First Instance (CFI) in Case T-69/89 [1991] 4 C.M.L.R. 586.

17 For example, *ibid.*, Joined Cases C-241/91P and C-242/91P, *RTP & ITP v. Commission*.

18 Case 40/70, *Sirena* [1971] E.C.R. 69; [1971] C.M.L.R. 260 at para. 16.

19 Case 78/70, *Deutsche Grammophon Gesellschaft v. Metro*, n. 2 above, at para. 16.

20 Case 40/70, *Sirena*, n. 18 above.

21 Case T-30/89, *Hilti AG v. Commission*, n. 12 above, confirmed on appeal in Case C-53/92P [1994] E.C.R. I-667.

22 Case T-83/91, *Tetra Pak International SA v. Commission* [1997] 4 C.M.L.R. 726 confirmed on appeal by the ECJ in Case C-333/94P [1997] 4 C.M.L.R. 662.

23 In Case T-504/93, *Tierce Ladbroke SA v. Commission* [1997] E.C.R. II-923; [1997] 5 C.M.L.R. 309, the Court stated that the "habits of bettors" were one of the factors in restricting the relevant geographical market to Belgium (at para. 28 of the judgment). The close links between those who take bets and those who place them makes it a local or regional market (para. 98 of the judgment).

24 Case 238/87, *AB Volvo v. Erik Veng* [1988] E.C.R. 6211; [1989] 4 C.M.L.R. 122.

25 Case 53/87, *CICRA v. Regio Nationale des Usines Renault* [1988] E.C.R. 6039; [1990] 4 C.M.L.R. 265.

In *Tierce Ladbroke*,[26] the Court of First Instance confirmed the Commission's assessment of the relevant market as the Belgian market for televised pictures of and information on horse races. It was unsuccessfully argued that the product market should have been narrowed to French sound and pictures of horse races and the geographical market widened to France, Germany, Austria and Belgium, since the French owners of the intellectual property rights had no presence in Belgium itself. This market, however, was held to be ancillary to the main betting market, which was national by nature as far as the users were concerned. This ruling shows again the importance of market definition in intellectual property cases. By deciding that the relevant market was ancillary to national betting markets, the relevant market was confined to sound and pictures in Belgium. The Court of First Instance did not really address the issue of dominance. In particular, the Court did not consider whether copyright owners might be dominant in Belgium over the supply of sound and pictures although they were not operating in that territory. This is clearly deduced from paragraph 110 of the judgment, where the Court states that, even if they were dominant, the Commission Decision would not be annulled unless an abuse within the meaning of Article 86 was established.

The exercise of an intellectual property right as an abuse

Article 86 is only concerned with the *abuse* of a dominant position. Thus, where the owner of an intellectual property right is found to be dominant within the meaning of the Article, the question which then arises is whether the exercise of his rights can constitute an abuse within the prohibition of Article 86. Intellectual property rights by their very nature prevent, restrict or distort competition. This does not *per se* amount to an abuse within the meaning of Community law.

The Court of Justice has always maintained that Community law does not affect the so called "specific subject-matter" of the right which is a matter to be determined by national law.[27] The concept of the "specific subject-matter" of the right has been discussed most often within the context of free movement of goods rules. Consequently, the approach has been refined over the last 30 years. The Court tends no longer to refer to it but rather to the "essence" or "function" of the right. Thus the *Magill* ruling was difficult to accept since the right concerned, a copyright, has in its essence the right to refuse to license. Can a legitimate or normal use of an intellectual property right, such as a refusal to deal or to license a third party, be found to be abusive?

The Court of Justice has made it clear that there is a need to establish an anti-competitive element additional to the normal use of the intellectual property right. As early as the case of *Parke Davis*[28] (1968), Advocate General Roemer stated that reliance on the exclusivity of the right in court (*i.e.* enforcement of the right) could not constitute an abuse of a dominant position within Article 86 since an action for infringement is part of the specific subject-matter of the right itself. The Advocate General, however, went on to state that whether or not the use of a patent infringes Article 86 depends on commercial realities—for example, fixing prices and terms, the existence of several licences restricting competition, the commercial value of the patent and the presence of substitute products on the market. The Court confirmed this position by ruling that, although ownership of a patent is not an abuse in itself, "the utilisation of the patent could degenerate into an improper exploitation of the protection".[29]

The position taken in 1968 has not really changed. In *Volvo v. Veng*, the Court stated that, although the right not to license is the essence of copyright, where the refusal is combined with market conditions generated by the intellectual property owner, such as a discontinuation of production of spare parts for models still in circulation, the charging of unfair prices for spare parts or a refusal to supply spare parts to independent repairers in an arbitrary manner, then there is a prima facie abuse. In these circumstances the abuse lies in an "improper" use/exercise of the rights as opposed to their proper (*i.e.* "normal") use in accordance with their nature. Thus a "proper" use of an intellectual property right, as a Community concept, can never as such be prohibited under Article 86.

A brief survey of the case law illustrates the point. A proper use of the intellectual property right arose in *Parke Davis* itself, where the Court ruled that "a higher price for the patented product as compared with that of the unpatented product coming from another Member State does not necessarily constitute an abuse".[30] Similarly, in ***Renault*** and in *Volvo v. Veng* a refusal to license *per se* was deemed not to be an abuse. In *Tierce Ladbroke*, it was stated that the mere fact that a party is prepared to pay a reasonable royalty does not mean that the refusal to license is arbitrary. In the absence of discrimination the refusal does not amount to sufficient evidence of abuse.[31] However, in *Hilti*, a demand by the patent owner for an "excessive" royalty was found to be an abuse. In *Tetra Pak*,[32] an abuse was found where a dominant undertaking took over a competitor and acquired additional intellectual property rights. In *Magill*, a refusal to license was ruled to be an abuse.

However when these cases are examined in more depth, the circumstances surrounding the use/exercise of the right show that the owner had not used his intellectual property right in a "normal use". In *Hilti* it was established as a fact that the sole object of demanding an excessive royalty was to block or, at least, unreasonably delay a licence of right which was available under the U.K. patent. In *Tetra Pak* it was found that it already

26 See n. 23 above. The case is on appeal to the European Court of Justice—C-300/97P.

27 The concept of "specific subject-matter" of intellectual property rights was first enunciated in the context of trade marks in *Consten & Grundig*, n. 3 above.

28 Case 24/67, *Parke Davis v. Probel* [1968] E.C.R. 55; [1968] C.M.L.R. 47.

29 *ibid.*, at 72.

30 See n. 28 above, at 73–74.

31 para. 26 of the judgment.

32 Case T-51/89, *Tetra Pak Rausing v. Commission* [1991] 4 C.M.L.R. 334.

had a substantial lead over competitors in the technological field and the additional property right related to a very significant development. In *Magill*, the primary business was broadcasting, not publishing. The publication of the TV listings was a mere consequence of the TV companies' primary business and thus the refusal to supply the listings except to its own publications was akin to a refusal to supply the spare parts themselves to users, the abuse envisaged by the Court of Justice in *Volvo v. Veng* which would justify an interference with the exercise of the intellectual property right. Furthermore, TV companies were the "sole source of information which was indispensable as the raw material for the production of a new product in a secondary market controlled by them and where the arbitrary refusal to supply was not justified".[33]

The recent case of *Tierce Ladbroke*[34] confirms the uniqueness of the "exceptional circumstances" of *Magill*. The Court of First Instance distinguished *Magill* on the fact that the refusal to license did not prevent Ladbroke from entering into another market. Furthermore, the refusal to license did not prevent a new product, nor was it indispensable to the betting agencies in exercising their main activity. The refusal could also have been said to be justified as the owners of the intellectual property rights had not operated in Belgium or licensed their rights to anyone in Belgium.

For the sake of completeness, some comment on the essential facilities doctrine should be made. According to the Commission, an essential facility is "a facility or infrastructure, without access to which competitors cannot provide services to their customers".[35] This is a doctrine which has its origins in the United States. The Commission is one of its great advocates. The European Court of Justice is less enamoured with it, which should not surprise anyone familiar with the Court's traditions. The Court has created and developed a unique legal order, a Community legal order, and has taken great care to introduce legal concepts and legal doctrines which have a Community law meaning. For example, there are Community meanings to familiar words such as "exhaustion of rights", "workers", "public policy" and "undertakings". There are also Community law doctrines or principles such as "proportionality", "direct effect" and "Community rights" which have been promoted by the Court in pursuit of ensuring effectiveness of Community law within the national legal orders. The Court is right in its approach. The objectives of the European Community and its law are very different from those of the United States. Community law needs to be developed to meet the Community's needs, not imported from other legal systems which were designed in a different environment for different agendas. The Court has shown that it does not need to import jargon and doctrines from across the Atlantic to deal with the practices of intellectual property owners in market circumstances which make those practices an abuse of a dominant position within the meaning of Article 86.

33 R. Greaves, "Magill est arrivé . . . " (1995) E.C.L.Rev. 244 at 246.
34 See n. 23 above.
35 Commission Decision 94/19, *Sea Containers/Stena Sealink* [1994] O.J. L15/8 para. 66.

Article 86 and the English Courts

What about the English courts? To what extent and in what circumstances do English courts consider Article 86 in the context of intellectual property rights? A Lexis search revealed, after considerable editing, a few relevant cases which provide the basis for an impressionist, non-scientific assessment. Predictably, Article 86 has come before English courts primarily on applications to strike out an Article 86 defence (and/or as a counterclaim) to an alleged infringement of an intellectual property right. This is often combined with a request to stay proceedings since the defendant is likely to have also complained to the European Commission.

To strike or not to strike out an Article 86 defence

A brief and non-exhaustive review of judgments in English courts on applications for striking out an Article 86 defence is not conclusive. According to Aldous J. in *Ransburg-GEMA*,[36] "a defence should only be struck out if it is clear that it raises no good ground for defending the action". In the context of an Article 86 defence to an infringement action of an intellectual property right, the situation facing the national judge is particularly difficult. Templeman L.J., in *Lansing Bagnall*, a 1984 Court of Appeal judgment in a copyright case, put it this way:

> If the enforcement by the plaintiffs of their copyright monopoly, including the enforcement by means of the present litigation against the defendants, amounts to an infringement of the Treaty of Rome, the English Court will be faced with the dilemma of preventing the infringement or upholding the copyright monopoly granted to the plaintiffs by the national law.[37]

Thus it is not surprising that the jurisprudence is not consistent.

In the early 1980s, Falconer J. in *Smith Kline & French* (1983, unreported) granted the injunction sought since the defendants failed to show that a defence based on Article 86 was sustainable. However, in *Lansing Bagnall Ltd v. Buccaneer* (1984) the Court of Appeal[38] allowed an appeal from the decision of the judge of first instance to strike out an Article 86 defence. However, at the end of the 1980s, while Hoffmann J. in *Pitney Bowes*[39] (1989) refused to strike out the defence, Blanco White Q.C. in *Yale Security Products*[40] (1990) and Aldous J. in *Quantel Ltd v. Electronic Graphics Ltd*[41] (1990) found there was no arguable case and struck it out.

In the 1990s, a consistent pattern of striking out the defence on the grounds of no nexus begins to emerge. The Court of Appeal, in *Chiron v. Murex*[42] (1993) upheld Aldous J.'s decision to strike out the defence since it could not be said the judge was "plainly wrong" in ruling that there was no arguable case that there was

36 [1989] 2 C.M.L.R. 712 at 714.
37 [1984] 1 C.M.L.R. 224 at para. 14 of the judgment.
38 Lawton L.J., Templeman and Fox L.JJ.
39 [1991] F.S.R. 72.
40 [1990] F.S.R. 320.
41 [1990] R.P.C. 272.
42 [1994] F.S.R. 187 (Balcombe, Staughton and Rose L.JJ.).

an effect on trade between Member States. On the issue whether a nexus existed between an Article 86 defence and a claim for patent infringement, only Staughton L.J. expressed the view that no nexus existed. The majority of the Court of Appeal avoided deciding the matter and tacitly approved the possibility by stating the first instance judge was not "plainly wrong" in concluding that there was a sufficient nexus.

However, in *IBM v. Phoenix*[43] (1993), three months after *Chiron v. Murex*, Ferris J. struck out the defence on the ground of no nexus since a breach of Article 86 was held to be no defence to a claim of passing off or for trade mark infringement. Ferris J. relied on the earlier decision of the Court of Appeal in *Lansing Bagnall Ltd v. Buccaneer* (1984), where their Lordships had approved Sir Robert Megarry's decision, in *IBM v. Berk*[44] (1981), to strike out an Article 86 defence to a passing-off action. Ferris J. was of the opinion that a trade mark entitlement is similar to passing off and therefore an Article 86 defence is inappropriate. He expressed the view that it was "unsafe to lay down a general rule as to when an infringement of Article 86 will, and when it will not, amount to a defence to a claim to enforce intellectual property rights".[45] He went on to state that "The one clear rule, it seems to me, is that there must be some nexus between the infringement complained of and the abuse which is said to constitute a defence to the claim of infringement".[46]

Before the Court of Appeal's ruling in *Chiron* (1993), Mervyn Davis J. in *Digital Equipment Corporation* (1992, unreported) did strike out the defence on the basis that there was no evidence of the alleged abusive conduct having an effect on trade between Member States. However, the ruling implies that if he had found otherwise he would have allowed the defence. Finally, *Intergraph Corp. v. Solid Systems* and *Philips Electronics v. Ingram Ltd* complete the survey.

Intergraph (1993, unreported) was concerned with an alleged breach of copyright where the issue turned on whether there was sufficient nexus between the plaintiff's claim for breach of copyright and the alleged infringements under Articles 85 and 86. Ferris J. quoted at length from Staughton L.J. in *Chiron*, where he had found that a nexus had not been established. However, Ferris J. followed the majority view in *Chiron*, namely that the judge was not "plainly wrong" to accept the sufficiency of the nexus, and so he decided not to strike out the defence. However, in *Philips Electronics* (1998, not yet reported) Laddie J. ruled that the Article 86 defence/counterclaim was not maintainable and struck it out, giving leave to appeal. The other defence based on Article 85 was allowed to proceed as a separate action.

So is there a path through these decisions? It has been suggested that there may be a different result depending on the type of intellectual property which is being enforced. If it is an action for passing off or for trade mark infringement, then the issue for trial is whether there has been a misrepresentation as to the origin of the goods, and therefore an Article 86 defence is not relevant since no nexus is established. Where the action is for patent or copyright infringement, Article 86 may offer a defence. This approach is not convincing. Only Ferris J. supports this distinction in not allowing the defence in a passing-off action (*IBM v. Phoenix*, 1993), but allowing it in a copyright action (*Intergraph*, 1993). Other judgments do not support this approach.

In *Pitney Bowes* (1989) and in *Chiron* (1993), the defence was allowed, but in *Smith Kline & French* (1983), *Quantel* (1990) and *Philips Electronics* (1998) the judge struck it out. These actions were for patent infringement. In *Lansing Bagnall* (1984) the Court of Appeal allowed the defence and so did the judge in *Intergraph* (1993) but not in *Ransburg-GEMA* (1989) nor in *Digital Equipment* (1992) which were actions for copyright infringement. Only in respect of passing off and trade mark infringement has there been consistency. The defence was not allowed in *IBM v. Berk* (1981), a passing-off action, nor in *IBM v. Phoenix* (1993), a trade mark infringement action. Aldous J. has shown consistency in both *Ransburg-GEMA* (1990) (copyright) and in *Quantel* (patent) in not allowing the defence.

Do the courts stay the proceedings when a counterclaim based on Article 86 is not struck out?

If the defence based on Article 86 is allowed to proceed and a complaint has been registered with the Commission then the nature of the E.C. Competition Rules support the view of English judges that the best way to proceed is to stay proceedings. Even though the judge has to balance two important principles, that is, on the one hand, that the plaintiff not be denied access to a court to protect its legal rights and, on the other hand, that the defendant not be required to argue its case simultaneously in two jurisdictions,[47] the rationale for staying the action is convincing. It would be onerous and a great waste of costs and court time to duplicate the appraisal of the same question simultaneously in proceedings before a national court and the Commission. This is more so in the case of the E.C. Competition Rules, where the Commission Decision is binding. For example, in the case of Article 85 proceedings, only the Commission has the competence to grant an individual exemption under Article 85 (3) for an agreement which would be otherwise unenforceable as infringing Article 85 (1).

Concluding Observations

First, the application of Article 86 to situations concerning the use of intellectual property rights remains limited to a few exceptional cases. Furthermore, the rulings of the European Court of Justice suggest that the Court will resist the invitation to treat an intellectual property right as an essential facility. However, where there is a natural monopoly, which for example may be argued to be the case with computer operational systems, there may well be a need to ensure access is

43 [1994] F.S.R. 251.
44 [1981] F.S.R. 1.
45 See n. 43 above, at 273.
46 *ibid.*

47 See, for example, Sir Godfrey Le Quesne sitting as Deputy Judge in the QBD in *ICS v. IPM* (unreported).

granted to dependent users (and perhaps to industries where the standards adopted by the dominant undertaking have become the international standard for that industry) so that innovation is not stifled and competition in ancillary markets is maintained.

Secondly, the practice of pleading Article 86 as a defence to infringement actions in domestic litigation is not appropriate. It raises unnecessary difficulties for the domestic court and leads to decisions on a motion to strike out the defence which are inconsistent and unsatisfactory. A prima facie case of infringement should lead the national court to grant the injunction requested. There is a tendency to assume that, since Articles 85 and 86 have the same objectives, namely the maintenance of a competitive market, they can be used in the same manner. However, an Article 85 defence to a breach of a licensing agreement may be appropriate because Article 85 (2) expressly states that the *agreement* is void if caught by Article 85 (1). Consequently, contractual obligations arising from that agreement are not enforceable. If the defence succeeds, the defendant has no enforceable obligation to discharge and thus the plaintiff loses the action. It is true that a party may bring an action for damages suffered as a consequence of the operation of that unlawful contract, but that is a separate cause of action. Article 86, however, does not nullify the market power of the dominant party. If the market power is due to the exclusivity granted by an intellectual property right, a successful Article 86 action does not affect the right itself. Damages may be awarded for conduct which is deemed abusive (*e.g.* excessive royalty, refusal to license, discriminatory licensing), not for holding a dominant position. A successful action under Article 86 does not deprive the owner of its property. It may limit the extent and/or the choice of the reward he will receive, not expropriate it.

Finally, the willingness of English judges to consider judgments of the European Court of Justice in this area is impressive. In several cases the judge quoted from ECJ's judgments and considered both the Advocate General's opinion and the judgment of the Court. England does appear to have a well-informed judiciary in this area of law.

Essential Facilities Doctrine

[17]

Essential Facilities Doctrine in EC Anti-trust Law: A Contribution to the Current Debate

Daniel Glasl

Market access for all competitors on equal terms is a controversial issue. In EC competition law and policy, third party access (TPA) to essential facilities is of increasing interest and importance. The following article discusses recent cases and regulatory works and intends to establish certain common parameters governing TPA cases. It will also contribute to the current debate on the so-called 'essential facilities doctrine' in the United States, which is laudably referred to as a 'useful analytic tool' by some,[1] and described in more critical terms by others.[2]

The Notion of 'Essential Facilities'

What are 'essential facilities'? The notion has not been mentioned by the Commission until quite recently. In academic works on EC competition law the question of third party access is normally treated under the abuse of a dominant position, however generally without referring to the concept of essential facilities.[3] Based on the *Magill* case, concerning the obligation to share intellectual property rights[4] and the *Sealink/B&I-Holyhead* case, concerning interim measures and equal treatment in port facilities,[5] the European discussion on TPA has been reinvigorated. First an attempt will be made to define the notion of essential facilities.

Essential facilities in EC law

The fact that there is only a very limited number of references to the essential facilities concept does not mean that TPA cases are rare—on the contrary: they are rather numerous. Some examples may illustrate this.

Recent EC cases

The four airlines Lufthansa, Air France, Cathay Pacific and JAL notified their agreements relating to the setting up of a computerised global logistics system (GLS)[6] containing schedules, rates and conditions for transport of air freight. Subject to certain undertakings given by these airlines, in particular with respect to the principles set forth in the block exemption for air transport computerised reservation systems,[7] the Commission has indicated a favourable decision. The GLS could be considered as an essential facility, the participation in which constitutes a precondition for other carriers entering into competition in the air freight market.[8] In *London European/Sabena*[9] the computerised reservation system for air transport services 'Saphir', owned and controlled by Sabena, was an essential facility for competing in the market for air transport on a given route. In *Lufthansa/Interflug*[10] the airport facilities such as air-traffic control and ground handling were considered as essential facilities for all users of the airports concerned. In *Telemarketing/CLT*[11] French-speaking television broadcasting by CLT was considered essential for competing in the neighbouring market of telemarketing services and could not be reserved to CLT's own subsidiary. In the case *Sealink/B&I-Holyhead*,[12] mentioned above, the Commission defined the essential facilities as 'a facility or infrastructure without access to which competitors cannot provide services to their customers'. In this case the port facilities, including the waterways, docks, loading and unloading infrastructure and related equipment, were considered as essential facilities.

Dr Daniel Glasl, Attorney-at-law, von Meiss Blum & Partners, Zurich.

Special thanks to the Alliance of European Lawyers, Brussels, especially Erik Pijnacker Hordijk and Gerwin Van Gerven, for their support, without which this article would not have been possible.

1 *See ABA Antitrust Section, Antitrust Law Developments*, American Bar Association, 1992 (3rd edn), at 241 footnote 258.
2 Philip Areeda, 'Essential Facilities: An Epithet in Need of Limiting Principles', (1990) *Antitrust Law Journal* Volume 58 at 841.
3 Ritter, *EEC Competition Law, a Practitioner's Guide*, Kluwer Law and Taxation Publishers, 1991, at 311 (Access to Infrastructure).
4 Discussed below; see Romano Subiotto, 'The Right to Deal with Whom One Pleases under EEC Competition Law: A Small Contribution to a Necessary Debate', [1992] 6 ECLR 234.
5 Discussed below; see Nick Maltby, 'Restrictions on Port Operators', [1993] 5 ECLR 223 and John Ratliff, 'EC Competition Law: The Impact on Ports', [1994] 22 IBL 182.

6 OJ 1993 C76/5.
7 Regulation 83/91/EEC, OJ 1991 L10/9. The undertakings assured that access for subscribers is granted on equal and non-discriminatory terms, and that participation and access to the GLS is not an impediment to participation in and use of other systems.
8 See also Encompass Europe (cargo logistics system) OJ 1992 C233/2.
9 OJ 1988 L317/47.
10 XXth Report on Competition Policy, (1990) point 114.
11 *CBEM-Telemarketing v CLT and IPB*, Case 311/84, [1985] ECR 3261.
12 Commission Decision IV/34.174, [1992] 5 CMLR 255; press release of 11 June 1992, IP/92/478; XXIInd Report on Competition Policy (1992), point 219; see also Nick Maltby, 'Restrictions on Port Operators', [1993] 5 ECLR 223.

Recent regulatory examples

Besides numerous individual competition law cases, some of which are mentioned above, there are regulatory issues concerning TPA. The block exemption for agreements on computerised reservation systems in the air transport market (CRS)[13] establishes certain principles according to which a participating airline can enter into and leave such a system without interference by a 'mother' airline which owns the system. The CRS is an essential facility. In the energy market, characterised by complex and costly infrastructure investments, pipelines and transmission grids often are the object of compulsory sharing with competitors. Both in electricity and in gas, the 'common carrier' directives establish standards for cross-frontier transmission.[14] Further integration and market access questions are in discussion.[15] A last example is the Commission paper in connection with the easier cross-border payments programme, where one reads that:

> as a general rule, co-operation agreements which embrace the majority of credit institutions of one country or are likely to process a significant part of payment traffic between different countries either totally or in a given market segment, may be considered to provide an *essential facility* and, therefore, should be open for further membership provided that candidates meet appropriate criteria . . .[16]

The question arises: are companies which own an essential facility required to 'share their assets with third parties simply in order to enable them to compete'?[17] To determine the right use of the notion of 'essential facilities' a look into US anti-trust law, which is 67 years of experience ahead in this area, might be useful.

Essential facilities in US case law

In US anti-trust law the essential facilities (or 'bottleneck') doctrine deals with a particular type of refusal to deal under the Sherman Act. The doctrine originates from a Supreme Court decision in the *Terminal Railroad* case.[18] The Terminal Railroad Association controlled passages into and out of St Louis, an important railroad junction. This monopoly facility was acquired by a combination of some, but not all, of the railroads transiting St Louis. This combination of railroads did not create anything new; it merely acquired an existing facility. The combination was now in a position to use the pre-existing monopoly to exclude or disadvantage competitors needing to pass through St Louis. The Court held that it was improper for the railways that jointly owned the only terminal in St Louis to deny their competitors access to the terminal on reasonable terms because such access was essential to their ability to compete. Recognising that the combination had obtained a monopoly through joint purchase, the Supreme Court concluded that the most efficient remedy was to admit non-member competitors to the consortium.[19] In this case both the junction infrastructure and the services related to it constituted the essential facility.

In *Associated Press*[20] (AP) 1,200 newspapers created AP, granting access to news generated by one member to the others and enabling creation of their own reporting and news-generating staff in areas where they were not previously present. Existing members were allowed to block the admission of competitors. It was considered a violation of the Sherman Act, discriminating against competitors, but the Supreme Court did not say that AP had to admit everyone. One judge used the essential facility doctrine comparing AP to a public utility, a business infused with the public interest that was required to serve all ('need for the maximum flow of information and opinion to preserve our democracy and Constitution').

In *Otter Trail*,[21] municipalities were refused the opportunity to sell electricity purchased from another supplier to their residents through Otter Trail's electricity network. The Supreme Court held that the refusal violated section 2 of the Sherman Act. The essential facility consisted in the cables and technical installations necessary for the local distribution of electricity. The conditions in the distribution market were already regulated by federal law. Otter Trail, being on the one hand a competitor in the distribution business and on the other hand owner of the facility, had to grant access to the municipalities on equal terms.

In *Hecht*,[22] the use of a stadium was considered essential to the operation of a professional football team in Washington. Based on the fact that a stadium of such size could not easily be duplicated by potential competitors and that the use of the stadium by another team was possible without interference to the existing team, the prohibition to share in the lease agreement was considered illegal by the Court.

In *Aspen*,[23] the Supreme Court held that an undertaking

13 See Note 7 above.
14 Council Directive 91/296/EEC, OJ 1991 L147/37 (natural gas); Council Directive 90/547/EEC, OJ 1990 L313/30 (electricity).
15 See below, 'Gas and electricity'.
16 Internal working document of the Commission, XV/31/91, 19 March 1991, at 16 and Annex 4.
17 See R. Subiotto, Note 4 above, at 234.
18 *United States v Terminal Railroad Association* 224 US 383 (1912).
19 Philip Areeda, 'Essential Facilities: An Epithet in Need of Limiting Principles', (1990) *Antitrust Law Journal* volume 58 at 842.
20 *Associated Press v United States* 326 US 1 (1945).
21 *Otter Trail Power & Co. v United States* 410 US 366 (1973).
22 *Hecht v Pro Football Inc.* 436 US 956 (1978).
23 *Aspen Skiing Co. v Aspen Highlands Skiing Corp.* 472 US 585 (1985).

with monopoly power has—under certain circumstances—a duty to continue a joint marketing arrangement with a smaller competitor. The defendant operated three of the four ski locations in Aspen, Colorado, the plaintiff one. For many years the parties had jointly offered an 'all Aspen' ski pass covering all four mountains. The defendant's refusal to continue this marketing co-operation and the absence of any valid business reasons for this conduct led to the defendant's liability.[24] This judgment encouraged many attempts for an expanded application of the duty to deal, including some too farreaching.[25] The Supreme Court reversed a jury decision based on *Aspen* by saying that:

> if *Aspen* stands for any principle that goes beyond its unusual facts, it is that a monopolist may be guilty of monopolisation if it refuses to co-operate with a competitor in circumstances where some co-operation is indispensable to effective competition . . .[26]

In the *Network* cases,[27] each television network monopolised its prime time. The access of independent producers was protected by restrictions on the networks to produce their own prime time programmes and by a prohibition of financial participation of networks in independent producers.

A leading case in the US essential facilities doctrine is *MCI Communications Corp. v AT & T.*[28] MCI claimed that AT & T should let it connect its telephone lines with their nation-wide telephone network in order to be able to compete in the long-distance business. Based on *Otter Trail* the Supreme Court acknowledged that it was technically and economically feasible for AT & T to have provided the interconnections and that AT & T's refusal constituted an act of monopolisation.[29] Four elements necessary to establish liability under the essential facilities doctrine have been identified:

(1) control of the essential facility by a monopolist;
(2) a competitor's inability practically or reasonably to duplicate the essential facility;
(3) the denial of the use of the facility to a competitor; and
(4) the feasibility of providing the facility.[30]

However, this decision has been criticised. Further limitations are suggested by Professor Areeda, according to which the following principles should be taken into account: there is no general duty to share; no-one should be forced to deal unless doing so is likely substantially to improve competition in the market-place; and not if it could chill desirable activity. And even when all these additional conditions are satisfied, denial of access should never *per se* be unlawful; legitimate business purposes may justify not sharing a facility.[31]

Definition of essential facilities in EC law

Based on these observations and considerations, the following characteristic criteria for essential facilities in EC anti-trust law may be suggested:

> (1) Facilities consist in infrastructure, or infrastructure combined with services related to them, which are of an auxiliary nature to an economic activity in a related but separated market. Tangible or intangible goods are unlikely to constitute such facilities.[32]
> (2) It is practically or reasonably impossible for any new competitor to duplicate such facilities.
> (3) Such facilities, access to which is necessary in order to compete, are considered essential facilities.[33]

These three elements are guidelines; they do not replace detailed knowledge of the market situation in each individual case. Furthermore it should be clear that the identification of essential facilities is nothing but a first step and not an equivalent to winning a TPA case.

Access to Essential Facilities

What conditions must a third party fulfil to get access to essential facilities? This section analyses some of the EC case law and regulatory works dealing with compulsory access.

24 Whereas the Court of Appeals had upheld the defendant's liability under both the intent and the essential facilities test, the Supreme Court found it not necessary to address the essential facilities test, after it had confirmed the defendant's liability under the intent test (a business is free to deal with whomever it pleases, so long as it has 'no purpose to create or maintain a monopoly').
25 Critical: Philip Areeda, Note 19 above, at 841.
26 *Olympia v Western Union Telegraph* 797 F. 2d 370 (7th Cir. 1986), *cert. den'd*, 480 US 934 (1987); see also ABA Antitrust section, Note 1 above at 244 footnote 276.
27 For example *United States v NBC, CBS, ABC* (1990) *Antitrust Law Journal* volume 58 at 875.
28 708 F. 2d 1081, 1132 (7th Cir.), *cert. den'd*, 464 US 891 (1983).
29 The Court said: 'A monopolist's refusal to deal under these circumstances is governed by the so-called essential facilities doctrine. Such a refusal may be unlawful because a monopolist's control of an essential facility (sometimes called a 'bottleneck') can extend monopoly power from one market into another. Thus, the antitrust laws have imposed on firms controlling an essential facility the obligation to make the facility available on non-discriminatory terms.' *Ibid.*, at 1132.
30 See ABA Antitrust Section, Note 1 above, at 246 footnote 292 (with further references).
31 See Philip Areeda, Note 19 above, at 841.
32 Exclusive products or industrial property may evoke the duty to deal issue, in a downstream market. The essential facility doctrine does not apply to such cases. See discussion of the *Magill* case, below.
33 See Kurt Ritter, 'EC Antitrust Law and Energy', in *Twentieth Anniversary Fordham Corporate Law Institute*, 21 to 22 October 1993, at p. 6/339.

TPA case law

The applicability of Community anti-trust law is in general not dependent on prior harmonisation of the competitive structures in the different Member States.[34] Thus the lack of harmonisation has never been accepted as a justification of the non-applicability of Treaty rules.[35]

Refusals to supply or to deal

Comments on essential facilities often include refusal to deal cases. But not all of these cases are in fact concerned with essential facilities. Some are worth mentioning for delimitation purposes. In *Commercial Solvents*,[36] the plaintiff had a monopoly position for the production and sale of certain raw materials which are necessary for the industrial production of ethambutol. Through a reselling company it had supplied this raw material to an Italian manufacturer of ethambutol until 1970. The subsequent refusal to supply that manufacturer was considered to be an abuse of a dominant position. The Court held that a manufacturer which has a dominant position in the production of a raw material and which, therefore, controls the supply to manufacturers of derivatives, may not refuse to supply the raw material when such refusal could lead to the elimination of all competition on the part of an important manufacturer of derivative products. The cases of *Hugin*[37] and *Telemarketing v CLT*[38] confirm that an undertaking which is dominant with regard to the production and supply of certain products which are necessary to compete in another market may not, without any objective necessity, refuse to supply these products and thereby reserve that market for itself. In *United Brands*[39] the Court put dominant firms under a positive duty to supply unless objective reasons justify the decision not to supply. The *CLT* decision is in fact concerned with an essential facility and therefore of particular interest. Telemarketing claimed to keep access to CLT's television broadcasting services, in particular its advertising programmes, in order to continue its telemarketing activities (which consist in advertising products on television by inviting consumers to call a specific telephone number). CLT was the only television broadcaster in French and decided to reserve this service for its daughter company. It refused to provide Telemarketing any longer with the services. Thus it eliminated any possibility of competition in the telemarketing market. Based on *Commercial Solvents* the Court held that it is abusive for a dominant undertaking to reserve an auxiliary service to itself or to a subsidiary without reasonable grounds, if such service can be supplied by another undertaking in another market and such reservation is able to eliminate competition.

The *London European/Sabena* case concerned access to Sabena's computerised reservation system Saphir, through which Sabena occupied a dominant position in the Belgian market for computerised air travel reservations. Based on the argument that London European's tariffs were too low and that London European appointed another company instead of Sabena for some of its ground handling services, Sabena refused to grant London European access to Saphir. The Commission stated that it is a misuse to impose a higher tariff level to a competitor as a precondition to get access to the reservation system. It condemned Sabena of an infringement of Article 86. The Commission stated also that the behaviour of Sabena can be considered as a deliberate reduction of production in the sense of Article 86(b), since it might have the consequence that London European must leave the market of air transport services between Brussels and Luton.

In *British Midland/Aer Lingus*[40] the Commission found that Aer Lingus had abused its dominant position by terminating its interline agreement with British Midland. New entrants should get some access to interlining facilities,[41] in particular in the initial stage of their business, but not indefinitely. Therefore the duty to interline should be limited to the time period which is objectively necessary for a competitor to become established in the market.

Tie-in/monopoly leverage

The *London European/Sabena* case made clear that, by making access to the reservation system conditional on prior agreement on the ground handling services, that is, two services not being linked together, Sabena committed an infringement of Article 86(d) EEC.

A related approach is what is referred to as 'monopoly leverage' in US anti-trust law. It can be found in *CLT*, discussed above, and in the case of *RTT*,[42] where the Belgian RTT was condemned for abuse of its monopoly

34 *Verband der Sachversicherer eV v Commission (Fire Insurance)*, Case 45/85, [1987] ECR 405; *Rendo v Commission (Ijsselcentrale)*, Case T–16/91, [1992] ECR II–2417; *RTE v Commission (Magill)*, Case T–69/89, [1991] ECR II–485, 518.
35 See Kurt Ritter, Note 3 above at 343.
36 *Commercial Solvents v Commission*, Case 7/73, [1974] ECR 223.
37 *Hugin v Liptons* OJ 1978 L22/23, *Hugin v Commission*, Case 22/78, [1979] ECR 1869.
38 *Telemarketing v CLT*, Case 311/84, [1985] ECR 3261.
39 *United Brands v Commission*, Case 27/76, [1978] ECR 207.
40 OJ 1992 L96/34; XXIInd Report on Competition Policy, No. 216.
41 Interlining is a traditionally used co-operation in the airline industry: it allows passengers to change flights on to the other airline's services and travel agents to issue tickets combining flights by both airlines. The withdrawal of interline facilities makes flights with that airline less attractive.
42 *RTT v GB-Inno-BM*, Case 18/88, [1991] ECR 5941.

position over an essential facility, namely, the telephone network, to expand into related markets. RTT, holding exclusive rights for the establishment and operation of the network, was also entrusted with the task of defining specifications for terminal equipment, monitoring their application and granting type-approval. The Court held that the Treaty precludes a Member State from granting to the undertaking which operates the public telecommunications network the power to lay down standards for telephone equipment and to check that economic operators meet those standards when it is itself competing with those operators on the market of that equipment.

Access to facilities on less favourable terms

In the case of *B&I v Sealink*[43] the Commission ordered interim measures to prevent irreparable damage to B&I, an Irish ferry operator. Sealink is a British ferry operator which is also the port authority at Holyhead. It had permitted changes to its own ferry sailing times which forced B&I to interrupt its loading or unloading every time a Sealink vessel passed a moored B&I ship, due to water rising. The Commission considered 'that a company which both owns and uses an essential facility, in this case a port, should not grant its competitors access on terms less favourable than those which it gives its own services'.

In the *Port of Genoa* case[44] the Court held that it is a breach of Article 86 to confer exclusive rights for the loading and unloading services at ports only to companies using Italian workers and that Italy was in breach of Article 90(1) of the Treaty. The ship's own crew could have unloaded the goods quicker and therefore on better terms. The Court did not deal with the market definition but simply relied on the significance of that port. Implicitly the Court applied the essential facilities doctrine. In such circumstances this approach might indeed replace the definition of the relevant geographical and product market.[45]

In *British Telecommunications–Italy v Commission*[46] the Court confirmed the decision taken by the Commission concerning access to telecommunication facilities.[47] It held that British Telecom infringed Article 86 by preventing private transmission agencies from providing certain services in the United Kingdom insofar as access to its telecommunication systems and services was made conditional on unrelated and exclusionary terms. The *ERT* case[48] is another example for essential facilities in the television broadcasting industry.

In the energy sector there is a number of actual and potential cases involving TPA to power lines and other facilities.[49] In the *VNG* case, the obligation imposed on VNG by the Bundeskartellamt to provide potential competitors with information on access conditions or to prove the lack of capacity and to grant the plaintiff access to its pipelines at reasonable fees was smashed by the Berlin Court.[50] According to the court decision, there was no legal base for a general duty to avoid any potential future abuse of a dominant position; concerning the pending application the refusal to grant access to its pipelines did not constitute an abuse of VNG's dominant position.

Article 85 cases

TPA to essential facilities has also been considered in connection with Article 85 of the Treaty. In *British Midland/Aer Lingus*[51] the participation of Aer Lingus at IATA conferences on tariffs, not allowing British Midland to participate in the IATA system on interlining and tariffs, constituted an infringement of Article 85 EEC.

In Ijsselcentrale[52] the Dutch company SEP, a joint venture of the four electricity generators in the Netherlands, owned and operated the international power lines through which all imports and exports of electricity must be transmitted. The four participants and SEP agreed on co-operation according to which all imports and exports of electricity had to be effected through SEP. The construction of own power lines are not considered a real alternative for industrial consumers. SEP's refusal to make power lines available to others made it practically impossible for them to import electricity themselves. The Commission held that such refusal can be considered as an infringement of Article 85 of the Treaty.[53] The power lines controlled by SEP can, therefore, constitute an essential facility, access to which is necessary for competition in electricity in the Netherlands.

There are also many precedents for the Commission's granting an individual exemption subject to conditions or undertakings concerning TPA. A particularly pertinent

43 Commission Decision IV 34.174, [1992] 5 CMLR 255; press release 11 June 1992, IP/92/478; see also Nick Maltby, Note 5 above, at 223. The case has since been appealed by Sealink.

44 Case C–179/90, [1991] ECR I–5889.

45 See also Michel Glais, 'Les concepts de "relevant market" et "dépendance économique" au regard de l'article 86 du traité de Rome', *Revue du Marché Commun*, 306, Avril 1987, at 203; and L. Hancher and P.-A. Trepte, 'Competition and the Internal Energy Market', [1992] 4 ECLR 149 at footnote 17.

46 Case 41/83, [1985] ECR 873.

47 Commission Decision of 10 December 1982, OJ 1982 L360/36.

48 Case C–260/89,[1991] ECR I–2925.

49 See Ritter, Note 33 above, at 353.

50 *VNG/Weissenborn*, decision of the Bundeskartellamt of 29 June 1992, annulled by the Kammergericht Berlin on 9 June 1993, WuW12/1993, 1037, second appeal pending.

51 See Note 40 above.

52 Commission Decision of 16 January 1991, OJ 1991 L28/32.

53 Recital 29 of the Decision.

example is *Eirpage*,[54] where the Irish Telecom monopoly and Motorola Ireland Ltd were granted a ten-year exemption for their joint venture for the promotion and operation of nation-wide paging services interconnected to the public telephone network. The exemption was in particular based on a written undertaking from Irish Telecom to treat new entrants on the same footing as Eirpage, that is, to make available to persons satisfying the relevant licensing and financial requirements the facilities necessary for operating such a paging service under the same conditions as those applying to Eirpage.[55]

Discussion

The current debate on the so-called essential facilities doctrine does not always concentrate on true access to essential facilities cases. In some cases the well established case law on the duty to deal may fully serve its purposes and nobody needs a new doctrine. However, some cases are not about the duty to deal but about sharing essential facilities. In such cases the access to and use of a facility rather than the supply of a tangible or intangible good are concerned.[56]

The *Magill* case concerns the duty to make available copyright protected information and is a clear duty to supply case, in the line of *Commercial Solvents*, *Hugin* and *United Brands*.[57] The difference was that the product Magill wanted was not tangible but intangible; and its supply was not withdrawn but refused in the first place.[58] In this line of case law, *Magill* certainly is important.[59] However, it does not contribute to the essential facilities doctrine, because the intellectual property concerned cannot be classified as an essential facility.

On the other hand access to broadcasting networks, power lines, CRS or port facilities are clear essential facilities cases. In these cases, the essential facilities doctrine might be a valuable approach.

Liberalisation of markets and reserved sectors

In the sectors of telecommunications, transport or energy the process of Community-wide liberalisation is not yet very advanced. However, strong impulses for market liberalisation and establishing an environment of free competition are originating from the Commission. Often characterised by monopolistic structures and exclusive rights, these markets tend to be covered by few but very strong companies even after liberalisation.[60] In order to play a competitive role as a service provider in these markets, a newcomer is often dependent on the use of an already existing infrastructure which cannot, at reasonable terms, be easily duplicated. On the other hand, in order to guarantee the supply of the so-called universal services, it is accepted that some restrictions of competition and thus of TPA are indispensable.

The analysis of how TPA to essential facilities is dealt with in the regulatory way[61] will provide an interesting contribution to the debate.

Gas and electricity

There is a general consensus that common market principles and free competition should apply as well in the energy sector.[62] However, the goals of a perfect internal market are by far not yet achieved.[63]

The first stage of liberalisation in the energy market[64] consists in the effective implementation of the 'common carrier' directives and that on the transparency of prices of 1990 and 1991,[65] which should have been implemented by the Member States in July 1991. The Commission has initiated a number of procedures under Article 169 against Member States concerning exclusive import and export rights in the electricity and gas market.[66]

54 Commission Decision of 18 October 1992, OJ 1992 L303/22.
55 Further examples for individual exemptions based on TPA guarantees are *DHL International* (XXIst Report on Competition Policy (1991), point 89), *KLM/Transavia* (*ibid.*, point 92), *Amadeus/Sabre* (*ibid.*, point 95), *UIP Distribution of film productions* (XIXth Report on Competition Policy, (1989), point 51), *Film purchases by German TV* (*ibid.*, point 52).
56 Facilities, often combined with related services are, for example, power lines (*Ijsselcentrale*), CRS, GLS, ports (*Sealink*, *Port of Genova*), airports (*Lufthansa-Interflug*), television networks (*CLT*), railway tracks (*St Louis*), electricity networks (*Otter Trail*), stadiums (questionable, *Hecht*), telecommunications networks (*MCI*), telephone networks (*RTT*).
57 The issue in these cases is whether and under what circumstances a refusal to supply—or to license—may constitute an abuse of a dominant position. In his opinion in *Magill*, joined cases C-241/91 P and C-242/91 P (delivered on 1 June 1994), Advocate General Gulman does not mention the essential facilities doctrine.
58 The equal treatment of refusal and withdrawal to deal was already applied in *Aer Lingus/British Midland*. However, justification of refusal remains easier than for withdrawal or termination of earlier supply contracts (see, for example, *CLT*).
59 In fact, this case reflects the conflict between national concepts of intellectual property rights which must be respected by EC law and the competition law-motivated duty to share which cannot take unlimited account of the underlying (national) reasons of natural monopolies. The questionable validity of the copyrights concerned and the lack of plausible reasons not to sell these rights to Magill might have had an influence on the judgment of the Court of First Instance.

60 For example British Telecom is, years after privatisation, still by far the most powerful company in the UK telecommunication sector.
61 In this respect the existence of essential services or facilities in the respective markets is presupposed.
62 See Kurt Ritter, Note 33 above at p. 4/337.
63 See, for example, XIXth Report on Competition Policy (1990), point 32.
64 See also L. Hancher and P.-A. Trepte, Note 45 above, at 149.
65 Council Directive 90/547/EEC on electricity transit, OJ 1990 L313/30; Council Directive 91/296/EEC on gas transit, OJ 1991 L147/37; Council Directive 90/377/EEC on price transparency, OJ 1990 L185/16.
66 See also *Ijsselcentrale*, Note 52 above.

Further liberalisation should be effected based on the draft directives concerning common rules for the internal market on electricity and natural gas.[67] They both contain provisions on TPA which can be examined together. The second stage of liberalisation should, according to these drafts, provide for a greater integration while respecting existing structures.[68] It consists of three issues:

> *firstly*: abolition of exclusive rights for the production of electric power and construction of electric power lines and gas pipelines by establishing an objective, transparent and non-discriminatory system for granting licences for the production of electricity and the building of lines and pipelines. The aim is to open up investment in production and transport to independent operators, in particular large industrial users. The criteria for granting a licence are in accordance with the vital concerns of national licence-granting systems and must exclusively relate to environmental protection, town and country planning, security and safety of the installation, and technical and financial capacity of the applicant. For reasons of environmental policy or security of supply, the Member States may supplement these criteria by criteria restricting the nature of the primary energy source that may be used for the generation of electricity.[69]
>
> *secondly*: establishing of vertical structures, i.e. separation of management and accounting of production, transmission and supply activities.
>
> *thirdly*: limited introduction of TPA to the network, according to which the transmission, supply and distribution companies are required to offer certain eligible entities access to their network at reasonable rates as long as there is transmission or distribution capacity available. The eligibility criteria should include:
> a) large industrial users whose consumption exceeds certain thresholds and
> b) distribution companies in such a way as to ensure that other industrial users and domestic users benefit indirectly from TPA.[70]

The third stage—intended to complete the internal energy market for gas and electricity—will, according to the present drafts, involve an enlargement of TPA, in particular by modified criteria of eligibility in the light of the experience gathered during the second stage, in all probability expanding it to all categories of consumers which can take advantage of these possibilities. This stage is intended to start on 1 January 1996.

The adoption of these draft directives has been postponed[71] and new approaches on negotiated access by third parties to the energy networks have passed the European Parliament.[72]

Telecommunication

Limited liberalisation of telecommunication services was established in 1990.[73] All data transfer services on the public network with the exception of telex, mobile telephone and satellite communication and radio and television services are liberalised. Extension of liberalisation for satellite, mobile telephony and telex is in preparation. The sector of voice telephony – with the exception of communication within closed user groups – has not (yet) been liberalised.[74] The Commission has recently outlined its views on what constitutes a universal service and how it can be financed.[75]

Since public networks must be available in cases of emergency, technical integrity must be maintained at all times of operation. Apart from the essential requirements, Member States can introduce or maintain conditions regarding public service requirements which constitute objective, non-discriminatory and transparent trade regulations regarding the conditions of permanence, availability and quality of the service. Any restrictions based on other grounds represent an infringement of Treaty provisions.

67 Electricity: OJ 1992 C65/4, as amended OJ 1994 C123/1; gas: OJ 1992 C65/14, as amended OJ 1994 C123/36.
68 See Chapter II (Access to the Market) of the draft directives.
69 Article 4(2) of the electricity draft Directive.
70 In view of the technical complexity and the innovative nature of giving third parties freedom of access to the networks, it is considered desirable for the Member States to be able to allow a period of gradual adaptation and for a while to start by restricting the right to use the interconnected network to a small number of economic operators who are the best situated to make use of it, that is, the major industrial consumers and the supply companies. Therefore the Commission proposals set certain thresholds for eligibility. Making access available to third parties has to be done in conditions which will guarantee reliability of operation of the networks and security of supply. Management and technical supervision of the electricity network and its links with other networks should be maintained by a network manager who is acting in an independent and non-discriminatory manner. To guarantee his neutrality he must be separate from any production and supply activities so as not to favour his own activities.

71 See European Report, No. 1897, 27 October 1993.
72 Electricty: OJ 1994 C329/182; gas: OJ 1994 C329/212.
73 Commission Directive 90/388/EEC, OJ 1990 L192/10.
74 Since the main financial resources for the development of the network still derive from the telephone service, it is agreed that the opening up of voice telephony to competition could threaten the financial stability of the telecommunication organisations responsible for the network.
The following criteria for liberalisation of telecommunication services can be named: As a general rule, Article 59 of the Treaty provides for the abolition of any restrictions on the freedom to provide services. However, such restrictions are, under Articles 66, 55 and 56 of the Treaty, allowed on certain non-economic grounds: exercise of official authority, public policy, public security and public health. The ECJ also recognises restrictions on the freedom to provide services if they fulfil essential requirements in the general interest and are applied without discrimination and in proportion to the objective. Such restrictions are consumer protection and protection of intellectual property, both of which are not considered endangered by the freedom to provide telecommunication services.
75 Commission communication of 15 November 1993, COM(93)543. According to the Commission, universal service includes the right for all customers to have a phone connected; to obtain service meeting defined quality standards; to benefit from clear procedures to sort out problems between the customers and the telecommunications operator; and progressively to have access to a range of new services.

Concerning TPA to networks, a Council Directive of 1990 provides for criteria for access to liberalised telecommunication sectors through the implementation of open network provisions (ONP).[76] Based on this framework, some ONP legislation has passed, such as in the sector of leased lines,[77] Packet-Switched Data Services, and harmonised Integrated Services Digital Network (ISDN) access.[78] Further ONP directives are expected in the voice telephony service, telex service, mobile telephone service and other areas.

Railways

In July 1993 two draft Council Directives were published concerning licences of railway undertakings and the sharing of railway infrastructure capacity.[79]

Licence

The first draft has the objective to define the criteria for granting of licences based on the right of access provided in a Directive of 29 July 1991.[80] The conditions must be determined in a non-discriminatory way. The granting of licences is based on elements of good standing,[81] of financial capacity[82] and professional capacity.[83] Furthermore the risk of financial liability must be covered. The licence should remain valid as long as the undertaking fulfils the conditions laid down in the directive. In cases of *non usus* for longer than six months the Member State could require a new licence granting procedure.[84]

A railway undertaking which satisfies the requirements of the directive should have a right to receive a licence; the licence itself does not grant any authorisation of access.[85]

Access to infrastructure and fees for use

Eligible companies are railway undertakings, which should have the traction available.[86] The access to free infrastructure capacity is granted by the Member States on an equal and non-discriminatory basis.[87] The Member States can privilege certain services in the public interest on infrastructure built specifically for those services (for example, high speed lines).[88]

For the use of existing infrastructure, the undertaking should pay a fee to the holder of the infrastructure. The Member States will have to establish the modalities of such payments based on the principles that the fees are fixed according to the characteristics and the time of the service and correspond to normal market conditions, that is, that they are not excessive.[89]

The draft directive also contains provisions on the procedure to determine free infrastructure access and for the application including remedies for such access.[90]

Discussion

It is evident that market liberalisation is, in particular in the sectors exemplified above, a difficult process. It is generally accepted that under certain conditions restrictions to free competition and full liberalisation remain justified. Such conditions are, for example, certain non-economic grounds of public interest that restrict the implementation of competition in a given sector to a certain extent.[91] Another example is the economic equilibrium of a service provider entrusted with a universal service obligation; his financial stability must be protected in order to achieve the policy objective in a specific market.[92]

Conclusions

These observations show that TPA to essential facilities is a matter of great detail and complexity. Differences in

76 Council Directive 90/387/EEC of 28 June 1990. The basic principles for open network provisions are: they must be based on objective criteria; they must be transparent and published in an appropriate manner; they must guarantee equality of access and they must be non-discriminatory, in accordance with Community law (namely security, maintenance, interoperability of services and data protection).

77 Council Directive 92/44/EEC of 5 June 1992 on the application of ONP to leased lines (OJ 1992 L165/27).

78 Council Recommendation 92/383/EEC of 5 June 1992 (OJ 1992 L200/1).

79 Draft Council Directive concerning licences to railway undertakings, OJ 1994 C24/2, as amended OJ 1994 C225/9; draft Council Directive concerning infrastructure capacities and user fees, OJ 1994 C24/6, as amended OJ 1994 C225/11.

80 Directive on Community railway development (91/440/EEC).

81 See Article 5 of the draft licence Directive: the applicant may not have prior penal condemnation, bankruptcy or infringement of railway law.

82 See Article 6 of the draft licence Directive.

83 See Article 7 of the draft licence Directive: a control organisation must be established, the applicant must be able to provide all rolling stock including traction and assure the maintenance of all rolling stock, and he must have qualified personnel.

84 See Article 10 of the draft licence Directive.

85 See Article 3(3) of the draft licence Directive.

86 See Article 2(a) of the draft infrastructure Directive.

87 See Article 4 of the draft infrastructure Directive.

88 See Article 5 of the draft infrastructure Directive.

89 See Article 13 of the draft infrastructure Directive.

90 See Articles 16 to 18 of the draft infrastructure Directive.

91 The following grounds may justify a restriction in competition in a given sector: safeguard of public order, security, and health, consumer protection, intellectual property protection.

92 Both in the postal and telecommunication services the policy of universal services has been established; such services should be:

- available everywhere (geographical coverage);
- available on request within reasonable time; and
- affordable to all, that is, on reasonable terms.

If such policy objective is endangered by full liberalisation, then certain restrictions by the establishment of reserved areas which confer some special and exclusive rights are justified in order to maintain the resources necessary to keep the provider of the universal services in good financial conditions. The determination of the reserved areas, where free competition does not exist, requires profound analysis of the conditions of the individual market concerned. Again, general criteria cannot be established.

the speed and intensity of liberalisation in the sector concerned add to these difficulties. Some might be better handled by applying elements of what is called the essential facility doctrine. Based on the individual case law and regulatory approaches discussed above these elements are:

(1) Access to facilities may be compulsory only if these facilities are essential facilities.[93]
(2) Only undertakings or groups of undertakings which are (alone or jointly) in a dominant position by controlling essential facilities can be obliged to grant TPA.
(3) Access may be denied if the applicant does not satisfy certain personal requirements such as being in good standing, creditworthy and financially independent. Furthermore the applicant must have the professional and technical skills and capacity required for the operation and security of the business. For this purpose the applicant must eventually provide for certain specially trained personnel or certain equipment.
(4) A duty to use the facility according to specific rules may be imposed on the applicant; this can include maintenance duties, presence or performing obligations. Failure in satisfying these duties may lead to access withdrawal or other sanctions.
(5) Access may be denied if the applicant does not satisfy payment obligations of a fee for the use of the infrastructure. Such fee must be fixed in a general, transparent, equal and non-discriminatory manner and the level of the fee must be reasonable and not excessive, however a reasonable profit margin is acceptable.
(6) Access can be denied if there is no free capacity for additional use of the essential facilities; capacity determination must be undertaken on a fair and transparent basis.
(7) Access can be denied if the granting may impede the dominant undertaking in performing its public service mission or endanger its economic stability and equilibrium.

In the regulatory approach to TPA issues the following observations were made:

(1) If TPA provisions are adopted by regulation or directive, these provisions must be general, transparent and published in an appropriate manner; they must be based on objective criteria; they must guarantee equality of access; they must be non-discriminatory, in accordance with Community law; they should provide for a transparent granting procedure with a right of appeal; they should provide for a monitoring and controlling system in order to ensure that granting conditions are maintained; and they may contain provisions for *non usus*.
(2) If a formal TPA application procedure is established such procedure must be equal and non-discriminatory and it must necessarily lead to access if the TPA requirements are fulfilled.

A dominant undertaking or group is, in essence, not forced to grant third parties access to its facilities, if the applicable TPA conditions listed above are not satisfied. There is no general duty to share essential facilities, but denial of access to essential facilities must be justified by qualified criteria. Unjustified denial may have liability consequences. If an access-granting contract is withdrawn by the dominant undertaking, liability is more likely to occur than in a case where TPA has never been granted in the first place.

93 As defined above, 'Definition of essential facilities in EC law'.

Abuse

[18]

LAW AND THE ABUSE OF ECONOMIC POWER IN EUROPE

DAVID J. GERBER*

* Associate Professor, IIT/Chicago-Kent College of Law. B.A., 1967, Trinity College (Conn.); M.A., 1969, Yale University; J.D., 1972, University of Chicago Law School. The author wishes to thank Professor Ulrich Immenga of the University of Göttingen, Germany, for helpful comments on a prior draft of this article and the Marshall D. Ewell Research Fund of IIT/Chicago-Kent College of Law for financial support in preparing this study. He also wishes to thank Andre Fiebig for his research assistance.

Translations are by the author unless otherwise indicated.

INTRODUCTION

Most industrialized countries treat the possession of significant economic power by individual firms as a potential societal harm and, therefore, apply legal controls to the conduct of firms having such power.[1] United States law utilizes the concept of monopolization to define the limits of permissible conduct for powerful enterprises,[2] but virtually all other competition law systems, including all significant European legal systems, utilize the concept of abuse of power to fulfill this function.

These two approaches to the problem of single-firm economic power share a common objective: each attempts to protect society against harms which may result from the use of economic power without unduly restricting the conduct of powerful enterprises. The two legal mechanisms are, however, fundamentally different. They have evolved from different conceptual and theoretical starting points; they are embedded in different legal traditions, especially in relation to the role of government in economic activity; they are shaped by different social and political pressures; and their enforcement is based on different assumptions about law as well as about economics.

Because of these differences, the concept of abuse of economic power is alien to American lawyers. It has been little studied in English, and what little attention has been paid to it has focused on its use in the competition law of the European

1. For a dated, but still useful, review of the various national statutes, see ORGANISATION FOR ECONOMIC COOPERATION AND DEVELOPMENT, MARKET POWER AND THE LAW (1970) [hereinafter O.E.C.D.].

2. For a leading discussion of the monopolization concept in United States antitrust law, see 3 P. AREEDA & D. TURNER, ANTITRUST LAW chs. 6-8 (1985).

Economic Community.[3] Consequently, American lawyers frequently misunderstand the concept, its legal context, and the factors influencing its use and interpretation.[4]

This lack of understanding has several harmful effects. It impairs the ability of American lawyers to render advice relating to business operations in most of the industrialized countries of the world. An understanding of the legal regime relating to the conduct of economically powerful enterprises is critical not only to those enterprises themselves, but also to all who would either deal or compete with such enterprises. In addition, this lack of understanding of the abuse concept tends to prevent meaningful evaluation in the United States of the European experience in controlling economically powerful enterprises. This is particularly important in light of long-standing dissatisfaction in the United States with the treatment of single-firm economic power under United States antitrust law.[5] Proper evaluation of the European experience can thus provide needed perspective on United States law.

The problems involved in understanding the abuse concept are exacerbated by the fact that in recent years the role and content of the concept of abuse have undergone significant and rapid change. In Germany, for example, the abuse concept primarily targets a substantially different type of conduct than was its principle aim only ten years ago.[6] Moreover, the nature and extent of these changes in the role of the abuse concept have been seldom recognized and little understood.

---

3. *See generally* R. JOLIET, MONOPOLIZATION AND ABUSE OF DOMINANT POSITION: A COMPARATIVE STUDY OF THE AMERICAN AND EUROPEAN APPROACHES TO THE CONTROL OF ECONOMIC POWER (1970). *See also generally* C. EDWARDS, CONTROL OF CARTELS AND MONOPOLIES 177-95 (1967); Edwards, *American and German Policy Toward Conduct by Powerful Enterprises: A Comparison*, 23 ANTITRUST BULL. 83 (1978). For a German comparison of U.S. and German antitrust law regarding powerful enterprises, see I. SCHMIDT, US-AMERIKANISCHE UND DEUTSCHE WETTBEWERBSPOLITIK GEGENÜBER MARKTMACHT (1973).

4. In 1956, Professor Wolfgang Friedmann wrote that "[h]ardly any topic requires more urgently a comparative survey and critical analysis than that commonly described as "anti-trust law." ANTITRUST LAWS: A COMPARATIVE SYMPOSIUM iii (W. Friedmann ed. 1956). Yet in the ensuing years there has been very little comparative work done in English. *See generally* Gerber, *Antitrust Law and Economic Analysis: The Swedish Approach*, 8 HASTINGS INT'L & COMP. L. REV. 1 (1984). *See also* Rittner, *Konvergenz oder Divergenz der Europäischen Wettbewerbsrechte*, in INTEGRATION ODER DESINTEGRATION DER EUROPÄISCHEN WETTBEWERBSORDNUNG (1983).

5. *See, e.g.*, 1 NAT'L COMM'N FOR THE REVIEW OF ANTITRUST LAWS AND PROCEDURES, REPORT TO THE PRESIDENT AND THE ATTORNEY GENERAL 141-74 (1979).

6. *See infra* pt. III *D*, p.74.

This article, therefore, responds to this lack of understanding by analyzing the legal concept of abuse of a market-dominating position.[7] Section I of the article presents some historical background for the development of the abuse concept. Section II describes the function of the abuse concept in competition law systems based on administrative control.[8] Sections III and IV examine, respectively, the concept's role in the competition law systems of the Federal Republic of Germany and the European Economic Community, analyzing in detail the factors which affect its interpretation and application. Section V then compares and assesses the role and development of the abuse concept in German and European Community law. The focus of this article is on understanding how meaning is ascribed to the vague notion of abuse.[9] In analyzing this process, however, the article also reveals characteristics of the general process of law creation in the legal systems involved.

I. Historical Background on the Abuse Concept

A. Pre-Modern Conceptions of Abuse

The concept of abuse of a market-dominating position has developed during the twentieth century in the context of modern antitrust law systems. The idea of imposing sanctions on certain forms of conduct by economically powerful enterprises can be traced back, however, at least as far as the Roman Empire,[10]

---

7. There has been little attempt to study the interrelations between antitrust law developments in the various European countries. For notable exceptions, see U. Bernitz, Marknadsrätt (1969); R. Joliet, *supra* note 3; and Rittner, *supra* note 4.

8. The term "competition law" is used here to refer to legal processes designed to protect against restraints of competition. In the United States the term "antitrust law" is used to refer to these issues, but that term has the disadvantage of being associated with the American system of competition law.

The term "competition law" is, however, also less then optimal, because its direct analogues in European languages (for example, *Wettbewerbsrecht* and *Droit de Concurrence*) also refer to the law of unfair competition.

9. The concept of abuse of a market-dominating position has two components—the concept of abuse and the concept of dominant position. The abuse concept provides conduct standards; the concept of dominant position identifies those enterprises whose conduct is subject to those standards. The central idea is that an enterprise is market-dominating where it is not subject to substantial competition in a particular market. For a review of approaches to defining market-dominance, see O.E.C.D., *supra* note 1. Market-dominance is roughly the equivalent of having a high degree of market power for purposes of applying § 2 of the Sherman Act. *See generally* L. Sullivan, Handbook of the Law of Antitrust 19-40 (1977). Due to space limitations, only the concept of abuse will be studied here.

10. *See generally* R. Piotrowski, Cartels and Trusts ch. 2 (1933); *see also* R.

where several separate laws established penalties for individuals or groups of individuals who "cornered" a market and used the power achieved by that monopoly position to drive up prices to consumers.[11]

Roman laws on this subject would be of limited interest, however, if it were not for the fact that provisions of these laws were included in the Corpus Juris Civilis, the repository of Roman legal learning which served as the basis for law and legal education throughout much of Europe from the eleventh century until well into the last century.[12] At least partially as a result of this fact, laws following the Roman pattern were frequently in effect from the early middle ages until the nineteenth century.[13]

During the medieval period the concepts of "usury"[14] and of "just price"[15] added an important dimension to the way Europeans viewed economic activity. First, they established the proposition that any given price was either "just" or "unjust" and that legal processes not only could, but should, make that determination. Second, they labeled the charging of "unjust" prices as morally wrong and abhorrent to the basic religious tenets of society.[16] These ideas have had a powerful effect on legal and popular thought relating to economic activity, and this effect can still be detected.[17]

Since the last century, the concept of fairness implicit in the notions of just price and usury has been developed within the

---

ISAY, DIE GESCHICHTE DER KARTELLGESETZGEBUNGEN 2-3 (1955); von Brunn, *Vom Kartellrecht der Roemer*, in RECHT UND WIRTSCHAFT: FESTSCHRIFT FÜR J.W. HEDEMANN 47 (1958).

11. *See generally* Trinkner, *Die Kartellgesetzgebung des Corpus Juris Justiniani im Vergleich zum modernen Recht*, 1973 BETRIEBS-BERATER 860.

12. For a discussion of the importance of the Corpus Juris Civilis in continental European legal education, see H. BERMAN, LAW AND REVOLUTION 120-65 (1983).

13. *See* R. PIOTROWSKI, *supra* note 10, at 118.

14. *See* BERMAN, *supra* note 12, at 248-50; *see also generally* B. NELSON, THE IDEA OF USURY (2d ed. 1969); J. NOONAN, THE SCHOLASTIC ANALYSIS OF USURY (1957).

15. *See, e.g.*, de Roover, *The Concept of Just Price: Theory and Economic Policy*, 18 J. ECON. HIST. 418 (1958); Kaulla, *Die Lehre vom gerechten Preis in der Scholastik*, 60 ZEITSCHRIFT FÜR DAS GESAMTE STAATSWESEN 579 (1904). *See also generally* H. SCHMIDT, DIE LEHRE VON DER SITTENWIDRIGKEIT DES RECHTSGESCHÄFTS IN HISTORISCHER SICHT (1973); Gordley, *Equality in Exchange*, 69 CAL. L. REV. 1587 (1981).

16. *See* J. GILCHRIST, THE CHURCH AND ECONOMIC ACTIVITY IN THE MIDDLE AGES 58-70 (1969).

17. *See, e.g.*, Korah, *Interpretation and Application of Article 86 of the Treaty of Rome: Abuse of a Dominant Position Within the Common Market*, 53 NOTRE DAME LAW. 768, 769 (1978).

framework of unfair competition law. Most European legal systems have developed a distinct body of legal principles that define standards of fairness in business behavior and provide private remedies for competitors injured by violations of these standards.[18] Moreover, these principles tend to be well-developed, much used, and highly important.[19]

This body of unfair competition law helped set the stage for the development of the abuse concept, because it expanded the idea that legal processes could determine whether a *price* was fair to include determination of whether particular *business conduct* was fair. From here it was a short step to the idea that conduct which normally would be fair might become unfair when engaged in by a firm with substantial economic power.[20]

B. *Initial Steps Toward Competition Law*

Although the idea of passing legislation to combat restraints on competition began to be discussed in Europe around the turn of the century,[21] such legislation was rejected as inappropriate for European conditions until after the First World War.[22] The proposals conflicted sharply with the then dominant conception that laws should not restrict freedom of economic activity, even in the name of protecting the process of competition.[23]

With the close of World War I, however, political changes

---

18. In the nineteenth century the French courts led this development. *See* Derenberg, *The Influence of the French Code Civil on the Modern Law of Unfair Competition*, 4 AM. J. COMP. L. 1, 2-4 (1955).

19. For a discussion of unfair competition law in Germany, see F. RITTNER, WIRTSCHAFTSRECHT 185-267 (1979).

20. The fact that there was a significant and effective body of law to protect competitors from unfair conduct eliminated an important impetus for the development of competition law in general and control over economically powerful enterprises in particular. In addition, it meant that competition laws did not need to be concerned with unfairness as such, but only with unfairness as a function of market dominance.

21. For discussion, see generally H. SCHULTE, DAS ÖSTERREICHISCHE KARTELLRECHT VOR 1938 (1979); Grossfeld, *Zur Kartellrechtsdiskussion vor dem ersten Weltkrieg*, in H. COING AND W. WILHELM, WISSENSCHAFT UND KODIFIKATION DES PRIVATRECHTS IM 19. JAHRHUNDERT 255 (1979).

22. *See* A. ROTTHEGE, DIE BEURTEILUNG VON KARTELLEN UND GENOSSENSCHAFTEN DURCH DIE RECHTSWISSENSCHAFT 76-78 (1982).

23. *See generally* F. WIEACKER, PRIVATRECHTSGESCHICHTE DER NEUZEIT, pts. 5 & 6 (2d ed. 1967). Closely associated with concepts of political liberty, economic liberalism held that entrepreneurs should be free to do as they wished and that state interference should be kept to a minimum. The process of emancipating economic activity from mercantilism and guild-based restrictions reached different stages at different times in different parts of Europe, but it dominated the century.

and severe economic adjustments led to attempts to control certain uses of economic power. The primary impetus to early competition legislation was the post-war inflation of the early 1920s.[24] Cartels and economically powerful enterprises were seen as contributing to inflationary pressures,[25] and the first European competition laws were designed to combat such price increases.[26] These initial measures aimed at controlling cartels and monopolies were, in general, tentative and quite limited, typically requiring powerful enterprises or groups of enterprises to provide information to governmental organizations.[27] Such measures were based on the belief that publicity would itself inhibit enterprises from engaging in conduct that was harmful to society.

In Germany, however, postwar economic problems led to more substantial measures.[28] In response to crisis-level inflation, the German government in 1923 issued a Regulation Against Abuse of Economic Power Positions ("Abuse Regulation"), which became the forerunner of modern European competition laws.[29] The immediate aim of the regulation was to limit the ability of cartels and market-dominating enterprises to manipulate shortages and thereby increase consumer prices.[30] It was thus conceived as a means of combating harms caused by hold-

24. For discussion, see H. HOLBORN, A HISTORY OF MODERN GERMANY: 1840-1945, at 595-601 (1969).

25. *See* R. ISAY & O. TSCHIERSCHKY, KARTELLVERORDNUNG 31-34 (2d ed. 1930).

26. This is particularly true for the Scandinavian countries. *See generally* W. VON EYBEN, MONOPOLER OG PRISER (1981).

An additional goal was economic growth. The newly democratic governments were compelled to produce results to justify their existence, and they saw improved economic performance as a source of legitimization.

27. *See, e.g.*, Wetter, *Swedish Antitrust Law*, 10 AM. J. COMP. L. 19, 20-21 (1961).

In Norway a more substantial competition statute, the Trust Law (*Trustlov*), was passed in 1926. It contained the basic elements of the administrative control model of antitrust law which was further expanded in other European countries after the war. It was also closely associated with price control objectives. It established registration requirements for cartel agreements and authorized a specially-created administrative body to intervene in cases of abuse of power. The law's substantive provisions were conceived as legal rules, embodying judicially applicable standards. The actions of this administrative body were subject to review by a special council which functioned on legal and judicial principles. For a description of the Norwegian legislation, see U. BERNITZ, *supra* note 7, at 394-98.

28. For the economic situation, see 2 H. KELLENBENZ, DEUTSCHE WIRTSCHAFTSGESCHICHTE 355-65 (1981).

29. Verordnung gegen Missbrauch wirtschaftlicher Machtstellungen, 1923 REICHSGESETZBLATT [RGBl.]I 1067 (W. Ger.). An English translation appears in R. LEIFMAN, CARTELS, CONCERNS AND TRUSTS 351-57 (1932).

30. R. ISAY & O. TCHIERSCHKY, *supra* note 25, at 35-36.

ers of economic power, and it identified the socially harmful use of power as an abuse of that power. The Abuse Regulation granted to the Minister of Economics the authority to bring actions before a specially-created cartel court in cases where economic power was used so as to "endanger the economy or societal welfare."[31] The court's sanctions were generally limited, however, to voiding contracts.[32]

The German legislation was applied, with varied effectiveness, throughout the 1920s,[33] but it was replaced in 1933 by National Socialist legislation which mandated the formation of cartels.[34] Moreover, during the depression of the 1930s European governments generally encouraged rather than discouraged cartels and other forms of anticompetitive activity.[35] Thus, the first European experiments with competition law did not lead to a lasting legal framework. They did establish, however, an identifiable European approach to competition law which shaped subsequent developments.

II. The Administrative Control of Economic Power

During the first decade after the close of the Second World War, most Western European governments considered the introduction of competition legislation. Such legislation was eventually enacted in all major states except Italy.[36] In part, this was a response to specific problems of the post-war period. Widespread shortages and cartelization led to strong inflationary pressures, and competition laws were often viewed primarily as means to combat these pressures. The development of competition legislation also resulted from dissatisfaction with the political and economic consequences of pre-war dirigistic economic policies. Against this background, competitive processes were seen as the

31. "Basically, the statute was the expression of a kind of syndicalistic cooperation between the state, on the one hand, and business on the other, oriented according to administrative, public-law categories. . . ." W. Möschel, Recht der Wettbewerbsbeschränkungen 19 (1983).

32. For example, according to § 10 of the regulation, the cartel court could invalidate contractual terms where they were likely to "endanger the economy or general welfare through the exploitation of a position of economic power . . . ."

33. For a description, see A. Rotthege, *supra* note 22, at 167-216.

34. Zwangskartellgesetz of July 15, 1933, RGBl.I 488 (W. Ger.).

35. *See generally* H. Friedländer, Die Rechtspraxis der Kartelle und Konzerne in Europa (1938).

36. For discussion, see generally Thorelli, *Antitrust in Europe: National Policies After 1945*, 26 U. Chi. L. Rev. 222 (1959).

preferable means of organizing economic behavior.[37]

The European competition laws formed during the post-war period—including those of the United Kingdom, the Netherlands, Sweden, Norway, Denmark and Belgium[38]—were based on what may be called the administrative control model of competition law, the essential components of which had been worked out by 1930.[39] The administrative control model is based on two related notions. The first is that no particular conduct—be it the formation of a cartel or the monopolization of a market—is necessarily "bad." There may always be circumstances which justify particular conduct, and, therefore, no conduct should be prohibited per se. Conduct should be prohibited only where it is "abusive"—i.e., where the socially harmful effects of the conduct are not outweighed by other benefits to society. This "abuse" or "public interest" standard was conceived and developed as a counterpoint to the "prohibition" model which is closely associated with United States antitrust law, and it continues to be so viewed.[40]

Related to this broad concept of the nature of the legal standard to be used is the assumption that competition law should be applied primarily by administrative bodies rather than by courts. Such institutions are considered more appropriate for determining whether conduct is socially harmful.[41] Consequently, in most administrative control systems a specialized governmental organ administers a system in which legal norms are viewed primarily as guides for administrative action. Private suits are generally not permitted, and judicial review of administrative action, if allowed at all, is assigned to specialized or administrative courts rather than to the regular courts.

The combined effect of these two concepts is that administrative control systems typically accept a high degree of discretion on the part of those administering the competition

37. For discussion of the objectives sought to be achieved through competition legislation, see C. EDWARDS, *supra* note 3, at 6-13.

38. For discussions of individual statutes, see *id.* and ANTITRUST LAWS, *supra* note 4.

39. These concepts were crystallized at least by 1930, when cartel issues were a focus of debate at an important meeting of the Interparliamentary Union. *See* UNION INTERPARLEMENTAIRE, COMPTE RENDU DE LE XXVI. CONFERENCE INTERPARLEMENTAIRE 33-34, 145-71, 335-73 (1930).

40. *See generally* Von Eyben, *Forbud eller misbrugskontrol i konkurrence og markedsforingsretten*, in TIDSKRIFT UTGIVEN AV JURIDISKA FÖRENINGEN I FINLAND 236 (1979).

41. *See, e.g.*, Gerber, *supra* note 4, at 5, 15-23.

legislation. Competition law thus tends to be subject to political influence, and its concepts often remain poorly defined.[42]

Since administrative control systems apply an "abuse" standard, violation of that standard by powerful enterprises is generally labeled "abuse of power" or "abuse of a market-dominating position." In some systems the concept is used in the legislation itself,[43] while in others it is used generally to refer to violations of the public interest standard by dominant firms.[44] In both cases, however, the abuse concept generally remains devoid of substantial analytical content. There has been a tendency in recent years to introduce judicial processes into administrative control systems in order to increase predictability in the application of the law. Typically, this has meant subjecting administrative decisions to review by a specialized court. In Sweden, for example, a so-called "Market Court" was created in 1974 to hear appeals from decisions of the administrative body which enforces the competition law.[45] This court is comprised of professionally-trained judges as well as economic experts and representatives of interest groups. With respect to the abuse concept, however, this type of change has yet to produce significant conceptual developments.

III. The Concept of Abuse in German Competition Law

A critical step in the development of the abuse concept was its inclusion in the German Law Against Restraints of Competition (GWB), which was enacted in 1957.[46] This statute created what has become the most developed and influential competition law system in Europe, and thus codification of the abuse concept in the GWB helped establish that concept as the main legal tool in Europe for dealing with economically powerful enterprises. In Germany, competition law has been the object of intensive and widespread legislative, judicial, and scholarly attention, and

42. *See generally* C. Edwards, *supra* note 3, at 32-35.

43. *See, e.g.*, Belgian Law of May 27, 1960 for Protection Against the Abuse of Economic Power, as described in Bellis, *Belgium*, in 2 World Law of Competition §§ 2.01-2.03 (J. von Kalinowski ed. 1987).

44. This is the case, for example, in the United Kingdom. *See, e.g.*, Barounos & Allan, *United Kingdom*, in 4 World Law of Competition § 2.02 (J. von Kalinowski ed. 1987).

45. For a description, see Gerber, *supra* note 4, at 21-23.

46. Gesetz gegen Wettbewerbsbeschränkungen [GWB], 1957 Bundesgesetzblatt [BGBl.]I 1081 (W. Ger.).

it is in this context that the abuse concept has been most vigorously applied and most intensively analyzed.

A. German Antitrust Law: The Context of the Abuse Concept

The development of the abuse concept in German competition law has been molded by the essentially judicial character of the legal process in which it has operated.[47] For the first time in Europe, the German system subjected competition law concepts to the full rigors of judicial scrutiny and legal science.[48]

As with most other European states, Germany began to consider modern competition legislation after the Second World War.[49] Drawing heavily on the Abuse Regulation of the 1920s,[50] the initial plans envisioned a system similar to the administrative control systems elsewhere being established. Germany did not, however, finally enact a competition statute until 1957, after a decade of often highly controversial efforts to achieve a politically acceptable system.[51] This longer gestation period, together with Germany's status as an occupied country, exposed the new system to outside influences, including, in particular, United States antitrust thinking.[52] The system that resulted was a hybrid. It combined basic elements of the administrative control model with other elements often drawn from American antitrust

47. *See infra* text accompanying notes 54-58.

48. The term "legal science" describes a conception of law that is characteristic of the Civil Law tradition. *See generally* J. MERRYMAN, THE CIVIL LAW TRADITION 65-73 (1969).

49. For discussion, see R. ROBERT, KONZENTRATIONSPOLITIK IN DER BUNDESREPUBLIK—DAS BEISPIEL DER ENTSTEHUNG DES GESETZES GEGEN WETTBEWERBSBESCHRÄNKUNGEN 97-110 (1976).

50. Verordnung gegen Missbrauch wirtschaftlicher Machtstellungen, *supra* note 29; *see also supra* notes 29-33 and accompanying text.

51. For a detailed discussion of early efforts, see generally R. ROBERT, *supra* note 49.

52. The GWB was greatly influenced, both directly and indirectly, by U.S. antitrust law experience. U.S. occupation forces insisted that the German government agree to pass antitrust-type legislation to curb the concentration of economic power that was widely believed to have aided Hitler's rise and which American authorities feared might subvert democratic institutions. *See* F. RITTNER, *supra* note 19, at 276. For a discussion of the decartellization laws in effect during the occupation, see Bock & Korsch, *Decartellization and Deconcentration in the West German Economy Since 1945*, in ANTITRUST LAWS, *supra* note 4, at 138-53.

Equally important, however, was the indirect influence. Many of those who had a significant impact on the GWB studied the U.S. experience with antitrust law. *See generally* Mestmäcker, *Diskriminierungen, Dirigismus und Wettbewerb*, 1957 WIRTSCHAFT UND WETTBEWERB [WuW] 21. For bibliography, see Fikentscher, *Die deutsche Kartellrechtswissenschaft 1945-1954*, 1955 WuW 205, 208 n.18.

law, chief among which was the notion that competition law should be subject to the judicial process.

Basic elements of the administrative control model are present in the German system. For example, an administrative body called the *Bundeskartellamt* (Federal Cartel Office or FCO) is primarily responsible for applying and enforcing the law.[53] Private antitrust suits are permitted only with respect to certain provisions,[54] and such suits generally play a limited role in enforcement of the statute.[55] Thus, administrative sanctions represent the primary means of enforcing the provisions of the GWB.

In other ways, however, the German system deviates significantly from the administrative control model. It does not treat competition law merely as an instrument of economic policy. The FCO is essentially independent and largely protected from the exercise of political influence.[56] Its role is not that of discretionary policy creation or implementation; rather, its function is to interpret and apply a detailed statutory enactment.[57] Accordingly, enforcement action is reviewed internally according to judicially-oriented procedures to determine whether it is based on a legally-justified interpretation of the GWB. In addition, the German system provides a critically important incentive for the FCO to operate according to judicially-oriented principles, because it makes the decisions of the FCO reviewable

53. For discussion in English of the enforcement activities and concepts of the FCO, see Haley, *Antitrust Sanctions and Remedies: A Comparative Study of German and Japanese Law*, 59 WASH. L. REV. 471 (1984).

54. Private suits may be instituted in the regular courts to secure damages or injunctions based on violation of certain provisions, namely, those which are considered to provide "individual protection" (*Individualschutz*). *See* GWB, *supra* note 46, at § 35. Private legal actions are an important means of enforcing certain provisions of the GWB, but they are far less important as an enforcement mechanism than is the case in the U.S.

55. In one area, however, private suits play a central role in enforcing competition law concepts. According to § 26(2) of the GWB, injured purchasers or competitors can bring suit in the regular courts against firms which engage in price discrimination or other forms of business discrimination. For discussion, see Gerber, *The German Approach to Price Discrimination and Other Forms of Business Discrimination*, 27 ANTITRUST BULL. 241 (1982).

56. For discussion of the role of the FCO, see Stockman & Strauch, *Federal Republic of Germany*, in 5 WORLD LAW OF COMPETITION 23-25 (1985); *see also generally* U. IMMENGA, DIE POLITISCHE INSTRUMENTALISIERUNG DES WIRTSCHAFTSRECHTS (1976).

57. *See generally* Rittner, *Das Ermessen der Kartellbehörde*, in BEITRÄGE ZUM WIRTSCHAFTSRECHT: FESTSCHRIFT FÜR HEINZ KAUFMANN 307 (1972); Weber, *Geschichte und Aufbau des Bundeskartellamtes*, in ZEHN JAHRE BUNDESKARTELLAMT 263 (1968).

by the regular courts.[58] In particular, the federal appeals court in Berlin (the Berlin Appeals Court or *Kammergericht*) and the Federal Supreme Court (*Bundesgerichtshof*) play a central role in the development of the law.

The judicial orientation of the system is underscored by the fact that the GWB's substantive provisions are drafted as legal norms rather than as administrative authorizations.[59] They require characterization of conduct and subsumation of fact patterns rather than administrative judgment about the welfare of society.

B. The Concept of "As-If" Competition and the Original Role of the Abuse Concept

The changes in the proposed system that were made during its ten-year gestation period were especially important for the development of the abuse concept because the changes in the system altered the function of the concept in that system. The original draft of the GWB, the so-called Josten draft,[60] was based on the ideas of the "Ordo-Liberal School" of economists.[61] The Ordo-Liberals believed that socialism and classical *laissez-faire* economics had been discredited, respectively, by the rise of authoritarianism and by the Great Depression.[62] They developed, therefore, a set of ideas about the relationship between political and economic institutions which combined classical *laissez-faire* economics with concepts of state intervention.[63]

58. The decisions of the FCO are appealable to the *Kammergericht*, which is the federal appeals court for Berlin, where the FCO is located.

59. Certain of the GWB's substantive norms also reflect the influence of the administrative control model. In addition to the concept of abuse of a market-dominating position, there are, for example, a large number of specific exceptions to the prohibition against horizontal agreements that permit cartels where they are considered likely to be in the public interest. In addition, several of the provisions relating to vertical restraints on competition are very broadly drafted and give the FCO substantial discretion in applying them.

60. Entwurf zu einem Gesetz zur Sicherung des Leistungswettbewerbs und zu einem Gesetz über das Monopolamt (Bundeswirtschaftsminister pub. 1949).

61. Among the leading representatives of this school were Walter Eucken and Franz Böhm. For general background discussion, see F. BÖHM, WETTBEWERB UND MONOPOLKAMPF (1933); W. EUCKEN, DIE GRUNDLAGEN DER NATIONALÖKONOMIE (1939). For discussion of the Ordo-Liberal school, see R. ROBERT, *supra* note 49, at 73-85; W. Möschel, Competition Policy from an ORDO-point of view (date unknown) (unpublished manuscript).

62. *See generally* Günther, *Die Geistigen Grundlagen des Sogenannten Josten-Entwurfes*, in WIRTSCHAFTSORDNUNG UND STAATSVERFASSUNG: FESTSCHRIFT FÜR FRANZ BÖHM 183, 189-93 (1975).

63. In their view, history had demonstrated that without government intervention

One of the central components of the Ordo-Liberal program was the idea that where competition was weak or non-existent, the state should require enterprises to conduct themselves *as if* there were essentially perfect competition. This concept of "as-if" competition rested on the assumption that economic science could determine with reasonable accuracy whether conduct was consistent with conditions defined as "competitive." This notion of "as-if" competition was closely associated with the concept of "performance competition" or "competition on the merits."[64] The Ordo-Liberals assumed that in enforcing the standard of "as-if" competition the state would be assuring that success in the marketplace was the result of better performance rather than of the use of economic power.

Under the competition law envisioned in the Josten draft, a governmental office was to require powerful enterprises and groups of enterprises to act "as-if" they were constrained by competition. In subsequent drafts the concept of abuse was then used to designate conduct by powerful enterprises which deviated from the competitive norm. Thus, for the first time, the abuse concept was associated with a defined standard rather than with a vague public interest standard.

Although the competition law system finally established in the GWB was significantly different from the system envisioned by the Ordo-Liberals, the abuse concept remained part of the legislation.[65] Consequently, a concept originally designed to authorize actions by an administrative agency now had to function as part of a system of legal norms that was to be applied according to the judicial process.[66] The concept of "as-if" competition was assumed, however, to continue to provide a means of giving content to the abuse concept.[67] If economic science could determine for a given market the parameters which com-

competitive processes tended to collapse, because enterprises preferred private (i.e., contractual) regulation of business activities rather than competition, and because market-dominating enterprises often acquired such power that they were not affected by competitive pressures. Thus, the state had to enforce competitiion. *See* R. ROBERT, *supra* note 49, at 78-82.

64. The title of the Josten Draft, *see supra* note 60, was, in fact, "Draft of an Act to Protect Competition Based on Performance and an Act Concerning the Monopoly Office."

65. For discussion of the various changes made in the development of the legislation, see R. ROBERT, *supra* note 49.

66. *See generally* Rittner, *§ 22 GWB im Spannungsfeld wirtschaftswissenschaftlicher Theorien und rechtsstaatlicher Postulate*, in FESTSCHRIFT FÜR GÜNTHER HARTMANN 251 (1976).

67. *Id.* at 259-62.

petition would create, the FCO and the judge could apply the statute by determining whether particular conduct was within those parameters. At least in theory, the abuse standard could be consistently and objectively applied.

In order to assure that the abuse concept would not be interpreted too broadly, however, the legislation did place limitations on its scope. According to section 22 of the GWB, as originally enacted, the FCO was authorized to take action against the abuse of power by market-dominating enterprises only in conjunction with (1) the establishment of prices, (2) the formulation of terms or conditions of sale, and (3) tying arrangements.

C. *Interpreting the Abuse Concept: Early Problems and Basic Principles*

For well over a decade after enactment of the GWB, section 22 was little used.[68] In part this was due to the fact that the FCO was a new governmental office with sometimes uncertain political backing.[69] This caused it generally to avoid potentially controversial issues, especially where there were likely to be significant conflicts with powerful interests. Consequently, it tended to avoid applying the abuse concept, at least in part because powerful segments of German industry were opposed to the potential government "interference" with business activity represented by that concept.[70]

The FCO's reluctance to enforce section 22 was also related to Germany's economic situation.[71] The process of post-war economic recovery was not yet complete. As a result, the international competitiveness of German industry was a dominant political concern of the period, and there was little support for any government activity that might hamper the activities of the

---

68. *See* W. MÖSCHEL, DER OLIGOPOLMISSBRAUCH IM RECHT DER WETTBEWERBSBESCHRÄNKUNGEN 134-37 (1974).

69. For discussion, see Günther, *Zehn Jahre Gesetzes gegen Wettbewerbsbeschränkungen: Rückblick und Ausblick*, in ZEHN JAHRE GESETZ GEGEN WETTBEWERBSBESCHRÄNKUNGEN 29 (1968).

70. For a discussion of the view of industry, see Riffel, *Industrie und Wettbewerbspolitik—Erfahrungen und Ausblick*, in ZEHN JAHRE GESETZ GEGEN WETTBEWERBSBESCHRÄNKUNGEN 53 (1968).

The FCO's reluctance to use the concept also meant that there was little opportunity for the courts to develop the law, because private suits cannot be brought under § 22.

71. *See generally* Küster, *Germany*, in BIG BUSINESS AND THE STATE: CHANGING RELATIONS IN WESTERN EUROPE 64-86 (R. Vernon ed. 1974).

major corporations that were viewed as the engines of economic recovery.[72]

Resistance to the abuse concept was particularly strong, however, because of the concept's vagueness. In German law a court must generally refuse to apply a statutory provision which is so vague that the accepted methods of legal reasoning cannot be used to interpret it—i.e., where the judge must "legislate" rather than interpret.[73] The vagueness of the abuse concept thus created a significant risk that the courts would overturn enforcement actions based on it and increased the FCO's reluctance to enforce the concept.[74]

In 1965, the legislature expanded the scope of application of the abuse concept in order to make section 22 a more effective tool in the hands of the FCO.[75] It eliminated reference to specific types of abuse and authorized the FCO to take action against any conduct which was determined to represent abuse of a market-dominating position.[76] The substantive scope of the provision has remained unchanged since then.[77]

Expansion of the scope of the concept generated often intense scholarly controversy during the latter half of the 1960s,[78] and only after this activity had generated a degree of clarity concerning basic principles to be used in interpreting sec-

72. *See id.* at 78-82.

73. K. LARENZ, METHODENLEHRE DER RECHTSWISSENSCHAFT 410 (5th ed. 1983).

74. Developments in economic thought were also undermining confidence in the applicability of the abuse concept. The assumption that the concept of "as-if" competition would provide clear guidelines for applying the abuse concept had been based on the proposition that economic science could effectively use "perfect competition" as a model against which to measure actual economic behavior. In the post-war period, however, economic thinking largely rejected the notion that a model of perfect competition could be used to evaluate actual economic conditions. The work of economists such as John M. Clark and Erhard Kantzenbach focused economic thinking instead on concepts of "workable competition." This development thus left the abuse concept without the reference framework which, it had been assumed, could give it content. For discussion, see the seminal article by Clark, *Toward a Concept of Workable Competition*, 30 AM. ECON. REV. 241 (1940). *See also generally* J. CLARK, COMPETITION AS A DYNAMIC PROCESS (1961); E. KANTZENBACH, DIE FUNKTIONSFÄHIGKEIT DES WETTBEWERBS (2d ed. 1967).

75. GESETZ ZUR ÄNDERUNG DES GESETZES GEGEN WETTBEWERBSBESCHRÄNKUNGEN, 1965 BGB1.I 1363 (W. Ger.).

76. *See* W. JÄCKERING, DIE POLITISCHEN AUSEINANDERSETZUNGEN UM DIE NOVELLIERUNG DES GESETZES GEGEN WETTBEWERBSBESCHRÄNKUNGEN (GWB) 38-42 (1977).

77. The legislature has, however, expanded the concept of market-domination. *See* Zweites Gesetz zur Änderung des Gesetzes gegen Wettbewerbsbeschränkungen, *infra* note 79.

78. For a description, see J. BAUR, DER MISSBRAUCHSAUFSICHT IM DEUTSCHEN KARTELLRECHT 43-54 (1972).

tion 22 did the FCO begin to apply that section on a regular basis. The FCO increased its application of the abuse concept during the early 1970s, and it has continued actively to apply it. Part of the reason for the increased activity has been increased popular and hence political concern about the power of large enterprises.[79] This has been manifested through repeated parliamentary urging of the FCO to increase its use of section 22 as well as through several expansions of the concept of a market-dominating position.[80]

By the mid 1970s, case law and legal scholarship had produced a general consensus regarding certain basic contours of the abuse concept. First, the guiding principle in applying the abuse concept is protection of the process of economic competition.[81] The central value is, therefore, freedom of enterprise. This notion is derived from the general principle that the GWB is to be interpreted according to the "ordering principles of a competitive economy."[82] Thus, guidance for interpreting the abuse concept is derived deductively from a more general principle of interpretation for the statute as a whole.

Related to this basic principle of interpretation and in part derived from it are several other basic principles. First, neither motive nor intent to harm are relevant to the application of the concept; it is to be applied solely with reference to the objective characteristics of the conduct involved.[83] Second, the concept of abuse does not involve moral or ethical values; its interpretation, therefore, is to be based solely on political and economic values and ordering concepts.[84] Third, in order to be abusive within

79. *See* W. JÄCKERING, *supra* note 76, at 127-65. Moreover, especially during the 1970s, the comparative strength of the German economy has reduced political opposition to efforts to control large enterprises.

80. For references to the legislature's appeals to the FCO for stronger enforcement, see Baur, *Missbrauchsaufsicht über marktbeherrschende Unternehmen*, in KONTROLLE VON MARKTMACHT NACH DEUTSCHEM, EUROPÄISCHEM UND AMERIKANISCHEM KARTELLRECHT 131, 133 n.14 (1981).

The most important expansion of the concept of market-domination occurred in 1973, when the legislature (1) included in the category of market-dominating enterprises those enterprises that merely had a superior market position, and (2) facilitated application of the concept by including a set of statutory presumptions. Zweites Gesetz zur Anderung des Gesetzes gegen Wettbewerbsbeschränkungen, 1973 BGB1.I 917 (W. Ger.).

81. *See generally* W. MÖSCHEL, *supra* note 31, at 294.

82. *See generally* F. RITTNER, *supra* note 19, at 281-84.

83. *See* U. IMMENGA & E. MESTMÄCKER, KOMMENTAR ZUM GWB: GESETZ GEGEN WETTBEWERBSBECHRÄNKUNGEN 678 (1981).

84. *See* V. EMMERICH, DAS WIRTSCHAFTSRECHT DER ÖFFENTLICHEN UNTERNEHMEN 133 (2d ed. 1971).

the meaning of the statute, conduct must be related to the firm's economic power. Either the firm's economic power must make possible the conduct, or such power must cause the harmful effects of the conduct.[85]

D. *Application of the Abuse Concept*

Analogizing from the basic conceptual structure of the GWB, German legal scholars quickly distinguished between two basic forms of abuse—namely, "exploitation abuse" (*Ausbeutungsmissbrauch*) which includes harm to those who either buy from or sell to market-dominating enterprises, and "impediment abuse" (*Behinderungsmissbrauch*) which includes harm to other enterprises, typically competitors of the dominant enterprise. During the past ten years, the focus of application of the abuse concept has shifted dramatically from the former to the latter category of abuse.

1. Exploitation Abuse

The concept of exploitation abuse is based on the Ordo-Liberal notion of "as-if" competition, and it is used to prevent dominant enterprises from "exploiting" those dealing with them, as, for example, where such enterprises raise prices beyond a level that a competitive market would allow, or force suppliers or purchasers to grant terms more favorable than those that would exist under competition.[86] Such conduct is seen as inconsistent with a competitive economy, for it allows powerful firms to use their power to "distort" the competitive process.[87]

This concept of exploitation abuse has been viewed primarily as a means of combating high consumer prices.[88] In order to apply section 22 in such cases, however, German law had to resolve a basic issue concerning the relationship between the substantive concept of abuse and the FCO's enforcement power. If the FCO could merely levy a fine against an enterprise for having charged a price above the "competitive" price, its ability

85. E. LANGEN, E. NIEDERLEITHINGER, L. RITTER & U. SCHMIDT, KOMMENTAR ZUM KARTELLGESETZ 680-81 (6th ed. 1982).

86. For discussion, see MONOPOLKOMMISSION, ANWENDUNG UND MÖGLICHKEITEN DER MISSBRAUCHSAUFSICHT ÜBER MARKTBEHERRSCHENDE UNTERNEHMEN SEIT INKRAFTTRETEN DER KARTELLGESETZNOVELLE 31-35, 415 (Sondergutachten 1, 1977).

87. *See* V. EMMERICH, *supra* note 84, at 123-24.

88. *See* U. IMMENGA & E. MESTMÄCKER, *supra* note 83, at 746.

to prevent such pricing abuses might be quite limited. On the other hand, if the FCO could order enterprises not to raise prices above a level that it determined to be "competitive," this might be viewed as economic dirigism and thus inconsistent with the GWB's basic goal of protecting economic freedom.[89]

The Federal Supreme Court faced this issue in 1976 in the *Vitamin B12* case.[90] The case involved the sale of vitamins in Germany at prices significantly above those in neighboring countries.[91] The FCO had found German prices to be above those which could have been charged in a competitive market and ordered the seller to reduce its prices by a specific percentage so as to bring them within the range of competitive prices.[92] The Berlin Appeals Court had confirmed the FCO's authority to take such action, while changing the percentage reduction required.[93]

The BGH held that the FCO could indeed order the defendant to reduce its prices.[94] According to the court, such an order did not represent administrative interference with the defendant's economic freedom. It merely established a limit beyond which prices would be considered abusive. The defendant could then determine how to respond to that specific order. The court emphasized that section 22 was not to be understood to justify ongoing control by the FCO of business activity; it could merely be used to determine whether specific conduct—such as setting prices above a specified level—was abusive.

The *Vitamin B12* decision clarified and strengthened the FCO's position in applying section 22, but on another key issue—namely, the standard of proof applicable in pricing cases—the BGH soon undermined that position. In order to apply section 22 in exploitation cases, it is necessary to utilize a hypothetical standard. One must posit a hypothetical "competitive" price range and then ask whether the prices at issue fall

89. For discussion, see Baur, *supra* note 80, at 138-40.

90. Judgment of July 3, 1976, Bundesgerichtshof [BGH], W. Ger., WIRTSCHAFT UND WETTBEWERB ENTSCHEIDUNGSSAMMLUNG [WuW/E] [BGH] 1435 (*Vitamin B12*).

91. *See* Markert, *Recent Developments in German Antitrust Law*, 43 FORDHAM L. REV. 697, 711-14 (1975).

92. Decision of March 21, 1974, Federal Cartel Office [FCO], W. Ger. WuW/E [BKartA] 1482 (*Vitamin B12*).

93. Judgment of March 19, 1975, Kammergericht [KG], W. Ger., WuW/E [OLG] 1599 (*Vitamin B12*).

94. Judgment of July 3, 1976, WuW/E [BGH] at 1437.

within that range. Thus, the question of how one establishes that standard is fundamental to application of the concept.

This issue came before the BGH in late 1976 in the *Valium* case.[95] In that case, the FCO had ordered the manufacturer of Valium and Librium to reduce the prices of those drugs in Germany. In order to establish that the prices were abusive, the FCO compared the prices on the German market with prices in neighboring Holland, where the market was more competitive.[96] The Berlin Appeals Court upheld the FCO's determination of abuse.[97]

The BGH approved the comparison market method of establishing abuse. Accordingly, abuse can be established by comparing the market results achieved by the dominant firm with the results of firms offering the same or similar goods on markets with a significantly higher degree of competitive intensity. The court held, however, that the FCO had not established the comparability of the markets. It analyzed the various adjustments which had been made by the FCO in order to take account of the structural differences between the dominated market and the comparison market and held that the FCO had not provided sufficient proof that the adjustments were proper. The case thus requires that in order to establish abuse by means of market comparison, the FCO must provide a detailed factual and theoretical analysis of every significant structural difference between the two markets. In addition, the court held that prices in the dominated market would be considered abusive only where they exceeded the comparison market price by a "substantial margin" and that the FCO would also have to provide a detailed analysis of the reasons for its standard of substantiality in each case.[98]

The *Valium* decision demonstrated the difficulty of applying the concept of exploitation abuse in a manner which satisfied judicial standards. The BGH was unwilling to allow the application of a hypothetical standard of conduct without adequate proof of each of the elements on which the derivation of the

95. Judgment of Dec. 16, 1976, BGH, W. Ger., WuW/E [BGH] 1445 (*Valium*).

96. Decision of Oct. 16, 1974, FCO, W. Ger., WuW/E [BKartA] 1526 (*Valium/Librium*).

97. Judgment of Jan. 5, 1976, KG, W. Ger., WuW/E [OLG] 1645 (*Valium/Librium*).

98. Judgment of Dec. 16, 1976, WuW/E [BGH] at 1452.

standard was based. The result was to make proof of abuse extremely difficult.

In an attempt to facilitate application of the exploitation abuse concept, the legislature in 1980 amended section 22 to provide that abuse exists where an enterprise demands terms or prices which deviate from those "which with a high degree of probability would exist if there were effective competition in the market."[99] This change has been interpreted to eliminate the requirement that prices exceed comparison market prices by a "substantial margin," but it does not significantly alter the general requirements established by the *Valium* case.[100]

The FCO has continued to apply section 22 to exploitation cases, but the problems of proof have reduced its effectiveness. Relatively few of these cases have reached the courts or even public hearings,[101] and there is a widespread belief that the concept of exploitation abuse is ill-adapted to judicial application.[102]

2. Impediment Abuse

While application of the exploitation abuse concept has been shown to be of limited effectiveness, interest and enforcement activity have increased in recent years with regard to impediment abuse.[103] The main objective here is to protect the process of competition by preventing dominant firms from using their power to harm competitors, but there is much controversy concerning the analysis to be applied in impediment cases.[104]

The central problem with this category of cases is how to distinguish "abusive" from competitive conduct. Competition assumes, by definition, that enterprises attempt to "win" the battle of the marketplace—i.e., to cause economic harm to competi-

99. Viertes Gesetz zur Änderung des Gesetzes gegen Wettbewerbsbeschränkungen, 1980 BGB1.I 458 (W. Ger.).

100. Niederleithinger, *Probleme der Missbrauchsaufsicht aus der Sicht des Bundeskartellamtes* in DIE MISSBRAUCHSAUFSICHT VOR DEM HINTERGRUND DER ENTWICKLUNGEN DER NEUEREN WETTBEWERBSTHEORIE 65, 72-73 (B. Röper ed. 1982).

101. *See* U. IMMENGA & E. MESTMÄCKER, *supra* note 83, at 675-76.

102. *See, e.g.*, Baur, *supra* note 80, at 132.

103. Among the leading works that have recently treated the subject are E. MESTMÄCKER, DER VERWALTETE WETTBEWERB (1984); K. MARKERT, DIE WETTBEWERBERBEHINDERUNG IM GWB NACH DER VIERTEN KARTELLNOVELLE (1982); O. TYLLACK, WETTBEWERB UND BEHINDERUNG (1984).

104. For an overview of the controversy, see Ulmer, *Kartellrechtswidrige Konkurrentenbehinderung durch Leistungsfremdes Verhalten marktbeherrschender Unternehmen*, in RECHT UND WIRTSCHAFT HEUTE: FESTGABE ZUM 65. GEBURTSTAG VON MAX KUMMER 565 (1980).

tors. The fact that conduct is intended to cause such harm and that such harm results cannot, therefore, be the criterion for abusive conduct; that criterion must be sought in the characteristics of the conduct or in its other effects. The early impediment abuse cases struggled to find an analysis which could identify conduct as abusive.[105]

An early example of this struggle can be found in the 1969 *Labeling Devices* case in which the Berlin Appeals Court was faced with competitor impediment in the form of a tying agreement.[106] The defendant, dominant in the market for hand-held labeling devices, required purchasers of its labelers also to purchase all of their labels from it during a 5-year warranty period. The court held that such tying arrangements violated section 22 "because they cement a market-dominating position other than by better performance and strangle future competition."[107] The central element in the court's reasoning was the concept of competition on the merits; increased sales of the tied product were achieved not because of improved performance but as a result of power derived from the market position of the tying product. The court also included, however, a balancing element in its opinion. It found that the tie-in was not necessary to the defendant's operations. If it had been found necessary, the court indicated that the arrangement might have been approved for reasons of fairness.[108]

These two basic approaches to applying the abuse concept to impediment abuse situations—the concepts of competition on the merits and balancing—have been further developed and modified, and they have become the focus of the controversy concerning the application of section 22.

The merit competition analysis was given a theoretical base during the latter half of the 1970s by Professor Peter Ulmer of the University of Heidelberg.[109] Ulmer developed a performance

105. *See, e.g.*, Judgment of March 3, 1969, BGH, W. Ger., WuW/E [BGH] 1027 (*Sportartikelmesse II*).

106. Judgment of Feb. 2, 1969, KG, W. Ger., WuW/E [OLG] 995 (*Handpreisauszeichner*).

107. *Id.* at 1000.

108. *Id.*

109. *See, e.g.*, Ulmer, *supra* note 104. *See also generally* P. ULMER, SCHRANKEN ZULÄSSIGEN WETTBEWERBS MARKTBEHERRSCHENDER UNTERNEHMEN (1977); Ulmer, *Der Begriff "Leistungswettbewerb" und seine Bedeutung für die Anwendung von GWB-und UWG-Tatbeständen*, 1977 GEWERBLICHER RECHTSCHUTZ UND URHEBERRECHT [GRUR] 566.

competition test which was quickly adopted by the Berlin Appeals Court[110] and which continues to represent that court's analysis. According to this test, the conduct of a dominant firm constitutes "abuse" where two conditions are met. First, the conduct must constitute "non-performance competition"—i.e., it must represent competition which is not "on the merits."[111] Second, the effect of the conduct must be to restrict competition remaining in the dominated market.

The central concept in this analysis is that of performance competition, which Ulmer borrowed from the German law of unfair competition.[112] It was introduced by scholars in the 1930s in order to help determine whether conduct was unfair for purposes of that statute.[113] Conduct which represents improved performance in the marketplace generally cannot violate the unfair competition law, whereas non-performance competition may violate that statute. For purposes of section 22 of the GWB, this performance competition concept is used to provide a higher standard of conduct for dominant firms than is required for other firms. Accordingly, non-performance competition that does not violate the unfair competition statute may be abusive under section 22, provided it also restricts competition in the dominated market.

The performance competition standard was first applied by the Berlin Appeals Court in the *Combination Price Schedule* case.[114] The FCO there had ordered a publishing company to discontinue use of a combination price schedule for advertising in two separate newspapers owned by the company in Berlin. One newspaper had a market-dominating position; the other was struggling financially. The combination price schedule listed advertising rates for the two newspapers only in combined form, and it was apparently presented to any potential advertiser who wanted to advertise in the dominant newspaper. The FCO argued that this was a tying arrangement and, therefore, an abuse under section 22.

110. Judgment of Jan. 26, 1977, KG, W. Ger., WuW/E [OLG] 1767, 1773 (*Kombinationstarif*).

111. For discussion of the performance competition standard in the context of § 22, see R. HAHN, BEHINDERUNGSMISSBRÄUCHE MARKTBEHERRSCHENDER UNTERNEHMEN 53-79 (1984).

112. For a general discussion of unfair competition law, see F. RITTNER, *supra* note 19.

113. *See* O. TYLLACK, *supra* note 103, at 188-213.

114. *See* Judgment of Jan. 26, 1977, KG, W. Ger., WuW/E [OLG] 1767.

The Berlin Appeals Court's analysis began with the proposition that the strengthening of a market-dominating position reduced the intensity of competition in the market and that, consequently, dominant enterprises should be subject to a standard of conduct higher than that of non-dominant firms. Conduct which did not represent "competition on the merits" was, under such circumstances, a particularly grave threat to the competitive process, for such conduct necessarily distorted competition and increased barriers to entry. Therefore, since the combined price schedule improved sales of the tied product by using the power of the tying product rather than through improved performance, it was classified as non-performance competition and a potential abuse under section 22.

A second part of the analysis required that abuse be found only where the conduct led to the destruction or serious impairment of the competition remaining in the dominated market.[115] According to the court, this limitation on the scope of the non-performance test was necessary in order not to interfere with the dominant enterprise's right to *use* its market power. The court found that the structural effects of the conduct had not been substantial enough to apply section 22.

The Berlin Appeals Court has consistently applied this basic analysis in its subsequent decisions.[116] In the *Rama-Mädchen* case, for example, it found that the use of fidelity rebates in an advertising campaign constituted non-performance competition for purposes of applying section 22.[117] Similarly, in its *Fertigfutter* decision it held that the use of a bonus rebate system for distributors based either on total firm revenues or on the extent of the distributors' requirements violated the performance competition standard.[118]

Despite this consistent application of the performance-competition analysis by the Berlin Appeals Court, the status of the analysis remains uncertain. The BGH has yet to take a position concerning the proper analysis of impediment abuse cases under section 22. Moreover, the performance competition analysis has not been widely accepted by legal scholars.[119] Although that

115. *Id.* at 1772.

116. *See generally* R. HAHN, *supra* note 111, at 33-37.

117. Judgment of April 14, 1978, KG, W. Ger., WUW/E [OLG] 1983 (*Rama-Mädchen*).

118. Judgment of Nov. 12, 1980, KG, W. Ger., WUW/E [OLG] 2403 (*Fertigfutter*).

119. *See, e.g.*, U. IMMENGA & E. MESTMÄCKER, *supra* note 83, at 681-82.

analysis admittedly identifies some conduct which is potentially harmful, its critics claim that with regard to many important fact situations it does not effectively distinguish between conduct which is economically justified and that which is not.[120] In addition, under this analysis economic power renders conduct illegal which would otherwise be legal, and critics claim that it is unclear how much power makes what kinds of conduct illegal. Finally, the performance competition concept does not deal directly with certain harms to which section 22 is thought to be addressed, and it does not relate to the restriction of competition.[121] For example, if a dominant firm intentionally injures competitors in an overt attempt to monopolize a market, this intentional injury would not necessarily be abusive under the performance competition analysis.

Such criticism of the performance competition analysis has led to substantial support in the legal literature for an alternative analysis of impediment abuse based on interest balancing.[122] According to this view, the conduct of a dominant firm is considered abusive when it impedes the competitive opportunities of another firm and cannot be justified by resulting improvements either in consumer welfare or in the structure or intensity of competition in the market. The courts must, therefore, weigh the harm to competitors against the expected economic benefits to society. Proponents of this approach argue that the abuse concept is so vague that it can be given content only through case-by-case analysis of the economic consequences of the dominant firm's behavior.[123] Moreover, they claim, conduct by dominant firms should lead to state interference only when harm to competitors clearly outweighs any resulting economic benefits to society.[124]

In an effort to clarify the legal situation relating to impediment abuse, the legislature in 1980 amended section 22 by adding a provision that finds abuse when a market-dominating enterprise "impedes, without a factually justified reason, the competitive opportunities of other enterprises in a way which is

120. W. MÖSCHEL, *supra* note 31, at 328-31.

121. *See* U. IMMENGA & E. MESTMÄCKER, *supra* note 83, at 726-27.

122. *See id.* at 681-82.

123. The main criticism of the balancing test also focuses, however, on its vagueness. Critics argue that it is so vague that it cannot provide effective guidance to economic decision-makers. *See, e.g.*, Ulmer, *supra* note 104, at 570-71.

124. W. MÖSCHEL, *supra* note 31, at 332.

significant for competition in the market."[125] These amendments establish that impeding conduct need only have a "significant" effect on competition in order to violate section 22;[126] it need not have the extensive effect which originally had been required by the Berlin Appeals Court.[127]

Beyond this, however, the amendments do not clarify the analysis required in impediment abuse cases. There is no reference to the concept of performance competition, although the concept was included in several drafts of the amendments;[128] nor is there direct reference to its alternative, the balancing test. Included within the statute is any impeding conduct, provided that it has a significant competitive impact and is not "factually justified."[129] This language does not, however, address the core analytical issue of how to distinguish impeding conduct from acceptable competitive conduct. Moreover, the amendments have created a new level of complexity, because the language "without a factually justified reason" now must also be interpreted and applied.

The German attempts to utilize the abuse concept to protect the competitive process against particular types of competitor-harmful conduct thus remain inconclusive. The interest shown in this issue in recent years reflects a widespread belief that the abuse concept should be used to accomplish this objective. Serious doubts remain, however, as to whether sufficient analytical content can be ascribed to the concept to allow it to perform this task effectively.

IV. The Concept of Abuse in the Competition Law of the European Economic Community

In 1958, the same year in which the German GWB became effective, the Treaty of Rome established the European Economic Community (EEC), and it included the abuse concept as one of two central competition law concepts.[130] This fact is sig-

125. Viertes Gesetz zur Änderung des Gesetzes gegen Wettbewerbsbeschränkungen, 1980 BGB1.I 458 (W. Ger.).

126. Judgment of April 14, 1978, KG, W. Ger., WuW/E [OLG] 2403, 2406.

127. *See supra*, note 115.

128. *See* Niederleithinger, *supra* note 100, at 74.

129. This term was borrowed from another section of the GWB—§ 26—which provides a private cause of action for firms harmed by economic discrimination. *See generally* Gerber, *supra* note 55.

130. Treaty Establishing the European Economic Community (Treaty of Rome), Mar. 25, 1957 (effective Jan. 1, 1958).

nificant for two main reasons. First, the Treaty's provisions are applicable wherever conduct affects trade between states of the Community,[131] and, as a result, the abuse concept is applicable to conduct throughout Europe. In addition, Community competition law has a major influence on the development of national antitrust regimes, for member states have a strong incentive generally to conform their own legal systems to Community law.[132] Several member states have adopted the abuse concept because it is part of Community law.[133]

A. *Community Competition Law: The Conceptual and Institutional Contexts*

The Treaty of Rome created a new legal system and new legal institutions.[134] On the one hand, this has provided freedom to find new solutions; conceptual development has not been confined by the traditions or doctrines of a particular legal order.[135] On the other hand, it also means that the institutions charged with interpreting and applying Community law do not have the benefit of having a well-established legal tradition that can serve as an authoritative source of ideas as well as of conceptual guidance.

Community competition law operates through one process and two institutions. In general, the law develops through the process of adjudication. The competition law provisions of the

---

131. Competition law concepts are applicable to conduct which either occurs within the territory of member states or has an effect within the community. *See, e.g.*, Beguelin Import Co. v. G.L. Import Export S.A., [1971-1973 Transfer Binder] Common Mkt. Rep. (CCH) ¶ 8149, at 7697 (Ct. J.E. Comm., Nov. 25, 1971), and Imperial Chem. Indus. v. E.C. Comm'n, [1971-1973 Transfer Binder] Common Mkt. Rep. (CCH) ¶ 8161, at 8001 (Ct. J.E. Comm. July 14, 1972).

132. In Italy, for example, the use of Community competition law by domestic courts has developed to such an extent that specific domestic legislation is considered unnecessary. For a study of the application of Community competition law in the French courts, see Behrens & Korb-Schikaneder, *Europäisches Wettbewerbsrecht vor Französischen Gerichten*, 48 RABELS ZEITSCHRIFT 457 (1984).

133. For example, France adopted its abuse provisions largely in order to be consistent with the Treaty of Rome. *See* J. BURST & R. KOVAR, DROIT DE LA CONCURRENCE 284 (1981). *See also* Rocas & Perakis, *Greece*, in 7 WORLD LAW OF COMPETITION GRE 1-1 (von Kalinowski ed. 1987).

134. For discussion of the system and its institutions, see generally T. HARTLEY, THE FOUNDATIONS OF EUROPEAN COMMUNITY LAW (1981).

135. The original signatories of the Treaty of Rome were all part of the civil law tradition, and all current members, except the United Kingdom and the Republic of Ireland, are part of that tradition. This does not, however, seem to have been a controlling factor in the development of the legal concepts. For a general description of the civil law tradition, see J. MERRYMAN, *supra* note 48.

Treaty itself have not been changed since its inception, and they could be changed only with great difficulty.[136] The European Commission can issue regulations regarding the application of the competition law provisions, but such regulations serve merely as administrative interpretations of the Treaty.[137] Moreover, the Commission has issued such regulations infrequently, preferring to rely on adjudicative procedures to develop competition law principles.

Community competition law is developed primarily by the European Court of Justice.[138] The decisions of this court are the sole authoritative interpretations of the Treaty,[139] and the Community legal system contains neither lower courts nor intermediate appeals courts.[140]

The Commission's role is to develop competition policy and to apply and enforce provisions of the Treaty.[141] Consequently, its decisions provide a substantial body of case law interpreting the Treaty. In addition, the Commission shapes Community competition law by determining the kinds of cases on which the European court has the opportunity to rule, because the court generally can take appeals (other than advisory appeals) only from Commission actions.[142]

B. The Abuse Concept in the Treaty of Rome

The EEC was created in order to reduce the barriers to trade between the member states and to establish an institutional framework by means of which the member states could more closely integrate their economies. The Treaty of Rome included competition law provisions in order to prevent private barriers

136. Substantive changes in the Treaty would require the unanimous consent of all members. *See* Treaty Establishing the European Economic Community (Treaty of Rome), art. 238, Mar. 25, 1957 (effective Jan. 1, 1958).

137. *See* L. BROWN & F. JACOBS, THE COURT OF JUSTICE OF THE EUROPEAN COMMUNITIES 91-117 (2d ed. 1983).

138. For a description of the court, its role and its mode of operation, see *id.*

139. The national courts of the member states apply community law under certain circumstances. Such applications are not, however, binding on Community institutions.

140. The role of the court is limited, however, by the fact that it can rule only where there is an application from a decision of the European Commission or a referral from a national court. For a discussion of the court and the referral mechanism, see L. BROWN & F. JACOBS, *supra* note 137, at ch. 9.

141. *See generally* 4 H. SMIT & P. HERZOG, THE LAW OF THE EUROPEAN ECONOMIC COMMUNITY 5-156.1-252 (1986).

142. *See* L. BROWN & F. JACOBS, *supra* note 137, at ch. 9.

to trade from obstructing these objectives.[143]

The Treaty contains two substantive articles relating to competition. Article 85 prohibits certain concerted actions to restrict competition,[144] while article 86 aims at unilateral actions,[145] prohibiting "any abuse by one or more undertakings

143. *See* A. GLEISS, COMMON MARKET CARTEL LAW 14 (3d Amer. ed. 1981).

144. According to article 85:

1. The following shall be deemed to be incompatible with the Common Market and shall hereby be prohibited: any agreement between enterprises, any decisions by associations of enterprises and any concerted practices which are likely to affect trade between the Member States and which have as their object or result the prevention, restriction or distortion of competition within the Common Market, in particular those consisting in:

a) the direct or indirect fixing of purchase or selling prices or of any other trading conditions;

b) the limitation or control of production, markets, technical development or investment;

c) market-sharing or the sharing of sources of supply;

d) the application to parties to transactions of unequal terms in respect of equivalent supplies, thereby placing them at a competitive disadvantage; or

e) the subjecting of the conclusion of a contract to the acceptance by a party of additional supplies which, either by their nature or according to commercial usage, have no connection with the subject of such contract.

2. Any agreements or decisions prohibited pursuant to this Article shall be null and void.

3. Nevertheless, the provisions of paragraph 1 may be declared inapplicable in the case of:

- any agreements or classes of agreements between enterprises;
- any decisions or classes of decisions by associations of enterprises; and
- any concerted practices or classes of concerted practices which contribute to the improvement of the production or distribution of goods or to the promotion of technical or economic progress while reserving to users an equitable share in the profit resulting therefrom and which:

a) neither impose on the enterprises concerned any restrictions not indispensable to the attainment of these objectives;

b) nor enable such enterprises to eliminate competition in respect of a substantial proportion of the goods concerned.

145. According to article 86:

To the extent to which trade between any Member States may be affected thereby, action by one or more enterprises to take improper advantage of a dominant position within the Common Market or within a substantial part of it shall be deemed to be incompatible with the Common Market and shall hereby be prohibited.

Such improper practices may in particular, consist in:

a) the direct or indirect imposition of any inequitable purchase or selling prices or of any other inequitable trading conditions;

b) the limitation of production, markets or technical development to the prejudice of consumers;

c) the application to parties to transactions of unequal terms in respect of equivalent supplies, thereby placing them at a competitive disadvantage;

d) the subjecting of the conclusion of a contract to the acceptance, by a party, of

of a dominant position . . . in so far as it may affect trade between Member states." The Treaty does not define the concept of abuse, and there are no official preparatory materials which might reveal the intent of the framers in drafting article 86. It does, however, designate four specific examples of abusive conduct: unfair prices or contract terms; limiting production, markets, or technical development to the prejudice of consumers; discrimination; and tying practices.

The Treaty's abuse concept derives from two main sources—the law of the European Coal and Steel Community (ECSC) and German law.[146] The 1951 treaty establishing the ECSC was envisaged as the first step in the development of the European Community.[147] It contains an abuse concept whose primary aim is to prevent dominant enterprises from extracting excessive prices or unduly favorable terms.[148] The influence of the German GWB derives primarily from the fact that the controversy surrounding its drafting was a focus of European competition law thinking during the period in which the EEC treaty was being considered. Reference is made to both of these sources in interpreting article 86 of the Treaty of Rome.[149]

C. Development of the Abuse Concept

The development of the abuse concept in Community law can be divided into three main phases. During the first, the Commission sought to establish a theoretical framework for interpretation of the concept; during the second, the European Court established basic interpretative principles; and during the third, the court has been developing application concepts—i.e., concepts which determine how the general principles are to be applied.

---

additional supplies which, either by their nature or according to commercial usage, have no connection with the subject of such contract.

146. *See* Focsaneau, *La Notion d'Abus dans le Système de l'Article 86 du Traité Instituant la Communauté Économique Européenne*, in REGULATING THE BEHAVIOR OF MONOPOLIES AND DOMINANT UNDERTAKINGS IN COMMUNITY LAW 324, 336-40 (J.A. van Damme ed. 1977).

147. Treaty of Paris, April 18, 1951, 261 U.N.T.S. 142. For a general discussion, see Bebr, *The European Coal and Steel Community: A Political and Legal Innovation*, 63 YALE L. REV. 1 (1953).

148. W. DIEBOLD, THE SCHUMANN PLAN 353-54 (1959); *see also* R. KRAWIELICKI, DAS MONOPOLVERBOT IM SCHUMANN PLAN 57-58 (1952).

149. *See, e.g.*, Europemballage & Continental Can Co. v. Comm'n of the European Communities, [1971-1973 Transfer Binder] Common Mkt. Rep. (CCH) ¶ 8171, at 8279-3, 8299 (Ct. J.E. Comm. Feb. 21, 1973).

1. The Period of Restraint: 1958-1968

During the EEC's first decade, article 86 was little used. The legal officers of the Commission as well as the judges of the European Court were trained in the civil law tradition and were, therefore, reluctant to apply overly vague legal concepts. In addition, Community economic policy during this period was focused on the creation of business enterprises of sufficient size to compete with American corporations, and the Commission hesitated to apply legal provisions which might reduce the ability of such enterprises to compete internationally. The lack of enforcement under article 86 led to concern in the early 1960s that it would simply remain a "dead letter."[150]

During this period, however, the Commission was attempting to establish a theoretical framework for interpreting the abuse concept. It created an advisory group composed primarily of professors and charged this group with working out basic principles. The conclusions of this group were then published in 1966 as the core of the Commission's first major statement concerning interpretation of the abuse concept, its *Memorandum on Concentration.*[151]

The method chosen by the Commission to develop the abuse concept reflects its civil law context. First, in relying on scholars for guidance as well as for legitimation,[152] the Commission obviously believed that conclusions reached by a group of professors would carry substantially more authority than its own conclusions. Second, the Commission sought to establish abstract principles of interpretation before attempting to apply the Treaty's provisions to specific facts.

The *Memorandum* contained two basic principles relating to the interpretation of the abuse concept. The first was that abuse occurs where a dominant firm utilizes the possibilities which flow from its position of dominance in order to obtain benefits which it could not obtain if it were exposed to "effective competition."[153] Accordingly, a direct causal link was required

150. *See, e.g.*, Samkalden & Druker, *Legal Problems Relating to Article 86 of the Rome Treaty*, 1965-66 COMMON MKT. L. REV. 158, 162 (1966).

151. European Economic Community Comm'n, Memorandum Sur le Probleme de la Concentration dans le Marché Commun (Dec. 1, 1965), *reprinted in* REVUE TRIMESTRIELLE DE DROIT EUROPÈEN 651-77 (1966) [hereinafter Memorandum on Concentration].

152. For a discussion of the role of legal scholars in the civil-law tradition, see J. MERRYMAN, *supra* note 48, at 59-65.

153. Memorandum on Concentration, *supra* note 151, at 670.

between the enterprise's power and its results in the market. This link was not intended as a definition of abuse, for such a definition obviously would be overbroad and would label as abusive virtually any conduct by a dominant firm. It represented merely a starting point for interpreting the abuse concept.

The second principle of interpretation utilized a different conceptual reference point. It claimed that abuse is found where a dominant firm's conduct is "wrong (*fautif*) in regard to the fixed objectives of the Treaty."[154] In defining abuse in relation to the objectives of the Treaty, the *Memorandum* merely was applying a basic method of interpretation—namely, the teleological method—to the abuse concept. The decision to do so was of crucial importance, however, for it established the framework within which subsequent development was to take place.

2. The Establishment of Basic Principles by the European Court

The European Court's first opportunities to interpret article 86 came in the late 1960s and early 1970s in a series of three cases that were referred to the court by national courts.[155] In each of these cases the court was asked for an advisory opinion as to whether a dominant firm possessing industrial property rights could violate article 86 by using those rights to increase its prices. The court took the position that "[t]he price level of a product is not in itself necessarily indicative of an abuse of a dominant position within the meaning of article 86, but it can be a decisive indication where it is particularly high and is not justified by the facts."[156] The court did not elaborate on what it meant by justification, nor did it discuss in detail any interpretative issues relating to article 86.

In 1972 the court, in its first regular (non-advisory) opinion under article 86, established a general principle which has guided its interpretation of abuse ever since. In the *Continental Can* case the issue was whether a corporate acquisition could

154. *Id.* at 676.

155. Sirena S.r.l. v. Eda GmbH, [1971-1973 Transfer Binder] Common Mkt. Rep. (CCH) ¶ 8101, at 7103 (Ct. J.E. Comm. Feb. 18, 1971); Deutsche Grammophon GmbH v. Metro-SB-Grossmärkte GmbH, [1971-1973 Transfer Binder] Common Mkt. Rep. (CCH) ¶ 8106, at 7183-3 (Ct. J.E. Comm. June 8, 1971); Parke, Davis and Co. v. Probel, Reese, Beintema-Interpharm, & Centrafarm Companies, [1961-1970 Transfer Binder] Common Mkt. Rep. (CCH) ¶ 8054, at 7810 (Ct. J.E. Comm. Feb. 29, 1968).

156. *Sirena S.r.l. v. Eda GmbH*, [1971-1973 Transfer Binder] Common Mkt. Rep. (CCH) ¶ 8101, at 7112.

constitute abuse under article 86.[157] The issue was politically charged because there was growing concern in Europe about excessive concentration of industry.[158] More importantly, however, there was great concern about the acquisition of European firms by American firms,[159] and article 86 was the only potential legal mechanism for attacking such acquisitions under the Treaty of Rome.

The Commission applied article 86 to prohibit the acquisition by Continental Can, a United States corporation, of controlling shares in a Netherlands company that had been a licensee of certain European patents held by Continental Can.[160] The Commission argued that an acquisition by a dominant firm of another market participant could severely damage competition in the market and, therefore, that the objectives of the Treaty could only be accomplished by interpreting abuse to apply to acquisitions which had that effect. On appeal, Continental Can argued that abuse could only be found where the dominant firm actually used its power to accomplish a result that it could not have achieved had there been competition.[161] Since Continental Can did not use its market power to make the acquisition, the conduct could not constitute an abuse of its power. This position had substantial support in the legal literature.[162]

The court was thus faced with a fundamental methodological choice. A technical legal analysis of article 86, as urged by Continental Can as well as by the Advocate General,[163] called for the conclusion that power could not be *abused* unless it was *used*. On the other hand, a teleological interpretation centering on the needs and objectives of the Community would allow the court to support the Commission's enforcement action.

157. Europemballage & Continental Can Co. v. Comm'n of the European Communities, [1971-1973 Transfer Binder] Common Mkt. Rep. (CCH) ¶ 8171, at 8279-3.

158. *See, e.g.*, O.E.C.D., *supra* note 1, at 13-14.

159. *See* Communication from the Commission to the Council (Nov. 8, 1973), Multinational Undertakings and Community Regulations, O.J. C114, *reprinted in* 19 ANTITRUST BULL. 555, 561 (1974). *See also generally* J. SERVAN-SCHREIBER, LE DÉFI AMÉRICAIN (1967).

160. Commission Decision of December 9, 1971, [1970-1972 New Developments] Common Mkt. Rep. (CCH) ¶ 9481, at 9020.

161. *Europemballage & Continental Can Co.*, [1971-1973 Transfer Binder] Common Mkt. Rep. (CCH) ¶ 8171 at 8285-8287.

162. *See* Focsaneau, *supra* note 146, at 247-52; Joliet, *Der Begriff der Missbräuchlichen Ausnutzung in Art. 86 EWG-Vertrag*, 8 EUROPARECHT 97, 120-23 (1973).

163. *Europemballage & Continental Can Co.*, [1971-1973 Transfer Binder] Common Mkt. Rep. (CCH) ¶ 8171, at 8303 (Conclusions of Advocate General K. Roemer).

The court sided with the Commission and held that in interpreting the abuse concept the primary guidelines were to be derived from the general objectives of the Treaty rather than from analysis of the language of article 86 itself.[164] In the court's view, article 86 was to be given content through analysis of its role in the Treaty scheme.

Using this teleological method to interpret article 86, the court turned to the Community goals as expressed in the Treaty, specifically to article 3(f), according to which the goals of the Community include "the establishment of a system ensuring that competition within the Common Market . . . not [be] distorted."[165] On the basis of this provision, the court held that article 86 was to be interpreted in such a way as to prohibit the distortion of competition. As a result, the concept of competitive distortion became the central source of guidance in applying article 86.

Applying this concept to the acquisition by Continental Can, the court stated that abuse may occur where an enterprise acquires a dominant position that undermines the objectives of the Treaty by substantially altering the supply situation and thus jeopardizing the consumer's freedom of action. This is necessarily the case where virtually all competition is eliminated.[166] Since the acquisition eliminated "virtually all competition" in the relevant market, it was held to violate article 86.

In the 1974 *Commercial Solvents* case, the court confirmed the central analytical role of the notion of competitive distortion and expanded its scope.[167] The case involved a refusal to deal in which a United States corporation, Commercial Solvents (CSC), was the target of Commission enforcement activities. CSC had a virtual monopoly on the world production of certain chemicals that it had been selling in the EEC through a joint venture in Italy. CSC then decided it would no longer supply the chemicals in Europe, except to the joint venture company for its own manufacturing uses; resale would no longer be permitted. The

164. *Instituto Chemioterapico Italiano S.p.A. & Commercial Solvents Corp.*, [1974 Transfer Binder] Common Mkt. Rep. (CCH) ¶ 8209, at 8299.

165. *Id.*

166. *Id.* at 8301.

167. Istituto Chemioterapico Italiano S.p.A. & Commercial Solvents Corp. v. Comm'n of the European Communities, [1974 Transfer Binder] Common Mkt. Rep. (CCH) ¶ 8209, at 8800 (Ct. J.E. Comm. Mar. 6, 1974). For discussion, see Scott, *The Concept of Abuse in EEC Competition Law: An American View*, 92 L.Q. REV. 242, 253-56 (1976).

effect of this decision was virtually to eliminate a former competitor of CSC from the market for certain products manufactured from those chemicals. The court held that this represented an abuse of CSC's market-dominating position.[168] It reasoned that where a dominant firm's refusal to supply a competitor would effectively eliminate the competitor from the market, this elimination of competition necessarily distorted the competitive structure of the market and, therefore, violated article 86, at least where the competitor was a major force in the market.

Having established in *Continental Can* that the actual elimination of a competitor through acquisition could constitute abuse, the court in *Commercial Solvents* also labeled as "abusive" conduct that destroyed the ability of a significant competitor effectively to compete. The court's conclusion was based on the conduct's "effect on the structure of supply of the market."[169]

3. Refinement of the Abuse Concept

Defining abuse by reference to the concept of competitive distortion created an extremely broad principle of interpretation: Any conduct which significantly affected the structure of competition could constitute a violation of article 86.[170] In its subsequent decisions, however, the court has been developing principles of application which determine when competitive distortion represents abuse.[171]

---

168. *Id.* at 8820.

169. *Id.*

170. *See, e.g.*, A. GLEISS, *supra* note 143, at 341: "[A]buse is an objective term. It comprises every conduct of a dominant enterprise which might adversely affect the structure of a market in which competition is weakened . . . ."

171. The term "application principle" is chosen here to make clear that these principles relate to the application of a more general principle—namely, that of competitive distortion—to specific fact situations. The European Court is not always explicit about the relationship between these principles and the concept of competitive distortion, but analysis of the cases indicates that this is the reasoning that the Court is using.

The discussion here does not include all such application principles but merely those most central to the development of the abuse concept. For discussions of the development of the abuse concept, using slightly different conceptual frameworks, see C. BELLAMY & G. CHILD, COMMON MARKET LAW OF COMPETITION 185-202 (1978); Korah, *supra* note 17; Lang, *Monopolization and the Definition of "Abuse" of a Dominant Position under Article 86 EEC Treaty*, 16 COMMON MKT. L. REV. 345 (1979).

a. Consumer Welfare, Potential Elimination of a Competitor, and the Protection of Small and Medium-Sized Firms

The court developed several important application principles in its 1978 *United Brands* opinion.[172] The case applied the abuse concept to three types of conduct—resale restrictions, refusal to sell to a former customer, and the charging of "excessive" prices.

According to the court, United Brands Company (UBC), a United States company with a dominant position in the European banana market, abused its dominant position by requiring European ripener/wholesalers not to sell bananas acquired from UBC to other ripeners, not to sell such bananas when still green, and, in some cases, not to sell such bananas unless they carried UBC brand names. The court held that these resale restrictions constituted an abuse "since they limit markets to the prejudice of consumers. . . ."[173] The court thus used a consumer welfare standard rather than the broader concept of competitive distortion that also would have been applicable. Accordingly, in analyzing resale restrictions the issue is whether they distort competition by significantly affecting the structure of supply on the market *and*, as a result, harm consumers.

The court also applied the abuse concept to UBC's refusal to deal with one of its former distributors. UBC had stopped supplying its former customer because the latter had cooperated with a major competitor of UBC in certain activities, including an advertising campaign. The court announced as a general rule that a dominant enterprise "cannot stop supplying a long-standing customer who abides by regular commercial practice if the orders placed by this customer are in no way out of the ordinary . . ."[174] at least where the sale is of a branded product with established goodwill. According to the court, such a practice constituted abuse because it limited markets to the prejudice of consumers and because it constituted discrimination which might eventually eliminate a firm from the relevant market.[175] Thus, whereas previous refusals to deal had been found abusive

172. United Brands Co. & United Brands Continental B.V. v. Comm'n of the European Communities, [1977-1978 Transfer Binder] Common Mkt. Rep. (CCH) ¶ 8429, at 7655 (Ct. J.E. Comm. Feb. 14, 1978).

173. *Id.* at 7713.

174. *Id.* at 7714.

175. *Id.* For discussion of the price-discrimination issue, see di Valgiurata, *Price*

where they necessarily eliminated a competitor from the market and thus posed an immediate threat to the structure of competition, UBC's refusal to deal was found abusive because it had the potential, if repeated often enough, to drive firms from the market.

The court buttressed its conclusions concerning UBC's refusal to deal by referring to its impact on the independence of small and medium-sized enterprises. It held that under the circumstances of the case a refusal to sell "amounts to a serious interference with the independence of small and medium-sized firms in their commercial relations with the undertaking in a dominant position . . . ."[176] The court thus introduced a concept of economic coercion into the law of abuse. At least where such coercion would have a "serious adverse effect on competition . . . by allowing only firms dependent upon the dominant undertaking to stay in business,"[177] a refusal to sell could not be used to coerce purchasers to adhere to a dominant firm's policies.

The court's reference to the independence of small and medium-sized firms reflected a growing concern throughout Europe about the economic position of smaller firms. This concern has focused on the issue of so-called "demand-side power"—i.e., the ability of large firms to extract unfair prices and terms from smaller enterprises.[178] It is also based on a conceptual development. In the 1960s the German economist Helmut Arndt began to analyze the economic consequences of dependency relationships between firms.[179] According to Arndt, a firm which is dependent on another firm for either supplies or sales is subject to the power of the dominant firm, and abuse of this power by the dominant firm could have negative consequences for both the dependent firm and the economy as a whole. This concept of relational power had been introduced

---

Discrimination under Article 86 of the E.E.C. Treaty: The United Brands Case, 31 INT'L & COMP. L. Q. 36 (1982).

176. *United Brands Co. & United Brands Continental B.V.*, [1977-1978 Transfer Binder] Common Mkt. Rep. (CCH) ¶ 8429, at 7714.

177. *Id.* at 7715.

178. *See, e.g.*, MONOPOLKOMMISSION, MISSBRÄUCHE DER NACHFRAGEMACHT UND MÖGLICHKEITEN ZU IHRER KONTROLLE IM RAHMEN DES GWB (Sondergutachten 7, 1977). *See also* Gerber, *supra* note 55, at 244-49.

179. For example, see generally H. ARNDT, MARKT UND MACHT (2d ed. 1973); H. ARNDT, RECHT, MACHT UND WIRTSCHAFT (1968); H. ARNDT, WIRTSCHAFTLICHE MACHT (3d ed. 1980).

into the German GWB in 1973,[180] and in *United Brands*, it became part of Community law as well.

b. *Abuse and "Excessive" Prices*

A third abuse issue in the *United Brands* case related to UBC's prices. Example (a) of article 86 specifies that abuse may consist in "directly or indirectly imposing unfair purchase or selling prices or other unfair trading conditions," and the court previously had held that excessively high prices could be sufficient to establish abuse.[181] The court had not yet established, however, a method by which the fairness of prices could be determined.

The Commission found that in certain countries UBC's prices for bananas were excessive and ordered a reduction of such prices.[182] It based this conclusion on the comparative market method that had been approved by the German Supreme Court in 1976.[183] The European Court did not accept the Commission's use of the comparison market approach, however, holding that the Commission had not proven its case.[184]

The court focused on the relationship between the dominant firm's costs and its prices and held that abuse occurs where a dominant firm charges a price which "has no reasonable relation to the economic value of the product supplied. . . ."[185] The court thus required that the firm's costs be compared to its prices. An "excessive" profit margin would be evidence of abuse. The court did not explain, however, what it meant by an "excessive" profit margin. Moreover, it indicated that other factors may have to be considered in determining whether an "excessive" price was, in fact, abusive, but it did not discuss what those factors were.

The court's analysis was impelled by its general analytical reference point—namely, the concept of competitive distortion.

180. Zweites Gesetz zur Anderung des Gesetzes gegen Wettbewerbsbeschränkungen, *supra* note 80.

181. *See supra* note 155.

182. Commission Decision of December 17, 1975, [1976-1977 Transfer Binder] Common Mkt. Rep. (CCH) ¶ 9800, at 9774.

183. *See supra* text accompanying notes 95-98.

184. *Id.*

185. United Brands Co. & United Brands Continental B.V., v. Comm'n of the European Communities, [1977-1978 Transfer Binder] Common Mkt. Rep. (CCH) ¶ 8429, at 7655, 7718 (Ct. J.E. Comm. Feb. 14, 1978). For discussion, see A. GLEISS, *supra* note 143, at 345-48.

If a firm's prices are "excessive" in relation to its costs, this necessarily "distorts" the competitive process. At the core of the analysis is a notion of transactional equivalence—specifically, the idea that a dominant firm acts abusively where it uses its economic power to achieve a gross disproportion between the respective performances required in a transaction.

This standard has proven to be as difficult to apply as its German counterpart.[186] It requires the Commission to engage in an expensive, complex and uncertain process of allocating costs in relation to specific products. Yet there is little guidance as to how great the disparity between costs and prices must be in order to be considered excessive. Moreover, the court has provided no guidance as to when "excessive" prices are also "abusive." As a result, the *United Brands* decision has discouraged efforts to use the abuse concept to reduce the prices charged by dominant firms.

c. *Dependency and Transactional Equivalence: Exclusive Dealing and Rebates*

In the 1979 case of *Hoffmann-LaRoche*, the European Court developed a new principle of application in order to analyze measures taken by a dominant firm to induce loyalty from its distributors.[187] The case involved exclusive dealing contracts and fidelity rebate systems used by Hoffmann-LaRoche, a Swiss chemical producer, in distributing its products within the EEC. The rebates found abusive by the Commission were of two kinds: loyalty rebates, which provided direct incentives for not purchasing from other suppliers, and total purchase rebates, which indirectly provided similar incentives by calculating rebates on the basis of total purchases of all drugs from Hoffmann-LaRoche rather than on the purchase of particular drugs.

The court found that Hoffmann-LaRoche's exclusive dealing contracts, as well as both types of rebates, constituted abuse under article 86. The first step in the court's reasoning was to analyze the agreements as well as the rebates according to their function. Therefore, an agreement by a distributor to purchase its requirements from Hoffmann-LaRoche was to be analyzed in

186. *See supra* text accompanying notes 95-102.

187. Hoffmann-LaRoche & Co. AG v. Comm'n of the European Communities, [1978-1979 Transfer Binder] Common Mkt. Rep. (CCH) ¶ 8527, at 7503 (Ct. J.E. Comm. Feb. 13, 1979).

the same way as rebates which created incentives not to purchase from other suppliers.

The court found the practices abusive because there was both a lack of equivalence in the transactions and a dependency relationship between Hoffmann-LaRoche and its distributors. According to the court, such practices are considered

> incompatible with the objective of undistorted competition . . . because . . . they are not based on an economic transaction which justifies this burden or benefit but are designed to deprive the purchaser of or restrict his possible choices of sources of supply and to deny other producers access to the market.[188]

Thus, the court spliced together two concepts used in *United Brands*—namely, the notions of transactional equivalency and of dependency—in order to produce a new test for abuse.

The court placed two limitations on the reach of its reasoning. First, in order to be abusive, such restrictive obligations and incentives must have "the effect of hindering the maintenance of the degree of competition still existing in the market or the growth of that competition."[189] Second, the dominant enterprise must use methods which are "different from those which condition normal competition in products or services on the basis of the transactions of commercial operators . . . ."[190] This commercial usage limitation appears to create a defense against abuse charges where the conduct would be normal business practice for firms not in a dominant position in similar markets.

In 1983, the court applied the same analysis in its *Michelin* decision.[191] At issue was the so-called "target rebate" system that Michelin used in its relationships with distributors of replacement tires for heavy vehicles. This system provided an annual variable discount to the dealers that was determined according to the dealer's attainment of targets for annual sales. The sales targets were discussed at the beginning of the year, but

---

188. *Id.* at 7553. For discussion, see Dhaeyer, *L'Article 86 du Traité de Rome et les Contrats d'Approvisionnement Assortis de Rabais de Fidelité*, 94 JOURNAL DES TRIBUNAUX 401 (June 16, 1979).

189. *Hoffmann-LaRoche & Co. AG*, [1978-1979 Transfer Binder] Common Mkt. Rep. (CCH) ¶ 8527, at 7553.

190. *Id.*

191. N.V. Nederlandsche Banden-Industrie Michelin v. Comm'n of the European Communities, [1983-1985 Transfer Binder] Common Mkt. Rep. (CCH) ¶ 14,031 at 14,488 (Ct. J.E. Comm. Nov. 9, 1983).

Michelin apparently provided written confirmation of the targets only on request.

The Commission argued that such a system had essentially the same effect as the loyalty rebates in *Hoffmann-LaRoche*.[192] The court agreed, finding that the rebate system distorted competition because it was "not based on any economic service justifying it."[193] Michelin received no cost savings from the scheme, and, therefore, there was no economic equivalency. Moreover, the scheme had the effect of restricting the dealer's "freedom to choose his sources of supply" by putting pressure on the dealer to purchase from Michelin.[194] The court explicitly rejected two arguments made to justify the scheme and concluded that "[n]either the wish to sell more nor the wish to spread production more evenly can justify such a restriction of the customer's freedom of choice and independence."[195]

The *Hoffmann-LaRoche* and *Michelin* cases thus designate as abuse any conduct which places significant pressure on an enterprise to deal with a dominant enterprise unless (1) there is economic equivalency in the transactions, (2) the conduct has no significant effect on the structure of competition, or (3) the conduct is normal for non-dominant firms.

d. Abuse and Competitive Fairness

Although Community abuse law has focused on vertical relationships, the Commission recently has begun to apply article 86 to horizontal abuse—i.e., conduct that does not involve transactions between the dominant firm and the firm seeking protection. The Commission's objective in such cases is to prevent the distortion of competition which may result from the use of economic power to eliminate or discipline competitors.

The Commission first applied a theory of horizontal abuse in its investigation of IBM's marketing practices in the early 1980s.[196] The Commission claimed, *inter alia*, that IBM violated article 86 where it failed to make public certain information about its computer hardware products which European

192. *Id.* at 14,519.

193. *Id.* at 14,520.

194. *Id.*

195. *Id.* at 14,521.

196. For materials relating to the investigation, including IBM's undertaking to modify its operations, see *Commission of the European Economic Communities Suspends Proceedings Against International Business Machines Corporation*, 26 HARV. INT'L L.J. 189 (1985).

firms would have had to receive in order to compete effectively with IBM in manufacturing and selling compatible equipment. The investigation did not lead to formal action by the Commission, because IBM consented to make such information available, but the proceedings did establish the Commission's position.[197]

The Commission's only formal decision on this issue was taken in 1985 against Akzo, a Dutch soap manufacturer accused of predatory pricing.[198] In that case the Commission levied its largest fine ever when it found that Akzo had systematically attempted to eliminate a competitor, primarily by lowering its prices to a point that it believed would drive the smaller competitor out of business. The Commission's theory was that a distortion of competition caused by the unfair use of power necessarily represented an abuse of that power. "Unfair or unreasonable behavior which tend(s) to exclude competitors from the market" may be an abuse, because it has a negative effect on the structure of competition and, therefore, on consumer welfare.[199] According to the Commission: "Any unfair commercial practices on the part of a dominant undertaking intended to eliminate, discipline or deter smaller competitors would thus fall within the scope of the prohibition of Article 86 if the other conditions for its application were fulfilled."[200] The effect of this reasoning is to introduce concepts of unfair competition into Community law via article 86.

The Commission's notion of what constitutes "unfair or unreasonable behavior" was based on the concept of "competition on the merits." It stated that:

> A dominant firm is entitled to compete on the merits. . . . The maintenance of a system of effective competition does, however, require that a small competitor be protected against behavior by a dominant undertaking designed to exclude it from the market not by virtue of greater efficiency or superior

197. For discussion, see Dryander, Hehn & Lohmann, *Entwicklungen im EWG-Kartellrecht im Jahr 1984*, in RECHT DER INTERNATIONALEN WIRTSCHAFT 352, 360-62 (1985).

198. Commission Decision of December 14, 1985, [New Developments] Common Mkt. Rep. (CCH) ¶ 10,748, at 11,733-34.

199. *Id.* at 11,733-23. For a discussion of predatory pricing prior to the *Akzo* decision, see Ashley, *Predatory Pricing Under Article 86 of the Treaty of Rome*, 32 INT'L & COMP. L.Q. 1004 (1983).

200. Commission Decision of December 14, 1985, [New Developments] Common Mkt. Rep. (CCH) ¶ 10,748, at 11,733-23.

performance, but by an abuse of power.[201]

According to the Commission, therefore, abuse occurs where a dominant firm utilizes its economic power to gain a competitive advantage other than by "competition on the merits" and where this conduct has a substantial effect on the structure of competition.

Community abuse law thus has been built around the concept of competitive distortion. The court has used this concept to provide a cohesive reference point for interpretation of article 86. The court has, however, refined the concept by developing a set of principles that determine its application in specific types of situations. The result has been a flexible, if not always completely predictable, approach to giving meaning to the concept of abuse.

V. Comparative Perspectives

The concept of abuse of a market-dominating position began as the expression of two simple ideas—one substantive, the other procedural. The substantive notion was that society must be protected against those uses of economic power which cause more societal harm than can be justified by their societal benefits; the procedural notion was that such protection should be provided through an administrative process. Important European competition law systems have abandoned or modified both of these ideas, and in so doing they have transformed the abuse concept.

The catalyst for this transformation has been the subjection of the abuse concept to the judicial process. The vagueness of the original substantive standard was intimately tied to its procedural role. Where the function of the concept is to authorize administrators to take action against dominant firms on the basis of a public interest standard, vagueness may be not only acceptable, but preferable. Where the concept must be judicially interpreted and applied, the responsible institutions must attempt to ascribe content to it in a rationally defensible and reasonably predictable manner. Moreover, under such circumstances, success in achieving the policy goals behind the abuse concept depends on the extent to which those institutions effectively perform this ascriptive function.

Judicial application of the abuse concept has been most

201. *Id.* at 11,733-25.

extensive under German and European Community law, and thus comparative analysis of their combined experiences reveals the extent of the concept's development, the impact of its transformation, and the likely direction of its future development.

A. Conceptual Structure

Certain basic principles are common to the conceptual structure of abuse under both German and Community law. For example, abuse is analyzed according to objective criteria in both systems, with state of mind generally playing little role. Moreover, neither moral nor ethical issues are considered relevant to the application of the abuse concept. The abuse standard is based either on the characteristics of the conduct or on its effects.

Apart from these shared principles, however, the two systems have conceptualized abuse law in quite different ways. In Community law the broad principle of competitive distortion is the central mechanism for giving content to the abuse concept. It is generally applied, however, according to a developing set of case-law principles fashioned to protect particular interests. These application principles protect, for example, the interests of consumers and small and medium-sized firms. They also protect dominant enterprises by providing that conduct which otherwise would be a violation of article 86 may be justified under certain circumstances. Analysis generally begins, therefore, with the issue of whether conduct "distorts competition" and then turns to case law to determine whether the competitive distortion harms interests whose protection is required under existing guidelines.

German law, in contrast, does not utilize an over-arching principle such as that of competitive distortion in interpreting the abuse concept. Rather, it has identified two basic forms of abuse—namely, exploitation abuse and impediment abuse—and the ideas used to give meaning to these two categories of abuse remain separate and distinct. Exploitation abuse, analyzed by reference to a hypothetical standard of competition, occurs where a dominant firm utilizes economic power to achieve a transactional result that is significantly more advantageous than it could have achieved under this standard. Impediment abuse occurs where a dominant firm impedes another firm's competitive activities; under current judicial interpretations, the determination of what constitutes impediment is made by reference to a performance competition standard. In order to be abusive, conduct must be brought within one of these two categories, and this conceptual bifurcation of abuse law has created significant difficulties in the development of German abuse law.

B. The Application of Abuse Law Concepts

Despite differences between the two systems in the concepts used to interpret abuse, there are important similarities in the results obtained—i.e., in the conduct which is identified as abusive and in the effectiveness of applying the abuse concept to particular types of conduct.

This is particularly true with regard to use of the abuse concept to protect consumers against high prices. Both systems originally focused on this use of the concept, and in both it has been ineffective. The basic theory of application is the same in both systems: where a dominant firm uses its economic power to raise prices significantly above levels that would be obtainable if there had been "effective" competition, this represents harm to those transacting business with the dominant firm as well as to the competitive process. The differences are in the means of proving abusive prices. In Community law abuse is determined by reference to the costs of the firm, whereas in German law abuse is primarily established by comparing prices on the dominant market to prices in comparable markets.

Both approaches to the problem have faltered on the inherent difficulty of proving a hypothetical standard. In each system the courts have established standards of proof which represent substantial disincentives to enforcement, and there is general agreement that the abuse concept has not been effectively applied to this category of conduct. The experiences of both systems suggest, therefore, that application of the abuse concept to deter dominant firms from using the bargaining advantages which inhere in their economic power is largely incompatible with the judicial process.

Both systems have also identified competitive unfairness as a category of abuse. Here the abuse concept is used to prevent dominant firms from using their power to achieve an unfair advantage in competition with other firms, such as, for example, through predatory pricing. In German law competitive unfairness is included within the concept of impediment abuse, whereas the European Commission applies article 86 to such conduct because it distorts competition to the detriment of smaller competitors and, in the long run, consumers.

Both systems have encountered, however, significant difficulties in conceptualizing competitive unfairness for purposes of judicial application. Each has turned primarily to the intuitively appealing idea of competition on the merits in order to provide a fairness standard, but this method of giving content to the abuse concept has not been finally accepted in either system, and there are many who doubt its viability.[202] These doubts relate to whether the merit competition notion has sufficient analytical power to make justifiable and reasonably predictable distinctions among the various types of conduct available to economically powerful firms. Neither system has yet had sufficient experience with this concept to warrant final conclusions about its effectiveness. Nevertheless, the fact that both systems have chosen to rely on it in using the abuse concept to combat competitive unfairness means that the future of the idea of unfairness as part of abuse law may well depend on the amenability to judicial application of the concept of merit competition.

A third category of practices that are considered abusive in both systems includes those by which dominant producers exercise control over firms that distribute their products. In both systems loyalty rebates, exclusive dealing contracts, and similar control measures may be abusive. With regard to this category of abuse, however, differences in analysis between the two systems have had a significant impact on the results achieved. Under Community law, such control mechanisms are found abusive when they distort competition to the detriment of consumers and interfere with the freedom of small and medium-sized firms. This analysis refers directly to the power that a dominant producer may have over distributors as well as to its effects. The result has been the development of flexible and judicially applicable principles to guide business behavior.

In Germany, on the other hand, the conceptual structure of abuse law has impeded effective application of the abuse concept to this category of conduct. Such conduct does not fit easily into either of the existing categories of abuse,[203] but bipartite conceptualization of abuse law requires that one or the other of these

202. *See supra*, text accompanying notes 119-22.

203. It does not fit easily into the category of exploitation abuse, because that category of abuse refers to a lack of transactional equivalence, and there is typically no imbalance in such transactions. It also does not fit easily into the concept of impediment

categories be used to analyze them. Thus, German law generally analyzes such conduct under the principles of impediment abuse. The principles of impediment abuse are primarily designed, however, to protect against harm to competitors. Consequently, they do not relate to the type of relational power which a producer has over its distributors, nor do they take into account the effects of the use of that power. Because these principles are poorly adapted to this type of conduct, the results of trying to apply the abuse concept in this area have been predictably awkward, and the law remains particularly unclear.[204]

C. *Methods of Interpretation*

A key factor in the conceptualization and application of abuse in German and Community law has been the choice of methods to interpret the concept. Neither German nor Community law has found interpretative guidance by reference to the abuse concept itself—i.e., neither linguistic nor grammatical analysis has been a significant factor in interpreting abuse. In both systems the concept has been viewed as too vague to allow such analysis.

In Community law the decision in *Continental Can* to interpret abuse teleologically—i.e., by reference to the objectives of the Community—has determined the structure and development of abuse law, because it established the concept of competitive distortion as the analytical starting point. In addition, the court often fashions its application principles according to its perception of the systemic needs of the Community. For example, the court's application of the abuse concept to loyalty rebates is based on the perceived need to protect the structure of competition by protecting the competitive freedom of small and medium-sized firms. Although the court occasionally also finds guidance by analogizing to the examples provided in article 86, the teleological method has been the dominant means of ascribing meaning to abuse in Community law.

Despite criticism for failure fully to utilize more predictable methods of interpretation, the European Court has fashioned a

abuse, because a producer typically does not seek to impede the competitive opportunities of its distributors.

204. German competition law does, however, contain other provisions which may be used to restrict this type of conduct by dominant firms, thus limiting the impact of the defect. The most important such provision is § 26 of the GWB. For discussion, see Gerber, *supra* note 55.

body of legal principles with sufficient integrity and coherence to have achieved general acceptance. Its success in doing so is clearly related, however, to a general consensus concerning the basic objectives of articles 85 and 86—principally, the elimination of barriers to trade within the Community—as well as to the articulation of Community objectives in the governing treaty.

In Germany there has been little agreement concerning the methods to be applied in interpreting the abuse concept, and this lack of a generally accepted frame of reference for interpreting the concept has been an obstacle to its development. Analogical and historical methods have been the primary sources of major interpretative concepts. For example, the analytically critical bifurcation of abuse into the categories of exploitation and impediment abuse was based on analogy to the division of the GWB itself into vertical and horizontal restraints and supported by reference to the legislative intent to use the abuse concept to protect both consumers and competitors. These methods generally have not provided effective guidance in developing the abuse concept. The impact of the historical method has been limited by the major changes which occurred in the process of drafting the GWB and by the relative lack of consideration of how the abuse concept would function in the system which finally emerged.[205] The general ineffectiveness of the analogical method results from the sharp differences in function between the abuse concept and most other sections of the statute.

German law also has utilized the teleological method. Although reference is often made to the role of the abuse concept in the system of the GWB,[206] lack of agreement concerning the objectives of German competition law has made use of this method much less effective than it has been in Community law. For example, in the controversy surrounding impediment abuse each side has argued that its interpretation best serves the GWB's general goal of maintaining an economy based on competitive freedom. This goal is, however, so vague that reference to it has yielded little interpretative clarity.

D. The Process of Legal Development

Comparison of the processes by which abuse law has been

205. *See supra* text accompanying notes 60-66.

206. *See, e.g.*, U. IMMENGA & E. MESTMÄCKER, *supra* note 83, at 676-79.

developed in the two systems helps explain differences in methodological and conceptual choices as well as in practical results.

Both systems have followed identifiably civil law, as opposed to common law, developmental patterns. Each has developed abuse law by first establishing abstract principles of interpretation and then concretizing these principles by reference to specific fact situations. Moreover, both systems have assigned important roles in the development of the law to university professors.

There are, however, important differences between the two developmental processes. Although basic principles of analysis in Community abuse law were provided through the authority of outside experts, the subsequent development of the law has been primarily the product of adjudication by the European Court. The court has established a basic framework for giving content to the abuse concept and has consistently applied this framework and the ideas generated thereby to new fact situations. Consequently, it is the court's central role that has dominated the developmental process.

The Commission has shaped this development through both policy and enforcement decisions. Its identification and articulation of Community policy goals has been particularly influential because of the court's focus on using the abuse concept to achieve the fundamental objectives of the Community. Moreover, not only has the Commission's enforcement policy determined the fact situations which would reach the court, but its decisions have also established lines of conceptual development which the court has later adopted.

Except during its formative stages, scholarly writing generally has had limited impact on the development of abuse law. There are recognized experts on Community competition law, but the group is small, and its impact is restricted by geographical dispersion and language variety. Moreover, neither the court nor the Commission generally cite scholarly writings in their opinions, thereby further limiting the role of such writing and reducing incentives for scholars to publish in the area.

In German law the process of developing the abuse concept has been more complex, with legislation and legal scholarship playing major roles in addition to those of the courts and the FCO. Scholars generally have provided the key ideas in the development of German abuse law. The notion of "as-if" competition, which created the conceptual framework for exploitation abuse, as well as the concept of performance competition, around which the law of impediment abuse has been shaped, were, for example, both derived from scholarly work. Scholarly debate has also played a major role in determining the success of legal ideas, with such ideas being accorded full status as law only where they have been generally accepted in the scholarly community. The concept of "performance competition," for example, has yet to be generally accepted by legal scholars, and, as a result, its future remains uncertain.

The courts generally have not developed new ideas, but they have shared with legal scholarship the role of determining the success of ideas generated elsewhere. In particular, the courts have shaped the development of the law by subjecting the application of the abuse concept to judicial standards of proof. The German Supreme Court's insistence, for example, that a finding of exploitation abuse under the comparison market method be based on rigorous analysis of all significant market differences was the critical factor in undermining development of what had been expected to be a major area of application of the abuse concept.

The legislature's role generally has been to consolidate and attempt to clarify developments made by legal scholarship or by the courts; it generally has not provided significant developmental impulses. Moreover, its efforts to clarify the law have not always been successful. In the 1980 amendments, for example, it did clarify principles relating to exploitation abuse, but its attempts to do the same regarding impediment abuse were largely unsuccessful and may even have created additional uncertainty.[207] The legislature also has repeatedly and publicly urged the FCO to utilize the abuse provisions to protect consumers, particularly against the pricing practices of dominant firms, and it is likely that such pressure has been reflected in the FCO's enforcement activity.

The FCO has influenced the development of abuse law primarily by shaping enforcement policy and thus determining the fact situations in which the concept's application would be tested and by carefully articulating the reasoning behind its enforcement decisions. Moreover, the fact that its own enforcement decisions are made according to judicially-oriented procedures

207. *See supra* text accompanying notes 128-29.

provides an important additional mechanism for testing the application of the abuse concept to concrete fact situations.

* * * *

The concept of abuse of a market-dominating position is the primary legal tool for regulating the exercise of economic power in Europe, and as such its interpretation and application are critically important to the relationship between government and private economic activity. To the extent that European legal systems succeed in ascribing content to the concept in a manner which is rational, predictable and otherwise in conformity with judicial standards and social and economic objectives, the concept is likely to play a key role in economic and legal life in Europe. To the extent that they do not, the interests that the abuse concept is expected to protect will be protected in other ways or not at all.

Because of the concept's vagueness, some have feared that it would be interpreted so broadly as to create significant discretionary interference with business conduct, while others have feared that it would be interpreted so narrowly that it would not protect interests generally considered to deserve protection. In some cases these apprehensions have resulted from failure to appreciate the transformation of the abuse concept that has been described in this article. Experience in applying the abuse concept according to judicial standards has significantly limited the scope of application of the concept, identified some areas in which the concept appears compatible with judicial application and other areas in which it does not, and generally provided evidence that the abuse concept can be effectively used as a legal tool.

[19]

Predation

Thomas Sharpe

Introduction

It has never been an objective of the UK, US or EEC anti-trust policy to condemn monopoly *per se* or necessarily to prevent the creation of monopoly. Instead, policy has been directed towards an evaluation of the behaviour of a monopolist in order to determine, respectively, whether such behaviour is contrary to the public interest, constitutes monopolisation or is an abuse of a dominant position.[1] It is true that in the UK, following an investigation by the Monopolies and Mergers Commission (MMC), a monopoly situation may itself be condemned as 'contrary to the public interest', but such instances are very rare. Predation by an undertaking in a dominant position is one example of behaviour that has been declared unlawful in all the jurisdictions referred to above.

The underlying concept of predation is that there are limitations to the manner in which competition should be conducted. Certain types of behaviour will almost universally be condemned, for example, blowing up a rival's factory or falsely disparaging a rival's product or expertise: the civil and criminal law has a well established rôle to play, even if only occasionally called upon to play it. The action of one rival serves to increase the costs of another rival without any corresponding overall gain in efficiency. But conduct which falls short of the obviously criminal or which does not fit into the conventional tort pigeon-hole is notoriously difficult to evaluate and English judges at least have strongly resisted taking responsibility for establishing limits on competitive business behaviour.[2] American law represents a stronger tradition with fewer judicial inhibitions and, as we will see, is much concerned about appropriate tests for the existence of predation. EEC law is only slowly embracing predation within the terms of Article 86.

The author wishes to acknowledge the great assistance received from Andrew Powell in the preparation of this paper.

1 Section 48(c)(d) Fair Trading Act 1973 (c.41); Section 2 Sherman Act 1890; and Article 86 (EEC).
2 *Mogul SS Co. v McGregor* [1892] AC 25.

54 PREDATION — [1987] ECLR

If limitations are to be imposed by law, such limitations should be determined by reference to the objectives that the anti-trust laws were designed to further. If anti-trust laws are a means by which a certain conception of economic policy is translated into law, and no more, then these limitations should reflect the underlying economics. Much of what follows is an attempt to analyse predation in the light of economics and, in particular, in the light of 'efficiency' — the simple view that it is more desirable than not to produce goods and services at the least cost to the community, and that anti-trust laws should encourage and not inhibit this objective. This view is often assailed as being too narrow and it is often stated that the laws should have a broader range of objectives, including the dissipation of economic power or, in the European setting, the integration of trade. The view which is often assailed is indeed a highly stylised and simplistic interpretation of economic principles and is easily characterised as 'static' or incapable of reflecting the realities of strategic decision-making by dominant undertakings. But as we will see, a test which aims to be sufficiently simple to define the standard of behaviour by undertakings and the basis of enforcement by officials, as well as being sufficiently comprehensive to accommodate the complexity of dynamic situations, has two objectives that are not immediately compatible.

In the UK, with the advent of privatisation, especially of undertakings formerly enjoying statutory monopoly, questions surrounding acceptable business conduct reappear and add interest to the proper definition and control of predatory behaviour. This is particularly true in relation to the behaviour of British Telecom plc, British Airways plc and British Gas, and the possibility of predatory conduct by the British Airports Authority is expressly envisaged in the Airport Act 1986.

At the outset it must be recognised that controversies between competitors over predation or 'ruinous competition' are an old and familiar theme in the rhetoric of nineteenth and twentieth century commerce, nevertheless, the perfect legal and economic test for predation has yet to be formulated. What follows will draw heavily on influential academic comment, as well as the case law of the most advanced anti-trust jurisdiction, the United States, and UK and EEC practice.

For the lawyer an allegation of 'predatory behaviour' presents difficulties chiefly owing to the complexity in distinguishing between low prices as an effect of healthy competition and low prices which are brought about for predatory purposes and which owe their profitability to the exclusion of competitors of equal or greater efficiency. This makes it hard to detect the base line below which prices become *unfairly* low. All forms of regulation are prone to error in greater or lesser degree, and enforcement with respect to predation is no exception. In the area of predation, however, the consequences of error are perhaps more significant than elsewhere. If the authorities employ a test which is too *relaxed* the predator will enjoy the fruits of his conduct and competitors of equal or greater efficency will be deterred from entering the market. In the short run prices will be low, and the consumer benefits thereby, but in the long run they will rise, insulated from the threat of entry. On the other hand, if too *stringent* a test is employed, consumers will be worse off owing to higher prices, and inefficient undertakings will be encouraged to enter and remain in the market confident that an efficient party will be unable to reduce prices and drive them out. Consumers are therefore deprived of competition's main benefit, lower prices. It should be noted, however, that if predation is permitted consumers are certain to benefit from lower prices in the short run and would only suffer detriment, if at all, in the long run. There is therefore justifiable sensitivity on the part of economists and lawyers toward the heavy-handed investigation of allegations of predation.

As we will see, certain lawyers and economists believe forcefully that the conditions to be satisfied for successful predation are so stringent that they are unlikely ever to be satisfied in the real world, and that the dangers of over-zealous enforcement policies towards predation are greater than any likely loss suffered by consumers as a result of predation. (The same people typically have an equally relaxed attitude to questions of dumping, the international analogue of domestic predation.) They conclude there should be little or no policy towards predation.

An alternative view starts from the proposition that an undertaking enjoying a strong market position benefits disproportionately in terms of increased profits associated with a marginal increase in its market share. Therefore, there is every incentive to engage in predatory activity and to do so at least cost to the undertaking, typically by highly selective or localised discriminatory actions.[3] In the few instances in which predation has been detected in the history of British competition policy, predation took place from a position of overwhelming dominance by the incumbent enterprise, with market shares frequently over 90 per cent of the relevant market.

The Economics of Predation

Predatory pricing may be defined as the temporary strategy of setting price below cost in order to drive competitors out of business and earn monopoly profits in the future. The reasoning behind this definition begins with an analysis of the differing profit motives of honest competitors and predators.

Firms in very competitive industries have only limited control over the prices they charge. They may 'set' their prices, in the sense that they post them on a price list or fare schedule but the prices they post are market determined. Vigorous competition drives prices close to the level of cost, where 'cost' includes only the additional or incremental expenses of production and sale caused by the incremental volume sold. These expenses include variable operating expenses,

3 Shepherd, 'Predatory Actions', XXXI *The Anti-Trust Bulletin* No.1 (Spring 1986) 1.

costs of extra capacities needed for the incremental volumes sold, and a competitive return on invested capital sufficient only to encourage adequate new investment as existing plant and equipment depreciates with use.

Even firms in very competitive industries may earn more than a competitive return. For example, they may run abnormal risks or they may enjoy the benefits of short-run technological advantages over other competitors. Generally, however, competitive market forces will pressure a firm to keep prices low, that is to say, close to cost — because prices even slightly higher than cost will result in a large loss of sales. In markets like these, the consumer is sovereign. Consumers are able to purchase goods or services at very nearly the economic cost of producing them. The primary motive of sellers in such markets is to stay efficient enough to maintain sales value and earn a profit at market determined prices. When non-predatory competitors do have some power over prices, their objective is to maximise present profits by widening the margin between price and cost. In a competitive market, however, the price sensitivity of customers limits their ability to do this.

A firm engaged in a predatory pricing campaign has a different goal. The predator's objective is a larger than competitive profit *in the future*, once rivals have been ejected from the market. To achieve this future profit the predator must endure losses *in the present*. To drive out equally efficient rivals he must set the price low enough for them to sustain losses and go out of business. To accomplish this he must run losses himself — and, unless the action is highly selective, the dominant undertaking will experience significant losses. Recouping those losses with future monopoly profits is what makes the strategy pay.

Predatory pricing would only work in a market which is not easy to enter and leave. If it were otherwise, defeating one rival would be pointless; others would crop up to take its place. Nevertheless, a dominant firm can itself make entry difficult by a threat of predation, but the threat will only be credible if all parties know that the threat will be carried out, for example, if it is known that excess capacity exists to meet the new demand at a lower price. This is why it is so important for undertakings in a dominant position to establish a reputaion in the market place which they will carry before them when making any future threat. In certain instances it would be sensible for an incumbent to accept the presence of a newcomer rather than risk an expensive price war. If, however, the incumbent is known to react violently to a new entrant the threat of a low post-entry price may well deter any entry. So the initial loss may be regarded as an investment, recouped over the time in which future entry is deterred. No rational undertaking will suffer losses unless these losses can be recovered sometime in the future. If it is known that entry cannot effectively be deterred in future, by threats or otherwise, predation is an empty threat.

These insights about the motivations of competitors and predators are the foundations of a general test that should distinguish predation from competitive pricing: does a given rate, price or fare owe its profitability solely to the exit or exclusion of competitors? If so, the price is predatory. Is a given rate, price or fare profitable to the firm in the absence of any future gain from reduced competition? If so, presumptively, the price is not predatory. Generally (but, as we will see, not exclusively) the basis against which to measure the profitability of a given price is marginal cost. As long as a firm earns sales revenue which exceeds cost, and the price can be sustained without subsidy, the firm's profit is increased. Recoupment does not enter into it, and there is no reason without more information to suspect predatory pricing. If low but profit making prices make competitors uncomfortable, that is an entirely desirable outcome. Furthermore, if less efficient competitors are forced to make losses, or even driven out of business, that too is an inevitable result of properly waged competition, and is an efficient outcome; on the other hand, prices which are loss making are suspect. If the revenue does not cover costs, then predation is a possible motive.

This does not mean that firms which suffer temporary losses on individual products or services are necessarily guilty of predatory pricing. Losses may arise from bad planning, inadequate demand, unexpected expenses or other reasons. It is anticipated *prices* and costs that count. But when a price fails to recover the cost of the product or service over time and a turnaround is not expected, a rational manager will increase the price or, if he cannot, rather than sustain continuing losses, he will leave the market altogether.

A familiar sequence of events is the arrival of a new competitor on the scene, followed by a reduction in prices by the incumbent. This is the most common circumstance in which claims of predatory pricing are invoked. The newcomer feels that the response is unfair and intended to drive him out of the market. In fact, when competition increases, sellers must either reduce prices or lose market share. Reducing prices is an appropriate, indeed necessary, competitive response, so long as the prices are not loss making.

In circumstances where competitors differ in efficiency, a price change by a low cost firm may be below the cost of the less efficient rival. Competition requires that the more efficient firm be able to exploit and pass on its advantage and, in the end, force competitors to reduce costs and prices or drop out of the market altogether.

Throughout the analysis it should be borne in mind that at least two conditions must be satisfied for successful predation to occur. First, the party complaining of predation must not have the resources to meet the alleged predatory conduct. Although a competitor or new entrant may be small in relation to a particular market, it does not follow that an undertaking is weak or under-financed. It could very easily be the subsidiary of a major company with substantial assets elsewhere. In such a situation, the predator must gamble that his investment in the form of sustained losses will pay off owing to his deeper pocket; this does not follow if the new entrant is sufficiently strong and determined and can draw on funds from its parent. If the situation is perceived correctly, predation is unlikely to be an attractive strategy for any party and the knowledge that price cuts can be matched and losses sustained on all sides is generally sufficient to prevent any party from considering predation as a sensible policy. For example, the knowledge that Mercury is owned and financed by Cable and Wireless plc, a substantial company, will not have been the least of the considerations affecting British Telecom's price response to Mercury's entry into UK telecommunications. Second, the object of the policy is to secure long term profits so the losses sustained by predatory pricing must be recouped, suitably discounted, sometime in the future. For this to occur the alleged predator must be satisfied that another prospective entrant will not enter the market and threaten the position of dominance acquired or sustained at such cost. While it is likely that any future competitor will be mindful of any predatory conduct which had taken place in the past, there can be no guarantee that the incumbent will enjoy a monopoly of the market forever. A risk factor must therefore be built into the predator's calculations in order to recover the investment represented by the losses which are likely to be suffered. As there are very few undertakings in the private sector which can sustain losses indefinitely, and fewer still which can guarantee that new competitors will not seek to enter the market at a later date, it is not surprising that so few examples of price predation have been sustained in practice.

It is perhaps important to recall that price–cost comparison is not the only way in which price predation can be approached but it is perhaps the most widely accepted approach.

In addition to predatory pricing, a further concept of *non-price* predation exists. By its nature this is less defined and well-developed than predatory pricing but rests on the observation that dominant undertakings are well-placed and equipped to effect strategic moves designed to induce competitors and prospective entrants to make choices more favourable to the dominant undertaking or incumbent than would otherwise be the case.

For example, a dominant undertaking might invest more than would otherwise be the case in excess capacity: a threat of low post-entry prices might deter a prospective entrant. An undertaking might introduce a phethora of new products by way of product differentiation so that, with advertising and other promotional devices, there is no obvious 'space' or niche for a new entrant, and no real alternative other than entry on a large scale (which may not be supported by the capital market). Similarly, a dominant undertaking might deny technology to a competitor by pre-emptive patenting or outright purchase at disproportionately high cost. It should be borne in mind that an incumbent will always pay more than a prospective entrant in order to deny technology to the entrant. The reason for this is that the incumbent's dominance persists if entry is denied. After entry, competition will exist which, by definition, is less profitable than dominance. Other examples of non-price predation consist of the payment of excessively high wages, which would increase the cost of entry to a newcomer, or the 'bundling' of equipment by way of new design, which would have the effect of excluding the independent manufacturer of the bundled product from the market. For example, manufacturers of independent disk drives will obviously lose if disk drives are incorporated as a matter of design into the computer.

This last example reveals one of the many difficulties associated with non-price predation. It is clearly advantageous to permit incorporation of disk drives, even at the expense of disk drive manufacturers. At what point, if at all, does such behaviour become unlawful? If, for example, the disk drive manufacturer announced an intention to enter the computer manufacturing market, and 'bundling' constituted the competitive response of the incumbent, a colourable argument could doubtless be made that the profitability of the design change was derived from inhibiting entry. But the ambiguity of the policy is obvious enough.

Tests of Predation

Much of the literature and case law in the area of predatory pricing comes from the United States. Under United States law, section 2 of the Sherman Act provides that:

> every person who shall monopolize, or attempt to monopolize, or combine or conspire with any other person, to monopolize any part of trade or commerce among the several states . . . shall be deemed guilty of a felony.

Although section 2 does not explicitly mention predatory pricing, it has been established by judicial precedent that predatory pricing is within the statute.[4]

As we have seen, the model case in which predatory pricing is claimed to constitute an attempt to monopolise an industry is that in which a dominant firm deliberately sacrifices present revenues for the purpose of driving rivals out of the market and then recouping the losses from higher profits earned in the absence of competition. It is unclear, however, what precise conduct constitutes predatory pricing. The United States Supreme Court, in its most recent reference to the issue, declared (in a footnote only) that 'pricing below some appropriate measure of cost' would define conduct that in certain circumstances could be claimed to be predatory.[5] Courts in predatory pricing cases have generally turned to imprecise formulae such as 'below cost' pricing,[6] ruinous competition,[7] or 'predatory intent',[8] in adjudicating liability.

4 See for instance, *Utah Pie Company v Continental Baking Company* 386 US 685 (1977).
5 *Matsushita Electrical Industrial Company v Zenith Radio Corp.*, US (No. 83–2004, March 26, 1986).
6 See for instance, *National Dairy Products Corp. v United States* 350 F.2d 321 (CA8, 1965).
7 *Porto Rican American Tobacco Company v American Tobacco Company*. 30 F.2d 234 (CA2, 1929).
8 *Forster Manufacturing Company v FTC*, 335 F.2d 47 (CA1, 1964).

60 PREDATION — [1987] ECLR

More recently, United States courts have attempted to analyse predatory pricing in terms of more concrete conceptions of cost, but no universal rule has emerged. What follows is a survey of some of the theories directed towards proposing and justifying rules which should be adopted in the area of predatory pricing and a survey of some of the relevant US, UK and EEC case law which purports to adopt the principles espoused in the literature.

Areeda and Turner were the first to analyse the predatory pricing offence in terms of its economic underpinnings. In their famous article[9] they summarised the theory of the firm, and then focused on the various measures of cost that should be applicable in adjudging a particular pricing policy to be predatory or not. The conclusions of their analysis set out the following principles:

(1) a short-run profit maximising (or loss minimizing) price [defined as the price at which marginal revenue will equal marginal cost for a producer with sufficient market power to face a downward sloping demand curve], even though it may be below average [total] cost, is non-predatory.
(2) a price at or above average [total] cost should be deemed non-predatory even though not profit maximising in the short run.

For instance, at high levels of production, marginal cost may exceed average total cost. In such cases, however, pricing at above or even below marginal cost, so long as price is above average total cost, will not eliminate equally efficient rivals or potential entrants in the market, since such rivals or entrants may restrict their output and thus make substantial profits at the monopolist's price. This would of course only be true for equally efficient rivals, defined as being those firms with similar cost curves to those of the monopolist.

(3) a price at or above reasonably anticipated short-run marginal cost should be deemed non-predatory even though not loss minimising in the short run.

This price would not be loss minimising in the short run if average total cost, which includes an element of normal profit, exceeded marginal cost at the point of production. However, where average total cost exceeds marginal cost, the theory of the firm implies that the monopolist would have excess capacity, and therefore to legislate to encourage entry into the industry in such circumstances would be inefficient. This principle is put forward on the proviso that any permitted price should be above average variable cost, since to sell a product for a price less than average variable cost would represent a situation when a firm would do better to cease operations.

9 Philip Areeda and Donald F. Turner, 'Predatory Pricing and Related Practices under Section 2 of the Sherman Act', 88 Harv. LRev. 697 (1975) (hereinafter 'Areeda and Turner').

(4) unless at or above average total costs, a price below reasonably anticipated (a) short-run marginal costs, or (b) average variable costs, should be deemed predatory.

Areeda and Turner point out that a monopolist would be both incurring private losses and wasting social resources when marginal costs exceed the value of what is produced. Pricing below marginal cost would thus greatly increase the possibility that rivalry would be extinguished or prevented for reasons unrelated to the efficiency of the monopolist.

Recognising that marginal cost data are typically unavailable, Areeda and Turner then suggested that average variable cost be used as a surrogate for marginal costs and summed up and rephrased their rules in terms of the following presumptions:

(a) a price at or above reasonable anticipated average variable cost should be conclusively presumed lawful;
(b) a price below reasonably anticipated average variable cost should be conclusively presumed unlawful.

In its simplest form the test does nothing to discourage strategic manipulation in that, for example, by investing heavily in fixed costs an undertaking could charge at above a very low figure of average variable cost.

Scherer's was the first response to Areeda and Turner's analysis.[10] Scherer starts from the premise that Areeda and Turner's rules would sometimes be too permissive and sometimes too restrictive. He points out, for instance, that while a price drop below average variable cost may be instigated as pre-emption or predation by a dominant firm, it may also be caused by an entrant flooding the market with new production, and in this latter situation it would seem wrong to hold the dominant firm legally culpable.

Scherer also questions the efficiency of a rule that would ever allow pricing below marginal cost (albeit above average total cost) or any rule that would encourage excess capacity. He accepts and explains the proposition that marginal cost pricing maximises welfare in the short run. However, he conducts his own analysis of the long-run welfare effects of so-called exclusionary pricing. In concluding that long-run welfare loss minimisation cannot be guaranteed by any general rule purporting to be based on such clear-cut cost standards as those of Areeda and Turner, he notes that long run welfare turns on the characteristics of the market and the behaviour and relative positions of the cost curves of the monopolist and fringe firms in each case; none of these can be predicted by any general formula. Consequently, Scherer inclines to a case-by-case analysis of the

10 F.M. Scherer, 'Predatory Pricing and the Sherman Act: A Comment', 89 Harv. LRev. 869 (1976).

factual background of any allegation of predation. His is essentially a rule reason approach which is of course no rule at all, and has been criticised as such.[11]

Posner analyses the predatory pricing issue similarly to Areeda and Turner, describing the offence as 'pricing at a level calculated to exclude from the market an equally or more efficient competitor'.[12] He then defines this practice as, firstly, pricing below short-run marginal cost and, secondly, pricing below long-run marginal cost. Posner's main disagreement with Areeda and Turner lies in the fact that he considers the former measure hard to derive and of only limited relevance in the real world. Consequently, he stresses long-run marginal cost as the relevant cost measure by which to define predatory pricing.

Baumol,[13] by way of criticising Areeda and Turner, characterises the problem of predatory pricing as dynamic rather than static. His central proposal is that any threat to competition and to the general welfare is not a function of the relationship between prices and costs, but rather a matter of the responsiveness of pricing to changing competitive developments. He maintains therefore that any rule against predatory pricing should address the firm's responses over time, rather than simply laying down a static standard.

By way of example he sketches out the problem of predatory pricing in the context of Laker's entry into the transatlantic air travel market. He points out that in the face of Laker's moves to undercut established carriers, policy makers had to decide between prohibiting established carriers from reducing their prices to those of Laker (and thereby effectively granting Laker a protective shield), or approving the responses of established carriers (which would probably have had the effect of driving Laker out of the market). Baumol's response to such dilemmas is to propose a third option, namely that established firms should be free to cut prices in order to protect their interests, but should not be permitted to revise those prices upwards (except in response to extraneous factors) if the entrant leaves the market or if the firm wants to subsidise price cuts of other products which are then threatened by competition. He justifies this rule as guaranteeing that an established firm would only reduce prices to levels that were profitable in the medium term. As a result, he maintains that an established firm will only adjust its price if the value of the resulting competitive gain exceeds the long run cost of a permanent reduction in price. He characterises this situation as 'true competition' and proceeds to analyse favourably the welfare effects that the succesful implementation of such a rule would have, when compared to the static standards of Areeda and Turner and others. However, Baumol does not satisfactorily meet the obvious objection, that the test is backward looking and

11 See for instance, John S. McGee, 'Predatory Pricing Revisited', 23 J. Law & Ec. 389 at 307 (1980).

12 Richard A. Posner, *Anti Trust Law, An Economic Perspective*, 1976, at 188.

13 William J. Baumol, 'Quasi Permanance of Pricing Reductions: A Policy for Prevention of Predatory Pricing', 89 Yale LJ 1 (1979).

affords relief primarily to liquidators of companies, by way of damages (in the USA), rather than grounding a basis of intervention in anticipation of harm befalling the plaintiff or complainant.

Williamson[14] also criticises the Areeda and Turner tests for being too preoccupied with a static economic model, and contests the proposition that marginal cost pricing will accurately reflect efficiency and maximise welfare in the long run when allowance must be made for strategic behaviour by firms. He compares a marginal cost rule with an average variable cost rule and with an output restriction rule, analysisng the effect of each rule on pre- and post-entry welfare. In light of his analysis, Williamson proposes the following rules:

(a) dominant firms reducing their output or holding their output constant in the face of new entry shall be deemed to be behaving in a non-predatory way, provided that the resulting market price is not less than average variable cost;
(b) dominant firms that expand their output in the face of new entry will be deemed to be engaged in predatory behaviour even if the resulting market price exceeds the dominant firm's average variable cost.

These rules have the effect of protecting a new firm's right to enter the market and leave the dominant firm an opportunity to reduce its output and accommodate the new entrant. The rules do not, however, guarantee to any new entrant the right to be accommodated. Rather, the new entrant must be prepared to compete with the dominant firm at a common post-entry price below prevailing pre-entry price. Williamson points out that in the absence of an output restriction, dominant firms may have an incentive to price higher and restrict supply in the pre-entry period since they would subsequently be able to increase output and depress price to levels that would not be profitable in response to the entry of a competitor.

Williamson thus adopts many of the principles articulated by Areeda and Turner, but objects to what he calls the 'straightforward application of settled micro-economic propositions to public policy'. He concludes that the output rule better maximises consumer welfare in light of the temporary strategic pricing practices likely to exist in the real world.

The Areeda and Turner test has frequently been criticised as focusing overly on the short-run micro concerns of the monopolist, and not sufficiently emphasising the long run impacts of certain pricing policies. Joskow and Klevorick[15] also focused on this shortcoming of the Areeda and Turner principles to formulate what they call a two-tier rule of reason approach to the diagnosis and remedy of predatory pricing practices.

14 Oliver E. Williamson, 'Predatory Pricing: A Strategic and Welfare Analysis', 87 Yale LJ 284 (1977).
15 Paul L. Joskow and Alvin K. Klevorick, 'A Framework for Analysing Predatory Pricing Policy', 89 Yale LJ 213 (1979).

64 PREDATION — [1987] ECLR

Joskow and Klevorick begin by suggesting that the authorities commence their inquiry by isolating certain market characteristics that may be conducive to successful predatory pricing practices and that may result in predatory pricing practices having long-run deleterious effects on the market. These factors include, *inter alia*, the elasticity of demand for the product in question, the ease with which new firms can enter, the availability of the necessary capital to enter, the time required to acquire the necessary sophistication to enter, the advertising predominance of an incumbent that must be overcome to enter, whether innovation in the industry would normally arise as a result of economies of sale or of increased competition, whether entry into one market is a necessary prerequisite for entry into various other industry sub-markets, and whether one firm that is dominant can control the flow of information about the market characteristics. The first tier of the two-tier test is designed to screen out from attention situations where truly predatory practices are unlikely to take place, and where, consequently, official intrusion would result in unnecessary constraints on the efficiency of the industry.

Having in the first tier test isolated environments in which predatory pricing may be profitably practised, Joskow and Klevorick then go on to apply a second tier of analysis, which effectively echoes, albeit in slightly modified form, the predatory pricing test criteria of Areeda and Turner, Baumol, Williamson, and others. They endorse, for instance, the conclusion of Areeda and Turner that a price cut to below average total cost should be the primary cost standard at the second tier level of analysis. Similarly, they pick up the sustained price reduction standard of Baumol in recommending that in the event of reversal of a price reduction, the burden of proof should shift to the dominant firm which would have to show that its subsequent price increase was justified by independent increases in the costs of production or independent changes in demand, rather than by a desire to recoup short term losses by charging monopoly prices after successful predation in the market. To a lesser extent, the Williamson output restriction rule is also reflected in Joskow and Klevorick's recommendation that a firm should not be allowed to defend against charges of predatory pricing by claiming that its increased production and lower prices were simply a result of using hitherto idle excess capacity. Joskow and Klevorick's rule would thus, essentially, be a case-by-case rule of reason, not unlike that proposed by Scherer, but it would also include a more rigid analytical framework through which to screen situations in which predatory practices were alleged to have taken place.

Another line of thinking questions the relevance of any legislation at all against the practice of predatory pricing. This thinking points to the fundamental tension between the ideas of preventing predatory price cuts and the central tenet of anti-trust law, namely to encourage competition at the lowest possible price thereby maximising benefits to consumers. Furthermore, it questions the likelihood of circumstances ever arising in which a firm could, with any certainty, embark on a course of predatory pricing in the knowledge that losses thereby incurred could be recouped by subsequent exploitation of a monopoly position.[16]

These commentators have also focused on the costly and imprecise means by which any anti-predatory pricing controls are likely to be implemented. One conclusion is that, despite the potential injury which theoretically can be caused by predatory practices, costs to society would probably be minimised by not having any anti-predatory pricing rule at all. In a detailed analysis of the total social costs incurred both through potentially undesirable maintenance of monopoly as well as the cost of enforcing any anti-predation rule, Easterbrook concludes:

> The total social costs of predation — welfare loss from monopoly plus the loss from deterring competition through an anti-predation rule and the costs of administering such a rule — would be minimised by declaring low prices lawful *per se*. The theoretical case for a rule against predation is too weak, the damages measures too inaccurate and the administrative costs too high to justify intervention designed to control the prices charged by rivals.

If there is any room in anti-trust law for rules of *per se* legality, one should be created to encompass predatory conduct. The anti-trust offence of predation should be forgotten.[17]

Summary

The literature can be summarised briefly as falling into the following categories: first, tests for predation which are based entirely upon costs; secondly, broader tests which can be grouped according to whether they look at 'net revenue price' patterns, or a mix of standards interpreted in accordance with rule of reason considerations.

Costs tests

Pure costs tests rely on some measure of cost to identify a price floor below which any price is deemed predatory. There are various schools of thought concerning whether the cost measure should be long run or short run and whether it should be based on average total cost, average variable cost or marginal cost. The distinction in relation to the time period is less an issue of time and more a matter of whether the firm is able freely to vary all of its inputs to produce a designated output at the lowest possible cost. Short run cost reflects the firm's inability to

16 See for instance R.H. Bork, *The Anti Trust Paradox*, 1978, at 144 to 160; F.H. Easterbrook, 'Predatory Strategies and Counterstrategies', 48 Chicago LR 263 (1981).

17 Easterbrook, *ibid*, at 336 to 337.

alter immediately some of its inputs; long run costs, by contrast, describe the minimum cost of producing at an output where all inputs are variable. Thus, the long run cost of any output level is unique but there is no unique short run cost since the level of short run cost depends on the nature and amount of inputs regarded as fixed. (On the relevance of what should be included in variable costs see the discussion of the EEC *AKZO* decision, below.)

Average total cost is often recommended as a price floor. Prices below average cost imply losses for the incumbent firm and their persistence may be evidence of intent to eliminate a competitor. But a price above average cost may still be aimed at preventing entry. Profit maximization normally means price at or above short-run marginal cost. If short-run marginal cost exceeds average cost, a price between the two (that is, less than short-run marginal cost) might reflect predatory intent. Similarly, a firm may have an incentive to lower a price below average total cost for reasons unrelated to any predatory intent, for instance in the presence of excess capacity. This circumstance is probably not uncommon in some situations, notably in telecommunications markets or in the provision of a new airport terminal or runway on the first day of its operation. Intermittent states of excess capacity are unavoidable in these and other markets. Pricing below average cost therefore may not be predatory if it coincides with states of excess capacity.

Marginal cost standards have been proposed to deal with some of the problems arising in the use of average cost. Any price which is greater than or equal to short-run marginal cost cannot lead to the elimination of a more efficient competitor. Furthermore, such standards avoid some of the problems associated with using average total cost as a price floor; in particular, it deals with pricing behaviour in the presence of excess capacity. A short-run marginal cost test, however, could be manipulated by a firm bent on predation by the firm, for example, electing to accept high fixed costs, reducing its variable cost and thus making its short-run marginal cost arbitrarily small.

Arching over all these conceptual objections is the very real practical question of whether a firm has the detailed knowledge of its cost structure to enable it to isolate its marginal cost or average variable cost. The problem is particularly acute where products are in joint supply and the allocation of overhead expenditure between the products must necessarily be arbitrary. This was an issue when the Office of Telecommunications considered complaints alleging that by incorporating bills for radiopaging with ordinary telephone bills, British Telecom was unfairly subsidising its radiopaging business from its monopoly telephone activities.[18]

But more fundamentally, reliance on cost based standards requires knowledge on the part of the complainant or plaintiff of the dominant undertaking's costs.

18 For a summary see OFTEL Report, HMSO, 1985, paragraph 3.19.

Since, to repeat, the incumbent may not itself know its costs, it is little wonder that few successful examples of predation have been proved in the absence of damning documentary proof of predatory intent. Moreover, costs will usually vary with output and output will be determined by price: a change in price will affect the cost at which the marginal unit is produced. It is a hard task for a prospective entrant to calculate the likely cost–price relationship following an anticipated price reduction as a result of its entry.

Net revenue tests

The net revenue test proceeds directly from the fundamental definition of predatory pricing: that any price cut whose profitability depends on the elimination of competitors is predatory. To pass this test the firm would have to demonstrate the profitability of a price reduction on the assumption that it does not cause any firm to depart from the market. Thus, the relevant demand curve would include the price response of competitors but would exclude contemplation of a rival leaving the market. The net revenue test, focusing as it does on a price *change*, is an attempt to distinguish between non-predatory profit maximising responses to new competition and pricing to exclude new competition.

For a multi-product firm, as most are, the question arises as to whether the net revenue in question should be that of the prices challenged as predatory or the net revenue of the firm's combined operation. If the demand for each of the firm's services is independent of prices charged for the other service, the choice is inconsequential since the two net revenues will change by equal amounts. But if the tested service is either a substitute or complement in demand for other services produced by the firm, the net revenue of the firm is the appropriate measure. This technique lacks nothing in complexity. In addition to the firm's costs, the firm's demand curve would have to be estimated and there may also be some difficulty in determining the appropriate time period in which the analysis should be conducted.

Price stability

A further approach examines the firm's pricing policies over time. If an initial decrease in price resulting in the exclusion or exit of competitors is followed by a subsequent increase in price, predatory pricing is suspected. But, as pointed out earlier, the test is reactive; it is applied after the damage is done so its success in preventing anti-competitive behaviour hinges critically on the existence of damages or suitably punitive fines to cause dominant undertakings to adjust prices only on the basis of sustainable profitability.

Rule of reason

The final method involves the application of a rule of reason, which provides for the assimilation of a number of factors and doing away with the economy of proof and information which 'bright line' cost based tests imply. After the preliminary screening of the market, an analysis of respective market shares, entry barriers and so forth, and a determination that predation could exist in such a market, the following guidelines are applied:

(a) a price below average variable cost or short-run marginal cost is sufficient to demonstrate predation;
(b) a price below average total cost should be presumed predatory unless the dominant firm can show that this price strategy maximises short run profits.

In practice such a defence is only likely to be valid when substantial excess capacity exists.

(c) a price decrease to a point above average total cost would not be presumed predatory unless exit occurs and is followed by considerable price increase soon thereafter.

If exit occurs and price increases, the dominant firm would have to show that the increase was justified by independent increases in the cost of production or independent changes in demand.

(d) other non-cost evidence of predatory intent, garnered perhaps from seized or discovered documents may be taken into account.

The proponents of the rule of reason approach argue that all the preceding standards for identifying and regulating predatory conduct are deficient. A rule of reason approach would take into account all the relevant variables on a case-by-case basis. This means measuring the economies of scale, the extent to which there is excess capacity, price patterns over time and all the other variables which might help to determine the existence of predatory behaviour. The rule of reason approach can therefore becomes extremely onerous and firms are not provided with clear signals of what behaviour would be deemed impermissible.

Law and Practice

The United Kingdom

In the United Kingdom the MMC has considered the issue of predatory pricing in a number of its reports on dominant firms but it has only contributed a part and sometimes only a minor part of the analyses. The overall conclusion drawn from study of all the MMC reports is that predatory pricing tactics are comparatively rare or, what is somewhat different, investigated rarely. In the report on the British Match Corporation,[19] the Commission was highly critical of the tactics used to sustain an already overwhelming position; BMC enjoyed 92 per cent of the UK market and indulged in selective price cutting which effectively excluded entry.

Similarly, where the report on the British Oxygen Company[20] was concerned, the company produced well over 90 per cent of UK supplies of oxygen and among the practices designed to maintain its monopoly was the use of 'fighting companies' to stifle and eliminate competition. The report concluded that it was:

> . . . contrary to the public interest when a monopoly such as BOC should take advantage of its position to eliminate competitors by making local and selective reductions in prices instead of extending to all consumers the benefits of any price reductions which may be possible.

A third example is found in the Report on Electrical Equipment for motor vehicles,[21] in which Joseph Lucas was a monopolist for certain items of equipment, but in respect of other equipment it faced strong competition. It was alleged that Lucas had practised selective price cutting and it was prepared to quote low and uneconomic prices for products for which there were alternative sources of supply. Unlike the earlier two examples, the Commission found that Lucas's action was not contrary to the public interest.

These cases are all somewhat dated and precede the important American anti-trust literature discussed above, which points to cost based tests for establishing the existence of predation. Only in *Electrical Equipment* was accounting data referred to and only then to demonstrate that Lucas's predatory policy was unsuccessful in the face of competition from a subsidiary of General Motors of America. In all three cases the alleged predator enjoyed market shares of 90 per cent or more and it is perhaps understandable that the Commission was reluctant in the face of such overwhelming dominance and documentary evidence to intrude too deeply into a cost related data. More recent MMC reports, on Domestic Gas Appliances[22] and the London Electricity Board[23] reveal the difficulties of allocating overhead costs as between retailing and other activities

19 Monopolies and Restrictive Practices Commission, Report on the Supply and Export of Matches and the Supply of Matches and the Supply of Matchmaking Machinery, HMSO, 1953.
20 Monopolies and Restrictive Practices Commission, Report on the Supply of Certain Industrial Medical Gases, HMSO, 1956.
21 Monopolies Commission, Report on the Supply of Electrical Equipment for Mechanically Propelled Land Vehicles, HMSO, 1963.
22 MMC, Report on the Supply of Certain Domestic Gas Appliances in the UK, HMSO, 1980.
23 MMC, Report on the Direction and Management by the London Electricity Board of its Business of Retailing Electrical Goods, Spare Parts and Ancillary Goods, HMSO, 1983.

but nevertheless point to costs, profits and the preservation of market share as important *indicia* in demonstrating the existence or otherwise of predation. In Concrete Roofing Tiles[24] the MMC declared that Redland did not sell below average variable cost and even in the most heavily discounted products prices were not clearly below the full cost of the plant at a high level of capital capacity utilisation. The MMC concluded that the elimination of a third competitor to the duopoly of Redland and Marley would be contrary to the public interest, and did not believe that the entrant was the least efficient producer, although the published evidence does little to sustain this conclusion. The market was heavily concentrated into two long established producers and was not prone to sudden and sustained entry by third party.

The possibility that British Telecom would abuse its dominant position in telecommunications was not lost on the framers of telecommunications legislation and the licence under which British Telecom conducts the bulk of its activities. Under section 8(1)(d) of the Telecommunication Act 1984 (C.12), the holder of a telecommunications licence must not show undue preference to, or exercise undue discrimination against, any person in respect of any specified service. Section 8(1)(e) further requires that all changes must be published. These provisions are expanded by Conditions 16 and 17 of the licence. As is clear, neither the Act nor the licence addresses expressly the question of predation. It is only when the terms and conditions offered to a particular class of user are unduly preferential or discriminatory that the powers granted to OFTEL's director under the licence can be invoked. While highly selective action in connection with British Telecom's licensed activities will probably be caught by the licence provision, not every example of predation will constitute undue discrimination, and therefore some examples will escape scrutiny under the provisions for enforcement of the licence. Such actions would, however, fail to be considered under the Competition Act 1980 even though enforcement procedures under that Act are less direct than under the licence. Oddly, the price control formula contained in the licence might encourage predatory pricing: observance of the constraint might require price reductions (below cost) for certain services in order to compensate for price increases elsewhere in the basket of services subject to price control.

The United States

The traditional American approach is represented by the following quotation from the Court of Appeals for the Third Circuit: 'Predatory intent can be shown by two means: (a) by express evidence; and (b) by inference from "below cost"

24 MMC, Report on the Supply in the United Kingdom of Concrete Roofing Tiles, HMSO, 1981.

pricing.'[25] As for the appropriate cost formula, the Court 'was inclined to accept the basic premise of the Areeda and Turner thesis that predatory intent may not be inferred from sales at or above average variable costs' and found it unnecessary to ramble through the thickets of economic theory because the record was barren of any substantial lessening of competition or any tendency to create a monopoly caused by the price cuts.[26] In another case, the Eighth Circuit refused to narrow the scope of the traditional test based on predatory intent to one which was simply determined by cost based considerations. The Court recognised that there could be instances in which a monopolist who reduced its prices to a point above marginal or average variable cost could still be held to have engaged in predatory actions.[27]

The traditional approach, however, is giving way somewhat to the use of presumptions, a technique which still falls short of the adoption of *per se* legality and illegality as espoused in the Areeda and Turner test. In *International Air Industries, Inc. v American Excelsior Company*[28] the Court stated that:

> . . . in order to prevail as a matter of law, a plaintiff must at least show that either (1) a competitor is charging a price below his average variable cost in the competitive market or (ii) a competitor is charging a price below its short run profit maximizing price and barriers to entry are great enough to enable the discriminator to reap the benefits of predation before new entry is possible.

Obviously, this formulation is short of an automatic inference of predatory conduct and may perhaps best be interpreted as holding that proof of below marginal cost pricing is a necessary element of establishing a *prima facie* case of predatory pricing rather than a sufficient condition for the existence of predatory pricing.

In *MCI Communications Corp. v American Telephone and Telegraph Company*, the Seventh Circuit stated that 'a strong presumption of lawfulness must attach when price is shown . . . to be above an appropriately derived measure of long running incremental costs.'[29]

The general tenor is that pricing below reasonably anticipated marginal costs will be presumed to be predatory, while prices above reasonably anticipated marginal costs will be presumed non-predatory. The presumptions are not conclusive but the presumption of predation is rebuttable if the defendant could offer an acceptable business justification for its pricing policy.

The realisation that a firm may change its prices in an effort to discipline competitors and establish a reputation for meeting competition, thereby

25 *O. Hommel Co. v Ferro Corp.* 659 F.2d 340, 347 (CA3, 1981) *cert. denied*, 455 US 1017 (1982).
26 Ibid. at 352 to 353.
27 *Super Turf, Inc. v Monsanto Co.* 660 F.2d 1275 (CA8, 1981).
28 517 F.2d 714, 715 (CA5 1975), *cert. denied* 424 US 943 (1976).
29 708 F.2d 1081, 1123 (CA7, 1983).

enhancing its long term ability to reap the benefits of monopoly, is found in the *Inglis* case.[30] In this case the court created a two-tier burden shifting device: (1) if the defendant's prices are below average total cost but above average variable cost, the plaintiff bears the burden of showing the defendant's pricing was predatory; (2) if, however, the plaintiff proves that the defendant's prices were below average variable cost, the plaintiff has established a *prima facie* case of predatory pricing and the burden shifts to the defendant to prove that the prices were justified without regard to any anticipated anti-competitive effect. In a subsequent case[31] the court added a third tier, which extended the burden of proof to prices *above* average total cost: (3) if the challenged prices exceed average total cost, the plaintiff must prove by clear and convincing evidence, that is, that which is highly probably true, that the defendant's pricing policy was predatory.

This third tier was explicitly rejected by the First Circuit in *Barry Wright Corporation v ITT Grinnell Corp.*,[32] and later by the Sixth Circuit.[33] These circuits require that liability should be contingent on evidence that a defendant had charged prices *below* its total cost for the product sold thus making the presumption of lawfulness irrebuttable, as in the Areeda and Turner test. In short, the theories regarding reputation and the disciplining effect of price movements accompanied by pricing above average total cost have not found favour with the influential First and Sixth Circuits, although judgment is divided elsewhere in the US Court of Appeals.

The EEC Case Law

In its only substantial confrontation with the issue of predatory pricing, in the *AKZO* case,[34] the European Commission has similarly not articulated a firm standard or mode of analysis. ECS alleged that AKZO had engaged in abusive conduct in violation of Article 86. Under Article 86 of the EEC Treaty any abuse by a firm in a dominant position in the Common Market which affects trade between Member States is prohibited as incompatible with the Common Market.

AKZO was judged by the Commission to occupy a dominant position in the organic peroxides and flour additives markets in the EEC. ECS was a smaller

30 *William Inglis and Sons Baking Company v ITT Continental Baking Company* 668 F.2d 1014 (CA9, 1981), *cert. denied* 459 US 825 (1982).
31 *Transamerica Computer Company v International Business Machines Corp.*, 698 F.2d 1377, (CA9, 1983), *cert. denied*, 464 US 955 (1983).
32 724 F.2d 227, 236 (CA1, 1983).
33 *Arthur Slangenderfer, Inc. v S.E. Johnson Co.*, 729 F.2d 1050, (CA6) *cert. denied* 105 S.Ct 510 (1984).
34 *ECS/AKZO*, Decision of 14 December 1985, OJ L 374, 31/12/1985. For interim measures: Decision of 29 July 1983, OJ L252, 13/8/1983.

competitor which in 1979 decided to expand from producing only flour additives into the more lucrative business of supplying organic peroxides to the plastics industry. When AKZO heard of this decision it announced that it would pursue pricing policies designed to undermine ECS's position in the flour additives market unless ECS withdrew from the plastics market. In the face of these threats, ECS applied for and was granted an *ex parte* injunction under Article 86 of the EEC Treaty following a hearing in the High Court in London. Throughout these proceedings AKZO denied any predatory intent.

After various interlocutory proceedings, AKZO gave an undertaking to the court that it would not reduce its prices 'with the intention of eliminating ECS as competitors'. This undertaking lasted for two and half years, until 1982. AKZO, according to ECS, nevertheless continued to undercut the prices offered by ECS, on a selective basis, to ECS's best customers, claiming that it was simply meeting the competitive threat posed by ECS. ECS complained to the Commission which then proceeded to investigate AKZO in the Netherlands and in the UK. An AKZO company memoranda discovered in the course of these inquiries revealed that it was the policy of AKZO to allow its flour additive business to be operated at a loss in order to eliminate ECS from the market. This documentation was not available in the earlier High Court proceedings. The Commission took interim measures which had the effect of controlling AKZO UK's profit margins.

When the matter was brought before the Commission on the substantive question of abuse of dominant position the Commission considered that three essential questions should be addressed:

(1) whether AKZO held a dominant position under the terms of Article 86;
(2) whether the alleged conduct of AKZO constituted an abuse of such dominant position;
(3) whether there was an appreciable effect on trade between the Member States.

The Commission answered questions (1) and (3) briefly in the affirmative, and focused on question (2) in more detail. Abusive conduct was defined to include the imposition of 'unfair purchase or selling prices' and the notion of unfair prices was defined to embrace prices which might damage consumers both directly and indirectly through detrimental impact on the competitive structure of an industry. At the same time, the Commission stressed that while deep and prolonged price cutting may be the principal means of achieving an illegal advantage in a competitive market, other aspects of AKZO's commercial conduct might be considered exclusionary and should as such be scrutinised as potentially abusive.

AKZO's principal defences were, first, that its prices had been reduced only to match those of other competitors, and second, that by virtue of being above variable cost AKZO's prices could not be considered to be predatory. In making this second claim AKZO apparently referred to the rules propounded by Areeda and Turner. The Commission, however, rejected AKZO's claim, noting that in the Areeda and Turner formulation variable costs included such direct manufacturing costs as labour, repair and maintenance, all of which had been (surprisingly) omitted from AKZO's calculation.

More significantly, the Commission rejected any notion of a *per se* standard based on cost–price relationships:

> Article 86 does not prescribe any cost based legal rule to define the precise stage at which price cutting by a dominant firm may become abusive and indeed the broad application of the concept of abuse to different forms of exclusionary behaviour would argue against such a narrow test.[35]

The Commission further took issue with the value of cost based tests on the grounds that they reflected only a notion of short term efficiency, which was not necessarily in line with the broader objectives of EEC competition policy. By way of comment the Commission noted that a dominant firm might achieve its aim of harming a competitor or deterring potential entrants by means of price cutting that would fall short of predatory pricing as defined by a variable cost standard.

Having rejected cost based tests, the Commission focused its analysis on what it termed 'unfair means differing from normal competition' as in principle falling under Article 86 'whatever the detailed mode of implementation'.[36] In defining unfairness the Commission appeared to fashion a standard based principally on the concept of intent, and applicable in all but the most self-evidently egregious circumstances. In the words of the Commission:

> . . . where low pricing could be susceptible of several explanations, evidence of an intention to eliminate a competitor or restrict competition might also be required to prove an infringement. Such evidence may exist in the form of internal documentation of the dominant company pointing to a scheme to damage competitors. In the absence however of direct documentary evidence an exclusionary intention might be inferred from all the circumstances of the case.[37]

In AKZO's case the evidence of intent was clear from company memoranda, and passing judgment in the case seemed consequently straightforward. The rather loose general observations of the Commission do not, however, imply how the Commission would analyse a case in which such evidence of intent was not to hand.

In concluding that AKZO's behaviour did indeed have an illegal exclusionary effect, the Commission was able to list certain specific actions of AKZO's which it considered abusive under Article 86. These included (1) making direct threats to ECS, (2) making direct approaches to ECS's customers, (3) offering to meet the

35 Ibid at paragraph 75.
36 Ibid at paragraph 85.
37 Ibid at paragraph 86.

needs of ECS's customers at unreasonably low prices, (4) making the above price quotations selectively to ECS customers while maintaining substantially higher prices to its own established customers, (5) using 'bait pricing' on certain items to lure ECS's customers, (6) exploiting its superior financial resources to keep prices generally at an uneconomic level over time, (7) deliberately seeking out and undercutting competitive quotations, and (8) doing all of the above with the express purpose of damaging or securing the withdrawal of ECS as a competitor. With evidence of such clear-cut malpractices to hand, the Commission did not have to get involved in detailed determinations of the economic harm threatened by conduct that could plausibly be defended as fair competition. The Commission was able to apply what was essentially a rule of reason and condemn practices which it was able to portray, given the documentary evidence, as flagrantly unreasonable and departures from normal modes of competition.

The Commission's decision, which is under appeal, does not, however, give much clue as to exactly how much a rule of reason would be applied in a closer run case. It is suggested that apart from documentary evidence the Commission will consider relative market shares and the selective character of dominant undertakings' actions. An undertaking enjoying a high market share has most to gain from successful predation, and highly selective price reductions is the least cost method of successful predation.

The concept of 'normal and reasonable pricing practices which can in no way be construed as predatory' recently reappeared in the terms of a reported undertaking given by British Sugar, a subsidiary of S and W Berisford, to the Commission following a complaint from the largest British independent sugar merchant, Napier Brown. The undertaking was accepted in place of threatened interim measures following a price war designed, it was alleged, to drive Napier Brown out of business.[38]

Conclusion

There is fragmented evidence (of which the *AKZO* case is the most recent) of predatory strategies adopted by dominant undertakings. This, in itself, is insufficient to require regulation if the burden of regulation and likely errors in enforcement outweight the competitive, long run detriment of the predatory activity. American experience, with extensive pre-trial discovery, depositions, non-trivial legal and expert fees, juries and treble damages, gives rise to caution in supporting a policy toward predation which is independent of the conceptual difficulties of distinguishing predatory from non-predatory conduct.

38 *Financial Times*, 22 August 1986, at 28.

76 PREDATION — [1987] ECLR

In the UK and EEC these protracted and expensive features of the American experience do not apply or apply to a lesser extent and, as the Napier Brown matter demonstrates, allegations of predation can be settled speedily if the parties consent. Furthermore, the absence of effective remedies or fines in the UK makes predation a riskless activity, a fact reinforced by the weakness of UK official powers of seizure and access to documentation — powers which cost based standards of predation place at a premium

What is important in any further analysis of predation is the understanding that all players in a market operate to some extent interdependently, and that it is *expected* or *anticipated* responses which are important. The decisions to accept or fight a new entrant, to develop a new product, adopt a particular technology, to price at a particular level, locate in a particular situation and so on, are taken with a view to their strategic impact on the market and on competitors. If done cleverly, the decisions are made to achieve the objectives of enhancing profitability or increasing competitors' costs. Taken to extremes either of these objectives can constitute predation; the point at which extremes are reached will continue to cause difficulty. Recourse solely to cost based standards does no more than simplify a complex issue. It does not conclude the debate.

Thomas Sharpe
Barrister
Lincoln's Inn
London

Efficiency Defence in Mergers

[20]

Efficiency Considerations in the Assessment of Horizontal Mergers under European and U.S. Antitrust Law

Pierre-Emmanuel Noël

A horizontal merger removes a competitor from the market and therefore creates a risk that the resulting undertaking may exercise market power.[1] On the other hand, such a transaction may also generate efficiencies (*e.g.* economies of scale, better integration, plant specialisation) which would ultimately be beneficial to society. The *efficiency defence* can be broadly defined as an argument available for parties to a merger seeking the clearance of their transaction notwithstanding the fact that the transaction may create a significant increase of the concentration in the relevant market by demonstrating that the merger will generate efficiencies.

Nowadays, mergers involving multinational corporations or likely to have a worldwide impact will often trigger the scrutiny of national or federal competition "watchdogs".[2] The purpose of this article is to compare the extent to which efficiencies are considered in the analysis of horizontal mergers in the United States and the European Union.

A short presentation of American and European merger enforcement and of the political and economic backgrounds of the efficiency defence will introduce a discussion of its treatment in both jurisdictions. In conclusion, a comparison will be drawn between the two approaches and some prospective developments related to the efficiency defence will be discussed in the light of new economic theories and of global competition concerns.

Merger Enforcement in the United States and the E.U. and Attitudes Towards Efficiency Arguments

Regulatory framework and enforcement authorities

The United States

Antitrust was an early concern for the American legislatures, with the enactment of the Clayton Act in 1914 to complement the Sherman Act of 1890.[3] Section 7 of the Clayton Act was redrafted in 1950 to boast merger enforcement, and currently provides that "No person . . . shall acquire . . . the whole or any part of the stock or . . . assets of another person . . . where in any line of commerce in any section of the country, the effect of such acquisition may be substantially to lessen competition, or to tend to create a monopoly".

The American antitrust laws can be enforced in different ways: by the *Antitrust Division of the Department of Justice*, which may bring civil or criminal cases against corporations or individuals before federal courts; by the *Federal Trade Commission* ("FTC"), with a concurrent power in civil cases[4]; by *State Attorney Generals* enforcing state (and, in certain circumstances, federal) antitrust laws;[5] and by *private parties*, entitled to sue in federal court for an injunction and for treble damages if they believe they have been harmed by a violation of the antitrust laws[6].

Pierre-Emmanuel Noël, de Bandt, Van Hecke & Lagae, Brussels. *The author would like to warmly thank Professor Michel Waelbroeck for comments and assistance. This article was made possible thanks to a Fellowship from the Belgian American Educational Foundation.*

1 Market power can be defined as "the power to restrict output in the market to less than the pre-merger level and to charge a higher price to consumers". See generally Hovenkamp, *Economics and Federal Antitrust Law* ¶1.2–1.3.

2 For example, the merger between Boeing and McDonnell Douglas has confronted the U.S. and E.U. approaches towards the efficiency arguments which were claimed by Boeing in support of the transaction: see De Jonquières and Baker, "Aerospace merger tests U.S.–E.U. harmony", *Financial Times*, December 23, 1996, at 3.

3 See Barnes, "Revolutionary antitrust: efficiency, ideology, and democracy", 58 U. Cin. L. Rev. 59, 69 (1989) ("Historically, antitrust has been perceived as a means for ensuring that the views of private citizens will not be lost in the 'thunder' of large, monopolistic business interests"). For a detailed historical overview, see, *e.g.* Elzinga, "The goals of antitrust: other than competition and efficiency, what else counts?," 125 U. Pa. L. Rev. 1191 (1977).

4 To prevent or settle jurisdictional disputes, a liaison agreement was worked out by the agencies, though overlapping jurisdictions still exist in some areas; see Roll, "Dual enforcement of the antitrust laws by the department of justice and the Federal Trade Commission: the liaison procedure", 31 *Bus. Lawyer* 2075 (1976).

5 For a description of the U.S. State/Federal enforcement and a comparison with the E.U. subsidiarity principle, see Hawk and Laudati, "Antitrust federalism in the U.S. and decentralization of competition law enforcement in the E.U.: a comparison", 20 *Fordham Int'l L.J.* 1, 19 (1996).

6 Section 4 of the Clayton Act at 15 U.S.C. §15; for a discussion of the problems posed by private merger enforcement, see Hovenkamp, "Merger actions for damages", 35 *Hastings L.J.* 937 (1984).

The Antitrust Division of the DOJ and the FTC periodically set forth their enforcement policy in guidelines, the latest being the 1992 Horizontal Merger Joint Guidelines.[7] The pattern of analysis described in these guidelines involves several steps, relying heavily on quantitative presumptions (market share and concentration).

First, a definition of the relevant market, a calculation of the market shares and of the degree of concentration are established for the tentative merger. When the market, calculated by summing the squares of the market shares of each firm in the market (Herfindahl-Hirschman Index, or HHI), is found "unconcentrated" (HHI below 1000), there is a strong presumption of legality; on the other hand, an HHI above 1800 is a proof of a "highly concentrated" market and triggers a presumption of illegality of the transaction; in between, the market is considered as "moderately concentrated".[8]

The inquiry will then focus on the increase of the HHI caused by the merger. If the increase is substantial (more than 100 in a moderately concentrated market, more than 50 in a highly concentrated one), the merger will be regarded as "raising significant competitive concerns", and the parties will have to rebut a presumption of illegality with specific categories of evidence listed in sections 2 to 5 of the Guidelines.

At this stage, the parties may establish that the expected anti-competitive effect of the large market share, which is indicated by the quantitative analysis, should actually be offset in view of specific qualitative factors. These factors are mainly the assessment of the risk of co-ordinated interaction or of unilateral effect (*e.g.* "power-buyer" defence[9]), the "entry analysis" as a guarantee that the new firm will be deterred from exercising market power, and the "failing firm" and "failing division" defences.[10]

If the competitive threat of the merger remains after this qualitative analysis, parties still have an argument if they can demonstrate that the otherwise illegal merger "may be reasonably necessary to achieve significant net efficiencies"[11] (*e.g.* economies of scale, integration of production or distribution facilities).

The E.U.

European merger control did not exist as such before the enactment of Regulation 4064/89,[12] which entered into force on September 21, 1990 in anticipation of the corporate moves likely to follow the 1992 liberalisation deadline.[13]

Article 2(3) of Regulation 4064/89 on the control of concentrations between undertakings prohibits as "incompatible with the common market" any merger which "creates or strengthens a dominant position[14] as a result of which effective competition would be significantly impeded in the common market or a substantial part of it". Under this Regulation, the Commission is vested with the exclusive power to control the concentrations with a "Community dimension",[15] while the national authorities retain jurisdiction over the smaller transactions in compliance with the one-stop shop and subsidiarity principles.[16] The Commission has created within its Competition Directorate General (DGIV) a Merger Task Force to handle the notifications of mergers and to investigate them.

As in the United States, the Regulation has adopted a pre-merger mandatory notification and a waiting period during which the operation is

7 4 Trade Reg. Rep. (CCH) ¶ 13, 104. Previous Merger Guidelines were issued by both Agencies in 1968 and 1982, and by the Department of Justice alone in 1984.

8 See Laine, "The Herfindahl-Hirschman index: a concentration measure taking the consumer's point of view", 40 *Antitrust Bull.* 423 (1995); Hawk and Veltrop, "Les développements du droit antitrust aux Etats-Unis: analyse raffinée; application agressive et internationale", R.I.D.E. 299, 322–323 (1994).

9 Steptoe, "The power-buyer defense in merger cases", 38 *Antitrust L.J.* 493 (1993).

10 Section 5 of the Guidelines.

11 Section 4 of the Guidelines.

12 Regulation of the Council 4064/89 on the control of concentrations between undertakings, [1990] O.J. L257/13.

13 Mergers were nevertheless indirectly subjected to the Commission's monitoring power, through Article 86 (and 85 in some situations like concentrative joint ventures) of the Rome Treaty. However, this provision was not really suited for such a control, as Article 86 was primarily enacted to prevent the *abuse* of a dominant position, and not the dominant position in itself.

14 A dominant position is "a position of economic strength enjoyed by an undertaking which enables it to hinder the maintenance of effective competition on the relevant market by allowing it to behave to an appreciable extent independently of its competitors and customers and ultimately of consumers" (*N.V. Nederlandsche Banden-Industrie Michelin/Commission*, [1983] E.C.R. 3461).

15 A discussion of the scope of Regulation 4064/89 is beyond this article. For an overview of the current situation and the future outcomes regarding the reach and enforcement of the merger regulation, see Broberg, "The E.C. Commission's green paper on the review of the Merger Regulation", [1996] 5 E.C.L.R. 289.

16 Only some European countries have established a merger control. For a discussion of the various national systems and their consistency with the European procedure, see Berlin, *Controle Communautaire des Concentrations* 116–128 (1992).

investigated and the parties may not close the transaction.[17]

In short, the Commission will analyse the effects of the contemplated transaction on competition in two steps: (i) definition of the relevant market[18] and (ii) assessment of "dominance". The Task Force will generally conduct an intense factual inquiry centred on the market-specific reasons why a particular merger may or may not create or enhance market power (or "dominance" in the European Union lexicon).

The concrete case-by-case approach of the Commission differs from the U.S. heavy reliance on presumptions based on market share and concentration data.[19] A study of the enforcement practice of the Commission shows that the criteria used to gauge "dominance" have been not only quantitative (market share and degree of concentration on the relevant market—although not used in a systematic way as in the United States), but qualitative as well[20] (barriers to entry,[21] customer or consumer buying power,[22] product substitutability[23]). However, and contrary to the U.S. approach, the efficiency analysis is not a formal part of the standards of appraisal embodied in the Regulation.[24]

As the Merger Task Force of the Commission has not issued guidelines defining its evaluation of mergers, its standards of appraisal must be found in its practice.

Settlements are allowed in both jurisdictions when antitrust concerns are present, which will result in a clearing of the merger in exchange for the parties' acceptance of binding remedies.[25] A major difference with the United States is that the Commission does not need to go to court to obtain the equivalent of a preliminary injunction and has the power to block the transaction by rendering a formal decision, which can be reviewed by the Court of First Instance or the European Court of Justice.[26]

The status of efficiency arguments in the U.S. and the E.U. antitrust policies

The acceptance of efficiency arguments to authorise a merger harming competition departs from an otherwise competition-driven analysis centred on market shares and numerical data. Such claimed benefits are indeed difficult to quantify and may be influenced by the political environment.

It is only recently that efficiency considerations have begun to play a significant role in merger analysis, especially in the United States. However, it is necessary to track down the policies underlying American and European antitrust, in order to properly define the status of the efficiency defence in their respective merger enforcement patterns.

The United States

Decentralisation and consumer welfare. Section 7 of the Clayton Act merely prohibits mergers which would "substantially . . . lessen competition" and gives no guidance for the definition of "competition". This broad provision has given birth to a huge literature, tracking Congress' intent in order to devise enforcement standards.[27]

According to the authoritative study of the legislative history of section 7 made by J. Ponsoldt and

17 The notifications are required when the firms involved have a turnover exceeding determined thresholds: in the United States, see Hart–Scott–Rodino Antitrust Improvement Act, adopted as section 7A of the Clayton Act, 15 U.S.C.A. §18A (requiring a filing with the FTC and the Department of Justice); in the European Union, see Art. 5 of Regulation 4064/89.

18 The analysis will be slightly different than in the United States, following a sequential rather than simultaneous procedure for product and geographic market definition; it will often result in an extremely narrow definition of the relevant market; see Neven, Nuttall and Seabright, *The Economics and Politics of European Merger Control* (1993), 101.

19 Leddy, "The 1992 U.S. Horizontal Merger Guidelines and some comparison with E.C. enforcement policy", [1993]1 E.C.L.R. 15, 20.

20 Waelbroeck and Frignani, 4 *Commentaire J. Megret – Le Droit de la CE (Concurrence)* (1997), 899. Downes and MacDougall, "Significantly impeding effective competition: substantive appraisal under the Merger Regulation", 19 E.L.R. 287, 293–296 (1994).

21 See, *e.g. Thomson/Pilkington*, Case IV/M.086 (Decision of Oct. 23, 1991).

22 See, *e.g. BA/TAT*, Case IV/M.259 (Decision of Nov. 27, 1992).

23 See, *e.g. VIAG/Continental Can*, Case IV/M.081 (Decision of June 6, 1991).

24 Neven, Nutall and Seabright, *The Economics and Politics of European Merger Control* (1993), 13.

25 See Bergmann, "Settlements in E.C. Merger Control proceedings: a summary of E.C. enforcement practice and a comparison with the United States", 62 *Antitrust L.J.* 47 (1993).

26 Regulation 4064/89, Art. 8. For an overview of the multi-levels enforcement schemes used in the E.U. and the U.S., see Hawk and Laudati, "Antitrust federalism in the United States and decentralization of competition law enforcement in the European Union: a comparison, 20 *Fordham Int. L.J.* 1, 18 (1996).

27 See, *e.g.* Barnes, "Revolutionary antitrust: efficiency, ideology and democracy", 58 U. Cin. L. Rev. 59 (1989) and "Federal and State philosophies in the antitrust law of mergers", 56 *Geo. Wash. L. Rev.* 263 (1988); Broadley, "The economic goals of antitrust: efficiency, consumer welfare and technological progress", 62 N.Y.U. L. Rev. 1020 (1987); Fisher and Lande, "Efficiency considerations in merger enforcement", 71 *Calif. L. Rev.* 1582 (1983).

28 Ponsoldt and Westerhausen, "Competition and/or efficiency: a review of West German antimerger law as a model for the proposed treatment of efficiency promotion under Section 7 of the Clayton Act", 9 *J. Int'l L. Bus.* 296 (1988).

C. Westerhausen,[28] the Clayton Act of 1914 and its amendment by the Celler–Kefauver Act of 1950 had two main purposes.

First, it promoted a "decentralisation" in the economy, based on the repugnance of Congress for concentrations, which was in turn a consequence of the widespread fear in the public that a totalitarianism would emerge from huge, powerful corporations, and, in addition, of an economical belief that mergers would reduce "business opportunities" for small firms by raising entry barriers. This objective of "decentralisation" was therefore considered as fundamental to attain, even at the price of economic efficiency.

The "prohibition of unfair wealth transfers" from consumers to monopolists was the second aim of these regulations. Indeed, Congress decided to favour "consumer welfare" above all and to ban supra-competitive pricing.[29]

However, the conflict between the realisation of economic efficiency and the dispersion of economic power was not squarely addressed by Congress, and in conclusion "one can only speculate whether [it] would have regarded the achievement of efficiencies as justification for mergers resulting in market power gains".[30]

The first decisions of the Supreme Court to interpret the scope of section 7 after 1950 relied on the "populist" (social, political and moral) goal of Congress to prohibit mergers, whether or not creating market power.[31] In the landmark case *Brown Shoe*, in 1962,[32] Chief Justice Warren emphasised the socio-political considerations which almost exclusively guided Congress in the 1950 Amendment, without regard for efficiency arguments.[33] The court held that even in an unconcentrated market, a transaction not resulting in a large post-merger market share (5 per cent in that case) may still be illegal. A tough approach of horizontal mergers was also endorsed in *Philadelphia National Bank*,[34] where a large market share in a highly concentrated market was deemed to constitute a presumption of anti-competitive effect, not rebuttable by evidence of incidental social or economic benefits. The numbers were thus virtually conclusive to make a merger anti-competitive, in this opinion.

Under this conception, which prevailed until the early 1980s, the efficiency defence was of course of no value and irrelevant in view of the emphasis on "democratic decentralisation". In some cases, enforcement agencies even weighed efficiencies *against* the legality of a merger, forcing defendants into the irrational argument that the merger in question would not benefit the firms involved.[35]

The emergence of the Williamsonian economics and the Chicago school. After more than half a century of populist antitrust, O. Williamson imposed his new analysis, asserting that efficiencies were a highly desirable result of mergers and therefore that enforcement policy should facilitate (by the introduction of an efficiency defence) the maximisation of overall efficiency in the economy.[36] Most importantly, he identified the standard to be used by the agencies as a *tradeoff between efficiencies* (*i.e.* the future gains resulting from the merger) *and market power* (*i.e.* the expected anti-competitive effects of the transaction).

Therefore, the early populist antitrust of the Supreme Court was questioned by the Chicago School's "new learning",[37] which considered that the administrative agencies and the courts should develop merger standards solely by reference to economic concerns, without regard for political goals. The Chicago approach was clearly at odds with the legislative history of section 7 and the *Brown Shoe*

29 Fisher and Lande, "Efficiency considerations in merger enforcement", 71 *Calif. L. Rev.* 1582, 1590–1591 (1983) (Congress' main economic goal was to prevent firms with market power from "victimizing consumers through monopoly pricing").

30 Ponsoldt and Westerhausen, "Competition and/or efficiency: a review of West German antimerger law as a model for the proposed treatment of efficiency promotion under Section 7 of the Clayton Act", 9 *J. Int'l L. Bus.* 296 (1988) (at note 40) (these authors disagree with the view, advocated by some commentators, that Congress decided to put a significant emphasis on efficiency as a goal of antimerger policy).

31 See Lande, "The rise and (coming) fall of efficiency as the ruler of antitrust", 33 *Antitrust Bull.* 429, 430–321 (1988).

32 370 U.S. 294 (1962).

33 For an overview of the "populist antitrust" doctrine see Barnes, "Revolutionary antitrust: efficiency, ideology, and democracy", 58 *U. Cin. L. Rev.* 59 (1989).

34 374 U.S. 321 (1963).

35 Fisher and Lande, "Efficiency considerations in merger enforcement", 71 *Calif. L. Rev.* 1582 (1983); for an example of such contentions, see: *In re Procter & Gamble*, 63 F.T.C. 1465 (1963).

36 Williamson developed his theory in five famous articles: "Economies as an antitrust defense: the welfare tradeoffs", 58 *Am. Econ. Rev.* 18 (1968); "Economies as an antitrust defense: correction and reply", 58 *Am. Econ. Rev.* 1372 (1968); "Allocative efficiency and the limits of antitrust", *Am. Econ. Rev. Papers & Proc.* (May 1969) at 105; "Economies as an antitrust defense: reply", 59 *Am. Econ. Rev.* 954 (1969); "Economies as an antitrust defense revisited", 125 U. Pa. L. Rev. 69 (1977).

37 Composed of economists and lawyers; their leading writings include Bork, *The Antitrust Paradox: a Policy at War with itself* (1978, reissued 1993); Posner, "The social costs of monopoly and regulation", 83 *J. Pol. Econ.* 807 (1976); McGee, *In Defense of Industrial Concentration* (1971).

holding, emphasising the increase of "aggregate social wealth" without consideration for wealth distribution between large businesses and consumers or small firms, or for the dispersion of economic power sought by Congress at that time.

The Supreme Court of the 1970s was quite receptive to the criticisms raised by its previous "populist" reading of section 7 and, in a conservative political landscape, adopted a more *economic-oriented* attitude. In *General Dynamics*,[38] *Marine Bancorporation*[39] and *Connecticut National Bank*[40] the court, under the leadership of Justice Stewart, endorsed a dynamic analysis of the relevant market: even if the market share is high, the "prima facie" case can be rebutted by qualitative factors (*e.g.* market history and future,[41] entry of potential competitors, new firm's ability to compete), evidencing the absence of real competitive harm.

Since then, lower courts and the administrative agencies have adopted new analytical methodologies and liability thresholds which have, to a large extent, departed from the old Supreme Court cases. Nevertheless, the *Philadelphia National Bank* holding that there is an irrebuttable presumption of illegality when market share and concentration exceed a certain threshold has not been overruled yet.

In the aftermath of the Chicago School, the Reagan administration endorsed this permissive philosophy based on the narrow view that efficiency is the only original and legitimate concern of antitrust.[42] This theory assumed that inter-firm rivalry is not a prerequisite for the improvement of productive and allocative efficiency, which in turn increase the total social wealth.[43]

During this period of "merger frenzy",[44] there was thus a shift in the competition policy of the agencies, followed by the courts,[45] and characterised by lenient, low-profile merger enforcement.

Enforcement policy under the Bush and Clinton administrations. Today, the Chicago School "laissez-faire" orthodoxy has been tempered by a new political landscape as well as the refinement of economic models.[46] The 1992 Joint Guidelines of the Agencies reflect this point of view:

> The primary benefit of mergers to the economy is their efficiency-enhancing potential, which can increase the competitiveness of firms and result in lower prices to consumers . . . Some mergers that the Agency otherwise might challenge may be reasonably necessary to achieve significant net efficiencies . . . The expected net efficiencies must be greater the more significant are the competitive risks. [Section 4]

Controversies have of course not disappeared but the goals of antitrust law, as expressed by J. Brodley, adequately reflect the current belief: "antitrust policy enunciates a distinct economic objective—a blending of efficiency and consumer welfare—to be achieved by a particular social instrumentality—interfirm rivalry".[47]

The new approach is therefore not a return to "activist antitrust" and remains within the scope of economic-oriented antitrust.[48] It only asserts that the first goals of antitrust laws were to give consumers the right to purchase competitively priced goods, to condemn the use of market power artificially to raise prices, and to prevent wealth transfers from consumers to cartels with market power, to ensure that the consumers would ultimately be the main beneficiaries of "the fruits of competitive capitalism".[49]

38 *U.S. v. General Dynamics Corp.*, 415 U.S. 486 (1974).
39 *U.S. v. Marine Bancorporation, Inc.*, 418 U.S. 602 (1974).
40 *U.S. v. Connecticut National Bank*, 418 U.S. 656 (1974).
41 This criterion had already been formulated in *Brown Shoe*: ". . . only a further examination of the particular market—its structure, history and probable future—can provide the appropriate setting for judging the probable anticompetitive effect of the merger": 370 U.S. 294, 322 (n. 321).
42 Lande, "Beyond Chicago: will activist antitrust arise again?", 39 *Antitrust Bull.* 1, 5 (1994).
43 Bork, *The Antitrust Paradox: a Policy at War with itself*, 57 (1978, reissued 1993).
44 For numerical data illustrating this trend in the U.S. industry, see Woodrow Eckard, "The impact of the 1980's merger movement on U.S. industrial concentration", 40 *Antitrust Bulletin* 397 (1995).
45 See, *e.g. Matsushita Elec. Indus. Co., Ltd v. Zenith Radio Corp.*, 475 U.S. 574, 106 (1986).
46 The Post-Chicago Economics includes the *game theory*, the *information economics*, the *contestable markets theory* and the *transaction costs analysis*; these theories use sophisticated mathematical models. The difference between Chicago and Post-Chicago thinking about competition and monopoly is related to the difference often noted between neoclassical and industrial organisation(IO) economics; see Sullivan, "Post-Chicago economics: economists, lawyers, judges, and enforcement officials in a less determinate theoretical world", 63 *Antitrust L.J.* 669 (1995); Salop, "Kodak as post-Chicago law and economics", in *New Directions in Antitrust Law* (A.L.I., 1993); Hawk and Veltrop, "Les développements du droit antitrust aux Etats-Unis: analyse raffinée; application agressive et internationale", R.I.D.E. 300, 302–304 (1994); Hovenkamp, "Antitrust policy after Chicago", 84 *Mich. L. Rev.* 213 (1985).
47 Brodley, "The economic goals of antitrust: efficiency, consumer welfare, and technological progress", 62 N.Y.U.L. Rev. 1020, 1023 (1987).
48 See Lande, "Beyond Chicago: will activist antitrust arise again?", 39 *Antitrust Bull.* 1 (1994).
49 Bingaman, "Antitrust enforcement, some initial thoughts and actions", Address before the Antitrust Section of the A.B.A., reprinted in 23 *Journal of Reprints for Antitrust Law and Economics* 747 (1993).

The Clinton administration has apparently no plans to amend the 1992 Guidelines and its enforcement of these guidelines seems to be no more aggressive than enforcement by the Bush administration.[50]

The European Union

Should the Commission only appraise concentrations on the basis of their influence on free competition, or should its analysis also take into account industrial, economic and even social considerations?

Unlike section 7 of the Clayton Act, the Rome Treaty expressly incorporates non-competition goals in its antitrust provisions, and, in particular, Article 85.[51] However, these provisions are no longer relevant since Regulation 4064/89 was intended to supersede them regarding the control of concentrations.[52] Defining the goals of the E.U. concentration control is therefore a prerequisite to determine the status of the efficiency defence in the Commission merger analysis.

Regulation 4064/89 did not explicitly refer to the same general objectives as Articles 85 and 86. Therefore, it remains to be seen whether it imposes a strictly competition-driven control (in the narrow sense, *i.e.* market shares, market concentration, barriers to entry), or instead allows other factors to be considered.[53] Of course, the efficiency defence does not mean the introduction of social or regional policy considerations in merger appraisal; it only uses an economic rationale to clear a merger harming competition.

The mere reading of Regulation 4064/89 may induce one to think that some kind of "efficiency defence" was implicitly included in the mandatory appraisal scheme. Indeed, Article 2[1] requires the Commission to appraise mergers on the basis of, among others, "the development of *technical and economical progress* provided that it is *to consumers' advantage* and *does not form an obstacle to competition*" ("technical and economic progress" factor), as well as the "actual or potential competition from undertakings located either within or *out[side]* the Community" ("global competitiveness" criterion).[54]

"Technical and economic progress" (Article 2(1)(b)). There is considerable confusion regarding the extent to which this factor should be construed as allowing the recognition of an "efficiency defence".[55] At first glance, the provision could be read as an authorisation to balance the cost savings or technical benefits against the finding of dominance to determine if the merger is compatible with the common market.[56] However, some commentators[57] and Commission officials[58] have regarded this provision as without real impact, in order to avoid the introduction of industrial policy considerations in merger enforcement, whose exclusive aim should be the preservation of effective competition through inter-firm rivalry.[59]

Aside of the fear of a politicisation of merger control, there are some arguments weighing against the admission of an efficiency defence which result from the structure and the legislative history of the Regulation. Indeed, Article 2(3) is widely construed as requiring an exclusively competition-based standard ("A concentration which creates or strengthens a dominant position as a result of which effective competition would be significantly impeded . . . shall be [illegal]") in view of the absence of "safe harbour" provisions, unlike in the U.S. Guidelines where "efficiency" and "failing firm/division" defences are admitted.

The fact that a provision included in the 1988 and 1989 drafts of the Regulation and allowing authorisation of mergers where they would "contribute to the attainment of the basic objectives of the Treaty in such a way that, on balance, their economic benefits prevail over the danger they cause to competition" was ultimately removed from the text has also

50 Thompson, "A proposal for antitrust merger enforcement reform: repudiating judge Bork in favour of current economic learning", 41 *Antitrust Bull.* 79, 83 (1996).

51 For example, Article 85(3) of the Rome (E.E.C.) Treaty, dealing with the monitoring of cartels, authorises exemptions based on non-competition justifications: it allows other factors to outweigh the anti-competitive effects, provided they enhance economic efficiency in society ("economic audit method").

52 Picat and Zachmann, "Community monitoring of concentration operations", [1993] 6 E.C.L.R. 240, 246.

53 For a recent overview of the merger appraisal under Regulation 4064/89, see *e.g.* Snelders, "Developments in E.C. Merger Control in 1995", 21 E.L.Rev. Checklist No. 2, 66 (1996).

54 Emphasis added.

55 Afonso, "A catalogue of merger defenses under European and United States antitrust Law", 33 *Harv. L. Rev.* 1, 32 (1992).

56 Jones and Gonzales-Diaz, *The EEC Merger Regulation*, 153 (1992).

57 See Hawkes, "The E.C. Merger Control Regulation: not an industrial policy instrument: the de Havilland decision", [1992] 1 E.C.L.R. 34.

58 Former Competition Commissioner Leon Brittan declared that "the control of concentrations is an economic and not a political matter" (quoted in Picat and Zachmann, "Community monitoring of concentration operations", [1993] 6 E.C.L.R. 240, 246.

59 This view was adopted by Germany and the United Kingdom, which strongly opposed factors such as industrial, social, and regional development policies being considered for merger appraisal.

been used in support of an exclusively competition-oriented merger control.[60]

To be sure, economic or technical benefits are referred to in Article 2(1)(b), but only as long as they "[do not] form an obstacle to competition", which clearly excludes any trade-off.

Until now, the Commission has been trying to avoid making a clear-cut choice between the two interpretations.[61]

The "global competitiveness of European industries" (Article 2(1)(a)). The text of this provision requiring the Commission to consider competition outside the Community in its appraisal seems to constitute another motive to allow otherwise anti-competitive mergers. It has also generated long discussions among Member States.

Once again, the debate highlighted the differences between the economic culture of southern European states, favourable to the emergence of European industrial groups with sufficient strength to contend with American and Japanese competitors, and the northern states, strongly attached to the principle of free trade.[62]

As of today, it seems that the advocates of a soft merger enforcement to permit the creation of "European champions" have not yet succeeded in imposing their views.[63]

In conclusion, in the current state of the Regulation there is no efficiency defence in the sense recognised in U.S. merger control; besides, until now no decision of the Commission has ever allowed social, industrial, technological or regional policy considerations to prevail on competition.[64]

60 1989 version, [1989] O.J. C22/14 (emphasis added). See also Article 13 of the Preamble: "Whereas . . . the Commission must place its appraisal within the general framework of the achievement of the fundamental objectives referred to in Article 2 of the [Rome] Treaty,[60] including that of strengthening the Community's economic and social cohesion, referred to in Article 130a" (of course, the Preamble does not have a legal value but it indicates the drafter's intent that can be used to interpret the scope of unclear provisions of the Regulation).

61 Cohen-Tanugi, Encaoua, Winckler, Siragusa and Brunet, *La Pratique Communautaire du Controle des Concentrations*, 80 (1996).

62 Picat and Zachmann, "Community monitoring of concentration operations", [1993] 6 E.C.L.R. 240, 246.

63 Leon Brittan claimed that "a competitive world market cannot justify a dominant position within the E.E.C.", quoted by Fine, "The appraisal criteria of the E.C. Merger Control Regulation", [1991] 4 E.C.L.R. 148, 150.

64 Waelbroeck and Frignani, 4 *Commentaire J. Megnet – Le Droit de la CE (Concurrence).* (1997), 898–900; Cook and Kerse, *E.C. Merger Control*, 167 (1996).

The Efficiency Defence in Merger Decisions

The United States[65]

The Supreme Court

Under the current case law of the Supreme Court, there is no efficiency defence and an otherwise objectionable merger may not be justified because of certain economic benefits such as lower costs from economies of scale.[66] The rationale for this position was clearly set forth in *Philadelphia National Bank*:[67]

> a merger the effect of which may be substantially to lessen competition is not saved because, on some ultimate reckoning of social or economic debits and credits, it may be deemed beneficial. A value choice of such magnitude is beyond the ordinary limits of judicial competence, and in any event has been made for us already by Congress when it enacted the amended section 7. Congress was determined to preserve our traditionally competitive economy. It has therefore proscribed anticompetitive mergers, the benign and the malignant alike, fully aware, we must assume, that some price might have to be paid.

In *Procter & Gamble*, the Supreme Court refused to consider promotional efficiency gains and held that "possible economies cannot be used as a defense to illegality. Congress was aware that some mergers which lessen competition may also result in economies but it struck the balance in favor of protecting competition".[68]

Of course, these decisions are characteristic of the "populist antitrust" which dominated the Supreme Court before the modern era of economics-oriented antitrust, announced by *Brunswick*[69] in 1977. Since the end of the 1970s, efficiency claims have had an increasing influence in the assessment of mergers by the lower courts and the agencies.

The Agencies

The conventional reading of the Supreme Court cases as prohibiting an efficiency defence was clearly

65 See generally Kattan, "Efficiencies and merger analysis", 62 *Antitrust L.J.* 513 (1994); Stockum, "The efficiencies defense for horizontal mergers: what is the government's standard?", 61 *Antitrust L.J.* 829 (1993); Yao and Dahdouh, "Information problems in merger decision making and their impact on the development of an efficiencies defense", 62 *Antitrust L.J.* 23 (1993); Gilbert and Sunshine," Incorporating dynamic efficiency concerns in merger analysis: the use of innovation markets", 63 *Antitrust L.J.* 569 (1995).

66 Kintner, *Federal Antitrust Law*, 180.

67 374 U.S. 321, 371 (1963).

68 *F.T.C. v. Procter & Gamble Co.*, 386 U.S. 568, 580 (1967).

69 *Brunswick Corp. v. Pueblo Bowl-O-Mat, Inc.* 429 U.S. 477 (1977).

overturned by the FTC in *American Medical International*,[70] where the Commission made a policy pronouncement regarding these precedents as obsolete and embraced efficiencies as an admissible defence in horizontal merger litigation.[71] The current formulation of the efficiency defence is located in Section 4 of the 1992 FTC/DOJ Joint Guidelines,[72] which has to be extensively quoted:

> The primary benefit of mergers to the economy is their efficiency-enhancing potential, which can *increase the competitiveness of firms* and *result in lower prices to consumers*. . . .
>
> Some mergers that the Agency otherwise might challenge may be *reasonably necessary to achieve significant net efficiencies*. Cognizable efficiencies include, but are not limited to, achieving economies of scale, better integration of production abilities, plant specialization, lower transportation costs, and similar efficiencies relating to specific manufacturing, servicing or distribution operations of the merging firms. The Agency may also consider claimed efficiencies resulting from reductions in general selling, administrative, and overhead expenses, or that otherwise do not relate to specific manufacturing, servicing, or distribution operations of the merging firms, although, as a practical matter, these types of efficiencies may be difficult to demonstrate.
>
> In addition, the Agency will reject claims of efficiencies if *equivalent or comparable savings can reasonably be achieved by the parties through other means*. The *expected net efficiencies must be greater the more significant are the competitive risks* identified in sections 1–3.[73]

In addition, the Federal Trade Commission Staff has issued a report defining the analytical framework to be used for the assessment of efficiency arguments.[74]

There follows an analysis of the enforcement of this provision by the Agencies when reviewing alleged efficiency gains.[75] Hospital merger cases[76] will illustrate the discussion, as they often involve efficiency arguments.[77]

Under Section 4 of the Guidelines, the parties to a merger "that the Agency otherwise might challenge" (mainly on the grounds of a quantitative analysis based on concentration data) may nevertheless obtain the approval of their transaction if they can demonstrate that the merger would actually generate net efficiencies (*evidences of net efficiencies* requirement), which are sufficient to offset the anti-competitive effect of the merger (*sufficient efficiencies* requirement) and cannot reasonably be achieved through any other means (*merger specific* requirement).[78]

Before going further, one should keep in mind the fact that, according to statistics, only a few mergers have been challenged under the first Clinton

70 *American Medical International*, 104 F.T.C. 1 (1984).

71 Berg, "Cost Efficiencies in the Section 7 calculus: a review of the doctrine", 37 *Case W. Res.* 218, 258 (1987).

72 For a review of the situation prior to the 1992 guidelines, see Afonso, "A catalogue of merger defenses under European and United States antitrust law", 33 *Harv. L. Rev.* 1, 53–55 (1992).

73 Emphasis added.

74 "Efficiencies and the failing firm in merger analysis—FTC staff recommendations", Report by the Federal Trade Commission Staff (May 1996), National Reports: [1996] 6 E.C.L.R. 158.

75 The national Association of States Attorney Generals (N.A.A.G.) has issued its own 1993 Horizontal Merger Guidelines, which adopts a significantly more sceptical attitude toward efficiency claims; see Barnes, "Federal and State philosophies in the antitrust law of mergers", 56 *Geo. Wash. L. Rev.* 263 (1988): "The antitrust policy of the states with respect to horizontal mergers and acquisitions reveals a markedly different philosophy of the role of government in antitrust enforcement from that underlying federal policy . . . the states' philosophy emphasizes concern for the distribution of wealth in society . . ., a greater skepticism regarding the benefits to be derived from mergers . . .".

76 See generally: Magleby, "Hospital mergers and antitrust policy: arguments against a modification of current antitrust law", 41 *Antitrust Bull.* 137 (1996); Matthew, "Doing what comes naturally: antitrust law and hospital mergers", 31 *Hous. L. Rev.* 813 (1993), Steptoe, "Efficiency justifications for hospital mergers", Remarks Before Practising Law Institute (F.T.C., 1994), Flynn,"Antitrust Policy and Health Care Reform", *Antitrust Bull.* 59, 104 (1994), Paulter and Vita, "Hospital market structure, hospital competition, and consumer welfare: what can the evidence tell us?", 10 *Journal of Contemporary Health Law and Policy* 117 (1994), Paschall, "Antitrust and hospital mergers: a law and economics rationale for exemption", 30:39 *Duquesne L. Rev.* 61, 77, and Rule, "Antitrust enforcement and hospital mergers", 21 *J. Health & Hosp. L.* 125 (1988). Among many others, the $3.45 billion acquisition of Health Trust by Columbia/HCA some years ago demonstrated the importance of the issue for this sector of the U.S. economy.

77 The banking industry may also provide an interesting field of research for the efficiency defence (see Quinn, "Practical aspects of defending bank mergers before the federal reserve board and the DoJ", 62 *Antitrust L.J.* 91 (1993); Guerin-Calvert, "Bank merger analysis and the 1992 merger guidelines: the view from the Justice Department", Speech given before the ABA Antitrust Meeting on April 1, 1993, in 23 *Journal of Reprints for Antitrust Law and Economics*, 1, 489.

78 It should be noted that, contrary to the Federal Policy, the N.A.A.G. Guidelines (relevant at the State level) consider efficiency arguments only where the post-merger HHI is lower than 1800 and where there is clear and convincing evidence of cost savings of 5 per cent or more.

administration.[79] Therefore, there is some uncertainty as to the exact standards of review which are actually relied upon by the Agencies in their efficiency analysis.[80]

Parties must provide evidence of net efficiencies. Operational and/or managerial efficiencies are the primary goal of almost every merger.[81] However, the Guidelines limit the admissible efficiencies by considering the *cost increases* and *quality decreases* that could result from the merger and which are *weighed against its potential benefits*.[82]

Some of the efficiency gains are listed as "cognizable" in the Guidelines: "economies of scale, better integration of production abilities, plant specialization, lower transportation costs". Economies not related to specific manufacturing, servicing or distribution operations, like a "reduction in general selling, administrative and overhead expenses . . ", may also be considered, but only as "claimed efficiencies". They will call for a more sceptical approach because "as a practical matter, these types of efficiencies may be difficult to demonstrate".

Among the category of cognisable efficiencies is the creation of improved research and development through the merger ("dynamic efficiency"). These R&D efficiencies are related to the "production efficiencies" and thus already plainly valid under the Guidelines,[83] though some commentators maintain that they should have a stronger presumptive impact on the assessment of mergers.[84]

Other cognisable efficiency gains are cost savings, but also quality improvements like the consolidation of two open-heart surgery departments which would allow the surgical team to practise more frequently, therefore keeping its skills sharp and achieving normal quality levels and mortality rates.[85]

The net efficiencies requirement also rejects cost savings resulting from a reduction in the quantity or quality of services provided to consumers, as opposed to producing the same level of service at lower cost.[86] This aspect was illustrated by *University Health*,[87] where the merging parties argued that the women in the relevant geographic market did not really need to have two women's centres (the merging parties had planned to upgrade their own facilities—working above the minimum efficient scale—before the transaction occurred).

In the hospital mergers, consultant reports are often presented as the principal support for the efficiency argument case of hospitals[88], but unduly downplay what is lost in achieving the savings; *e.g.* a study might quantify the savings created by the centralisation of two inventories or laboratories at one of the facilities, but ignore the resulting transport costs.[89]

The third factor in the "net efficiencies" requirement is that a merger which might achieve scale economies cognisable under the Guidelines may nevertheless not be efficient if the benefits from operating at a more efficient scale are offset by the capital costs involved in bringing the merged entity to that scale, as was ruled in *Adventist Health System*,[90] where the economies of scale generated by the combination of the two small hospitals (operating below

79 See Paulter and O'Quinn, "Recent empirical evidence on mergers and acquisitions", 38 *Antitrust Bull.* 741 (1993).
80 In most cases where no challenge is made, the reviewing enforcement agency will not enunciate publicly the reasons underlying the decision not to initiate an enforcement action, so the potentially dispositive role that efficiencies play in these prosecutorial decisions cannot be ascertained (see Fisher, Johnson and Lande, "Mergers, market power and property rights: when will efficiencies prevent price increases?", FTC Working Paper No. 130 (Sept. 1985), 3–7).
81 Paulter and O'Quinn, "Recent empirical evidence on merger and acquisitions", 38 *Antitrust Bull.* 741, 742 (1993). It is generally agreed that improved operating efficiency and management control were driving the wave of takeovers of the 1980s (see Romano, "A guide to takeovers: theory, evidence and regulation", 9 *Yale J. on Reg.* 119 (1992).
82 Steptoe, "Efficiency justifications for hospital mergers", Remarks Before Practising Law Institute (F.T.C., 1994), at 9.
83 Gilbert and Sunshine, "Incorporating dynamic efficiency concerns in merger analysis: the use of innovation markets", 63 *Antitrust L.J.* 569, 594 (1995) (for a discussion of the effects of competition on innovation and of the incorporation of innovation in merger analysis).
84 See Yao and DeSanti, "Innovation issues under the 1992 Merger Guidelines", 61 *Antitrust L.J.* 505 (1993).
85 Steptoe, "Efficiency justifications for hospital mergers", Remarks Before Practising Law Institute (F.T.C., 1994), at 13.
86 Quinn, "Practical aspects of defending bank mergers before the federal reserve board and the DoJ", 62 *Antitrust L.J.* 1, at 126 (1993) ("efficiencies gained from reducing redundant and excess capacity in the banking system" is an often-invoked benefit of bank mergers, and typically requires "a demonstration of the extent of the redundant facilities that can be eliminated without a reduction in output or service to customers and the costs that will be saved by doing so").
87 *FTC v. University Health*, 938 F.2d 1206 (1991).
88 Stockum, "The efficiencies defense for horizontal mergers: what is the government's standard?", 61 *Antitrust L.J.* 829, 838 (1993); see also Whalley, "After the Herfindahls are counted: assessment of entry and efficiencies in merger enforcement by the Department of Justice" (Dec. 1, 1989), reprinted in *Collaboration Among Competitors: Antitrust Policy and Economics* 625 (E. Fox and J. Halverson eds, 1992).
89 Steptoe, "Efficiency justifications for hospital mergers", Remarks Before Practising Law Institute (F.T.C., 1994), at 9.
90 *Adventist Health System/West and Ukiah Adventist Hospital*, F.T.C. Docket No. D-9234 (April 1, 1994).

efficient scale) into one were counterbalanced by the costs that such expansion would require.

Difficulty of producing such evidence. Even the efficiency-oriented supporters of the "new learning" were sceptical about the efficiency defence as such, mainly because of the difficulties of demonstrating the realisation of efficiency gains *ex ante*[91] or, in other words, the difficulty of providing the agencies with strong evidence that the tentative merger will achieve efficiencies.[92] The burden of proof rests on the parties to the merger, but it seems that the 1992 Guidelines have lowered the standard of proof by deleting from the 1984 version the additional requirement of "clear and convincing" evidence; this is at least the view endorsed by the FTC Staff,[93] although it seems that at the Department of Justice, the new text does not entail any departure from the previous heightened evidentiary standard.[94]

The typical documents used to support the efficiency claim will be engineering and financial evaluations of cost savings to be achieved and management internal plans and cost studies that preceded the decision to merge.[95] The type of evidence presented to the Agencies has a significant impact on the strength of the argument: the most persuasive documents will be business documents created in the ordinary course of business and clearly identifying the efficiency gains sought by the merger; on the other hand, studies prepared *post hoc* by consultants in order to convince the Agencies will be of little relevance.[96]

Certain efficiencies may thus pose a problem as a matter of evidence and therefore will often not pass muster under the Agencies' inquiry. Among these are managerial and advertising efficiencies. The former type, which postulates that the merger will bring more quality in the management, is virtually impossible to assess (how to quantify the efficiency of a manager?) and, besides, can be achieved otherwise than through a merger, by searching in the labour market for qualified executives (thus not meeting the *merger-specific* requirement).[97] The latter is based on the idea that the enhanced bargaining power[98] of the combined entities and their new corporate image will result in a better promotion; but this argument, too, is unlikely to be persuasive in most cases.[99]

The efficiencies must be sufficient to offset the anti-competitive effect of the merger. The Guidelines provide that "the expected net efficiencies must be greater the more significant are the competitive risks".[100] This requirement suggests a *sliding scale approach* to efficiencies, *i.e.* efficiencies can save an otherwise anti-competitive merger, but the higher the competitive risk, the greater the efficiencies needed to save the transaction.[101]

This view was adopted by the FTC in its *Honickman*[102] decision, where it held that the efficiency claim of the acquiring firm had substantial merit and was sufficient to offset the anti-competitive potential of the transactions[103] while stressing that "only an extremely strong showing of net efficiencies could outweigh the competitive risks" of a proposed transaction involving a high risk to competition.[104]

91 Bork, *The Antitrust Paradox: a Policy at War with itself* (1978, reissued 1993), 124–129; Posner, *Antitrust Law: an Economic Perspective*, 112 (1976); Bork, "Section 7 of the Clayton Act and the Merging of law and Economics", 74 *Harv. L. Rev.* 226, 318–321 (1960).

92 Yao and Dahdouh, "Information problems in merger decision making and their impact on the development of an efficiencies defense", 62 *Antitrust L.J.* 23 (1993).

93 "Efficiencies and the failing firm in merger analysis—FTC staff recommendations", Report by the Federal Trade Commission Staff (May 1996, National Reports: [1996] 6 E.C.L.R. 158 ("the Staff would not require that [efficiencies] be proved by clear and convincing evidence, pointing out that that burden of persuasion was removed by the Guidelines").

94 See the contradictory declarations of D.O.J. and F.T.C. officials on the issue in: Yao and Dahdouh, "Information problems in merger decision making and their impact on the development of an efficiencies defense", 62 *Antitrust L. J.* 23, 29 (1993) (and the declarations quoted in footnote 18) ("it is fair to say that notions similar to the "clear and convincing" evidentiary standard . . . will continue to influence assessments of efficiencies claims"); Stockum, "The efficiencies defense for horizontal mergers: what is the government's standard?", 61 *Antitrust L. J.* 829, 833 (1993) (the new text "appears to signal a more sympathetic attitude toward efficiency claims, because relevant efficiencies are referred to as 'expected' rather than 'establish[ed] by clear and convincing evidence'").

95 Kattan, "Efficiencies and merger analysis", 62 *Antitrust L. J.* 513, 533 (1994).

96 Steptoe, "Efficiency justifications for hospital mergers", Remarks before Practising Law Institute (F.T.C., 1994), at 26.

97 *ibid.*, at 19–20.

98 Such an argument was used in *Procter & Gamble* (386 U.S. 568), but rejected by the Supreme Court.

99 Kattan, "Efficiencies and merger analysis", 62 *Antitrust L. J.* 513, 532 (footnote 79) (1994).

100 Horizontal Merger Guidelines, Section 4.

101 Kattan, "Efficiencies and merger analysis", 62 *Antitrust L. J.* 513, 518 (1994).

102 *Harold A. Honickman*, F.T.C. Docket No. 9233 (Nov. 16, 1992) 5 Trade Reg. Rep. (CCH) ¶ 23, 286 (Letter from F.T.C. Secretary D. Clark to P. Greene).

103 The case involved acquisitions by H. Honickman of soft-drink franchises in New York and New Jersey. Only the New Jersey purchases were authorised by the Commission, which considered the competitive risks in New York to be too important.

104 at ¶ 22, 964.

Theoretically, a two-step "critical magnitude" test could therefore be applied to alleged efficiency gains:

- *expected value*, which is their magnitude (quantitative and/or qualitative) multiplied by their likelihood.[105] This concept, not explicit in the Guidelines, entails a probabilistic approach of the efficiencies defence, balancing probable efficiencies against probable anti-competitive effects.[106]
- *sufficient value*, which is the determination of "how much of an efficiency is enough to offset an apparent anti-competitive effect".[107] As the Guidelines have built into their analysis the expectation that some efficiencies occur as a result of any merger, only significant, specific efficiencies will be pertinent; the parties must thus ground their argument by "itemising" instead of simply relying on opportunities to reduce personnel or overhead expenses, which are routine and modest cost savings.[108]

When can efficiencies be regarded as "sufficient"? The determination of the "sufficient value", *i.e.* the required amount of cognisable efficiencies necessary to authorize the merger, is controversial.

T. Muris suggests that, as they are difficult to quantify, only proof of "*substantial*" efficiencies should be necessary.[109]

The *efficiency standard*,[110] requiring that efficiencies only be sufficiently large to offset the deadweight loss[111] resulting from anti-competitive behaviour, appears to be most popular among economists.

The *consumer surplus (or "price") standard* is met if the marginal cost reduction due to the efficiency is sufficient to offset the incentive to increase prices due to increased market power, *i.e.* if the efficiency is large enough to prevent prices from increasing.[112] It seems the most appropriate in view of the Congress' intent in enacting the Clayton Act and its amendment.

This aspect of the efficiency defence is at the core of the traditional policy debate surrounding efficiency. Indeed, the *efficiency standard* is only concerned with societal welfare,[113] while the *price standard* calls for a distributional approach, favouring consumers over producers.[114]

The Williamson ("efficiency") standard has been rejected by authoritative commentators,[115] though the issue is still debated.[116] The agencies seem to have adopted the price standard, which is "implicit in the Guidelines".[117]

The practice of the Agencies under the 1992 Guidelines has been consistent with the policy expressed above, allowing efficiencies to be balanced against market power provided that the merger will result in lower prices for consumers.

In the past, the FTC and the DOJ views with respect to the requirement that the benefit of the efficiencies must be passed through to consumers was slightly different, the FTC appearing to be more demanding than the DOJ on this point.[118] However, with the appointment of R. Pitofski as Chairman of the FTC, this may not be the case anymore.[119] At the State level, the N.A.A.G. Guidelines have

105 Stockum, "The efficiencies defense for horizontal mergers: what is the government's standard?", 61 *Antitrust L. J.* 829, 838 (1993).
106 This approach is suggested by Professor Pitofsky, "Proposals for revised United States merger enforcement in a global economy", 81 Geo. L.J. 195, 206 (1992).
107 Stockum, "The efficiencies defense for horizontal mergers: what is the government's standard?", 61 *Antitrust L. J.* 829, 840 (1993).
108 Steptoe, "Efficiency justifications for hospital mergers", Remarks Before Practising Law Institute (F.T.C., 1994), at 18.
109 Muris, "The efficiency defense under Section 7 of the Clayton Act", 30 *Case W. Res. L. Rev.* 381, 420 (1980).
110 Also called *Williamson* (or "*consumer welfare*") *standard*, because it was evidenced by the researches of O. Williamson (see note 36).
111 In Williamson's view, anti-competitive pricing will result in a reduction in consumer purchases (output restriction), causing an absolute (*i.e.* for society in the aggregate) loss of "welfare" (called "deadweight loss").
112 Stockum, "The efficiencies defense for horizontal mergers: what is the government's standard?", 61 *Antitrust L. J.* 829, 841 (1993).
113 There will be efficiency gain for the society "if the amount gained by all who gain from the change is greater than the amount lost by all those who lose" (see Hovenkamp, "Merger action for damages", 35 *Hastings L.J.* 937 (1984).
114 See Barnes, "Revolutionary antitrust: efficiency, ideology, and democracy", 58 *U. Cin. L. Rev.* 59, 66–67 (1989) (illustrating the issue of efficiency v. wealth distribution in a hospital merger case).
115 See Fisher, Johnson and Lande, "Price effects of horizontal mergers", 77 *Cal. L. Rev.* 777 (1989); Lande, "Wealth transfers as the original and primary concern of antitrust: the efficiency interpretation challenged", 34 *Hastings L.J.* 65 (1982).
116 See Pitofsky, "Proposals for revised United States merger enforcement in a global economy", 81 Geo. L.J. 195, 208 (1992), considering that "In short requiring . . . that efficiencies be passed along to consumers is a way of preventing consideration of an efficiencies defense in most cases where it would make a difference".
117 Steptoe, "Efficiency justifications for hospital mergers", Remarks before Practising Law Institute (F.T.C., 1994), at 17.
118 Catvani and Todd Miller, "31 merger policy questions—still lingering after the 1992 guidelines", 38 *Antitrust Bull.* 602, 634 (1993).
119 Mr. Pitofsky had indeed criticised this requirement, "Proposals for revised United States merger enforcement in a global economy", 81 Geo. L.J., 195, 208 (1992).

adopted the very demanding requirement that the parties should "demonstrate that the efficiencies will ensure that consumer prices will not increase despite any increase in market power due to the merger".[120]

While efficiencies technically do not constitute a *defence* under the Guidelines, as a practical matter if the Agencies were to accept efficiencies as justification for an anti-competitive merger, then their net effect would be the same as a valid defence, *i.e.* the merger will not be challenged.[121]

But it is still unclear whether Agencies only regard efficiencies as a "plus factor" used to tip the balance in close cases, an element to assess the likely competitive effects of the transaction,[122] or finally a real, full-fledged argument operating outside the measurement of the competitive effects and capable of counterbalancing potential anti-competitive effects to redeem an otherwise illegal merger.

In practice, the FTC appears very reluctant to acknowledge an *explicit* trade-off of potential anti-competitive risk against efficiencies gains. Indeed, the position of the FTC has been set forth recently on this issue:

> In evaluating the merged firm's probable effect on competition, the efficiencies justification would depend on the answer to two questions: (1) is the merger likely to result in credible efficiencies, and (2) if so, how are these efficiencies likely to change the merged firm's ability and incentives so as to deter the likelihood of lessened competition post-merger or increase competition in a relevant market? *The answers to these questions do not allow parties to justify an otherwise anti-competitive merger, they permit parties to demonstrate that the overall effect of the merger will increase, not lessen competition.*[123]

Therefore, the threshold level of efficiencies necessary for an effective affirmative defence remains undefined, which may have a chilling effect preventing some potentially efficient hospital mergers.[124]

The efficiencies may not reasonably be achieved through other means. As stated in the Guidelines, "the Agency will reject claims of efficiencies if equivalent or comparable savings can reasonably be achieved by the parties through other means". This requires a showing that the efficiencies be merger-specific, and could not be attained by other means (*e.g.* by internal expansion, joint venture or licensing).[125]

A good example of an argument ignoring this requirement is the consolidation of hospital's laundry services, because even if one or both parties are unable to manage their laundry rooms at efficient volume, a whole hospital merger is not the only way to solve such minor inefficiency: they can combine their laundry operations with a non-hospital facility or even set up a joint venture.[126]

This requirement creates, according to some authors, "a substantial and perhaps impossible test" for hospital mergers.[127]

Nevertheless, the possibility of an alternative means to achieve the alleged efficiencies will weigh against the transaction only when the alternatives would not have been unduly costly ("reasonable" requirement). In considering the parties' appreciation of potential alternatives, the Agencies may use a less demanding evidentiary standard than for the proof of the existence of efficiencies (heightened standard), because of the information problems arising in such analysis and also to avoid Agencies making a normative judgment by "second-guessing" business decisions to merger rather than combine in ways short of a merger.[128]

The lower courts

The litigation stage is reached when the Agencies have found the merger to be illegal. Consequently, efficiencies arguments will be denied by the Agencies when they are in court[129] and some commentators

120 N.A.A.G. Merger Guidelines, at ¶ 5.3.
121 Vakeriks, *Antitrust Basics* ¶ 9.04[6][c] (1994).
122 Kattan, "Efficiencies and merger analysis", 62 *Antitrust L. J.* 513, 514 (1994).
123 "Efficiencies and the failing firm in merger analysis—FTC staff recommendations", Report by the Federal Trade Commission Staff (May 1996), National Reports: [1996] 6 E.C.L.R. R-1548 (emphasis added).
124 Magleby, "Hospitals mergers and antitrust policy: arguments against a modification of current antitrust law", *Antitrust Bull.* 137, 173 (1996).
125 This requirement differs from the one occasionally imposed by the courts that the merger should be the least restrictive way of achieving the efficiencies (see: "Efficiencies and the failing firm in merger analysis—FTC staff recommendations", Report by the Federal Trade Commission Staff (May 1996), National Reports: [1996] 6 E.C.L.R. R-158.
126 Steptoe, "Efficiency justifications for hospital mergers", Remarks Before Practising Law Institute (F.T.C., 1994), at 13.
127 Magleby, "Hospitals mergers and antitrust policy: arguments against a modification of current antitrust law", *Antitrust Bull.* 137, 174 (1996).
128 Yao and Dahdouh, "Information problems in merger decision making and their impact on the development of an efficiencies defense", 62 *Antitrust L. J.* 23, 35–41 (1993) (these authors also suggest a lower evidentiary standard for the requirement that efficiency will be passed through to consumers).
129 In their statements, Agencies officials often limit the scope of the efficiencies defence to the prosecutorial discretion.

have even suggested that efficiency issues should only be presented before the Agencies.[130]

In the exercise of their prosecutorial discretion, the Agencies may give efficiency considerations a more important role, but as they do not disclose the reasons why they permitted the transactions to go forward, the importance of these considerations is difficult to estimate.[131] This first, non-public review could explain why efficiencies are not so important in court: when they are compelling, they are likely to be accepted at the agency level.[132]

Therefore, considering the evidentiary problems raised by the efficiency defence at the litigation stage, courts have been reluctant to make the formal trade-off between competitive effects and efficiencies.[133] Besides, the efficiencies provision of the Guidelines are legally irrelevant for the judges, who may still rely on the Supreme Court's restrictive standards of review.[134]

Despite these considerations, courts have in some instances been receptive to efficiency considerations.

The major case formally recognising the existence of an efficiencies defence is *University Health*.[135] In this hospital merger case, the 11th Circuit held:

> The appellees argue that the proposed acquisition would generate significant efficiencies and, therefore, would not substantially lessen competition. The FTC responds that the law recognizes no such efficiency defense in any form. We conclude that *in certain circumstances, a defendant may rebut the government's prima facie case with evidence showing that the intended merger would create significant efficiencies in the relevant market*. Here, however, the appellees have failed to . . . demonstrate that their transaction would yield any efficiencies.[136]

However, as the court was aware of the Supreme Court's restrictive precedents,[137] instead of using a trade-off approach (efficiencies v. anti-competitive effect), it fudged the issue by aligning efficiency with competition:

> It is clear that whether an acquisition would yield significant efficiencies in the relevant market in predicting [the competitive impact of the acquisition] . . . market share statistics . . . are not an end in themselves; rather, they are used to estimate the effect an intended transaction would have on competition. Thus, evidence that a proposed acquisition would create significant efficiencies benefiting consumers is useful in evaluating the ultimate issue—the *acquisition's overall effect on competition*.[138]

In *Carilion Health System*,[139] the court admitted defendants' evidence that the proposed merger would lead to at least a $40 million savings in capital avoidance and clinical and administrative efficiencies.[140] But its analysis is not informative because it is cursory and based on incomplete financial information by the court's own admission.[141] Besides, *Carilion* was not published and therefore lacks precedential authority.

The *Rockford*[142] case also dealt with a hospital merger, in a setting comparable to *Carilion*. The defendants argued before the District Court that the merger would generate benefits, both qualitative (the Rockford community would be provided with a state-of-the-art regional tertiary referral center) and quantitative (elimination of duplicative services and consolidation of programmes and insurance coverages).[143]

But the court, though recognising the reality of the efficiencies created by the merger,[144] refused to clear the transaction: relying on *Philadelphia National Bank*,[145] it considered "the defendants'

130 Williamson, "Economies as an antitrust defense revisited", 125 U. Pa. L. Rev. 699, 729–731 (1977). This standpoint is not accurate anymore: see: "Efficiencies and the failing firm in merger analysis—FTC staff recommendations", Report by the Federal Trade Commission Staff (May 1996), National Reports: [1996] 6 E.C.L.R. R–158 ("merging parties may be permitted to submit efficiency arguments favouring a merger at the agency review stage as well as in any court challenge").

131 Berg, "Cost efficiencies in the Section 7 calculus: a review of the doctrine", 37 *Case W. Res.* 218, 222 (1987).

132 Kattan, "Efficiencies and merger analysis", 62 *Antitrust L. J.* 513, 521 (1994).

133 *ibid.*

134 The Horizontal Guidelines are not binding for courts, though in some cases judges have strongly relied on them; the issue of whether the Agencies can depart from them—in litigation or even in the exercise of their prosecutorial discretion—is debated.

135 938 F.2d 1206 (1991).

136 *ibid.*, at 1221 (emphasis added).

137 The court, quoting *Procter & Gamble* and *Brown Shoe*, acknowledged the uncertainties surrounding the existence of an efficiencies defense (*ibid.*, at 1222).

138 *ibid.*, at 1222 (emphasis added).

139 707 F. Supp. 840 (W.D.Va), *aff'd without opinion*, 892 F.2d 1042 (4th Cir. 1989).

140 at 845–46.

141 See Matthew, "Doing what comes naturally: antitrust law and hospital mergers", 31 *Hous. L. Rev.* 813, 865 (1993).

142 *U.S. v. Rockford Memorial Corp.*, 717 F. Supp. 1251 (N.D. Ill. 1989), *aff'd*, 898 F. 2d 1278 (7th Cir.), *cert. denied*, 111 S. Ct. 295 (1990). For comments on *Rockford* and other not-for-profit hospital mergers cases, see Kopit and McCann, "Towards a definitive antitrust standard for nonprofit hospital mergers", 13 *Journal of Health Politics, Policy and Law* 635 (1988).

143 717 F. Supp. 1251, 1288.

144 *ibid.*

145 374 U.S. 321 (1963).

intention to create a state-of-the-art tertiary referral center and all its corresponding benefits in quality and community development as irrelevant for the present section 7 inquiry"[146] and also that the quantitative gains, described in a study "hastily commenced well after the announcement of the merger", were falling short of some Guideline requirements like the consideration of net efficiencies (the study showed a "lack of consideration for the expenses brought on by the proposed merger").[147]

However, the court did actually acknowledge the principle of an efficiency defence, although not applicable in that particular case in view of the fact that "the defendants have failed to clearly and convincingly demonstrate that the merger will, in fact, create a net economic benefit for the health care consumer".[148] In short, *Rockford* may be read as admitting the efficiency defence, but using a strict approach: "clear and convincing evidence" of the efficiencies has to be brought, sustained by precise dollar figures;[149] the extent of the "sufficient" efficiencies has to be determined under the more demanding "price standard". Besides, the court also held that the efficiencies had to be made possible through the merger and "in no other manner".[150]

Taken together, these cases offer little guidance concerning the operation of the efficiency defence in general and in hospital merger cases in particular, and "[its] judicial treatment has been inconsistent at best, and in some case plainly inaccurate".[151] The picture gets even murkier with the (isolated) *Imo Industries* case, which deviated from the general pattern adopted by lower courts: relying on *Philadelphia National Bank*, it enjoined a merger that would make the merging firms' production more "cost effective".[152]

Efficiency considerations in the legal literature

The status of the efficiency defence in U.S. antitrust is far from clear, as illustrated by the numerous disparate decisions of the courts and the Agencies. The current attitude of the federal enforcement authorities with respect to horizontal mergers seems thus open to efficiency arguments, but not as an absolute justification for anti-competitive mergers.

The various approaches of the efficiency defence are echoed in the doctrine, where numerous viewpoints on the issue have been expressed by antitrust commentators:

– Fisher and Lande ("implicit incorporation model"): these authors consider that a case-by-case evaluation of efficiencies v. anti-competitive effects of each transaction would be far too complex and impractical and instead propose an *implied efficiency defence*: firms should be granted the opportunity to realise efficiencies through mergers, which could be achieved by substantially raising the concentration thresholds above which a merger is presumed illegal (as, they think, did the 1982 Guidelines) or by the Agencies using their prosecutorial discretion to favour efficiency-boosting mergers.[153]

– Brodley: also noticing the problem of quantifying efficiencies, this author proposed another solution: a two-stage efficiency review, where an *ex post* inquiry would occur after a sufficient time had passed to allow the parties to realise the asserted efficiencies, accepted on their face at the initial stage.[154]

– Muris ("presumptive model"): this approach defends the idea that, as efficiencies cannot be adequately quantified, they should be presumed sufficient to overcome a presumption of illegality based on market shares, provided that they are "substantial"; therefore, an efficiency defence should be incorporated directly into Agencies' and judicial analysis of mergers.[155]

– Williamson ("naive trade-off model"): having observed that efficiency and concentration are only loosely correlated, O. Williamson defined the task of antitrust enforcers as a case-by-case determination of the efficiencies to result from the merger, and then a balance of these gains against the likely reduction of consumers' welfare, identified as the potential for price increase and/or quality decrease caused by the market power of the new entity. But the author argues, through the controversial "partial equilibrium" model, that a merger resulting in even small

146 717 F. Supp. 1251, 1288.

147 *ibid.*, at 1289.

148 *ibid.*, at 1291.

149 Matthew, "Doing what comes naturally: antitrust law and hospital mergers", 31 *Hous. L. Rev.* 813, 865 (1993).

150 at 1289; this merger-specific requirement is also present in Section 4 of the Guidelines.

151 Matthew, "Doing what comes naturally: antitrust law and hospital mergers", 31 *Hous. L. Rev.* 813, 865–866 (1993).

152 *FTC v. Imo Indus. Inc.*, 1992–2 Trade Reg. Rep. (CCH) ¶ 69,943 at 68,560 (D.D.C. 1989).

153 Fisher and Lande, "Efficiency considerations in merger enforcement", 71 *Calif. L. Rev.* 1582, 1650 (1983).

154 Brodley, "The economic goals of antitrust: efficiency, consumer welfare, and technological progress", 62 N.Y.U.L. Rev. 1020, 1048.

155 Muris, "The efficiency defense under Section 7 of the Clayton Act", 30 *Case W. Res. L. Rev.* 381 (1980).

average cost decreases (5 to 10 per cent) can produce societal benefits as long as price increases are not greater than 20 or 40 per cent, depending on the elasticity of demand.[156]

– Pitofsky: appointed at the FTC under the Clinton Administration, Robert Pitofsky is open to the efficiency defence on a "probabilistic tradeoff approach" resembling the one used in the *Honickman* decision.[157] In his view, the defence should be allowed "where the likelihood of realizing efficiencies is maximized and the likelihood of consumer injury as a result of an increase in market power is minimized". The author proposes an absolute efficiency defence "in any market where postmerger concentration is moderate, and the combined company after the merger would hold less than thirty-five per cent of the market", but "only if the defendants can clearly support the claim that production efficiencies leading to a substantial reduction in unit costs will result and these efficiencies could not be achieved through a much less restrictive alternative".[158] The requirement that parties must prove that efficiencies will be passed along to consumers should therefore be rejected, Mr. Pitofsky arguing that it would prevent consideration of an efficiencies defence in most cases where it would make a difference.[159] Without surprise, this is also the current position of the FTC.[160]

The European Union

The relevant decisions of the Commission

As discussed above, there is no "efficiency defence" as such in the E.U. Merger Regulation, and it is not clear to what extent the Commission may consider "technical and economic progress" when appraising a merger.[161] Until now, there has been no decision from the Court of Justice on this issue and this factor has only played a minor role in the Commission enforcement, with only a few rulings discussing whether a concentration will achieve such progress.[162]

In its few relevant decisions, the Commission efficiency arguments were inconsistently handled, sometimes as a potential source of dominance, and maybe in one case as a potential (if practically negligible) defence.[163]

In the *AT&T/NCR* case,[164] possible synergies between the merging parties (the development of "more advanced communication features at a lower cost") were considered as potentially "creat(ing) or strengthen(ing) a dominant position".[165] Efficiencies were thus viewed as a negative factor[166] but their role was not addressed, as dominance was not found in that case.[167]

The landmark case on efficiencies remains the *Aérospatiale–Alenia/de Havilland*,[168] in which the counsel for the parties argued that one of the objectives of the merger was to reduce costs.[169] The Commission held that:

> The potential cost savings . . . amount to only some ECU 5 million per year. According to the estimates of the parties' economic consultants, these cost savings to the combined entity would arise from rationalizing parts procurement, marketing and product support. *Without prejudice as to whether such considerations are relevant for assessment under Article 2 of the Merger Regulation*, such cost savings would have a negligible impact on the overall operation of ATR/de Havilland, amounting to around 0.5% of the combined turnover. The parties have identified (although not quantified) costs savings which could be made by de Havilland's internal operation. *These cost savings*

156 Williamson, "Economies as an antitrust defense: the welfare tradeoffs", 58 *Am Econ. Rev.* 18, 21–23, (1968).
157 *Harold A. Honickman*, F.T.C. Docket No. 9233 (Nov. 16, 1992) 5 Trade Reg. Rep. (CCH) ¶ 23, 286 (Letter from F.T.C. Secretary D. Clark to P. Greene).
158 n. 159 below, at 207.
159 Pitofsky, "Proposals for revised United States merger enforcement in a global economy", 81 Geo. L.J. 195, 217 (1992).
160 "Efficiencies and the failing firm in merger analysis—FTC staff recommendations", Report by the Federal Trade Commission Staff (May 1996), National Reports: [1996] 6 E.C.L.R. R–158 ("the proposed framework does not require proof that efficiency related savings be passed immediately on to the customer").
161 Neven, Nuttall and Seabright, *The Economics and Politics of European Merger Control* 116 (1993).
162 Hawk and Huser, *E.C. Merger Control: a Practitioner's Guide* 265 (1996).
163 *ibid.*, at 77.
164 Case IV/M.050 (Decision of January 18, 1991).
165 On this issue, see Jenny, "EEC merger control: economies as an antitrust defense or an antitrust attack?", in 1992 *Fordham Corp L. Inst.* 591 (B. Hawk ed., 1993), and Cohen-Tanugi, Encaoua, Winckler, Siragusa and Brunet, *La Pratique Communautaire du Contrôle des Concentrations* 83 (1996). Comp. with the *Brown Shoe* decision of the Supreme Court, quoted above.
166 A similar concern was expressed in cases where joint ventures were providing a competitive advantage to the venturers (see, *e.g.* the *Dräger/IBM/HMP, Pan Am/Delta* and *Sextant/BGT–VDO* cases).
167 Jones and Gonzales-Diaz, *The EEC Merger Regulation* 157 (1992).
168 Case IV/M.053 (October 2, 1991), [1991] O.J. L334/42.
169 One could wonder why the counsel raised such an argument despite the existing hostile approach of the Commission toward efficiencies.

> *would not arise as a consequence of the concentration per se*, but are cost savings which could be achieved by de Havilland's existing owner or by any other potential acquirer. . . . For the above reasons, the Commission does not consider that the proposed concentration would contribute to the development of technical and economic progress within the meaning of Article 2(1)(b) of the Merger Regulation. Even if there was such progress, this would not be to the consumers' advantage. The consumers will be faced with a dominant position which combines the most popular aircraft families on the market. Choice will be significantly reduced.[170]

This holding has been subject to various interpretations by commentators. Some saw the decision as a clear rejection of the "technical and economic progress" argument (or *progress test*) of Article 2(1)(b) in merger analysis and an affirmation that "competition is the central yardstick according to which (the Commission) will interpret the Merger Regulation".[171]

Based on the text of the decision, though, it seems possible to infer that the Commission did not rule out the possibility of efficiency arguments in its appraisal of mergers ("Without prejudice as to whether such considerations are relevant for assessment under Article 2 . . ."). Furthermore, the Commission gives some indications of the requirements that this type of defence would face:

- cost savings should be substantial:[172] the parties claimed cost savings amounting to 0.5 per cent of the combined turnover.
- the burden of proof should rest on the parties:[173] cost savings were merely identified ("although not quantified") by the consultant hired by the merging firms.
- efficiencies should be "merger specific": the fact that "these cost savings would not arise as a consequence of the concentrations *per se*" and could be achieved through other means was retained as a negative factor.
- efficiencies should be "at consumers' advantage": this requirement is expressly mandated by the text of Article 2(1)(b) of the Merger Regulation. The Commission correctly noted that the dominant position which would be obtained as a result of the transaction would result in less choice for consumers and an incentive to raise prices.

Interestingly, the decision mentions that "the parties have not claimed that cost savings will arise from combining the research and development activities . . .",[174] and therefore the alleged economies would have mostly consisted of rationalisation of basic operational costs ("parts procurements, marketing and product support") without enhancing the potential for innovation of the new entity.

The last decisions on the issue do not really help to further define a consistent standard for the consideration of efficiencies.

In *Accor/Wagon-Lits*,[175] the "technical and economic progress" factor was invoked by Accor, which claimed that the merger would enable it to improve personnel training and modernise certain facilities.

The Commission dismissed this argument because (i) there was insufficient evidence of the efficiencies; (ii) even assuming such effects, there was no claim or showing that these benefits would outweigh the anti-competitive effects of the concentration; and (iii) given the highly inelastic demand of customers for motorway catering services, there was no indication that these purported benefits would be passed on to consumers.

In its *MSG/Media Service* decision[176] the Commission again confirmed that the reference in Article 2(1)(b) to the development of technical and economic progress was subject to the reservation that no obstacle is formed to competition.[176a]

The rather short rationale used to dismiss this argument was that the technical progress likely to be achieved (this point was acknowledged by the Commission) would in fact be offset by the hindering of the competition resulting from the "sealing-off" and "early creation of a dominant position" foreseeable on the market for pay-TV as a consequence of the merger.

In *Mercedes-Benz/Kässbohrer*,[177] the Commission briefly dismissed, without evaluative comment, the parties' claim that the merger would produce

170 at 65 (emphasis added).
171 Hawkes, "The EC Merger Control Regulation: not an industrial policy instrument: the de Havilland decision", [1992] 1 E.C.L.R. 34, 37.
172 Jones and Gonzales-Diaz, *The EEC Merger Regulation* 158 (1992).
173 *ibid*.
174 at 66.
175 Case IV/M.126 (April 28, 1992), [1992] O.J. L204/1, at ¶ 26(2)(f).
176 Case IV/M.469 (November 9, 1994), [1994] O.J. L364/1, at ¶¶ 100–101.
176a Waelbroeck and Frignani, 4 *Commentaire J. Megret – Le Droit de la CE (Concurrence)* (1997), 901.
177 Case IV/M.477 (Feb. 14, 1995), [1995] O.J. L211/1, at ¶ 66.

several economic synergies (R&D, production, purchasing and administrative cost savings).

The rejection was mainly a consequence of the lack of sufficient evidence to establish that the alleged synergies would in fact have been obtained as a result of the transaction.

Finally, in the *Mannesmann/Vallourec/Ilva* decision[178] (joint-venture for the production of seamless stainless steel tubes), it seems that the Commission implicitly relied on efficiency and industrial policy considerations, and also paid attention to the competition from undertakings located outside the E.U. (*in casu*, Japanese and East European competitors). Indeed, the Commission noted as *obiter dictum* that the merger would help the parties to reduce production overcapacity and achieve plant specialisation.[179]

In conclusion, it seems that for the time being, economic efficiencies are unlikely to play a decisive role in the vast majority of the merger reviews conducted by the Commission.[180]

However, they remain "a potential weapon to defend a merger or acquisition raising competition concerns, at least in those circumstances where there is strong evidence of substantial synergies that can only be realized as a result of the proposed concentration"[181] and maybe "in cases raising oligopolistic dominance issues".[182] Besides, the need for restructuring may also be taken into account by the Commission if it is supported by convincing evidence,[183] as was probably the case in *Shell/Montecatini*[184] or *ICI/Du Pont*.[185]

178 Case IV/M.315 (Jan. 31, 1994), [1994] O.J. L102/15.
179 See Cohen-Tanugi, Encaoua, Winckler, Siragusa and Brunet, *La Pratique Communautaire du Contrôle des Concentrations* 82–83 (1996) (the authors note that in this case, there may have been a disagreement between the MTF/DGIV and the Commissioners, the former advocating a strong competition-driven analysis while the later were more receptive to industrial policy considerations).
180 Cook and Kerse, *E.C. Merger Control* 167 (1996) ("there seems to be no scope for such benefits to be taken into account in the appraisal process. However, a well-proven case explaining the need for restructuring could well persuade the Commissioners, if not the Merger Task Force, to give the undertakings concerned the benefit of the doubt or to feel disposed to accept remedial undertakings in order that the transaction can proceed").
181 Hawk and Huser, *E.C. Merger Control: a Practitioner's Guide* 269 (1996).
182 See Warner, "Efficiencies and merger review in Canada, the European Community and the United States: implications for convergence and harmonization", 26 *Vanderbilt J. Transnat'l L.* 1059, 1099 (1994).
183 Cook and Kerse, *E.C. Merger Control* 167 (1996).
184 [1994] O.J. L332/48.
185 [1993] O.J. L7/13.

In the future, the standards for assessing efficiency arguments should be expressed more clearly[186] and could be derived from the holding of *Alenia/de Havilland*. But as is the case in the United States, the requirement that benefits should ultimately be passed on to consumers may be the greatest obstacle to the admission of an efficiency defence.

Indeed, former Commissioner Leon Brittan once expressed the view that in the cases where there will be a *clear* finding of dominance, the "debilitating effect" of monopoly will generally prevent product innovation and charge a "monopoly rent" on consumers.[187] In the other situations where dominance would be less obvious, the merger should normally be cleared without special justifications and allow the transaction to generate efficiencies, because only concentrations as a result of which competition would be "significantly" impeded are deemed illegal.[188]

Conclusion

Comparison between U.S. and E.U. approaches towards efficiency arguments

The efficiency arguments apparently play a sharply different role in the two jurisdictions. While the efficiency defence is increasingly prevalent and explicitly acknowledged in the assessment of mergers by the U.S. courts and agencies, the European Commission has been reluctant and even hostile to such claims.

Both American and European authorities have been carrying out merger enforcement rather leniently. This is in line with the philosophy embodied in the relevant provisions, prohibiting only mergers "the effect of (which) may be to *substantially* lessen competition"[189] in the United States, or "as a result of which effective competition would be *significantly* impeded"[190] in the European Union.

But to exercise this control they have used divergent patterns of analysis which in turn have shaped the role and strength of efficiencies arguments.

186 See Cohen-Tanugi, Encaoua, Winckler, Siragusa and Brunet, *La Pratique Communautaire du Contrôle des Concentrations* 83 (1996) (*"les considérations de politique industrielle et d'efficience économique peuvent parfois, dans des circonstances exceptionnelles, être également prises en compte. Il est toutefois dommageable que de tels objectifs ne soient pas clairement explicités et interviennent de manière inavouée dans la décision d'autorisation"*).
187 See former Competition Commissioner Sir Leon Brittan, Speech at the Centre for European Policy Studies (Brussels, September 24, 1990), reported in [1990] E.L.R. at 351.
188 Regulation 4064/89, Article 2(3).
189 Section 7 of the Clayton Act (emphasis added).
190 Regulation 4064/89, Article 2(3) (emphasis added).

As they place a great emphasis on market shares as a presumption of illegality, the U.S. Horizontal Guidelines had to pay attention to other factors in order to rectify or recalibrate their assessment when a merger represents the only possibility of achieving significant efficiencies, provided that these efficiencies are sufficient to offset the anti-competitive effects resulting from the increase in concentration.

European control deals with mergers in a more flexible fashion by performing an ad hoc, factual inquiry to review a wide range of factors affecting competition in the relevant market; and it is only when the competitive harm is blatant that the transaction will be barred; accordingly, the efficiency argument only arises in cases where there is a clear risk that the post-merger firm would be in a position to exercise market power.

It can therefore be concluded that, despite appearances, efficiencies may play a roughly identical role in the future in the two systems, though under different forms:[191] in the United States, they can redeem an otherwise objectionable merger according to a sliding-scale standard, making it practically impossible to triumph when the post-merger market is extremely concentrated; in the European Union, they would only appear at the end of the scale, where the transaction raises significant competitive concerns.[192]

In the latter situation, there could arguably be room for an efficiency defence which would be weighed by the Commission according to standards comparable to those set forth in the U.S. Horizontal Guidelines. The *Aérospatiale-Alenia/de Havilland* decision, though declaring the merger incompatible with the common market, entertained the (weak) efficiencies argument sustained by the parties and briefly alluded to a series of factors which could augur the future content of an efficiency defence: that the efficiencies be proved by the parties, significant, merger-specific and to consumers' advantage.

One Commission official once suggested that the Commission should, in the exercise of its prosecutorial discretion and as a matter of public policy, have regard for the "progress factor" in close cases, "when it is unclear whether a concentration creates or strengthens a dominant position or significantly impedes effective competition" and when the progress is substantial or strategically important for the European industry.[193] Yet this standpoint remains out of step with the prevailing view that merger control is purely competition-driven.[194]

Although both the U.S. and the E.U. approaches towards efficiency make sense when one takes into account the differences in the appraisal procedures, we have seen that the status of the efficiency defence in the analytical framework and its policy grounds remain rather unclear.[195]

The reasons for this inconsistency, *i.e.* whether cognisable efficiencies should serve as an absolute defence to antitrust enforcement against mergers, or as a mitigating factor that could influence a finding of illegality in a close case, have been explored by some authors in the United States:

The trade-off may not be fully understood. The tendency to align competitive and efficiency effects in particular cases "may be a useful analytical device so long as it is understood that the two effects are linked only loosely, as Williamson has shown that *a merger may both reduce competition and enhance efficiency* . . . in other words, *at least some cases may call for a tradeoff between a competitive market structure and . . . efficiency*".[197]

Politically sensitive implications of the tradeoff. Explicitly yielding competition and inter-firm rivalry for expected efficiencies may be politically difficult in some cases and therefore courts or agencies may have an incentive to disguise the trade-off by using the efficiency gains to bolster the appreciation of the competitive risks.

Uncertainties surrounding the efficiencies analysis. A reliable theoretical model for the evaluation of efficiencies has not been proposed yet, though economists have been working steadily on the issue.[198]

191 It is important to note, however, that the assessment of the role of efficiencies in merger appraisal is made difficult by the lack of transparency in the decision-making process of the enforcement authorities in both the E.U. and the U.S.

192 There is an analogy between the E.U. procedure and the implicit incorporation model of Fisher and Lande ("Efficiency considerations in merger enforcement", 71 *Calif. L. Rev.* 1582 (1983)) which suggested that by raising the concentration thresholds, the Agencies would implicitly admit an efficiency defence by allowing the parties to achieve the efficiency gains inherent to all mergers.

193 Langeheine, "Substantive review under the EEC Merger Regulation", paper presented to 1990 Fordham Corporate Law Institute, at 15.

194 Fine, "The appraisal criteria of the EC Merger Control Regulation", [1991] E.C.L.R. 148, 155.

195 Pitofsky, "Proposals for revised United States merger enforcement in a global economy", 81 Geo. L.J. 195, 205 (1992).

196 Stockum, "The efficiencies defense for horizontal mergers: what is the government's standard?", 61 *Antitrust L. J.* 829, 849 (1993).

197 Kattan, "Efficiencies and merger analysis", 62 *Antitrust L. J.* 513, at 519 (1994) (emphasis added).

198 Stockum, "The efficiencies defense for horizontal mergers: what is the government's standard?", *61 Antitrust L. J.* 829, 841–855 (1993).

Some commentators have suggested that Congress should enact legislative guidelines to settle the treatment of the efficiency defence, to reduce the differences between the Agencies' and courts' approaches[199] (resulting in lower uncertainties and thus lower transaction cost) and to prevent the Agencies from being influenced by current political thinking.[200] Besides, it could prevent the emergence of extraneous industry-specific factors or exemptions in the merger assessment (advocated by some industries and authors[201]), by reconsidering the way efficiencies are being dealt with.[202]

These inconsistencies in the theoretical definition of the efficiency defence may, in this writer's view, be reconciled if one tries to figure out what is the essence of antitrust. As Judge Bork once observed, "antitrust policy cannot be made rational until we are able to give a firm answer to one question: what is the point of the law, what are its goals? Everything else follows from the answer we give . . . Only when the issue of goals has been settled is it possible to frame a coherent body of substantive rules."[203]

The bottom line of my reasoning is that *consumer welfare* must be regarded as the very purpose of the current competition policies in the United States and the European Union.[204]

The consequence to be drawn from this assumption is that mergers must be allowed as long as they do not result in higher prices and/or lower quality for consumers. The instrument the European and American legislators retained to fulfil this objective was *inter-firm rivalry*, because concentrated markets were precisely found to generate price increases and/or quality decreases.[205] Inter-firm rivalry can be equated with the technical definition of *competition*, as determined by market share and other numerical data.

But although the welfare of consumers will often be secured by a vigorous inter-firm rivalry,[206] in some circumstances competition can prevent firms from achieving *efficiencies* they could otherwise realise. Sometimes, this may be at consumers' detriment, and especially when these efficiencies would have resulted in better product or services through synergies or integration between firms engaged in the same business.

Therefore, when a merger is potentially anti-competitive, a *trade-off* between competition and efficiencies should be accepted, but only in limited cases: when the efficiencies are substantial, cannot be obtained through other means and, more importantly, *will be passed on to consumers*. This last requirement imposes on the merging firms the burden to prove that the operation will entail benefits for consumers, like lower prices, better products or improved service. Such evidence should preferably result from *ex ante* corporate documents rather than from outside counsel reports prepared after the completion of the transaction.

This understanding of the mechanism and goal of competition by American and European authorities seems to comply with the relevant provisions and could help the efficiencies defence play an expanded role in the future.[207] The remaining issues are: up to what level of concentration should an efficiency defence be accepted, and should it depend on the type of industry involved? Nowadays, these questions are strongly debated among authors.

The current debate about the scope of efficiency defense

The position of the Agencies towards efficiency arguments is, as we have seen, intermediate: efficiencies are considered as a qualitative factor for merger appraisal, but they may not explicitly redeem an otherwise prohibited merger. Some

199 Berg, "Cost efficiencies in the Section 7 calculus: a review of the doctrine", 37 *Case W. Res.* 218, 266 (1987).
200 *ibid.*, at 269.
201 See Matthew, "Doing what comes naturally: antitrust law and hospital mergers", 31 *Hous. L. Rev.* 813 (1993) (proposing a natural monopoly standard for hospital mergers).
202 Stockum, "The efficiencies defense for horizontal mergers: what is the government's standard?", 61 *Antitrust L. J.* 829, 849 (1993).
203 Bork, *The Antitrust Paradox: a Policy at War with itself*, 50 (1978, reissued 1993).
204 This assumption has been made by several authors: see Afonso, "A catalogue of merger defenses under European and United States antitrust Law", 33 *Harv. L. Rev.* 1, 32 (1992); 4 Phillip Arreeda & Donald F. Turner, *Antitrust Law* ¶ 940 (1980).
205 In either monopoly or oligopoly situations, as in the first the monopoly can charge supra-competitive prices, and in the second illegal co-ordination among competitors (like price-fixing) is favoured.

206 There is evidence that where the markets are concentrated, the prices tend to be higher, although it is still difficult to determine if the profits are strongly related to the concentration: see Pautler and O'Quinn, "Recent empirical evidence on mergers and acquisitions", 38 *Antitrust Bull.* 741, 770–772 (1993); for a survey of mergers in the U.K., Hughes, "Mergers and economic performance in the U.K.: a survey of the empirical evidence 1950–1990, in *European Mergers and Merger Policy* (Oxford University Press, 1993).
207 Kattan, "Efficiencies and merger analysis", 62 *Antitrust L. J.* 513, 534 (1994). Some countries have already adopted a bold approach of efficiencies and expressly permitted a full-fledged efficiency defence, like Canada or Germany.

authors have criticized this approach as being too restrictive, others as too lenient.

Supporters of a full-fledged efficiency defence consider that in some instances efficiencies may justify allowing a merger that creates market power because the merger is demonstrably necessary to sustain incentives for innovation or to bring the benefits of significant innovation to market more quickly.[208] In the same direction, a recent study by G. Robert and S. Salop concluded that efficiency gains resulting from mergers have consistently been overlooked: the argument is that the efficiencies achieved by the new firm are often "emulated" by competitors, and the "diffusion" of the progress generated by the merger constitutes a clear benefit for society as a whole, including consumers; consequently, one should be more open to efficiency claims in considering the effects of mergers on competition.[209] The "innovation market" approach in merger analysis could thus help sharpen the focus on technological advancement, so critical to the continued growth of the economy.[210]

Furthermore, the wave of industry restructuring (*e.g.* health care, defence, banks, high technology) has put some pressure on the Agencies, calling into question the relevance of antitrust enforcement and seeking legislative relief. It is sometimes argued that economies of scale and scope are so great in these industries that, as a matter of fact, mergers should be allowed even though they contravene normal antitrust standards.[211]

However, this view is strongly opposed by authoritative authors, who consider that "antitrust policy for high-technology industries does not require the overhaul of the familiar analytic principles of antitrust", because the public policy focus should be on preserving and fostering competition for the ultimate benefit of consumers.[212] Other antitrust lawyers and economists have proposed a more aggressive enforcement, based on recent economic researches showing that mergers may lead to market power and misallocation of resources even when concentration is moderately high, and, in addition, that "it does not appear that mergers are particularly successful in attaining efficiencies".[213] For Sherer and Ross, "statistical evidence supporting the hypothesis that profitability and efficiency increase following mergers is at best weak".[214]

In conclusion, current economic analysis makes it impossible to show with mathematical precision that more generous treatment of efficiency claims would offset anti-competitive effects from a merger.[215] Therefore, and until legal or economic analysis becomes more adequate to the task, it is difficult to decide on the merits of the efficiency defence. At the current stage, one could only suggest the adoption of an absolute efficiency in moderately concentrated markets, allowing mergers where "the likelihood of efficiencies is extremely high and the likelihood of anticompetitive effects relatively low".[216]

The efficiency defence in a global market

American and European firms will increasingly be confronted by aggressive foreign firms in global markets where success depends critically upon

208 See Sunshine (Deputy Assistant Attorney General, Antitrust Division-DoJ), "Initiatives in merger and joint venture analysis", Address before the 33rd Antitrust Conference, reprinted in 23 *Journal of Reprints for Antitrust Law and Economics* 531 (1994).

209 Quoted by Kattan, "Efficiencies and merger analysis", 62 *Antitrust L. J.* 513, 527 (1994); see also Stockum, "The efficiencies defense for horizontal mergers: what is the government's standard?," 61 *Antitrust L. J.* 829 (1993) (study concluding that very modest efficiency gains can outweigh competitive losses from mergers).

210 Gilbert and Sunshine, "Incorporating dynamic efficiency concerns in merger analysis: the use of innovation markets", 63 *Antitrust L. J.* 569, 601 (1995) (for a review of the economic literature on the topic).

211 Paschall, "Antitrust and hospital mergers: a law and economics rationale for exemption", 30:39 *Duquesne L. Rev.* 61, (arguing that in view of the unique nature of the hospital market, the enforcement authorities should "permit all hospital mergers under a general exemption as *per se* legal"); Afonso, "A catalogue of merger defenses under European and United States antitrust Law", 33 *Harv. L. Rev.* 1, 53–55 (1992) (the author writes that the advantage of pooling extremely expensive R & D resources in the telecommunication and integrated circuits market seems to have been a decisive consideration in the Commission's approval of the 1989 takeover bid of Plessey by GEC and Siemens).

212 Ordover, "Competition policy for high-technology industries", 26 *Busin. Lawyer* 479 at 481 (1996).

213 Thompson, "A proposal for antitrust merger enforcement reform: repudiating judge Bork in favor of current economic learning", 41 *Antitrust Bull.* 79, 136 (1996). The author proposes a return to the 1968 Guidelines approach, considering efficiencies only "in exceptional circumstances" (*id.*, at 122).

214 Sherer and Ross, "Industrial market structure and economic performance", 174 (3rd ed. 1990). See also Mueller, "U.S. merger policy and the 1982 guidelines", 8 *Rev. Ind. Org.* 151, 153 (1993).

215 Mueller, "US merger policy and the 1982 merger guidelines", 8 *Rev. Ind. Org.* 151, 153 (1993 (for evidence that mergers may lead to a *decrease* in efficiency).

216 Pitofsky, "Proposals for revised United States merger enforcement in a global economy", 81 Geo. L.J. 195, 250 (1992).

productivity and innovation.[217] To what extent must foreign competition be taken into account when assessing mergers? May firms be authorised to merge to be more efficient on international markets or, as some have contended, is antitrust antagonistic to competitiveness?[218]

The European Union Merger Regulation provides that among the relevant factors for merger appraisal there is "the actual or potential competition from undertakings located either within or outside the Community".[219] This criterion has created some controversies among Member States,[220] some arguing that this language implies the possibility of increasing the competitiveness of European enterprises at the expense of competition within the European Union.[221]

But the creation of such "European champions", favoured by southern European states, has been rejected by northern countries as an undesirable intervention of industrial policy considerations in a free trade, competition-driven control.[222] This last view triumphed in the *Aérospatiale-Alenia/de Havilland* decision, reflecting the view of Sir Leon Brittan that a competitive world market cannot justify a dominant position within the Community.[223]

Competition Commissioner Van Miert seems to have adopted a more flexible view than his predecessor Brittan: he has said that "competition should evolve and develop in close relationship with the legal, economic, political and social context in which it is found. Community competition policy should not be seen as an end in itself, but rather as an instrument for the development of the objectives of the Treaty of Rome".[224] However, many companies still complain that Mr Van Miert's enforcement policy "works to the disadvantage of European businesses trying to survive in the global marketplace".[225]

In the United States, concerns about a potential negative impact of antitrust on international competitiveness of American businesses arose in the 1980, with some scholars supporting the creation of broad "safe harbours" to allow co-operation among competitors.[226] Others have criticised this position, considering that contemporary antitrust allows efficiency-driven competitor collaboration, *i.e.* promotion of efficiencies in the field of R&D (but not naked horizontal price fixing, production and territorial restraints or boycotts).[227] As Mr Pitofsky notes, Chairman of the FTC:[228]

> There is a widespread belief that American R&D efforts have not kept pace with other countries, particularly Japan and Germany. Surprisingly, a leading scapegoat for these failures is antitrust enforcement. The charge is surprising because American antitrust enforcement aimed at R&D alliances has been extremely lenient. For example, in the 102 years since the Sherman Act has been on the books, there has been exactly one government challenge to an R&D joint venture.

Furthermore, empirical evidence seems to refute the belief that "big is better" and instead shows that decentralised economic structures are important to stimulate innovation,[229] and excessive yielding of domestic rivalry has even been identified as a cause of loss of national advantage.[230]

In the recent Boeing/McDonnell merger, the latter position was endorsed by the FTC, which denied speculation that it cleared the $13.3 billion merger

217 The globalisation of the markets also triggers important jurisdiction issues which are beyond the scope of this article; for a good overview, see Halverson, "Harmonization and coordination of international merger procedures", 60 *Antitrust L.J.* 531 (1992); for a statement of the current Agencies' policy, see Department of Justice, Draft Antitrust Enforcement Guidelines for International Operations, 59 Fed. Reg. 52,810 (October 1994). See also Griffin, "Special international antitrust doctrines and defenses", 60 *Antitrust L. J.* 543 (1992).

218 See Goldschmid, "Is antitrust antagonistic to American competitiveness? antitrust, innovation, and competitiveness" (book review), 93 *Colum. L. Rev.* 1572 (1993).

219 Article 2(1)(a).

220 National authorities may adopt a specific view on the issue, and allow international competition to be considered as a factor justifying the merger (*e.g.* in Belgium: see 93–94 Activity Report of the Competition Council, at 53–54).

221 Fine, "The appraisal criteria of the E.C. Merger Control Regulation", 4 E.C.L.R. 148, 154 [1991].

222 Picat and Zachmann, "Community monitoring of concentration operations", 6 E.C.L.R. 240, 246 [1993].

223 Brittan, "The law and policy of Merger Control in the EEC", 15 E.L.R. 351 (1990).

224 Quoted by Picat and Zachmann, "Community monitoring of concentration operations", E.C.L.R. 240, 246 [1993].

225 Murray, "Will EU really split off antitrust powers?", *Wall Street Journal Europe*, May 28, 1996.

226 See Goldschmid, "Is antitrust antagonistic to American competitiveness? antitrust, innovation, and competitiveness" (book review), 93 *Colum. L. Rev.* 1572 (1993), quoting Jorde and Teece. Another way of looking at the issue is to consider the size of the relevant market and, by expanding it, to reduce the market share of the post-merger firm.

227 *ibid.*

228 Pitofsky, "Proposals for revised antitrust enforcement in a global economy", 81 Geo. L. J. 195, 241 (1992).

229 See Shepherd, "Antitrust repelled, inefficiency endured: lessons of IBM and General Motors for future antitrust policies", 39 *Antitrust Bulletin* 203 (1994) (concluding that antitrust leniency toward concentration during the 1980s was a mistake because, as IBM and GM problems illustrate, structure has mattered and X-inefficiencies have exceeded scale economies in importance).

230 Porter, *The Competitive Advantage of Nations* 169 (1990).

because the United States needed a "national champion" to compete internationally, and stated: "we do not have the discretion to authorize anticompetitive but 'good' mergers because they may be thought to advance the United States trade interests".[231]

At the end of the day, one may express the wish that the world's two main antitrust jurisdictions will ultimately move towards an international framework of competition rules,[232] in which efficiency analysis would be handled in a coherent and politically sound fashion, in order to ensure consumers' welfare on a global scale.

231 Dunne and Tucker, "Boeing and McDonnell merger approved", *Financial Times*, July 2, 1997.

232 See Brittan and Van Miert, "Towards an international framework of competition rules", 24 *Bus. Lawyer* 454 (1996) and Fox and Ordover, "Internationalising competition law to limit parochial state and private action: moving towards the vision of world welfare", 24 *Bus. Lawyer* 458 (1996).

Part IV
Competition Law and the Global Economy

[21]

The Dilemma of Regulating International Competition under the WTO System

Ignacio De León

Introduction

The increasing interdependence and globalisation of the world economy has decisively influenced the nature of international relations among states. Particularly, the notion of sovereignty that emerged with the rise of the national state during the sixteenth and seventeenth centuries has tended to become blurred as a consequence of the marked economic integration among domestic economies occurring since 1945.

New communication technologies have erased former barriers to economic exchange; as a consequence, governments are increasingly running into difficulties in exercising their formerly uncontested powers of sovereignty.[1] Indeed, the evaluation of conflicts whose causes are ultimately originated abroad has induced some states (most notably, the United States) to exercise their jurisdiction beyond their borders, thus creating a conflict with the conventional principle of territoriality under international law. In sum, economic integration and globalisation of the world economy has led to a redefinition of the boundaries of sovereign powers, as described by Pescatore.[2]

Increasingly, the new reality has brought about the need to revise those regulations simultaneously affecting multiple jurisdictions. Ultimately, the issue at stake is whether states can co-ordinate their surveillance over international economic transactions, and whether it is convenient to do so.

The need to reconsider international regulation over economic transactions inevitably uncovers significant problems stemming from the particular nature and importance attached by policy makers to these regulations. These ideas entail entrenched principles about state intervention and individual freedom, and are therefore doomed to conflict. Additionally, the very nature of the phenomenon creates further challenges to the task of harmonising these views. The international economic order, like any other economic order, emerges from the consensus of its participants. This is frequently ignored by policy makers, who assume that public policy goals may be set and reached independently from the will of those affected by these rules.

The problems are increased because the international order lacks a supranational authority to which to refer the conflicts that might arise among its participants. At best, there are sets of imperfect rules loosely defining their terms of enforcement as well as the conditions by which economic agents may reasonably expect others to honour their commitments.[3] These gaps and imperfections in the legal setting encourage opportunistic behaviour from its participants, particularly in the form of protectionism; they can only be resolved through complex and tiresome international negotiations.

This article explores these problems in the light of the challenges arising from the proposed international regulation of competition through antitrust rules.[4] In particular, it examines the proposals aimed

Ignacio De León, Attorney, LL.M. (Lon), M. Phil. (Lon).

1 An explanation of the process of globalisation and its consequences over the international legal system is found in A. Avila, J. Castillo-Urrutia and M. Diaz-Mier, *Regulación del Comercio Internacional tras La Ronda Uruguay*, Editorial Tecnos, Madrid, 1994, pp. 170–179, 209. See also E. J. Mestmacker, "Maintaining Competition", in *International Harmonization of Competition Laws*, C.-J. Cheng *et al.* (eds.), Martinus Nijhoff Publishers, London, 1995, pp. 3–9.

2 P. Pescatore, *Le droit de l'intégration: émergence d'un phénomène nouveau dans les relations internationales selon l'expérience des Communautés Européennes*, A. W. Sijthoff, Leiden, 1972.

3 Such imperfection allows Doern, for example, to distinguish between two different sets of rules in the international sphere, which he names as "regimes" and "institutions". He defines the former as the "array of informal co-operative relationships not centered on specific formal organizations and do not involve binding rules and dispute settlement", whereas the latter "refer to the more entrenched system of values more often centred around organizations." (B. Doern, "The Internationalization of Competition Policy", in *Comparative Competition Policy: National Institutions in a Global Market*, G. B. Doern and S. Wilks (eds.), Clarendon Press, Oxford, 1996, pp. 303–305. Yet even the more integrated set of institutions are frequently characterised by a lesser degree of enforceability if compared to domestic jurisdictions. This is precisely the dilemma of regulation in international economic relations.

4 In this work, we use the term "antitrust policy" as it is traditionally referred to by U.S. authorities and following the practice of the majority of OECD countries, as "the body of laws and regulations governing business practices (horizontal or vertical agreements between enterprises, abuses of dominant positions, monopolization, mergers and acquisitions)." (M. Rowat, *Competition Policy in Latin America: Legal and Institutional Issues*, The World Bank, Washington, D.C.,

to replace current anti-dumping legislation by antitrust rules and their likely effects on international commerce. Therefore, it explores the rationality behind these rules, as well as their intellectual origins. The thesis of the article is that the current proposals promoting antitrust rules to regulate international transactions would regulate rivalry among firms, introducing a disincentive to competition. We argue that these rules do not strengthen the international institutional framework but instead undermine it, as they reintroduce, albeit in new ways, sources of discretion and uncontrolled behaviour that could seriously diminish the expectations of the participants in the international economic order.

The first part of this work describes the current approach upon which the proposals for antitrust rely; in the second part, we propose an alternative approach, in the light of the insufficiencies of this policy to promote competition.

The Problem of Competition in International Trade

Market failures and international trade

The conventional theory holds that there is a need to introduce public interest measures to prevent or to correct the monopolistic manipulations of firms enjoying market power aimed either at increasing prices or excluding competitors from the market. The ultimate goal is to prevent them from extracting monopolistic rents from helpless consumers as well as to ensure their access to a wider array of products than otherwise.

This perspective emerged out of a lengthy process of evolution in economic theory, where eventually positive economic theory began to draw normative conclusions about public policy which were immediately accepted by legislators and policy makers alike. In the beginning, there was a widespread acceptance of the benefits of free trade and free markets in promoting social wealth. Generally, the economics profession agrees that the division of labour and economic exchange arising thereof are the key to economic development. Public policy should not interfere with market functioning, and therefore should be limited to ensuring peace and order. Yet under the influence of the positivistic intellectual climate dominant during the nineteenth century, economic science came to adopt a different view that eventually led them to reconsider their former expectations about market functioning as well as their normative conclusions about public policy to sustain them towards public interest.[5] In particular, this new appraisal (which still dominates the design and implementation of public policy) stressed the structural weakness of markets in producing social wealth, owing to the existence of inherent "failures" that prevent them from achieving a social optimum. Such failures induce markets to depart from a state of "equilibrium" where otherwise they would allocate resources most efficiently throughout society according to their most valuable uses. For this reason, public policy was called on to regulate the conduct of market participants, in order to ensure that none of them introduced distortions into the system. It is easy to see why this regulation was regarded as introduced to protect a "public interest".[6]

As they inevitably departed from the model of "equilibrium" predicated under the new paradigm of thought, the restrictions that market participants introduced to competition became almost immediately regarded contemptuously, as they were assumed to produce a misallocation of social resources for the benefit of unscrupulous rent-seeker monopolists. Consequently, a new concern arose demanding the control of abusive practices addressed to limit and to exclude competitors. In the international arena, these views challenged the former beliefs about the benefits of free trade, already put into question by the old mecantilist views

4 *continued*
1995.Internet:http://www.worldbank.org/html/lat/english/papers/trade/cmp_plcy.pdf.) For the purposes of this work we use the term "competition policy" in a wider sense as compared to the sense attributed in some jurisdictions, notably in Europe. Here, competition policy refers to *any* policy aimed at enhancing competition, regardless the form that it adopts. Consequently, deregulation, liberalisation of trade and the elimination of licences, to name a few, are also measures regarded as part of a competition policy since they promote competition in the marketplace.

5 Although the formation of this true "paradigm" (in the Kuhnian sense of the word) was influenced by several intellectual sources, scientific positivism was perhaps the most noticeable trend. According to its premises, positivism relies on empiricism as a tool for the analysis of reality. The influence of the positivist method still dominates "mainstream" economics to a large extent, as argued by De Alessi (L. De Alessi, "Nature and Methodological Foundations of some Recent Extensions of Economic Theory", in *Economic Imperialism: The Economic Approach Outside the field of Economics*, G. Radnizky and P. Bernholz (eds.), Paragon House Publishers, New York, 1987, p. 52). About the influence of positivistic thinking over the public law paradigm of regulation, see, M. Louglin, *Public Law and Political Theory*, Clarendon Press, Oxford, 1992.

6 A summary of the public interest theory of regulation is found in W. Mitchell and R. Simmons, *Beyond Politics: Markets, Welfare and the Failure of Bureaucracy*, Westview Press, Boulder, 1994, pp. 3–37.

towards international trade implemented through protective tariff barriers. Free trade alone was no guarantee that competition would accrue spontaneously.

This view is widely shared by policy makers and scholars alike. For example, at the 1993 Ministerial Meeting of the OECD countries, the Committee on Competition Law and Policy and the Trade Committee submitted a joint progress report on trade and competition policies. They agreed that globalisation should produce more efficient production and marketing, lower prices and improved product quality and variety, but will fail to do so unless market access and competition can be preserved and enhanced.[7]

Similarly, scholars such as Hoekman and Mavroidis argue that "while a free trade stance greatly reduces the scope of the task facing competition authorities, it does not imply that the need for competition rules disappear. Many products are non-tradeable (*e.g.* many services), or, even if tradeable, competition may be limited to local markets for other reasons. Free trade must therefore be complemented by the freedom of entry, including the possibility to contest markets through foreign direct investment. Even then, certain products may be produced by (natural) monopolies, by firms with global market power, or by firms where natural or 'unnatural' (government-made) barriers to entry restrict contestability."[8] Indeed, in their opinion, free trade could be a risky business: "the more open markets are to foreign products, the greater potential vulnerability to anti-competitive practices of foreign monopolists or cartels."[9]

7 OECD Working Papers, Trade and Competition Policies, No. 35, Paris, 1994, p. 2.

8 B. M. Hoekman and P. C. Mavroidis, Linking Competition and Trade Policies in Central and East European Countries, Policy Research Working paper 1346, The World Bank, Washington, D.C., 1994, p. 3.

9 *ibid*. Further, Trebilcock argues that "While some have argued that completely unrestricted international trade largely obviates the need for domestic competition laws, there are reasons for scepticism about this claim. First, even in the traded goods sector, depreciated exchange rates and transportation costs may often attenuate the impact of import competition, and in the non-traded goods sector, especially the service sector which is an increasingly important element in many domestic economies, import competition will not often be an effective competitive threat, and restrictions on foreign investment (an effective market presence rather than effective market access) may be more salient impediments to offshore competition." (M. Trebilcock, "Reconciling Competition Laws and Trade Policies: A New Challenge to International Cooperation, in *Comparative Competition Policy: National Institutions in a Global Market*, G. B. Doern and S. Wilks (eds.), Clarendon Press, Oxford, 1996, pp. 269–270.

Finally, the "public interest" view of competition policy views the rules regulating competition as a necessary complement to the rivalry introduced by a liberal trade policy. The implicit premise is that markets alone may create obstacles to their functioning. For this reason, antitrust supporters argue that it is necessary to distinguish between "fair" and "unfair" market behaviour, and to minimise the negative effects of the latter.

Origins of the rules for the protection of international competition

In order to translate into positive law the former theoretical premises, governments began to introduce legislation addressed to restrictions to competition and other unfair practices of market exchanges, both domestically and internationally. The connecting thread between both antitrust legislation and unfair trade practices legislation is evident, as both sets of legislation aimed at the ultimate goal of preserving the "purity and transparency" of market transactions. They emerged in the wake of a generalised trade protectionism, being regarded as a "second best solution" for the lack of competition arising from the foreclosure of international markets to foreign competition. In this sense, they both represented official attempts to administer competition according to some "public standard". Antitrust was merely regarded a complement to trade protectionism, to which unfair trade legislation belonged.[10] It is important to grasp the connection between both policies in order to understand why the proposal aiming for the substitution of antitrust rules for anti-dumping rules would not introduce a true reform to the policy of promoting competition but would merely amount to a restatement of the old policy, albeit supported by a more elaborate theoretical framework, and with a somewhat different scope. In turn, this will lead us to the conclusion that a different approach is needed if policy makers sincerely strive to promote competition.

10 For example, Trebilcock argues: "Competition laws were enacted in Canada and the USA late in the last century at the same time as their governments were adopting high tariff policies. Thus, for a good past of the ensuing century, competition laws in these two countries were interpreted and applied in a deep 'second-best' world, where domestic competition was promoted in contexts where foreign competition was often severely restrained by self-imposed protectionist trade policies." n. 9 above, p. 269.

Dumping and subsidies as "unfair" trade practices under international commerce

In the realm of international relations, where trade was fragmented and obstructed by government (tariff and non-tariff) barriers the goal of a policy aimed to promote competition was relatively straightforward: this policy should ensure that commercial relations were conducted in such a way as to reflect the "true" competitive advantages of its participants. It was therefore on the grounds of defining the true competitive advantage of nations that policy makers could ultimately isolate those cases regarded as "unfair" under international trade. Only by protecting trade flows from business or government manipulation could trading countries reasonable expect that imports introduced into their respective domestic markets would truly enjoy a fair advantage over their national production and not be the subject of any artificial support from governments or from monopolistic firms interested in excluding domestic competitors by undercutting prices.

However, it was only in 1947 that these unfair practices in international trade became the subject of multilateral regulation for the first time. The GATT introduced specific legislation dealing with "dumping" and "export subsidies".[11] Conventionally, dumping is defined as "exporting at prices below those charged on the domestic market (or, if none, on a third-country market) or at prices insufficient to cover the cost of the goods sold".[12] On the other hand, export subsidies comprise any help "paid to an industry on products that are exported".[13]

11 This regulation is developed in the following way: In regard to anti-dumping, Article VI of the GATT comprises a general definition of dumping and regulates the use of anti-dumping measures; the Uruguay Round Code on Anti-dumping specifies the general framework laid down by GATT's Article VI. In connection with export subsidies, the original GATT agreement regulated subsidies on four levels: 1) Article XVI, paragraph 1 set a loose reporting requirement; 2) Article XVI, paragraphs 3 and 4 regulated the restraints on export subsidies; 3) Article XXIII regulated the restraints over new domestic subsidies; and 4) Article VI governed the imposition of countervailing duties. The Uruguay Round Agreement on Subsidies and Countervailing Measures developed these provisions in a systematic way.

12 J. Jackson, W. Davey and Alan Sykes, *Legal Problems of International Economic Relations*, West Publishing Co., St Paul, Minn., 1995, pp. 671–672.

13 *ibid.*, p. 758.

Limitations of the unfair trade legislation to deal with the complexity of competition

The GATT rules on dumping and subsidies represent a first attempt at multilateral control over business conducts regarded as "unfair". However, that these endeavours were insufficient to promote fair competition and even counterproductive became evident as soon as the effects of other forms of trade barriers over commerce decreased in significance, particularly tariff barriers. These obstacles, by allowing an unchecked power on authorities to regulate commerce, disguised the potential effects of unfair trade measures as non-tariff barriers. Such dangers became quite obvious as soon as governments realised the advantages of replacing tariff protection (subject to reduction and relatively easy multilateral surveillance) by more subtle means of trade protection.

To avoid this problem, governments aimed to improve the rules governing multilateral trade. Unlike former rounds of negotiations, mostly addressed to achieve tariff reductions through the most-favoured-nation clause, the Uruguay Round was primarily devoted to improving the rules governing the commercial conduct of its participants. Although the aftermath of the process evidenced a clear improvement in the definition of the rules dealing with export subsidies, it did not solve the problems associated to the exercise of government discretion in the field of anti-dumping. Indeed, the round succeeded in notably improving the ex-ante definition of those ("red") subsidies forbidden under the international rules and those permitted ("green"), thus reducing considerably the number of grey cases of subsidies subject to an ex-post determination of injury ("yellow") which formerly enabled a great deal of discretion on behalf of national trade authorities.[14]

However, in the case of dumping, the round did not succeed in eliminating effectively the substantive sources of administrative discretion which remained almost untouched. Instead it was content merely to deal with the procedural shortcomings of the current legislation, in the expectation of reducing administrative discretion to a tolerable level.[15]

14 *ibid.*, pp. 769–770. See also GATT Focus Newsletter, GATT Secretariat, Dec. 1993, at 10–11.

15 To name some procedural improvements, the Uruguay Round unified the criteria followed for the determination of injury in both anti-dumping and countervailing cases; it also committed countries to follow an "injury determination" formerly set aside unilaterally by some countries (notably, the U.S.) benefiting from their grandparent's rights; further, the

Thus, the round failed to challenge the key issue, namely, the nature of dumping as an "unfair" behaviour. In this regard, Ordover *et al.*, for instance, argue that selling exports at prices below the home market price is not necessarily indicative of "unfairness", and instead may show a healthy strategy of business rivalry.[16]

Indeed, the unavoidable vagueness in the determination of "dumping" invites national trade authorities to exercise their discretion in determining what imports will be regarded as being sold at a dumping price. This vague character emerges from the very determination of the dumping margin, which is used as the basis of calculation of anti-dumping duties. To calculate the margin of dumping it is necessary to determine the "normal value" of the merchandise; to do so, three alternative rules are followed. The normal value will be calculated on the basis of the price of sale of a similar merchandise in the country of origin, deducting transport and other similar expenses. If this price is not ascertainable, the normal value will be determined by reference to the sale price of a similar merchandise in a third market, again making similar deductions. If it is impossible to ascertain these values, the normal value will be constructed on the basis of its estimated production costs, less deductions.[17]

It is easy to see why these rules amount to absolute uncertainty as to the rights of importers and other participants in international trade. Indeed, it is evident that uncontrolled discretion is granted to the administrative agencies by virtue of these rules. This is so because the determination of what is a normal value in a specific case depends upon the construction of inevitably arbitrary assumptions. For example, what is a "similar product"? Strictly speaking, the production of one firm will inevitably be different from the rest, particularly if one considers the subjective nature of the costs involved. Thus, "similarity" must be by definition arbitrary. For this reason, it is not surprising that in most cases, anti-dumping authorities find no "similar product" available, and thus determine the normal value of the products with reference to the constructed value. Needless to say, this "constructed value" measure is an even more misleading and arbitrary rule, based upon the false assumption that it is possible to determine objectively the costs involved in producing the goods. Again, similar caveats apply to this case.[18] Finally, there are further minor substantive shortcomings in the anti-dumping legislation, such as the determination of expenses incurred to be considered in the respective deduction.[19]

These circumstances left regulatory gaps to be used by anti-dumping agencies to exercise trade protectionism, which in turn has led to mounting criticism over the rules.[20]

Enforcement of antitrust rules over international trade

Owing to the shortcomings mentioned in the preceding section, commentators are increasingly in

15 *continued*
new code introduced a special concern over the transparency and publicity of procedures, and also states general criteria to follow in the submission of evidence, setting minimum limits of dumping margin to open procedures, and so forth (A. Avila *et al.*, n. 1 above, p. 154).

16 These authors correctly point out that a firm may exercise monopoly power in its home market, and sell at lower prices to the export market. This lower price could still be above marginal cost (otherwise, it would be predation, and therefore unfair). The fact that such price *above* marginal costs may still be regarded as dumping, and subject to prosecution by anti-dumping agencies, reveals that the regulation is incapable of making a proper distinction between truly unfair and healthy competitive business behaviour. (J. Ordover, A. Sykes and R. Willig, *Unfair International Trade Practices*, PP–19, C.V. Starr Center for Applied Economics, New York University, Department of Economics, Sept. 1982, pp. 6–16).

17 See Agreement on Implementation of Article VI of GATT, Article II paragraph 2.1 (normal value calculated on the basis of sales made in domestic markets) and Article II paragraph 2.2 (normal value calculated on the basis of sales to a third country, and normal value calculated on the basis of costs of production).

18 The lure of objective costs is indeed one of the most entrenched notions in the models from mainstream economics. This notion is inconsistent with the subjective nature of costs. Indeed, costs represent first and foremost the value foregone as a consequence of adopting a certain course of action. This value cannot be ascertained by anyone other than whoever makes such decision. For an explanation about the subjective nature of value, see T. Taylor, ***The Fundamentals of Austrian Economics***, Adam Smith Institute, London, 1980, pp. 14–15, 26–34.

19 A. Avila *et al.*, n. 1 above, pp. 138–139.

20 For example, Messerlin regards anti-dumping rules as "undesirable and perverse" (P. Messerlin, "Should Antidumping rules be replaced by National or International Competition Rules?", 18 *World Competition Law and Economics Rev.* [1995], p. 37). On the other hand, Trebilcock argues: "While the trade liberalization that has occurred in the post-war period under GATT and under various regional trading arrangements—such as the E.C., the FTA (Free Trade Agreement), and now NAFTA (North American Free Trade Agreement)—has mitigated these tensions, many trade restrictions still remain. Such restrictions are now less likely to be in the form of tariffs, and instead take the form of quantitative restrictions and the increasing utilization of trade remedy laws, in particular anti-dumping laws, with many countries adopting anti-dumping regimes for the first time during the 1980s, and utilization rates world-wide growing dramatically during the 1990s." (Trebilcock, n. 9 above, p. 269.) A more extended analysis about the protectionist use of anti-dumping remedies is found in M. Leidy, ***Antidumping: Unfair Trade or Unfair Remedy?***, Finance & Development, IMF–World Bank, March 1995.

favour of replacing anti-dumping provisions by a more elaborated set of rules enabling a more proper regulation of the problems associated to competition in international trade. A sophisticated framework is increasingly perceived as necessary to deal with the greater complexity of transnational business transactions in the contemporary world. This initiative is far from being new.[21]

Antitrust rules appear an ideal substitute for anti-dumping legislation for several reasons. First, unlike the attention paid by anti-dumping rules to the protection of domestic competitors, antitrust rules proclaim the promotion of competition in the market place as their foremost goal. In the conventional wisdom, this focus somehow directs legal enforcement towards the "right" goal, namely, the protection of economic efficiency and consumer sovereignty, rather than inefficient domestic producers.[22] In other words, antitrust partisans assume that policy goals, once declared, will inexorably lead to enforcement, at least if the "right" people enforce the policy according to the declared goals. Second, antitrust is attractive to these scholars because it apparently diminishes government discretion associated to the substantive definition of "dumping", vaguely described under the current anti-dumping statutes. In this regard, the concepts of both discriminatory and predatory pricing[23] appear to provide grounds for more elaborate analysis, and therefore less discretion in the hands of enforcement agencies. Finally, antitrust would allow the incorporation of a cluster of behaviours not covered under the current regulations, which nevertheless constitute expressions of "unfairness" in international trade. For example, F. S. Scherer lists the following conduct deserving international antitrust surveillance, not covered by present unfair trade practices legislation: price fixing or other output restrictions among exporting firms; economic concentration through merger and acquisition; voluntary export restraint;[24] as well as others.[25]

Thus, the present inadequacy of unfair trade legislation in dealing with these issues, and the numerous exemptions to antitrust prosecution allowed to "export" cases, lead to the conclusion that it would be beneficial to adopt international antitrust rules.[26]

However, assuming the need for international antitrust rules, the question emerges: which set of rules should apply? In this connection, scholars frequently regard domestic antitrust legislation as insufficient to deal with international restrictions,

21 The introduction of antitrust rules in international trade is not recent, nor are efforts to develop multilateral antitrust rules. The Havana Charter incorporated specific rules to regulate restrictive business practices, such as the prohibition of price agreements among competitors, fixing sale or purchasing quotas, the limitation of production or fixing production quotas. The Havana Charter would have obliged the members of the proposed International Trade Organization to take appropriate measures to prevent private commercial enterprises that had "effective control of trade" from "restrain[ing] competition, limit[ing] access to markets, or foster[ing] monopolistic control in international trade." (Art. 46, Ch. 5, Havana Charter for an International Trade Organization, U.N. Doc. E/Conf. 2/78 (1948), reprinted in U.N. Doc. ICITO/1/4 (1948).) Later, during the 1970s, much attention on international antitrust was related to the control of multinational enterprises. The aftermath of this focus was the adoption, in 1980, by the U.N. Assembly, of the Set of Equitable Principles Multilaterally Agreed for the Control of Restrictive Business Practices. More recently, the attention on international antitrust has been aroused again, this time associated to the extension of trade disciplines to new areas of regulation, in the Uruguay Round. The history of international antitrust is well explained in N. Yacheistova, "The International Competition Regulation", 18 *World Competition Law and Economics Rev.* [1994]. See also E. Fox, "Competition Law and the Agenda for the W.T.O.", in *Antitrust: A New International Trade Remedy?*, J. Haley & H. Iyori (eds.), Pacific Rim Law & Policy Association, Seattle, 1995, pp. 2–7.

22 In this regard, Trebilcock argues: "Tensions between the objectives and application of domestic competition laws, and international trade policy have a long genesis." (Trebilcock, n. 9 above, p. 269.) Further, Hoekman and Mavroidis state the following: "Trade policy is consequently often inconsistent with the objectives underlying competition policy. The way this inconsistency is frequently put is that competition law aims at protecting competition (and thus economic efficiency) while trade policy aims at protecting competitors (or factors of production)." (n. 8 above, p. 2.)

23 According to Ordover and Willig, there is evidence of predatory objectives whenever the exclusion of competitors increases the monopoly power of incumbent firms in the market. To be predatory, such increase in monopoly power must be the ultimate cause of the rival's exit from the market (Ordover and Willig, "An Economic Definition of Predation", 91 Yale L.J. 8 [1981]).

24 The proposed inclusion of these agreements under the scope of antitrust is somewhat puzzling, as they are concluded between governments and not firms. Further, they refer not only to dumping situations, but also imports enjoying subsidies, or simply a competitive advantage. About the nature and effects of these agreements in international commerce, see generally *Competition and Trade Policies: their Interaction*, O.E.C.D., Paris, 1984, pp. 16–17.

25 F. M. Scherer, *Competition Policies for an Integrated World Economy*, The Brookings Institution, Washington, D.C., 1994, pp. 43–88.

26 See *Los Nuevos Temas del Comercio*, SP/CL/XXI.O DT No. 13, XXI Reunión Ordinaria del Consejo Latinoamericano, Sistema Económico Latinoamericano. Traditionally, it is assumed that antitrust discretion would work in such way to favour their unenforceability to domestic producers in "export cases". This is the reasoning which leads to the adoption of international antitrust rules. (See, *e.g.* A. Haagsma, "An International Competition Policy as a Means to Create an Open Global Market Place", in *International Harmonization of Competition Laws*, C.-J. Cheng *et al.* (eds.), Martinus Nijhoff Publishers, London, 1995, pp. 409–426.

owing to the numerous exceptions granted to export cartels, as well as other loopholes enabling infringing firms to avoid prosecution in their domestic jurisdictions. Also, and no less important, there are several problems associated with the extraterritorial enforcement of domestic antitrust provisions in various cases. For example, the United States has attempted to exercise its antitrust provisions to prosecute domestic subsidiaries of foreign corporations allegedly involved in manipulations to restrain competition.[27] Despite the rise of a more flexible trend in court decisions which regard the principle of extraterritorial effects in the light of international principles of comity, it is unlikely that such problems will disappear.[28]

For this reason, there is an increasing tendency for commentators to advocate the development of international standards to regulate competition internationally. There is a variety of alternative solutions.

First, the negotiation has been proposed of an international set of ad hoc rules which would be imposed "from the top" into the legislation of states. This solution has already been attempted (albeit unsuccessfully) by a group of trade and competition experts from the Max Planck Institut in Munich; it adopted the form of a Multilateral Antitrust Code, to be celebrated within the framework of GATT.[29] According to this proposal, there would be a set of five basic principles of consensus which would be incorporated into the domestic legislation of each member country:

1) national enforcement of antitrust laws;
2) observance of a principle of equality as between foreign and domestic competition;
3) enforcement of minimum standards in the regulation of domestic antitrust against restrictive conduct of international dimension;
4) the use of GATT sanctions to ensure the non-discriminatory use of international rules of competition;
5) the Code would apply to transnational cases exclusively.[30]

27 The U.S. courts have been particularly active in extending the jurisdiction of the Sherman Act over cartels formed abroad. The principle of extraterritoriality had already been established in the *ALCOA* case (*United States v. Aluminium Co. of Am.*, 148 F.2d 416, 443 2d Cir. 1945). However, it was the Uranium case (*Westinghouse Elec. Corp. v. Rio Algom Ltd. in re Uranium Antitrust Litigation*, 617 F.2d 1248 7th Cir. 1980) which evidenced the difficulties of enforcing the principle, as shown by the diplomatic protest of several states who consequently enacted blocking statutes, such as the Canadian Uranium Information Security Regulations of 1976, or the Australian Foreign Proceedings Act. Furthermore, the claw-back provision of the U.K. Protection of Trading Interests Act of 1980 provides for the recovery of the non-compensatory portion of treble damage awards made by U.S. courts.

28 Decisions such as *Timberlane Lumber Co. v. Bank of America* (574 F. Supp. 1453, 1466 N.D.Cal. 1983) or *Manington Mills Inc. v. Congoleum Corp.* (595 F.2d 1287, 1297 3d Cir. 1979), established a rule of reason based on the principle of "international comity", which lessened the stringency of the extraterritorial principle. As a result of this trend, according to Trebilcock, the U.S. Department of Justice adopted its "DOJ International Antitrust Guidelines" comprising the principles and conditions that the agency would consider before ascertaining its jurisdiction over an extraterritorial case. (Trebilcock, n. 9 above, p. 275; also U. Immenga, "Export Cartels and Voluntary Export Restraints between Trade and Competition Policy", in *Antitrust: A New International Trade Remedy?*", J. Haley & H. Iyori (eds.), Pacific Rim Law & Policy Association, Seattle, 1995, pp. 112–113.)

However, the matter is far from being settled and the objection to allowing a rule of reason in this field still persists, as evidenced in *National Bank of Canada v. Interbank Card Association* (666 F.2d 6, 8 2d Cir. 1981), *Laker Airways Ltd v. Sabena* (731 F.2d D.C.Cir. 1984).

29 BNA Antitrust & Trade Reg. Rep., vol. 64, no. 1628 (Aug. 19, 1993) More recently supporting the idea of an international antitrust code, see Y-P. Chu, "Towards the Establishment of an Order of Competition for the International Economy: With References to the Draft International Antitrust Code, the Parallel Imports Problem, and the Experience of Taiwan, ROC," in *International Harmonization of Competition Laws*, C.-J. Cheng, L. S. Liu and C.-K. Wang (eds.), Martinus Nijhoff Publishers, London, 1995. An alternative view is presented by W. Fikentscher, "On the Proposed International Antitrust Code", in *Antitrust: A New International Trade Remedy?*, J. Haley & H. Iyori (eds.), Pacific Rim Law & Policy Association, Seattle, 1995, pp. 345–357.

30 Scherer also proposes some guidelines that could be incorporated into such an international antitrust code. His proposals are as follows: 1) Following ratification of an international compact, an International Competition Policy Office (ICPO) will be created within the ambit of the new WTO. It will have both investigative and enforcement responsibilities; 2) A year after the new Competition Policy agreement is ratified, all substantial single-nation export and import cartels and all cartels operating across boundaries must be registered, and the mechanisms of their operation must be documented with the ICPO. "Substantial" comprises cartels exceeding $100 million in sales a year. Also, all enterprises originating 40% or more of world exports must register with the ICPO, providing details of their annual sales and the locations of their principal operations; 3) Following a petition of a signatory nation that trade has been restricted or distorted by a monopolistic practice, the ICPO will study the alleged practices, publishing the results of its investigation and recommendations for correction; 4) Within three years after the creation of the ICPO, representatives of the signatory nations will agree upon a common format for reporting information on the supply and international trading activities of substantial enterprises that propose to merge. A previous notification must be filed. The ICPO will distribute the information of the competition agencies of all affected nations; 5) Within five years after the creation of the ICPO, all signatories will enact legislation prohibiting export cartels; 6) Within six years after the creation of the ICPO, all signatories will enact legislation prohibiting import cartels; 7) After seven years, the ICPO will accept complaints about the alleged abuse of monopoly powers by cartels or by any substantial enterprise (40% world's output). 8) After seven years, the ICPO will accept complaints about notified substantial mergers with probable

Secondly, there are proponents of the harmonisation of domestic antitrust standards with international standards; this process would develop international legislation "from the bottom", by means of bilateral or multilateral co-operation agreements negotiated to solve specific problems. This solution has already been followed in agreements entered into by the United States with Canada,[31] Australia,[32] Germany[33] and more recently the European Union.[34]

Third, some scholars assume that endorsing multilateral competition standards is an impractical or difficult goal, and therefore concentrate, perhaps more pragmatically, on the use of the current instruments of control. Under these proposals, they either assign domestic antitrust authorities the task of reviewing the effects of anti-dumping standards when examining a case,[35] or propose an extended interpretation of certain key GATT provisions and principles, which would eventually allow for coverage of restrictive conduct not encompassed by express provisions.[36]

Finally, Fox proposes a more "constitutional" approach which would identify those strengths and limitations of competition as applied to international commerce in order to identify an international agenda of action. This proposal, in her opinion, would overcome the limitations of all the former proposals, either too ambitious or unrealistic (*i.e.* negotiating an international antitrust code) or too narrowly focused (*i.e.* harmonising domestic antitrust criteria) or no solution at all (*i.e.* the use of current GATT provisions).[37]

Shortcomings of Antitrust Policy in Promoting Competition

The different proposals outlined above of antitrust enforcement in international trade are unable to solve the fundamental flaws implicit in the basic assumption of its supporters, namely, that antitrust laws do in fact promote competition, and therefore that they should be enforced in order to promote international trade relations.

Indeed, these proposals present deficiencies on three different levels. First, the model of *perfect* competition and *static* markets underlying antitrust policy bears little resemblance to competition as it

30 *continued*
effects (concentrations of more than 40% of world trade). 9) Should a substantial firm continue to control 40% of world trade for a period longer than twenty years on the basis of validly issued patents or copyrights, any signatory nation may require the compulsory licensing of the firm's patents or copyrights within its jurisdiction at reasonable royalties. 10) After seven years, the ICPO will receive complaints concerning monopolistic practices which distort international trade that are not expressly covered above. 11) None of this prevents any signatory nation from implementing more stringent rules within its own national market. (F. M. Scherer, n. 25 above, pp. 91–97.)

31 23 I.L.M., 275.

32 20 I.L.M., 702.

33 Agreement between the Government of the United States of America and the Government of the Federal Republic of Germany relative to Mutual Co-operation on Restrictive Business Practices (1976).

34 Agreement between the Commission of the European Communities and the Government of the United States of America relative to the Enforcement of their Competition Laws, Washington, Sept. 23, 1991.

35 B. Hoekman and P. Mavroidis, Antitrust-based Remedies and Dumping in International Trade, Policy Research Working Paper No. 1347, The World Bank, Washington, D.C., 1994. The goal sought under this proposal is to ensure that domestic markets remain contestable notwithstanding the enforcement of anti-dumping.

36 B. Hoekman and P. Mavroidis, Competition, Competition Policy and the GATT, Policy Research Working Paper No. 1228, The World Bank, Washington, D.C., 1993. Under this proposal, the authors suggest that current GATT rules and case law provide scope for disputes to be brought before the GATT that relate to the application and the non-application of existing domestic competition laws of GATT Contracting Parties. In particular, they propose to overcome the limitation that by definition GATT mechanisms apply to private entities by treating anti-competitive measures as resulting from government

36 *continued*
behaviour, either in the form of official approval (*e.g.* an antitrust exemption) or other support (*e.g.* trade barriers). The point is that if a Contracting Party supports business practices leading to a *de facto* if not *de jure* discrimination against foreign products GATT dispute settlement procedures may be invoked. Thus, measures inconsistent with Article III (National Treatment) or with complementary rules on state-trading enterprises and quantitative restrictions (Articles XVII and XI), may give rise to a "violation" complaint under Article XXIII:1 (a). Measures that are not inconsistent with the General Agreement, but nullify or impair an existing concession, may give rise to a so-called "non-violation" complaint under Article XXIII:I (b).

On the other hand, Trachtman holds that theoretically GATT could apply to those restrictions of competition not enforced or exempted from domestic legislation. These cases could be regarded as domestic subsidies, under GATT's provisions; consequently, they could promote commercial compensation. However, there is little control of the use of domestic subsidies; indeed, GATT provisions deal foremost with the effects of "export subsidies", against which it allows the use of countervailing measures. (J. Trachtman, "International Regulatory Competition, Externalization and Jurisdiction", 34 *Harvard International L.J.*, pp. 47–104.).

In such a framework, antitrust complaints would be presented as government disputes. In other words, they would be brought only if they are supported by a Contracting Party. The conduct must also violate some GATT obligation. Hence, for example, a cartel agreement exemption would not be immediately void, unless the government supports the operation of the cartel through other policies.

37 E. Fox, "Competition Law and the Agenda for the WTO", in *Antitrust: A New International Trade Remedy?*, J. Haley and H. Iyori (eds.), Pacific Rim Law & Policy Association, Seattle, 1995, pp. 1–36.

is in the real world; hence the pretension of antitrust supporters to use this model as a normative landmark is completely unfounded and misleading for public policy purposes. Secondly, antitrust partisans overlook the actual negative effect of antitrust policies, in the light of the incentives that political actors face when designing and enforcing this policy. Thirdly, antitrust policy introduces an *absolute* uncertainty upon the transactions of economic agents, as the discretionary powers of enforcing agencies cannot be submitted to judicial review effectively, owing to the nature of economic evidence as well as to the arbitrary implications of positive economic models upon which antitrust theories are constructed.

Inability of the perfect competition model to deliver adequate normative conclusions

As Petermann aptly observes, the conglomerate of economic activities from different actors in the international sphere comprises an "international economic order".[38] The nature of this order is essentially "dynamic" in the sense that it results from the interaction of its participants. As put by Taylor, "The process of interaction and co-operation is the essence of the market; the market is not something physical but a process."[39] Owing to its nature as process, market events take place in "real" time; they are in constant "disequilibrium". Further, individuals interact in the market in order to unfold hidden information about consumer tastes, to develop cheaper means of production, more effective techniques of distribution, more capable technologies, and in general to overcome their "ignorance" about opportunities of profit. They do so by collaborating and competing one against another.[40]

By contrast, the model of perfect competition underlying antitrust theory depicts efficient markets in exactly the opposite way: complete information (present and future) about consumer preferences, tastes, available resources and technologies; comprising multiple sellers and buyers; and characterised by the presence of a constant "equilibrium" or static relationships among its elements. These conditions ensure that markets allocate resources most efficiently, allocating resources to their best valuable use among members of society.

Under this view real markets are represented as "imperfect" structures chronically departing from the stringent conditions set up by the model, or, to put it differently, subject to "failures" that lessen the level of efficiency which otherwise would accrue. Consequently, there is no wonder that the model possess a normative inclination to hold government intervention necessary to correct these failures. Antitrust policy appears in this context as a single case of justified intervention to put things in order.[41]

While it is true that this positive model is useful to express the mathematical relationships among the variables of the model in order to understand how market forces work, it seems incapable of delivering an accurate picture of competition in the real world. In fact, by assuming a perfect knowledge among market participants, the model eliminates the need of competition to obtain such information.[42]

38 E.-U. Petersmann, *Constitutional Functions and Constitutional Problems of International Economic Law*, PUPIL 3, University Press Fribourg, Switzerland, 1991.

39 He also adds: "The tendency to ascribe to the market economy the characteristics of being something other than the events caused by the choices and actions of individuals is incorrect." (Taylor, n. 18 above, p. 35.).

40 On the dynamic nature of competition, see F. A. Hayek, "The Meaning of Competition", in *Individualism and Economic Order*, The University of Chicago Press, Routledge, London, 1948, pp. 92–106. Similarly, J. M. Clark, "Toward a Concept of Workable Competition", *The American Economic Review*, Vol. XXX, June 1940; F. Machlup, "Competition, Pliopoly and Profit", *Economica*, Vol. IX (1942), No. 33. More recently, the Austrian School of Economics has developed these seminal ideas and consequently has attempted an alternative explanation of markets and competition as processes performed in the course of time. (See C. Taylor, *The Fundamentals of Austrian Economics*, Adam Smith Institute, London, 1980; also, R. Langlois, "Economics as a Process", Introductory Paper for a Liberty Fund symposium, October 13–15, 1982, pp. 29–44; an

40 *continued*
extensive discussion about the fundamentals of the Austrian view over markets is found in I. Kirzner, *The Meaning of Market Process: Essays in the Development of Modern Austrian Economics*, Routledge, London, 1992. The dynamic view of competition is explained in I. Kirzner, *Competition and Entrepreneurship*, University of Chicago Press, Chicago, 1973.

41 As Langlois argues: "[The conclusions of the perfect competition model] consist in comparing real-world states of affairs with the hypothetical states of affairs that, in the general-equilibrium model, can be shown to be Pareto optimal. It is in this practice—and it is a widespread one—that Demsetz [H. Demsetz, "Information and Efficiency: Another Viewpoint", 12 *Journal of Law and Economics*, [1969], p. 1] branded the 'nirvana' approach, the comparison of actual situations with an impossible ideal. And, to the extent that the failure of competition to live up to this hypothetical standard is taken as justification for government intervention, the welfare comparison necessarily implies a hidden value judgement that such government intervention is the more efficient institutional arrangement." (Langlois, n. 40 above, p. 41).

42 See also generally I. Kirzner, n. 41 above, and G. O'Driscoll, "Monopoly in Theory and Practice", in *Method, Process and Austrian Economics*, I. Kirzner (ed.), Lexington Books, Toronto, 1982, pp. 189–214. The insufficiency of the perfect competition model is thoroughly explained in G. B. Richardson, *Information and Investment: A Study in the Working of the Competitive Economy*, Oxford University Press, London, 1960. A recent work by Machovec explains the origins of the change in the paradigm dominating the study of

Further, the use of this model as a normative yardstick to judge real markets is excessive. This is particularly noticeable in the lack of attention that the model gives to the behaviour of the firm, which is regarded as a "black box". Antitrust policy draws normative conclusions about the behaviour of entrepreneurs, yet its underlying theory completely neglects the analysis of their behaviour in the real world. Obviously, this theoretical limitation seriously undermines the consistency of the policy of developing normative conclusions about business behaviour.[43]

From another viewpoint, these conclusions lead to a new normative appraisal over traditionally suspected restrictive practices. From such a new perspective, such conduct, which currently appears "negative" and restrictive of "perfect competition" (in the sense of departing from the model) would be regarded as positive initiatives displayed by businessmen to facilitate the process of discovery of scattered information and to improve the imperfect assignment of rights granted by the state.[44]

Government failures in the exercise of antitrust policy

A second misconception by supporters of antitrust policy arises from their unfounded assumption that the policy in question is developed and enforced following a "public interest" objective, in principle, the promotion of competition.[45] Empirical evidence presented increasingly shows that such an assumption of benevolence on behalf of governments is proving to be unwarranted, as political agents (bureaucracy, legislators, policy makers, etc.) have clear incentives to diverge from such public welfare, and instead to promote their own welfare.[46] In particular, the empirical studies in the field of antitrust policy are increasingly leading to the following conclusions.

First, that the emergence of the policy is closely related to the protection of local interests in the agricultural sector and some specific industries (*e.g.* railways) which cannot compete with new entrants as the result of the introduction of new technologies reducing production costs.[47]

42 *continued*
economics as a result of the introduction of the perfect competition model: F. Machovec, *Perfect Competition and the Transformation of Economics*, Routledge, London, 1995.

43 Critics of the perfect competition model's ability to deliver normative conclusions are numerous. See, for example, F. A. Hayek, *Law, Legislation and Liberty, Vol. 3: The Political Order of a Free People*, University of Chicago Press, Chicago, 1973, chapter 2; also, R. Cordato, *Welfare Economics and Externalities in an Open Ended Universe: A Modern Austrian Perspective*, Kluwer Academic Publishers, Boston, 1992; also, G. B. Richardson, *Information and Investment*, n. 42 above.

44 This occurs, for example, when private parties negotiate dealings to prevent "free riding" from unauthorised parties who would unjustly benefit from the investments made by the contracting parties, with no effort. There are numerous forms of opportunistic behaviour arising from a poor assignment of rights that market participants seek to correct through contractual dealings regarded by antitrust legislation as "restrictive". See H. Lepage, *La nouvelle économie industrielle*, Pluriel (Inédit), Hachette-Librairie Générale Française, Paris, 1989, Chapter "La Théorie Économique des Contrats"; also, B. Klein and K. Leffler, "The Role of Market Forces in Assuring Contractual Performance", *Journal of Law and Economics*, [1979] pp. 297–326; and B. Klein, R. Crawford and A. Alchian, "Vertical Integration, Appropriable Rents, and the Competition Contracting Process", 89 *Journal of Political Economics* [1981], pp. 615–641.

45 The discussion about the goals of antitrust policy involves one of the most debated issues concerning this policy among scholars and policy makers. In this connection, there are two clear trends of thought. On the one hand, there are those that regard antitrust as pursuing economic efficiency, consumer welfare and the promotion of competition. In their view, antitrust should limit itself to ensuring the protection of competition and avoiding any measures that could impair efficient market functioning. On the other, there are those who regard antitrust as a policy guided by socio-political goals, besides the proper functioning of markets. Under this view, the policy should be enforced to protect small and medium enterprises, product diversity and equity in the market place. The concerns under this view are related to the size of modern industrial corporations. The crucial issue here is that there has been no reconciliation between these two conflicting views, and therefore it cannot be stated that antitrust, as it is under positive law, can provide any guidance as to the goals of the policy in international economic relations.

46 A thorough explanation of Public Choice theory is found in W. Mitchell and R. Simmons, n. 6 above, pp. 41–84. The most salient feature of regulation according to this theory is the "capture" of the regulator by regulated industries. (G. Stigler, "The Theory of Economic Regulation", 2 *Bell Journal of Economics and Management Science* [1971], pp. 3–21.) This theory is generally applied to the case of "natural monopolies". In the field of antitrust, the capture occurs too, albeit in more subtle ways. Perhaps the best explanation is found in further refinements of the Capture Theory, arguing that rents are spread among several competing groups and do not benefit only one constituency group, such as the producer: S. Peltzman, "Toward a More General Theory of Regulation", 19 *Journal of Law and Economics* [1976], pp. 211–240. This might explain that antitrust is likely to be shaped by the combined *private* interest of less efficient competitors, government attorneys seeking fame and experience in the field, economists expecting high income from their professional advice as court experts, bureaucracy, litigants, and the like. Several studies dealing with each of these interests have been presented in F. McChesney and W. Shughart (eds.), *The Causes and Consequences of Antitrust: The Public-Choice Perspective*, The University of Chicago Press, Chicago, 1995.

47 T. Di Lorenzo, "The Origins of Antitrust: An Interest-Group Perspective", 5 *International Review of Law and Economics* (1985), pp. 73–90. Also, D. Boudreaux, T. DiLorenzo and S. Parker, "Antitrust before the Sherman Act", in *The Causes and Consequences of Antitrust: The Public-Choice Perspective*, n. 46 above, pp. 255–270.

Secondly, that the policy is enforced in a way that has little to do with the promotion of competition, and is more related to the protection of particular interests, such as the creation of more bureaucracy and the welfare of law firms and litigants.[48]

Thirdly, that the policy is frequently used by less efficient competitors as a deterrent to competition in order to keep more efficient firms in line or force their exit from the market.[49] In sum, antitrust policy generates costs of enforcement associated to the promotion of grossly inefficient activities and rent-seeking behaviour that are probably more expensive to society than the benefits allegedly brought about by antitrust in terms of enhanced social efficiency.

Discretion of antitrust enforcement and the lack of effective judicial review

Perhaps the most severe limitation of antitrust policy in promoting trade and economic transactions stems from the uncertainty that arises from the discretion exercised by enforcing antitrust agencies. Such discretion is inherent to the nature of antitrust policy,[50] and further it is not possible to exercise judicial control to limit its scope and intensity beyond proper limits. In other words, by its very nature, discretion associated to antitrust enforcement must always be excessive and arbitrary. The lack of control emerges from the impossibility of exercising thoroughly a judicial review of decisions imposing fines or penalties on allegedly misbehaving firms.

Antitrust laws cannot thoroughly define *ex ante* conduct forbidden by legislation; at best they can only describe certain formal features that obscure, rather than clarify, the truth about the restrictive nature of the conducts involved. For example, when listing an exclusive dealing as suspected restrictive behaviour (since it excludes potential competitors otherwise "enjoying" the possibility of, say, distributing products of a given manufacturer), antitrust statutes cannot determine in advance which of those dealings represents monopolistic behaviour and which is the exercise of a normal business dealing aimed at enhancing efficiency by eliminating the opportunistic behaviour of potential "free-riders" in the market.[51] Antitrust supporters must always resort to *ex post* economic analysis in order to determine, case by case, whether such practices are truly monopolistic and should be eliminated, or whether they are efficient and should be upheld.

The fact that antitrust legislation cannot identify properly what practices are subject to prohibition should already send a signal of warning about its possible negative effects.[52] Nevertheless it is the analysis of the economic evidence that shows the arbitrary character of the antitrust process as a whole. Indeed, the question here is, how do positive economic analysis and evidence enable us to distinguish proper from improper competitive behaviour in the marketplace? In this regard, it must be noticed that the premises upon which antitrust theory builds its normative assumptions about the true nature of restrictive behaviour have been increasingly subject to reappraisal and criticism. In particular, both the doctrine of concentration and the doctrine of barriers to entry, which formerly upheld the economic determinism of the structure-conduct-performance paradigm,[53] have been challenged by new empirical evidence. This new evidence shows that concentration does not determine the fate of competition in markets, and that barriers to entry may be evidence of efficiencies developed by entrepreneurs in highly competitive environments.[54] The models of market behaviour traditionally employed by antitrust supporters cannot serve as normative yardsticks for

48 S. Weaver, *The Decision to Prosecute: Organization and Public Policy in the Antitrust Division*, M.I.T. Press, Cambridge, Mass., 1977.

49 A. Rodriguez and M. Coate, "Antitrust Policy for Reforming Economies", 18 *Houston Journal of International Law* [1996], pp. 337; also, W. Baumol and J. Ordover, "Use of Antitrust to Subvert Competition", 28 *Journal of Law & Economics* [1985], pp. 247–266. This is similar to what Bork refers to as "predation through governmental processes" (R. Bork, *The Antitrust Paradox: A Policy at War with Itself*, Basic Books Publisher, New York, 1978, pp. 347–349.)

50 In this regard, I am not alone. See Sir G. Borrie, Q.C., "The Need for Discretion in the Application of Competition Law", in *International Harmonization of Competition Laws*, C.-J. Cheng *et al.* (eds.), Martinus Nijhoff Publishers, London, 1995, pp. 255–267.

51 On the problem of free riding and its contractual solutions, see for example B. Klein and K. Leffler, "The Role of Market Forces in Assuring Contractual Performance", *Journal of Law and Economics*, [1979] pp. 297–326; also, B. Klein, R. Crawford and A. Alchian, "Vertical Integration, Appropriable Rents, and the Competitive Contracting Process", 89 *Journal of Political Economics* [1981], pp. 615–641.

52 F. A. Hayek, *Constitution of Liberty*, Routledge & Kegan Paul Ltd., London, 1960, pp. 205–220. See also S. Selinger, "The Case Against Ex-Post Facto Laws", 15 *Cato Journal* [1995–1996], pp. 191–213. On the consequences of the retroactive laws on individual rights and the Rule of Law, see J. Jowell, "The Rule of Law Today", in *The Changing Constitution*, J. Jowell and D. Oliver (eds.), Clarendon Press, Oxford, 1994, pp. 57–78.

53 J. S. Bain, *Barriers to New Competition*, Harvard University Press, Cambridge, Mass., 1956.

54 See, for example, D. T. Armentano, *Antitrust and Monopoly: Anatomy of a Policy Failure*, The Independent Institute, San Francisco, 1990, p. 1.

policy purposes because economic theory is not really sure about their truthfulness and accuracy.[55]

Further, these shortcomings show the relative value of economic evidence in confirming the existence of restrictive monopolistic behaviour. Economic data can merely state that past actions occurred in a definite way; it cannot predict how economic agents will behave in the future. In this regard, positive economics, upon which antitrust policy relies, cannot attach to a given case under review the consequences predicted by the models of positive economics.[56]

Finally, the very limitations of positive economics in determining with certainty the monopolistic content of a given restrictive practice arise from the impossibility of ascertaining in a particular case whether the conduct subject to analysis is efficient or inefficient. In this regard, the Pareto standard is above all a test measuring interpersonal values, or to be more precise, "assuming" interpersonal values. In other words, it is a test designed to measure "social" efficiency, not individual. For this reason, its operative form entails an assumption that is not possible under antitrust analysis, namely, that the gains and costs of one restrictive agreement can be contrasted with the gains and costs of all other agreements of the same kind. By definition, the standard demands that these *individual* costs and benefits be contrasted with the individual costs and benefits of other similar arrangements in fact entered into by other firms in order to have a *social* account of their convenience.

55 In fact, as stated by Langlois, if these models were taken seriously, they would lead to disastrous results. (Langlois, n. 40 above, p. 40).

56 This observation was made by Mises, who correctly pointed out that this premise is a consequence of the false belief according to which economic behaviour can be assimilated to that of natural phenomena. Physical and natural events are dominated by "laws", since they behave according to patterns of behaviour or regularities easy to predict using empirical evidence. Therefore, past events could somehow "predict" future ones. Yet in the case of economics, this is not possible, as individuals behave purposely, that is, pursuing individual goals that cannot possibly be predicted. (L. Mises, *The Ultimate Foundation of Economic Science: An Essay on Method*, Van Nostrand Company, Inc., Princeton, New Jersey, 1962.) Of course, the positive method has been extremely useful in detecting relationships among its elements, particularly to the idealistic perfect competition model, whose logic, as we have seen, is based upon mathematical *impersonal* relationships. Nevertheless, it is necessary to acknowledge the limitations of the positive model beyond these boundaries, and to apply it cautiously in public policy matters, as Friedman himself agreed. (M. Friedman, "The Methodology of Positive Economics", *Essays in Positive Economics*, M. Friedman (ed.), University of Chicago Press, Chicago, 1953.)

Such condition is unrealistic in terms of evaluating the personal liability arising from a specific undertaking. Antitrust cannot determine that the efficiencies (and costs) of agreement A are better or worse than those found under agreements B and C. All behaviour (restrictive or not) does bring new improvements over former stages; otherwise the parties would not undertake it.

The question involved in the Pareto standard of whether such individual arrangements bring about efficiencies to third parties (creating positive externalities compensating the negative ones brought by the restriction), to consumers or to society as a whole cannot be solved by balancing the efficiencies and restrictions of the agreement itself. Even within one class of undertakings (say, exclusive distribution agreements) the parties may be motivated to enter into such agreements for various reasons, changing in space and time: the changing preferences of customers may determine that these agreements are more "cost saving" in certain cases as compared to other cases; also, particular products may be likely to be distributed more efficiently by imposing extended periods of time.

The number of examples in this connection is infinite; not to mention those possible examples that could arise if we compare the efficiencies delivered by different kinds of agreements. For example, how can we argue that a franchise is "better" or "worse" (more efficient or less efficient) than another arrangement, say an exclusive supply agreement? That will obviously depend upon the subjective costs involved in the operation to the parties concerned; not on interpersonal ones.

As Rothbard puts it, there is no way that an outside observer can distinguish between purely restrictive behaviour and an efficiency-increasing operation. Efficiency can be increased not only as a result of the advantages resulting from an enhanced plant capacity. The size of the factory is not the only factor the efficiency of which can increase; marketing, advertising, distribution, etc. could also improve. In sum, their difference does not arise from their impact over competition in the marketplace. The difference between these various forms of corporate organisation relies primarily on their permanent or transitory corporate form and not on their profitability. This is why it becomes so difficult

57 M. Rothbard, *Monopoly and Competition* in "Man, Economy and State: A Treatise on Economic Principles", Vol. II, D. Van Nostrand Company, Inc., Princeton, New Jersey, 1962.

for antitrust rules to distinguish between acceptable and non-acceptable forms of organisation.[57] As Bork emphatically states: "efficiency cannot be studied directly and quantified."[58]

For these reasons, Calabresi finds "pointless" a social welfare test for normative purposes extending to any *ex ante* premise guiding policy attempts: "the set of Pareto superior changes which would make no one worse off and at least one person better off must *ex ante* be a void set. For if strict or fanatical Pareto is the criterion, why wouldn't any change that belonged in the set have already been made? Since, by definition, no one would in any way be hurt by the change, why would anyone object?" He concludes: "the Pareto criterion is of no general use as a normative guide."[59]

For these reasons, it is unreasonable to expect that judicial review can deliver sufficient control over antitrust activity by government officials. For this reason, depending on the level of review allowed under each legislation, judges either state their lack of jurisdiction over the merits of the decision, limiting themselves to a mere formal revision of its procedural aspects,[60] or end up making statements of social policy, to which they are not

58 Bork, n. 49 above, p. 192.

59 G. Calabresi, "The Pointlessness of Pareto: Carrying Coase Further", 100 *The Yale Law Journal*, p. 1216. In fact, the attempt to use the Pareto standard in antitrust "efficiency" analysis reveals a misconception about the original use of the standard. The Pareto test is above all an *ordinal* concept of efficiency, and therefore does not reveal any intensity of preference, interpersonal comparability of utilities or conmensurability of different inputs or outputs for its definition. In other words, not even Pareto himself would have agreed to use his test for normative purposes, to make interpersonal comparisons of value: Pareto himself was a convinced ordinalist, who believed that the utilitarian concept of introspective utility was unscientific. Indeed, individuals perceive value differently, as their hierarchy of personal preferences obviously differ. (V. Pareto, *Manual of Political Economy*, Macmillan, London, 1971, p. 113.) In fact, determining an ideal state of affairs following social welfare measures represents an impossible task. Further, while it provides a ranking of allocations of economic goods between individuals, the Pareto test does not permit a ranking of all such allocations. That is to say, there are many different allocations that are Pareto-optimal and which differ with respect to the distribution of real income (*i.e.* utility) among the individuals in society. Therefore, it becomes impossible for the would-be interventionist (antitrust) agency to determine the most adequate allocation considering the distribution of income. (B. Lockwood, *The New Palgrave in Economics: A Dictionary of Economics*, Vol. 3, J. Eatwell, M. Milgate and P. Newman (eds.), Macmillan Press Ltd., 1987, p. 811.) For an extended critique on the use of efficiency as normative yardstick, see M. Rizzo, "The Mirage of Efficiency", 8 *Hoftra Law Review* [1980], pp. 641–658; and M. Rizzo, "Law Amid Flux: The Economics of Negligence and Strict Liability in Tort", 9 *Journal of Legal Studies* [1980], pp. 291–318. In these articles, the author clearly shows the theoretical contradictions of those who pretend to use economic efficiency as a normative yardstick to measure the functioning of the law.

60 This is frequently the case with European laws, where the judicial review of government acts has been traditionally limited to a mere revision of legal formalities due to the continental understanding of the principle of separation of powers which prohibited any interference on the functioning of the executive power. As a result, the understanding of legal rights became severely constrained by the limits provided under positive law, in the absence of an effective judicial protection over government intervention on individual rights. (On the development and consequences of this process, see E. Garcia de Enterria, *La Lengua de los Derechos: La formacion del Derecho Publico europeo tras la Revolucion Francesa*, Alianza Universidad, Madrid, 1994.) It was only after the Second World War that a new constitutionalism emerged, particularly in Germany and those countries which suffered most the positivism of the law as applied by totalitarian regimes. (See Lon. L. Fuller, "Positivism and Fidelity to Law—A Reply to Professor Hart", 71 *Harvard Law Review* [1958], pp. 630–672; also U. Everlin, "El Tribunal de Justicia de las Comunidades Europeas como Tribunal Administrativo", in *La Justicia Administrativa en el Derecho Comparado*, Edit. Civitas, Madrid, 1993, pp. 647 *et seq*.) Yet the pace of judicial control even in these countries is still slow and dominated by formalism. This is the case, for example, of the French judicial review over administrative acts within a special jurisdiction. As argued by Everlin, "In France the Public Administration enjoys a considerable margin of appraisal . . . the courts seem to let themselves become influenced by the allegations of the Public Administration, presuming that it has appraised properly the relevant facts. And of course, they do not review those facts which require a technical or economic analysis." (Everlin, *ibid*., p. 648.) Furthermore, European scholars highlight the diversity of national jurisdictions in regard to judicial control; as an ex-judge from the European Court of Justice argues: "it is in this area particularly that national interests show their differences". (Lord Mackenzie Stuart, *The European Communities and the Rule of Law*, The Hamlyn Lectures, Stevens and Sons, London, 1977, p. 64.) As contrasted with the French experience, Germany has attempted to develop a more ambitious judicial review. In this country, the emergence of the theory of "essential core of rights" has attempted to provide some protection for individual rights. They have also developed the theory of "unspecified legal concepts" whereby certain concepts contained in statutes lacking a proper legal sense (*e.g.* "competition", "relevant market", "dominance", "market power"), must be interpreted in accordance with social conventions, not according to the whim of the judge. Yet these theories still deny the possibility of questioning the way in which economic theories permeate "social conventions" to influence the judge's appraisal in a given case. Indeed, as we have seen, the "public interest" view of antitrust entails a true paradigm in the Kuhnian sense of the word. These limitations are noticeable in the rulings on European competition policy, notwithstanding certain cases where the European courts have cautiously examined the merits of the cases presented before them, albeit from the models of perfect competition and the "public interest" paradigm of competition policy. (Decision of 17 November 1987, concerning Case 142 and 156/84, *BAT/Phillip Morris*, Rep., 1987, 4487; Decision July 3, 1991, Case C–62/86, *AKZO*. For a different view, see Lord Mackenzie Stuart, *ibid*., pp. 64–68.)

61 Indeed, it is the legislative power, where the interests of groups within society are balanced and levelled, and not the judicial power which is the proper forum for the discussion of such matters, as rightly observed by Bork (Bork, n. 49 above, pp. 79–80). This is the case in countries where judicial review has few limits (*e.g.* the U.S.).

allowed under the constitutional principle of separation of powers.[61]

From another perspective, it is easy to see that the impossibility of identifying what conducts should be regarded as "unfair" or "restrictive of competition" poses an insurmountable problem to any endeavours of harmonising domestic antitrust substantive criteria and/or to develop an international set of antitrust rules. At best, harmonisation is possible in those procedural aspects surrounding the implementation of these rules, as they involve areas of law where consensus has already been built, such as the right not to be condemned without being heard, or the right to submit evidence, and so on. Unlike the *ex post* nature of substantive antitrust issues, such as the definition of a restrictive or inefficient exclusive dealing, these principles involve rules which it is possible to define in advance and can be known by all participants. It is not surprising that the international efforts made so far have been mostly oriented in this direction.

As a consequence of these reasons, it must be concluded that if applied to economic transactions and international trade, antitrust policy bears a high risk of obstructing such transactions. Under such conditions, it is very likely that if implemented to regulate international trade, antitrust will simply reproduce the protectionism of present anti-dumping rules, constituting a new non-tariff barrier. This is not surprising, considering the enormous and uncontrolled degree of discretion vested upon enforcing agencies. It is to be expected that such agencies would be inclined to find anti-competitive the aggressive conduct of foreign firms undermining the position of local firms as a result of what would otherwise be understood as healthy competitive behaviour.[62]

Indeed, the transparency of international trade is endangered by the proposals calling for antitrust intervention. The danger lies in introducing, as part of the institutional framework governing international trade relations, rules and principles that could increase the opportunities for countries to develop opportunistic behaviour and disguised trade protectionism. Indeed, given the considerable (to say the least) amount of discretion entertained by antitrust provisions, there is the risk that by incorporating these provisions into the set of institutions governing trade, the latter will be severely hampered, rather than being fostered. These terms are easily confused, as shown, for example, by the opinion of Hoekman and Mavroidis in this regard: "We argue that efforts might more productively center on ensuring that current GATT (or post-Uruguay Round) rules and principles enhancing competition are actually applied by contracting parties, and on further attempts to eliminate the 'loopholes' in the GATT allowing contracting parties to impose trade restrictions."[63] In the light of these considerations and the discretion entertained, it is naive to believe that antitrust principles would eliminate "loopholes" of the institutional rules governing trade. Instead a new, large, and unchecked source of discretion would be created.

In the light of the above, it is easy to see that the promotion of competition requires above all a reliable and predictable set of rules enabling participants in international trade to anticipate their strategies in order to obtain information most efficiently. Institutional predictability is the most important ally of any policy truly committed to fostering competition. To this we now focus our attention.

Alternative Proposal for the Promotion of Competition in International Trade Relations: Strengthening Institutions

Regulating competition does not necessarily guarantee its promotion, as antitrust supporters assume. Yet this evidence should not lead us to conclude pessimistically that public intervention is irreconcilable with the promotion of competition and market transactions. Markets can only function within a defined framework of rights, and this is a responsibility of governments, not particular. Hence, advocating against antitrust policy does not belittle government's involvement in promoting competition. On the contrary, it is unthinkable to imagine economic transactions occurring in an institution-free setting. Yet, it should be immediately realised that such intervention bears a different sign and purpose.

The question, then, is what sort of competition policy is compatible with market functioning? This section aims to define an alternative proposal of competition policy.

An alternative competition policy as applied to international transactions acknowledges the para-

62 This is, of course, far from embracing antitrust policy as the Magna Carta of economic freedom, as proclaimed naively by the U.S. Supreme Court in cases such as *Northern Pacific Railways v. United States* 356 U.S. 1, 6, 8–9, 10 N.8 (1958) or *U.S. v. Topco Associates Inc.* 405 U.S. 596, 610 (1972).

63 Hoekman and Mavroidis, Competition, Competition Policy, and the GATT, n. 36 above, pp. 2–3.

mount significance of controlling government discretion over trade and economic transactions. Administrative discretion potentially harbours new forms of trade protectionism. In turn, discretion develops in the presence of regulatory gaps; these "loopholes" are used opportunistically by governments to apply non-tariff barriers to trade.

Why does the absence of multilateral rules governing trade generate such restrictions? As it is argued elsewhere,[64] governments tend to behave strategically in their international trade relations. Such strategies are currently based in the mercantilist assumption that exports are praiseworthy, whereas imports should be discouraged.

Based on the "prisoner's dilemma" situation developed under the models of game theory,[65] it is possible to predict that governments will be inclined to favour their "own" national firms against their foreign counterparts. Yet the existence of multilateral commitments prevents them from making such distinctions and from discriminating against foreign firms. They will do so only in the presence of regulatory loopholes enabling them to decide according to discretion. Therefore, government discretion should be kept to a minimum and any institution developed to promote trade transactions and business competition should be designed with this goal in mind.

From the perspective of individuals, there are two further conditions that must be met: first, a proper delimitation in the sphere of individual rights, which would encompass not only clarity in the initial assignment of rights over things, but also clear rules on the transmission of such rights. Secondly, it calls for an expedite and efficient dispute settlement mechanism allowing to eliminate any source of interference and uncertainty in the initial allocation or transfer of rights. An efficient dispute settlement system would allow to solve *ex post* conflicts over the use of resources due to a poor *ex ante* identification and assignment of rights.

By no means such initiatives would call for a government retreat of its commitments. There are particular several instances where the formulation of policies addressed to make rights and legal relations more transparent demands particular active government involvement. Consider the case of the legislation dealing with intellectual property. This legislation aims to identify and protect certain sorts of (intellectual) entitlements over things, whose intangible nature makes them difficult to grasp, let alone to enjoy legal protection. In these cases, governments must entertain into the difficult task of detecting the infringement of these rights, whose legal qualification makes them particularly subtle. For example, how to determine that a product has been reproduced up to the point of creating a confusion in the consumers' perceptions as to the identity of the rightful producer? How to establish that a negative opinion spread about a competitor's product constitutes the denigration of his reputation and therefore a legal wrong? The delimitation of individual rights is frequently difficult and therefore requires particular care and commitment from the government in its enforcement.

The question is therefore, that there are two ways in which government intervention is necessary for market functioning and competition: First, in the *ex ante* definition of entitlements and individual spheres of action, and secondly in the *ex post* intervention aimed to clarify, albeit in an imperfect way, the content of such spheres of action in cases where initial entitlement proves difficult. The ultimate goal of defining rights and entitlements lies on the public interest to prevent unauthorised subjects ("free riders") from obtaining undeserved benefits out of the investments made by legitimate owners. This is a task that governments can perform themselves, or allow individuals to perform: another reason to repeal antitrust policies.[66]

These elements provide the blueprint for the formulation of an adequate competition policy: to ensure economic freedom to market participants in international trade, in order to provide them effective market access which is frequently denied to satisfy the interests of particular groups seeking protection from international trade. This sort of intervention would warrant positive results for the promotion of competition, in a more effective way than chasing elusive monopolistic practices.

In sum, the goal of an alternative competition policy in international trade is to enhance the predictability of market participants through the

64 I. De León and M. Morales, "From Aid to Trade: A new appraisal in the economic relations between the European Union and Latin America", *European Foreign Affairs Review* (forthcoming). Also, Ordover *et al.*, n. 16 above, pp. 10–16.

65 See A. Dixit and B. J. Nabeluff, *Thinking Strategically*, W. W. Norton & Company, New York, 1991.

66 Indeed, antitrust generally subjects contractual arrangements to exclude "free riders" (*e.g.* exclusive dealings) to a rule of reason analysis, in order to determine their restrictive effects. It is overlooked that by their very nature, these agreements are aimed to exclude ("free riding") competitors from the market. Once more, antitrust analysis reveals itself as lacking touch with reality.

reduction of uncertainty on their individual rights. This is possible if, as Petermann suggests,[67] there is an economic constitution in the international economic order, fundamentally integrated by GATT principles to which international trade participants could refer for the protection of their economic rights, in case they are harmed or lessened by trade protectionism.

Indeed, such protection would do more for individual rights and trade than any well-intentioned set of international antitrust rules.

Conclusions

Understanding the problems put forward by the promotion of competition in the contemporary world extends beyond the substitution of a well-intentioned yet inefficient policy by another based on similar premises. Nor the essence of the problem involved here is to "level the playground", and harmonise domestic legislation into a single set of multilateral antitrust principles. The question is, alas, more complex and rejects such easy answers.

The essence of this problem has to do with the nature of the restrictions to commerce and the most expedient way to avoid them. As it is shown, there are conflicting views in this sense, but some views are more realistic than others. It is clear that the role of institutions cannot be ignored, as it has been from the conventional neo-classical analysis nourishing antitrust predictions and theories. A constructive and more profound perspective must not attempt to isolate social reality and market functioning from those sets of rules that enable them to function. Constructing public policies on the basis of ideal worlds cannot lead but to contradictions and institutional failures. The theoretical shortcomings and the enforcement experience of antitrust policy show the possible consequences of these rules as applied to international trade relations. In fact, more than anything, the concerns about restrictive trade and business practices in international trade relations show, in the words of Godek, "an unhealthy anxiety about the imagined ills of capitalism".[68]

So one must be particularly wary about the claims of scholars, particularly (but not exclusively, it is fair to say) in the legal field, who take these policies at their face value without regarding the economic theory and the implications behind resulting from their implementation. It is not possible, but to agree wholeheartedly with Ackerman, when he sarcastically put the matter in these terms: "When they speak so resonantly of 'public policy', do lawyers have the slightest idea what they're talking about?"[69]

67 E.-U. Petersmann, n. 38 above.

68 P. Godek, "One U.S. Export Eastern Europe doesn't need", *International Merger Law*, September 1991, p. 3. Also, Regulation, Winter, 1992.

69 B. Ackerman, *Reconstructing American Law*, Harvard University Press, Cambridge, 1984, p. 22.

[22]

Neo-Realism and the International Harmonization of Law: Lessons from Antitrust

Spencer Weber Waller *

TABLE OF CONTENTS

---

* Associate Professor of Law, Brooklyn Law School. B.A., 1979, University of Michigan; J.D., 1982, Northwestern University Law School. Special thanks to Bailey Kuklin, Anthony Sebok and Joel Reidenberg for their comments on earlier drafts and to Elizabeth Stern, Michael Goldstein, Michelle MacGregor and Mark Radom for their research assistance.

I. INTRODUCTION

Five great attempts have been made to achieve a true international harmonization of competition law in the twentieth century.[1] None has been successful. Despite the failures of the League of Nations,[2] the proposed International Trade Organization (ITO),[3] the Economic and Social Council of the United Nations,[4] the Organization for Economic

---

1. For a discussion and definition of harmonization as applied to legal endeavors, see Martin Boodman, *The Myth of Harmonization of Laws*, 39 AM. J. COMP. L. 699, 702-08 (1991). Professor Boodman states:

> [H]armonization is a process in which diverse elements are combined or adapted to each other so as to form a coherent whole while retaining their individuality. In its relative sense, harmonization is the creation of a relationship between diverse things. Its absolute and most common meaning, however, implies the creation of a relationship of accord or consonance.

Id. at 702. The harmonization and unification of law generally has been an aspiration of the international legal community since the fall of the Roman Empire. *See* Hessel E. Yntema, *Comparative Research and Unification of Law*, 41 MICH. L. REV. 261, 265 (1942). The harmonization of competition law is part of the periodic attempts to achieve general harmonization of law across cultures. The full extent of such efforts and the forces propelling such attempts are beyond the scope of this Article, but have waxed and waned over the course of the twentieth century. For a particularly optimistic view of harmonization, see Mario Sarfatti, *Comparative Law and the Unification of Law*, 26 TUL. L. REV. 317 (1952).

2. The work of the League of Nations on cartels has received the least attention of any of the international organizations that have worked in this area. A series of reports by experts was generated, none of which was adopted by the League itself. The attitudes in the reports did not universally condemn cartels and often praised such agreements as instruments of peace, international cooperation and prosperity. *See* Henri Decugis et al., *Review of the Legal Aspects of Industrial Agreements*, League of Nations Doc. E.529(1) 1930.II.11 (1930); Antonio St. Benni et al., *General Report of the Economic Aspects of International Industrial Agreements*, League of Nations Doc. E.736 1931.II.B.21 (1931); Paul de Rousiers, *Cartels and Trusts and Their Development*, League of Nations Doc. C.E.C.P.95 1927.II.21 (1927); D.H. MacGregor, *International Cartels*, League of Nations Doc. C.E.C.P.93 1927.II.16 (1927); Gustav Cassel, *Recent Monopolistic Tendencies in Industry and Trade: Being an Analysis of the Nature and Causes of the Poverty of Nations*, League of Nations Doc. C.E.C.P.98 1927.II.36 (1927). *See generally* Dale B. Furnish, *A Transnational Approach to Restrictive Business Practices*, 4 INT'L LAW. 317 (1970) (offering a historical review of attempts to impose a system of international controls on anticompetitive behavior).

3. Havana Charter for an International Trade Organization, Mar. 24, 1948, art. 46, U.N. Doc. E/Conf.2/78 (1948), *reprinted in* U.S. DEP'T OF STATE, PUB. NO. 3206, COMMERCIAL POLICY SERIES 114, at 86-87 (1948). *See generally* Furnish, *supra* note 2, at 322-26 (discussing the proposed ITO); Earl W. Kintner et al., *Groping for a Truly International Antitrust Law*, 14 VA. J. INT'L L. 75, 86-89 (1973) (discussing the Havana Charter). For a contemporaneous discussion of the proposed ITO, see John E. Lockwood, *Proposed International Legislation with Respect to Business Practices*, 41 AM. J. INT'L L. 616 (1947).

4. *Report of the Ad Hoc Committee on Restrictive Business Practices to the Economic and Social Council*, U.N. ESCOR, 16th Sess., Supp. No. 11, U.N. Doc. E/2380 (1953). For differing views of the Report, compare Sigmund Timberg, *Restrictive Business Practices as an Appropriate Subject for United Nations Action*, 1 ANTITRUST BULL. 409 (1955) with Gilbert H. Montague, *Limitations on What UN Can Do Successfully: The Proposed UN Program on Restrictive Business*

Cooperation and Development (OECD)[5] and the United Nations Conference on Trade and Development,[6] the groundswell for a new round of harmonization efforts has begun. The 1990s blueprint for international harmonization of antitrust law includes proposals for changing the jurisdiction over transnational anticompetitive behavior,[7] the procedures for investigation of transnational competition matters[8] and the substance of competition law,[9] and suggestions for promoting

---

Practices, 1 ANTITRUST BULL. 441 (1955).

5. OECD: Guidelines for Multinational Enterprise, June 21, 1976, *reprinted in* 15 I.L.M. 969 (1976). For discussions of the OECD's efforts, see 2 BARRY E. HAWK, UNITED STATES, COMMON MARKET AND INTERNATIONAL ANTITRUST: A COMPARATIVE GUIDE 1020-30 (2d ed. Supp. 1990); Barry E. Hawk, *The OECD Guidelines for Multinational Enterprises: Competition*, 46 FORDHAM L. REV. 241 (1977); Kintner et al., *supra* note 3, at 94-95; Richard Schwartz, *Are the OECD and UNCTAD Codes Legally Binding?*, 11 INT'L LAW. 529 (1977).

6. Set of Multilaterally Agreed Equitable Principles and Rules for the Control of Restrictive Business Practices, Apr. 22, 1980, U.N. Doc. TD/RBP/CONF/10 (1980), *revised by* U.N. Doc. TD/RBP/CONF/10/Rev.1 (1981) [hereinafter RBP Code], *reprinted in* 19 I.L.M. 813 (1980). For a survey of the efforts of all of these organizations to develop international antitrust rules, see Diane P. Wood, *The Impossible Dream: Real International Antitrust*, 1992 U. CHI. LEGAL F. 277. For specific discussions of the RBP Code, see HAWK, *supra* note 5, at 1001; Timothy B. Atkeson & David G. Gill, *The UNCTAD Restrictive Business Practices Code: A Step in the North-South Dialogue*, 15 INT'L LAW. 1 (1981); Stuart E. Benson, *The U.N. Code on Restrictive Business Practices: An International Antitrust Code is Born*, 30 AM. U. L. REV. 1031 (1981); Thomas L. Brewer, *International Regulation of Restrictive Business Practices*, 16 J. WORLD TRADE L. 108, 109-12 (1982); Philippe Brusick, *UN Control of Restrictive Business Practices*, 17 J. WORLD TRADE L. 337 (1983); Joel Davidow, *The UNCTAD Restrictive Business Practices Code*, 13 INT'L LAW. 587 (1979-80); David P. Fidler, *Competition Law and International Relations*, 41 INT'L & COMP. L.Q. 563, 578-82 (1992); David G. Gill, *The UNCTAD Restrictive Business Practices Code: A Code for Competition?*, 13 INT'L LAW. 607 (1979-80); Debra L. Miller & Joel Davidow, *Antitrust at the United Nations: A Tale of Two Codes*, 18 STAN. J. INT'L L. 347, 348, 351-56, 366-71 (1982); Dale A. Oesterle, *United Nations Conference on Restrictive Business Practices*, 14 CORNELL INT'L L.J. 1, 2-9, 28-55 (1981); Cynthia Day Wallace, *International Codes and Guidelines for Multinational Enterprises: Update and Selected Issues*, 17 INT'L LAW. 435, 438-39 (1983). *See also* Schwartz, *supra* note 5, at 531-36 (discussing the enforceability of codes like the RBP Code).

7. *See* Liad Whatstein, *Extraterritorial Application of EC Competition Law—Comments and Reflections*, 26 ISRAEL L. REV. 195, 236-37 (1992); A. Paul Victor, *Export Cartels: An Idea Whose Time Has Passed*, 60 ANTITRUST L.J. 571, 577-81 (1991).

8. *See, e.g.*, James F. Rill & Virginia R. Metallo, *Convergence of Premerger Notification and Review: A Case Study*, 28 WAKE FOREST L. REV. 35 (1993) (discussing the need for further harmonization of procedures to enforce transnational mergers); *see also* Eleanor M. Fox, *Harmonization of Law and Procedures in a Globalized World: Why, What, and How?*, 60 ANTITRUST L.J. 593, 597 (1991); James T. Halverson, *Harmonization and Coordination of International Merger Procedures*, 60 ANTITRUST L.J. 531 (1991); James F. Rill, *Antitrust in a Global Environment: Conflicts and Resolutions; Commentary I*, 60 ANTITRUST L.J. 557 (1991).

9. *See* Committee on the United States in a Global Economy, Association of the Bar of the City of New York, Harmonization of International Antitrust Enforcement (Nov. 16, 1993 draft) (on file with author).

antitrust enforcement in foreign markets as a means to enhance United States export and investment opportunities.[10]

The most recent attempts have proceeded very differently from past efforts in this area. First, the growing recognition of links between competition policy and trade policy has focused attention on competition as a fitting topic for consideration by national trade policy planners and international trade institutions like the General Agreement on Tariffs and Trade (GATT).[11] Second, the growing number of countries that enforce reasonably comprehensive and sophisticated systems of competition law has produced pressure from the business community and national governments to work toward more uniform systems of notification by private parties and greater cooperation between national authorities, and has created a desire for more uniform rules of both jurisdiction and substantive law. Third, continuing conflict between nations over the investigation and enforcement of competition provisions that affect important national interests provides a further impetus for harmonization. Finally, the adoption of new competition regimes in the developing market economies in eastern Europe, the former Soviet Union and throughout the developing nations of the world has invited discussion about the most appropriate content for such laws in new and diverse settings.

The United States government and many segments of the bar apparently view these developments as an export opportunity for the Sherman Act. Both the Antitrust Division of the Department of Justice and the Federal Trade Commission have worked with foreign governments on the development of competition regimes and have detailed lawyers and economists for long-term assignments abroad to work

---

10. *See* Harry First, *Selling Antitrust in Japan*, ANTITRUST, Spring 1993, at 34.

11. General Agreement on Tariffs and Trade, Oct. 30, 1947, T.I.A.S. No. 1700, 55 U.N.T.S. 187 [hereinafter GATT]. For references to the GATT in the context of competition policy discussions, see Edwin A. Vermulst, *A European Practitioner's View of the GATT System: Should Competition Law Violations Distorting International Trade Be Subject to GATT Panels?*, 27 J. WORLD TRADE No. 6, at 55 (Dec. 1993); *National Economic Strategies for a Global Economy: Hearings Before the Senate Comm. on the Judiciary*, 102d Cong., 2d Sess. 70, 73 (1992) (statement of Prof. John H. Jackson), *prepared statement reprinted in* 26 J. WORLD TRADE No. 5, at 111 (Oct. 1992); Whatstein, *supra* note 7, at 237; *EC's Brittan Calls for Countries to Re-Examine Global Antitrust Rules*, 9 Int'l Trade Rep. (BNA) 500 (1992). For example, a working group at the Max Planck Institute in Munich, Germany has prepared a draft international antitrust code for use in a GATT framework. *See* International Antitrust Code Working Group, Draft International Antitrust Code as a GATT-MTO-Plurilateral Trade Agreement, July 10, 1993, *reprinted in* 64 Antitrust & Trade Reg. Rep. (BNA) No. 1628, Special Supp. (Aug. 19, 1993); *see also* Eleanor M. Fox, *Antitrust, Trade and the Twenty-First Century—Rounding the Circle*, 48 REC. ASS'N B. CITY N.Y. 535 (1993) [hereinafter Fox, *Rounding the Circle*]; Eleanor M. Fox, *The End of Antitrust Isolationism: The Vision of One World*, 1992 U. CHI. LEGAL F. 221, 230 [hereinafter Fox, *The End of Antitrust Isolationism*].

closely with the foreign governments.[12] The American Bar Association through its Central and Eastern European Law Initiative has provided comments and analysis from American practitioners and academics on the development of new market-based legal regimes, including comments on draft competition legislation.[13] The question of harmonization of competition policy has been addressed directly by a recent American Bar Association task force,[14] ongoing efforts by the Association of the Bar of the City of New York[15] and a growing body of academic literature.

In this Article, I look at the transferability of law from one nation and culture to another in the context of the current movement both to harmonize and to internationalize competition law, particularly as it has developed in the United States and the European Union. Part II analyzes the transferability of national law from a number of historical and philosophical perspectives, focusing on the ideas first developed by Montesquieu and debated by comparative law scholars from Montesquieu's time to our own. Parts III, IV and V critically examine the explicit and implicit assumptions that United States antitrust law can or should serve as a model for competition law for the rest of the world. Part VI offers suggestions for the process that central and eastern European nations, and other developing market economies, should use in developing indigenous competition regimes.

Finally, I end with a call for a neo-realist approach to harmonizing international economic law. Such an approach applies much of the teaching of the legal realism movement in American jurisprudence to identify the values and governance norms underlying technical rules of competition law. Neo-realism also requires a new conception for the expert in comparative competition law and a new focus on the harmonization of values and norms in place of a wasteful search for a common global text of competition law.

---

12. *See* James Langenfeld & Marsha W. Blitzer, *Is Competition Policy the Last Thing Central and Eastern Europe Need?*, 6 AM. U. J. INT'L L. & POL'Y 347, 348-49 (1991); James F. Rill, *Creating and Maintaining Competition in a Common Market: The Future of Antitrust in an Integrated World Economy*, 1992 U. CHI. LEGAL F. 263, 274-75; *see also* A.E. Rodriguez & Mark D. Williams, *The Effectiveness of Proposed Antitrust Programs for Developing Countries*, 19 N.C. J. INT'L L. & COM. REG. 209 (1994).

13. Section of Antitrust Law, American Bar Association, Comments on Draft Bulgarian Antitrust Law (Apr. 11, 1991), *reprinted in* 60 ANTITRUST L.J. 245 (1991).

14. *See* Abbott B. Lipsky, Jr., *Deterring Cartel Behavior: Harmonies and Disharmonies, Problems and Solutions*, 60 ANTITRUST L.J. 563, 563, 568-69 (1991) (summarizing recommendations of the American Bar Association Special Committee on International Antitrust); *see also* Victor, *supra* note 7, at 577-81 (same).

15. Harmonization of International Antitrust Enforcement, *supra* note 9.

II. THE TRANSFERABILITY OF NATIONAL LAW

> Laws should be so appropriate to the people for whom they are made that it is very unlikely that the laws of one nation can suit another.[16]

The transferability of national law has been one of the classic questions of comparative law. One of the earliest examinations of this question was undertaken by Montesquieu in his master work *The Spirit of the Laws*.[17] First published in 1748, *The Spirit of the Laws* represented a twenty-year effort by Montesquieu[18] and has become a classic of political science, jurisprudence and sociology. Montesquieu, while nominally paying lip service to a natural law tradition,[19] analyzes the effect of governmental structures on the resulting legal structures of the society. He uses a model of three basic governmental structures—a republic, a monarchy and a despotic regime—from which he derives the characteristics that the supporting legal regime must possess.[20] A republic requires virtue, a monarchy honor, and a despot fear.[21] The laws under each style of government are laboriously analyzed as to their method of creation and content, using then contemporary and historical examples.

While the development of theories of comparative law is not central to Montesquieu's intent, or to the subsequent use of his writings,[22] he discusses the transference of law between states at great length. Montesquieu relies on the nature of a government to determine the nature of the law implemented by that government. He identifies such indigenous characteristics as climate, terrain, population and religion as

---

16. MONTESQUIEU, THE SPIRIT OF THE LAWS 8 (Anne M. Cohler et al. eds. & trans., 1989) (pt. 1, bk. 1, ch. 3).

17. *Id.*

18. *See* Anne M. Cohler, *Introduction* to MONTESQUIEU, *supra* note 16, at xi.

19. *See* Melvin Richter, *Montesquieu*, *in* 10 INTERNATIONAL ENCYCLOPEDIA OF THE SOCIAL SCIENCES 467, 468, 470-71 (David L. Sills ed., 1968).

20. MONTESQUIEU, *supra* note 16, at 10 (pt. 1, bk. 2, ch. 1).

21. *Id.* at 28 (pt. 1, bk. 3, ch. 9).

22. While Montesquieu's political agenda appears to have been primarily to defend hereditary aristocracy as a check on the power of a monarch and to praise the system of constitutional monarchy in Great Britain, his writings became an important source of support for the creation of a federal republic in the United States and for the system of checks and balances and separation of powers embodied in the United States Constitution. *See* THE FEDERALIST No. 9, at 66-67 (Alexander Hamilton) (Charles A. Beard ed., 1948); *id.* No. 43, at 188-89 (James Madison); *id.* No. 47 (James Madison); *id.* No. 76, at 323-25 (Alexander Hamilton). Montesquieu was cited with equal passion by the Anti-Federalist forces. *See* THE ANTI-FEDERALIST PAPERS AND THE CONSTITUTIONAL CONVENTION DEBATES 102, 232, 242, 245, 251, 275, 320, 338 (Ralph Ketcham ed., 1986). For a general discussion of republican principles expounded by Montesquieu and his contemporaries as implemented by the American colonies, see Gordon S. Wood, *Classical Republicanism and the American Revolution*, 66 CHI.-KENT L. REV. 13 (1990).

the keys to determining governmental structures and to understanding the diverse practices of nations in matters of public and private law.[23] Based upon this analysis, Montesquieu concludes that culture and law are not readily transferable among nations with radically different endowments and governmental structures.[24]

Montesquieu addresses this theme directly in his chapter "On the Way to Compose the Laws."[25] He explains how the passage of identical laws in different cultures may result in one law being socially useful and the other disastrous and cruel.[26] He critiques the wholesale adoption of another country's laws that may look suitable, but were created for very different motives.[27] He concludes "[t]hat laws must not be separated from the purpose for which they are made,"[28] or "from the circumstances in which they were made."[29]

On the specific question of the transferability of law, Montesquieu states:

> As civil laws depend on political laws because they are made for one society, it would be well if, when one wants to transfer a civil law from one nation to another, one examines beforehand whether they both have the same institutions and the same political right.[30]

He criticizes the idea of uniformity among laws as one that sometimes seizes great spirits such as Charlemagne, but "infallibly strike[s] small ones,"[31] and offers the presumably rhetorical question: "[D]oes not the greatness of genius consist rather in knowing in which cases there must be uniformity and in which differences?"[32]

Montesquieu's methods, rather than his specific conclusions,[33] have survived and prospered in the work of subsequent and more rigorous comparative law scholars. Montesquieu was influential, although not

23. MONTESQUIEU, *supra* note 16, at 231-336 (pt. 3), 468-78 (pt. 5, bk. 24, chs. 14-26).

24. *Id.* at 477-78 (pt. 5, bk. 24, chs. 25-26), 494-518 (pt. 5, bk. 26).

25. *Id.* at 602-18 (pt. 6, bk. 29).

26. *Id.* at 604-05 (pt. 6, bk. 29, ch. 6). Montesquieu's specific example compares the passage of a law in ancient Rome limiting the amount of silver coin that could be kept in one's home, which had the effect of promoting the circulation of money, and a later similar law in France that amounted to confiscation by the state. Montesquieu also examines the radically different effects of the law of ostracism in ancient Athens, Argos and Syracuse. *Id.* at 605 (pt. 6, bk. 29, ch. 7).

27. *Id.* at 606 (pt. 6, bk. 29, ch. 8).

28. *Id.* at 609 (emphasis omitted) (pt. 6, bk. 29, ch. 13).

29. *Id.* at 611 (emphasis omitted) (pt. 6, bk. 29, ch. 14).

30. *Id.* at 610 (pt. 6, bk. 29, ch. 13).

31. *Id.* at 617 (pt. 6, bk. 29, ch. 18).

32. *Id.*

33. The substance of Montesquieu's conclusions about the effects of climate on national character tends to strike a late twentieth century reader as somewhere between quaint and offensive. *See, e.g.*, *id.* at 231-49 (pt. 3, bk. 14, bk. 15, chs. 1-4) (discussing the effect of climate on physiology and national character).

universally followed, in the development of the wave of legal historical research undertaken in the nineteenth century by such figures as Friedrich von Savigny[34] in Germany, Frederic Maitland,[35] Frederick Pollock[36] and Henry Maine[37] in Great Britain, and Oliver Wendell Holmes, Jr.[38] in the United States.

Montesquieu's observations regarding the transferability of law were debated more directly in the legal academy in the 1970s in an exchange between Professors Alan Watson and Otto Kahn-Freund.[39] Kahn-Freund relies on Montesquieu for the proposition that law is so closely linked to its environment that it can hardly ever change its habitat.[40] His central thesis is that in the two hundred years since Montesquieu, the geographic, economic and social differences between nations may have narrowed, but the political differences have greatly expanded.[41] He points to three political factors prohibiting the transfer of law and true reception in another country. First, he points to the gulf between the communist and the non-communist world,[42] which is a less important factor today. Second, he cites the "seemingly endless series of variations" of democratic governments.[43]

Finally, and most importantly, Kahn-Freund relies on the differing role played by organized groups and interests—business, cultural and religious—in the making and maintenance of legal institutions.[44] He states that the success of a legal transplant depends on:

---

34. *See* FRIEDRICH C. VON SAVIGNY, OF THE VOCATION OF OUR AGE FOR LEGISLATION AND JURISPRUDENCE 30 (Abraham Hayward trans., 1831) (discussing the connection of a body of law with the character of its people).

35. *See* 1 FREDERICK POLLOCK & FREDERIC W. MAITLAND, THE HISTORY OF ENGLISH LAW 111-35 (2d ed. 1898) (discussing interplay and borrowing among Roman law, civil law and canon law in twelfth and thirteenth century England).

36. *See id.*; FREDERICK POLLOCK, The History of Comparative Jurisprudence, Farewell Lecture in the University of Oxford (Jan. 24, 1903), *in* ESSAYS IN THE LAW 1, 19-20 (1922).

37. *See* HENRY S. MAINE, ANCIENT LAW (John Murray 1920) (1861).

38. *See* OLIVER WENDELL HOLMES, JR., THE COMMON LAW (1881) (tracing the history of the common law). *See generally* OLIVER WENDELL HOLMES, *Montesquieu*, *in* COLLECTED LEGAL PAPERS 250 (1921) (introducing a 1900 reprint of *The Spirit of the Laws*).

39. Most American audiences were introduced to this debate through an article by Professor Eric Stein describing this exchange of views between Kahn-Freund and Watson. *See* Eric Stein, *Uses, Misuses—and Nonuses of Comparative Law*, 72 NW. U. L. REV. 198 (1977).

40. *See* O. Kahn-Freund, *On Uses and Misuses of Comparative Law*, 37 MOD. L. REV. 1, 7 (1974).

41. *Id.* at 8; *cf.* John H. Merryman, *On the Convergence (and Divergence) of the Civil Law and the Common Law*, 17 STAN. J. INT'L L. 357, 372 (1981) (discussing decentralization of political decisionmaking as an additional force working against harmonization).

42. Kahn-Freund, *supra* note 40, at 11.

43. *Id.* at 11-12.

44. *Id.* at 12.

> how closely it is linked with the foreign power structure, whether that be expressed in the distribution of formal constitutional functions or in the influence of those social groups which in each democratic country play a decisive role in the law-making and the decision-making process and which are in fact part and parcel of its constitutional and administrative law.[45]

He further states:

> All rules which organise constitutional, legislative, administrative or judicial institutions and procedures, are designed to allocate power, rule making, decision making, above all, policy making power. These are the rules which are closest to the "organic" end of our continuum, they are the ones most resistant to transplantation.[46]

Although speaking about labor law, he concludes in words quite apropos to the antitrust context:

> It would indeed be an almost unbelievable "hazard," an unexpected coincidence if substantive rules wrenched out of their American, constitutional, political and industrial context could successfully be made to fit the needs of a country with institutions and traditions so different from those of the United States.[47]

In his brief response, Professor Watson does not dispute that law is deeply embedded in its political context, but he argues that Kahn-Freund and Montesquieu seriously underestimated the amount of successful transplantation of legal ideas, both historically and in the modern era.[48] Watson argues that successful borrowing can be accomplished from very different legal systems, even without a systematic knowledge of the law or political structure of the donor system.[49] He concludes:

> What, in my opinion, the law reformer should be after in looking at foreign systems was an *idea* which could be transformed into part of the law of his country.[50]

Professor Watson repeats his belief in the successful transplantation of ideas, but takes a more extreme position, in a subsequent article,

---

45. *Id.* at 13 (footnote omitted).

46. *Id.* at 17.

47. *Id.* at 26-27 (emphasis omitted).

48. *See* Alan Watson, *Legal Transplants and Law Reform*, 92 LAW Q. REV. 79, 80-84 (1976). *See generally* ALAN WATSON, LEGAL TRANSPLANTS (1974); Christopher Osakwe, Book Review, 62 TUL. L. REV. 1507 (1988) (reviewing K. ZWEIGERT & H. KOTZ, AN INTRODUCTION TO COMPARATIVE LAW (Tony Weir trans., 2d ed. 1987)) (emphasizing extent of borrowing and transplantation even in advanced legal systems). For a discussion of the view that human nature is substantially more stable than portrayed by Montesquieu, see MAINE, *supra* note 37, at 125-26.

49. Watson, *supra* note 48, at 79. Watson does concede that "a law reformer with such knowledge would be more efficient." *Id.*

50. *Id.* (footnote omitted).

Comparative Law and Legal Change.[51] In this article, Watson again points to a lengthy history of legal transplantation from Roman times to the present and directly challenges the link between law and social structures. He writes:

> [T]o a large extent law possesses a life and vitality of its own; that is, no extremely close, natural or inevitable relationship exists between law, legal structures, institutions and rules on the one hand and the needs and desires and political economy of the ruling élite or of the members of the particular society on the other hand. If there was such a close relationship, legal rules, institutions and structures would transplant only with great difficulty, and their power of survival would be severely limited. Changes in societal structure would always entail changes in the law.[52]

Even Watson eventually admits a certain correlation between law and society.[53] He masks that admission, however, by positing a series of seemingly exogenous factors influencing legal change—such as judicial and legislative sources of law, interest groups, and the level of generality and discretion in a particular legal system—without explicitly acknowledging or analyzing the social components of these factors.[54]

Few have followed Watson's extreme banner. Bernard Grossfeld has worked to analyze the role of comparative law and the transferability of national law in terms of the same types of factors and national endowments—climate, geography, population, religion—identified by Montesquieu.[55] Grossfeld argues that "law, culture, and society are indissolubly linked"[56] and "[t]he culture and law of a country are as dependent on its geography as is its very terrain."[57] He cautions against assuming that the general framework for a foreign legal system is the same as the home system of the person engaged in the comparative law analysis.[58] He points to the need to understand the social, political and cultural background of the foreign law in order to comprehend not just its text, but its social context, euphemisms, taboos, camouflages and conspiracies of silence about underlying motivations.[59] Accordingly, he rejects the notion that ideas are universal, or

---

51. Alan Watson, *Comparative Law and Legal Change*, 37 CAMBRIDGE L.J. 313 (1978).

52. *Id.* at 314-15.

53. *Id.* at 321.

54. *See id.* at 321-32.

55. *See* BERNHARD GROSSFELD, THE STRENGTH AND WEAKNESS OF COMPARATIVE LAW (Tony Weir trans., 1990); Bernhard Grossfeld, *Geography and Law*, 82 MICH. L. REV. 1510, 1511 (1984).

56. GROSSFELD, *supra* note 55, at 41.

57. *Id.* at 76.

58. *See id.* at 41-49.

59. *See id.* at 45-48. Grossfeld offers the example that a textual analysis of the United States Constitution as drafted in 1789 would be unilluminating in interpreting provisions regarding "'the

are capable of easy transplantation and reception across national boundaries.[60]

Grossfeld is no foe of the proper use of comparative law. Essentially, he believes that good ideas are in short supply and should be seized whenever possible. As a devoted scholar and practitioner of the art of comparative law, he merely understands its limitations:

> The only way to decide on the probable success of importing a foreign idea, once we have understood it, is to find out how the foreigners have fared with it. The difficulty here is that their experience took place in a natural and cultural context quite different from our own. On the other hand, a sense of this distance may help us appraise ideas which are vaunted as especially suitable. These points are all the more important when an entire legal institution rather than an isolated idea is in issue. Then it is not enough just to ascertain the rules in the foreign system, we have to find out how this system operates in actual practice, and evaluate the probable results of a transplant.[61]

Ultimately Grossfeld offers comparative law as a kind of "early warning system," alerting countries to impending social changes and how other systems are coping with those changes.[62] He also defends comparative law as encouraging knowledge, acceptance and responsibility for each country's legal culture. Specifically, he notes the value of comparative law in defending against the imperialism of other systems and in promoting the indigenous legal culture through greater self-awareness and insight into the nature of law itself.[63]

Another set of scholars has focused on the transformative power of legal transplants. These scholars typically have focused on the adoption of Western law in twentieth century Africa.[64] They echo the teach-

---

peculiar institution'" without a knowledge of the treatment of slavery in colonial times. *Id.* at 47; *see also* Stephen C. Hicks, *The Jurisprudence of Comparative Legal Systems*, 6 LOY. L.A. INT'L & COMP. L.J. 83, 102 (1983) (need to explore "realities" of foreign law); F.S.C. Northrop, *The Comparative Philosophy of Comparative Law*, 45 CORNELL L.Q. 617, 617-18 (1960) (importance of "living law" expressing normative customs of people).

60. *See* GROSSFELD, *supra* note 55, at 45-47.

61. *Id.* at 46; *cf.* Hicks, *supra* note 59, at 88 (value of comparative law is not adoption of any single solution but the teaching of a variety of potential solutions to domestic problems).

62. GROSSFELD, *supra* note 55, at 112.

63. *See id.* at 112-13.

64. *See* ROBERT B. SEIDMAN, THE STATE, LAW AND DEVELOPMENT (1978); Antony Allott, *The Unification of Laws in Africa*, 16 AM. J. COMP. L. 51 (1968); John H. Beckstrom, *Transplantation of Legal Systems: An Early Report on Reception of Western Laws in Ethiopia*, 21 AM. J. COMP. L. 557 (1973); Jack A. Hiller, *Language, Law, Sports and Culture: The Transferability or Non-Transferability of Words, Lifestyles, and Attitudes Through Law*, 12 VAL. U. L. REV. 433 (1978); Robert A. Sedler, *Law Reform in the Emerging Nations of Sub-Saharan Africa: Social Change and the Development of the Modern Legal System*, 13 ST. LOUIS U. L.J. 195 (1968); *cf.* Henning Wegener, *Cultural Relativism, and Aid in the Legal Development of New Nations*, 9 NAT. L.F. 95 (1964) (discussing the role of Western lawyers in devising and

ings of Montesquieu, Kahn-Freund and Grossfeld in formulating a "Law of Non-Transferability of Law,"[65] but appear to be more interested in the unintended cultural changes that accompany the reception of foreign law in a developing country. For example, one scholar working in this tradition has suggested:

> that while any developing country can probably adopt and adapt any law or body of laws from another culture, if necessary, and can even translate such laws or rules into its indigenous language, such laws or body of laws carry with them so much imperceptible and incommensurable cultural "baggage" that the receiving country will inevitably experience far more internal cultural change than it either realized, intended or would have intended.[66]

Modern sociology sheds further light on the transferability of law. The social construction of reality is a concept derived from the sociology of the early twentieth century[67] and is made more prominent in its radical form by the French philosopher Michel Foucault.[68] Both the mainstream and radical forms of this concept tell us that ideas and theories are not universal, but are embedded in a specific temporal, physical and social setting that permits them to flourish.[69]

While rarely applied directly to the study of antitrust doctrine,[70] such teachings suggest that the Sherman Act,[71] like any intellectual construct, is heavily particularized rather than being a universal norm readily applicable to other social systems. Like Montesquieu and comparativists such as Kahn-Freund, sociologists and philosophers working in this social construction tradition suggest that an idea divorced from its context is not much of an idea at all.

Similarly, post-modern legal theory, in particular the application of analytical techniques from literary criticism, suggests that law cannot be easily transferred for a different reason. Post-modernism suggests that

---

modernizing law in African and Asian countries).

65. SEIDMAN, *supra* note 64, at 29; Hiller, *supra* note 64, at 433-35; *cf.* Northrop, *supra*, note 59, at 657 (arguing that imposition of Western legal and political systems on lesser developed countries will be unsuccessful unless basic aspects of receiving countries' traditions are incorporated).

66. Hiller, *supra* note 64, at 434.

67. *See* PETER L. BERGER & THOMAS LUCKMANN, THE SOCIAL CONSTRUCTION OF REALITY: A TREATISE IN THE SOCIOLOGY OF KNOWLEDGE 4-12 (Anchor Books 1967).

68. *See generally*, MICHEL FOUCAULT, THE ARCHAEOLOGY OF KNOWLEDGE AND THE DISCOURSE ON LANGUAGE (A.M. Sheridan Smith trans., Barnes & Noble Books 1993).

69. *See* BERGER & LUCKMAN, *supra* note 67, at 18-46; FOUCAULT, *supra* note 68, at 135-40.

70. Professor Rudolph Peritz of New York Law School consistently has applied the teaching of Foucault toward a penetrating analysis of the early history of the Sherman Act and the genealogies of the contending streams of argument that permeate current antitrust discourse. *See, e.g.*, Rudolph J. Peritz, *The "Rule of Reason" in Antitrust Law: Property Logic in Restraint of Competition*, 40 HASTINGS L.J. 285, 289 n.18 (1989).

71. Sherman Antitrust Act, 15 U.S.C. §§ 1-7 (1988 & Supp. IV 1992).

texts are not authoritative statements of either an author's intent or objective plain meaning. Such theories attack the notion that a text can effectively convey the author's intent or any stable meaning to a reader.[72] Under post-modern analysis, the focus shifts to the reader's construction of the text based on the reader's life experience and social setting. A post-modern approach would therefore deemphasize concern over the receiving country being transformed against its will and would suggest, along with Montesquieu, Kahn-Freund and Grossfeld, that a text speaking to competition principles in a particular historical and social setting will rarely transfer to another setting with its message intact.

III. SHERMAN ACT FOR SALE

The events since 1989 in eastern Europe and the former Soviet Union have been a gold mine for American attorneys and legal academics. The development of new competition regimes has been an important part of the reformation and regeneration of commercial law in these newly emerging market economies.

The United States government has been a principal player in offering its expertise to develop American-style antitrust law in eastern Europe and elsewhere where the allure of state planning has faded. The private sector has not been far behind. Attorneys with personal and family ties to the new market economy countries have been influential in the process of legal reform. Several law firms have advised foreign governments on both a fee and pro bono basis regarding the drafting of new constitutions and statutes. The American Bar Association has organized a Central and Eastern European Law Initiative to provide long-term assistance on legal questions as well as to provide comments on draft legislation. State and local bar associations also have participated with exchange programs, pro bono legal advice and the establishment of longer term relationships with foreign bar associations.[73]

These efforts have been particularly noticeable in the field of competition law. Both the Department of Justice and the Federal Trade Commission have consulted with foreign governments regarding the development of antitrust law and have stationed attorneys and econo-

72. *See generally* RICHARD WEISBERG, POETHICS: AND OTHER STRATEGIES OF LAW AND LITERATURE (1992); RICHARD H. WEISBERG, THE FAILURE OF THE WORD; THE PROTAGONIST AS LAWYER IN MODERN FICTION (1984); Anthony D'Amato, *Aspects of Deconstruction: The Failure of the Word "Bird"*, 84 NW. U. L. REV. 536 (1990).

73. For example, the Illinois State Bar Association has formed a "twining" project with the Warsaw Bar Association.

mists abroad to consult more closely and on a longer term basis with the new competition authorities in many countries.[74]

Much of the effort appears to be aimed at selling the Sherman Act as an appropriate model for other countries that are drafting new competition provisions. James Rill, the former Assistant Attorney General in charge of the Antitrust Division, has offered American antitrust law as a model for eastern Europe, and has analogized the task of restoring competition in Poland to that faced by the United States in 1890 when it passed the Sherman Act.[75]

Another approach has been to perceive the Sherman Act as competing with the competition law of the European Union (EU) for the hearts and minds of eastern Europe. Here, the adoption of the Sherman Act is advocated against the EU's approach to competition law, which may be favored by the developing market economies in Europe due to geographic proximity and a desire for closer ties and eventual membership in the EU.[76] Janet Steiger, the former Chairman of the Federal Trade Commission, has recommended the adoption of Sherman Act-style provisions in eastern Europe, and has cautioned against the adoption of provisions modeled after EU competition provisions, which she claims "'may do too much to protect individual competitors rather than the competitive process.'"[77]

A final approach has been to conceive of foreign competition law as a means of transforming and reinvigorating United States antitrust law. Professor Eleanor Fox has argued for an interesting twist on the theme of the competition between United States and EU competition policy. She has advocated the international harmonization of competition law more along the lines of EU competition policy as a means of injecting

74. Langenfeld & Blitzer, *supra* note 12, at 348-49; *Justice Department, FTC Receive Funds to Support Competition Counseling Aid*, 8 Int'l Trade Rep. (BNA) 871 (1991) [hereinafter *Justice Department*].

75. *Polish Businesses 'Have Nothing to Fear' on Joint Ventures, Justice Official Says*, 7 Int'l Trade Rep. (BNA) 746 (1990).

76. *See* Langenfeld & Blitzer, *supra* note 12, at 353; *EC Agreements with Eastern Neighbors Seen as First Step to EC Membership*, 8 Int'l Trade Rep. (BNA) 1853 (1991); *Eastern Europe Importing EC Antitrust Rules as Part of Trade Access Pacts*, 8 Int'l Trade Rep. (BNA) 1815 (1991). Poland, Czechoslovakia (prior to partition) and Hungary each has signed an association agreement with the European Union that includes the obligation to apply EU-style competition policy. The association agreements are published in 1992 O.J. (L 114) (Poland); 1992 O.J. (L 115) (Czechoslovakia); 1992 O.J. (L 116) (Hungary). For a discussion by FTC economists nominally advocating a hybrid of U.S. and EU approaches for Latin American countries, but urging adoption of a strict law-and-economic version of recent U.S. antitrust policy as the preferred solution for each antitrust issue analyzed, see Malcolm B. Coate et al., *Antitrust in Latin America: Regulating Government and Business*, 24 U. MIAMI INTER-AM. L. REV. 37 (1992).

77. *FTC's Steiger Says U.S. Has Responsibility to Help New Democracies in Eastern Europe*, 7 Int'l Trade Rep. (BNA) 1070 (1990).

back into United States antitrust law non-economic values that were rejected or downgraded during the last fifteen years.[78]

Private efforts also have been bullish on international harmonization based upon the Sherman Act.[79] The Antitrust Section of the American Bar Association provided a fifty-six page analysis of the Bulgarian draft antitrust law.[80] The report contained numerous specific comments and recommendations, but concluded that Bulgaria should "'stress the importance of preserving the freedom of firms to engage in competition, even hard competition that may hurt less efficient competitors, lest the law undercut the benefits of competition to the consumer, to the growth of efficient enterprise, and to the economy.'"[81]

A secondary goal of these efforts stems from the perception that the adoption of U.S.-style antitrust law will aid U.S. export competitiveness. Janet Steiger has stated: "Reform in these areas will not only benefit the citizens of the region but will enhance the competitiveness of American industry by helping to open new markets and investment opportunities."[82]

This concept of antitrust salesmanship as a trade weapon has been particularly prominent in the area of U.S.-Japan trade. Following the threat of trade sanctions by the United States, the United States and Japan announced an agreement on June 28, 1990 on a series of measures designed to eliminate structural barriers and distortions in the Japanese market.[83]

---

78. *See* Fox, *The End of Antitrust Isolationism*, *supra* note 11, at 221-22, 238-40.

79. *See, e.g.*, *ABA Section Forms International Committee Aimed at Creating Antitrust Harmonization*, 8 Int'l Trade Rep. (BNA) 29 (1991).

80. *Bulgarian Parliament Considering Revisions in Draft Legislation on Competition Law*, 8 Int'l Trade Rep. (BNA) 870 (1991).

81. *Id.* at 871.

82. *Justice Department*, *supra* note 74, at 871.

83. Joint Report of the U.S.-Japan Working Group on the Structural Impediments Initiative, June 28, 1990 [hereinafter Joint Report on the SII] (unpublished report, available from the U.S. Dep't of the Treasury). For a summary of the policy commitments contained in the Joint Report, see *Key Elements of U.S.-Japan Structural Impediments Initiative Joint Report Released by USTR, June 28, 1990*, 7 Int'l Trade Rep. (BNA) 1014 (1990). The measures set forth in the agreement go beyond traditional trade liberalization measures and seek to alter structural aspects of the Japanese economy perceived as constituting barriers to United States trade and investment. The so-called Structural Impediments Initiative (SII) measures include changes in Japanese saving and investment patterns, land policy, distribution system, exclusionary business practices, *keiretsu* relationships (discussed *infra* text accompanying notes 87-90) and pricing mechanisms. The Report also addresses aspects of United States competitiveness, including savings and investment policy, corporate behavior, government regulation, research and development, export promotion and work force education and training. *See United States-Japan Structural Impediments Initiative (SII): Hearing Before the Subcomm. on International Trade of the Senate Comm. on Finance*, 101st Cong., 2d Sess., pt. 3 of 3 (1990).

Amending and enhancing the enforcement of the Japanese Antimonopoly Act is an important aspect of the U.S.-Japan agreement, with at least the implicit assumption by the United States that in order to constitute true competition law, Japanese law should more closely resemble our own.[84] The final agreement calls for increased funding of the Japanese Fair Trade Commission (JFTC) to enforce the Japanese Antimonopoly Act through more formal investigations and prosecutions, increased use of criminal sanctions and enhanced use of private damage actions.[85] The agreement also calls for the JFTC to formulate guidelines covering areas such as vertical distributional restraints, resale price maintenance and anticompetitive dealings between parents and subsidiaries.[86]

There also has been increased attention to the competitive significance of the Japanese *keiretsu* system. *Keiretsu* refers to a system of loose vertical integration through long-term relationships and partial

---

84. *See* First, *supra* note 10, at 36-37.

85. Report by the Japanese Delegation, pts. IV-V, Joint Report on the SII, *supra* note 83.

86. *Id.* pt. III, at 12-13. On July 11, 1991, the JFTC issued its final guidelines. Executive Office, Fair Trade Commission, The Antimonopoly Act Guidelines Concerning Distribution Systems and Business Practices (July 11, 1991) (on file with author). While the Guidelines responded to many of the concerns raised by critics, Japanese competition policy remains the focus of substantial attention in the SII talks and the surrounding diplomacy, with increasing attention to the actual enforcement efforts of the JFTC. *See Structural Impediments Initiative (SII) Review: Hearing Before the Subcomm. on International Trade of the Senate Comm. on Finance*, 102d Cong., 2d Sess. (1992); *Review of Ongoing Trade Negotiations and Completed Trade Agreements: Hearing Before the Subcomm. on International Trade of the Senate Comm. on Finance*, 102d Cong., 1st Sess. (1991); *Reviewing Structural Impediments Initiative (SII): Hearing Before the Subcomm. on International Trade of the Senate Comm. on Finance*, 102d Cong., 1st Sess. (1991); *see also Japanese Banking Group Develops Draft Antitrust Compliance Program*, 9 Int'l Trade Rep. (BNA) 767 (1992); *U.S. Increases Pressure on Japan to Curb Anti-Monopoly Act Exemptions*, 9 Int'l Trade Rep. (BNA) 765 (1992); *Hills Urges Japan to Step Up Antitrust Enforcement and Increase Maximum Fines*, 9 Int'l Trade Rep. (BNA) 761 (1992); *U.S., Japan Affirm Commitment to Enforcing Competition Policies, Rill Says*, 9 Int'l Trade Rep. (BNA) 727 (1992); *U.S. Makes a 20-Point Demand of Japan for Structural Changes, Officials Say*, 9 Int'l Trade Rep. (BNA) 433 (1992); *U.S. Seeks New Commitments from Japan Under Structural Impediments Initiative*, 9 Int'l Trade Rep. (BNA) 400 (1992); *Expanded Role Is Expected for Antitrust Enforcement Officials*, 9 Int'l Trade Rep. (BNA) 244 (1992). In response, the JFTC apparently has assumed a more active role through such measures as expanding its authority over the Japanese economy, recommending increases in the maximum fines under the Antimonopoly Act, more aggressively investigating violations and seeking fines, and bringing its first criminal proceeding in seventeen years. *Japan's FTC Says It Will Loosen Rules on Business Tie-Ups with Japanese Firms*, 9 Int'l Trade Rep. (BNA) 490 (1992); *Japan's FTC Is Investigating Charges of Price Maintenance in Consumer Goods*, 9 Int'l Trade Rep. (BNA) 597 (1992); *Japanese Panel Recommends Increasing Fines for Corporate Antitrust Violators*, 9 Int'l Trade Rep. (BNA) 397 (1992); *Expanded Role Is Expected for Antitrust Enforcement Officials*, 9 Int'l Trade Rep. (BNA) 244 (1992); *Japan's FTC Files Charges Against Plastic-Wrap Firms For Alleged Collusion*, 8 Int'l Trade Rep. (BNA) 1650 (1991).

common stock ownership.[87] Most *keiretsu* combine manufacturers, parts suppliers, a major financial institution, other service providers and often a major export trading company.[88]

Keiretsu will continue to attract much attention from both antitrust and international trade policymakers. The United States will have difficulty prohibiting or limiting the operation of *keiretsu* on antitrust grounds, however, because of the increased tolerance of vertical restraints in U.S. antitrust policy[89] and the encouragement of vertical integration on efficiency grounds. Unless these attitudes change, it will be difficult to justify exporting U.S. antitrust law as a means of attacking a uniquely Japanese version of practices that U.S. firms themselves are encouraged to undertake.[90]

The tensions between the United States and Japan are an excellent illustration of the problems and assumptions underlying recent attempts at harmonizing competition law. Much of the frustration in the United States stems from the assumption—at least implicit—that competition law in Japan should work in a similar fashion as in the United States given the textual similarities between the two sets of legal rules and the role of the United States in the promulgation of the Japanese Antimonopoly Act at the end of World War II. Instead, Japan, without an indigenous tradition of competition as a value to enforce through legal mechanisms, began amending its antitrust laws as soon as politically possible. Although Japan today has an Antimonopoly Act and a Fair Trade Commission to enforce it, the Act is enforced much less frequently than the comparable laws in the United States. Furthermore, the Act is often perceived more as an instrument of industrial development and a barrier to market access than a true antitrust system. Japan thus was successful in shaping its antimonopoly law to meet indigenous societal needs, but may have eliminated the core of a competition law

---

87. *See* MICHAEL E. PORTER, THE COMPETITIVE ADVANTAGE OF NATIONS 153-54 (1990); Michael Gerlach, Keiretsu *Organization in the Japanese Economy: Analysis and Trade Implications*, *in* POLITICS AND PRODUCTIVITY: THE REAL STORY OF WHY JAPAN WORKS 141, 142 (Chalmers Johnson et al. eds., 1989).

88. *See* PORTER, *supra* note 87, at 153-54; Gerlach, *supra* note 87, at 143; Angelina Helou, *The Nature and Competitiveness of Japan's* Keiretsu, 25 J. WORLD TRADE No. 3, at 99 (June 1991).

89. *See, e.g.*, Business Elecs. Corp. v. Sharp Elecs. Corp., 485 U.S. 717, 724-25, 735-36 (1988).

90. *See* MICHAEL L. DERTOUZOS ET AL., MADE IN AMERICA: REGAINING THE PRODUCTIVE EDGE 99-105 (1989); Kevin Kelly et al., *Learning from Japan*, BUS. WK., Jan. 27, 1992, at 52; Alan S. Blinder, *A Japanese Buddy System That Could Benefit U.S. Business*, BUS. WK., Oct. 14, 1991, at 32; *cf.* Thomas E. Kauper, *Antitrust in 1992: The Year of the Storyteller*, 61 ANTITRUST L.J. 347, 364 (1993) (noting hypocrisy in U.S. stance toward *keiretsu* and questioning extent to which increased Japanese antimonopoly enforcement will aid U.S. exports).

system in doing so. In reality, the United States and Japan are not even discussing the same topic when they discuss competition policy.

IV. THE UNIQUELY AMERICAN CULTURAL MYTH OF THE SHERMAN ACT

> [M]yth is unsuccessful in giving man more material power over the environment. However, it gives man, very importantly, the illusion that he can understand the universe and that he *does* understand the universe. It is, of course, only an illusion.[91]

What then is the role of the U.S. antitrust laws embodied in the Sherman Act[92] in light of the debate over the transferability of national competition law? Can the Sherman Act be exported? Will either foreign or U.S. interests be served if it is adopted by post-socialist and developing countries as part of a package of market-based reforms and privatization? The unique and mythical role the antitrust laws play in American law and culture suggests not.

A. The Contrasting Narratives of the Sherman Act

There are at least six conventional narratives to describe the passage of the Sherman Act and the goals it supposedly implements. The principal "story" for the Sherman Act over the last twenty years has been the efficiency-consumer welfare model promulgated by economists, lawyers and policymakers associated with the price theorists at the University of Chicago. The "Chicago school" story of antitrust suggests that the antitrust laws should be primarily or exclusively concerned with the promotion of consumer welfare, defined as aggregate wealth maximization.[93] The strongest version of this story has been told by Robert Bork who argues that this goal was, in fact, the exclusive legislative goal of the United States Congress in enacting the Sherman Act in 1890.[94] Another version of the history of the antitrust laws closely linked to the consumer welfare model has been the argument that the federal antitrust laws were intended to federalize the common law of restraints of trade and confer a broad jurisdiction on the

---

91. CLAUDE LÉVI-STRAUSS, MYTH AND MEANING 17 (1978).

92. Besides the Sherman Act, U.S. antitrust laws include the Clayton Act, 15 U.S.C. §§ 12-27 (1988 & Supp. IV 1992), section 5 of the Federal Trade Commission Act, 15 U.S.C. § 45 (1988), the Wilson Tariff Act, 15 U.S.C. §§ 8-11 (1988), and the Antidumping Act of 1916, 15 U.S.C. § 72 (1988).

93. *See* Frank H. Easterbrook, *The Limits of Antitrust*, 63 TEX. L. REV. 1 (1984); Richard A. Posner, *The Chicago School of Antitrust Analysis*, 127 U. PA. L. REV. 925 (1979).

94. ROBERT H. BORK, THE ANTITRUST PARADOX: A POLICY AT WAR WITH ITSELF 50-51 (1978).

federal courts to create a continuing common law of antitrust,[95] which proponents of this history often argue follows the same normative values of wealth maximization through productive and allocative efficiency.[96]

The influence of the Chicago school has been enormous at both a doctrinal and an enforcement level. In recent years, the enforcement efforts of the Antitrust Division have focused almost entirely on price fixing, bid rigging and related types of horizontal collusion.[97] As a result of the narrow economic reasoning the Divison has applied in its decision-making process,[98] enforcement actions in the Reagan and Bush Administrations virtually ceased against vertical restrictions, restrictions in the creation or licensing of intellectual property rights, and most mergers and joint ventures.

A principal counternarrative has been the political story of antitrust. Scholars such as Lawrence Sullivan,[99] Eleanor Fox[100] and Robert Pitofsky[101] have argued that the goals of antitrust are, and always have been, far broader than the promotion of a narrow type of allocative efficiency, and that they encompass the overtly political goals of controlling the accumulation of private economic power and enhancing the freedom of individuals and enterprise to engage in market activity.[102]

95. HANS B. THORELLI, THE FEDERAL ANTITRUST POLICY 228 (1955).

96. Frank H. Easterbrook, *Is There a Ratchet in Antitrust Law?*, 60 TEX. L. REV. 705, 706, 715 (1982).

97. *See* Timothy Brennan, *Content, Controversy, and Control: Politics and the Evolution of Antitrust Enforcement*, 14 LAW & POL'Y 107, 109 (1992).

98. *See id.* at 108-09.

99. For some examples of Sullivan's work, see Eleanor M. Fox & Lawrence A. Sullivan, *Antitrust—Retrospective and Prospective: Where Are We Coming From? Where Are We Going?*, 62 N.Y.U. L. REV. 936 (1987); Lawrence A. Sullivan, *The Viability of the Current Law on Horizontal Restraints*, 75 CAL. L. REV. 835 (1987); Lawrence A. Sullivan, *Monopolization: Corporate Strategy, the IBM Cases, and the Transformation of the Law*, 60 TEX. L. REV. 587 (1982); Lawrence A. Sullivan, *Antitrust, Microeconomics, and Politics: Reflections on Some Recent Relationships*, 68 CAL. L. REV. 1 (1980); Lawrence A. Sullivan, *Economics and More Humanistic Disciplines: What Are the Sources of Wisdom for Antitrust?*, 125 U. PA. L. REV. 1214 (1977).

100. For some examples of Fox's work, see Fox, *Rounding the Circle*, *supra* note 11; Fox, *The End of Antitrust Isolationism*, *supra* note 11; Fox, *supra* note 8; Fox & Sullivan, *supra* note 99; Eleanor M. Fox, *The Politics of Law and Economics in Judicial Decision Making: Antitrust as a Window*, 61 N.Y.U. L. REV. 554 (1986); Eleanor M. Fox, *The Modernization of Antitrust: A New Equilibrium*, 66 CORNELL L. REV. 1140 (1981).

101. *See* Robert Pitofsky, *The Political Content of Antitrust*, 127 U. PA. L. REV. 1051 (1979).

102. For further discussions of the political aspects of antitrust, see THORELLI, *supra* note 95, at 227; Richard Hofstadter, *What Happened to the Antitrust Movement?*, *in* THE PARANOID STYLE IN AMERICAN POLITICS AND OTHER ESSAYS 188 (1965); Louis B. Schwartz, *"Justice" and Other Non-Economic Goals of Antitrust*, 127 U. PA. L. REV. 1076 (1979); *cf.* Donald I. Baker, *Antitrust*

While the principal debate has been between a political and a consumer welfare model of antitrust,[103] other more eclectic voices have been heard as well. Many scholars who accept the need to apply the antitrust laws in economic terms dispute whether the Chicago school applies the correct insights and methods.[104] In a different vein, Rudolph Peritz, in a series of articles, describes the dynamics of this early period of antitrust law as an ongoing struggle—which continues even today—between the promotion of competition and the protection of property rights.[105]

More cynical scholars perceive the antitrust laws as an ineffective system shrewdly accepted by the American business community as a fundamental validation of free enterprise and a nearly costless compromise that heads off any serious efforts to promote greater corporate accountability, comprehensive regulation or the growth of public enterprise.[106] Another commentator views the antitrust laws as not related to the regulation of competition at all, but as the last gasp of nineteenth century restrictions on the creation and operation of enterprises in corporate form.[107] Others have perceived the rise of antitrust as a reflection of deep spiritual and cultural values regarding the importance of competition and individual entrepreneurship in the American psyche.[108]

---

and Politics at the Justice Department, 9 J.L. & POL. 291 (1993) (discussing political component of decision to proceed or refrain from government antitrust enforcement action).

103. The sources on both sides of the traditional debate are collected in Barbara A. White, *Black and White Thinking in the Gray Areas of Antitrust: The Dismantling of Vertical Restraints Regulation*, 60 GEO. WASH. L. REV. 1 (1991).

104. *See* 1 PHILLIP AREEDA & DONALD F. TURNER, ANTITRUST LAW ¶ 105 (1978); Jonathan B. Baker, *Recent Developments in Economics That Challenge Chicago School Views*, 58 ANTITRUST L.J. 645 (1989); Thomas G. Krattenmaker & Steven C. Salop, *Anticompetitive Exclusion: Raising Rivals' Costs to Achieve Power over Price*, 96 YALE L.J. 209, 214 (1986).

105. *See* Rudolph J.R. Peritz, *Foreword: Antitrust as Public Interest Law*, 35 N.Y.L. SCH. L. REV. 767 (1990); Rudolph J. Peritz, *A Counter-History of Antitrust Law*, 1990 DUKE L.J. 263; Peritz, *supra* note 70; Rudolph J. Peritz, *A Genealogy of Vertical Restraints Doctrine*, 40 HASTINGS L.J. 511 (1989); *see also* Martin J. Sklar, *Sherman Antitrust Act Jurisprudence and Federal Policy-Making in the Formative Period, 1890-1914*, 35 N.Y.L. SCH. L. REV. 791 (1990).

106. *See* THORELLI, *supra* note 95, at 319-26; Hofstadter, *supra* note 102, at 190-91, 198.

107. *See* DUDLEY H. CHAPMAN, MOLTING TIME FOR ANTITRUST: MARKET REALITIES, ECONOMIC FALLACIES, AND EUROPEAN INNOVATIONS 1-41 (1991). Chapman views the passage of the Sherman Act in 1890 as a great irony, it having occurred just after New Jersey authorized the existence of holding companies. *See id.* at 45. This authorization ended the need for the trust device, which had spawned the perception that antitrust laws were needed in the first place. *See id.*

108. Hofstadter, *supra* note 102, at 209-11. For a further discussion of this important mythic undercurrent expressed in American competition policy, see *infra* notes 110-32 and accompanying text.

The power and impact of U.S. antitrust law has ebbed and flowed in accordance with the strength of the prevailing "story" of the Sherman Act. In the 1970s and 1980s, the Chicago school and its story first captured the academy, and then largely captured the governmental enforcement mechanisms and the judges who interpret the statutory language. The Chicago school's influence will remain pervasive but its dominance, to the exclusion of other interpretations of the language chosen by Congress, will persist only if its normative values remain persuasive to policymakers, law enforcers and commentators.[109]

B. The Sherman Act as Cultural Myth

The enduring debate over the meaning of the Sherman Act suggests several conclusions that diminish its utility in other settings. First, there is no single Sherman Act to use as a model for the United States, or any other legal system, for problem solving. Second, if there ever was such a thing as a true history of the Sherman Act, it has long since been shrouded in the majestic but imprecise language chosen by Congress. Third, any discourse about the proper meaning and interpretation of the Sherman Act today is a rhetorical exercise in favor of a particular normative vision of the importance and definition of competition, and not a meaningful dialogue about original intent and legislative purpose.

Finally, considering only the expressly suggested purposes of the Sherman Act may fail to inform the American observer, let alone a foreign observer, of the key symbolic and mythic roles served by having an antitrust law. Viewed in mythic terms,[110] American antitrust law is a remarkably resilient, if empty, vessel. It is simply indestructible at this stage of American jurisprudence. In describing the Sherman Act as a "charter of freedom" of nearly constitutional dimension[111] the Supreme Court has accurately stated both its

109. For example, the Supreme Court's recent opinion in *Eastman Kodak Co. v. Image Technical Services, Inc.*, 112 S. Ct. 2072 (1992), already has been analyzed as the beginning of the post-Chicago school of antitrust. *See* Jean Wegman Burns, *Vertical Restraints, Efficiency, and the Real World*, 62 FORDHAM L. REV. 597, 637-51 (1993); Michael S. Jacobs, *Market Power Through Imperfect Information: The Staggering Implications of* Eastman Kodak Co. v. Image Technical Services *and a Modest Proposal for Limiting Them*, 52 MD. L. REV. 336 (1993); Lawrence T. Festa, III, Comment, Eastman Kodak Co. v. Image Technical Services, Inc.: *The Decline and Fall of the Chicago Empire?*, 68 NOTRE DAME L. REV. 619 (1993); Lisa Meckfessel Judson, Note, Kodak v. Image Technical Services: *The Taming of* Matsushita *and the Chicago School*, 1993 WIS. L. REV. 1633.

110. *See* Peritz, *supra* note 70, at 312-13; *cf.* Fidler, *supra* note 6, at 565-70 (discussing antitrust law as defining national identity and image both internally and in relation to other societies).

111. Appalachian Coals, Inc. v. United States, 288 U.S. 344, 359-60 (1933), *overruled on unrelated grounds by* Copperweld Corp. v. Independence Tube Corp., 467 U.S. 752, 777 (1984).

centrality and its durability in American jurisprudence. Although the antitrust laws occasionally will be amended and clarified by legislation, and exemptions will be added and subtracted by both congressional and judicial pronouncements, the Sherman Act has about as much chance of being comprehensively rethought and redrafted as the United States Constitution.

The mythic aspects of atomistic competition in private markets substantially predate the Sherman Act. In *The Protestant Ethic and the Spirit of Capitalism*,[112] Max Weber linked the rise of private capitalism to the Protestant doctrines of a worldly calling and the importance of worldly deeds as a sign of predestination, grace and true belief.[113] Although Weber cautions against simplistic causalities,[114] he notes the influences of Puritan and Calvinistic dogma on the promotion of open markets and on the dissolution of the great concentrations of economic power that form the core of modern antitrust:[115]

> Calvinism opposed organic social organizations in the fiscal-monopolistic form which it assumed in Anglicanism under the Stuarts, especially in the . . . alliance of Church and State with the monopolists on the basis of a Christian-social ethical foundation. Its leaders were universally among the most passionate opponents of this type of politically, privileged commercial, putting-out, and colonial capitalism. Over against it they placed the individualistic motives of rational legal acquisition by virtue of one's own ability and initiative. And, while the politically privileged monopoly industries in England all disappeared in short order, this attitude played a large and decisive part in the development of the industries which grew up in spite of and against the authority of the State.[116]

In fact, Weber compares the struggle against the privileged position—legal and actual—of the sixteenth and seventeenth century trading companies to the late nineteenth century struggle against the trusts.[117]

Weber is actually speaking far more to the American experience than the British. The battle that Weber describes in Britain evolved into a battle against crown monopolies, not all special economic privileges. It was merely a battle over who had the power to confer monopoly grants, which was won early on by Parliament.[118] But the wisdom of

---

112. MAX WEBER, THE PROTESTANT ETHIC AND THE SPIRIT OF CAPITALISM (Talcott Parsons trans., 1930).

113. *See id.* at 91-180.

114. *See id.* at 91, 181-83.

115. *See id.* at 179-80.

116. *Id.* at 179. For a similar discussion of the links between the Reformation and capitalism, see BROOKS ADAMS, THE EMANCIPATION OF MASSACHUSETTS: THE DREAM AND THE REALITY 484-87 (rev. ed. 1919).

117. WEBER, *supra* note 112, at 82.

118. Statute of Monopolies, 21 Jac. 1, ch. 3 (1623); *see also* Darcy v. Allein (The Case of Monopolies), 77 Eng. Rep. 1260, 1260 (K.B. 1602) (voiding Crown grant of monopoly over

such grants was never in serious dispute. The colonial and foreign trade of Britain continued to be dominated by statutorily authorized monopoly trading companies well into the late nineteenth century.

Great Britain, therefore, never experienced an indigenous impetus for the development of true antitrust law. By Weber's own time, British competition law had evolved away from the promotion of a competitive equilibrium model and allowed lawful and enforceable cartels as a means of maximizing the property of the owners, even at the expense of competitors and consumers.[119]

The American colonial and revolutionary experience is the better and more fertile ground for testing Weber's thesis.[120] American independence was threatened by foreign control of international trade by the colonial powers. As early as the Washington Administration, Thomas Jefferson, as Secretary of State, devoted substantial time to ending monopoly privileges that restricted American trade with and exports to France.[121]

The history of the enforcement of the Commerce Clause illustrates the federal government's continuing struggle against the monopoly grants of state governments,[122] which retarded the expansion and completion of the U.S. national economy until the mid-nineteenth century. Even so, the development of antitrust principles to control the abuses of private economic power was largely irrelevant until the completion of a true national economy in the late nineteenth century, following the fruition of the industrial revolution, the military subjugation of the South and the West, and the development of transportation and communication systems linking buyers and sellers in urban and rural areas in an impersonal dependence on market forces.

The forces that produced the Sherman Act, however, also contradicted the vision upon which it was based. Even at the time Congress passed the Sherman Act, it was unclear whether the antitrust laws promoted an atomistic vision of the national economy that was still possible.[123] In *The Folklore of Capitalism*,[124] Thurman Arnold described the growth and role of antitrust in Weberian terms, namely as demonizing individuals who fail to conform to the prevailing social and

---

importation and manufacture of playing cards).

119. *See* TONY FREYER, REGULATING BIG BUSINESS: ANTITRUST IN GREAT BRITAIN AND AMERICA, 1880-1990, at 196-212 (1992).

120. *See* GORDON S. WOOD, THE RADICALISM OF THE AMERICAN REVOLUTION 188, 318-19 (1992) (discussing aversion of colonial America to monopoly grants).

121. *See* DUMAS MALONE, JEFFERSON AND THE RIGHTS OF MAN 328-30 (1951).

122. *See, e.g.*, Gibbons v. Ogden, 22 U.S. (9 Wheat) 1, 33 (1824) (holding New York law granting exclusive navigation rights repugnant to Commerce Clause).

123. *See* Hofstadter, *supra* note 102, at 196.

124. THURMAN W. ARNOLD, THE FOLKLORE OF CAPITALISM (1937).

religious mythology.[125] He states: "When John D. Rockefeller built an empire in a world which was supposed to be composed of competing individuals, he violated the mythology and folklore which pictured what the great businessman was supposed to do."[126] Arnold then proceeds to describe antitrust as a ceremonial vehicle for attacking the personifications of unreasonable "bigness" without actually interfering with the process of consolidation.[127] He concludes:

> In this atmosphere the antitrust laws were the answer of a society which unconsciously felt the need of great organizations, and at the same time had to deny them a place in the moral and logical ideology of the social structure. They were part of the struggle of a creed of rugged individualism to adapt itself to what was becoming a highly organized society.[128]

The hunt for a single coherent narrative thread to the antitrust laws is thus impossible if they are premised on unexpressed and unexpressible social myths. Similarly, the true force of the antitrust laws cannot be undermined or weakened with factual or logical assaults on the surface premises for their enactment. The political consensus supporting the antitrust laws has survived unscathed "proof" of what Congress supposedly meant in the Sherman Act,[129] that monopolies may be beneficial and not necessarily bad,[130] that Standard Oil never engaged in predatory pricing[131] or that predatory pricing cannot even exist in the real world.[132]

Thus, American antitrust law fails to offer a single or stable vision in either the internal or external debate over the importance and nature of competition policy. It remains tied to specific social and historical events that other countries may never experience, or at least never experience in synchronization with the events in the United States that

125. *See id.* at 207-29.

126. *Id.* at 4.

127. *See id.* at 207-08. The irony, of course, is the role played by Arnold in the years that followed as head of the Antitrust Division in revitalizing antitrust following America's explicit flirtation with enforced cartelization under the National Recovery Act.

128. *Id.* at 211; *see also* JOHN K. GALBRAITH, THE NEW INDUSTRIAL STATE 184-88 (2d ed. 1971); JOHN K. GALBRAITH, AMERICAN CAPITALISM: THE CONCEPT OF COUNTERVAILING POWER 50-53 (1952).

129. *See* BORK, *supra* note 94, at 19-20, 50-51 (identifying the policy of advancing consumer welfare as the overriding goal of the Sherman Act).

130. *See* D.T. ARMENTANO, THE MYTHS OF ANTITRUST 42-49 (1972).

131. CHAPMAN, *supra* note 107, at 38 (1991); John S. McGee, *Predatory Price Cutting: The Standard Oil (N.J.) Case*, 1 J.L. & ECON. 137, 138 (1958).

132. *See* Frank H. Easterbrook, *Predatory Strategies and Counterstrategies*, 48 U. CHI. L. REV. 263 (1981); John S. McGee, *Predatory Pricing Revisited*, 23 J.L. & ECON. 289 (1980); Roland H. Koller II, *The Myth of Predatory Pricing: An Empirical Study*, 4 ANTITRUST L. & ECON. REV. 105 (1971).

propel antitrust law and policy. American antitrust law cannot be sold to other countries, which create and live by their own myths.

V. THE INDIGENOUS ROOTS OF FOREIGN COMPETITION LAW

> We have become rather accustomed since the War to treating the United States as the source of anti-trust law, but the roots of our law lie elsewhere.[133]

One final myth surrounds U.S. antitrust law. That myth tells us that the Sherman Act was the direct or indirect source of all the foreign competition systems that developed later. Supposedly, antitrust flowed from the United States either as part of victor's justice after World War II or by its sheer persuasiveness as part of the capitalistic ethic.

The best comparative work on competition law has sought to dispel this myth and to identify the indigenous historical and cultural conceptions for foreign competition law. Apart from the United States, the most analyzed body of competition law is that of the European Union (EU). The EU's competition law is a sophisticated and effective system that serves the unique needs of the EU by creating and enhancing a single European market that can promote prosperity and peace through the integration of several national economies.[134]

The search for the indigenous roots of EU competition law and the competition law of its member states has just begun. Professor David Gerber has addressed these issues most directly, in a series of articles tracing EU and European national competition provisions to their roots.[135] His most recent article debunks the notion that the German adoption of a stringent competition law in the 1940s was merely victor's justice imposed by the Allies.[136] He points instead to the legal and economic ideas of the Freiberg school—which preceded and largely survived the horrors of the Nazi regime—as giving legitimacy to a social market economy, including strict legal provisions for the maintenance of competition.[137] Gerber's analysis supports the notion that the enthusiasm for the enforcement of competition by law had to have indigenous roots or would not have survived, let alone thrived, in post-war Germany.

---

133. GROSSFELD, *supra* note 55, at 17.

134. *See generally* Spencer Weber Waller, *Understanding and Appreciating EC Competition Law*, 61 ANTITRUST L.J. 55 (1992).

135. *See infra* notes 136-40 and accompanying text.

136. *See* David J. Gerber, *Constitutionalizing the Economy: German Neo-Liberalism, Competition Law and the "New" Europe*, 42 AM. J. COMP. L. (forthcoming 1994) (manuscript on file with author).

137. *See id.*

Similarly, in an earlier article, Professor Gerber identifies the roots of EU competition law in nineteenth century neoclassical economics rather than assuming a comprehensive borrowing from U.S. antitrust laws.[138] He analyzes the cultural, historical, intellectual, political and economic theories and forces that shaped the proposals for competition law in nineteenth century Austria[139] and observes the influence of the resulting Austrian model on European competition law, particularly on the adoption of the competition provisions of the Treaty of Rome in 1958.[140]

In less historical terms, I have traced elsewhere the need to analyze EU competition law as a separate and distinct body of law with its own unique goals and values, and I have pointed out the dangers of making superficial comparisons between EU competition law and nominally similar U.S. antitrust statutes designed to accommodate another country in another century.[141] EU competition law is a meaningful and important system with many lessons to be learned from its successes, because it achieves the unique goals of the European Union in promoting the continued integration of a Union-wide common market. Whether EU competition law prohibits the same practices as the Sherman Act or whether EU decisionmakers work in the same analytical tradition as U.S. competition officials and courts are questions that are irrelevant and misleading. EU competition law works because it ultimately serves the Union's interests, regardless of whether it would serve U.S. interests or those of another society.[142]

VI. THE LESSONS FOR EASTERN EUROPE

> The laws must also prohibit nobles from engaging in commerce; merchants with such rank would set up all sorts of monopolies. Commerce is the profession of equal people, and the poorest despotic states are those whose prince is a merchant.[143]

---

138. *See* David J. Gerber, *The Origins of European Competition Law in Fin-de-Siècle Austria*, 36 AM. J. LEGAL HIST. 405, 406 (1992).

139. *See id.* at 406-20, 431.

140. *See id.* at 437-40; *see also* David J. Gerber, *Law and the Abuse of Economic Power in Europe*, 62 TUL. L. REV. 57, 82-86 (1987) (discussing influence of European Coal and Steel Community and German Law on competition provisions of the Treaty of Rome).

141. *See* Waller, *supra* note 134.

142. This analysis suggests that U.S. antitrust law cannot profit from the adoption of EU-style antitrust as an antidote to the narrow vision of the Chicago school. *Cf.* Fox, *The End of Antitrust Isolationism*, *supra* note 11, at 237-38 (advocating a "One World" competition policy based on the EU's "One Europe" policy). While Professor Fox and I share a similar vision of antitrust law and policy, I do not believe that vision can be achieved through transference of another system's law, but only through the domestic assertion of a political consensus for change.

143. MONTESQUIEU, *supra* note 16, at 53 (pt. 1, bk. 5, ch. 8).

Competition principles can be of great value to the emerging market economies of central and eastern Europe. As symbols of a commitment to a free market, laws reflecting these principles provide a vivid and public rejection of the former central planning system.[144] Antitrust also can play an important, but secondary, role in the privatization process. Competition law cannot privatize an economy or directly promote the growth of a stable, liberal, democratic political structure, but it can assist these goals by making the disposition of state property more attractive through rules for stable, efficient and fair private markets after privatization.

A. Competition and Government Action

The focus must be on the diminution of state power and the acceleration of a privatization process to promote both political and economic pluralism, lest the winds of change reverse themselves once again. Unfortunately, the unique attributes of U.S. antitrust law are virtually powerless to control public anticompetitive conduct. Not only are the Sherman and Clayton Acts silent on the regulation of public market power, but United States law affirmatively exempts such behavior from antitrust scrutiny.[145] United States antitrust law is geared only toward the prevention of private agreements and single *private* actor conduct that restrict market activity.[146]

Most federal government market activity and regulation is exempt from antitrust scrutiny. The anticompetitive conduct of entities owned by the federal government normally is exempt from the operation of antitrust law.[147] In addition, Congress can expressly create exemptions from the antitrust laws, and has done so on many occasions.[148] Finally, doctrines of implied preemption and immunity permit courts to approve actions contrary to the existing tableau of antitrust statutes and provide a blanket of implied immunity for at least the bare minimum of

144. *See* David J. Gerber, *Integration, Disintegration and the Protection of Competition: Of Images, Stories and Myths*, 68 CHI.-KENT L. REV. 229, 230-31 (1992).

145. *See* Sessions Tank Liners, Inc. v. Joor Mfg., Inc., 17 F.3d 295, 300 (9th Cir. 1994); *see also infra* notes 147-53 and accompanying text.

146. *See Sessions Tank Liners, Inc.*, 17 F.3d at 300; *see also infra* notes 154-58 and accompanying text.

147. *See, e.g.*, Sea-Land Serv., Inc. v. Alaska R.R., 659 F.2d 243, 244-45 (D.C. Cir. 1981), *cert. denied*, 455 U.S. 919 (1982) (holding that the United States and its instrumentalities are not subject to Sherman Act constraints).

148. *See generally* SECTION OF ANTITRUST LAW, AMERICAN BAR ASSOCIATION, ANTITRUST LAW DEVELOPMENTS 599, 619-23, 631-40 (2d ed. 1984) (discussing statutory exemptions for organized labor, government contracts and small business, insurance, agricultural cooperatives).

conduct necessary to achieve the legislative scheme mandated by Congress.[149]

State and local governments also enjoy immunities deriving from the scope of the antitrust laws as contemplated by Congress in 1890 and the federalism implications of our constitutional structure. Under the state action doctrine enunciated in *Parker v. Brown*,[150] states are not subject to antitrust liability for governmental actions that may have the effect of eliminating or diminishing market competition among private actors.[151] Local governments enjoy the same immunity when they are acting pursuant to powers delegated by the states.[152] Private parties acting in reliance on such state and local government action also may be immune, at least if the anticompetitive conduct is clearly articulated and actively supervised by the governmental unit.[153]

Private parties also have substantial antitrust immunity in seeking approval of anticompetitive conduct from all levels and branches of the government. Under the *Noerr-Pennington* doctrine,[154] private persons may petition the government and seek anticompetitive results from government action under one of two theories. One rationale for such immunity is a view of the Sherman Act as limited to the market behavior of private actors and not applicable to political action and governmental processes.[155] The second, and somewhat related, view is that applying the Sherman Act to the seeking of government action would implicate and contravene important First Amendment rights related to free speech and the petitioning of the government.[156] The *Noerr-Pennington* doctrine has evolved through judicial interpretation to protect virtually all forms of petitioning aimed at the legislative branches regardless of the tactics used,[157] and to protect all but

149. *See* United States v. National Ass'n of Sec. Dealers, Inc., 422 U.S. 694, 725, 735 (1975); Pan American World Airways, Inc. v. United States, 371 U.S. 296, 309 (1963).

150. 317 U.S. 341 (1943).

151. *Id.* at 367-68.

152. *See* Local Government Antitrust Act of 1984, 15 U.S.C. §§ 34-36 (1988) (exempting local government entities from liability for damages arising under §§ 4, 4A, 4C of the Clayton Act, 15 U.S.C. §§ 15, 15a, 15c (1988 & Supp. IV 1992)); *see also* Community Communications Co. v. City of Boulder, 455 U.S. 40, 51-52 (1982); City of Lafayette v. Louisiana Power & Light Co., 435 U.S. 389, 416-17 (1978).

153. FTC v. Ticor Title Ins. Co., 112 S. Ct. 2169, 2176 (1992); California Retail Liquor Dealers Ass'n v. Midcal Aluminum, Inc., 445 U.S. 97, 105 (1980).

154. *See* Eastern R.R. Presidents Conf. v. Noerr Motor Freight, Inc., 365 U.S. 127 (1961); United Mine Workers v. Pennington, 381 U.S. 657 (1965).

155. *Noerr Motor Freight, Inc.*, 365 U.S. at 135-38.

156. California Motor Transp. Co. v. Trucking Unlimited, 404 U.S. 508, 513-15 (1972).

157. City of Columbia v. Omni Outdoor Advertising, Inc., 499 U.S. 365, 381-84 (1991).

narrowly defined "sham" uses of judiciary and administrative processes.[158]

This elaborate set of interlocking doctrines speaks little to the needs of central and eastern Europe. The most important threat to the nascent competition among private actors is the state itself. The strictest rules relating to cartel behavior and dominant firm behavior are meaningless if the anticompetitive behavior of the state is not checked. The structure of the market, and the behavior that flows from the market structure, are in the hands of the state as it decides the extent and speed of privatization and the competitive relationship between state and private enterprise in the economic markets.

Regulation of public market behavior therefore must precede regulation of private behavior. American competition policy has never grappled with the issue of how to use competition law to diminish and control public economic power and anticompetitive behavior. The American system of focusing *exclusively* on private market behavior as the only appropriate subject for antitrust liability presupposes fully developed markets and is an ineffective solution for eastern and central Europe's nascent economies.

The European Union (EU) approach to public anticompetitive behavior better addresses the real problems facing these countries. The Treaty of Rome includes elaborate rules regulating competition, not just for the sake of promoting economic competition, but because of the important role competition plays in achieving the EU's primary goal of creating a fully integrated and prosperous continental-wide market and community of diverse nations.[159] In addition to the competition provisions, the Treaty of Rome includes rules of free movement of goods, services, capital and people, and elaborate institutional mechanisms to create a true Common Market in Europe.[160]

Distortions of competition by the member states are just as important an impediment to the achievement of the EU's goals as private agreements and the abusive behavior of dominant firms. The EU therefore applies its competition rules to both private and public entities,[161] and includes in its competition rules prohibitions on

158. Professional Real Estate Investors, Inc. v. Columbia Pictures Indus., Inc., 113 S. Ct. 1920, 1928 (1993) (defining "sham" litigation as a lawsuit that is objectively baseless and which conceals an effort to interfere directly with a competitor's business relationships).

159. Treaty Establishing the European Economic Community, Mar. 25, 1957, art. 3(f), 298 U.N.T.S. 11, 15-16 [hereinafter EC Treaty] (entered into force Jan. 1, 1958) (stating that "the activities of the Community shall include . . . the establishment of a system ensuring that competition shall not be distorted in the Common Market").

160. EC Treaty, *supra* note 159, arts. 3, 30-36, 48-51, 59-65, 67-73, 137-88, 298 U.N.T.S. at 15-16, 26-29, 36-37, 40-44, 67-68.

161. EC Treaty, *supra* note 159, art. 90, 298 U.N.T.S. at 50.

subsidies and other state aids that would distort market conditions.[162] While these rules may not be completely congruent with the needs of central and eastern Europe, they offer several decades of experience to examine and to utilize if found to be applicable.

B. Competition and Other Social Policies

American antitrust law is applied with a peculiar set of blinders designed to prevent the consideration of any factor outside the narrow question of whether an agreement or practice unduly restricts competition. Even the "rule of reason" used in the application of Section 1 of the Sherman Act[163] is deceptive in this regard. Under the mainstream view of the "rule of reason," the courts have analyzed alleged antitrust violations under two distinct standards. Certain agreements have been found to be so inherently anticompetitive that they are per se unreasonable, and hence unlawful.[164] Other agreements—those that are not inherently pernicious to competition—will be prohibited only if a comprehensive analysis of their purpose and effect indicates that, on balance, the agreement unreasonably restrains competition.[165]

From the very beginning of Sherman Act enforcement, the Supreme Court rejected defenses that cartels were reasonable because of industry conditions or because the prices set by the members were fair.[166] In *National Society of Professional Engineers v. United States*,[167] the Court rejected the argument that such factors as health, safety or general public welfare could even be considered, and held that the sole focus was whether the challenged practice promoted competition or unreasonably restrained competition.[168] The Court stated:

> The Sherman Act reflects a legislative judgment that ultimately competition will produce not only lower prices, but also better goods and services . . . . [A]ll elements of a bargain—quality, service, safety, and durability—and not

162. EC Treaty, *supra* note 159, arts. 92-94, 298 U.N.T.S. at 51-52.

163. *See* Standard Oil Co. v. United States, 221 U.S. 1, 61-62 (1911).

164. *See, e.g.*, United States v. Socony-Vacuum Oil Co., 310 U.S. 150, 223 (1940) (declaring price fixing per se illegal); *see also* United States v. Trenton Potteries Co., 273 U.S. 392, 396-98 (1927) (declaring price fixing per se illegal even when prices set are reasonable).

165. *See* Broadcast Music, Inc. v. Columbia Broadcasting Sys., Inc., 441 U.S. 1, 24 (1979); Board of Trade v. United States, 246 U.S. 231, 238 (1918).

166. United States v. Trans-Missouri Freight Ass'n, 166 U.S. 290, 327-42 (1897).

167. 435 U.S. 679 (1978). *Professional Engineers* concerned a rule of the professional society of civil engineers that prevented price competition in the quotation of prices for the construction of bridges and other public works. *Id.* at 681-84. The defendants contended that the agreement was reasonable because of the possibility that unscrupulous firms would underbid projects and build public works with substandard material. *Id.* at 684-85.

168. *Id.* at 693-95.

just the immediate cost, are favorably affected by the free opportunity to select among alternative offers.[169]

The Court dismissed all the proffered social justifications for the agreement not to compete on price, holding that the statutory policy underlying the Sherman Act "precludes inquiry into the question whether competition is good or bad."[170]

The Supreme Court has rejected social justifications for price fixing even more appealing than those in *Professional Engineers*. In *FTC v. Superior Court Trial Lawyers Ass'n*,[171] the Court declared per se unreasonable an agreement by criminal defense lawyers to refuse to accept further court appointments to represent indigent criminal defendants in the District of Columbia until hourly compensation was raised by legislation.[172] The Court concluded that the boycott by the defense bar was a naked restraint of trade by competitors seeking to raise price by concerted action.[173] The Court rejected all attempts to justify the concerted action on the basis of promoting societal values other than competition:

We may assume that the preboycott rates were unreasonably low, and that the increase has produced better legal representation for indigent defendants. Moreover, given that neither indigent criminal defendants nor the lawyers who represent them command any special appeal with the electorate, we may also assume that without the boycott there would have been no increase in District [Criminal Justice Act] fees at least until the Congress amended the federal statute. These assumptions do not control the case, for it is not our task to pass upon the social utility or political wisdom of price-fixing agreements.[174]

The U.S. approach is premised on the preservation and enhancement of competition as the paramount and overriding goal of the antitrust laws to be applied by the courts, while an active Congress stands ready to pass subsequent specific statutes when it wishes to achieve some other result or promote a different social or policy goal. Such compartmentalization reflects basic separation of powers notions fundamental to the United States, but is meaningless in other contexts and potentially detrimental to the achievement of the national priorities of other countries.

---

169. *Id.* at 695.

170. *Id.*; *see also* NCAA v. Board of Regents of the Univ. of Okla., 468 U.S. 85, 117-20 (1984) (rejecting proffered defenses that competition was not appropriate for amateur sports and that competitive balance among teams justified fixing of price for television broadcast rights).

171. 493 U.S. 411 (1990).

172. *Id.* at 414, 436.

173. *Id.* at 422-23.

174. *Id.* at 421-22.

C. Competition and Enforcement Mechanisms

American antitrust law represents first and foremost an abiding faith in courts, juries and the litigation process to resolve complicated disputes directly affecting public policy and national welfare. The Federal Trade Commission (FTC) represents one of the few limited experiments America has undertaken in creating expert administrative bodies to regulate competition policy.[175] Nevertheless, the FTC's competition jurisdiction is circumscribed by and shared with the Antitrust Division of the Department of Justice. The FTC's remedies are quite modest, and frequently the agency must resort to the courts to enforce its cease-and-desist orders and civil penalties. In contrast, the Antitrust Division has a relatively limited regulatory role,[176] and depends almost entirely on the litigation process—or the threat of litigation—to enforce the antitrust statutes and competition policy.[177]

The backbone of the system remains private litigation seeking treble damages and injunctive relief for persons injured in their business or property by reason of a violation of the antitrust laws. Despite the formulation of restrictive doctrines of liability,[178] standing[179] and antitrust injury,[180] as well as the resurgence of procedural devices to prevent or overturn a jury verdict,[181] antitrust litigation remains alive

---

175. *See generally* STEPHANIE W. KANWIT, FEDERAL TRADE COMMISSION (1979) (analyzing the goals and procedures of the FTC in administering various trade and antitrust laws).

176. The Antitrust Division is one of two agencies that grant certificates of review under the Export Trading Company Act of 1982, 15 U.S.C. §§ 4011-4021 (1988). The Division also grants immunity pursuant to the Newspaper Preservation Act, 15 U.S.C. §§ 1801-1804 (1988), and registers filings under the National Cooperative Research and Production Act of 1993, 15 U.S.C.A. §§ 4301-4306 (West Supp. 1994).

177. The Antitrust Division also publishes guidelines, issues business review letters in response to specific requests for its likely enforcement position regarding specified conduct, and acts as an advocate for competition policy within the Executive Branch and before independent regulatory agencies.

178. *See, e.g.*, Business Elecs. Corp. v. Sharp Elecs. Corp., 485 U.S. 717, 723-36 (1988) (holding termination of price-cutting dealer per se illegal only if some actual agreement on price or price levels exists); *see also* Jefferson Parish Hosp. Dist. No. 2 v. Hyde, 466 U.S. 2, 27 (1984) (condemning tying arrangements only if defendant has substantial market power).

179. *See* Kansas v. Utilicorp United Inc., 497 U.S. 199, 207-19 (1990) (refusing to allow indirect purchasers standing to sue antitrust law violators in utilities cases); Illinois Brick Co. v. Illinois, 431 U.S. 720, 746-48 (1977) (allowing only direct purchasers to bring suit for overcharges due to price fixing).

180. Atlantic Richfield Co. v. USA Petroleum Co., 495 U.S. 328, 335-41 (1990) (holding that a vertical, maximum-price-fixing conspiracy causes antitrust injury only if predatory pricing results); Cargill, Inc. v. Monfort of Colo., Inc., 479 U.S. 104, 115-17 (1986) (finding no antitrust injury where damages were due only to increased price competition); Brunswick Corp. v. Pueblo Bowl-O-Mat, Inc., 429 U.S. 477, 489 (1977) (requiring proof that the type of injury was one the antitrust laws were designed to prevent and one that flows from anticompetitive activity).

181. Matsushita Elec. Indus. Co. v. Zenith Radio Corp., 475 U.S. 574, 585-87 (1986)

and well. It is sustained by the self-interest of both plaintiffs and counsel through devices such as class actions,[182] contingent fee arrangements, liberal discovery,[183] the availability of treble damages, attorney's fees and costs,[184] the ability to couple antitrust claims with other state and federal causes of actions, and the ability to take advantage of the collateral estoppel effect of prior government criminal and civil cases.[185]

These procedural and litigation aspects of American antitrust are as important to the ethos of the Sherman Act as its substantive rules. A per se rule against price fixing would be unrecognizable without a government prosecutor vigilantly seeking to bring felony charges and a private bar acting as private attorneys general to supplement government actions and litigate when the government fails to act.

It is unlikely that these conditions can be duplicated as part of the "adoption" of U.S.-style antitrust anywhere else in the world. Central and eastern Europe may not have a tradition of competition law, but they have long traditions of civil and criminal practice and procedure that will not be jettisoned just to accommodate the enhancement of competition as part of privatization and democratization. There is no rush to adopt the criminalization of anticompetitive behavior, truly effective private rights of action, or any of the other distinctive features of American litigation, as part of a move toward competition law. While any country has the freedom to pick and choose what features it finds admirable in foreign legal systems, a successful transplantation of the Sherman Act seems unlikely unless matched with a compatible set of substantive and procedural rules and supported by a bench and bar with the confidence, independence and competence to implement it.

Nor for that matter is EU-style enforcement possible without the tradition of a bureaucratic elite with a substantial body of expertise to review agreements submitted by private parties and to distinguish between anticompetitive agreements and classes of agreements meriting challenge, on the one hand, and those that are competitively neutral or positive.[186] The European Commission is a specialized creature of

---

(standards for summary judgment in antitrust case); Monsanto Co. v. Spray-Rite Serv. Corp., 465 U.S. 752, 760-64, 768 (1984) (standards of proof necessary to sustain a jury verdict).

182. FED. R. CIV. P. 23.

183. FED. R. CIV. P. 26-37.

184. 15 U.S.C. § 15 (1988).

185. 15 U.S.C. § 16 (1988).

186. *See* Council Regulation 17/62, art. 4, 1959-1962 O.J. SPEC. ED. 87, 88, *amended by* Council Regulation 59/62, 1959-1962 O.J. SPEC. ED. 249, Council Regulation 118/63, 1963-1964 O.J. SPEC. ED. 55, Council Regulation 2822/71, 1971 O.J. SPEC. ED. 1035 (implementing EC Treaty, *supra* note 159, arts. 85, 86, 298 U.N.T.S. at 47-49); *see also* Commission Regulation 556/89, 1989 O.J. (L 61) 1 (on block exemption of know-how license agreements); Commission

treaty law among twelve member states no more duplicable in another setting than is the litigation process in the United States.

Enforcement procedures should be as indigenous as the substantive rules they enforce. Private rights of action are meaningless where the judicial process has no experience, independence or integrity. Purely administrative solutions have no credibility where the administrators have no substantial expertise or resources. Procedure must be the art of the possible, illuminated through knowledge of the indigenous system, not copied from foreign systems with their own histories and logics.[187]

VII. THE ROLE FOR COMPARATIVE COMPETITION LAW

> Not all monopolies are contrary to the law of nature.[188]

The push for a universal and transcendent ideal of competition law that transfers effortlessly across national borders and social and political institutions seems like an unexpected and unwelcome reappearance of the brand of formalism heavily criticized since the pragmatism movement of the late nineteenth century,[189] personified by Charles Peirce in philosophy[190] and Oliver Wendell Holmes, Jr. in jurisprudence.[191] As Judge Richard Posner has observed: "[T]he essence of formalism is to conceive of law as a system of relations among ideas rather than as a social practice."[192]

Regulation 4087/88, 1988 O.J. (L 359) 46 (on block exemption of franchising agreements); Commission Regulation 417/85, 1985 O.J. (L 53) 1 (on block exemption of specialization agreements); Commission Regulation 418/85, 1985 O.J. (L 53) 5 (on block exemption of research and development agreements); Commission Regulation 123/85, 1985 O.J. (L 15) 16 (on block exemption of motor vehicle distribution and servicing agreements); Commission Regulation 2349/84, 1984 O.J. (L 219) 15 (on block exemption of patent licensing agreements); Commission Regulation 1983/83, 1983 O.J. (L 173) 1 (on block exemption of exclusive distribution agreements); Commission Regulation 1984/83, 1983 O.J. (L 173) 5 (on block exemption of exclusive purchasing agreements).

187. *See* Spencer Weber Waller & Rafael Muente, *Competition Law for Developing Countries: A Proposal for an Antitrust Regime in Peru*, 21 CASE W. RES. J. INT'L L. 159 (1989).

188. HUGO GROTIUS, THE LAW OF WAR AND PEACE 353 (Francis W. Kelsey trans., 1925).

189. *See* JOHN E. SMITH, PURPOSE AND THOUGHT: THE MEANING OF PRAGMATISM (1978).

190. *See* THE PHILOSOPHY OF PEIRCE: SELECTED WRITINGS (Justus Buchler ed., 1940).

191. *See* RICHARD A. POSNER, THE PROBLEMS OF JURISPRUDENCE 15-28 (1990); Thomas C. Grey, *Holmes and Legal Pragmatism*, 41 STAN. L. REV. 787 (1989). *See generally* Richard A. Posner, *What Has Pragmatism to Offer Law?*, 63 S. CAL. L. REV. 1653 (1990).

192. POSNER, *supra* note 191, at 454.

A. *Neo-Realism and the Harmonization of Law*

What is needed is a neo-realist approach to the harmonization of competition law that recognizes both the unique social construction and the embedded governance norms present in the competition provisions of the state being used as a model for either transference or harmonization. The suggested approach also would recognize the need to develop a pragmatic feel for how well these norms might work in new and unfamiliar settings where the prevailing norms are unknown or are disguised from the view of outsiders. Neo-realism in this context looks behind the formal texts of rules and is skeptical of grand attempts to harmonize substantive bodies of law such as competition policy, commercial law, data flows and other traditionally private areas of law that reflect deeply embedded governance norms and underlying political and social values. Successful transference or harmonization ultimately hinges on values, norms and actual behavior, not rules and texts.[193]

In this discussion, I am deliberately echoing the labels promulgated in the 1920s and 1930s by the legal realist movement and first used to advocate analysis of the social policies and interest groups underlying seemingly neutral legal doctrines.[194] The application of these principles in the international arena has been associated most frequently with the writings of Myres McDougal, who was a legal realist[195] before he

193. As Professor Joel Trachtman has noted: "[U]nceasing policy analysis and political discourse remain necessary, to define those areas that are appropriate for international discipline, and those areas that should be left to competition." Joel P. Trachtman, *International Regulatory Competition, Externalization, and Jurisdiction*, 34 HARV. INT'L L.J. 47, 51 (1993).

194. Karl Llewellyn, Jerome Frank and Leon Green each has produced seminal writings in the legal realist canon. *See* JEROME FRANK, COURTS ON TRIAL: MYTH AND REALITY IN AMERICAN JUSTICE (1949); JEROME FRANK, LAW AND THE MODERN MIND (1930); LEON GREEN, THE LITIGATION PROCESS IN TORT LAW (2d ed. 1977); KARL N. LLEWELLYN, JURISPRUDENCE: REALISM IN THEORY AND PRACTICE (1962) [hereinafter LLEWELLYN, JURISPRUDENCE]; KARL N. LLEWELLYN, THE COMMON LAW TRADITION (1960); K.N. LLEWELLYN, THE BRAMBLE BUSH (1930), *reprinted in* KARL NICKERSON LLEWELLYN: ON LEGAL REALISM 1 (1986). For a discussion and analysis of Llewellyn's early German language writings, see Michael Ansaldi, *The German Llewellyn*, 58 BROOK. L. REV. 705 (1992). For further discussions of the legal realist movement, see LAURA KALMAN, LEGAL REALISM AT YALE, 1927-1960 (1986); WILFRID E. RUMBLE, JR., AMERICAN LEGAL REALISM (1968); ROBERT S. SUMMERS, INSTRUMENTALISM AND AMERICAN LEGAL THEORY (1982); WILLIAM TWINING, KARL LLEWELLYN AND THE REALIST MOVEMENT (1973); Felix S. Cohen, *Transcendental Nonsense and the Functional Approach*, 35 COLUM. L. REV. 809 (1935).

195. *See* Harold D. Lasswell & Myres S. McDougal, *Legal Education and Public Policy: Professional Training in the Public Interest*, 52 YALE L.J. 203 (1943). For a discussion of the distinctions between McDougal's policy science and the traditional legal realism that preceded it, see Edward McWhinney, Book Review, 87 AM. J. INT'L L. 335, 338 (1993) (reviewing HAROLD D. LASSWELL & MYRES S. MCDOUGAL, JURISPRUDENCE FOR A FREE SOCIETY: STUDIES IN LAW,

assumed his stature in the field of public international law and world order.[196] Similar principles were used later in the work of his followers and disciples who formed the so-called New Haven school.[197]

SCIENCE AND POLICY (1992)).

196. *See, e.g.*, MYRES S. MCDOUGAL & W. MICHAEL REISMAN, INTERNATIONAL LAW IN CONTEMPORARY PERSPECTIVE: THE PUBLIC ORDER OF THE WORLD COMMUNITY (1981); *see also* MYRES S. MCDOUGAL ET AL., HUMAN RIGHTS AND WORLD PUBLIC ORDER (1980); MYRES S. MCDOUGAL ET AL., THE INTERPRETATION OF AGREEMENTS AND WORLD PUBLIC ORDER (1967); MYRES S. MCDOUGAL & FLORENTINO P. FELICIANO, LAW AND MINIMUM WORLD PUBLIC ORDER (1961); MYRES S. MCDOUGAL ET AL., STUDIES IN WORLD PUBLIC ORDER (1960). Many of McDougal's shorter seminal writings, in the fields of both jurisprudence and international law, are reprinted in HAROLD D. LASSWELL & MYRES S. MCDOUGAL, JURISPRUDENCE FOR A FREE SOCIETY: STUDIES IN LAW, SCIENCE AND POLICY (1992). *See also* John N. Moore, *Prolegomenon to the Jurisprudence of Myres McDougal and Harold Lasswell*, 54 VA. L. REV. 662 (1968); W. Michael Reisman, The View from the New Haven School of International Law, Panel Discussion, The Jurisprudence of International Law: Classic and Modern Views, *in* 86 AM. SOC'Y INT'L L. PROC. 108, at 118-25 (1992) [hereinafter View from New Haven]; Panel Discussion, McDougal's Jurisprudence: Utility, Influence, Controversy, *in* 79 AM. SOC'Y INT'L LAW PROC. 266 (1985) [hereinafter McDougal's Jurisprudence].

197. For a sample of works espousing the views of the New Haven school, see LUNG-CHU CHEN, AN INTRODUCTION TO CONTEMPORARY INTERNATIONAL LAW: A POLICY-ORIENTED PERSPECTIVE (1989); RICHARD FALK, REVITALIZING INTERNATIONAL LAW (1989); TOWARD WORLD ORDER AND HUMAN DIGNITY: ESSAYS IN HONOR OF MYRES S. MCDOUGAL (W. Michael Reisman & Burns H. Weston eds., 1976); W. Michael Reisman, International Lawmaking: A Process of Communication, Luncheon Address (Apr. 24, 1981), *in* 75 AM. SOC'Y INT'L L. PROC. 101 (1981); View from New Haven, *supra* note 196; W. Michael Reisman, Remarks, McDougal's Jurisprudence, *supra* note 196, at 273-80.

While Chen and Reisman were consistent followers of McDougal and collaborators with him on many projects, the intellectual relationship between the work of Falk and McDougal is more complex. *See* Richard A. Falk, *The Adequacy of Contemporary Theories of International Law—Gaps in Legal Thinking*, 50 VA. L. REV. 231, 233-34, 239-40, 263 (1964) [hereinafter *Gaps*]; Richard A. Falk, Remarks, McDougal's Jurisprudence, *supra* note 196, at 280-83; *see also* McWhinney, *supra* note 195, at 338; Phillip R. Trimble, *International Law, World Order, and Critical Legal Studies*, 42 STAN. L. REV. 811, 820-21 (1990).

As Professor Tom Farer has observed: "[Anthony] D'Amato is not a direct descendant of Lasswell and McDougal, [but] he employs an epistemology very much like theirs and therefore can be said to reside within realism's intellectual domain." Tom J. Farer, *Human Rights in Law's Empire: The Jurisprudence War*, 85 AM. J. INT'L L. 117, 119 n.8 (1991); *see also* ANTHONY D'AMATO, INTERNATIONAL LAW: PROCESS AND PROSPECT (1987); Anthony D'Amato, *The Relation of Theories of Jurisprudence to International Politics and Law*, 27 WASH. & LEE L. REV. 257 (1970).

For a discussion praising the process introduced by McDougal and Lasswell for analyzing norms, see Jordan J. Paust, *The Concept of Norm: A Consideration of the Jurisprudential Views of Hart, Kelsen, and McDougal-Lasswell*, 52 TEMP. L.Q. 9 (1979). For a discussion of realist and functionalist work in international law unrelated to the New Haven school, see Douglas M. Johnston, *Functionalism in the Theory of International Law*, 1988 CAN. Y.B. INT'L L. 3.

The legal realist movement was primarily, but not exclusively, an American movement. *See* Rosalyn Higgins, *Policy Considerations and the International Judicial Process*, 17 INT'L & COMP. L.Q. 58, 58-63 (1968). For a discussion of the work of Professor Julius Stone at the University of Sydney echoing many of the themes of realism applied to international law, see James

Legal realism has not been a prominent part of international law scholarship,[198] especially in international economic law, for a number of related reasons. First, international law as an autonomous discipline faced the devastating challenge of the political realists, who asserted that international law did not constrain nations' behavior and that only politics, power and self-interest governed relations between sovereign states.[199] Although such a position is consistent with an extreme form of legal realism,[200] the defenders of international law were forced to downplay the subordination of law to other societal forces, a phenomenon they might emphasize in other contexts.[201] In addition, the influence of political realism was so direct and all-consuming that the nomenclature of "realism" in the international arena became exclusively associated with Hans Morgenthau and those who followed and expanded upon his ideas.[202]

To achieve a penetrating analysis of the issues underlying the harmonization of international economic law, it is better to invent a new form of international legal realism rather than attempt to revive or extend the work of the New Haven school. Legal realism, as applied to international law by the New Haven school, has always been subject to telling criticisms. It often assumed a single international community sharing like values and interests. The supposedly shared values and interests, it has been charged, matched those of only a small segment of American intellectuals devoted to Western liberal ideology and a particularly idealistic view of the post-World War II world order.[203]

Crawford, *Realism, Scepticism and the Future World Order: Some Thoughts on Julius Stone's Contribution to International Law*, 13 SYDNEY L. REV. 475 (1991).

198. For a discussion of the rise and fall of legal realism in public international law, see Farer, *supra* note 197; Martin A. Rogoff, *International Law in Legal Theory: The New Positivism*, 1970 U. TOL. L. REV. 1; Trimble, *supra* note 197. For a variety of substantive and tactical reasons, the New Haven school has continued to portray itself as a marginal and radical force in opposition to an entrenched and mainstream classical, rule-oriented tradition. McDougal's Jurisprudence, *supra* note 196, at 286-87. For a recent use of realist techniques in international law, see CHRISTOPHER R. ROSSI, EQUITY AND INTERNATIONAL LAW: A LEGAL REALIST APPROACH TO INTERNATIONAL DECISIONMAKING (1993).

199. *See, e.g.*, HANS J. MORGENTHAU, POLITICS AMONG NATIONS: THE STRUGGLE FOR POWER AND PEACE (5th ed. rev. 1978); *see also* DEAN ACHESON, FRAGMENTS OF MY FLEECE (1971); GEORGE F. KENNAN, AMERICAN DIPLOMACY 1900-1950 (1951); Hans J. Morgenthau, *Positivism, Functionalism, and International Law*, 34 AM. J. INT'L L. 260 (1940).

200. The relationship between the legal realists and the political realists, as part of a more general exploration of the relationship between international law and international relations theory, is discussed in Anne-Marie Slaughter Burley, *International Law and International Relations Theory: A Dual Agenda*, 87 AM. J. INT'L L. 205 (1993).

201. *See, e.g.*, LOUIS HENKIN, HOW NATIONS BEHAVE 1-98, 313-39 (2d ed. 1979); *see also* Johnston, *supra* note 197, at 17.

202. *See supra* note 199 and accompanying text.

203. *See* Trimble, *supra* note 197, at 815-18; Oran R. Young, *International Law and Social*

Further, the peculiar language of the New Haven school made its work overly obscure and complicated. The indeterminacy of the language opened the New Haven brand of legal realism to manipulation.[204] While a specialized "meta-language" is appropriate for specific purposes,[205] the language adopted by the New Haven school was particularly dense. As a result, most scholars and policymakers who took the time and effort to master the vocabulary for active use were already members of the New Haven school, limiting its spread within the legal community.

Equally important, the New Haven school never focused on international economic law as its main topic of interest. Instead, most adherents focused on the classic issues of public international law shaped by the end of World War II and the onset of the Cold War, such as the use of force, the law of the sea, the role of the United Nations and the interpretation of treaties.[206]

In the area of unification and harmonization of law, neither the New Haven school nor any other segment of the legal realist movement has been well represented. At one end of the spectrum, those influenced by the political realists perceived harmonization simply as inherently political and doomed to failure when requiring states to act against their self-interest.[207] The real work occurred at the other end of the spectrum where the "functionalists" attempted to harmonize and unify law through institution building, emphasizing technical expertise in areas that normally were perceived as apolitical, or below the explicit level of political or normative scrutiny, and therefore ripe for harmonization.[208]

The remaining explanations for the dormancy of legal realism in international economic law relate to timing. Historically, jurisprudential movements have entered international law ten to twenty years after their introduction in traditional domestic areas of the law. By the time legal realism entered international law after the Second World War, members

---

Science: The Contributions of Myres S. McDougal, 66 AM. J. INT'L L. 60, 72-76 (1972); *see also Gaps*, *supra* note 197, at 239-40.

204. *See* Trimble, *supra* note 197, at 818-19; *see also Gaps*, *supra* note 197, at 234-35.

205. *See* Moore, *supra* note 196, at 665.

206. *See supra* notes 196-97.

207. *See generally* JAMES E. DOUGHERTY & ROBERT L. PFALTZGRAFF, JR., CONTENDING THEORIES OF INTERNATIONAL RELATIONS 66-69 (2d ed. 1981) (discussing various "geopolitical" theories of the struggle among states for survival).

208. *See* Johnston, *supra* note 197, at 21-23. A more extreme form of functionalism offered the not-so-hidden agenda of making states so dependent on one another in so-called technical areas that more overtly political forms of cooperation would be possible, and eventually inevitable. *See* ERNST B. HAAS, BEYOND THE NATION-STATE: FUNCTIONALISM AND INTERNATIONAL ORGANIZATION 47-48 (1964).

of the general academic community either had accepted legal realism but moved past reliance on the insights it offers, or had rejected its indeterminacy in favor of natural law theories, which attacked the moral legitimacy of the Nazi regime in Germany and the implications of the Holocaust,[209] or in favor of the teachings of the legal process school, which offered a more autonomous view of law grounded in specific kinds of procedure and reasoned explanation.[210]

The field of international economic law achieved its prominence long after the first flower of legal realism had come and gone.[211] The legal academy had long since assimilated legal realism and moved on to critical legal studies, a variety of interdisciplinary studies and the contributions of post-modernism. Legal realism was far from cutting edge, if not actually passé. Few scholars continued to work within that tradition, and even fewer were willing to stake a tenure application upon its banner.

International economic law began with two strikes against it as a discipline. First, there was the general view that international law as a whole was a peripheral subject matter.[212] To compound matters, the field of international economic law was itself marginalized within the academy due to the perceived advantages of the more theoretical study

---

209. *See* Anthony J. Sebok, Legal Positivism and the Growth of Modern American Jurisprudence (1993) (unpublished Ph.D. dissertation, Princeton University, on file with author); *see also* LON L. FULLER, THE LAW IN QUEST OF ITSELF 122 (1940); Oscar Halecki, *The Natural Law and International Affairs Today*, 23 FORDHAM L. REV. 1 (1954); Francis E. Lucey, *Natural Law and American Legal Realism: Their Respective Contributions to a Theory of Law in a Democratic Society*, 30 GEO. L.J. 493, 513 & n.41 (1942); Carlos P. Romulo, *On Natural Law and International Law*, 35 VA. L. REV. 1052 (1949); Samuel E. Stumpf, *International Law: The Testing Ground of Theory*, 7 NAT. L.F. 120 (1962). Natural law theories also had an impact on the realists themselves, particularly Llewellyn and Frank, who sought in their later writings to portray legal realism and natural law theories as compatible. *See* LLEWELLYN, JURISPRUDENCE, *supra* note 194, at 111, 115; JEROME FRANK, FATE AND FREEDOM: A PHILOSOPHY FOR FREE AMERICANS 295 (1945); K.N. Llewellyn, *On Reading and Using the Newer Jurisprudence*, 40 COLUM. L. REV. 581, 593, 603 (1940); *see also* EDWARD A. PURCELL, JR., THE CRISIS OF DEMOCRATIC THEORY: SCIENTIFIC NATURALISM AND THE PROBLEM OF VALUE 173-74 (1973) (discussing movement by Frank and Llewellyn toward natural law school).

210. *See* HENRY M. HART, JR. & ALBERT M. SACKS, THE LEGAL PROCESS: BASIC PROBLEMS IN THE MAKING AND APPLICATION OF LAW 2-6 (tent. ed. 1958); James Boyle, *Legal Realism and the Social Contract: Fuller's Public Jurisprudence of Form, Private Jurisprudence of Substance*, 78 CORNELL L. REV. 371, 376-78 (1993).

211. *See* SUMMERS, *supra* note 194, at 281 (indicating that realist scholarship was at a standstill by the 1950s). For a recent application of legal realist scholarship, see Robert J. Martineau, *Craft and Technique, Not Canons and Grand Theories: A Neo-Realist View of Statutory Construction*, 62 GEO. WASH. L. REV. 1 (1993).

212. *See* John K. Gamble, Jr. & Natalie S. Shields, *International Legal Scholarship: A Perspective on Teaching and Publishing*, 39 J. LEGAL EDUC. 39, 40-41 (1989) (noting failure of general law reviews to publish more than one percent of articles on public international law).

of public international law.[213] This marginalization continued as long as private international law was seen as something only practitioners did.[214] Consequently, scholarship in the area often did not rise above the level of "Doing Business in Country X."

The current rise of international economic law among a generation of younger academics has been as natural as the prior generations' interests in international organizations following World War II and the preservation of world order during the Cold War. It is where the action is. The result has been a bounty of scholarship bringing great theoretical insights and analyses to bear on international economic problems, including innovative approaches that span the previous distinctions between public and private law.

The new scholarship is more theoretical, more eclectic and more willing to draw upon traditional jurisprudence, including legal realism, for frameworks to analyze economic behavior and regulation. The critical legal studies movement also has contributed to the renewed interest in an updated version of realism by refocusing attention on institutions, the need to analyze the political and social interests underlying legal rules, the illusion of neutral principles, and the indeterminacy of legal doctrine.[215]

The neo-realist approach I suggest calls for a middle ground between a hopelessly political sphere and an unrealistically apolitical technical sphere of law. The neo-realist examining a question of harmonization of law would consider the value- and norm-sensitive aspect of lawmaking, which is particularly important when attempting to harmonize law across national borders. The neo-realist is inclined, however, to accommodate a more heterogenous group of norms expressed by the legal systems of different states than has been acceptable under the relatively limited application of critical legal studies principles in the international law area.

B. The Role of the Competition Law Expert

Under the neo-realist approach, the role of the competition law expert becomes that of an expert in her own competition law system, not

---

213. Joel R. Paul, *The Isolation of Private International Law*, 7 WIS. INT'L L.J. 149, 154 (1988).

214. *See id.* at 163, 177-78; *see also* David Kennedy, *A New Stream of International Law Scholarship*, 7 WIS. INT'L L.J. 1, 4-5 (1988).

215. *See generally* ROBERTO M. UNGER, THE CRITICAL LEGAL STUDIES MOVEMENT (1986); Nigel Purvis, *Critical Legal Studies in Public International Law*, 32 HARV. INT'L L.J. 81 (1991); G. Edward White, *The Inevitability of Critical Legal Studies*, 36 STAN. L. REV. 649 (1984); *see also* THE POLITICS OF LAW: A PROGRESSIVE CRITIQUE (David Kairys ed., rev. ed. 1990) (presenting various essays on progressive approaches to the law).

others. This does not mean that there is no role for her to play in the creation and propagation of competition law in other systems, but suggests that comparative competition law and comparative lawyers must play a different role than conceived under current practice.

The competition lawyer can do little to identify the values that a foreign state or international system should promote through a system of competition law. This determination must come from within, as all effective competition law systems have demonstrated. To transplant or graft in the absence of this indigenous consensus produces, in the words of Professor Kahn-Freund, "the risk of rejection"[216]—or merely symbolic and rhetorical uses of competition law to achieve norms other than the stated purpose of promoting economic competition through law.

For example, a developing country might adopt principles similar to those advanced by the Sherman Act using the following false syllogism: all developed market economies have antitrust law; therefore, the actual or perceived development of a market economy will be furthered by the adoption of antitrust laws. Similarly with the currently developing market economies of eastern Europe, it is unclear whether any of the countries with antitrust laws intend them as anything other than a potent symbol of the rejection of state planning or a concession to the EU in order to obtain valuable benefits of association.

The competition law expert can best serve another state *after* that state has developed and articulated the norms most conducive to its social and political structure, institutions and principles. Once these norms have been established, the true comparative work can begin. The foreign expert can contribute the most by demonstrating how her own system promoted similar norms, or sought to achieve completely different ends, through the rules it adopted, and by explaining the consequences that resulted from the adoption of particular rules and institutions. Thus, this process is more about particularizing competition rules than universalizing them.

C. Harmonizing Values, Not Rules

The neo-realist model suggests a different vision of harmonization than merely a process through which people of good faith from different nations come together for the creation of common rules. Even if such an effort were successful,[217] it would be meaningless if the rules were translated through various national and regional systems into a discordant symphony of differing texts implemented according to

216. Kahn-Freund, *supra* note 40, at 27.
217. *See supra* notes 2-6 and accompanying text.

differing attitudes regarding the desirability of economic competition. This type of breakdown has occurred even in the context of attempts to harmonize seemingly private areas of law by creating an optional system of international law available for selection by the parties. One example is the United Nations Convention on Contracts for the International Sale of Goods.[218] The intent of the drafters[219] has been frustrated by the Convention's effective exclusion in favor of more familiar, although not necessarily more favorable, national law,[220] or by the interpretation of its provisions through inappropriate reference to familiar national law concepts antithetical to the principle of harmonization that the treaty sought to achieve.[221] Such contradictions can be explained only by reference to the important traditions and cultural, social and legal values underlying seemingly private commercial law provisions.[222]

The most extreme example comes from the field of customs law. National regulators and private actors were plagued by a lack of uniformity in the valuation for customs purposes of merchandise entering a country. The total customs duties to be paid on any given item were a percentage of the "value" of the item as set by national customs authorities. The existing provisions of the GATT[223] were perceived as inadequate in constraining contracting parties from using discretionary valuation of merchandise to reintroduce international trade barriers—barriers that were thought to have been eliminated by progressive reductions of ad valorem custom duties achieved through several rounds of multilateral tariff negotiations.

---

218. United Nations Convention on Contracts for the International Sale of Goods, Apr. 11, 1980, U.N. Doc. A/CONF.97/18, 19 I.L.M. 668, 671 (entered into force Jan. 1, 1988).

219. *See id.* art. 7(1), 19 I.L.M. at 673 (calling for uniform application of the Convention).

220. Jim Middlemiss, *Opting Out Best Way to Go on UN Treaty*, FIN. POST, Oct. 20, 1992, at 24, *available in* LEXIS, Nexis Library, FINPST File; *Convention on International Sale of Goods Expected to Aid Contract Dispute Resolution*, 4 Int'l Trade Rep. (BNA) 677 (1987).

221. *See* Filanto, S.p.A. v. Chilewich Int'l Corp., 789 F. Supp. 1229, 1240 (S.D.N.Y. 1992), *appeal dismissed*, 984 F.2d 58 (2d Cir. 1993); *see also* Ronald A. Brand & Harry M. Flechtner, *Arbitration and Contract Formation in International Trade: First Interpretations of the U.N. Sales Convention*, 12 J.L. & COM. 239, 241 (1993); Helen E. Hartnell, *Rousing the Sleeping Dog: The Validity Exception to the Convention on Contracts for the International Sale of Goods*, 18 YALE J. INT'L L. 1 (1993); Maureen T. Murphy, Note, *United Nations Convention on Contracts for the International Sale of Goods: Creating Uniformity in International Sales Law*, 12 FORDHAM INT'L L.J. 727, 738-39 (1989).

222. This view is not shared by those who regard the law merchant as a universal transnational force seeking to break free of mandatory national rules through promotion of private autonomous choice of law and the development by merchants of optional rules to suit their own needs. *See* Mark Garavaglia, *In Search of the Proper Law in Transnational Commercial Disputes*, 12 N.Y.L. SCH. J. INT'L & COMP. L. 29 (1991).

223. GATT, *supra* note 11, art. VII, 55 U.N.T.S. at 216.

The attempted solution was the passage of a harmonized system of tariff classifications and the creation of a Customs Valuation Code.[224] The goal of these side agreements was to achieve uniform customs duties for the same item entering any country by developing a single valuation methodology.

Even this seemingly arithmetic exercise has not achieved its desired goal. Divergence has been narrowed but not eliminated. The failure to achieve uniformity is not just the result of bad faith, lack of clarity or misunderstanding of the common text. It is the product of a more fundamental disagreement about what it means to "value" something.[225]

A candid discussion of norms and values, rather than the enactment of specific legal rules, would provide a better chance of meaningful, but slower, international harmonization. A dialogue of this type would serve as a "truth-in-labeling" measure to determine whether nations are actually discussing the same topic, or whether they are discussing very different topics but using overlapping vocabularies.

Such an approach would help avoid the fate that befell the UNCTAD Set of Multilaterally Agreed Equitable Principles for the Control of Restrictive Business Practices.[226] When that code was negotiated, the United States and many other developed market economies were talking about antitrust, or something close to it.[227] The unaligned nations were using the rhetoric of antitrust to talk about development needs and the transfer of technology.[228] It was unclear what, if anything, the socialist bloc thought it was discussing, other than a set of principles that might disadvantage the West.[229]

A candid normative discussion would also affect the choice of the forum or institution for the harmonization of competition law. None is perfect. For example, the GATT is an extremely heterogenous organization with a membership rapidly approaching that of the United Nations, but with a limited institutional structure.[230] Although

---

224. Agreement on Implementation of Article VII of the General Agreement on Tariffs and Trade, Apr. 12, 1979, T.I.A.S., No. 10,402, *reprinted in* H.R. Doc. No. 153, 96th Cong., 1st Sess., pt. 1, at 3-65 (1979). For a discussion of the code process and the legal status within the GATT framework of side codes implemented by less than the full membership of the GATT, see John H. Jackson, *The Birth of the GATT-MTN System: A Constitutional Appraisal*, 12 LAW & POL'Y INT'L BUS. 21 (1980).

225. *See* Saul L. Sherman, *Reflections on the New Customs Valuation Code*, 12 LAW & POL'Y INT'L BUS. 119 (1980).

226. RBP Code, *supra* note 6.

227. *See* Miller & Davidow, *supra* note 6, at 351-56.

228. *See id.* at 352, 354.

229. *See id.* at 352.

230. JOHN H. JACKSON, RESTRUCTURING THE GATT SYSTEM 9-30, 81-87 (1990).

structural aspects of the GATT and the new World Trade Organization will be strengthened if the successful completion of the Uruguay Round of multilateral negotiations is ratified by the United States and its key trading partners,[231] certain key weaknesses remain. The GATT is, for all practical purposes, unamendable.[232] Furthermore, its dispute resolution mechanism is clumsy, with sanctions limited to the withdrawal of concessions previously extended to the offending party.[233]

The GATT's greatest success has come in the area of tariff reduction, with a zero tariff world for many goods likely in the near future. In contrast, the GATT has had only qualified success in addressing nontariff barriers. For example, the GATT merely has achieved a consensus on the nature of nontariff barriers such as dumping and subsidies, and on the countermeasures authorized to be taken by injured parties.[234] Likewise, the GATT has achieved only limited reductions in nontariff barriers involving technical standards[235] and government procurement,[236] and has done so only on a reciprocal basis, which does serious violence to the most-favored-nation principle enshrined in Article I of the GATT.[237] For more explicitly value-laden areas, such

231. *See* Final Act Embodying the Results of the Uruguay Round of Multilateral Trade Negotiations, Dec. 15, 1993, *reprinted in* 33 I.L.M. 9 (1994); Agreement Establishing the Multilateral Trade Organization [World Trade Organization], *adopted* Dec. 15, 1993, 33 I.L.M. 15. *See generally* Symposium, *The Uruguay Round and the Future of World Trade*, 18 BROOK. J. INT'L L. 1 (1992).

232. *See* GATT, *supra* note 11, art. XXX, 55 U.N.T.S. at 282.

233. Understanding on Rules and Procedures Governing the Settlement of Disputes, Dec. 15, 1993, *reprinted in* 33 I.L.M. 114 (1994); GATT, *supra* note 11, art. XXIII, 55 U.N.T.S. at 266; *see also* Miquel Montañà Mora, *A GATT With Teeth: Law Wins over Politics in the Resolution of International Trade Disputes*, 31 COLUM. J. TRANSNAT'L L. 103 (1993) (discussing proposals for revising GATT dispute resolution procedures). For a discussion of the relationship between the improved dispute resolution procedures proposed in the Uruguay Round and the prospects for a GATT competition code, see Vermulst, *supra* note 11, at 65-69.

234. *See House Implementing Language Proposed for New GATT Antidumping, Subsidy Codes*, 11 Int'l Trade Rep. (BNA) No. 5, at 178 (Feb. 2, 1994); *GATT and the Uruguay Round*, 11 Int'l Trade Rep. (BNA) No. 3, at 102 (Jan. 19, 1994); Agreement on Interpretation and Application of Articles VI, XVI and XXIII of the General Agreement on Tariffs and Trade, Apr. 12, 1979, T.I.A.S. No. 9619, *reprinted in* 18 I.L.M. 579 (1979) (GATT Subsidies Code); Agreement on Implementation of Article VI of the General Agreement on Tariffs and Trade, Apr. 12, 1979, T.I.A.S. No. 9650, *reprinted in* 18 I.L.M. 621 (1979) (GATT Antidumping Code).

235. Agreement on Technical Barriers to Trade, Apr. 12, 1979, T.I.A.S. No. 9616, *reprinted in* 18 I.L.M. 1079 (1979).

236. Agreement on Government Procurement, Apr. 12, 1979, T.I.A.S. No. 9788, *reprinted in* 18 I.L.M. 1052 (1979).

237. The codes are often described as interpretations and clarifications of language found in the GATT, rather than as creating new benefits or obligations. This characterization avoids the criticism that the codes circumvent both the amendment process and the unconditional most-favored-nation provisions found in the GATT itself.

as antitrust, labor and environmental issues, the GATT has no real record at all.[238]

Side codes have been the vehicle for whatever progress has been achieved in implementing the provisions of the GATT. These codes were negotiated as part of the recent rounds of multilateral trade negotiations conducted under the auspices of GATT. Although all contracting parties are invited to participate in the process of code creation, a contracting party does not assume the obligations or obtain the benefits set forth in these side agreements unless it signs them. As a result, the code process has attracted a varying number of participants and signatories, as dictated by their perceived self-interests.

All the great successes of the Uruguay Round merely are necessary, but not sufficient, conditions for work in the competition field. Candid normative discussions would provide different and better solutions than a GATT side code on competition. This approach would eliminate the laborious task of attempting to fashion global rules on technical antitrust principles, such as rules on price fixing, export cartels and resale price maintenance, or standards for unlawful mergers and acquisitions. Before "price fixing" can be defined and regulated by a carefully crafted legal rule, a more fundamental consensus must be developed: that a plurality of economic actors, private or public or both, is an important part of a liberal democratic political order. A consensus also must be developed as to the meaning and desirability of the competition that would ensue.

Even assuming that consensus has begun to manifest itself in these respects, states need to understand how their own and other states' competition policies reflect unexpressed governance norms before the question of common competition rules becomes a fruitful inquiry. Scholars and policymakers of each state might consider carefully the following inquiries before directly proceeding to the actual drafting of a code:

---

238. The closest the GATT has come to dealing with competition issues is the "TRIPs agreement" in the Uruguay Round. Agreement on Trade-Related Aspects of Intellectual Property Rights, Including Trade in Counterfeit Goods, *adopted* Dec. 15, 1993, 33 I.L.M. 83. The agreement permits signatories to regulate the use of intellectual property rights to prevent anticompetitive abuses, but does not define what constitutes anticompetitive conduct in the first place. *See id.* art. 40, 33 I.L.M. at 98-99.

A recent GATT-based decision examining the trade implications of national environmental legislation has been severely criticized. In that case, a GATT dispute settlement panel held that United States legislation relating to tuna fishing was inconsistent with the GATT. *See* General Agreement on Tariffs and Trade: Dispute Settlement Panel Report on United States Restrictions on Imports of Tuna, GATT Doc. DS21/R (Sept. 3, 1991), *reprinted in* 30 I.L.M. 1594, 1623 (1991); *see also* Jeffrey L. Dunoff, *Reconciling International Trade with Preservation of the Global Commons: Can We Prosper and Protect?*, 49 WASH. & LEE L. REV. 1407 (1992).

1) Where does the promotion of economic competition for its own sake rank on the hierarchy of social values?

2) Does the emergence of winners and losers inherent in the promotion of economic competition threaten the general social, political or economic stability of the country?

3) Should persons normally have the right to be heard regarding their government's adverse regulatory and law enforcement decisions of an economic nature?

4) Should persons normally have the right to invoke judicial action to challenge adverse government regulatory or law enforcement action in the economic sphere?

5) May persons invoke private rights of action when the government takes no action or has an interest adverse to the claim?

6) Should the government be subject to legal constraints on its behavior in economic markets, or will government action always trump private market forces?

7) Can private actors invoke governmental processes to restrict competition and, if so, what processes and with what limits?

8) How will other social interests be taken into account in the enforcement of competition by law?

9) Are there administrative or judicial bodies with the respect, integrity, ability and resources to uphold effectively legal norms related to the enforcement of competition law?

10) Should competition rules incorporate only narrow nationalistic concerns, or should the interests of foreign actors, other states and the international system be incorporated as factors in decisionmaking and case resolution?

Without a consensus on these and other explicitly normative issues, no workable agreement on rules will be possible. If agreement could be reached, it would be an exercise in papering over differences and selecting ambiguous language so that each state could pursue its self-interest and still remain nominally in compliance with any rules generated through the process. The world does not need another such ambiguous voluntary code.

The world may not need an agreement at all, at least not the type that has been forged in the past. As values converge, if they do converge, statements of the norms to be implemented may be more useful than the enunciation of a rule. Norms need not be implemented through any single rule. They can be implemented by individual states through a variety of legal mechanisms in the manner that suits each state's unique historical and social factors. Rules need not be uniform as long as they implement, rather than subvert, the norm in question. Diversity and flexibility can thus be maintained, and dominant states cannot use harmonization as a means of legal hegemony or cultural imperialism—intended or unintended. Such a regime would allow each state to implement its own vision of the values of economic competition without buying wholesale those of another system. In sum, this approach values pluralism,[239] which hardly has to be defended to proponents of political and economic competition.

VIII. CONCLUSION

A push for facile harmonization is upon us once again in the area of competition law. The pressure has begun for another attempt to find a common text and a single institution to bring together the diverse laws governing competition between economic actors. More often than not, the Sherman Act is offered by United States commentators and policy-makers as the appropriate model for transference to and adoption by other nations and as a guide for the development of multilateral competition codes. Occasionally, the Sherman Act and the competition provisions of the European Union are viewed as rivals for the affections of emerging market economies. Rarer still, international harmonization is viewed as an opportunity to reverse unwanted trends in United States antitrust law.

Neither the transfer of existing national laws nor the international harmonization of competition law offers any realistic prospect for the desired outcomes. The law transferred is not likely to be the law that is received. There is even less reason to believe that it should be. United States antitrust law is a peculiar and unique social and historical construct of events and themes that are difficult for a U.S. observer to perceive and unfathomable to all but the most diligent foreign observer. Transferring our law to another setting produces only a set of words ill-suited for another legal culture, a symbolic adoption of antitrust for some other purpose, or a foreign gloss on familiar words that creates unintended friction.

Attempts to harmonize competition law on an international basis produce similar results. In the past, these exercises have ended either in the failure to adopt a common text, the adoption of rules of the lowest common denominator that were subsequently neglected, or the adoption of a text with no common interpretation. Future attempts by people of the utmost good faith will produce nothing different if the emphasis remains on the negotiation of common rules and agreements.

239. *See* Trachtman, *supra* note 193, at 66 (noting the intrinsic value of diversity).

Such agreements, even if attainable, are meaningless without a consensus as to the values and norms underlying the rules. Technical rules about price fixing, vertical agreements, monopolization and mergers are part of a broader view about the benefits and meaning of competition. Competition policy broadly construed is the jurisprudence of capitalism, and it speaks to a society's view of the role and the relationship of the individual, the enterprise and the government in a pluralistic society and economy. Societies do not speak with a single voice about these critical issues. Each society should implement its unique vision with a set of carefully considered indigenous laws, not a set of rules that represents the vision and voice of another.

Name Index